Social Origins of Educational Systems

Dedication

To the memory of my father
Ronald Archer

Social Origins of Educational Systems

Margaret Scotford Archer
University of Warwick, UK

$\textcircled{\$}$ SAGE Publications Ltd · London and Beverly Hills

For information address

SAGE Publications Ltd
28 Banner Street
London EC1Y 8QE

SAGE Publications Inc
275 South Beverly Drive
Beverly Hills, California 90212

International Standard Book Number
8039 9876 7 Cloth

Library of Congress Catalog Card Number
77-084072

First Printing

Printed in Great Britain by
Biddles Ltd, Guildford, Surrey

CONTENTS

Part I:

THE DEVELOPMENT OF STATE EDUCATIONAL SYSTEMS

Part II:

EDUCATIONAL SYSTEMS IN ACTION

Acknowledgement

My thanks to the Trustees of the Nuffield Foundation for their generous award under the Social Sciences Small Grants Scheme during 1977-78 which enabled me to complete Part II of this study.

1 THINKING AND THEORIZING ABOUT EDUCATIONAL SYSTEMS

The questions dealt with here are macroscopic ones: how do educational systems develop and how do they change? The nature of these problems means that our approach to them must be both historical and comparative. If sociology is to add to the work of the educational historian and the comparative educationalist it must be by developing theories which over-arch their findings. This is what the present study attempts to do — to account for the characteristics and contours of national educational systems and their processes of change. However, it goes about this in a particular way because of the conviction that macroscopic educational problems can best be approached through macro-sociological theory.

The first question about the characteristics of education can be broken down into three subsidiary ones: Who gets it? What happens to them during it? Where do they go to after it? These enquiries about inputs, processes and outputs subsume a whole range of issues, many of which have often been discussed independently. They embrace problems about educational opportunity, selection and discrimination,

1

about the management and transmission of knowledge and values, and about social placement, stratification, and mobility. At the same time they raise the two most general problems of all, namely those about the effects of society upon education and about the consequences of education for society.

Thus the fundamental question here is why does education have the particular inputs, processes and outputs which characterize it at any given time? The basic answer to it is held to be very simple. Education has the characteristics it does because of the goals pursued by those who control it. The second question asks why these particular inputs, processes and outputs change over time? The basic answer given here is equally simple. Change occurs because new educational goals are pursued by those who have the power to modify previous practices. As we shall see, these answers are of a deceptive simplicity. They are insisted upon now, at the beginning, because, however complex our final formulations turn out to be, education is fundamentally about what people have wanted of it and have been able to do to it.

The real answers are more complicated but they supplement rather than contradict the above. It is important never to lose sight of the fact that the complex theories we develop to account for education and educational change are theories about the educational activities of people. This very basic point is underlined for two reasons. Firstly, because however fundamental, much of the literature in fact contradicts it and embodies implicit beliefs in hidden hands, evolutionary mechanisms, and spontaneous adjustments to social change. There education is still seen as mysteriously adapting to social requirements and responding to demands of society not of people. Secondly, and for the present purposes much more importantly, our theories will be *about* the educational activities of people even though they will not explain educational development strictly *in terms* of people alone.

The basic answers are too simple because they beg more questions than they solve. To say that education derives its characteristic features from the aims of those who control it immediately raises problems concerning the identification of controlling groups, the bases and processes upon which control rests, the methods and channels through which it is exerted, the extensiveness of control, the reactions of others to this control, and their educational consequences. Similarly, where change is concerned, it is not explained until an account has been given of why educational goals change, who does the changing, and how they impose the changes they seek. To confront these problems is to recognize that their solution depends upon analyzing complex forms of social interaction. Furthermore, the nature of education is rarely, if ever, the practical realization of an ideal form of instruction as envisaged by a particular group. Instead, most of the time most of the forms that education takes are the political products of power struggles. They bear the marks of concession to allies and compromise with opponents. Thus to understand the nature of education at any time we need to know not only who won the struggle for control, but also how: not merely who lost, but also how badly they lost.

Secondly, the basic answers are deceptively simple because they convey the impression that education and educational change can be explained by reference to group goals and balances of power alone. It is a false impression because there are other factors which constrain both the goal formation and goal attainment of even the most powerful group — that is the group most free to impose its definition of instruction and to mould education to its purposes. The point is that no group, not even for that matter the whole of society acting in accord, has a blank sheet of paper on which to design national education. Conceptions of education are of necessity limited by the contemporary state of knowledge, and their implementation by the existing availability of skills and resources. Another way of stating this is to say that cultural and structural factors constrain educational planning and its execution. Since this is the case, then explanations of education and educational change will be partly in terms of such factors.

Moreover, only the minimal logical constraints have been mentioned so far: in practice educational action is also affected by a variable set of cultural and structural factors which make up its environment. Educational systems, rarities before the eighteenth century, emerged within complex social structures and cultures and this context conditioned the conception and conduct of action of those seeking educational development. Among other things the social distribution of resources and values and the patterning of vested interests in the existing form of education were crucially important factors. Once a given form of education exists it exerts an influence on future educational change. Alternative educational plans are, to some extent, reactions to it (they represent desires to change inputs, transform processes, or alter the end products); attempts to change it are affected by it (by the degree to which it monopolizes educational skills and resources); and change is change of it (which means dismantling, transforming, or in some way grappling with it).

These considerations introduce important refinements to the basic answers and at the same time specify the theoretical problems to be solved in answering the basic questions properly. A macro-sociology of education thus involves the examination of two things and the relations between them. On the one hand, complex kinds of social interaction whose result is the emergence of particular forms of education: on the other, complex types of social and educational structures which shape the context in which interaction and change occur. The sociological task is thus to conceptualize and theorize about the relationship between these two elements. Its aim is therefore to provide an explanation of how social interaction produced specific kinds of education in different countries and how, from within this context, further interaction succeeded in introducing change.

It is a complicated task because it involves separating out the factors which impinge upon education from the wider social structure and network of social relationships in which it is embedded. This means that we have to differentiate continuously between those things in society which influence education and those which may be ignored at any given time because they do not then impinge upon it. It also follows that the factors which are included are themselves treated as unproblematic — for instance, in incorporating the educational consequences of economic organization we do not try to explain the nature of the economy, but treat it as given. This procedure is unavoidable for there is no such thing as an educational theory (which explains education by things educational), there are only sociological theories of educational development and change. Equally, there is no such thing as a unified sociological theory which can be applied to education, whilst simultaneously explaining the nature of and relationships between every other relevant element.

It is a task worth doing in its own right but also because, if such theories are developed, they can point to the best ways of going about changing our educational systems. There is nothing more pointless than the debates which have now lasted for centuries about the ideal nature of education. The only function they serve is in helping individuals and groups to clarify their educational goals, to recognize the implications of their chosen aims, and sometimes to get others to share them. They remain sterile unless and until they are harnessed to an understanding of the processes by which present education can be changed to conform to the ideal.

However, we are proposing to go about this task in a particular way and to develop a particular type of sociological theory to deal with the two major problems. It will be clear by now that both a pure action approach and a purely structural approach have been rejected in favour of a macro-sociological perspective which blends the two. Action theory is held to be incomplete because it has to take the social context of action for granted, and structural theories are considered equally inadequate if they make no reference to social interaction, but instead perpetuate an empty form of determinism. Nevertheless, rejection of these two types of theories does not involve abandoning all of their core premises. Indeed the notion that relations between education and other social institutions condition social interaction and in turn influence educational change is crucially important. But, equally essential to explaining the origins of educational systems and the processes of educational change are propositions about the independent contributions made by social interaction. In other words, it is argued that an adequate sociology of education must incorporate statements about the structural conditioning of educational interaction and about the influence of independent action on educational change.

Weber's analysis which gave equal emphasis to the limitations that social structures impose on interaction and to the opportunity for innovatory action presented by the instability of such structures is the prototype of this theoretical approach. The kind of macro-sociology advocated here is seen as following the mainstream of the Weberian tradition. Pedigrees, however, can always be disputed and are no substitute for justifying the adoption of a particular approach. The rest of the chapter will be devoted to just that: to spelling out the nature of macro-sociological theory, to examining the principal objections brought against it, and to disabusing serious misapprehensions about it.

IN DEFENCE OF MACRO-SOCIOLOGY

From the beginning of the discipline sociologists have been concerned with the explanation of large-scale, complex social phenomena. From its earliest origins too there has been disagreement about the nature of such phenomena and the proper method of explaining them. The debate about their nature has been conducted between those who describe the major components of social structure in holistic terms versus those who employ individualistic terms. It is thus a controversy about the nature of sociological concepts, or, to put it another way, about the definition of the 'social'. Those maintaining that supra-individual group properties can be meaningfully attributed to social phenomena are usually termed descriptive holists. On the other hand descriptive individualists insist that, in principle at least, all group concepts can be redefined in terms of individual behaviour (although group properties like stratification and centralization may be quite different from those possessed by individuals).[1] It is only a slight exaggeration to claim that we are all descriptive individualists now, i.e., that we all accept as a matter of logic that groups are made up of nothing more than individuals and the relations between them, whatever the practical difficulties of defining our concepts in this way. Because descriptive individualism is so general this particular debate has lost its sting and will not be re-entered here.

However, even if we agree in principle about the *nature* of the 'social', this does not involve consensus upon how we can *explain* large-scale events and things. This is a distinct problem: whilst some have adopted a macro-sociological approach as appropriate for the explanation of complex phenomena, others have denied that the scale of events studied calls for a distinctive body of sociological theory. It is with this denial that the rest of the chapter will be concerned. The issues involved have of course been the subject of considerable philosophical as well as sociological controversy, and reference will frequently have to be made to the former in discussing the latter. However, the philosophical debate will not be entered into here except to show that the conclusions reached by many philosophers do not constitute *practical* injunctions to develop one kind of sociological theory rather than another.

First, however, macro-sociology must be defined and the nature of the claims made about its special appropriateness for the explanation of complex social structures and large-scale social processes need to be outlined. Historically the origins of the discipline are synonymous with the origins of macro-sociology — most of the early founding fathers asked big questions to which they gave equally big answers. Yet initially there was not thought to be anything distinctive or difficult about, for example, explaining political instability by reference to sedentary culture (Ibn Khaldun) or social order by religious organization (Maistre and Bonald). The reason for this seems to be that these thinkers did not simultaneously address themselves to the explanation of smaller phenomena: for when, in the nineteenth century, various writers sought to treat both small group interaction and events of the largest scale together, the problem of scope became immediately apparent and, with it, the nature of macro-sociology was clarified.

The work of Simmel and Weber contains a recognition of the fact that there is frequently little similarity between the behaviour of a complex and that of its component elements. Correspondingly both acknowledged that the laws developed to cope with one level of complexity were not directly applicable to a higher or lower level. Thus Simmel appears to have become increasingly uneasy about the appropriateness of applying statements concerning dyadic or tryadic relations to, for instance, the behaviour of political parties or religious organizations, because of the 'unending complexity' of these large-scale phenomena.[2] To him the problem of transition from micro- to macro-sociological considerations appeared insuperable and in consequence he tended to endorse a dualistic position in which micro explanations were provided for small-scale events and macro ones for the large-scale. The distinctive characteristic of such macro-sociological explanations is the assumption that the laws explaining large group behaviour are emergent with respect to laws about individuals. Macro-sociological laws contain *group* variables like 'ruling class ideology', 'political stability', 'legitimacy', or 'social stratification' and often state relations between them. While such variables are defined in terms of properties of and relations between individuals, they only pertain to certain sizes of groups. For example, 'racism' can develop in the tryad, but logically cannot emerge from dyadic interaction.

However, while Simmel's dualism led him to treat macro-sociology as an undertaking distinct from studies of smaller phenomena, rather than simply a distinctive type of theory, Weber took the opposite view. Though equally concerned to account for large-scale problems, (relations between social institutions, cross cultural differences in social structure and value systems), he nevertheless sought to transcend Simmel's implicit dualism. One of the most important aspects of Weber's work is the attempt to chart a 'methodological path leading from the "understanding" of individual behaviour to the analysis of larger interactional combinations, processes and structures'.[3] In his attempt to make the transition from the discussion and explanation of action to the discussion and explanation of civilizations, Weber tried to reduce statements about social structures to ones in terms of their component action elements. Here, as Rex has recently argued,[4] it was unfortunate that Weber seemed to consider his macro-sociology dependent upon certain rather unhelpful propositions about *verstehen* and positivism. At the same time no major improvement upon this attempt has been made and the transcending of dualism remains problematic.

With greater and lesser awareness of this problem, twentieth century sociologists have broadly divided into those who take 'groups and institutions as their study',[5] and in turn generate statements about them involving group variables, and those who study actors and situations and provide explanations which are fairly easily reduced to laws about individuals. The distinction between micro- and macro-sociology thus reflects a pragmatic acceptance of dualism by many sociologists and their use of a very different type of theory and methodology according to the respective size of problems tackled. However, just as unease had developed in the nineteenth century over *defining* society as something more, or other, than its component members and the relations between them (descriptive holism), so dissatisfaction grew in the twentieth century about *explaining* society by reference to group variables (explanatory emergence).[6]

Currently then there are many who, under the flag of 'methodological individualism', deny that macro-sociological explanations are full, real or 'rock-bottom'[7] explanations of large-scale complex phenomena. Their arguments are too well known to require detailed recapitulation here. The position adopted by those endorsing this view is summarized in the following quotation from Watkins:

> according to this principle, the ultimate constituents of the social world are individual people who act more or less appropriately in the light of their dispositions and understanding of their situation . . . There may be unfinished or half-way explanations of large-scale social phenomena (say, inflation) in terms of other large-scale phenomena (say, full employment); but we shall not have arrived at rock-bottom explanations of such large-scale phenomena until we have deduced an account of them from statements about the dispositions, beliefs, resources and inter-relations of individuals.[8]

In other words, for macro-sociological explanations to count as complete explanations they must somehow be reduced to a series of statements about individuals — that is to microscopic terms. Were this reduction to be accomplished there would of course remain no distinctive macro-sociology or, for that matter, micro-sociology, for dualism would be transcended as soon as the problem of scope was solved.

Yet the problem of dualism remains outstanding. Indeed, rather than working towards its solution by searching for ways of bringing about reduction, many theorists instead engage in displacement of scope[9] — i.e., the assumption that society is simply the small group writ large (the most notorious version of this being the 'dyadic fallacy'), or the opposite assumption that there is a homology between the social system and the miniaturized system — the small group. However, the methodological individualist is not arguing that satisfactory means for accomplishing reduction *have* been found, or even that promising solutions are in sight, but only that *in principle* such reduction is possible. Discussion about how this might be achieved *in principle* has largely centred on one possible method — the development of 'composition laws'.

Here to reduce macroscopic laws we require statements about individual dispositions together with a specification of how people's behaviour differs according to the size and kind of group in which they are participating. This specification means establishing a series of relevant empirical generalizations, the composition laws, which would then enable one to compute complex situations involving more people from simpler ones involving the behaviour of smaller numbers. Provided the group variables in the macroscopic laws are *defined* in individualistic terms (descriptive individualism) and composition laws are known, then reduction can take place and complex group behaviour be explained in terms of the behaviour of individuals in groups.[10]

The problem of scope remains precisely because we do not yet possess this armoury of empirical generalizations, the composition laws necessary for reduction, and thus are unsure whether or not they break down at some given point of complexity. It remains possible, given appropriate laws of behaviour in small groups in addition to composition laws, that observed behaviour will not conform to predictions made on this basis, once the size of the group exceeds a certain number. If the search for explanations is not to be abandoned, a new composition law has to be discovered which has a different form or includes additional variables irrelevant in smaller groups, (e.g. *esprit de corps* or *anomie*). Whenever breakdown occurs we have a case of explanatory emergence, and, since composition laws are no more than empirical generalizations, the possibility of breakdown cannot be excluded.

These breakdowns, far from being unusual, are vastly more common than cases in which reduction has been accomplished. Even when the group variables contained in macro-sociological laws are defined individualistically, these laws 'are still not derivable from the laws, including whatever composition laws there are, about individual behaviour. This is *in fact* the case at present'.[11] Despite this fact the methodological individualist argues that the task of reducing macro-sociology to micro-sociology is possible *in principle.* At the same time he asserts that macro-sociological laws are not complete or 'rock-bottom' explanations *until* such reduction is accomplished. Since this task is beyond us at present, what then is the status of our current macro-sociology? The answer given by individualists is that at best it provides 'unfinished' or 'half-way' explanations,[12] which are methodologically dubious. In other words, the argument about reduction being possible *in principle* is used to condemn current macro-sociology: it is thus the basis of a *practical injunction* to abandon this type of theorizing.

What then about the explanation of our large-scale complex social phenomena? Methodological individualism undoubtedly involves what Gellner[13] has termed 'programmatic implications for historians and social scientists' – that is for those investigating macroscopic problems. Watkins, for example, is quite explicit when he states that he will 'consider how regularities in social life, such as the trade cycle (a macroscopic problem) should be explained according to a methodological individualism. The explanation should be in terms of individuals and their situations.'[14] In replacing the study of groups and institutions by that of individuals and their situations, he clearly expects that we will find it possible to move from the micro-to the macroscopic level. Yet this task involves precisely the same difficulties as the attempt to reduce macro to micro explanations, for 'construction' and 'reduction' involve one and the same activity – the search for composition laws. If these break down in practice for the one they also do so for the other. Thus upon the first incidence of explanatory emergence the methodological individualist of integrity must shut up shop before he has explained the particular complexity in question. This being the case, the explanation of macroscopic phenomena must be left in abeyance until the reductionism which we are told can be accomplished in principle has been achieved in practice.

Hence the explicit injunction to abandon a form of theorizing (macro-sociology) appears to carry with it a more implicit injunction to abandon for the time being a certain kind of problem (macroscopic). This prospect is undoubtedly unacceptable to many sociologists, and most of all to those who share the individualists' moral conviction about the desirability of human control over social development. In fact, however, such a 'principle' cannot serve as the basis for practical injunctions of this kind: for the denial of explanatory emergence cannot be decided upon 'in principle' on logical grounds. Whether or not there are composition laws is, as Brodbeck argues, a matter of fact, and 'matters of fact cannot be legislated into existence'.[15] It is interesting in this connection to note that the unfounded injunction of individualism to abandon macro in favour of micro-sociology has in the past been paralleled by an equally unfounded injunction of holism (based on the conviction that reduction is logically impossible) to treat the microscopic as epiphenomena of the macroscopic. As McIntyre argues,

> nothing but the progress of scientific enquiry in the formulation of scientific theories can decide whether individual properties are always to be explained by reference to social properties, or social by reference to individual, or sometimes one and sometimes the other. As mutually exclusive theses both methodological individualism and holism are attempts to legislate *a priori* about the future progress of the human sciences.[16]

Thus it appears from the philosophical debate that the macro-sociological undertaking is not one which can be outlawed at the present time. And here in one sense the discussion could and does end. However, while consistency demands that no attempt is now made to establish the superiority of macro-sociology 'in principle', there remain some important points to be made in the *pragmatic* defence of its continuation and development at the moment.

THE AUTONOMY OF THE PRESENT TENSE?

The first element of this defence of macro-sociology hinges on a point for which the individualists have regularly been taken to task; namely that in practice they often find it difficult to eradicate group variables from their own explanations. However, what I want to accentuate here is that the solutions they suggest for getting rid of such group variables depend on a curiously deliberate suspension of the time scale. This is curious in that the present is cut off from the past and severed from the future: it is deliberate because their proposed solutions actually necessitate an ahistorical approach to social problems.

In other words, I shall argue that without assuming the autonomy of the present tense, individualists cannot consistently eliminate reference to social facts. At the same time to speak exclusively in the present tense appears to involve a number of counterfactual assumptions about the nature of society. One implication of this is that the examples individualists supply in illustration of their methodological procedure are convincing only when they refer to small-scale situations, lacking in historical depth. They are peculiarly unconvincing when dealing with large-scale complex problems whose study has typically been the forte of macro-sociology.

As we have seen the opponents of macro-sociology assert that any attempt to explain social phenomena must be rejected unless it refers exclusively to facts about individuals. This means, at its simplest, that any direct reference to groups or institutions must be excluded from the statement of general laws and the statement of initial conditions (the explicans). What I want to underline here is not the general difficulty of executing such a policy, for this has been done convincingly by Gellner and Lukes.[17] Instead, I wish to stress how both the plausibility of this undertaking and its ultimate weakness derive from the exclusive use of the 'present tense'. This is equally clear whether one considers the way methodological individualists treat man or his social context — whether we focus on their discussion of general laws or initial conditions.

The bedrock of such explanations is individual dispositions. An event is explained when this outcome has been related to motives, aims, expectations, beliefs etc., that is to some intelligible reaction of man to his circumstances, on the part of individuals involved or of typical actors. However, as we have seen, any reference to groups or institutions must be eliminated for this to count as a complete explanation. The general difficulty involved here is of identifying such attitudes without reference to these social terms. Can we, for example, account for electoral success in terms of certain diffused political attitudes without presupposing statements about 'Parties' and 'Voting'? Can we explain educational attainment by achievement motivation without entailing propositions about 'examinations', 'standards of excellence', and 'ascription'? In such cases the problem is that the explanatory attitude itself depends upon, and is only identifiable in relation to, certain facts about groups or institutions. What the individualist seems to be asserting is that it will always be possible to eliminate the social terms by isolating a more elementary disposition which is independent of them. Thus 'achievement motivation', which entails reference to (and in fact is measured against) social standards of excellence, could be reduced to something more elementary, like a desire to display personal competence or to master new problems, which do not depend on social terms – or do they?

Here, as Gellner has pointed out, is the real difficulty of the procedure, for it supposes the possibility of isolating more elementary dispositions 'as they are prior to their manifestations in a social context. The real oddity of the reductionist case is that it seems to preclude *a priori* the possibility of human dispositions being the dependent variable in an historical explanation – when in fact they often or always are'.[18] This is the first aspect of what I have termed 'the autonomy of the present tense'. It is as if, in explaining any contemporary phenomenon, we were constantly starting afresh since it is assumed that we can detect dispositions which influence the explanandum without their being dependent upon it or on other earlier social phenomena. Not only is past historical conditioning discounted, but so too, in an odd way, is the future cut off from the present. For if dispositions can never be the dependent variable, then the things which today we explain as the unintended results of independent, elementary attitudes, cannot influence tomorrow's attitudes.

Protagonists of methodological individualism have replied to criticisms like this[19] and have sought to dissociate their approach to explanation from such implications. Thus Watkins has argued that

> it has been objected that in making individual dispositions and beliefs and situations the terminus of an explanation in social science, methodological individualism implies that a person's psychological make-up is, so to speak, God-given, whereas it is in fact conditioned by, and ought to be explained in terms of, his social inheritance and environment. Now methodological individualism certainly does not prohibit attempts to explain the formation of psychological characteristics: it only requires that such explanations should in turn be *individualistic*, explaining the formation as the result of a series of conscious or unconscious responses by an individual to his changing situation.[20]

Discussion of this defence thus involves an examination of the social context of attitude formation and action and how far it can be construed in 'human terms' – that is without reference to groups or institutions. Unless this is possible the explanation of attitude formation will not be fully individualistic.

Explanation of this context and examination of how it conditions action has always been the subject matter of macro-sociology. The two major categories of group variables employed in this connection are traditionally labelled 'structural' and 'cultural' factors. It is their systematic influence in a variety of specific situations which has been held to account for observed regularities in social behaviour and processes. However, statements about 'structure' and 'culture' are also statements about 'groups' and 'institutions' in the macro-sociological tradition. To the individualist the problem is to eliminate reference to all these four terms from his explanations (i.e., from both his statements of general laws and of initial conditions), while at the same time allowing for environmental influences upon the individual. Failure to make such an allowance would involve commitment to psychologism – a doctrine which most methodological individualists repudiate and consistently so. Psychologism implies the search for a very different type of explanation from the one the latter are at pains to offer (a quest for cross-cutting not composition laws). The general solution advanced is common to protagonists of this doctrine; it concerns the attempted reduction or translation of environmental factors into individualistic terms.

This can be approached in several ways – for example the neo-phenomenological school seeks to eliminate references to structure and culture by reducing the environment and its influence to a series of negotiated intersubjective constructs. Such a strategy simultaneously excludes any possibility of the social context exerting an objective and constraining influence on social interaction. The difficulties involved have been discussed elsewhere[21] and will not be re-entered here since the advocates of this sociological perspective are increasingly willing to admit that their procedures involve a switching of attention to extremely small-scale studies of everyday activities.[22] Of greater relevance is a second strategy, more common among philosophers of science, which seeks to allow for objective environmental constraint and conditioning, while at the same time remaining faithful to the doctrine of methodological individualism. In the present context this latter procedure is more important than the phenomenological approach because its advocates show a much greater concern to explain large-scale social regularities and obviously believe that they can do so.

The clearest exposition of this strategy is found in Watkins' discussion of regularities in social life and their explanation in terms of individuals and their situations. To him cultural conditioning can account for the widespread occurrence of certain dispositions and the social context can constrain various actions — provided both of these processes are explained in an 'innocent' not a 'sinister' fashion. Innocent explanations are ones which do not impute causation to impersonal sociological factors: that is to groups, institutions or relations between them. Such terms are excluded by defining the social context as made up of nothing more than other people.

> The methodological individualist only insists that the social environment by which any individual is confronted and frustrated and sometimes manipulated and occasionally destroyed is, if we ignore its physical ingredients, made up of *other people*, their habits, inertia, loyalties, rivalries, and so on. What the methodological individualist denies is that an individual is ever frustrated, manipulated or destroyed or borne along by irreducible sociological or historical *laws*.[23]

What we are arguing here is not a defence of historicism (which makes a principle out of irreducibility) but only that there are difficulties in reducing references to things like structure and culture to statements about 'other people'.

For this strategy of 'personalization' to work its protagonists have to show that *all* aspects of the social context, which figure in explanations (either in the statements of the general laws or of initial conditions), refer to nothing more than the behaviour of other people. To do this Watkins begins with a statement of *descriptive* individualism and employs this as an argument for *explanatory* individualism. Since society is made up of people there is nothing in the environment (although it may appear to be non-people) which people in turn cannot change, leaving aside its physical components. 'The central assumption of the individualistic position — an assumption which is admittedly counter-factual and metaphysical — is that no social tendency exists which could not be altered *if* the individuals concerned both wanted to alter it and possessed the appropriate information'.[24]

Thus social contexts and the constraints they exert, it must be underlined, have now become the effect of *contemporary* individual behaviour. It follows that what constitutes our social context are things that the 'people concerned' do not want to change/do not know how to change/do not think about changing. This is the second aspect of the autonomy of the present tense: whatever the origins of the social tendencies and characteristics we observe, their present existence is due in some way to the people present. A big jump has thus been taken from the truistic descriptive statement 'no people, no society' to a much more contentious explanatory one, 'this society because of these people'. Furthermore, this 'central assumption' is not metaphysical, in Popper's use of the term; it is an hypothesis which can be tested empirically *provided* the time dimension is reintroduced. It becomes testable if we specify that all existing social tendencies can be reversed immediately or within some specified period — it remains metaphysical only if the time involved is left indefinite and the statement therefore refers to ultimate reversibility. Yet it is a vital assumption for this strategy of dealing with the social context individualistically. Because of it references to social tendencies and characteristics can now figure in explanations, as each statement about the environment can now be personalized in terms of the desires and knowledge of the relevant people for its maintenance. But the strategy is only as good as the assumption on which it is based.

There are many situations in which this method of 'personalization' appears to work quite well or to have a strong *prima facie* validity. For example, one might think that the sanctions of 'community approval' which are influential in small villages could be boiled down to the activities of some particularly censorious individuals — to what certain specific 'neighbours might say'. Similarly it might be thought that status differentials depend on the evaluations given by some definable 'constituency'. Here the point is not to deny the existence of a category of cases in which this procedure can be effective, but to show by further reference to the above examples that it is smaller than it initially appears. If this is so, then the strategy is not universally applicable.

Firstly, although it is logically necessary that 'community approval' is something made up of what individuals think, say and do (for only people can disapprove), this example shows that descriptive individualism is not a good argument for explanatory individualism. If we take the experiments on the Autokinetic effect[25] as a prototype of how individual decisions are constrained by the judgements of others, we find that the subject is in fact influenced by the pressure of the group and not by its component individuals (i.e., he will not alter his judgement if contradicted by any *one* other member). Confusion arises because the individualist would argue that the group norm of light movement which develops over time is nothing more than a rough average of individual assessments. In fact, however, this is a case of explanatory emergence since this phenomenon only occurs when groups of naive subjects exceed a given size. Although it would not be difficult in this case to specify the composition rules involved, the same is not necessarily true for the two examples cited above. For instance, individuals may be motivated to accept village norms and sanctions by something like fear of losing their 'standing in the community' which is, as Gellner has argued, to imply that individuals themselves act and think in structural and cultural terms.

However, even if such difficulties do not arise and we succeed, let us say, in showing that someone's achievement of high status was dependent on receipt of positive evaluations from specified others for their distinctive life style, another problem follows. Here a complex social fact (social differentials) would have been traced back to its individualistic origins. Thus the methodological individualist has no difficulty in viewing such complexity as the final result of social interaction. On the contrary, this is his aim. If such is the case, then it seems strange that these factors cannot operate as initial conditions for *subsequent* action. Thus, as Weber showed, individuals can trade on status acquired at a particular time in one context to monopolize and usurp privileges in different situations on *future* occasions. However, since the individualist does not allow for such factors carrying over from time 1 to time 2, the 'present' (wherever it is situated historically) is always cut off from the future and the past. This is, of course, unless individualists can vindicate their 'central assumption' that every aspect of the social context is the result of *contemporary* behaviour, whatever its origins.

In terms of the present example this would involve showing that high status acquired at time 1 has no effect at time 2 *unless* other people (and they may be a new constituency) continue to award it, thus maintaining status differentials. The difficulties of this can be illustrated by taking the cases of certain nobility who are fast losing status at home but who successfully attain equivalent status positions abroad, or entertainers who are in the process of losing popularity but can be 'sold' abroad because of their (past) status at home and may well be 'unsaleable' without it. The individualist *is* quite right in arguing that such effects are reversible (for the *maintenance* of status does depend on continuing receipt of status honour); he *may* be quite right in arguing that such transfer effects will be short lived (for various reasons the new constituency might quickly reject the evaluations of the old). But who is to say that *meanwhile* some of the monopolistic practices mentioned by Weber will not have occurred, and, if they have, who is to deny that they could effect social change in important ways? To pursue our examples let us suppose that titles cease to impress and that acting is eventually judged by merit not repute, at time 3. It is quite possible that *between* time 2 and time 3, stars contract exclusive marriages and aristocrats favourable business contracts. These may continue to have important social consequences in themselves long after the status honour through which they were achieved has been withdrawn.

If we move on to the larger-scale it appears even more difficult to operate this strategy and to personalize every element of structure and culture. For there appear to be some structural and cultural tendencies which cannot be eliminated at will (given any amount of information, thought, or desire) by contemporary individuals − at least not for a considerable period of time. Such tendencies are the unintended consequences of past actions: their effects may be those of aggregates (like demographic structures) or of emergent properties (like systems integration). If we consider the existing age structure, the relevant population of child-bearing couples, (a) cannot significantly modify it for several years, (b) cannot eliminate its effects for very many years, and, most important of all, (c) are constantly influenced by it since it has determined the size of the initial 'relevant population' to which they belong. Similarly, a given level of national education presents the same problems, if of shorter duration. These social tendencies are about other people − a demographic structure is simply N people of different ages − this none save the descriptive holist denies, but their influence *in the short run* cannot be attributed to other people, their desires or levels of information. There are then some aspects of our environment which obstruct us (certain military recruitment policies are impossible with a particular kind of demographic structure) and which cannot be attributed to the sustaining behaviour of 'other people'.

Furthermore, there is nothing 'sinister' about such elements figuring in explanations. If, for example, it is argued that the development of an efficient administrative body in modernizing countries is hindered by low levels of national education, we are not discussing something imposed 'from above' or which cannot *ultimately* be changed by human action. All we are saying is that *while* such environmental factors endure, which are (temporarily) independent of any and all current behaviour, they can constrain or facilitate various activities and may have consequences which are not trivial for future social change. The individualist, however, makes the opposite assumption. In effect he is arguing that because such tendencies are ultimately reversible, nothing of importance will happen *before* they are reversed.

Empirical questions of this kind cannot be decided by theoretical fiat. Indeed Watkins appears to be rather uncomfortable about this and admits that his basic metaphysical assumption is of a counter-factual nature. We have argued here that all sociologists, (except perhaps those committed to the experimental study of extremely small groups) are interested in the very counter-factuality of his 'stop-the-world-while-we-get-off-and-change-it' assumption. Especially when dealing with the macroscopic, most sociologists are less concerned with metaphysics than with examining how it is that once 'relevant populations' have *been* defined, their (structured) interests in sustaining or reformulating such definitions in turn condition social interaction and change. In fact most macro-sociological work does not entail a denial of Watkins' metaphysical assumption; its advocates are simply a lot more interested in tracing the reasons why it does not work in practice — for, as Etzioni has argued, the ratio of guided to unguided social change is still low.[26]

Adequate explanations of large-scale phenomena cannot be based on assumptions about the autonomy of the present tense. Cohen makes this point clearly when he states that

> in all sociological enquiry it *is* assumed that some features of social structure and culture are strategically important and enduring and that they provide limits within which particular social situations can occur. On this assumption the action approach can help to explain the nature of the situations and how they affect conduct. It does not explain the social structure and culture as such, except by lending itself to a developmental enquiry which must start from some previous point at which structural and cultural elements are treated as given.[27]

The strength of this criticism does not depend on the infinite regress argument as is sometimes thought. It lies in the fact that by moving *one* stage further back in time, in order to explain the *present* social context, one has to take into account the *previous* social structure from which it developed. In other words, the moment the individualist turns historian he also becomes a structuralist.

This appears to be the logical consequence of 'bringing time back in', and, as we have seen, it is almost impossible to keep it out. The only consistent way in which this can be done is not through 'methodological individualism', but by the 'situational individualism' advocated by Popper and Wisdom. In the latter[28] the structural and cultural factors moulding situations are explicitly treated as given: here the object is not to explain the context itself but what goes on within it. In fact there is probably less difference between these two versions of individualism than is intimated by the posturings assumed in the methodological debate. As Watkins states when discussing a macroscopic problem, '. . . in the explanation of regularities the same situational scheme or model is used to reconstruct a number of historical situations *with a similar structure* in a way which reveals how typical dispositions and beliefs of anonymous individuals generated, on each occasion, the same regularity'.[29] Only the historicists and holists would disagree with that: it concedes the macro-sociologists' main point.

It does so, however, in a manner which is particularly unhelpful. Since the methodological individualist *seeks* to reduce the social context to the activities of other people he consistently blurs the distinction between man and his environment. Because the 'personalization' strategy involves the 'desperate incorporation of complex and diffuse relations into the related terms of individuals'[30] it precludes the possibility of focussing upon *their* relationship, which is of course that of the individual to society. Not only is this extremely important for the study of many problems but also its absence seems to have unexpected implications for the value-orientation of those endorsing the doctrine. In the same vein, the perfectly legitimate position adopted by the situational individualists always takes as given precisely those aspects of society which are problematic to the macro-sociologist. This is especially the case in historical studies (which examine the development of structural and cultural factors over time and their subsequent influence on interaction) and comparative ones (which focus on the systematic effect of these factors across different geographical areas). The fact that situational individualists consistently treat structural factors as unproblematic does have the cumulative, though purely subjective, effect of making them seem immutable. In normative terms, treating things as 'givens' over a long time period encourages a passive helpless attitude towards large-scale change.

MACRO-SOCIOLOGY AND SOCIAL VALUES

The second element in this defence of macro-sociology concerns the support which is often given to methodological individualism because of its supposed value-orientation. Frequently these values are held to stand in opposition to those endorsed by macro-sociologists. Thus it is common to find advocates of individualism arguing that there is a value-conflict which parallels the methodological controversy between the two schools. These views are also expressed in the recent manichean doctrine, according to which there is a sociology accentuating men controlling society and another stressing society controlling men.[31] The former denies the language of externality and constraint, while the latter, in speaking it, reveals its concern for the so-called Hobbesian problem of order. This dichotomy is superficially neat but completely deceptive in this context. The relationship between values and methodology is too complicated to be captured by distinguishing between 'the two sociologies'. This is the case especially where the (neglected) relationship between means and ends is concerned. Two arguments will be used in support of this viewpoint: the first will seek to establish that the methodology advocated by individualists does not lend itself to the development of an analytical framework which would be useful in the practical pursuit of the values endorsed — the simple denial of society as either a prison or a puppet-theatre does not help us gain control over social institutions; the second will claim that on the contrary it is macro-sociology which provides the practical tools for getting out of prison and off the marionette strings.

Individualism and Utopia

The extent to which different types of individualists do, in fact, share a common value-orientation is debatable, but it is probably true that 'man-over-society' represents the lowest common denominator of their views. What is questioned here is how far, in relieving us from the burden of 'social facts' and 'in bringing the men back in', they have succeeded in developing a method of analysis which is helpful in the practical assertion of human control over man-made institutions. Paradoxically, it is precisely those aspects of their methodology which reflect this value-orientation most clearly which also appear to militate against its practical utility in this connection.

The first aspect concerns the systematic overestimation of man's degree of freedom in the conception and conduct of action. It is the reverse face of the minimisation of constraints, which we have seen are limited to the obstructive activities of 'other people'. The second aspect concerns the precarious nature accorded to social institutions[32] — the result of viewing them simply as patternings which are changeable at will depending only on certain levels of information and combination. Both these elements reflect Utopian assumptions which have no strategic utility. To value man's freedom highly and to stress society's fragility is ultimately self-defeating if it simultaneously precludes an analysis of the how, when, or where of social change. To do this depends upon more than knowledge about information flow and combinatory potential. It requires an analysis of the relations between men and various forms of social organization — a specification of the degrees of freedom and the stringency of constraints in any situation. Without this we are left with bold assertions about the malleability of social institutions but deprived of the tools for detecting and inducing mutability at any given time and under any given conditions.

However, both these elements — the underconstrained view of man and the overplastic view of society — militate against such a specification. As we have seen the reductionism on which these are based involves the 'desperate incorporation' of social phenomena, (seen as a series of external constraining factors in other theories), into individual terms. Although this indeed implies a repudiation of the 'society-over-man' orientation, at the same time it hinders attempts to investigate the effects of society *upon* individuals and vice versa. This is the case even within the methodological individualists' own definition of social phenomena. It means in practice that any phenomenon, whether behavioural or institutional, which might be related to highly individualistic characteristics, (personality factors or charismatic qualities for example), could not be distinguished as such in a procedure which has burdened the individual with so many inalienable social properties.

Similarly, the influences of social phenomena (seen as a combination of the intended and unintended consequences of past actions) could not be shown to vary independently of the bundle of psychological attributes to which they have been assimilated. Yet their effect may be unrelated to such attributes since, for example, the consequences of past demographic changes for present age-structure and future population growth are independent of any and all contemporary attitudes — (though the reverse is not necessarily true). It is not only that there is a category of such phenomena, but also that for many problems it is important to know whether one is dealing with a psychologically 'supported' or 'unrelated' factor.[33]

The crucial difficulty which arises because 'personalization' prevents the separation of individual from social factors is that it also prevents the investigation of their respective weightings in any given situation. In other words, the specification of how much contextual constraint versus how many degrees of individual freedom is blocked by this procedure. The unhelpfulness of the value-oriented assumptions to the development of an analytical framework useful in their attainment now becomes apparent. For the 'control' of institutions or, more accurately, their guided change, depends on a framework which can help specify areas of most and least resistance, together with degrees of individual freedom and combinatory possibilities at each of these points. Such a framework would enable one to distinguish the irreversible (maximally constraining) from the mutable and to indicate optimal investment patterns for combination in relation to expected returns of institutional change. This kind of analysis would be strategic in that it pin-points the where, when, and how of social change; it is incompatible with an approach whose underlying assumptions are rather those of 'anytime', 'anywhere', and 'anyhow'. Compared with this, idealistic postulates about man's control and society's plasticity seem a poor substitute.

Before considering macro-sociology in this context it is important to note that the elements in individualism which clearly reflect the 'man-over-society' orientation are themselves dependent on the 'autonomy of the present tense': for it seems that these thinkers are only able to stress our freedom and society's plasticity *because* they constantly remain in the present tense. In other words, the value-orientation itself stems directly from the ahistorical perspective of methodological individualism.

On the one hand freedom is inflated by viewing all the consequences of previous history as reversible at the present time (given the appropriate co-operative acts, knowledge, inclinations, etc.). It is simultaneously exaggerated in the sense that the contemporary enjoyment of freedom has no deterministic consequences for the future. Yet as Martin argued in relation to the phenomenological version of individualism, 'the problem of freedom is not, except in a limited sense, a time problem simply because the past is completed and the future appears open'.[34] On the contrary, our open future is the next generation's constraints; just as the things constraining us are the product of the previous generation's freedoms. In both cases the complex un-intended consequences resulting from the exercise of choices can be irreversible (depletion of natural resources), or changeable, provided the appropriate tactics are employed to eliminate them. 'And this is not something to conjure away or to regret; historical determination is partly the obverse of necessary continuity, just as arbitrariness and constraining externality are partly the *results* of desirable freedom'.[35]

On the other hand society's malleability is similarly exaggerated since the repudiation of enduring structural influences is dependent upon neglecting the time scale. Problems arise from the complementary neglect of the interval it takes to eliminate unintended consequences inherited from the past, of the influence they exert whilst their reversal is taking place, and of the inescapable effect they have upon those guiding change and the strategies they employ. Because of this there is a fundamental confusion between malleability and mutability in individualism. Mutability is not malleability; although structures are not immutable facts of nature they are, nevertheless, only more or less changeable, and the process of change is itself affected by that which it is designed to eliminate. This, after all, is what we mean when we say that structure conditions interaction.

To insist that the complex net of unintended consequences stemming from past actions unavoidably affects contemporary action is not to deny that most of these can be changed eventually. Nor is it to discourage efforts to shorten the period of their influence. On the contrary, mutability can be accelerated provided one starts in *the right place and in the right way*. Any approach which presented guidelines for social change of this kind would simultaneously contribute to the increase of individual freedom through releasing the grasp of the dead hand. It is suggested that macro-sociology is useful in this connection precisely because of its concentration upon factors which affect freedom of action and reduce the plasticity of the social structure.

This seeming contradiction — that a framework which clearly accentuates limitations on individual freedom should at the same time be conducive to the increase of human control over social institutions — is apparent, not real. It does, however, account for the current orthodoxy according to which the macro-sociological preoccupation with factors restricting or directing action is automatically taken to reveal its practitioners' prime concern with the 'Hobbesian problem of order'.[36] The contradiction is resolved once it is understood that a precise knowledge of limitations on action and of interconnections between institutions is conducive to the development of strategies for social guidance. At the very least, to know where constraints are greatest is also to know where they are weakest. The maximization of individual freedom and the acceleration of social change are not achieved by denying the existence of constraints or the differential mutability of different parts of society, but by specifying the processes by which, and points at which, change can be produced most effectively.

Furthermore, the macro-sociological framework, in providing this kind of specification, avoids one of the most serious difficulties which characterizes the individualist perspective. There, the minimization of social constraints and interconnectedness leads one to expect hyper-activity on the part of actors (taking advantage of their freedoms), and hyper-changeability on the part of social structures (whose plasticity yields to manipulation). Both expectations are counter-factual.[37] The importance macro-sociologists attach to analyzing limitations on man's efforts to attain certain ends no more involves normative endorsement of 'society-over-man'[38] than does a defence of voluntarism depend upon a denial of structure.

Macro-sociology and Strategy

Although macro-sociology tends to be a blanket term, it is used here for those who employ explanatory emergence together with descriptive individualism (i.e., descriptive holists are specifically excluded). Nevertheless, the category remains broad and unites theorists of very diverse origins (neo-marxism, general functionalism, systems theory, structuralism, exchange theory, etc.), without however eliminating the debate between them. There is no one macro-sociology — only a set of shared methodological assumptions — and it is the implications of these rather than the merits of any particular theory which will be examined here. Thus in drawing largely from the work of Lockwood, Gouldner, Eisenstadt, Buckley and Blau it will be their similarities rather than differences which are stressed.[39] The common denominator which defines this category and distinguishes it from individualism is the study of groups and institutions rather than actors and situations. Connections between parts of the social structure are analyzed before proceeding to investigate inter-group relations — as opposed to the preliminary examination of the actors' perspectives and the subsequent study of social organization, which is characteristic of individualists. This methodological approach reflects the conviction that 'the properties of social structures and systems must be taken as given when analyzing the processes of action and interaction',[40] because of the conditional influence exerted by the former on the latter. It will be argued that the same is true of any attempt to control the nature and direction of social change.

The type of macro-sociology discussed here can contribute to the reversal of unintended and undesired consequences of past actions by indicating the best place at which to start and the best way to go about it.[41] Its contribution to the elaboration of practical strategies for social change consists in the specification of differential institutional mutability and degrees of individual freedom. The former involves pinpointing the areas of greatest and least resistance to change within the social structure, and outlining the relations between them. The latter involves the analysis of processes conducive to stability and change in relation to the position of groups in the social structure and the projects entertained by them. Both elements are of strategic utility and neither, it will be argued, need imply reification.

Analysis of the location of institutional instability (least resistance to change) is based on the assumption that the various elements making up social organizations make differential contributions to system change at any given time. Although macro theorists differ about how these distinctions should be made, there is general agreement upon the basic mechanism accounting for them. Derived jointly from Mertonian functionalism (where referred to as functional incompatibilities) and from Marxism (where discussed as structural contradictions), the mechanism consists in the development of strains between different parts of the social structure. A typical expression of this point is Blau's statement that 'many incompatible requirements exist in complex social structures, and . . . social processes that meet some requirements frequently create impediments for meeting others'.[42] Strains themselves are emergent properties — they are the unintended consequences of two sets of operations,[43] processes, and related conditions which had been independently developed to meet different goal requirements, then turning out to be non-complementary.

It is where such contradictions occur within the social structure that the loci of potential change are detected by macro-sociologists. This is neither to argue that change will occur there (for contradictions are conditional influences) or to exclude the possibility of its appearance elsewhere (for conditioning is not determinism). Nor is it to assume that if change does result it will necessarily affect more than the elements involved in the initial contradiction (for this depends upon the existence of further interrelations with other elements, and on the disruption of these other structural relations by the change taking place). To consider that such 'strains' exert an influence over the locus of change does not appear to involve reification because these emergent factors have no effect unless mediated through the activities of people.

If we take a simplified hypothetical example of a social structure in which educational operations are partly geared to the inculcation of pacificism, and military operations to territorial expansion, strain exists as an objective emergent property. It is not contained in either of the elements (education or army), but it cannot exist apart from them — it is the unintended consequence of their *relationship*. This is not a case where obstruction is simply made up of 'other people' — for it is the *level* of learned pacificism which can impede military operations. If the level is high it might be held unwise to publicize victories for fear of 'public outcry', and following this, army 'morale' could be lowered, thus further reducing territorial expansion. Reification would only be involved were it argued that the existence of objective contradictions directly induces change, independent of and unmediated by social interaction. This is not the case because, regardless of the different ways in which macro-sociologists conceptualize the occurrence of strains, as conditional influences upon stability and change, all depend upon these structural relations shaping actors' situations.

A basic mediatory mechanism is postulated which carries out this shaping process. It consists in the structural relations of contradiction or complementarity distributing frustrating or rewarding experiences to different situations in which actors find themselves. Where contradiction characterizes relations between elements, strains are experienced as exigencies by groups associated with the impeded operations. In other words, operational obstructions are translated into practical problems which frustrate those upon whose day-to-day situations they impinge. In terms of our earlier example, typical exigencies would be crises of military recruitment, problems of mobilization, falling morale, insubordination, etc., which would be experienced as problems by those in positions which deal with these aspects of military operations. On the other hand, where operational complementarity prevails, this is transmitted to the relevant action situations as a series of rewarding experiences. It means that for the actors involved, the tasks they undertake by virtue of their positions will (*ceteris paribus*) be easy to accomplish: the contexts in which they work will be problem-free. For example, the complementarity which characterized the operations of the reformed public schools and the reformed civil service in the latter half of the nineteenth century meant that those responsible for the recruitment of administrators were dealing with the 'right kind' of applicant from the 'right kind' of background and possessing the 'right kind' of skills.

In turn it is argued that rewarding or frustrating experiences condition different action patterns; groups having experienced exigencies seeking to eradicate them (thus pursuing institutional change), those having experienced benefits seeking to retain them (thus defending institutional stability). The 'neutral' category which has been left aside, specifies the likely non-participants in any struggle over the institutional relations in question. By this route macro-sociologists view the points of strain within the social structure as representing the loci of support for institutional change, whereas complementarity conditions maintenance pressures. Here the spectre of reification makes a brief reappearance. After all, it might be argued, frustration forces no-one to do anything about it and rewards are not universally received with gratitude, yet is not the opposite assumed here?

This is not the case. Individuals' interpretations of their situations are important in macro-sociology; its advocates simply insist that there are things about these (disagreeable and rewarding) situations which encourage certain interpretations of them. These things which are implicit in relations of compatibility or contradiction are usually called 'constraints' but the term 'predisposition' is preferred here. For it is their predispositional influence which accounts for the coincidence between observable trends in group support or opposition and the complementarity or contradiction prevailing between institutional operations.

'Predispositions' consist in the simple fact that opportunity costs are associated with different situational interpretations. Such costs constitute the final link between the shaping of actors' situations and their subsequent action patterns. Groups opposing the source of rewarding experiences risk harming their own operations (damaging the operations through which their goals can be achieved); groups supporting the source of frustrating experiences invite further impediment to their own operations, (as would a military elite which favoured the expansion of pacifist instruction). There is, therefore, a structured distribution of costs and benefits for given interpretations. It is wholly objective. These force no-one; they simply set a price on acting against one's self-declared interests and a premium on following them. Some groups will sometimes be willing to pay this price — to assert the existence of a conditional influence is not to deny this, it is only to assume that much of the time most groups will not tolerate too great a disparity between their values and their self-declared interests. Other groups may not be fully aware of the relations between the two — in which case they pay the price uncomprehendingly.

This attempt to isolate a common mechanism has of course greatly over-simplified the approach of macro-sociologists to this problem. In particular it has simplified by concentrating on the unilateral effects of strains, upon relations between independent elements, and by ignoring the great importance of differences in power and in value systems. Although necessary for ease of presentation at this stage, more detailed examination of the treatment of these issues by macro-sociologists, which will be taken up in later chapters, reveals nothing more sinister than this Weberian assumption about the rough compatibility of values and interests.

This attempt to specify points of least and greatest resistance to change does not mean that a simple distinction is being made between the mutable and the unchangeable at any given time. Neither does the specification of degrees of individual freedom to combine in supportive or oppositional activities in given contexts mean that a simple distinction is being made between the defenders of the status quo and the bearers of change in any period. To begin with, such knowledge provides a tactical guide to the points at which large-scale structural modifications can most successfully and economically be introduced, and to the groups best placed to initiate such changes. However, just as the potential for change is not exhausted once the initial contradictory character of certain elements has been exploited, so the strategic utility of the macro-sociological framework is not limited to the detection of 'starting points'.

Because in complex societies the number of cross-cutting interdependencies between parts is so high, any change induced in one element will have repercussions for others. These will be greater the lower the autonomy between parts. Blau has expressed this in terms of equilibrating processes in one area creating disequilibria in others and thus precipitating a new potential for change.[44] In other words, changes introduced at points of least resistance usually have wider ramifications, such that other areas are rendered less resistant because of new strains set in train. Such ramifications can also, of course, engender new compatibilities (by bringing certain operations into line with one another) and relations of neutrality (by making certain operations neither mutually beneficial nor harmful). In turn, this conditions new types of maintenance activities.

This can be illustrated by returning to the hypothetical example of a conquest army and a pacifist educational system. Suppose some of the groups who experience frustrating situations (graduates subject to military drafting, teachers hindered in their work by military propaganda available to pupils, parents subject to conflicting expectations about their children's future), combine and exploit the contradiction politically. Assuming too that they are successful in changing governmental military policy, then army activities could be redirected towards peace-keeping duties. If, previously, economic operations had been highly dependent on imperialist expansion, this earlier complementarity with army activities would be disrupted as military operations changed. A new contradiction would now be generated and would be experienced as a series of frustrations by the economic elite (reduced capacity to off-load surplus production etc.) Such economic exigencies may in due course stimulate group interaction to change the mode or relations of production.

Knowledge of these implications can be employed strategically in social guidance. The modifications introduced at points of least resistance could theoretically be designed in relation to their consequences for other parts of the social structure. The ideal here would be the introduction of a modification whose ramifications manufactured new strains at points where further change was sought. It would do this by disrupting a relationship between elements which had previously been complementary. Simultaneously it would engineer supportive pressures where maintenance was required.

Obviously this ideal is rarely if ever approached, precisely because institutional parts are not all mutually dependent nor arranged like standing dominoes. Interdependence is problematic and not given between elements comprising a social structure; degrees of autonomy and subordination vary between them, and if only because of this the extent to which a given modification has repercussions beyond the elements initially involved, is variable but always limited in reality. However, the fact that in some cases these effects will not be very extensive, that in others a mixture of strategically desirable and unwanted consequences will result, that in still others it may be impossible or unacceptable to introduce that modification which is tactically optimal — none of these affect the basic principle. Namely, it is always advantageous to have the effects of structural conditioning working on one's side, even if the extent to which they can be manipulated in practice does not approximate to the theoretically defined ideal.

Having outlined the strategic utility of the macro-sociological approach it seems profitable to try to dispel three commonly voiced fears about the sinister nature of this enterprise. All of them raise the spectre of 'society-over-man' as an orientation held to be implicit in macrotheory. The first and most pervasive is that discussion of 'properties of social structures' and their 'influence upon interaction' introduces supra-human factors and forces to account for observed regularities. In fact the properties so distinguished are emergent ones — they refer to relationships between elements in a social structure, where these relationships are not contained in the elements themselves although they have no existence apart from them.[45] They are therefore factors which pertain to groups of a particular size — in this case to very large groups — societies. These relationships in turn define the social structure and represent its organization.

To macro-sociologists the origins of complex organization reside in simpler processes of association. Large-scale organization is generated from the (largely) unintended consequences of these more primary forms of interaction. As yet there is no fully adequate account of this derivation, precisely because the problem of micro-macro dualism *does* still remain to be transcended. Nevertheless, its conceptualization in terms of a structurating exchange process by Blau,[46] or as a morphogenic process by cybernetic systems theorists like Buckley,[47] indicates the divide which separates their views from the supra-human mechanisms favoured by nineteenth century holism. Such emergent organizational properties may ultimately prove susceptible of reduction — this we do not know — but until then the macro-sociologist does not want to exclude them from his explanations. And here the second difficulty begins, for whilst few are worried by talk about relations between parts, concern is often aroused by mention of organizational effects or influences.

The fear appears to be that such influences, often described as constraints, involve something separate from and superordinate to human interaction. This is not the case. They are not separate because such properties only exist if the parts exist. All that is assumed about complex social organizations is that, 'their fates *qua* fates of complexes can nevertheless be the initial conditions . . . of a causal sequence'.[48]

Nor are they superordinate, because structural influences are inherent in the relations between parts of society and these derive from social interaction.[49] One way of putting it then is that constraints are the results of the results of interaction. At its simplest, constraints derive from the influence that prior emergent factors exert on contemporary action patterns. To discuss them does not imply the introduction of superordinate forces, it merely follows from abandoning the autonomy of the present tense. For constraints *ultimately* derive their effects from the activities of people (although not necessarily from living ones or by interpersonal influence) and they *ultimately* exert their effects through people (although not necessarily through individual action or through direct interpersonal influence).

Perhaps it is because the readiest word-association for 'constraint' is 'limitation', and those for 'control' are equally restrictive, that the assimilation of macro-sociology to the 'society-over-man' outlook has proved so tempting. But in this perspective 'constraints' are not just things which prevent or discourage people from doing what they want to do, they also have the opposite effect. The kinds of influences we are discussing can also facilitate the achievement of certain projects. It is for this reason that such influences were referred to as 'predispositions' because this covers their positive as well as negative implications, whilst 'constraint' highlights only the latter.

This distinction between positive and negative predispositions helps to dispose of the final misapprehension which concerns an underlying conservatism, often supposed to be characteristic of this approach. This misconception derives from a one-sided accentuation of constraints as maintenance, regulatory, or structure-restoring mechanisms — and a complementary neglect of the predispositions which condition structural elaboration. This bias, which is to some extent justified in terms of the Durkheimian tradition, has no basis in Marxian 'structuralism' where the intensification of contradiction in a given area is clearly seen to have positive repercussions in others. The influences which amplify deviations from the initial organizational structure are themselves generated by, not separate from, the effects of human interaction,[50] (although it is rarely 'contemporary behaviour' alone which is responsible). They derive from the interrelations between parts because these relationships in turn generate contradictions and exigencies (e.g. failures in goal attainment, contradictory expectations, conflicts of interest, frustrating experiences, etc.) which stimulate social change.

These effects which stem from the interconnectedness of parts can be examined without any of the assumptions about superordinate equilibration dear to neo-organic systems theorists.[51] The language of structural elaboration developed in modern macro-sociology is quite different from that used in steady-state theory, although the latter is frequently held against the former by its opponents.[52] It is, as Weber indicated in his macroscopic religious studies, through stressing both the restrictions that social organization imposes on people, and the opportunities for action that are rooted in the internal instability of social structures, that we arrive at detailed theories of change.

The practical and analytical advantages of such a macro-sociological approach over the various types of interactionism have been summarized by Lockwood; they consist in the capacity to distinguish conflictual·interaction likely to produce change (because related to lack of systems integration) from that which simply reflects group antagonisms (lack of social integration). Its advantage over the normative functionalist and neo-organic perspective has been summarized by Gouldner; it consists in the capacity to distinguish those relations between systems parts which make for change from those which make for stability, rather than assuming an inter-relatedness and equilibrium in which every element influences every other and all things work together for adaptation.

MACRO-SOCIOLOGY AND THE PROBLEM OF DUALISM

So far the level and type of theory that will be used to deal with education and educational change has been outlined, and an attempt made to clarify certain misapprehensions about its nature. Finally, then, I wish to suggest that there are good reasons for supposing that it is through the continued development of both macro and individualistic sociological theory that progress will be made towards transcending dualism.

This is of particular importance in the field of education where the pragmatic acceptance of dualism has meant that an (unbridged) gulf separates small-scale studies of the classroom, community, and school from those of larger-scale phenomena. Since the Second World War the latter have concentrated on empirical investigations of a predominantly static variety — that is they have sought statistical relationships between a range of variables, most frequently those associated with social stratification and educational selection. With notable exceptions these macroscopic studies have either ignored the smaller-scale problems or assumed that there is some sort of homology between the two, e.g. school streaming is a miniaturized version of social selection. On the other hand, many of those working on classrooms, communities and school organization have been equally willing to ignore the larger questions and to take as given the definition of achievement, the distribution of authority, the prescribed curricula, the nature of occupational outlets and the relations between social groups; or they have extended vague hopes that an accumulation of case studies will somehow 'add up' to an understanding of the educational system as a whole.

In other words, much of the sociology of education has been founded upon an acceptance of dualism or upon the displacement of scope. The unsatisfactory nature of this divide is increasingly recognized and there also appears to be a growing awareness that the displacement of scope is no solution at all. On the microscopic side, the extent to which many had previously taken existing definitions of school achievement as given, (passing the 11+, gaining a certain number of 'O' and 'A' levels, gaining competence in high status knowledge), is increasingly criticized. It is argued that 'givenness' becomes construed as immutability and that this in turn has misled some sociologists into casting around for methods of 'compensatory education'. This critique concludes that the thing to change may not be the children, the home, the community or the linguistic code, but the definition of achievement itself. So far so good — as a critique — but whether one agrees with it or not the implementation of its recommendations depends on understanding the processes by which definitions of instruction are imposed and changed. It asks therefore that micro- and macroscopic problems cease to be considered in isolation. This is what lies behind every appeal to understand educational achievement in terms of privilege, organization in terms of authority, and curriculum in terms of power.

Similarly, those who had taken up the larger issues and examined the connections between stratification and selection have been criticized for the abstract and non-explanatory nature of their statistical studies. Here it is argued that the search for further correlations with additional variables can continue indefinitely without increasing our understanding of the precise forms of home and classroom interaction, which underlie, produce, and explain the coefficients detected. Again the plea is for dualism to be transcended.

In this context I want to stress the contribution that macro-sociological theory can make to the problem of dualism and to indicate that studies of educational systems, conducted from this perspective, can be helpful in bridging the gap to smaller-scale events. One of the reasons for its constructiveness in this connection is that macro-sociology, unlike the various forms of holism to which some of the large-scale statistical studies were uncomfortably akin, does not neglect the importance of social interaction. Nor, on the other hand, does it ignore or treat as given, (i.e. unexplainable within the perspective adopted) major characteristics of the phenomenon studied, as was the case with small-scale studies of interaction. Instead it seeks to link the two.

In defence of macro-sociology we have been arguing not for its superiority over other approaches but for its indispensibility to them, at the present time, both in terms of its contribution to theories dealing with large-scale phenomena and its practical contribution to the pursuit of guided social change. Indispensibility, however, cuts both ways; equally macro-sociology cannot dispense with the action perspective, as its modern proponents, unlike the holists, recognize. They reject the holistic assumption that social structure dominates individual action in favour of a moderate notion of emergent power, 'according to which social wholes influence individuals so that individual action is determined by a combination of two factors, social wholes and individual purposes'.[53]

This recognition of the importance of action (uninfluenced by structural conditioning) is quite explicit in the analytical cycle employed by the macro-sociologists under discussion. Each of them distinguishes three broad analytic phases consisting of (a) a given structure (a complex set of relations between parts), which conditions but does *not* determine, (b) social interaction. Here (b) also arises in part from action orientations *unconditioned* by social organization, and in turn it leads to (c), structural elaboration or modification − that is to a change in the relations between parts. The cycle is then repeated.[54] Transition from state (a) to (c) is not direct, precisely because structural conditioning is not the sole determinant of interaction patterns. Only holism conceptualizes a movement straight from (a) to (c), without mediation.

What methodological individualists claim is that action alone, (b), constitutes the necessary and sufficient conditions for the explanation of (c). To them (a) can be eradicated. Macro-sociologists do not deny that the actions of individuals are the causal origin of complex pheno-mena (which include both unintended and emergent consequences): they simply maintain that because at present we are unable to know what this causal chain is, we must acknowledge this non-deducibility and thus consider individual actions to be necessary but not sufficient conditions.[55] Therefore, to account for the occurrence of structural change (c), interactional analysis (b) is essential, but inadequate unless undertaken in conjunction with (a) the study of structural con-ditioning.

This conjuncture between the two is sometimes accomplished by welding an existing form of action theory onto macro-sociology. This is the procedure adopted by both Lockwood and Buckley. The former appears to regard modern conflict theory as providing a satisfactory conceptualization of social interaction, once supplemented by and harnessed to the systems integration perspective. The latter links socio-cybernetics systems theory to a revised interactionist approach. Alter-natively, an appropriate form of action analysis can itself be developed in conjunction with a specific macro-sociological framework. This is the procedure employed by Blau and Gouldner. While Blau develops a detailed theory of action, based on power and exchange processes, Gouldner contents himself with rather sketchy indications of inter-actional principles, like the marginal utility of gratifications.

The point at issue at the moment is not the respective or compara-tive merits of these particular procedures, but rather that each theorist (in rejecting structural determinism) acknowledges the inadequacy of macro-sociological explanations of complex phenomena if they do not incorporate reference to social action. Here, of course, we are talking about theories of social change and not about the formulation and testing of discrete hypotheses. The latter is quite feasible without this conjunction between structural and interactional analysis, while the former is not. As Jessop has argued, 'a complete sociological theory needs to consider not only social structure but also culture and personality. However, it is possible to generate a number of testable hypotheses from a purely structural conceptual framework with the aid of assumptions about the nature of man and culture'.[56]

Regardless of whether they work with existing action theories or attempt to develop new approaches to interaction, macro-sociologists can make a direct contribution to the problem of micro-macro dualism. Thus, for example, the work of Blau and Buckley deliberately confronts the dualism issue, for both are unwilling to treat emergent factors as elementals[57] or to forget the constant interplay between complex and simpler forms of association and structuration. The importance of this confrontation lies in the fact that instead of seeking to derive social organization from elementary laws of psychological or inter-personal behaviour, they avoid displacement of scope by attempting to 'understand how the very processes of interpersonal interchange may give rise, through their own dynamics and dialectics, to some basic structural problems and exigencies which are not, however, simple extrapolations from such informal behaviour'.[58] In both the search is not for micro-macro homologies, but for the points of meeting and transition from one to the other. Although neither is fully satisfactory they both represent a quest for composition laws and an attempt to indicate where they break down.

Not all macro-sociologists make this kind of direct contribution to the problem. Both Lockwood and Gouldner, for example, tend to adopt dualism as a matter of practical expediency. Both, at least as far as the works in question are concerned, restrict their attention to problems about the stability or change of complex organizations and refer exclusively to large-scale group interaction in this connection. Consequently they themselves appear to take little interest in the derivation of either from simpler processes of association. Nevertheless the existence and refinement of this type of theory does make an important, though possibly unintended, contribution to the transcending of dualism.

The final point I wish to suggest is that the most promising method for overcoming dualism consists in the continuing (though preferably conjoint) development of both micro and macro-sociology. It is inadmissible for action theorists to consider that their approach provides the necessary and sufficient conditions for explaining complex phenomena simply because they place what Wagner has called, 'a big etcetera' after their micro-sociological expositions.[59] As he argues, they will have to demonstrate 'more than that their theory works well on the micro-sociological level. They will have to perform the transition from small-scale situational interpretations (to) all those cultural and institutional factors which "shape situations", without sacrificing the subjective-interactional approach'.[60] To overcome dualism in this way is impossible at present — we do not possess the necessary armoury of empirical generalizations by which the task might be accomplished, nor can we be certain that these will not break down at some point(s). The problem seems least well disposed of by simply abandoning the investigation of complex phenomena. Instead there appear to be good reasons for thinking that the micro-macro dichotomy can best be overcome if both kinds of theorizing continue to develop side by side.

Firstly, as we have seen, the practical consequence of denying explanatory emergence is simply a retreat from examining large-scale complex problems on grounds of purism. Simultaneously the activities of macro-sociologists are condemned. If this was taken to heart the individualist would be deprived of a large pool of what he considers to be 'unfinished' or 'half-way' explanations. However, were micro-sociologists to take Wagner's injunction seriously and were they to begin working out their 'big etcetera' by confronting more complex phenomena than those presented in small group situations, it seems that they would greatly miss this fund of 'half-way' explanations. The reason they would do so is because, almost of necessity, they would be engaging in an exercise of reduction (reducing statements about groups to statements about individuals in groups) rather than of deduction (deducing statements about groups from statements about individuals in groups). Reductionism implies the pre-existence of a set of macroscopic concepts and laws, (i.e. it involves some kind of dependence on the macro-sociological enterprise, however informal), whereas deduction does not.

To clarify this let us consider what would happen if the micro-sociologist did set about the task of deduction — if, for example, he sought to deduce statements about educational systems from statements about the behaviour of people in them. This exercise appears quite feasible when the numbers involved are small and the conditions under which interaction takes place are simple. Bales' 'law' — which is really an empirical generalization — about the division of group leadership into instrumental and affective roles in decision-making situations is a case in point.[61] (The same is not true of its Parsonian extensions because these invoke a micro-macro homology and thus involve displacement of scope). However, when dealing with an educational system and its thousands of actors and multiplicity of conditions, Bales' type of procedure is no longer possible.

Its impossibility is not simply due to the interactive combinations being so vast and multiplied, as it were, by the variety of conditions under which they take place — although this enters into it. The point is that in dealing with large-scale phenomena of considerable complexity, our observations have to be selective and are selected in relation to hypotheses. This, of course, is equally true when working with the smallest group, (Bales obviously had some sort of hypotheses in mind in experimentally setting up a *decision-making* group and recording verbal interaction under certain headings), but there is an important difference. Hypotheses about educational systems are *about* educational systems: hypotheses about small groups are about face-to-face interaction. In extending his scope to cover the educational system, the individualist must start thinking about systems of education since we deduce consequences from hypotheses, not from crude data.

In doing so it will be a strange researcher who deliberately turns his back on the statistical associations already established, on the 'unfinished' or 'half-way' macro-sociological explanations available. For this kind of 'incomplete' knowledge provides a preliminary sorting of the wood from the trees — a source of hypotheses and a fund of things to be explained. In practice it appears that individualists do not abandon such findings: on the contrary, they draw upon them for their own purposes. Thus, for example, the statement that 'social class affects school achievement' is used as a starting point for unravelling those forms of social interaction whose result is early leaving, truancy, failure in examinations, employment in different jobs, etc. In other words, what the individualist is doing much of the time (and with varying degrees of explicitness) is trying to *reduce* statements containing group variables to ones without them. Here, if an increase in scope is achieved it has been through reduction not deduction, and macro-sociology has helped not hindered.

Paradoxically it is macro-sociology which has provided the definition of the (macroscopic) situation — and this is more than just a play on words. So far it has been argued, on pragmatic grounds, that established macro-sociological findings will be consulted when individualists are confronted with a morass of data, and that certain methodological consequences stem from this. However, the individualist can make his usual reply, namely that manifest utility forces no-one to do anything and that therefore he is perfectly free to ignore existing 'half-way' explanations. This is true, but it does not mean that what is being done instead is deduction. If we attempt to think up 'fresh' hypotheses about educational systems we often find in formulating them that we are dealing in terms of group concepts, even if these disappear in the final version of the theory. This is partly because our non-sociological vocabulary about educational systems is full of them, (e.g. 'academic community', 'centralization', 'binary system', 'streaming', etc.). As Gellner has argued, we do think in holistic terms, and this is partly because there are some things we cannot express without them. It is not argued that no hypotheses about educational systems can be thought up without employing group-concepts — only that some are precluded in their absence: and, what is much more important, that many hypotheses which are eventually stated in individualistic terms are ones from which the group-concepts have been eliminated — by reduction.

In other words, it is argued that in dealing with large-scale phenomena one is usually engaging in a process of reduction, either informally (via our language usage) or formally (via the findings of macro-sociologists). If this is the case, then the existence and development of macro-sociology can only be of assistance to the micro-individualist who is seeking to increase his scope. Even if it turns out eventually that the individualists were right in their denial of explanatory emergence — it will, oddly enough, be macro-sociology which has helped them to discover it. Their progress towards increased scope will, partly at least, be due to the insights and connections provided by macro-sociologists.

On the other hand, macro-sociology can itself make an important contribution to transcending dualism, for there are two ways in which this type of theory contributes to reduction. Firstly, since macro-sociologists are also descriptive individualists, the group variables contained in their explanations are defined in terms of individual behaviour. Thus 'political legitimacy' refers behaviourally to various people considering that others have the right to use force, make decisions, mobilize resources, etc. Such definitions *can* in turn suggest relevant psychological laws about why some people accept others as 'superiors', 'leaders', 'authority figures' etc. Alternatively they can indicate profitable areas of psychological investigation, if the type of behaviour involved has not previously received attention. Blau's work abounds in suggestions of this kind and, in terms of the present example, invites an examination of the characteristics and conditions leading people to believe that their compliance is being recompensed by rewards received.[62]

Secondly, macro-sociology also contributes to the development of the composition laws which are needed in conjunction with psychological laws, if reduction is to be accomplished. By outlining connections between group variables, macro-sociologists may help to suggest the appropriate composition rules of individual behaviour in groups.[63] They do this by suggesting series of behaviour stemming from different types of orientation to other actors, by indicating different patterns of association under different conditions, and by detailing certain consequences of interaction. These can be regarded as hypotheses about the behaviour of individuals in groups or be trans-lated into such, and are interesting in that they say something both about association and about the conditions under which it takes place. Such hypotheses are clearly articulated in the work of certain macro-sociologists (Blau, Buckley and sometimes Eisenstadt), whereas in others (Lockwood and Gouldner) they remain implicit but are not lacking. It is holism, not macro-sociology, which is barren in this respect.

While it is rare to find that such hypotheses are actually tested by macro-sociologists, their work is usually suggestive of the kind of evidence required for testing. In this way they are very much the heirs of the Weberian tradition. As Rex has argued about his studies of complex phenomena,

> Weber did not believe that every reference to a social relationship should be justified by complete proof of the relevance of the hypotheses offered for the action orientation of each of the participant actors. The possibility of proof remains in the background, *but the model of a social relationship would in any case suggest its own verifiers.* These might refer to sequences of behaviour hypothesized in terms of action orientation but it might also refer to beha-viour, events and things, *which arise, not so much in action, as in inter-action.*[64]

None of this is to say that reduction can or will be achieved — only that if it can, then macro-sociology is a means to this end and, if it cannot, then macro-sociology helps to specify the points at which it breaks down. The problem of making an effective transition from the inter-actionism of micro-sociologists to the analysis of large-scale phenomena remains, as Weber presented it, to be solved. Whether or not it turns out that this will involve acceptance of explanatory emergence will be decided by future research. It cannot be decided in advance on logical grounds and the resolution of this problem will be severely retarded if one kind of research is prescribed.

It has become fashionable in the last few years to distinguish between 'the two Webers'; micro-sociologists accentuating the mid-Weber, concerned with the analysis of subjective meaning; macro-sociologists stressing the late-Weber, devoted to the comparative study of social systems. Yet, to 'dualize' Weber in this way, by minimizing either his micro or macro concerns, is to deny the integrality of his work and the significance of his own efforts to link the two. It is a failure to recognize the problem of dualism as Weber confronted it, just as to proscribe one kind of theorizing is a retreat from solving it.

MACRO-SOCIOLOGY AND EDUCATIONAL SYSTEMS

This study as a whole is devoted to the development of educational systems and to explaining the processes of educational change. Its aim is to provide a theoretical framework which will account for the major characteristics of national education and the principal changes that such systems have undergone. Its problem is to capture those factors which historically have moulded education in different countries, and to develop a set of propositions which explain these national patterns. Its methodology involves the extension of general macro-sociological theory, just discussed, to these macroscopic educational problems. Its frame of reference in this connection will be the educational systems of England, Denmark, France, and Russia.

These countries were selected for three reasons. Firstly, it is generally agreed that their present systems of education are very different and that they have undergone dissimilar forms of historical development. Admittedly various authors reach this conclusion on different grounds and by accentuating different characteristics. Admittedly, too, such judgments often exaggerate superficial dissimilarities. Nevertheless, in the absence of other criteria, they have been used as guidelines in selecting a group of countries which may reasonably be thought to cover a substantial range of variation in national education. This is an important check against developing theories which only work for special cases as it increases the range of data against which they are tested. The second reason concerns the diversity of history, culture, and social structure in these countries, and here again one is seeking to maximize variability for the same reason.

The final reason is of a different nature because it involves something that these countries have in common, and which separates them from the majority of others. In none was the initial emergence of an educational system the result of foreign domination or territorial redistribution. This is not to argue that foreign influence, example or experience were unimportant in these nations at the time. It is simply that their different forms of national education developed in response to internal pressures not to external imposition. Foreign *influence* has to be assimilated by and mediated through national groups, but foreign *intervention* imposes a given form of education on them. Freedom from foreign educational domination (like the extension of the Napoleonic *Université* to other countries by military means and the experience undergone in most colonial territories) is important, for the theory we seek to develop is a theory about the *autonomous* emergence of educational systems in different countries. In other words, the theoretical task is limited to specifying the conditions which result in the independent development of national education in different places. The problems surrounding retention, rejection or adaptation of externally imposed educational systems warrant a study in their own right but are too vast to be entered into here.

The two parts of the book deal with different substantive issues and historical periods. Part One is devoted to the development of state educational systems in the countries concerned — to questioning why, as they first emerged, these national systems had different structures and different relationships to other parts of the respective societies. Part Two examines subsequent educational change in the light of these variations. Since the major concern is to provide a comparative analysis, it is comparable events which will be discussed, rather than the same historical period for each country. There is, of course, no compelling reason why the subject should be divided in this way: to do so reflects not only the desire to investigate large-scale developments comparatively but also certain core premises of the theoretical perspective adopted. Those working on different problems may with good reason advocate alternative divisions: those of other theoretical persuasions may very well do so. However, the criterion for judging such subdivisions is ultimately that of utility in generating acceptable explanations.

This division between the two parts reflects the conviction that the emergence of state systems represented a crucial break, because of the change in structural relations between education and other social institutions which accompanied it. The development of state education universally spelled its connection to the political centre and to a plurality of other institutions in terms of the services it provides. These two changes are general, (they characterize educational systems which may be strikingly different in other respects), and, it is argued, they profoundly affect the subsequent social processes which produce stability and change in education. These are different from the types of interaction which brought about change (and in fact led to the emergence of state systems) in the antecedent period. Thus, because the theoretical perspective employed is one which attaches importance to the structural conditioning of interaction, the two parts deal with education when its position in the wider social structure exerted very different influences on social groups trying to change it.

However, it should be noted that to accentuate this break in no way necessitates a belief that educational institutions are converging, either during or after the emergence of state systems. The importance of this break, for analytical purposes, lies in the changed processes involved, *not* their outcomes (whose convergence or divergence will depend *inter alia* on differences in the systems established and in other parts of the respective social structures, which may themselves be either convergent or divergent). In other words, the features common to all countries possessing national educational systems, supersede the similarities which characterized them in the antecedent period.

The two parts are continuous, and in fact represent two analytical cycles each of (a) structural conditioning, (b) social interaction, and (c) structural elaboration. (Cycles are analytic in the sense that the historical sequence is an unbroken series of interaction – structural development – structural conditioning – interaction – structural elaboration etc.) In Part One, the complex forms of group interaction, partly conditioned by education being owned and monopolized by a restricted section of the population, are analyzed and their unintended consequences – the emergence of state educational systems – are examined. Part Two opens with the elaborated structures, these new systems of education, which now represent the new conditional influences upon interaction. Modern educational change is thus interpreted as the joint consequence of such effects in conjunction with other and independent sources of social interaction.

Of course there are historical cycles which preceded the one leading to the emergence of state systems, which constitutes our starting point here. In other words, we open up with the results of *prior* interaction. Here, for the purposes of analysis, such phenomena have been treated as elemental – that is, no attempt is made to account for how the structure we take as our starting point had developed from previous interaction between groups and individuals in the context of antecedent structures even further back in history. The decision to do this was governed by the need to avoid ultimate regress to historically distant and sociologically complex inter-relationships. Quite simply, one has to break into the historical sequence at some point, and that point was chosen with reference to the problems in hand. Some things always have to be taken as given — ultimate regress is and probably always will be beyond us, even if reference to it were considered necessary and desirable. Thus we start by examining that cycle which is considered to have most bearing on the phenomenon that we seek to explain, but accept that its own origins figure as elements of 'givenness' in our theories.

A final decision remains, namely about the most appropriate phase with which to begin each cycle. Here we have started with 'structure'. Part One opens with that structure which conditioned educational interaction immediately prior to the development of state systems. It does so for two reasons. Firstly, there is the obvious need, in any study devoted to change, to describe the entity which undergoes modification. And this is what is being done, although it is not the only reason for doing so. The second reason again hinges on the theoretical conviction that the properties of social structures and institutions must be taken as given when analyzing the processes of action and interaction, precisely because of the influence exerted by the former on the latter, within cycles as well as between them.

In other words, the organization of the study literally takes its shape from the theoretical approach adopted. The first three chapters each deal with one phase of the (a)-(b)-(c) sequence, (structural conditioning — interaction — structural elaboration), outlined earlier. The next four chapters follow the same format, although the examination of 'interaction' has been sub-divided because of its bulk. Thus the two parts of the book deal with two consecutive sequences, two continuous cycles, in the history of educational change.

NOTES

1. Cf. May Brodbeck, 'Methodological Individualisms: Definition and Reduction', in May Brodbeck (ed.), *Readings in the Philosophy of the Social Sciences*, New York, 1971, pp. 280-303.

2. Cf. H. R. Wagner, 'Displacement of Scope: A Problem of the Relationship between Small Scale and Large Scale Sociological Theories', *American Journal of Sociology*, Vol. LXIX, No. 6, 1964, pp. 572-74.

3. Ibid., p. 574.

4. J. Rex, 'Typology and Objectivity: A Comment on Weber's Four Sociological Methods', in Arun Sahay (ed.), *Max Weber and Modern Sociology*, London, 1971, p. 24 ff.

5. Ernest Gellner, 'Holism versus Individualism', in May Brodbeck, *Readings in the Philosophy of the Social Sciences*, op. cit., p. 255.

6. Cf. May Brodbeck, 'Methodological Individualisms: Definition and Reduction', op. cit.

7. J. W. N. Watkins, 'Methodological Individualism and Social Tendencies', in May Brodbeck, *Readings in the Philosophy of the Social Sciences*, op. cit., p. 271.

8. Ibid., pp. 270-71.

9. H. R. Wagner, 'Displacement of Scope', op. cit.

10. May Brodbeck, 'Methodological Individualisms: Definition and Reduction', op. cit., p. 299.

11. Ibid., p. 301.

12. J. W. N. Watkins, 'Methodological Individualism and Social Tendencies', op. cit., p. 271.

13. Ernest Gellner, 'Holism versus Individualism', op. cit., p. 268.

14. J. W. N. Watkins, 'Methodological Individualism and Social Tendencies', op. cit., p. 278.

15. May Brodbeck, 'Methodological Individualisms: Definition and Reduction', op. cit., p. 302.

16. Alasdair MacIntyre, 'On the Relevance of the Philosophy of the Social Sciences', *British Journal of Sociology*, Vol. XX, No. 2, 1969, p. 225.

17. Steven Lukes, 'Methodological Individualism Reconsidered', *British Journal of Sociology*, Vol. XIX, No. 2, 1968, pp. 119-29.

18. Ernest Gellner, 'Holism versus Individualism', op. cit., p. 260.

19. See also Leon J. Goldstein, 'The Inadequacy of the Principle of Methodological Individualism', *Journal of Philosophy*, Vol. 53, 1956.

20. J. W. N. Watkins, 'Methodological Individualism and Social Tendencies', op. cit., p. 274.

21. John H. Goldthorpe, 'A Revolution in Sociology?', *Sociology*, Vol. 7, No. 3, 1973, pp. 449-62.

22. Jeff Coulter, 'Decontextualised Meanings: Current Approaches to Verstende Investigations', *Sociological Review*, Vol. 19, No. 3, 1971, p. 314.

23. J. W. N. Watkins, 'Methodological Individualism and Social Tendencies', op. cit., p. 278.

24. Ibid., p. 271.

25. Cf. D. Krech, R. S. Crutchfield and E. L. Ballachey, *Individual in Society*, New York, 1962. In discussing M. Sherif's study on the autokinetic effect in conjunction with more recent work on the social influences upon conformity, Krech, Crutchfield and Ballachey make the following statement: '. . . the amount and kind of conformity induced by group pressure depends upon the nature of the situation . . . Another set of crucial determinants has to do with the nature of

the group – its size, composition, unanimity, extremeness of judgment, coercive force', p. 512.

26. A. Etzioni, *The Active Society*, London, 1968.

27. P. S. Cohen, *Modern Social Theory*, London, 1968, p. 93.

28. J. O. Wisdom, 'Situational Individualism and the Emergent Group-Properties', in R. Borger and F. Cioffi, *Explanations in the Behavioural Sciences*, Cambridge, 1970, p. 294.

29. J. W. N. Watkins, 'Methodological Individualism and Social Tendencies', op. cit., p. 279. Emphasis added.

30. Ernest Gellner, 'Holism versus Individualism', op. cit., p. 267.

31. E.g., Alan Dawe, 'The Two Sociologies', *British Journal of Sociology*, Vol. XXI, No. 2, 1970, pp. 207-18.

32. P. Berger and T. Luckman, *The Social Construction of Reality*, New York, 1966; '*All* social reality is precarious', p. 96.

33. Ernest Gellner, 'Holism versus Individualism', op. cit. Gellner has noted this difficulty: 'The differentia, which as the distinctive component in a complex set of conditions will be worthy of the investigator's attention, may well be something institutional and not psychological. It is perfectly possible, for instance, that there are no psychological differences of any importance between two European countries of widely divergent institutions, and that to explain the differentiation is only possible in sociological not psychological terms. Of course, psychological differences may be significant. The harm done by the kind of Individualism discussed, if taken seriously by investigators, is that it leads to a conviction that such differences must always be present and be significant', p. 267.

34. David Martin, 'The Sociology of Knowledge and the Nature of Social Knowledge', *British Journal of Sociology*, Vol. XIX, No. 3, 1968, p. 339.

35. Ibid., p. 341.

36. G. Runciman, 'What is Structuralism?', in his *Sociology in its Place*, Cambridge, 1970.

Salvador Giner, *Sociology*, London, 1972. 'The question whether one should or should not be a structuralist is meaningless, for all sociologists must have a structural view of the problems they study: social phenomena, taken in isolation, are sociologically meaningless', p. 83.

37. Most of the explanations advanced to account for this are unsatisfactory. They hinge on formulae like, 'Dead-weight of tradition' or 'Laziness' or 'Taken-for-grantedness' or 'Blinkering effect' – all of which beg the question since they do not account for the *object* towards which people hold such orientations. This in turn requires reference to an earlier period where once again structural relations have to be treated as given.

38. M. Ginsberg, 'The Individual and Society', in *The Diversity of Morals*, London, 1956, p. 161.

39. The main works drawn upon in this section are: P. Blau, *Exchange and Power in Social Life*, New York, 1964; Walter Buckley, *Sociology and Modern Systems Theory*, New Jersey, 1967; S. N. Eisenstadt, 'Social Change, Differentiation and Evolution', in N. J. Demerath and R. A. Peterson, *System, Change and Conflict*, New York, 1967; A. W. Gouldner, 'Reciprocity and Autonomy in Functional Theory' in N. J. Demerath and R. A. Peterson, op. cit., pp. 141-69;

and S. N. Eisenstadt 'Institutionalisation and Change', *American Sociological Review*, Vol. 29, No. 2, 1964, pp. 235-47. D. Lockwood, 'Social Integration and Systems Integration', in G. K. Zollschan and H. W. Hirsch, *Explorations in Social Change*, London, 1964.

40. P. S. Cohen, *Modern Social Theory*, op. cit., p. 205.

41. J. Rex, 'Typology and Objectivity: A Comment on Weber's Four Sociological Methods', op. cit., p. 39.

42. P. Blau, *Exchange and Power in Social Life*, op. cit., p. 338.

43. The term 'operations' is used to cover the 'social processesses' and 'social conditions' associated with, and the activities and goals collectively pursued in, institutionalized spheres. These aspects receive different amounts of attention from the authors considered.

44. P. Blau, *Exchange and Power in Social Life*, op. cit. 'In complex social structures with many interdependent, and often interpenetrating substructures, particularly, every movement towards equilibrium precipitates disturbances and disequilibria and thus new dynamic processes', p. 314.

45. Cf. W. L. Wallace, *Sociological Theory*, London, 1969, pp. 41-49.

46. P. Blau, *Exchange and Power in Social Life*, op. cit. Instead of extrapolating structural organization from elementary laws of psychology or interpersonal behaviour, Blau attempts to show how these simpler associative processes give life, through their own dynamics and dialectics to the emergence of complex social organization. To him the problem is to derive complex from simpler processes without committing the reductionist fallacy of ignoring emergent properties in collectivities, institutional sectors, and total societies.

47. Walter Buckley, *Sociology and Modern Systems Theory*, op. cit. Morphogenesis refers 'to those processes which tend to elaborate or change a system's given form, structure or state', p. 58. It is contrasted with morphostasis which refers to those processes in complex system – environment exchanges that tend to preserve or maintain a system's given form, organization or state. 'Just as the concept of negative feedback has provided insight into the mechanisms underlying homeostatic processes, the concept of positive feedback provides insight into the mechanisms underlying structure-building, or morpho-genesis', p. 59.

48. Ernest Gellner, 'Holism versus Individualism', op. cit., p. 263.

49. Walter Buckley, *Sociology and Modern Systems Theory*, op. cit. ' "Social control" is not a separate part of a system – something "set up" by or imposed upon a system – but is inherent in the interrelations and interactions of elements that make up the system', p. 165.

50. These are discussed as 'exigencies' by Lockwood, Eisenstadt and Buckley, whilst they are called 'disturbances', 'disequilibria' or 'imbalances' by Blau and Gouldner.

51. Even those macrosociologists closest to the neo-functionalist tradition make this distinction, the following point of view of Gouldner being typical in this connection. 'It makes a good deal of difference whether "interdependence" and "equilibrium" are treated as undifferentiated attributes, or whether they are viewed as dimensions capable of significant variation', A. W. Gouldner, 'Reciprocity and Autonomy', op. cit. p. 155.

52. A typical example is provided by D. Silverman's *The Theory of Organizations*, London, 1970, where the general term, 'systems approach' is employed as synonymous with 'organic systems theory'.

53. J. O. Wisdom, 'Situational Individualism and the Emergent Group-Properties', op. cit., p. 294.

54. For a clear example of the use of this cycle see S. N. Eisenstadt, 'Social Change, Differentiation and Evolution', op. cit.

55. R. Brown, 'Reply' (to J. O. Wisdom), in R. Borger and F. Cioffi, *Explanations in the Behavioural Sciences*, op. cit., p. 298.

56. R. D. Jessop, 'Exchange and Power in Structural Analysis', *Sociological Review*, Vol. 17, 1969, p. 429.

57. Cf. W. L. Wallace, *Sociological Theory*, op. cit., pp. 48-49.

58. S. N. Eisenstadt, Review of Blau's, *Exchange and Power in Social Life*, *American Journal of Sociology*, Vol. LXXI, No. 3, 1965, p. 333.

59. H. R. Wagner, 'Displacement of Scope', op. cit., p. 583.

60. Loc. cit.

61. R. Bales, *Interaction Process Analysis: A Method for the Study of Small Groups*, Cambridge, Mass., 1950.

62. P. Blau, *Exchange and Power in Social Life*, op. cit., pp. 191-93.

63. A suggestion advanced by May Brodbeck, 'Methodological Individualisms: Definition and Reduction', op. cit., p. 303.

64. J. Rex, 'Typology and Objectivity: A Comment on Weber's Four Sociological Methods', op. cit., pp. 28-29. Emphasis added.

Part I

THE DEVELOPMENT OF STATE EDUCATIONAL SYSTEMS

2 STRUCTURE: Education as Private Enterprise

The countries examined here have long and diverse educational histories. France provides an example of remarkable continuity in education, which mirrored the fortunes of the Catholic Church and its various orders until the late eighteenth century. In the two Protestant countries, England and Denmark,[1] the Reformation represented a single, crucial, and early break in educational history, which was followed by a long period in which new continuities developed. On the other hand, Russia is distinctive in that the history of formal education only dates back to about the beginning of the sixteenth century.[2]

However, our concern here is not to discuss the whole span of educational history or the various forms that instruction has taken in different nations at different times, but instead to examine that *type of formal education which gave way in each country to the development of state systems.* Immediately, this raises questions of definition and problems of identification. The two are closely related, for to define a social phenomenon clearly is to be able to identify occurrences of it unambiguously. Thus the important term to clarify is the concept of a 'state educational system', because for our present purposes the antecedent forms of instruction can be defined negatively in relation to it (i.e. those which do not yet display the characteristics distinctive of state systems). The definition adopted is one which follows the everyday meanings of the words in the phrase 'state educational system'.

Hence a state educational system is considered to be a *nationwide and differentiated collection of institutions devoted to formal education, whose overall control and supervision is at least partly governmental, and whose component parts and processes are related to one another.* It should be noted that this definition stresses both the political and the systemic aspects, and insists that they should be present *together* before education can be considered to constitute a state system. This is important because the appearance of either characteristic *by itself* is not uncommon in educational history. In Russia, for example, the Tsarist bureaucracy exerted control over higher education (part of the Petrine policy of working 'from the top down'[3]), long before the various levels and types of educational establishments were integrated into a system during the latter half of the nineteenth century. Similarly, relations between different establishments or levels can develop independently of central political control, as was sometimes the case in the educational networks operated by the Catholic Church in Europe, where a boy could learn his first letters from the monks and eventually proceed through various schools and seminaries to ordination. Finally, it is equally important to underline the fact that very dissimilar types of education can conform to this basic definition.

Definition of a state system helps to distinguish it from earlier forms of education, but it does not remove all the problems about identifying the type of instruction which *gave way to it*. The definition enables us to say when each nation acquired an educational system, (and almost a century separates their emergence in the four countries), but this only indicates that the nature of education prior to that date should be examined; it does not tell us when to examine it. The problem is that the struggles to reform instruction lasted for varying periods of time in different countries and as they proceeded, education was often being gradually transformed. Thus it is unacceptable simply to examine the form taken by education immediately preceding, (or some fixed number of years before), the date at which the state system was consolidated. Instead it is necessary to go back for variable periods of time in order to understand how this came about in different countries.

It is suggested that these attempts to change education, these processes of interaction which ultimately resulted in the emergence of state systems, must be traced back to their origins. In other words, it is necessary to back-track to the context, both educational and socio-cultural, within which such interaction first developed. Without this it is impossible to explain either the interaction or its consequences, for mention of the very situations that people were trying to change are thus omitted. It is this which provides the guide to identifying those prior forms of education which, in different countries, eventually gave way to state systems. These are located via groups of actors who sought to change them — they are identified as being those which various such parties wanted to transform. Thus the statements of historical actors indicate *what to examine* (that which they sought to change) and *when to investigate it* (immediately before they started to pursue educational change).

Although the statements of historic actors are used for purposes of identification and location, they cannot be employed as a substitute for analysis. The prior educational context is not assumed to be exactly as contemporary actors described it. This is not merely owing to the lack of objectivity, the bias, or the inaccuracy of historical commentators. It is because, as was argued in the introduction, social contexts cannot simply be reduced to what contemporary actors think, or thought about them, for this would be to endorse the 'autonomy of the present tense'. Actors react to the situations in which they find themselves; they may remain unaware of the factors which moulded such situations or of some of their properties. These socio-educational contexts must be investigated independently, and in doing so the sociological task is not just to record how they were viewed by people at the time but also to conceptualize how this broader context structured the actual situation in which each group found itself vis à vis education, helped them to view it in a particular way, and led them to seek change. The rest of the chapter will be devoted to this task.

These considerations mean that we shall be looking at education and society at different dates for the countries concerned, because we will concentrate upon similar social processes rather than the same historical epoch. Indeed, when the relevant forms of education are identified along the lines described above, they are found to span a substantial period of time between the various countries. Hence it is the educational and social structures of late eighteenth century England which will be compared with those of France in the 1750s, and of Russia at the end of the seventeenth century. Denmark, which underwent an exceptionally protracted period of educational conflict before the development of its state system, must be examined no later than the beginning of the seventeenth century, and perhaps slightly earlier.

At this point it might be objected, on one of two grounds, that the task is wrongly conceived because it does not really compare like with like. The first type of objection might consist in arguing that some of the factors which are known to be important in educational change, (e.g. mode and level of economic production, nature of social stratification, or type of political organization) vary considerably in the four social contexts to be examined. Because such factors are not controlled, (they are not present, or absent, or the same for all), the contexts themselves are very different. It might then be argued that any educational changes observed later on simply reflect these initial variations. Such an argument would be unanswerable were the problem in hand the examination, for example, of economic influences upon educational development. It is not; on the contrary, the aim is precisely to see whether general sociological propositions about educational change can be formulated in the presence of such variations. The existence of socio-economic differences cannot therefore be used as a basis from which to prejudge the outcome of this theoretical undertaking.

Exactly the same criticism could be made from the point of view of education. It could be argued that the substantive differences between education in, say, Romanov Russia and post-Reformation Denmark are so great that subsequent educational change simply mirrors these diverse origins. This indeed appears to be the underlying assumption of many educationalists who content themselves with studying the working out over time of national traditions in instruction. From this perspective comparative education is reduced to a description of different practices and procedures in various countries. Any attempt to provide explanations is abandoned or, even less acceptably, pseudo-explanations are advanced in terms of dubious variables like national character. The reply to this sort of criticism is similar to the one given above. If it is possible to develop general theories about education, then they have to be ones which embrace cross-cultural differences, for this is the nature of the subject-matter about which we are trying to theorize. There appear to be no grounds or precedents in the history of science for deciding *in advance* that particular phenomena are so intractable as to defy explanation.

FORMAL AND SUBSTANTIVE DIFFERENCES IN EDUCATION

The much more important point here is that substantive differences in national education, though very great, do not preclude the existence of formal similarities between them: and it is possible to theorize about the latter despite differences in the former. This is exactly what Max Weber did when showing how the structural similarities obtaining between the societies of ancient China and India had the same effect of restraining innovative processes in both countries, despite the great substantive differences in culture between the two at that time. It is by referring to such formal similarities (in the relations maintaining between education and social structure in all four countries) that it is possible to theorize about general effects on interaction patterns. Neither in Weber's historical studies nor in the present case does this mean that substantive variations are seen as unimportant influences upon action. In both it is merely that their effects co-exist with the patternings conditioned by common structural factors.

In the countries considered one feature at least was shared by the different types of education which prevailed in the antecedent periods already identified. *In all of them those who controlled education also owned it*, in the sense of providing its physical facilities and supplying its teaching personnel. Moreover, in each country this ownership was limited to a very restricted section of the population. In all, the overwhelming tendency was for educational control to be concentrated in the hands of a single group — but the educationally dominant group came from different parts of these societies. Each one had a virtual monopoly of the educational resources upon which its control rested and all appeared to be concerned, though to differing degrees, to protect their dominant position in instruction.

It is beyond the scope of the present study to explain why education was dominated by the Catholic Church and its component religious orders in mid-eighteenth century France, the Orthodox Church and its associated Brotherhoods in late seventeeth century Russia, the Lutheran Church in Denmark by mid-sixteenth century, and the Anglican Church in England at the end of the eighteenth century. Although the religious elites owned and dominated education in the four nations studied, control by this particular institutional sphere is not universal, and was, for example, the preserve of the political elite of Tokugawa Japan in the corresponding period, the late eighteenth century. How these situations came about, why dominant groups were based on different social institutions in different societies, why they valued educational control and were prepared to make considerable investment of resources to obtain it, and why they defined the content of instruction in particular ways – the answers to all these questions could only be provided by historical analysis. Only by the same kind of analysis could one explain why this situation proved so lasting in Europe, why challenges to educational control were so slow to develop, and why governing elites consistently tolerated the independence of education from the polity and its domination by others. Speculatively four factors could be suggested as important for leaving the ecclesiastical ownership groups unopposed for several centuries. Firstly, in the feudal and post-feudal periods, education was essentially a minority activity, involving a small proportion of the population, and having little effect on the majority of institutionalized activities, e.g. ascriptive systems of stratification and agrarian or mercantilist modes of production. Certainly these and other institutional operations could be obstructed by socialization practices and the universalization of religious values, but the target of any organized opposition to this was the Churches themselves as the defenders of these symbolic systems, rather than the clergy as the group dominating *formal* education. Secondly, the slow development of relatively autonomous groups in the cities of medieval Europe in conjunction with the powerful influence the Churches exerted to legitimate their educational hegemony, probably delayed the emergence of opposition. Various sections of society engaged in different forms of self-help which were often expressly defined as being other than 'education', the preserve of the clergy. Thus the secular professions slowly began to develop rudimentary training and certification procedures, urban craftsmen the apprenticeship system, the legal body its own centres and the military its own forms of officer training. Thirdly, some important institutional areas, including the polity and governmental bureaucracy, often derived certain benefits from religious education. Wherever and whenever compatibility prevailed, the polity received a free supply of adequately trained statesmen, of dynastic legitimation, and of some degree of popular socialization. When public administration began to be differentiated from the royal courts from the twelfth century onwards, it initially was wholly advantageous to gain the services of classically trained clerics whose celibacy precluded the acquisition of hereditary rights to posts. While this situation lasted, to seek to control education would have been an expensive and unnecessary luxury. Finally, some allowance should be made for the stabilizing effects of small transactions between the Churches and other elites, for these would have strengthened the ecclesiastical position in education, if only by removing some of its potential critics. Perhaps the clearest example of this is the Elizabethan transaction between State and reformed Church which impinged on the field of education.

Such factors are only tentatively advanced as reasons for the endurance of religious domination. These questions properly fall outside the scope of this study since their answers require a detailed analysis of institutional activities and elite goals during earlier centuries. The facts of religious ownership have to be taken as given here, for it is not they themselves, but their consequences for subsequent educational change which are of interest.

EDUCATION AND SOCIETY: OWNERSHIP, MONO-INTEGRATION AND SUBORDINATION

The fact that in all these countries educational control rested with a dominant ownership group has a series of important implications which will be examined in turn. Each of them is universal for they stem from formal characteristics shared by the four types of education, regardless of their substantive differences. First and foremost, the very existence of a dominant ownership group meant that education was related to the social structure in similar ways. All the other implications follow from this — for it conditions interaction and affects the processes required to change education. However, many of these consequences are far from obvious since they result from emergent properties of the socio-educational structure. It is these which will now be examined and traced through to their influence upon patterns of interaction and processes of change.

The fact that a particular group virtually monopolized educational ownership meant in turn that education was firmly linked to only one part of the total social structure. This part was, of course, the social institution with which the dominant group was associated, i.e. the institutional sphere in whose role structure they held positions (as ordained clergymen, priests, members of Brotherhoods etc.), with whose operations they were involved (by executing the obligations associated with these positions), and whose goals they helped to define and to attain. Another way of putting this is to say that education only had relations of interdependence with one other social institution.

The term 'interdependence' indicates that there is an interchange of resources and services between two social institutions. In all four countries interdependence involved the same thing — a flow of physical, human and financial resources from the ownership sphere to education and the counter flow educational services. The latter was made up of those kinds of educational outputs (people socialized into the values and having learned the skills) which were of use in the other institutional sector. Where Churches constituted the ownership groups this meant that those undergoing instruction emerged with a certain level of religious knowledge and at least a formal commitment to religious values, whilst some among them would have acquired the skills necessary for direct recruitment into the religious organization. (Similarly, in cases like Japan where the political elite was the dominant group, it received educational outputs which facilitated political socialization, political recruitment, and political integration). Interdependence between social institutions does not imply that this situation is equally advantageous for both parties, nor does it involve the assumption that the 'interchange' between them was freely determined. Instead, as we shall see, this is closely associated with differences in power between the two parties which emerge in their relationship. Finally, to talk of interdependence is not to argue that it necessarily contributes to the persistence of the two parts concerned or that of the wider social system.

In complex social structures there are a great number of cross-cutting interdependencies between the various institutional orders — indeed this is the principal reason for their complexity. Although in the countries examined their social structures displayed varying degrees of complexity, in all of them education was only related to one other social institution because of the monopolistic character of ownership displayed in all four. The term *'mono-integration'* will be used to indicate this common structural characteristic. Mono-integration thus refers to one of the possible relationships which could be maintained between an institutional sphere (education) and all the others that exist at a particular stage of social differentiation. Potentially any given institution could be related to all the others, to some of them, or to none at all; mono-integration is the term used when education is related to only one of these. This is not, therefore, a property of any institution as such but a characteristic of the relations *between* institutions. This kind of relational characteristic is also a group variable; it is something displayed by collectivities of a certain size but not by their component members, though it is a consequence of their actions. Its subsequent influence will be seen to be that of an emergent property.

When used adjectively, mono-integration implies that education is only related in this way to one other institutional sphere, i.e. it signifies that A (education) is only interdependent with B, but *not* that B in turn is only interdependent with A. Finally, it should be noted that this definition of mono-integration excludes cases where the *consequences* of operations conducted independently in one institutional order prove beneficial for another, as no interchange has taken place to ensure these services. The existence, however, of such adventitious benefits constitutes an important structural variable which has to be introduced into the analysis later on.

The fact that education was a mono-integrated institution in all four countries carries with it two major implications which will now be discussed in turn — the first is of concern to education itself, and the second to all other social institutions apart from the one with which education is integrated through ownership.

Effects on Education

Recently several sociologists have argued that there are certain things about mono-integration which affect the nature of the relationship between the two parts involved. As Gouldner has rightly argued, (in connection with a broader systems framework which does not concern us here), interdependence between two elements does not necessarily imply reciprocity in the interchanges between them.[4] Leaving aside the importance Gouldner attaches to reciprocity for persistence of a structural relationship, he advances two extremely significant conditions under which imbalance in exchange can arise and be sustained. Firstly, one part can continue to benefit from another without fully reciprocating, if it can constrain services from the former, and secondly, if no third party with which A and B are both integrated is present to operate as a compensatory mechanism controlling imbalance. In mono-integration there are of course no such third parties to perform this policing role. Thus there is some reason for anticipating that lack of reciprocity will characterize the interchanges between the two institutions involved.

If such imbalances do arise they are important because not only does one party end up serving the other for little or no return, but correspondingly it also suffers a loss of autonomy. Low autonomy means that it is difficult to pursue goals which have been arrived at within that sphere; instead, institutional operations are defined externally by the party which constrains its services. It is not interdependence as such which results in loss of autonomy but rather, as Blau has argued[5] the emerging capacity of one part to direct and organize the other in accordance with its own operations. This is rather similar to Gouldner's point about constraining services by power, but as will be seen there are differences.

The sub-category of integrative relationships where severe imbalances do occur will be termed *subordination* and defined as the case in which *one social institution has low autonomy for the internal determination of its operations because of its dependence on the other*. Again it should be noted that subordination is a characteristic of relationships between institutions and is not the property of any one social sphere. So far it has been argued that in relations of mono-integration one of the parties is likely to be subordinate, but this of course indicates nothing about which party this is likely to be. To determine this in particular cases, both Gouldner and Blau rightly recommend an examination of power differentials between the parts. By following this procedure it may be possible to make certain generalizations about the position of education in mono-integrated relationships.

However, Gouldner's treatment of power differentials has the deficiency of treating power as a generalized capacity for control and thus subordination cannot be held to emerge directly from the interdependence of two social institutions.[6] Instead, such an outlook invites a general investigation of the distribution of power between substructures in society. On the other hand, Blau's discussion of power differentials,[7] as themselves emerging from interdependence, is directly applicable to the analysis of mono-integrated institutions. For here the subordination of one party is held to result from its dependence on another for the supply of resources or services. When A contributes to the operations of B this represents some loss of autonomy for A and is the price it 'pays' for continued supplies from B. The more dependent A is on the supplies B provides, the greater the services A has to give B in order to secure them, and the bigger the loss of A's autonomy to determine the nature of its own activities. Whereas Gouldner sees power differentials as making for imbalance in interchange, to Blau the process is exactly the reverse and the latter accords better with the relations which emerge between education and its suppliers in the period under examination.

As a mono-integrated institution education was always the subordinate partner in the relationship because of its total dependence on the flow of resources from the other institution. Education has high material and physical resource requirements for its operations and these make it vulnerable to its source of supply, which is unitary where education is mono-integrated. Historically there appears to be a built-in, short-run, asymmetry between the dependence of educational operations on resources and the reliance of those supplying them on educational services. Quite simply, the operations of another institution can do without new educational outputs longer than education can function without resources. Thus the former can obstruct the latter more than education can impede other spheres. This fundamental source of imbalance in the relationship between education and its suppliers was translated into differences in power and reflected in lack of educational autonomy. Thus had those working within the educational field attempted to assert any autonomy, had they sought to redefine its intakes, processes or outputs, they could swiftly have been checked by withdrawal of pay, closure of buildings, changes in personnel and the use of a multiplicity of sanctions against them, including their own redeployment. Hence it is not simply that the dominant group's ownership of educational resources gave them control over instruction, but that the dependence of education precluded it from ever threatening this non-reciprocal relationship in the absence of alternative suppliers of resources.

The most important consequence to derive from the subordinate status of education in the periods considered is that *educational change could not be initiated endogenously*. In other words, the activities of teachers, pupils, dons and others engaged in instruction could not be an important source of educational innovation and change because of their stringent control by the dominant group. This is not to imply a lack of desire for change on the part of such groups — it is not necessary to assume this when arguing that constraints existed to prevent the realization of any aims of this kind.

Change could not be initiated endogenously because *subordination never involves lower autonomy than when it occurs in a relationship of mono-integration*. Dependence on a single supplier of resources makes education extremely vulnerable and highly responsive to control by the ownership group. The latter, who invest in instruction only because they require some particular kind of educational output which they perceive as essential to their (religious, political etc.,) operations, do all they can to get value for their money. The dominant group defines education in relation to its goals and monitors it closely to ensure that it serves these purposes. Close control means weak boundaries between education and the institution with which the dominant group is associated. It is reflected in a low level of differentiation between the two institutions.

Typically this means that there is no distinctively educational role structure, but instead an overlapping of roles between both institutions: hence the combined roles of priest-teacher, samurai-teacher etc. Those working in the educational field in no sense constituted a relatively autonomous professional body but instead could be manipulated by religious or political sanctions, depending on the nature of the ownership group. Typically too there were no distinctively educational processes, for the content of instruction, the definition and the management of knowledge as well as teaching methods, were 'confused' with the values and norms of the dominant group. Hence the inter-related 'Bun and Bu', the military and literary skills of Tokugawa Japan; whence the equation between theology and knowledge in much of Europe, and the use of catechisation and disputation as methods of teaching and learning. Correspondingly, educated persons acquired a set of skills whose limited relevance encouraged their employment in the dominant group's institutional sphere.

Taken together, these consequences of subordination and mono-integration — extremely low educational autonomy and little internal definition of goals — have further implications for the explanation of educational change. They mean that *such explanations will focus on social interaction outside the educational field and among groups of actors who are not employed or engaged in it.* Unlike the present day, when any explanation of change would be incomplete if it neglected the independent contribution of professional groups of teachers and organized groups of students, large scale educational transformation in this earlier period can be examined in terms of exogenous influences without loss of explanatory power.

Effects on Other Institutions

So far some of the consequences of mono-integration and subordina-

tion have been traced through for education itself, but of equal importance are their repercussions upon other social institutions. The fact that
education is integrated with only one institutional sphere has significant
consequences for others, for it indicates that they are not being directly
served by education. However, this does not mean that all social
institutions, other than the one in which the ownership group is
embedded, are in the same position vis-à-vis the education available in
that society. On the contrary, it seems clear that the nature of their
own institutional operations mediates the impact of education, as
defined by the dominant group, upon them. In other words the activities of those other groups help to determine their compatibility with
existing education. Potentially there are three major categories into
which other institutions can fall in these respects, although each one
need not be represented wherever and whenever education is found in a
mono-integrated and subordinate relationship.

Firstly, then, there may be some institutional spheres which
although not directly served by education are unimpeded by it. This is
not to say that they would not have been more efficient, better
adjusted, etc., were the available educational outputs of relevance to
them. It is simply that the existence of structurally induced strains or
impediments is dependent upon the *actual* obstruction of operations,
not *ideal* operative efficiency. Such an institution is neither helped nor
hindered by the form of education that the dominant group provides.
For example, it neither receives pre-trained, pre-socialized graduates nor
does it miss them and find itself confronting a recruitment crisis in
terms of lack of suitable people with appropriate skills and values.

Some might object to the existence of such a category on the
grounds that in any social system no institution can dispense with
cultural reinforcement (unless extreme cultural pluralism or social disintegration are posited) and therefore that the absence of positive
educational services is not synonymous with the lack of negative ones.
Historically, however, formal educational institutions have not been the
major agencies for the transmission of social values. Magico-religious
domination of formal culture together with family, community, and
guild control over socialization and occupational induction meant that
education played a limited role in normative conservation, transmission,
or elaboration. It might still be argued that other parts of society
require a negative service from education, namely that the latter does
not undermine their form and content, if the two are to co-exist. For
instance, a stratification system would be incompatible with a form of

instruction which opposed discrimination and hierarchy. Although insisting on the *logical* possibility of educational neutrality towards a particular sphere (i.e. of educational values being different from those of certain other institutions, without them in any sense undermining the latter, by denying the legitimacy of their operations), in practice it is not necessary to refute this objection. Cases in which such normative support is demonstrably present can be assimilated to the second category, outlined below, and cases where normative undermining clearly does occur belong in category three.

It is not of course possible to determine analytically which institutional spheres are most likely to be represented in this neutral category. This varies jointly with the nature of the given institution at any time, and the compatibility of education (as designed by the dominant group) with its operations. Sometimes even those institutions which historically and comparatively have shown most reliance on educational services have occupied this neutral category because of variations in the above respects. Hence it is not difficult to find examples of religious and legal subsystems or even forms of bureaucracy which at different times have been little impeded by lack of educational support. In general these relations of neutrality have to be identified by comparing educational outputs with institutional operations at any given time. Only occasionally does one find supplementary evidence, like the townsmen and artisans of early eighteenth century Russia petitioning the Tsarist government for a reprieve from scholarization because book learning was irrelevant to their activities:[8] their only objection to prevailing education being that they were forced to undergo it.

Those sectors of society which fall into this neutral category are not expected to be loci of educational change. Since they are neither served nor obstructed by education they are, in structural terms, neutral towards it. In other words, the structural relations between these institutions and education are neither ones of strain nor of complementarity. Because of this there are no structural factors which predispose these sectors to be loci of support of or opposition to the prevailing form of education. This, however, clearly does not prevent actors associated with these institutions from participating in educational conflict, either in pursuit of change or in defence of the status quo. It is simply to argue that such interaction on their part is not structurally conditioned by the relationships discussed.

The second category of institutions consists of those mentioned earlier which derive *adventitious benefits* from it. They do so exclusively because their own operations happen to be facilitated by the educational outputs offered, but determined elsewhere. Again it is impossible to decide analytically which sectors of society will fall in this category — for the receipt of adventitious benefits often depends upon an accidental compatibility between the definition of education and operational requirements. For example, legal systems, based upon Roman law, were quite well served by the classical education conducted by the most important Catholic teaching Orders in Europe.

Sometimes, though not necessarily, this coincidence is explained by inter-dependencies between the adventitious beneficiary and the single institution with which education is integrated. Here A (Education) is mono-integrated with B (an institution which subordinates it), but B is also integrated with C (the adventitious beneficiary). Here C is served indirectly by A as it does not engage in interchange with it. However, this only arises where B, which subordinates education, is itself highly dependent upon C because of an imbalance of exchange between *them*. Then C may negotiate with B for a certain type of educational service. The relations between the Anglican Church (B) and the political elite (C) were of this type in eighteenth century England. Because of its erastian position, the governing elite could gain important amounts of political socialization, legitimation and recruitment from Anglican education. In other words, because of its legal dependence upon the State, the established Church defined educational inputs, processes and outputs to provide some political services alongside the predominantly religious ones. These included an intake policy replicating the prevailing form of social stratification, a tuition process reproducing politico-cultural values, and an output of larger numbers than the Church itself could reabsorb, but who were acceptable for state service.[9]

Institutions in this category will tend to be loci of 'support' for the prevailing form of education and hence for its controllers. They will be areas from which support is forthcoming because benefits are received while no investment has to be made for these services. Because they gain something desirable for nothing, they seek to maintain the situation which gives this 'bonus'. Again this is only a conditional influence and in any case such pressures are tenuous since compatibility can be reduced over time.

Responsive to a variety of influences which lie outside the scope of this analysis, each institutional sphere is subject to changes in its operations which can render them less compatible with existing educational outputs. Providing education remains unchanged, such sectors will then decline in importance as loci of support. On the other hand the operations of such a sphere may remain unaltered but those of the institution subordinating education may undergo modification. In this case its elite will modify instruction in accordance with its changed operations. These new services or outputs could now be less advantageous to the previous beneficiaries. (However still further institutional sectors might profit from the educational changes and thus enter this supportive category for the first time). If either of these processes occurs, there will be a tendency for the institution involved to move out of the category of adventitious beneficiaries, either to become neutral or to enter the third category.

This third category consists of those institutions which are neither integrated with education nor served by it, but whose operations are clearly *obstructed* by educational outputs because they are incompatible with them. The precise nature of the obstruction can be very varied. It may be that those associated with a given institution require instruction but for some reason are denied access, that the values and skills disseminated are irrelevant or harmful to their activities, or that the graduates who are produced are deficient in either quantitative or qualitative terms. Sometimes an institutional sphere will be impeded in several different ways simultaneously as was the case with the expanding industrial economy in early nineteenth century England. The entrepreneurial elite had limited access to secondary and higher education due to social and religious discrimination, the Test Acts erecting a barrier to dissenters; the classical nature of secondary instruction was irrelevant to capitalist development while the catechistic nature of popular elementary instruction was an inadequate form of economic socialization for workers and was considered to endanger private property.[10] In sum, those leaving elementary school did not have the right values, those leaving secondary school did not have the right skills, and those leaving higher education had neither the right skills nor the right values: at all levels the wrong social groups had access and those most in need of instruction or of being instructed were debarred.

There is no reason of course why there should only be a single institution in this category (or either of the preceding ones) at any given time. Indeed, historically, it seems more common to find several different spheres simultaneously suffering from obstructions of varying degrees of severity. In Russia, for example, at the time of Peter I's accession, the very limited education provided by the Orthodox Church and Brotherhoods meant that *military* operations were impeded by lack of technical competence and training – the effective core of the army being made up of 'troops of foreign formation'[11] while the Streltsy regiments were unfitted for serious fighting and unreliable in terms of political loyalty; *civil bureaucracy* suffered at all levels from lack of training among officials and clerks due to the circumscribed religious definition imposed in the sole source of civic instruction, the Slavonic-Greek-Latin Academy at Moscow, and policy implementation was impeded by the absence of a cadre of trained jurists; *commercial activities* were obstructed by the Byzantine use of letters of the alphabet for the notation of figures which made accounting difficult; and finally, the *Nobility* in its search to become a polite European aristocracy of leisure was blocked by serious theology taught through dead languages when its goal required secular frivolity conveyed in French. This example also illustrates the important point that the parties jointly obstructed by a given form of education need not be allies but can have interests in complete opposition to one another.

When considered comparatively, different institutions are found in this category for the various countries discussed. In England, for example, it was the developing industrial economy and associated system of class stratification; in France the post-revolutionary polity and governmental bureaucracy. These cases will be examined in detail in Chapter 3, but in terms of the present argument what these social institutions have in common is a structured predisposition to be loci of opposition to the respective forms of education available in those societies. However, before examining supportive and oppositional activities stemming from these different loci, it is first necessary to examine the influence that mono-integration and subordination exert upon processes of educational change.

Effects on Processes of Educational Change

It is here that the significance of the subordinate status of education begins to be clarified. If education possessed some autonomy for the internal determination of its operations, then in theory change could be initiated, structure differentiated, and services diversified to offset a plurality of strains. Further relationships of interdependence could thus be established with a variety of institutional operations without repudiating the initial integration. However, the lack of autonomy implicit in subordination means that such solutions are precluded. Earlier it was argued that very low autonomy means that very little change could be initiated endogenously. It has the further consequence that transactions cannot take place between internal professional groups and external interest groups associated with institutions in category three. The profession lacks the independence and power to negotiate directly with the exterior. Thus the effect of subordination for those seeking change is that *instead of direct transactions taking place with education these have to be conducted indirectly with the party which has subordinated it.*

This is a result of the structural relations in which education is embedded. In this particular network of relationships some parts affect others more than they in turn are affected by them — the existing form of education induces strains which arise from the incompatibility between it and the operations of other institutional spheres, yet education itself is only *directly* affected by its subordinator. Because of this, attempts to overcome strains and remove obstacles will be directed towards the single institution with which education is integrated for it is *this which is* the source of obstruction. The ownership group has moulded education to serve its operations alone, and only by interacting with its members can the definition of instruction be changed.

However, these structural relations of subordination and mono-integration exert a further influence upon the type of process most significant for transforming education during this period. In other words, we will seek to demonstrate that they affect the *kind of transactions* taking place between the dominant group and those seeking educational change, and that one form of transaction is vastly more important than others in accounting for large-scale transformations.

So far it has been argued that the major source of opposition to existing education will originate from the category of obstructed institutions. This is because the definition given to instruction by the group which provides it severely hinders the attainment of other goals. Now the dominant ownership group's heavy investment in education is an acknowledgement of its indispensibility. Because ownership and control are exclusively theirs, they can define and monitor instruction to suit their own ends. Whatever impediments the relevant inputs, processes, and outputs constitute for other sections of society, they represent the form and content of education that its owners want. This is not tantamount to saying that this type of education optimally meets their requirements, only that this is the type that they *think* serves them best. If this is a serious impediment to others, it means that other groups require a very different kind of instruction. In other words *those suffering the greatest obstruction therefore need the greatest changes in education in order to remove these obstacles.*

Yet the magnitude of the changes required to relieve existing strains precludes their resolution by certain processes. Since the ownership group already has exactly the kind of education it (thinks it) wants for its particular operations, any *major* change away from this definition would be contrary to its declared interests. That these interests are both conscious and extremely strong cannot be doubted considering the resources that have voluntarily been laid out to meet them. Thus major educational change would represent an equally major shift away from their ideal — a move which if fully accomplished would place the ownership group itself in category three! Change of this magnitude is therefore the last thing that will be freely conceded; but if it does not occur, severe obstruction continues for other institutions. *The net result is that those concerned to introduce the most far reaching educational changes are least able to do so by peaceful negotiation with the controlling ownership group.* And the minor changes which might be produced by a process of transaction are inadequate for resolving the strains experienced in the impeded sectors. Thus the only way large-scale educational change can be brought about is by imposing it, not through voluntary negotiation, but via a *process of involuntary coercion.*

When negotiation is precluded, strains are only resolved by one party overcoming the other and thus removing the source of obstruction, which otherwise continues with all its negative consequences. Thus large-scale change only occurs if the existing structural relations are destroyed, and replaced by new ones. Any major changes in the form and content of instruction, observed during this period, are therefore expected to follow from equally fundamental changes in educational control. For inputs, processes and outputs will be modified to reinforce the operations of other institutional spheres only when the old relationships have been destroyed.

It is not that this is the sole process of educational change — the argument is more limited and maintains that this is the only process leading to *macroscopic* change. Our case will be strengthened if good reasons can be given to account for other processes leading to nothing but minor modifications which leave the existing definition of education largely intact. There appear to be two such alternative processes and these will be examined in turn.

Firstly, there is negotiation itself which, although precluded as a method for resolving the greatest strains, may still be open to parties seeking lesser modifications. But this is precisely the point. A party which suffers some hindrance but not severe obstruction can increase its rate of exchange with the sector subordinating instruction (or may initiate this for the first time) to produce a change in education such that it becomes more compatible with both sets of operations. However, this mutual compatibility does set a limit on the amount of change which can result from such a process. Again this is because the institution subordinating education is getting the maximum support possible from it and would begin to lose this if major modifications took place. Thus the changes produced by negotiation are not far-reaching, for by definition such negotiations are conducted with the ownership group as the controlling group. The latter will cease trading at the point where the benefits it receives would be bought at the price of damaging itself educationally. If the modifications in instruction which can be transacted before this point is reached are considered satisfactory, then small changes are clearly all that was wanted anyway. If this is not the case, negotiation breaks down and the other party must seek change through a different process — and one which is not based on the assumption of continuity in control.

Secondly, there are the changes that the dominant group itself chooses to introduce into education, either because of changes in its operations or in the pursuit of the optimal educational formula for its purposes. Although these may be extremely important they do not involve changes in structural relations. By definition they occur without a change in control and do nothing (unless fortuitously) to alleviate strains and pressures for radical educational transformation from other parts of society. Furthermore, such modifications as are introduced will represent adjustments to, and not reformulations of, the definition of instruction. This is partly because so much has been invested in legitimating a given definition that total reformulations will be avoided, but largely because it is the same general type of operations (religious, political etc.) which continue to be served and education will mirror their continuities.

So far in discussing structural influences upon patterns of support and opposition and upon processes of change we have been highlighting various aspects of systems integration with only the most sketchy indications of their significance for social interaction. It is, of course, an underlying assumption of this study that structural influences only exert their effects through people. Thus a complete discussion of the importance attaching to mono-integration and subordination involves an examination of how such factors condition interaction. Equally vital to the explanation of macroscopic educational change is an analysis of the independent contribution made by social action, (i.e. action free from structural conditioning).

Structural Relations Conditioning Educational Interaction

The fact that education is a mono-integrated institution creates a distinction between the ownership group and all others. Its implication is that there is only one group in society which is *assured* of educational services, whereas *all* the rest are not. Since, as has been seen, this situation does not mean that no other groups actually receive such services, this distinction is based on differential capacity to control and not upon differential rates of benefit. The existence of mono-integration thus dichotomizes the population vis-à-vis education. It structures two quasi groups – the first consisting of all those associated with the ownership sphere, and thus possessing some capacity to determine the nature of educational outputs; the second of all groups not so associated and thus deprived of this capacity. But this constitutes the limits of the structural influence of mono-integration, considered in isolation from other aspects of the relations between education and society. It indicates nothing about the capacity of this quasi-group to determine educational output, beyond the fact that this exists to some unspecified degree.[12] This is clarified, however, when the subordinate position of education is considered in conjunction with mono-integration. Since subordination derives from education's dependence on another institution for the supply of resources or services, then those groups associated with that institution have power over education since they alone can determine its operations. When subordination coincides with mono-integration, this *structures a single educationally dominant group in society* – all other groups are dominated because this power *is not based* on the receipt of educational benefits, but on the supply of indispensible resources to education.

Two important implications follow from this. Firstly, it is obvious that some of the educationally dominated groups will themselves be dominant in other parts of society, because the ownership group only embraces the elite of one particular institution. Perhaps less obviously, some of the educationally dominated may constitute the overall socio-political elite, for during this period there is no theoretical or empirical reason whatsoever to suppose that the educational ownership group occupies or shares this position. In other words, it is unlikely that the dichotomy of educational roles between dominant and dominated corresponds to the more general social division into elites and masses.

Secondly, since domination is based on the supply of resources to education, then their abundance, availability, and distribution in society provide a key to the security of the ownership group's control over education. Maximum security coincides with monopolization of such resources, although this does not guarantee it since coercion can be brought to bear by dominated groups.

In itself the structuring of these two quasi groups in terms of possession or lack of educational control indicates little about their interests, organization and interaction. That only one group has the capacity to control educational processes does not necessarily entail an opposition of latent interests between the two quasi groups. For this would involve the assumption that all groups at all times have an interest in, and see advantages deriving from, the control of education – and historically this has simply not been the case. Yet it would appear mistaken to assume that the relationships which develop between members of the two quasi groups simply vary unsystematically with empirical conditions. Instead it is argued that the compatibility or incompatibility between the definition of education and different kinds of operations, affects the interests, organization, and interaction of different institutional groups. Although these are only conditional effects it seems that the nature of the structural influence is such that *it is unlikely that the two quasi-groups, defined by possession or lack of educational control, will 'convert' into opposing interest groups*.

It was shown earlier that the relation between the kind of education supplied in a society and the type of operations conducted in different institutional spheres led to variations in the objective fit between them – thus producing strains as well as complementarities. While the existence of such factual strains and tensions constitutes objective obstructions to operations of various institutions, they exert an influence on interaction only because of the ways in which such factors structure action-situations for different groups. Incompatibilities and complementarities are transmitted to different social roles in different parts of the social structure. For those occupying such positions they will be experienced as frustrating or rewarding situations. As was argued in Chapter 1, rewards do not compel support nor does frustration dictate antagonism to its source. Nevertheless, although structural factors do not force anyone to do anything, they do render certain actions and interpretations distinctly advantageous, and others correspondingly disadvantageous.

Three categories of institution, all unintegrated with education, have been distinguished whose operations are affected differently by the education available. In the first are those whose activities are neither impeded nor reinforced by the existing definition of instruction, and thus the groups associated with them are not predisposed by structural influences either to support or to oppose the dominant educational group. This is because the roles they occupy and the tasks to be accomplished by occupants of these positions are unaffected by the prevailing form of education. Thus, for example, the Muscovite artisanat of the early eighteenth century recruited from its own ranks and transmitted its own skills — the frustrations experienced by craftsmen were due to the market situation and to political control, not to Orthodox or Tsarist educational activities. If such influences were deterministic and if all institutions fell into this category, then the educationally dominant group would remain totally unopposed (and unsupported too), as groups associated with other spheres would remain educationally inactive. However, there are several reasons why such groups may nonetheless engage in educational action. Firstly, some or all of their component members may endorse a normative system which places a high value on education regardless of its instrumental irrelevance to the operations with which they are involved. Secondly, while the available form of education does not impede present operations, groups closely associated with operational management may foresee or seek changes which would require educational services. Thirdly, in an institution whose associated groups are highly stratified, the 'managerial group' may remain uninterested in education but subordinate groups could perceive it as a means of enhancing their position. Nevertheless, it is groups associated with institutions in the other two categories who are expected to play the most important part in educational interaction.

Where institutions derive adventitious benefits from education, structural influences predispose groups associated with them to support the prevailing type of education and thus to buttress the position of those dominating it. Actors engaged in different aspects of institutional operations receive a variety of rewards. Although the nature of these may vary from institution to institution, most adventitious beneficiaries find the tasks of recruitment and replacement to be problem-free. Recruitment is facilitated by the availability of suitable candidates, training is shortened by the prior acquisition of relevant skills, and occupational socialization is made easier by antecedent acceptance of appropriate values. Apart from this, rewards might also consist, for example, in public legitimation of institutional activities, which will further the attainment of operational goals. Here roles concerned with external relations will be satisfying and the efforts made by their holders will show a good return.

Nevertheless, the values endorsed by such a group, or simply their ignorance, can lead either to an underestimation of the objective advantages derived from this type of education, or to a repudiation of them despite their contribution being correctly perceived. However, groups associated with these institutions are in a different *situation* from those in the neutral category, for here endorsement of educational values opposed to those of the dominant group carries opportunity costs. Oppositional activities risk harming the operations of the institutions with which these groups are associated by depriving them of the current 'cost-free' service received. Thus even if the advantageous character of available education had passed unperceived, it may well become evident at precisely the point when the dominant group is most threatened and other operations begin to suffer through attrition of adventitious benefits. Thus, for example, the English Tory Party's rather half-hearted support of Anglican educational domination in the first part of the nineteenth century (until the 1860s), increased throughout the remainder of the century: the benefits of religious instruction for social integration and popular quietism were fully acknowledged just as educational control gradually began to pass out of the hands of the traditional religious ownership group.

All these structural effects condition interaction through the influence they exert on the action situation. To deduce that such groups have a high probability of playing a supportive role in educational interaction, it is only necessary to assume that substrata do not support too great an incompatibility between their interests and their values — that the majority of their members do not bite the hand that feeds them. Even where the adventitious nature of educational benefits appears too tenuous to certain groups, these are more likely to seek greater interdependence by negotiating with the dominant group than to oppose it directly.

From the point of view of structural influences, groups associated with institutions whose operations are hindered by the education available find themselves in situations which are the reverse of those just discussed. It is obviously in the interest of the dominant educational group to legitimate its position to other social groups, and it usually employs instruction itself for this purpose. The more acceptable this source of legitimation is found to be by various dominated groups, the better domination is buttressed and the more universal is its definition of education. Crystallization of opposition depends on dominated groups rejecting claims to legitimacy and redefining the functions of education. There is nothing which compels obstructed groups to do this, it is simply that their members are in situations where penalties accrue for not doing so.

It is quite possible for some members to be convinced by the legitimatory arguments advanced by the dominant group and the very form taken by education may induce mental limitations about the services thought to be available from any kind of instruction. But such attitudes are maintained at a price and it is this cost which places these groups in a completely different position from those already discussed. Members of obstructed institutions suffer inconvenience and frustration in their role situations: to support the dominant group is to incur the penalty of continuing frustration. If the obstruction is severe, such support automatically threatens operational goal-attainment. Sometimes this can be circumvented, by the development for instance of in-service training or by attempts to increase the ideological self-consciousness of a group, but only at the expense of additional time, effort and money. On other occasions this is impossible, especially where personnel and resources are inadequate, as was the case with the Danish peasant proprietors in the nineteenth century who could not provide schooling related to agricultural life and based on folk culture, on the scale they required.[13] Sometimes too resources and efforts alone are inadequate to remove the frustrations undergone by group members. The English entrepreneurs could develop factory-based training and informal systems of recruitment but they could not remove the stigma attaching to 'trade' (reinforced by dominant educational values) nor the embargo it placed on certain life chances and styles for the middle classes themselves.

It is argued that groups in this category will be prone to engage in oppositional activities because of the structured opportunity costs involved in *not* doing so. As in the previous discussion of supportive groups, the only psychological assumption made here is that, on the whole, groups do not tolerate large discrepancies between their *declared* interests and the values they endorse. This assumption is not predicated on 'universal enlightenment': in making it and drawing conclusions from it one is not implying that every group member unerringly detects the source of his frustrations, that every actor in other words is a good sociologist. (Of course in many cases the correct diagnosis is difficult to avoid; e.g., Why do new recruits not have the appropriate skills? Where did they learn inappropriate values?) However, initially at least, the oppositional group is likely to be much smaller than the institutional membership and it may well remain so — partly through the ignorance of some, the value commitments of others and the preference of further members for getting on with the job in hand. For assertion to develop it is not necessary for all members in the same obstructed position to perceive the reasons for it and actively engage in it — any more than class conflict requires the active support and participation of all class members. Instead it is merely being argued that some members will identify and seek to overcome the source of the frustrations and contradictions they experience. In turn this will lead to a different patterning of educational activities amongst this group compared with that displayed by members of other groups whose operations are unobstructed. To maintain otherwise would involve a much more dubious psychological assumption: namely that the existence of objective obstructions makes no difference to people's actions and that the objective costs attaching to certain interpretations have no effect upon people's attitudes.

Determinants of Educational Interaction

What has been discussed so far is not simply group conflict or antagonism, for the groups involved are representatives of different institutions. However, in examining the conditioning of supportive and oppositional pressures, the structural relations of education have been artificially isolated from the wider social structure and culture in which they occur. Yet the latter will critically influence interaction to the extent that people hold roles in more than one or two institutions and share values which are not narrowly educational. Thus to improve our account of organized educational interaction, the impact of wider structural influences and broader value systems have to be introduced.

Here the crucial element is the extent to which such factors reinforce or counteract the structural influences conditioning the formation of supportive or oppositional groups which have been discussed in this Chapter. As had been indicated throughout, the values endorsed by different groups are extraordinarily important, if not decisive elements in the emergence of oppositional or supportive activities. The social distribution of values — and the extent to which a central value system can be said to exist — will seriously influence the articulation of educational demands. As we have seen, the actualization of assertive groups partly depends upon their rejection of the dominant group's justification for controlling education. This will be easier the more pluralistic social values tend to be because other values provide an established, acceptable alternative with which to resist the ownership group. It is not impossible to advocate radical educational change from within the same broad value system[14] as endorsed by the dominant group, but the debate then loses a clearcut character; changes of stress and redefinition take time to elaborate and the ideological positions adopted can become rather too intricate and involved for 'popular' appeal.[15]

However, it is not simply pluralism as such which facilitates the emergence of oppositional groups, it is the social distribution of values which is more important. In particular the degree of overlap between the values endorsed by leaders of the rudimentary oppositional group and those held in other parts of society has significant consequences for the consolidation of assertion. Firstly, if the embryonic assertive group has more in common with the values of other powerful groups in that society than does the educationally dominant group, this fosters the emergence of opposition. It does so for several reasons: this value consensus increases external receptivity to educational innovation, and simultaneously it reduces internal resistance among potential members. It helps overcome the inertia of those placed in frustrating situations (because of the prevailing type of educational output) by showing that the dominant group's outlook is not the only, or the only socially acceptable, perspective from which to approach educational problems. Above all this particular distribution of values helps to provide allies, allies help to produce results, and results help to consolidate opposition. This was very much the case with the French eighteenth century Parliamentarians in the early days of assertion against Catholic domination. They successfully represented to the political elite that their own nationalism and the polity's gallicanism were much closer to one another than to the Catholic ultramontanism of the major teaching Order. The ensuing expulsion of the Jesuits in 1762 and prohibition of their members from teaching furthered the development of assertion.[16] Where the overlap works the other way round and emerging opposition confronts normative solidarity between the ownership group and other powerful social groups, the consolidation of assertion is impeded. Thus the secularism and socialism of the English working class leaders deprived them of external allies and of numerous potential participants from among their own class members, many of whom retained religious affiliations. This was a contributory factor to the slow actualization of educational assertion after the decline of Chartism.[17]

Thus far, only the effects of what could be termed 'vertical' value consensus have been discussed. However, it is not only the tripartite relations between the values of dominant, assertive, and elite groups which are of importance. Equally significant is the degree of 'horizontal' overlap between the normative position adopted by assertive leaders and the value systems shared by the much wider (non-elite) groups to whom they appeal for support. The gross generalization which can be made here is that the consolidation of opposition will be more certain the greater the coincidence between assertive values and those shared by the majority of members of that society. Correspondingly, the more the dominant group legitimates its educational control by reference to minority social values, the weaker its position. However, both statements are gross over-simplifications for the *impact* of value consensus and overlap cannot be discussed exclusively in quantitative terms nor as a purely cultural phenomenon. Of equal importance are structural considerations about the positions held by those endorsing particular values, the resources which they have at their disposal, and, above all, the relationships which exist between them. It is to these considerations that we now turn.

To discuss the influence exerted by the wider social structure on educational interaction is very similar to the above analysis of the distribution of cultural values. Fundamentally the same points arise, only here they concern the social distribution of resources and the overlap of social ties. Extra-institutional involvements on the part of both oppositional and supportive groups may modify their commitment to educational change (or stasis) as well as the resources they can mobilize to these ends. Here we are on Dahrendorf's familiar ground, where cross-cutting ties minimize conflict and overlapping ones reinforce it — without, however, adopting his implicit assumption that the former prevail over the latter.

Firstly, there is the question of social ties linking the educationally dominant group to other parts of the social structure. As far as adventitious beneficiaries are concerned, close ties in terms of kinship, overlapping membership of the two institutions, or exchange of goods and services between them, encourage the emergence of supportive pressures. Reference has already been made to the close relations between Anglican Church and Tory Party members in this connection. If similar links exist between members of obstructed institutions and the ownership group, these may be strong enough to minimize opposition. If, for example, the dominant group is a clerical elite and its potential opponents are members of the same church, then religious sanctions can be used to discourage assertive activities. It was certainly the case in England that the Oxford Movement and Broad Church Party condemned attacks on Anglican educational control as *morally* wrong,[18] and equally true that the emergence of opposition was facilitated because many members of obstructed institutions also belonged to Dissenting denominations.[19] Again, however, the quality and the specificity of ties with the dominant group is crucially important. It was after all quite possible for the French Parliamentarians firmly to oppose the Jesuit Order without (initially) adopting an anti-clerical or anti-Catholic position.[20]

Secondly, vertical ties with elite groups, rich in different kinds of resources, can help or hinder the consolidation of assertive or supportive groups. For either group the absence of such ties can make it impossible to mobilize resources from these sectors with which to reinforce support or opposition. Similarly, however, if strong links exist between members of an obstructed institution and another which is favoured by the existing form of education, opposition will be enfeebled as no resources are transferred to aid it. Again, where there is an overlapping role structure, assertive potential is reduced because although people experience frustration in one position, they receive rewards in another — from the same education. (Where there is overlapping membership, sanctions may be applied within the adventitious beneficiary to protect its educational interests against what members might do in other contexts, and where there are kinship ties, personal loyalties may restrain conflict.) Exactly the opposite occurs when the elite with which opposition is linked is itself impeded by education. Assertive group formation is likely to be accelerated and additional resources to be forthcoming from the other sector to advance its cause.

The same points can be made in reverse for the consolidation of supportive groups.

Such relationships are highly complex because they occur simultaneously and thus cross-cut, neutralize, or accentuate one another. They are themselves heavily conditioned by the nature of the social structure in which they occur. The degree of systems integration, the extent of centralization, the superimposition or segregation of elites, all affect the kind of social ties observed in different societies and their impact upon educational interaction. Such complexity does not defy analysis but the intricacies involved mean that, apart from the few broad generalizations already advanced, such factors will be treated as empirical variations when discussing interaction in the next chapter.

Thirdly, 'horizontal' ties represent an important variable in the formation of alliances and mobilization of resources for supportive or oppositional activities. Groups associated with different institutions may themselves be highly stratified, and social ties linking those of different levels *across* society frequently of course prove more salient than sectoral involvements. Ties based on common class, rank or ethnic interests can further the cause of both assertion and support. This is particularly important where there is a superimposition of the grievances (or the advantages) shared by class group members. For it is here that the 'horizontal' ties can over-ride some of the influences exerted by the 'vertical' links already discussed. Educational interaction would then become part of a more broadly based group conflict and would benefit from the resources of the wider movement. Generally the 'vertical' and the 'horizontal' effects occur simultaneously. This is not a zero-sum situation although the relative importance of the two varies from society to society at different times.

Finally, a full account of educational interaction must incorporate the contribution of independent factors. It has been stressed throughout that the structural factors outlined only condition action, they do not determine it. Analysis of interaction must thus make full allowance for the (unconditioned) choice of particular goals, the avoidance of, or affinity for, given allies, the development and appeal of new ideas etc. Factors like group antagonism, as opposed to structured opposition, can sometimes be as important as the conditioning influences. Because of this the educational change which results must be viewed as the joint product of both these sources of interaction. Discussion of these independent influences belongs to Chapter 3. They are stressed now, partly as an antidote to creeping determinism and partly to complete

FIGURE 1

The Structural Conditioning of Educational Interaction

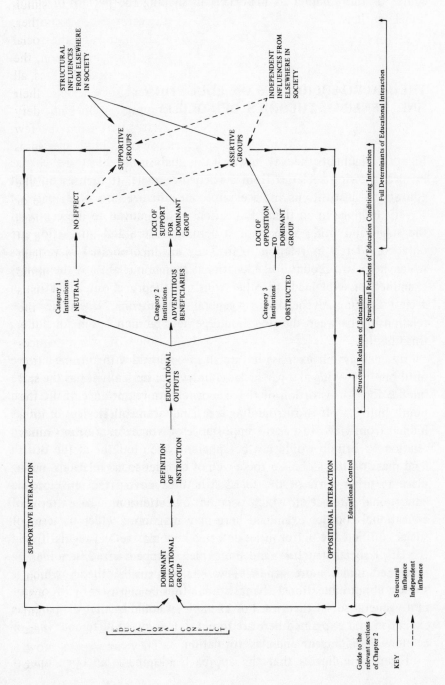

the picture of forces shaping educational interaction. Figure 1 on Page 83 summarizes the structural factors which have been underlined in the course of this Chapter as important in shaping the pattern of educational conflict.

THE MACRO-SOCIOLOGY OF EDUCATION AND GENERAL THEORIES OF SOCIETY

Figure 1 highlights the way in which this analysis of educational change involves viewing societies from a particular angle. It focuses on their educational institutions and seeks to conceptualize how other parts of society impinge upon them. Education is thus moved to the centre of the stage and other aspects of structure, culture and interaction are only considered in relation to it. They are incorporated as variables which help to account for educational change but are not themselves examined or explained. In other words, a theory about education in society is being advanced, not a general social theory. Nevertheless, the relationship between the two should perhaps be spelt out in concluding this Chapter.

By analogy our exercise has much in common with turning a globe until one is looking at a particular country, for optically it has the same implications — distortion of the size or relative importance of the focal point, blurring off of surrounding areas and, above all, neglect of things hidden from view. Just as the importance of North America or China in relation to Britain would not be apparent when looking at the British land mass on the globe, so too a web of broader social relations, taking place in other parts of the social structure, may in fact envelop the educational interaction which occupies our attention. The patterns of educational conflict examined here may map onto wider patterns of social conflict; the uniformities detected here may reflect regularities in the larger social structure, and the explanations advanced here may be subsumed under more general laws. As a specialist theory which is strictly about educational change it may thus be consistent with one or more general social theories. For example, it could be that the patterns examined and explained here are found to map on to different types of economic conjuncture and class formation.

Figure 1 indicates that the approach adopted is an open one; if group interaction is heavily structured in other parts of society then this enters our analysis (though is not explained by it) *at the point* where it intersects the educational-field. This approach allows any such factor freely to filter in, but is neutral in the sense that it excludes none in advance, nor does it give preferential treatment to any particular type of factor. Therefore whilst it is compatible in principle with larger scale general theories of society, it remains to be seen whether in practice any of these theories *are* capable of subsuming the educational propositions advanced here. Indeed one way of viewing this type of specialized analysis is as a testing ground for theories which make claim to a higher level of generality. Macro-sociological work does not itself presuppose a total system of sociological theory,[21] hence the onus is on those who feel that they do command such a theory to demonstrate that it holds the key which can unlock these subsidiary educational problems[22] as part of its general explanatory capacity.[23]

NOTES

1. Willis Dixon, *Education in Denmark*, Copenhagen, 1958, Ch. 1.

2. William H. E. Johnson, *Russia's Educational Heritage*, Pittsburg, 1950, pp. 1-15.

3. B. H. Sumner, *Peter the Great and the Emergence of Russia*, London, 1950. The following reply was made by Peter I to criticisms of his decision to establish the Academy of Science *before* founding secondary schools . . . 'I have to harvest big stooks, but I have no mill; and there is not enough water close by to build a water mill; but there is water enough at a distance; only I shall have no time to make a canal, for the length of my life is uncertain, and therefore I am building the mill first and have only given orders for the canal to be begun, which will the better force my successors to bring water to the completed mill', p. 209.

4. A. W. Gouldner, 'Reciprocity and Autonomy in Functional Theory', in N. J. Demerath and R. A. Peterson, *System, Change and Conflict*, New York, 1967, pp. 141-69.

5. P. M. Blau, *Exchange and Power in Social Life*, New York, 1964, p. 303 ff.

6. For a brief discussion of this theme see R. Robertson, 'The analysis of social and political systems', *B.J.S.*, Vol. XVI, No. 3, 1965, pp. 252-59.

7. P. M. Blau, *Exchange and Power in Social Life*, op. cit., Ch. 5.

8. Patrick L. Alston, *Education and the State in Tsarist Russia*, Stanford, 1969, p. 5.

9. Such considerations are good reasons for not assuming that low interdependence automatically leads to the high functional autonomy of a particular part as is maintained by Gouldner. In any case certain difficulties arise in Gouldner's discussion because he retains a neo-Parsonian framework in the sense that he is still assessing the interaction of parts *from the point of view* of the whole system. Because of this Gouldner assigns a particular part to a category of 'high functional autonomy' when it engages in interchange with only one other element. Consequently he must regard the mono-integrated institution as the most functionally autonomous — the most free therefore to resist further integration and to pursue its own operations rather than serving those of others. However, it is considered to be the most autonomous because it has the least *number* of relationships of interdependence with other parts. Thus functional autonomy is being defined quantitively from the point of view of the whole system and not qualitatively in terms of the nature of its relationship to the one part with which it is integrated. When these conclusions are compared with his earlier discussion of reciprocity and imbalance some rather curious inconsistencies arise. In that analysis he had initially confronted two interdependent structural parts (i.e. the number of their other interdependencies was not introduced) and shown how under certain conditions imbalance could develop in their interchange so that one could end serving the other, and consequently would have reduced autonomy. Here, of course, loss of autonomy results from the quality of their relationship. Also one of the very conditions under which such imbalance (and subsequent loss of autonomy for one part) was likely to occur was in the *absence* of a third part with which both others were interdependent. In other words, here the lower the number of interdependencies the greater the likelihood of autonomy loss and therefore the mono-integrated institution will be most prone to it . . . and hence the least autonomous! Such contradictions are dispelled by focussing on the *qualitative* interdependence of the parts themselves.

10. Michalina Vaughan and Margaret Scotford Archer, *Social Conflict and Educational Change in England and France 1789-1848*, Cambridge, 1971, Chap. 5 'Assertive Ideologies in English Education'.

11. B. H. Sumner, *Peter the Great and the Emergence of Russia*, op. cit., p. 13.

12. Logically there are three possible relationships which could pertain between the two institutions and thus influence the degree of educational control enjoyed by their respective members. Groups associated with Institution A (Education) may be subordinated by Institution B (here groups associated with B have a high capacity to determine educational output); A and B may engage in interchange which is sufficiently reciprocal to prevent the subordination of either, (here groups associated with B have some capacity to influence educational operations); B may be subordinated by A (a historically improbable but logically possible case) in which groups associated with B have a very low capacity to influence educational activities. Each of these potential relationships could of course be modified by further interdependencies between B and the wider social structure.

13. Willis Dixon, *Education in Denmark*, op. cit. 'The *Fri* school movement, which was entrenched in the countryside, had not expanded as fast as expected. Premises were often rudimentary and the teachers poorly paid; indeed the difficulty was often to secure the necessary financial support from parents. In 1895 there were 139 schools with 5,383 children', p. 91.

14. Indeed Gouldner (again as part of his functionalist heritage) analyses all oppositional values as arising from reinterpretations of the central value system. Cf. 'Reciprocity and Autonomy', op. cit. It should be plain that no such assumptions are made here.

15. This is well illustrated by the attempts to undermine the legitimacy of Tokugawu education in Japan, where most groups either defended or attacked it from within the broad framework of Confucianism. Cf. Albert Craig 'Science and Confucianism in Tokugawu Japan', in Marius B. Jansen (ed.), *Changing Japanese Attitudes towards Modernization*, New Jersey, 1965.

16. Cf. A. Dansette, *Religious History of Modern France* (3 Vols. Freiburg, 1961), Vol. 1; C. Falcucci, *L'Humanisme dans l'enseignement secondaire en France au 19è siècle*, Toulouse, 1939; J. Delvaille, *La Chalotais: educateur*, Paris, 1911; and G. Compayré, *Histoire des doctrines de l'éducation en France*, Paris 1879.

17. Cf. Brian Simon, *Studies in the History of Education: 1780-1870*, Vol. 1, London, 1960.

18. Michalina Vaughan and Margaret Scotford Archer, *Social Conflict and Educational Change in England and France 1789-1848* op. cit., Ch. 6 'The Defensive Ideologies of Anglican Domination'.

19. Cf. J. Murphy, *Church, State and Schools in Britain, 1800-1970*, London, 1971; and M. Cruickshank, *Church and State in English Education*, London, 1964.

20. The Parliamentarians as exponents of Gallicanism challenged the religious orders rather than the Church directly. As Compayré noted 'La Chalotais is a determined Gallican . . . He is otherwise sincerely religious. But he wants a national religion which does not subordinate the interests of the country to a foreign power. He wishes above all that the Church, keeping for itself the teaching of "divine truths", relinquishes to the state the teaching of morality and the direction of studies which are purely human', G. Compayré, *Histoire des doctrines de l'Education*, op. cit., p. 249.

21. Cf. Robert K. Merton 'On Sociological Theories of the Middle-Range', in his *On Theoretical Sociology*, New York, 1967, p. 60.

22. Equally, of course, this type of approach is consistent in principle with other theories which pertain to the *same* level of specialization, i.e. whose own focal point is a different social institution. An example of the latter might be David Martin's recent discussion of the comparative relations of organized religion to various parts of social structures. Cf. his 'The Religious Condition of Europe', in S. Giner and M. S. Archer (eds.), *Contemporary Europe: Social Structures and Cultural Patterns*, London, 1978, pp. 228-87.

23. For a more detailed discussion of this theme in general, see my essay 'The Theoretical and the Comparative Analysis of Social Structure', in S. Giner and M. S. Archer (eds.), *Contemporary Europe: Social Structures and Cultural Patterns*, op. cit., pp. 1-27.

3 INTERACTION: Competition for Educational Control

The previous chapter concentrated upon structural relationships, and how these condition which groups will be involved in educational interaction and which processes of interaction will lead to large-scale changes in education. Considered in isolation, the preceding type of analysis simply presents a static and artificial description of interdependencies, contradictions, and complementarities between different social institutions. It is static because it only deals with the elements of 'givenness' in situations concerning education, and artificial because, in reality, the relationships which have been isolated co-exist with a variety of independent factors which are equally important as influences on individual and group interaction. As Lockwood has argued, the gap between the elements of 'givenness' in situations and the individual or group action taking place within them must be bridged by a sociological appreciation of the ways in which motives are structured both normatively and factually.[1] In other words, to understand educational interaction means grasping how structural factors shape action situations and why in turn these are interpreted in particular ways by the people involved. To explain educational change means theorizing about these joint determinants of interaction, at their point of intersection.

Thus the basic theoretical assumptions made are that educational interaction cannot be fully explained without reference to antecedent structural conditioning, but that equally it is impossible to give an adequate account of structural change in education without examining prior forms of social interaction. This chapter thus attempts to theorize about the struggle for educational control before the development of state systems. Earlier it was argued that concern with struggle, rather than non-competitive forms of interaction (like negotiation), is appropriate when education is mono-integrated and subordinate. However, it should ɔe underlined that the justification for examining educational interaction in terms of conflict analysis is itself a structural one. Its use here does not stem from a general conviction that competitive conflict is the universal motor of educational change but from the fact that there are good reasons to think it the most important mechanism *during this period.* The exception of course is change initiated outside a given society and originating from conquest or territorial redistribution, but as already stressed, the concern here is with autonomous processes which transformed national education in the countries studied.

DOMINATION

When education is a mono-integrated and subordinate institution we have seen that its control and the power to define the nature of instruction rests in the hands of a single group which has been called the educationally dominant group.[2] This has been chosen as a neutral term which designates the educational powers once enjoyed by a particular social group and which differentiated them from other members of that society. Domination, following Max Weber,[3] is defined as the opportunity to have a command concerning education obeyed by a given group of persons. As such it may be quite distinct from other forms of social dominance: those with educational control may or may not be the ruling class, the political elite, or the military leaders etc. When compared cross-culturally, dominant groups are very different from one another. They may originate from different parts of their respective social structures and the possession of educational control could be their only common denominator.

It was argued in the last Chapter that prolonged educational stability, (which refers to the structural relations between education and other social institutions remaining unchanged and the definition of instruction showing a high degree of continuity) corresponds to the lasting domination of a particular group. Thus stability may endure either because the dominant group remains unchallenged or because it successfully overcomes threats to its control. Such challenges have been called assertion and defined as the sum of efforts made by another group, which does not have the opportunity to issue educational commands, to overthrow the existing form of domination. It is therefore by investigating the main prerequisites of successful domination and assertion that one can account for educational stability and change at the macro-sociological level. This involves specifying two sets of characteristics, those necessary for a group for it to be able to subordinate education (through rendering its operations dependent on the resources supplied), and those necessary for another group to be able to change this structural relationship.

As far as domination is concerned, it is less the question of obtaining than of maintaining control which is of interest here. When education is both subordinate and mono-integrated, the dominant group owns and supplies resources of a kind which are indispensible for instruction. Basically these consist in plant and personnel together with related capital expenditure (maintenance of school buildings, purchase of texts and materials, payment of teachers) and auxiliary services (administration, training, etc.). Because domination had been achieved by a particular group which owned and mobilized these supplies at some earlier point in history, this by no means implies that their control is secure and can be maintained over time. For other social groups may possess surplus resources which *could* be diverted towards the foundation of schools and converted into a trained teaching body. Indeed the dominant group may initially have gained control simply because no other party was interested in investing in education at that time — as appears to have been the case with the Church in mediaeval Europe. Where this is so, enduring domination and lack of large scale change merely reflect the absence of opposition. The prerequisites of educational domination become more complex once one is concerned with the maintenance of control and the continuity of a given definition of instruction *in the face of* opposition.

For the dominant group to retain its position of exclusive control it must continue to be the only supplier of the resources upon which educational operations *depend*. Yet as we have seen it is impossible for any one social group completely to mobilize the resources themselves, even if they are very unequally distributed in society. In other words, the dominant group must preserve its *monopoly of supplying* educational resources — it must in some way prevent others from converting financial and human assets into schools and teachers. This can be done in two ways simultaneously. Other groups can be discouraged from such actions by convincing them that they lack the right, the ability, or the experience to engage in educational activities, or instead that the type of instruction provided and defined by the dominant group is the best, the proper, or the only form possible. Thus an *ideology* legitimating this monopoly on traditional, charismatic, or rational grounds, can be used by the dominant group to defend its exclusive control. Secondly, a series of *constraints* can be employed to prevent other groups from supplying the facilities for imparting instruction. These may vary from the symbolic to the coercive, depending largely upon the nature of the dominant group itself. Use of either is conditional on members of the dominant group wishing to maintain control and the structural relations on which it is based. It is not necessary to assume that this desire is universal when seeking to specify the conditions for the maintenance of domination, for without it the pre-requisites will simply not be developed.

All three factors — monopoly ownership of educational facilities, protective constraints and legitimatory ideology — are together considered to be the necessary but not the sufficient conditions for maintenance of domination. The latter two elements may only be developed once a group has attained exclusive educational control, and their emergence can be delayed until domination begins to be challenged. Without constraints the monopoly is vulnerable; without an ideology recruiting positive support rather than enforced compliance, it is even more vulnerable. For the maintenance of domination the three elements ideally should be mutually reinforcing. Some resources should be devoted to the development of constraints and the universalization of the ideology; in turn the type of constraints should not run counter to the major ideological postulates; and the ideology should legitimate not only the monopoly on which domination is based but also the constraints employed to protect it from incursions.

Turning to the countries considered, the four dominant groups were concerned to defend their control of instruction but showed variable degrees of success in developing the three pre-requisites for its maintenance. In France, for example,[4] the Catholic Church and its multiplicity of teaching orders early acquired a monopoly of educational facilities. The Reformation had acted as a spur to the Catholic clergy and convinced them that religious conformity must be taught not assumed. Considerable progress was made during the following two centuries towards developing a countrywide network of confessional schools. Ownership was ecclesiastical, although it might consist in a religious order opening a school or the local priest holding classes on church premises. Certain fees and occasional community contributions helped with maintenance, but teaching was closely controlled by the Church. It was generally undertaken by clergy themselves but in other cases the regional Bishop certified a catholic lay teacher. Post-elementary education was the preserve of the religious orders and various types of *collèges* were owned, operated, and staffed by Jesuits, Barnabites, Doctrinarians etc. Here the scholastic Jesuit model prevailed, 'characterized by a concentration on Catholic doctrine and literary classicism; the former led to religious conformity, the latter to the intellectual homogeneity of the ruling elite'.[5] University instruction, which was not clearly distinguishable from the work of the collèges, was entirely dominated by the religious orders who had succeeded in directing it away from the pattern intended by mediaeval founders. The fact that universities retained a private collegiate structure meant that clerical staff could impose their own definition of instruction which gradually replaced the general education of the deserving poor, for which they were originally endowed.

This substantial monopoly was reinforced by an ideology based on traditional legitimation. Appeal was made to the supreme moral authority of the apostolic church, whose priests had the exclusive right to pronounce on ethical matters. Since every academic subject and issue was held to have moral implications, the clergy was presented as the only body which could properly teach. Thus the educational ideology was fundamentally religious, but included strong elements of social elitism and political conservatism, which broadened its appeal beyond the strictly theological.[6] Symbolic constraints were also available within the Church, which did not restrict itself to the use of the pulpit for disseminating its ideology. Religious sanctions were imposed on parents to ensure the catechization of children, on pupils in the boarding schools to induce doctrinal orthodoxy, and on recalcitrant communities harbouring schismatics who might be tempted to enter the educational market to perpetrate heresies.

The strong monopoly which had been slowly consolidated was protected by the use of religious constraints originating within the controlling group itself. Now all dominant groups share common access to certain constraints, namely those which derive from education itself. Discrimination and exclusion of potential critics from instruction, promotion of potential supporters through giving privileged educational access, and the use of tuition for spreading supportive values, were generally employed by every dominant group. But educational sanctions alone were never considered sufficient to protect control; groups which had other constraints at their disposal used them, as in the French case; those without such sanctions sought to obtain them from elsewhere.

Denmark provides an interesting case where a relatively weak monopoly was eventually reinforced and protected through a successful ideological appeal to another section of society. Despite certain formal expressions of interest in educational control on the part of the Monarchy, lack of physical and human resources meant that the Reformation did not present a break in the institutional sphere dominating instruction. Control passed directly from the Catholic Church into the hands of the Danish Lutheran clergy. Initially this spelt continuity in control, for the same (ex-Catholic) personnel continued to teach and administer schools in the sixteenth century. Nevertheless, confiscation of dissolved Catholic foundations meant that Lutheran domination was more dependent on its monopoly of human resources than had previously been the case.

This supply of teaching and administrative personnel for education continued to form the basis of Lutheran domination in the seventeenth century. As instruction in Latin schools was classical and theological as well as tightly geared to ordination, the clergy were indisputable curricular experts and the training, appointment, and supervision of teachers rested with Bishop and Dean. Similarly in Rural Schools, Church Deacons were the resident school masters and this minor office of the Church was used to support them. In Town Schools the holder was examined for competence and suitability by the clergy before certification. Although the church was the only organization capable of providing a countrywide network of educational administration, its relative weakness in terms of physical resources meant a patchy national coverage, making it easy for others to enter the educational market. It was still difficult at the beginning of the century to contain the threat posed by the continuation of Jesuit schooling and subsequently to prevent private enterprise from establishing unauthorized practical schools in the towns,[7] towards 1700.

It was the emergence of the latter, and especially the development of the secular mercantilist Writing Schools, which encouraged the quest for more stringent constraints than symbolic ones alone. This external threat to control coincided with the development of the Pietist movement within the Danish Lutheran Church and led to a corresponding reformulation of educational ideology. Control of schooling by the clergy was now justified by the vital role instruction could play in bringing about efficient catechization, in stressing the importance of personal salvation, and in encouraging universal confirmation – the major concerns of the Pietist movement. Simultaneously, during the main phase of the movement between 1675 and 1739, Denmark had a succession of kings who strongly supported Pietism against Lutheran orthodoxy. In addition, the Monarchy was increasingly in need of educational services for social control, especially in urban areas since agricultural failures between 1691 and 1735 led to rural depopulation, a doubling of the size of Copenhagen and other cities, and the social unrest typically associated with rapid population movements. The Pietist values shared by clergy and monarchy meant that the latter did not extract educational change as the price for the constraints and resources it offered the Church – its return was simply to be an increased volume of educational services, especially in urban areas, for religious instruction appeared a most acceptable and desirable form of social control. This then is another example of the B-C relationship described in Chapter 2, where two interdependent institutions negotiate the educational policy that B will execute for their mutual satisfaction.

It is not surprising then that the main thrust of educational development at the beginning of the eighteenth century centered on the Town Schools. The Monarchy stepped up the flow of resources and provided subsidies from the Poor Law, Customs returns, and from the municipalities, in order to build new schools and provide free schooling for poor pupils. Although it was impossible to keep all independent initiative out of this charity school movement, the Church acquired sufficient constraints from the State to guarantee its control over all urban establishments. Since schoolholders had to subscribe to the Augsburg Confession, be examined by the parish parson, and use only those texts approved by the Theology Faculty of the University, the clergy retained tight control over the definition of instruction: 'The whole instruction was under the supervision of the parish parson, who superintended all education, public and private alike, when the bells called to catechism, all schools were being called'.[8]

The high water mark of monarchic Pietism was reached with the accession of Christian VI in 1730, a king who wanted to extend the compact reached on the urban education of the poor to the rest of the country and to other levels of instruction — and who was willing to provide additional resources and constraints to this end. Confirmation was made compulsory in 1736 and paved the way towards the universal provision of rural schools under episcopal supervision and staffed by lower clergy.[9] Together with the reform of the Latin Schools which was to take place simultaneously, these exchanges were to leave the Church dominant over a much larger educational network and with much stronger constraints to reinforce its control. In return it had only been asked for a quantitative increase in teaching and administrative personnel, not a qualitative change in its definition of instruction.

In England the position of the Anglican Church was not altogether dissimilar, although historically it was less dependent on the receipt of protective constraints from elsewhere in order to defend its control at all levels. At the end of the eighteenth century the majority of facilities were owned by the Church and represented a thin network of parish and charity schools.[10] Already, however, in rural and urban areas lacunae were being filled by Dame schools and Schools of industry. The Established Church's response to the growth of Dissent took the form of expanding the Sunday School movement, since Anglican interest at this level was catechistical, rather than a tightening of the elementary network itself. As Brougham's Royal Commission of 1820 branded England the worst educated country in Europe,[11] the Anglican monopoly was clearly not extensive at elementary level. If domination was strong it was only by virtue of it not being opposed on an organized basis, for the Church had only symbolic constraints to protect its position and nothing but rather vague formulae with which to justify it.[12]

Their control of secondary and higher education was more firmly based. Not only were many of the endowed schools religious foundations, but also the clergy enjoyed a complete monopoly of educational personnel. It supplied the vast majority of staff and controlled the profession as a whole since an ecclesiastical licence was needed to become a teacher. The classical curricula of public and endowed schools, reflecting the state of knowledge at their foundation, was a definition of instruction upheld by the Church because of its relevance to ordination. The same was true of the universities where an entirely Anglican teaching and student body meant that higher education was permeated with religious orthodoxy[13] and largely geared to recruiting for the Church itself — between 1800-1850 nearly half of those matriculating at Oxford were subsequently ordained.[14] Clerical control over the loose agglomeration of privately endowed colleges and their governing organs was ensured through the system of closed scholarships which meant that the Anglican oligarchy reproduced itself over time.[15] Here symbolic constraints and appeals to traditional sources of legitimation were considerably more powerful than with the urban masses who were increasingly disaffected from the established Church. However, these sanctions were reinforced, as in Denmark, by a series of legal provisions provided by the governing elite, the most important being the Test Acts for university graduation, and the legal upholding of the statutes of the endowed foundations. In England a supportive ideology was not properly elaborated until Anglican domination came under attack.

Tsarist Russia perhaps represents the clearest example of a case where the domination of the Orthodox Church rested largely on lack of opposition, for although it possessed the three pre-requisites for maintaining control they were neither strong nor extensive. Formal education in Russia does not date back much further than the sixteenth century,[16] and domination by the Orthodox Church seriously began with the annexation of Southwestern Russia to the Muscovite domain. For in the more westernized Ukraine, whose capital Kiev had been a cultural centre from the twelfth century onwards, not only was neophyte instruction provided in Church and Latin Schools but also the religious Brotherhoods gave some teaching to the community. 'The way lay open to increasing Ukrainian influences in the Church which spelt both increased literacy and better training of the clergy and an element of secular education'.[17] Nevertheless, the definition of instruction and its purpose remained exclusively religious — thus the Lavr School (1631) had as its aim 'to teach free knowledge in Greek, Slavonic and Latin, at the same time preserving the Christian truths of Eastern Orthodoxy', while the object of the Lutsk Brotherhood School (1624) was simply 'to rear devout children'.[18]

Theological disputes with the Church, centering on the rites and doctrines distinguishing Russian from Greek orthodoxy and culminating in the excommunication of schismatic Old Believers (Raskol) in 1667 had important consequences for educational control. It stimulated the expansion of educational provisions, the development of constraints, and elaboration of an ideology. The desire of the Russian Church to centralize the power to define religious dogma found immediate educational expression in the Moscow Slavonic-Greek-Latin Academy, licensed by the Patriarch in 1682. It was devoted to the maintenance of the strictest orthodoxy and its staff propagated the defence of the faith as the major justification for ecclesiastical control of instruction in general. As an independent power within the State, Orthodoxy had a number of constraints at its disposal besides the purely symbolic. Rules were issued forbidding heretical books and severing contact with western science; within the schools the Church enjoined the burning of heretical staff and the enrolment of Orthodox pupils alone.

Nevertheless, the internal religious dispute had negative as well as positive consequences for the dominant group. Clarification of the Church's theological and ideological position intensified both the religious and the educational debate. Ultimately this resulted in a diversification of religious instruction, for in opposition to the Moscow academy and other institutions embodying the same values, the Old Believers developed a rural type of school, supported by parents, with peripatetic teachers giving schismatic tuition. Thus internal religious dissension contributed to diminishing the public impact of Orthodox ideology, to revealing the practical inefficacy of constraints, and to weakening monopoly ownership.

Thus in each of the four countries, the dominant group sought to retain its control by rendering education dependent on resources it alone supplied — strengths and weaknesses in monopoly, ideology, and constraints hinged upon the nature of the ownership group; its relations with other parts of society, its degree of internal unity, and its past history. From these too stemmed substantive differences in types of constraints available and the kind of educational ideology disseminated.

The Effects of Domination
on Other Parts of the Social Structure

The nature of the dominant group's definition of instruction gave rise to specific kinds of educational outputs in the countries examined. As we have argued these outputs can be either a help or a hindrance to contemporaneous operations taking place in other parts of society. It is to these that we must now turn in order to investigate what supportive pressures the dominant group's activities in the educational field generated from other sectors of society, and where they met with the greatest opposition. Although this only represents a preliminary and conditional structuration of parties whose interests lay in the maintenance of domination and those whose lay in its overthrow, it bears an important though imperfect relationship to subsequent patterns of educational interaction. This we will seek to demonstrate is not simply a matter of correlation but a structural influence on group interaction, which in turn is modified or reinforced by other influences. If this is the case, then the fact that the distribution of adventitious benefits and obstructions was very different in the countries concerned is of corresponding importance for understanding the educational conflict which took place.

In all the countries examined we have seen that the dominant group's definition of instruction was narrow (it embraced very few subjects and excluded much contemporary knowledge) and undifferentiated (those who were educated received a similar instruction to one another). Mirabeau's condemnation of the Catholic definition of French education is equally applicable to the other countries – 'There is no choice possible between courses in various subject-matters. A single one-way avenue is open to all types of intelligence. The homogeneity which is the result desired is, at the same time, the precondition of this result'.[19] Because of their supreme control over education all the dominant groups were able to design the form of learning which best served their purposes, with almost complete disregard of the requirements of others. It is not surprising then that the narrowness of instruction and the homogeneity of its outputs everywhere obstructed more activities than those which it accidentally aided. A broader more differentiated education could instead have produced more adventitious beneficiaries, each of whom gained something from different parts of instruction. However, it is not the number of parties who were obstructed or aided which is crucial, but rather the qualitative characteristics of groups in these categories – who they were, what resources they had at their disposal and how willing they were to engage in support of, or opposition to, the dominant group.

Orthodox education in Russia provided the clearest example of a definition which was so restrictively religious that school outputs were too specialized to have any spin-off for other institutional operations. The early internal wranglings about Greek versus Latin and the later ones over the schism question increased concern for teaching dogma and inducting the doctrinally pure into the priesthood, but simultaneously decreased the utility of such education to other parts of society. Although some operations like traditional agriculture and craft production were neither helped nor hindered by it, this definition of instruction was beginning to represent a severe obstruction to others by the end of the seventeenth century — in particular the military, the Tsarist bureaucracy and the aristocracy.

The content and values of religious instruction both helped to undermine military efficiency and reliability, as two events underlined at the end of the century. The crushing defeat of the army massed against Sweden at Narva in 1700 stressed the inability of untrained soldiers, officered by foreigners, to provide adequate national defence. The revolt of certain Streltsy regiments, during Peter I's absence in England, underlined the contribution of schismatism to political opposition.[20] Similarly governmental bureaucracy suffered from lack of competence among officials at all levels. The circumscribed religious curriculum of the Moscow Slavonic-Greek-Latin Academy was irrelevant to public administration, but as the only form of civil training available, had further deleterious effects upon specialized administrative activities. The absence of a cadre of trained jurists inhibited implementation of government policy; the (Byzantine) use of letters for notation of figures, as taught in schools, made calculation difficult[21] and impeded fiscal administration; medical training for civil and military purposes had no place in Orthodox instruction and devolved on the Moscow pharmacies which lagged centuries behind western progress.[22] At lower levels of officialdom shortage of clerks and scribes hindered the execution of governmental business.

Since the start of the Romanov dynasty, serious theology conveyed in dead languages in the Orthodox academies was incongruent with the nobility's aim of becoming a European aristocracy of leisure. It was not an impediment while this group could import private tutors and export its sons to foreign universities to acquire the polite secular instruction geared to status confirmation. It became obstructive in the late seventeenth century when the Church developed its constraints and limited the circulation of Western literature, condemned modern language learning, and segregated foreigners in a residential quarter of Moscow.[23] Since the acquisition of status honour is fundamentally a matter of usurpation it is very sensitive to countervailing influences from the educational sphere. Both the values and content of Orthodox instruction were inimical to aristocratic activities.

In France too Catholic domination sponsored a tradition of scholastic classicism which served its own purposes but increasingly meant that 'The University stagnated. A gap widened between it and society'. Diderot summed this up when he argued that it was only useful to the most useless of occupations — the priesthood and the professoriat.[24] Similarly, in the mid eighteenth century, Rolland stressed its incompatability with public administration and went on to underline its disservice to military and commercial activities . . . 'are public schools destined only to produce clergymen, judges, physicians and men of letters? Are soldiers, sailors, tradesmen and artists unworthy of the attention of the Government, and because Literature cannot maintain itself without classical studies, should these studies be the sole preoccupation of an instructed and enlightened people?'[25] Even for the *ancien régime* Monarchy, the benefits received in certain important areas of its activities were neutralized by the obstruction of others. The major service consisted in reinforcement of the stratificational system upon which the ancien régime rested — for the Catholic definition of instruction hindered social mobility; educational selection confirmed social privilege and tuition stressed duties associated with station in life. Nevertheless Jesuit Ultramontanism was antithetic to the Monarchy's Gallican policy in religious matters, and its scholasticism was decreasingly useful to government service. It was only with the expulsion of the Jesuits and their replacement by the more modernistic Oratorians as the leading teaching Order, that the Monarchy eventually became an unambiguous adventitious beneficiary.

As far as loci of support were concerned, a very similar situation prevailed in Denmark. The benefits the Monarchy derived from Lutheran educational outputs were in direct proportion to political Pietism. Again the absolute monarchy was an adventitious beneficiary in terms of one aspect of its political operations alone — political socialization on the basis of religious values — important because of the priority accorded to this by a succession of Pietist kings. However, political operations are multiple, and the relationship between the Lutheran definition of education and both political recruitment and integration remained potential sources of strain. This was to come to the fore as the Church increased the constraints at its disposal in the early eighteenth century. Until then the feudal forces in the countryside had remained in the neutral category. Agricultural operations were traditional and farming skills acquired in the family and on the estate. But the introduction of religious penalties for non-attendance and the imposition of land taxes for school building (introduced in 1739), represented severe impediments to peasants and landlords alike. To the former the labour and materials they were to provide toward school-building, plus the fees to be paid in kind to teachers, had the effect of adding religious taxation to the civil taxation extracted by landowners and thus endangered the peasant and small-holder economy. To land-owners schooling diminished the peasant workforce, and attendance at schools, whose location was determined by clerical convenience, reduced the time spent on the land still further. Land taxes for school-building and maintenance represented another outgoing which had to be paid before the landowners could start calling their revenues their own. All these were unmitigated impediments to traditional agricultural practice and landed interest – for any gentling of the peasantry via religious instruction was counteracted by the unrest that their growing impoverishment stimulated.

Simultaneously the restrictive religious definition of instruction and the constraints imposing it on all schools hindered urban commercial expansion.[26] The colonial wars between England and France benefited the international trade of neutral Denmark, which rapidly established new commercial links with the West Indies and the Asiatic. The growing complexity of mercantile operations made the educational outputs of *børnelærdom* a serious obstacle, when commercial practice required book-keeping and accountancy skills for import-export activities and modern languages, geography and navigation for trading.

In England the developing capitalist economy was similarly impeded by the Anglican definition of instruction and the values it embodied. It taught deference to squire and clergy but not to entrepreneur and merchant, it defended hereditary privilege but not newly acquired property, it preached catechism and constitution but not industrial skills and the spirit of capitalism, it taught classics and pure mathematics but not accountancy and applied science.[27] If the hindrances it presented to factory production were somewhat indirect, its penalization of other religious organizations was clear and obviously damaging. Constraints prevented dissenters from attending many endowed schools, from university graduation, and from entering the teaching profession, thus in turn hindering a range of denominational operations.

On the other hand, the Anglican dominant group had a clear adventitious beneficiary in the political elite. Increasing working-class unrest in the early nineteenth century made the contribution of religious instruction to social quietism proportionately valuable. Equally complementary with the goals of both political parties was the social exclusivity of Anglican secondary and higher education – for the status characteristics which were confirmed through education were the same as those employed by the governing elite when making ascriptive political appointments. Finally, the universities were an important part of the political establishment, as the *Westminster Review* was to over-emphasize in 1831 — 'the University of Oxford has long ceased to exist except for the purpose of electioneering'.[28] This was untrue; its major purpose remained the production of Churchmen, but that was in no way incompatible with the production of Statesmen or the inter-mingling of religious and political activities within the same organiza-tions.

Support for the Dominant Group

Adventitious beneficiaries do not convert directly into supportive groups. Indeed they may not move in this direction at all since other factors may neutralize or counteract the structural pre-disposition towards their becoming loci of support. To recap, those receiving rewards must be aware of it, and must not have social ties, values, or any other source of allegiance which militates against solidarity with and defence of the dominant group. In arguing that a conditional influence, favouring support, is exerted by virtue of receiving benefits, it is not claimed that this over-rides other influences upon interaction. In the countries examined there are cases where other factors re-inforced, diluted, or indeed counteracted the influence of educational relations on the formation of alliances for the maintenance of domina-tion.

In France conditional influences originating from *other* social rela-tionships reinforced the educational predisposition for an alliance between clergy and nobility. As enlightened thought simultaneously became more secular and more radical, the nobility were not slow to recognize the rewards they received from clerical instruction. Further-more, the Clergy and the Nobility constituted the two privileged Estates — they were united by social ties and similar vested social interests in the retention of privilege — a link which went far beyond their educational relations.[29] Once the Jesuits had been expelled in 1762 and the Oratorian Order, with its Gallican outlook and more modern curriculum, had stepped into the gap, then social, religious, political and educational factors encouraged the nobility to act in a supportive capacity.

In England too the educational alliance between Anglican Church and political elite was cemented by other factors, although this was obviously complicated by party politics. Tories and Whigs alike acknowledged the services of the Church in secondary and higher education, their contribution to maintaining the status quo, to making political recruitment unproblematic, and to legitimating elitist government. Although the Tories were initially less aware of the way in which a free supply of religious socialization facilitated social control, they gradually abandoned their view that the best form of education for the poor was no education at all. By the early nineteenth century they were sharing the Whig lead in supporting the National Society for promoting the Education of the Poor in the Principles of the Established Church. Social ties of family and class linked Anglican leaders to members of both political parties. Nevertheless the traditional 'Church and King'[30] outlook was more prominent among Tories than in the Whig Party, which increasingly received the Dissenting vote after 1832. Thus while the Whigs remained consistent in their support of *religious* instruction, it was the Tories who finally emerged as strong allies of *Anglican* education.

In Denmark, the Monarchy, as adventitious beneficiary, did not convert into a supportive group for the maintenance of domination but in fact came to play an important role in challenging it. For here two opposite conditional effects impinged on *the same social group*. The large landowners who were hindered by Lutheran education, and the Court who received benefits from it were to a significant extent the same people. Only the institution of personal absolutism firmly separated the adventitious beneficiary from the obstructed party. Furthermore, other structural influences reinforced solidarity between the Monarchy and the landowners. The ties linking the two were not simply those of kinship, connection, and affinity, for they also involved both political and economic interdependence. Royalty relied on the landed group to fill certain political and administrative offices and for ensuring provincial loyalty to the Crown: equally they depended on the landowners to provide state revenues by collecting taxes from the leasehold peasantry. In return the landowners were themselves exempted from taxation and given legal rights to extract unpaid peasant labour to work their estates.

This economic relationship was responsible for deflecting the Monarchy from its generous support of Lutheran domination, fostered by kingly Pietism. With a period of agricultural failure just over, central government finances were at low ebb, and the poorer the State the less it was able to resist pressures from the financial infrastructure, the landowning group. Their opposition to the 1739 proposals was immediately accepted by the king who reversed the original plan and instead left any provision of rural schooling to the initiative of the landowners themselves — 'who can best understand the possibilities of their estates and the circumstances of the peasants'.[31]

This economic dependence on the feudal forces of the countryside had even prevailed, as an influence upon educational policy, with Christian VI, the strongest Pietist among Danish monarchs. It was to grow in importance after the high tide of Pietism passed in the first half of the eighteenth century. Increasingly economic dependence on the landowners was supplemented by political dependence on them, once personal absolutism gave way to enlightened despotism with the accession of Crown Prince Frederick in 1784. At this time the improvement of agricultural prices coupled with the expansion of foreign trading led progressive landowners to advocate the commercialization of farming to increase agricultural exports abroad. The king's principal political advisors were leading members of this group and their plan to develop agricultural production through breaking up the open-field system and ending villeinage had educational implications. A practical instruction for the peasantry geared to commercial farming was seen as essential to back up the new economic and political programme. Thus dependency on the landowning group, coupled with changes in political operations and monarchic values, jointly resulted in the withdrawal of governmental support for Church domination.

In Russia too the domination of the Orthodox Church was without a supporting group committed to its maintenance. As we have seen the prevailing definition of education produced no adventitious beneficiary and other social links and influences were not strong enough to override the predisposition towards opposition. Even Tsardom, with its formal political ties with Orthodoxy, only modified the stringency of its attack upon the Church but did not reverse its attitude of hostility in educational matters, founded upon the incompatibility between school output and political operations.

ASSERTION

Educational conflict need not prove damaging to the dominant group or lead to any change in its definition of instruction if the constraints and ideological pressures it develops succeed in containing or eliminating opposition. Furthermore, the support that dominant groups receive from other parts of the social structure may be sufficient to protect their control and to maintain the structure of existing educational relationships. Having discussed the pre-conditions for the endurance of domination and analyzed the specific types of support accorded it in the four countries, we must now perform the same task for assertion. In other words, a parallel specification is required of the conditions under which an assertive group can seriously challenge domination.

Only the necessary conditions for successful assertion are outlined, and these consist in the factors required to overcome domination — to evade its constraints, to reject its ideology, and to damage its monopoly. In themselves these are necessary but not sufficient conditions for educational change. Without them there will not be far reaching changes, but conflict may be resolved in favour of existing domination, for this depends on the outcome of interaction itself. What is being specified then are only the factors without which latent opposition cannot be transformed into assertion and an assertive group cannot overcome the dominant group.

Firstly opposition must acquire *bargaining power*, i.e. sufficient numerical support and organizational strength to challenge domination. Both involve a desire for concerted action to transform educational control which over-rides social ties with the dominant group and any conviction that its legitimatory ideology may have carried. In other words diffuse discontent must be consolidated into organized assertion, which recruits further support, if constraints are to be subverted. To this end a counter *ideology* is required, partly to inform the movement of its goals, to recruit participants from the obstructed institution(s), and support from a wider audience, and ultimately to justify using the bargaining power at their disposal. But above all the ideology of the dominant group has to be challenged and negated by a separate philosophy which legitimates the goals and activities of the assertive group and specifies their new definition of instruction. Finally the assertive group must successfully engage in *activities* which are *instrumental* in devaluing the dominant group's monopoly.

Instrumental activities can take two different forms — *substitution* or *restriction*. These incidentally correspond to two of the ways that Blau outlines through which power can be challenged.[32] *Substitution* consists in replacing the supply of educational facilities, which the dominant group had monopolized, by new ones. In practice this means devaluing their monopoly by building and maintaining new schools and recruiting, training, and paying new teachers to staff them. Here domination is challenged by competition on the educational market — the aim of the assertive group being to price the dominant party out of it or to relegate it to a small corner of the market. In either case a transfer of control takes place and macroscopic changes are introduced. *Restriction* on the other hand consists in removing some of the facilities owned by the dominant group, or preventing it from supplying these resources to the educational sphere. Thus the monopoly is devalued coercively, buildings may be appropriated, educational funds confiscated, or personnel excluded from teaching and administration. Here domination is challenged, not by market competition but by coercive power — the aim being the forcible transfer of educational control.

Ideally, as with the pre-requisites of domination, these preconditions of assertion should be mutually reinforcing. The nature and timing of confrontation between domination and assertion depends upon the balance of factors present on the two sides. There are two limiting cases: unchallenged domination, when no group has acquired any of the factors necessary for assertion, (which corresponds to institutional stability) and, on the other hand, a situation where the prerequisites of domination are matched by the pre-conditions of assertion (which corresponds to overt institutional conflict). The three components of assertion may be developed simultaneously or over a period of time, but for analytical purposes they will be examined sequentially for the different countries.

The Consolidation of Bargaining Power

Bargaining power is essentially a matter of numbers and organization; it can obviously vary in strength and plays an important part in determining the relative success of different assertive groups. Several elements jointly contribute to influencing the bargaining power acquired. These can be classified as factors which restrain the development of a large and committed assertive group versus those which further its actualization. When the obstructions stemming from the prevailing definition of instruction all focus upon the same social group, a higher proportion of its members are likely to be active in the pursuit of educational change. Equally if frustrations are experienced by different social groups which are nevertheless closely linked by other kinds of social ties, their alliance increases overall bargaining power. Both of these represent a particular type of actualization, where a single assertive group develops with a large number of potential activists. Here there will be a polarization of conflict between domination and assertion. On the other hand, if frustrations are diffused among a number of different social groups which are not linked to one another, pluralistic assertion is more likely and each group will have a more limited pool of potential participants. Because each will have greater difficulties in acquiring strong bargaining power, educational conflict will be complex and protracted.

Other factors can operate in a cross-cutting or reinforcing fashion as was discussed in Chapter 2. Strong links, on grounds other than educational, with the dominant group or its supporters, can reduce the number of those actively opposing it. Similarly the existence of social antagonisms between the assertive group and other sections of society reduces the probability of recruiting allies and thus fulfils a similar restraining function. Bargaining power then will be stronger the greater the independence of the obstructed group from the dominant group and the greater its links with other parts of society, especially if these in turn are ill-disposed towards the dominant group on other grounds. So far only the structurally conditioned and independent influences of group relations have been considered as influential. Equally important of course are cultural and ideological influences which can restrain participation or add to the support recruited by the assertive group as well as the resources and abilities which these people bring to opposition. These ideational factors will be examined separately but it is important to underline that this is an artificial distinction of analytical convenience. What will be examined here for our four countries are a set of major influences upon the consolidation of bargaining power, but further considerations will have to be introduced before the strength of assertive alliances can be assessed relative to those of the dominant group.

France provides a striking example of a country where the polarization of educational conflict was not restrained by other social ties and allegiances and the consolidation of bargaining power by the assertive group was correspondingly easy. Most important here was the fact that obstructed operations gave rise to frustrations which were experienced cumulatively in one group — the bourgeoisie. Not only was Catholic education irrelevant to their activities in commerce and finance but their school enrolment and graduation placed them in a position of anomie for they could not gain appointments commensurate with their qualifications. 'Each year instructed, ambitious and intelligent young men graduated . . . but their legitimate ambition came up against unscaleable obstacles; money, titles . . . The Army, high positions in the Church, judicial offices were all the prerogatives of rich and noble families'.[33] These multiple grievances led to the recruitment of activists committed to educational change from all sections of the bourgeoisie.

Here too there were few links between the bourgeoisie and the privileged Estates to restrain participation in assertive activities. On the contrary social, economic, and political factors conditioned opposition to privilege itself – that is to the first and second Estates, the Dominant group and its noble supporters. Simultaneously, the bourgeoisie could recruit allies from among the people. As a group the latter were subject to indoctrination by clergy, repression by nobility, and financial exploitation by the State. The urban masses, who were less amenable to social control than the peasantry, were thus antagonistic to privilege and hence predisposed towards alliance with the bourgeoisie – political unity temporarily over-riding social diversity within the Third Estate. Thus predispositions towards educational assertion and support were superimposed on other sources of social division and political opposition.[34] Far from participation in educational conflict being restrained by other social ties it was encouraged by them, and assertive bargaining power was augmented proportionately. Educational conflict thus harnessed itself to social conflict structured by legal privilege.

In Russia, Denmark and England the various influences on the acquisition of bargaining power were complex and cross-cutting. In all of them two distinct assertive groups emerged and in each country this greatly lengthened the time taken for the three preconditions of assertions to develop. In particular the existence of more than one assertive group made the consolidation of bargaining power more difficult for each of them, for they had to recruit participants and supporters to oppose the dominant group *and* the other assertive group. It is this which accounts for educational conflict being much more protracted in these countries than in France.

In Russia, of the three institutional operations most seriously obstructed at the turn of the seventeenth century, two of these (the military and the bureaucratic) were part of and subordinate to the Tsarist State. The frustrations experienced by occupants of these two different role structures were undoubtedly important for the emergence of opposition, but even more crucial was the double frustration experienced at their intersection by Tsardom itself. With an army unable to back up foreign policy and a government service incapable of executing domestic policy, the Tsarist political elite was doubly penalised by the prevailing type of educational output. This impediment to military and administrative efficiency was immediately detected and Peter I informed the Patriarch of the country's need for schools 'from which people could go forth into Church service, civilian service, and ready to wage war, to practice engineering and medical art'.[35] Thus the political elite early defined its interest in a broader, practical, and multi-purpose definition of instruction.

On the other hand, the aristocracy's frustrations were rooted not in lack of practical training but of normative reinforcement. Made to feel undercultivated in the Courts of Europe, the cultural aspirations of the nobility were denied by the Church at home and their private educational initiatives were condemned by Orthodoxy. Again they were quick to advocate change, but just as the hindrance to the nobility differed from that suffered by the Tsarist bureaucracy, so too did the modifications demanded by them, with the aristocracy seeking the polite not the practical arts.

Thus the influence of educational relations conditioned the emergence of two separate forms of assertion, and relations with the dominant group did nothing to prevent their actualization. Both the secular rationalism of the Tsarist bureaucracy and the secular frivolity of the nobility burst the restraining bonds of religious conviction. Tsardom, however, had political ties of dependency with the Church which distinguished its position from that of the nobility. Unbridled attacks upon the Church would simply have played into the hands of the schismatics who 'found support and breeding ground far and wide among the under-privileged. Opposition on religious grounds to the State and the official Church became merged with opposition on economic and social grounds'.[36] On the other hand, unqualified support would have had political as well as educational drawbacks, for many looked to the Patriarch 'as a second sovereign, equal in power to the autocrat himself, or even above him'.[37] Peter I initiated the Tsarist policy of expediency towards Orthodoxy, a strategy which involved reducing the official church to a position of dependency upon the State while it was too weak to resist. The replacement of the Patriarch by the erastian Holy Synod in 1724 and the confiscation of some of its resources increased ecclesiastical dependency, limited Church autonomy, reduced reciprocity, and subordinated Church to State. It opened the way to deposing the Orthodox Church from educational control whilst retaining the (forced) alliance between official religion and Tsarist government. However, far from solving the question of educational control, this simply made the struggle to define instruction between Tsarist bureaucracy and nobility more crucial than their conflict with the Church.

Yet initially social links and mutual dependence between these two potential assertive groups had the effect of restraining their emergence as strong and separate forms of educational opposition. At the beginning of the eighteenth century social ties meant that the nobility and Tsarist bureaucracy overlapped. Despite the fact that Tsarist 'absolutism functioned less through aristocratic than through bureaucratic channels',[38] the attempt to gain an efficient civil service and army did not imply a break with social conservatism. Autocrats have few allies and the Tsarist bureaucracy, based on oppression of rural serfs and fierce taxation of urban freemen, could not for a century see any alternative to forcing 'the nobility back into lifelong labour for the Crown'.[39] This dependence on the nobility meant that efficiency was to be attained within the context of social conservatism by scholarizing the aristocracy and subsequently selecting the most able for civil and military posts. Equally the nobility was ultimately dependent upon the State for confirmation of its status and was made very aware of this when various Tsars manipulated the Table of Ranks in an attempt to make privilege depend upon educational qualification and state service.

Such interdependence had the initial effect of predisposing towards negotiation and minimizing outright conflict between the two parties. Peter I left a Titular channel to ennoblement open; Anna established exclusive military academies and Elizabeth diluted the academic content of courses required for government office. But in periods of political weakness, Tsarist reliance on aristocratic support could be exploited to widen the rights and reduce the obligations of nobility – as during the interregnum and the rule of Peter III when the Manifesto of Liberation (1762) released them from compulsory duties to the State. For over a century the nobility resisted attempts to scholarize it for state service; it evaded every measure to make rank dependent on state education and countered every initiative to impose a Tsarist definition of instruction.

The conflict between the two parties was based on the contradiction between defence of neo-feudal social relations on the one hand and the pursuit of those required for bureaucratic autocracy on the other. By the beginning of the nineteenth century mutual dependence could no longer contain this conflict of interests. Each educational concession made to the nobility had an equal, opposite, and detrimental effect on bureaucratic and military efficiency. The Tsarist elite had to choose between retention of the traditional stratification system and the operational requirements of modern statecraft. It chose, and opted for the loosening of social barriers commensurate with appointment by merit. Henceforth nothing restrained the Tsarist bureaucracy in its repressive actions against the nobility of leisure in the first decades of the nineteenth century. But at the onset of overt hostility between the two groups and their crystallization as distinct parties in educational assertion, both were desperately short of allies and were attempting to consolidate bargaining power from within very limited sections of society.

In terms of structurally conditioned alliances, both the political elite and the nobility were lacking in support for their educational aims. As far as economic ties were concerned both Tsardom and Aristocracy stood in the same exploitative position vis à vis other social groups: the closed society also precluded social links of any magnitude with the lower orders. The similarity of their positions contributed to prolonging educational conflict, for neither group could mobilize sufficient bargaining power to damage the other seriously. Such alliances as were formed were limited in nature, opportunist in motivation, and temporary in duration. For both the short-lived alliance between Tsardom and *Raznochintsy* (townsfolk of assorted rank) who gradually filled the State schools, and the putative alliance between nobility and serfs during the Decembrist uprising, over-rode structured group antagonisms between the parties involved. While temporarily augmenting bargaining power, both alliances were artificial products of the deadlock between assertive groups and were ultimately damaging to them. The concessions made to gain the support of townsfolk and serfs in fact aided their emergence as sources of opposition to autocracy and privilege alike.

Russia has been examined in detail because it graphically illustrates the problems which pluralistic assertion generates for the consolidation of bargaining power, problems which were shared by England and Denmark to some extent. In Denmark too obstructions affected different social groups. Obviously those frustrated in day-to-day activities as urban merchants were different people from those hindered in carrying out agricultural activities. Equally in the countryside peasants, smallholders, and landlords occupied discrete and non-overlapping parts of the feudal role structure and the actual difficulties experienced were as dissimilar as their positions – an increased problem of subsistence for the peasantry; an increased difficulty in extracting free labour for the landowner. This lack of superimposition of grievances within one or even two groups helps to account for the greater importance of other structural factors in shaping educational interaction in Denmark.

The alliance between Monarchy and landowners for the commercialization of agriculture involved land redistribution, whose unintended consequence was to open the way for the rise of the peasant proprietor group. This increased concern for agricultural production but simultaneously it restructured the feudal cleavage between landlord and peasant into a clash of interests between big and small farmers, the political manipulators versus those deprived of political influence. Peasant concern to improve their own farms was reflected in a desire for practical education related to rural life: opposition to the landowners was mirrored in the different definitions of instruction advocated by these two rural groups and precluded alliance between them. Furthermore the urban commercial class who had early indicated their preference for practical instruction geared to business life, did not have social ties which encouraged their alliance either with the assertion of landowners or of peasant proprietors. Although sharing much the same political position as the small farmers, the usual tensions between rural producers and urban middlemen interfered with the possibility of joint action, despite certain similarities in educational goals. Thus all three assertive groups had severe difficulties in consolidating bargaining power and ideological influences were to be especially important in tipping this balance of power.

The English case was slightly different for initially it appeared that middle class assertion was not to experience great difficulties in consolidating its bargaining power. Two of the major operations impeded by Anglican instruction – the development of the capitalist economy and the progress of dissenting denominations – affected many of the same people. The entrepreneurial and dissenting groups were not perfectly superimposed, but there was a large overlapping sector where frustrations were doubled. Here not only were they compelled to become self-taught scientists, to experiment with industrial applications on a trial and error basis, to develop in-service training for mechanics, operators and accountants, but also if they envisaged a polite education for their children they were largely debarred by religious affiliation and trade connections.

Unrestrained by ties with either the dominant group or its supporter, the political elite, the recruitment of middle class participants appeared unproblematic, even though many were themselves Anglican and deterred from outright hostility to Church control of education. Furthermore, during the first decades of the nineteenth century it appeared that alliance with the working class would considerably augment bargaining power. Shared opposition to the Church as the educationally dominant group, and to its supporter, the political elite as the ruling class, together with certain educational goals held in common, seemed to cement their assertive alliance. Increasingly however, the middle class experienced difficulties. The non-enfranchisement of the working class in 1832 accentuated the divergence of political and economic interests between industrial workers and entrepreneurs and signalled the emergence of independent educational assertion on the part of the former. This in itself severely damaged the bargaining power acquired by the middle class and threw it back on itself for the recruitment of participants. The middle class was always a diverse social group, and educational activists were not forthcoming in numbers from those who were still committed Anglicans or those factory owners afraid to lose child labour.[40] Again deadlock was reached and encouraged the search for further allies in order to consolidate bargaining power.

The Elaboration of Ideology

The possession of an ideology performs three vital functions for an assertive group. It is a central factor in challenging domination, since the legitimation of educational control must be negated by unmasking the interests served, thus reducing support for the prevailing definition of instruction. Secondly, it is crucial in legitimating assertion itself and is thus related to the consolidation of bargaining power. Finally, it is vital for the specification of the alternative definition of instruction, the blue-print which will be implemented in schools if the assertive group is successful. The elaboration of assertive ideologies can, as we have seen, be facilitated or hindered by cultural factors and the distribution of social values in a given country.

The analysis of educational ideologies is important for two reasons. On the one hand, ideological factors exert an independent influence upon educational interaction. As Weber argued, struggle in the realm of ideas parallels rather than reflects group conflict and although related to the structured interests of participants, contributes something of its own to determining the outcome between them. Here we will see that educational ideologies played an important role in the recruitment of support and formation of assertive alliances, sometimes over-riding differences of interest, sometimes introducing cleavage within an interest group. On the other hand, educational ideologies are vital to the understanding of educational change. The precise definition of instruction advocated by a group cannot be derived directly from its interests. These interests do not dictate the content of the ideology adopted, (for more than one educational philosophy may be compatible with them), nor within it the exact nature of the blue-print advanced, (for more than one specific curriculum, type of school, etc. may serve group interests and contribute to the attainment of group goals). Thus to account for the ends pursued in assertion and the changes introduced if successful, the ideological source of the new definition of instruction must be examined.

Here less attention will be given to the content of assertive ideology in England and France, for these were discussed in detail in *Social Conflict and Educational Change*;[41] but brief mention should be made of the differing effects that educational values had on interaction in the two countries. In France these encouraged polarization between domination and assertion and cemented the assertive alliance against the Catholic Church. In England, however, ideological influences had the opposite effect, especially as far as the consolidation of bargaining power is concerned. But in both countries a high degree of cultural pluralism made the elaboration of assertive ideologies unproblematic.

Initially restricting themselves to anti-clericalism, rather than anti-Catholicism, the bourgeois assertive group appealed to French Enlightened thought and especially to the educational philosophy of Diderot.[42] His stress upon utilitarianism, nationalism, and meritocracy captured their aims perfectly, specified precisely the type of education desired and negated the Catholic definition of instruction so successfully that even the Monarchy supported the expulsion of the Jesuit order. This particular strand of thought was however too explicitly elitist (though on meritocratic not traditional grounds) to recruit popular support, which the bourgeoisie needed in the educational struggle as in political conflict. To gain it involved papering over the divisions which threatened the unity of the Third Estate by legitimating educational assertion to the people as an inextricable part of their battle for political rights. This in itself involved overcoming a certain degree of popular religious affiliation and the thought of Condorcet and Sieyès contributed much to legitimating assertion on a wide social basis.

Condorcet[43] was important in showing that the source of artificial inequalities and the accompanying oppression of and discrimination against the non-privileged could be traced back to the role of the clergy in history. Even more polemical and appealing was the contribution of Sieyès[44] which linked the political attack on nobility to the educational assault on clergy, and blended the two into a single attack on privilege itself. In stressing that privilege prevented the enjoyment of natural rights and promoted an unfair distribution of rewards, he underlined that its abolition in all respects could only be achieved by the united action of the Third Estate.

In England on the other hand, cultural and ideological influences complicated alliances and prevented the clear-cut polarization of educational conflict. The existence of Dissent was initially helpful in crystallizing opposition to Anglicanism, for it represented pluralism in religious values. Almost immediately, however, strong denominational commitment reduced unity within the embryonic assertive group because of clashes with the secular utilitarian element. This strain was apparent during the early years of the British and Foreign School Society where schism developed between the secular and Quaker elements, eventually leaving the Society in Dissenting hands and destroying one of the earliest middle class organizations, the West London Lancastrian Association. However, although Utilitarianism represented an attack of secular ethics upon religious morals and appealed to an important section of the middle class, this ideological divide did not ultimately split the dissenter-entrepreneurial alliance. Initially the reason for this was restraint on the part of utilitarians themselves, who were cautious not to advance overt agnosticism and thus to antagonize the dissenting sub-group. More important later on were the practical advantages of religion for popular control, which became increasingly attractive to Radicals when working class unrest in the 1830s cast doubt on the restraining power of classical economics and secular ethics.[45] In other words, the alliance was kept intact at first by compromise, then by the concessions on the part of the secular section of the movement and their public endorsement of the values held by the more numerous dissenting element.

In turn, however, this contributed to losing the support of another section of this tenuous opposition group — the working class leadership to whom the the secular strand of middle class thought had appealed. It had done so because it harmonized with the intellectual traditions most influential in popular educational thought, the secular rationalism of the French revolution and early English anarchism. Ideologically the working classes were as tenacious in their adhesion to secularism as was dissent in its defence of denominationalism. It took other factors to precipitate the final breakaway — in general the crude and overt attempts to indoctrinate by middle class educationalists, and in particular working class exclusion from the provisions of the 1832 Reform Bill — but secular socialist values then played a major role in the crystallization of an independent popular assertive group and the corresponding reduction in middle class bargaining power.[46]

In Russia there was no cultural impediment to the elaboration of assertive ideologies and one of the most striking features of the educational debate was the importance of independent values imported from abroad to legitimate oppositional activities. The intense religious conflicts of the seventeenth century undermined anything approximating to a central value system in Russian society and may itself have contributed to a normative pluralism which soon came to include secular as well as religious alternatives. On the other hand the Orthodox affiliations of serfs, and the role Orthodox values played in political legitimation, were serious obstacles to the elaboration of the Tsarist assertive ideology, which had no parallel in the case of the Nobility. Thus throughout the eighteenth century the Tsarist bureaucracy contented itself with a pragmatic negation of the Orthodox definition of instruction (religious education was not wrong but was simply not expedient); it legitimated its own assertion on nationalistic grounds, and specified an alternative blue-print, geared to 'etatist' requirements. Thus Peter I 'looked on education as training for some specific form of state service: if men went abroad to learn economics, it was for the sake of his new tariff; if they were trained in languages, it was in order to act as translators or to serve as diplomats'.[47] This was reinforced by the utilitarian nationalist strand of French Enlightened thought (especially that of Diderot), during the reign of Catherine the Great, and the same etatist justification was advanced in almost the same words by Alexander I in 1803 — 'National Enlightenment in the Russian Empire is a special function of the State'.

The effect of the Napoleonic invasion was a repudiation of the West which led to the recasting of these tennets in a slavonic form. The new formula, 'Nationality, Orthodoxy, Autocracy' was only original in its middle element which signalled the re-establishing of links between the Tsarist State and Eastern Church. The monopoly of the latter had by then been seriously devalued and given the control of the Church by erastian government, the Tsarist bureaucracy could now use religious values[48] to underwrite its nationalism and to broaden its legitimatory appeal among the faithful. As such their revised educational ideology bore some resemblance to that used by Napoleon himself to justify the Imperial University.

Throughout the whole period the Nobility continuously drew upon foreign values, accessible to them because they intermingled with the European aristocracy, when elaborating their assertive ideology. Initially the definition of instruction they advocated was little more than an imitation of aristocratic practices abroad, weakly reinforced by reference to the status these conveyed. Although this probably stimulated participation within the nobility itself, it was eminently unsuited to recruiting wider support. Gradually towards the close of the eighteenth century the nobility broadened its ideological appeal by incorporating elements from the more radical stream of enlightened thought. When this went so far as to include advocacy of constitutional government and liberation of the serfs during the Decembrist uprising, polarization between the two assertive groups was complete. The Tsarist bureaucracy blamed this political instability on the 'deadly growth of semi-knowledge' and the fact that the nobility was prey to 'bloody and insane ideas' from the West.[49] Pushkin completed the governmental assault by attacking the aristocratic nature of their definition of instruction. Their infatuation with Western ideas was itself a by-product of the defective education in 'fashionable etiquette and recreation, that the nobility provided for itself'. Ideological differences which had always been great now intensified as the two groups seeking diametrically opposed changes made appeal to antithetic values to gain wider support for their assertion. In this the Tsarist readoption of traditional religious values probably did more for the consolidation of its bargaining power than did the Nobility's toying with European radicalism.

In Denmark, ideological influences played an important role in polarizing two distinct assertive alliances out of the plurality of oppositional groups that were examined earlier. As we have already seen, while ever Pietist enthusiasm gripped the country there was extra-ordinarily little educational debate. Even those consistently advocating educational change during this period, the urban commercial class, developed no alternative ideology but simply justified opposition on the grounds of practicality. They were pragmatists not utilitarians, they had no counter-ideology with which to negate the values legitimating control by the dominant group and consequently recruited little support for extending assertive activities. On the other hand, the universalization of religious values was furthered by the temporal authority until the mid eighteenth century.

It was the landed economic elite who first succeeded in elaborating an alternative educational ideology, which negated church control, legitimated assertion and specified a new definition of instruction. The ideas they endorsed were drawn from independent foreign sources, especially France and Germany, which were accessible to this group who travelled abroad extensively. From the mid eighteenth century onwards those who spread enlightened thought in Denmark used it as a direct attack on Pietism. Thus Holberg's denunciation of religious instruction as the inculcation of prejudice ('children must become persons before they become Christians'), was typical, but equally signi-ficant was his attempt to negate religious domination in terms of its dysfunctions to the State.[50] This was echoed by Count Reventlow, the most influential of the king's progressive landed advisors — the clergy 'looked at education from the religious and church point of view without considering the civic'.[51]

Much of the legitimation for assertion was therefore etatist and the new definition of instruction elaborated by enlightened land-owners was one that would jointly serve the political as well as the economic elite and would reinforce the existing system of social stratification. In a bifurcated system of instruction the lower orders would be schooled for 'life and work' while the Latin Academies, joining the mainstream of European culture, would prepare the traditional elite for positions of leadership. Napoleon I and Catherine II were not the only ones to draw the same conclusion from Diderot's educational philosophy, but the Danish ruling class also had the advantage of witnessing the Imperial University in action. Enlightened thought cemented this assertive alliance, and the withdrawal of monarchic support from the dominant group ceased to be a mere reflection of dependence upon landed interest but became a matter of etatist conviction.

The reaction to this attack upon the Church was very similar to that of the Anglican dominant group when challenged – an attempt to reformulate their ideology in order to justify continuing educational control. The intricacies of these theological debates cannot be examined here, but two strands of them were of particular importance for educational interaction. A majority party within the Lutheran Church appeared to dissociate itself from Pietism and to stress instead the national role of the Church in Denmark and its service to the State. A minority party, not unlike the English Christian socialists, reaffirmed Pietism, condemned 'official' Lutheranism and the culture it disseminated as being socially divisive, and instead advocated a Scandinavian education related to life which would restore the organic society. These views, expressed chiefly by N. Grundtvig in the 1830s, found little favour within the Church itself, for few would gamble on destroying formal ecclesiastical control over instruction so as to increase the informal influence of religion on popular awakening. But the violence of its rejection by official Lutherans[52] did much to enhance its appeal to the rural population – pietist by religious inclination and anti-clerical through political experience.

'Grundtvig's civil and religious ideas provided a suitable framework for the farmer's growing social consciousness',[53] and supplied the peasant proprietors with a ready-made educational ideology, which combined the three elements in a highly acceptable form. Grundtvig had launched a two-pronged attack on existing education – on compulsion in elementary instruction and on the culture of secondary education. In the former he was traditionally Lutheran: the education of the young was the responsibility of the family, not of Church nor of State – an assertion which was as appealing to those seeking community control as to those wanting to keep their children on the land. More important was the stinging assault on high culture, which the Church had propagated and the ruling class was now advocating in a modernized version. Classicism was condemned at the 'Black School of Death' and the germanization of the cultural elite, its universalism and cosmopolitanism was held to kill the spirit of the 'folk' and had divided the elite from the people in cultural terms. Grundtvig posed the alternative – 'Die in German or live in Danish' – and proceeded to advocate the school related to life, based on the oral Scandinavian folk culture, and concerned with personal awakening. 'Avec la notion de l'éveil, l'idéologie grundtwigienne avait trouvé un critère pour définir une culture qui fût accessible au peuple. L'éveil s'était substitué au savoir at aux connaissances, qui réservaient la culture à quelques privilégiés'.[54]

How far Grundtvig was right that Nordic culture (the paganism of the Icelandic sagas) was still alive among the people in the North is debatable. What is uncontestable was the acceptability of this notion of the folk as true guardians of the Scandinavian heritage as a source of legitimation. For it dramatically inverted the educational picture, and in terms of assertion replaced the self-image of an illiterate peasantry, hostile to a culture it could not comprehend, by one of the people restoring national culture to the whole country. As such Grundtvig's ideas helped to consolidate the peasantry and to unite them to a considerable extent with the townsfolk behind the *Kulturkamp* banner. They therefore helped crystallize popular assertion in pursuit of an education related to life, to the social, economic, and political concerns of the lower classes and to over-ride differences of interest within them. Paradoxically these ideas, which their originator saw as the formula for restoring the organic society, intensified the divide between the ruling class and the ruled as competing assertive groups.

The Development of Instrumental Activities

The choice of either a restrictive or a substitutive strategy by which to devalue the monopoly of the dominant group is conditioned by the social distribution of resources. Their allocation between dominant group, one or more assertive groups, and their respective supporters, exerts a strong influence on the strategy adopted. Thus few assertive groups have freedom of choice between the alternative strategies – for there are both positive and negative constraints on the availability of the two kinds of instrumental activities to different groups, although these can vary in strength.

The major positive factor which must be present for a group to begin its assertion by employing a *restrictive* policy is that it has some degree of access to the national legislative machinery. The social distribution of political power therefore structures the availability of restrictive strategies to different assertive groups associated with various institutions. However, the fact that some degree of legislative influence must be present does not imply that any group *initiating* a restrictive strategy is synonymous with the political elite itself. There is a tendency for this to be the case when political power is highly concentrated, but the degree of political influence possessed need not be extensive for an assertive group to engage in this type of instrumental activity, especially if substitutive strategies do not represent an alternative.

Where such influence is small, the use of restriction to damage the dominant group's monopoly is dependent on a concordance of goals between the assertive group and the political elite. However, this is something which can develop during the course of assertion; it need not be present at the start. As we have seen assertive ideologies can win the support of governing elites by convincing them that existing educational control is politically undesirable and specifying an alternative definition of instruction, which is more conducive to the goals of the polity.

If, however, the political elite cannot be recruited as a supporter or if a divergence of educational aims subsequently develops between it and the assertive group, then the latter has little chance of executing its restrictive strategy. That is it will not be able to engage in activities instrumental to devaluing the monopoly of the dominant group, unless changes occur which considerably increase its political power. Although educational conflict undoubtedly contributes to change in political institutions and in the power distribution this only occurs in conjunction with broader processes of social interaction. If these do not intervene after the adoption of a restrictive policy by an assertive group, their strategy is most unlikely to succeed. It is because such political changes can occur in the course of interaction that the initial degree of access to governmental machinery does not determine the success or failure of assertive groups. However, ultimately it is only when the assertive group is very closely allied to, or in fact coterminous with, the political elite that restrictive strategies can be successful and engender macroscopic educational change.

The basic positive factor that must be present for a group to begin its assertive activities by employing a strategy of *substitution* is access to some degree of economic surplus which can be directed to devaluing the existing monopoly of educational facilities. Although substitution represents market competition with the dominant group, the initiation of such a strategy does not depend upon economic affluence within the assertive group, nor is success proportional to the original distribution of wealth among the competing groups. Although this distribution certainly conditions the differential availability of this strategy to various assertive groups, it does not determine the outcome of assertion for at least three reasons. Firstly, the crucial factor in developing this kind of instrumental activity is not the absolute amount of wealth at a group's disposal, but the proportion of it which can be mobilized for educational purposes. Thus relative bargaining power is significant here; for an assertive group with a smaller economic surplus but higher bargaining power than another may inflict greater damage on the monopoly of the dominant group. Secondly, as we have seen, a major function of the assertive ideology is to legitimize opposition among a wider audience of potential supporters. If successful, one of its consequences will be an increase in the resources made available to this end. There appears to be little reason to suppose that the appeal of educational ideologies is directly proportional to the initial affluence of the groups diffusing them. Thirdly, while the provision of alternative physical facilities in education is a capital-intensive process, groups engaging in substitution can make considerable progress through concentrating on competition in the field of human resources. One of the clearest examples of this was the development by so many different assertive groups of the Monitorial method of teaching.[55] Although grossly deficient as a means of instruction, it was strategically ideal since it meant maximum educational encroachment for minimum investment.

Thus it can be seen that the economic distribution exerts an influence on the selection and development of substitutive strategies which exactly parallels that exerted by the power distribution on restrictive strategies. In both cases the initial adoption of a strategy is influenced by the original resource distribution, but the outcome cannot be predicted from it. However, in substitution, as in restriction, if the policy is to succeed, resources must be accumulated in the course of interaction. This has the further implication that *just as the political elite was considered to be the type of assertive group most likely to succeed in restriction, so the economic elite is best placed to carry through substitution*. Indeed the assertive groups which have the greatest probability of failing to develop either kind of instrumental activity are those which occupy the lowest position on both the wealth and power dimensions simultaneously. These in fact are usually the only groups who can be said to have a free choice between the two strategies, though negative constraints make progress with either difficult, but not impossible.

In France we have seen that a variety of factors helped to structure a single assertive alliance and here the distribution of resources encouraged the pre-revolutionary bourgeoisie to follow a restrictive strategy. As a predominantly professional-commercial group rather than an industrial middle class, it was not poor but was far from being in an economic position to compete with the resources of the Catholic Church, and it is the *distribution* of wealth which is crucial in substitution. Furthermore, the assertive alliance with the popular section of the Third Estate was not one which substantially added to the *financial* resources of opposition. On the political dimension, however, the bourgeoisie only had influence in the provincial Parliaments which were consultative rather than decision-making bodies. Nevertheless these could be employed as platforms for the expression of bourgeois views and the success of certain Presidents (especially Rolland and La Chalotais) in initiating the expulsion of the Jesuits confirmed the adoption of a restrictive strategy against the Church. It encouraged the search for allies and the attempt to unite the Third Estate in order to strengthen bargaining power and exert greater political pressure, for in France political power would have to be augmented during educational interaction if assertion was to succeed. However, the superimposition of grievances within a very large group made this a not unrealistic project, and thus the pursuit of a restrictive strategy was favoured by the association between educational assertion and strong pressures for political change induced by other factors.

The English case presents a complete contrast, for the middle class alliance of entrepreneurs and dissenters represented a group whose respective economic and political positions clearly favoured the adoption of a substitutive strategy. In terms of financial surplus they were, as their economists never failed to underline, the group making the greatest contribution to national wealth. However, despite having largely taken over from the landed interest as the economic elite, their political participation was minimal before large scale enfranchisement in 1832: after it, their parliamentary representation and cabinet influence remained small for several subsequent decades. It is not surprising then that in the first half of the nineteenth century this group concentrated on devaluing the Anglican monopoly by substituting new establishments at all levels, either on a proprietary basis or through voluntary subscription.

On the other hand, working class assertion came from a group which had neither political influence nor economic surplus and thus lacked the factors predisposing towards selection of either strategy. Indeed the tactical debate about whether to engage in educational substitution as a basis for subsequent political change or whether to seek franchise reform first as a means for obtaining educational change later on, was to divide the Chartist movement.[56] Nevertheless, it was the substitutive strategy which was adopted immediately after and largely because of political disappointment in 1832. The chance of being in a position to manipulate legislative machinery for educational reform then appeared remote; substitution could be immediate, and the argument of Lovett that an instructed class had a better chance of enfranchisement was influential. Relative to working class resources the sums mobilized for substitution — for elementary schools, halls of science, and Mechanics Institutes were impressive — but more as an index of class commitment to educational change than as a serious threat to the dominant group or the growing network of institutions founded by the assertive section of the middle class.

Denmark and Russia were, like England, countries where pluralist-assertion developed. However, they differed from the latter because in both nations the two assertive alliances each followed different strategies from one another. In Denmark the alliance between large landowners and the political elite represented a unique combination of those best placed for conducting a substitutive strategy and those best placed for carrying through a restrictive one. It is rare for an assertive group to be in a position to choose its instrumental activities, but unsurprising that in this situation it is restrictive tactics which are adopted. In these circumstances restriction has two advantages over substitution: it appears both a quicker and a cheaper course of action. The possibility of imposing legal limitations on the monopoly of the dominant group promises their speedy overthrow and the ability to mobilize public resources for replacement rather than drawing on the private surplus of the assertive group itself has the attraction of economy. It might be thought that with such advantages the assertive coalition could not fail to succeed rapidly, but this example cautions us not to view the outcome of educational interaction as determined by the initial distribution of resources among the parties involved.

The other assertive alliance of peasant proprietors and merchants had no such choice as to strategy. Already a wealthy group in the eighteenth century, the commercial townsmen were completely without political influence. Gaining no response from petitions to the King about the irrelevance of religious instruction, (which meant that 'none of the middle classes have been able to educate their children to earn their daily bread by commerce'),[57] they began to substitute their own instruction in towns. By the end of the century they had opened a considerable number of private proprietary schools geared to business careers, and the *Real* schools in Copenhagen had completely evaded the ecclesiastical licensing system. Despite their irregular status this *Fri* School movement continued to develop and only suffered a set-back when the Napoleonic wars temporarily brought Danish trade to a standstill and reduced the resources of this sub-group correspondingly.

Peasant proprietors too were without political influence and did not acquire suffrage (for the lower house) until 1866. After the reallocation of land the small proprietors remained poor and were limited to subsistence farming until well into the nineteenth century. This largely accounts for the tardy emergence of their substitutive activities relative to those of the urban middle class. The event which led to improvement in farmers' incomes and accumulation of a surplus with which to engage in substitution was the repeal of the English corn laws, which resulted in a general rise of world prices and favoured Danish grain producers. During 1830-80 agriculture accumulated more capital than it consumed and for the first and only time[58] Denmark became a creditor country. This coincided almost exactly with the period of active substitution on the part of the small farmers.

The interesting and possibly unique thing about educational interaction in Tsarist Russia was that the two assertive groups were in fact the political and the economic elite and that the two strategies were thus pursued simultaneously by the parties best placed to execute them. It is this which accounts for the marathon contest for educational control and for conflict remaining unresolved long after the dominant group's monopoly had been devalued. The two assertive groups were well matched and the strength of the one's strategy was the weakness of the other's. The nobility could found schools,[59] recruit better teachers,[60] attract a higher class of pupil, and generally substitute a private sector of education which checked and blocked public instruction at every turn. They could rarely, however, except in times of political weakness, gain official recognition for their establishments, evade the growing number of legal restrictions on private instruction and independent schools, or fully withstand the link that the Tsarist bureaucracy imperatively forged between public appointments and state education. On the other hand, the political elite could use the whole armoury of restrictive and repressive measures against Church and Nobility, but for over a century was unable to mobilize the resources necessary to replace Orthodox or Aristocratic facilities by public education.

EDUCATIONAL CONFLICT

Organized conflict rather than uncoordinated opposition occurs when the three prerequisites of domination are matched by those of assertion, as was the case in all the countries examined. The nature, length and intensity of educational conflict is influenced by a variety of factors, many of them non-educational, and these have been incorporated into the discussion but obviously cannot themselves be explained within the present analysis. They are taken as *given* in our theoretical approach, which is more concerned with their *consequences* for educational interaction. Hence the points at which they impinge upon educational groups have been indicated and it now remains to examine the combined impact of all the factors discussed on the course of educational conflict. It will only be possible to do this in the briefest terms; only the most salient features will be accentuated and most attention will be given to the final state of play between dominant and assertive groups at the point when macroscopic change begins to take place in education. Discussion of these changes themselves are reserved for the next chapter.

France and Russia are cases where an assertive group succeeded in devaluing the monopoly of the dominant group and gained educational control on the basis of restrictive strategies. For the Tsarist bureaucracy this also involved defeating another assertive group, through use of the same tactics, before it could assume control. Both countries clearly illustrate the fact that the possession of political power alone does not confer the ability to define instruction, although control of the legislative machinery is a necessary condition for restricting others and preventing them from doing so. For on the basis of this kind of strategy there are two stages involved in attaining educational control — one negative, the other positive. The first is restriction itself which is essentially a *destructive phase* comprising the closure of schools, proscription of teachers, and dismantling of the previous apparatus for educational administration. It is not synonymous with educational control (although it is a precondition of it), precisely because it is negative and may merely destroy the functioning of education altogether for a time. The second stage, where control is attained and a new definition of instruction is imposed, involves the *replacement* of educational facilities. For this to occur not only requires access to legislative machinery but also the political capacity to mobilize sufficient resources.

In France the Revolution itself only increased the instrumental activities of the assertive alliance; it gave the Third Estate legislative control through which to devalue the dominant group's monopoly, but it was not synonymous with successful assertion. The bourgeoisie was now politically powerful but still dependent on the support of the people in education as in politics. In both, the problem was to define a common denominator of reform acceptable to the diverse sections of the Third Estate. In effect this meant that whilst restriction against the Church was comparatively easy, the development of an acceptable blueprint for replacement was a problem which none of the three Revolutionary Assemblies solved.[61]

The need to retain popular support imposed two different kinds of constraints on replacement. Firstly, it meant that the bourgeois definition of instruction had to be modified to make concessions towards equality in educational opportunity and to shift its concern away from the secondary and higher levels towards the provision of elementary schooling for all. This had the undesirable effect of allowing private initiative to move into the field at the post primary level. Yet when an attempt was made in 1795 to found a national network of *écoles centrales* (secondary establishments), subsidised from public funds, with an intake of the best pupils from the elementary schools, it was impossible to found and maintain schools on anything approximating to the national scale planned. For the second constraint consisted in the fact that popular support was incompatible with high levels of popular taxation, however indirect these might be.

The shift from Assembly to Consular and finally to Imperial government meant that military coercion replaced popular support as the basis of political stability. With the return to strong government came educational etatism; the immediate resurgence of the bourgeois ideology of the Parliamentarians with its nationalism, vocationalism and gallicanism as the definition of instruction endorsed by the imperial political elite. On a coercive basis progress could finally be made towards replacement – of a kind which embodied these values.

In Russia the situation was complicated by the activities of the Nobility as an assertive group engaging in substitution on its own account. Its basic effect was greatly to prolong the period between restriction of the Orthodox Church's monopoly and educational replacement by the Tsarist bureaucracy. By the end of the eighteenth century the Church was no longer the controlling group – the State now educated as many pupils, the schools of the Holy Synod were ultimately subject to erastian supervision, and its ownership monopoly had been completely undermined by a series of confiscatory measures — but the Tsarist bureaucracy was unable to assume control. Its attempts to develop public education were blocked by competition from the private sector and aristocratic refusal to enrol in State Schools.[62] From the School Commission onwards the State ceased its assault on Orthodoxy and bent its restrictive powers to the suppression of aristocratic substitution. Alexander I's initial attempt to found a 'unified school system', to place all private establishments under the Commission, and to recruit a lower class of pupil, failed completely. In Count Stroganov's words, instead of a coherent Tsarist system, Russia's education was 'un tableau d'une bigarrure extrème'.[63] Instruction of the rural masses and unemancipated serfs was still consigned to the Church and at secondary level the nobility continued to operate its extensive private network.

Aristocratic resistance owed much to the fact that prestige could still be gained through the Ceremonial Table of Ranks. In 1809 this was abolished and an Education Act passed which associated rank with civil service grade and linked entry to governmental administration with production of a certificate from a *Russian* university. Despite the Nobility branding Speransky, the author of these reforms, a French agent, Tsarist policy was beginning to bite. Although the flow of 'latin babbling officials recruited from the sons of priests and government clerks'[64] increased, so did the number of noble pupils enrolled in public gymnasia. Nevertheless, private schooling did not diminish and in 1824 *pensions* and academies of the Moscow gentry received 2,000 pupils whilst the equivalent State gymnasia were training 450 and the university 51.

The uprising of westernised officers to prevent the accession of Nicholas in 1825 issued in the 'Nationality, Orthodoxy and Autocracy' phase, and with it the firmest commitment to restriction. Although ministerial directives sought to punish serfs for their recent political unreliability by excluding them from the democratic educational ladder, the main teeth of the legislation were directed towards the elimination of aristocratic substitution, now that it had proved a threat to political stability as well as to administrative efficiency. In 1835 all schools were placed under central administration and inspection, private schools had to observe the same rules as public ones in moral instruction, teacher selection, curricula, examination etc., and this included family tutors in private homes. Although the law and the directives issued between 1828-35 had not eliminated private education, but only brought it under state control in certain crucial respects, they killed its distinctiveness and prevented it from functioning as an alternative definition of instruction. From then on the long drawn out and double-barrelled restrictive phase was complete.

However, an unintended consequence of the repression used against aristocratic assertion was to delay the replacement phase still further. Part of the Tsarist success had derived from their willingness to rupture the traditional alliance between the political and the social elites, by opening state schools and public careers to talent. The unlooked for effect of this was the emergence of the intelligentsia.[65] Despite later attempts to stem the flow of commoners into gymnasia and universities, 'by 1840 that system that had been fashioned to prepare "humble" and "obedient" candidates for the state administration was becoming the seedbed of opposition to government' and a source of internal educational opposition to 'Nationality, Orthodoxy and Autocracy'. Attempts to expand public instruction to meet growing administrative requirements after the Crimean war[66] increased the size and organization of the student intelligentsia whose contempt for the modernization policy of the governing elite was branded as 'nihilistic'. Despite repression their politicization continued, and intensified in 1861 when the terms of the settlement for emancipation of serfs[67] led students to encourage the peasantry to 'take up axes' and 'seize land and liberty'. When they moved into the countryside and developed over 500 Sunday Schools for peasant literacy this was a clear anti-governmental threat. A student attack on the life of the Tsar convinced the political elite that top priority must be given to the development of educational control, whatever the competing claims on the national budget. On a fiercely coercive basis and with much forced public funding the full replacement phase finally got underway.

The cases of England and Denmark are very different for both had strong forms of assertion on a substitutive basis which led to the development of separate and alternative educational networks, outside the control of the dominant group. In both too, however, educational conflict did not result in a clear-cut transfer of control to an assertive alliance as occurred in France and Russia. Instead deadlock developed between the parties involved – the dominant group was threatened but not eliminated – the assertive alliance evaded constraints and entered the educational market, but could not monopolize it. Competition was fierce but since neither party could fundamentally damage the other, their respective educational networks continued to develop in parallel. Although the parties engaged in conflict in the two countries were very different, their reactions to deadlock in market competition were in fact identical — an attempt to form alliances which could undermine the market itself — activities whose rough economic equivalent would be cartelism.

English middle class substitution at the elementary level began early in the nineteenth century. Its immediate effect was to stimulate Anglican efforts to retain control and the National Society was the organization designed for this defence. The assertive group counter-attacked with the foundation of a parallel organization, the British and Foreign Schools Society, geared to undenominational instruction. A combination of factors reinforced this partitioning of the elementary field among the competing parties. Anglican fear, Tory repudiation, and Dissenting distrust of state intervention coupled with Whig commitment to educational expansion, represented a parallelogram of forces whose outcome was the voluntary system — where schools were financed through the two rival societies. In effect, control of the elementary level was left (and this itself was a product of substitutive conflict) to be determined by competition on the educational market. The factors which had produced the voluntary system, (and the religious difficulty was only partly responsible), ultimately had the effect of entrenching it. The wealth of the middle class allowed them to make considerable progress in founding schools and recruiting teachers, whilst Anglican appeals enabled the Church to increase its educational resources. Thus strong, differentiated, and autonomous networks of elementary schools continued to develop in parallel.

Although the middle class undoubtedly possessed a financial surplus, which if mobilized could have severely damaged the Anglican monopoly, two factors caused its substitution to falter in the 1840s. Both hinged on the fact that it is not the absolute availability of resources which is important, but the proportion of them devoted to assertion. On the one hand, the entrepreneurial element was too concerned with short-term profits derived from child labour to participate seriously in substitution, and the ambivalence of the ironmasters threw the economic burden of assertion onto the less wealthy sections of the alliance. On the other hand, the defection of the working class after 1832 presented the middle class with a fight on two fronts. Popular independent substitution, in depriving them of an ally and adding to their enemies, stretched their available resources and made them hesitate at precisely the point when they could have really damaged the Anglican monopoly.

At secondary and higher levels the same kind of stalemate occurred, for although the entrepreneurial-dissenting alliance succeeded in founding commercial, denominational, and proprietary schools in large numbers, this was countered by the revival, reform, and extension of the public schools under Anglican control. Similarly, the foundation of University College was matched by the establishment of King's College and Durham University as Anglican institutions, and the Test Acts remained in force.

Response to this deadlock was identical for the various parties concerned. After the decline of Tractarianism the Broad Church party increasingly turned towards the State for political intervention in defence of Anglican control and to further Church influence over the sectarian forces of dissent.[68] Partly because denominationalists feared the consequences of this, partly because closed corporations at secondary and higher level were outside the reach of competitive pressures, and partly due to their increased political influence, the middle class alliance was drawn into the political struggle in order to overcome market stalemate. Since working class assertion, with its limited resources, had recognized the impossibility of educational reform without political change during the second stage of the Chartist movement, all the parties engaged in conflict looked to political action for its resolution. The quest for politico-educational alliances which would exert pressure on political parties in Parliament developed in the 1860s. But it occurred when none of these groups had the exclusive prerogative of political influence and it took place in the context of two well-developed networks of national education. What all parties sought from the State was defence and expansion of what they had already achieved, and the extent to which they got it depended upon a lengthy and complex process of political interaction which lasted until the end of the century.

As far as Denmark was concerned, the obvious question is why the politico-economic elite, with all its advantages, failed to make rapid headway with its restrictive strategy, but also reached deadlock with other parties in the struggle for educational control. The intervening factors were both economic and political and involved the effects of foreign policy and internal changes which transformed the structure of government.

The first major attempt at restriction on the part of the politico-economic elite was the establishment of the Great School Commission (1789). This accepted that the clerical monopoly must be undermined if the new political goals were to be accomplished and saw that 'the keynote for success was . . . the provision of trained schoolmasters'[69] – an attack on the main basis of clerical control. Rural and town schools would be governed by Commissioners, a body so constituted as to prevent giving 'the parson too much authority'.[70] These proposals involved heavy public financing of teacher-training and salaries, the establishment of a secular system of educational administration, and the provision of school buildings. National economic depression intervened to prevent their implementation, for Denmark had supported Napoleon and been at war for seven years. At the end of this period trade had come to a standstill, corn prices had fallen so low that little progress could be made with the commercialization of agriculture, and the national bank was declared insolvent. The effect of government foreign policy had been to block its domestic educational policy. During the years of economic stagnation that followed, with agricultural prices continuing to fall between 1813 and 1830, there were neither the central nor the local resources available to mobilize for this purpose.

It was the worst of times at which to attempt major educational reform, and the financial situation accounts for so little of the assertive programme being accomplished by the legislation passed in 1814. In fact, since the Law made school attendance compulsory its unintended consequence was to consolidate the clerical monopoly in the country-side. 'In general there was a steady development of control by the clergy, who were often the only learned persons in a rural area and were perhaps the only persons able to carry out effective local administration'.[71] In urban areas legislation was marginally more successful, teacher training colleges being established despite the outcry of local taxpayers, but nevertheless staffing depended on the Lancastrian method. Town School Commissions with mercantilist patrons were responsible for local supervision, and they linked upwards to the School Directorate and finally the Chancery. Some centralized scrutiny was therefore established, especially for the appointment of school masters, but this was a far cry from successful restriction, for Church, Poor Law and Private schools remained under their own governing bodies. Some progress was made at the post-elementary level where the university was to supply staff for the Learned schools and the Directorate to scrutinize their appointment. But none of this seriously damaged the clerical monopoly, especially in the rural areas which the assertive group was most concerned to control. In other words, the politico-economic elite was neither able to exclude the dominant group from the educational market nor to prevent new assertive groups from entering it at the beginning of the nineteenth century. By 1845 two-thirds of the children in Copenhagen attended private schools, and substitution was under way in the countryside.

By 1848 peasant proprietors had made considerable progress in founding Folk High Schools for adults[72] and these now outnumbered the Learned Schools under the Directorate.[73] Increasingly the movement broke out of the Grundtvigian mould and became more closely related to peasant demands in other spheres, to the *Landboforeinger* seeking economic revindication, and to the agricultural co-operative movement. This 'alliance conclue entre la spiritualité grundtvigienne et le matérialism paysan',[74] increased resources available for substitution and the bargaining power of the group united under the ideological umbrella of popular Kulturkamp. Simultaneously the movement became allied with political organizations for the extension of peasant rights. Already in 1849 Sørensen had founded a school at Uldum which united tuition for practical agriculture with anticipatory preparation for political leadership.[75] After 1865 links developed with *Bondevennerne*, the peasant party demanding political participation and further land reform.

The powerful thrust of substitution between 1850 and 1870 frustrated attempts of the (now constitutional) elite[76] to push forward with its restrictive strategy. Certain concessions were made to peasant anticlericalism, children at Fri schools were exempted from examination in religious knowledge, the position of the Parson on School Commissions was weakened by increased community representation. Similar concessions were made to urban middle class initiative: the private schools were given legal recognition. If these were intended to reduce commitment to assertion through removing two of its original causes, the policy was a failure. For by now the Kulturkamp movement, which had always opposed the cultural elite, was determined to prevent the political elite from assuming educational control. Nevertheless, substitution became more difficult at the end of the 1860s when cheap corn from the USA and Canada, together with Baltic grain surpluses, damaged Danish agricultural exports. Although the co-operatives were to be extremely successful in reorienting production towards dairying and husbandry, these new capital requirements absorbed much of the economic surplus of small farmers.[77] Thus the rural Fri school movement faltered, and the war with Bismark, which hindered Danish trade and reduced middle class revenues, had a similar effect on the Real School movement in towns.

By about 1870 deadlock had been reached between the two assertive groups. The ruling class could not push forward with its restrictive strategy; 'in the political circumstances of the time, there was no future for any proposals to reform more drastically the school system, particularly when they contained any extension of State control'.[78] It thus remained firm only at the higher level. On the other hand, economic events had placed a firm brake on substitution at a time when the lower classes had made substantial progress only at the elementary level.[79] To break the deadlock the Kulturkamp movement became increasingly politicized, and not unlike their English equivalents, looked to political change to accomplish the redefinition of instruction. There was a difference, however, for Kulturkamp was far more extensive than English socialism in the mid-nineteenth century, and class conflict between the two Danish assertive groups had the advantage of being polarized. As the journalist Holm expressed it, 'Il n'y a chez nous que deux tendances principales qui s'opposent dans une lutte à mort. L'une trouve son expression dans la vieille culture classique, l'autre dans la nouvelle culture nationale, ou, pour les définir autrement, dans la culture qui a pour siège l'Université et dans celle dont la *højskole* est le centre'.[80]

This meant that educational interaction was to have a much greater influence upon political alignment in Denmark than was the case in England. The attacks launched against the National Liberal Party branded its protection of higher culture as a defence of upper class interests. This assault was virulent enough to promote an alliance between Liberals and Landowners in 1870 to constitute the Union of the Right. Correspondingly the Kulturkamp movement united with the Peasant Party to found the Union of the Left, *(Venstre)*, in the same year. This was led by Høgsbro, an ex-headmaster of the first Grundtvigian school, and was committed to educational change and the pursuit of parliamentary democracy.[81] The cultural battle had become a matter of class politics and in the words of a Venstre deputy in the *Folketing* (lower house), 'le véritable Kulturkamp a pour programme de préparer la voie à la liberté, à l'égalité, à la fraternité'.[82] Resolution of the educational conflict therefore depended on resolution of the political conflict, and until the end of the century political deadlock was to parallel the earlier educational stalemate. Meanwhile the separate educational networks retained their autonomy and continued to expand slowly.

NOTES

1. D. Lockwood, 'Some remarks on "The Social System"', in N. J. Demerath and R. A. Peterson, *System, Change and Conflict*, New York, 1967, p. 288.

2. The following discussion utilizes the theoretical framework developed in an earlier joint study of educational change in two countries before the advent of state systems. Cf. Michalina Vaughan and Margaret Scotford Archer, *Social Conflict and Educational Change in England and France, 1789-1848*, Cambridge, 1971, Ch. 2. This earlier book gives a much more detailed analysis of educational conflict itself, especially at the ideational level, and should be consulted as an example of the expanded application of the theoretical framework. However, this book stops short of the final consolidation of state systems in the two countries.

3. Max Weber, *Basic Concepts in Sociology*, London, 1962, p. 117.

4. This is discussed in greater detail in Michalina Vaughan and Margaret Scotford Archer, *Social Conflict and Educational Change in England and France, 1789-1848*, op. cit. Chs. 7-10.

5. Ibid., p. 134. See also F. Vial, *Trois siècles d'histoire de l'enseignement secondaire*, Paris, 1936, p. 48 ff.

6. Cf. F. Ponteil, *Histoire de l'enseignement en France: Les grandes étapes 1789-1964*, Paris, 1966 p. 32 ff. on Jesuit attempts to justify and strengthen their educational position.

7. Willis Dixon, *Education in Denmark*, Copenhagen, 1958, Ch. 1.

8. Ibid., p. 19.

9. Willis Dixon, *Society, Schools and Progress in Scandinavia*, Oxford, 1965, Ch. 1.

10. For an estimate of their extensiveness at the beginning of the nineteenth century see H. B. Binns, *A Centenary of Education, being the Centenary History of the British and Foreign School Society (1808-1908)*, London, 1908.

11. Select Committee on the Education of the Lower Orders in the Metropolis, appointed in 1816. (Its terms of reference subsequently included the whole country.)

12. A. O. J. Cockshut, *Anglican Attitudes*, London, 1959. See also D. Voll, *Catholic Evangelicalism*, London, 1963 and G. Faber, *Oxford Apostles*, London, 1954.

13. W. R. Ward, *Victorian Oxford*, London, 1965.

14. Cf. J. Sparrow, *Mark Pattison and The Idea of a University*, Cambridge, 1967, Ch. 3. During the period 1800-50, 25,000 matriculated from Oxford, and over 10,000 of them were later ordained.

15. M. Pattison, *Memoirs*, London, 1885, pp. 74-5.

16. W. H. Johnson, *Russia's Educational Heritage*, Pittsburg, 1950, Ch. 1. N. Hans, *The Russian Tradition in Education*, London, 1963, Ch. 1.

17. B. H. Sumner, *Peter the Great and the Emergence of Russia*, London, 1950, p. 16.

18. W. H. Johnson, *Russia's Educational Heritage*, op. cit., p. 20 and 21.

19. Quoted by F. Vial, *Trois siècles d'histoire de l'enseignement secondaire*, op. cit., p. 48. See also G. de Mirabeau, *Travail sur l'éducation publique*, Paris, 1791.

20. 'Military needs, above all, had necessitated the hiring of foreigners, and had emphasised dependence on trade and contact with the West. Bitter experience had proved how ineffectual the army usually was in any prolonged operations or in any offensive campaign. The Streltsy, part Palace guard, part standing army and police force . . . were more addicted to armed outbursts than fitted for serious military operations . . . They were a hereditary, privileged force, recruited for the most part from townsfolk, partly engaged in trade and handicrafts, living part in their own quarters, an inevitable hotbed of superstition, pride, reaction and religious dissent', B. H. Sumner, op. cit., p. 11 ff.

21. K. Waliszewski, *Le berceau d'une dynastie: les premiers Romanovs 1613-1682*, Paris, 1909. 'Empruté à Byzance, l'emploi des lettres de l'alphabet pour la notation des chiffres en rendre la pratique singulièrement difficile . . . et Krijanics aperçoit là avec raison une cause d'infériorité au point de vue commercial', p. 475.

22. 'Maîtres et disciples ne paraissent cependant y avoir connu que de très loin les éléments d'anatomie et de physiologie . . . Le livre de Vesale fut bien traduit en 1650 . . . mais pour l'usage du tsar seul, et l'unique examplaire de ce travail ne semble pas être sorti des mains du souverain. Le public était réduit à un manuel dont l'original latin, imprimé au quinzième siècle et de composition probablement plus ancienne, lui transmettait ces indications sur la vertu curative des pierres précieuses', op. cit., p. 477.

23. W. H. Johnson, *Russia's Educational Heritage*, op. cit., p. 16 ff.

24. 'The ancient tongues are only useful now to some specific sectors of society', D. Diderot, 'Plan d'une université pour le gouvernement de Russie ou d'une éducation publique dans toutes les sciences' in *Oeuvres complètes* (Assezat-Tourneux ed.) Paris, 1875, p. 441. Also see E. Caro, *La fin du 18è siècle*, Paris, 1880, pp. 255-56.

25. President B. G. Rolland, *Compte-rendu aux Chambres Assemblées des différents mémoires envoyés par les universités sises dans le ressort de la Cour*, Paris, 1786, p. 60.

26. In 1773 urban merchants petitioned the king that the exclusively religious nature of education meant that 'None of the middle classes have been able to educate their children to earn their daily bread by commerce', Willis Dixon, *Education in Denmark*, op. cit., p. 29.

27. Cf. Michalina Vaughan and Margaret Scotford Archer, *Social Conflict and Educational Change in England and France 1789-1848*, op. cit., pp. 60-79.

28. *Westminster Review*, Vol. XV, No. 29, (July) 1831.

29. An admirable contemporary account of the links between clergy and nobility is found in the polemic by E. J. Sieyès, *Essai sur les privilèges*, Paris, 1788.

30. A. O. J. Cockshut, *Anglican Attitudes*, op. cit.; T. W. Bamford, *Thomas Arnold*, London, 1960.

31. Willis Dixon, *Education in Denmark*, op. cit., p. 26.

32. P. M. Blau, *Exchange and Power in Social Life*, op. cit., pp. 117-141. See also W. Buckley, *Sociology and Modern Systems Theory*, op. cit., pp. 200-02. To Blau a group can avoid imbalances of obligations from occurring, in one of four ways:

(a) It can obtain benefits from X by providing services needed by X in return;
(b) It can suppress the need for such benefits;
(c) It can obtain these benefits from a source other than Group X;
(d) It can secure such benefits by force.

In this study we have seen that (a) and (b) are not feasible strategies for assertive groups for they cannot negotiate the scale of educational changes required nor renounce the need for them because of the continuation of obstructions. Hence the present study concentrates on strategies which coincide with Blau's (c) and (d) for gaining the educational benefits needed. Alternative (c) 'leads to the study of competitive processes, of the exchange rates that become established in social structure and of monopolisation' (p. 140). These are in other words precisely the issues examined here for SUBSTITUTIVE strategies. Alternative (d) calls attention to the differentiation of power in society, to organizations in which it is mobilized and to political processes and institutions. Again these are the crucial elements analyzed here for RESTRICTIVE strategies.

33. F. Ponteil, *Histoire de l'enseignement en France*, op. cit., p. 46.

34. G. C. Hippeau, *La révolution et l'éducation nationale*, Paris, 1883; M. Gontard, *L'enseignement primaire en France de la Révolution à la Loi Guizot, 1789-1833*, Lyons, 1959; A. Duruy, *L'instruction publique et la Révolution*, Paris, 1882; and L. Liard, *L'enseignement supérieur en France 1789-1889*, (2 Vols.) Paris, 1888.

35. P. L. Alston, *Education and the State in Tsarist Russia*, op. cit., p. 4.

36. B. H. Sumner, *Peter the Great and the Emergence of Russia*, op. cit., p. 18.

37. Ibid., p. 145.

38. Ibid., p. 6.

39. P. L. Alston, *Education and the State in Tsarist Russia*, op. cit., 4.

40. An apathy which led Engels to declare 'So stupidly narrow-minded is the English bourgeoisie in its egotism, that it does not even take the trouble to impress upon the workers the morality of the day, which the Bourgeoisie has patched together in its own interests for its own protection'. F. Engels, *The Condition of the Working Class in England in 1844*, London, 1892, p. 114.

41. M. Vaughan and M. S. Archer, *Social Conflict and Educational Change in England and France, 1789-1848*, op. cit.; see especially Chapter 5 'Assertive Ideologies in English Education', Ch. 6 'The Defensive Ideologies of Anglican Domination', Ch. 9 'Assertive French Educational Ideologies' and Ch. 10 'French Ideologies legitimating Educational Domination'.

42. His most important work in this connection is his 'Plan d'une université pour le gouvernement de Russie', op. cit. Cf. M. Tourneux, *Diderot et Catherine II*, Paris 1899, and J. Oestreicher, *La pensée politique et économique de Diderot*, Paris, 1936.

43. His most important work in this context is M. J. A. de Condorcet, *Sur l'instruction publique*, Paris, 1792. C.f. F. Vial, *Condorcet et l'éducation démocratique*, Paris, n.d.; J. Bouissounouse, *Condorcet, le philosophe dans la Révolution*, Paris, 1962; F. Alengry, *Condorcet – guide de la Révolution Française*, Paris, 1904. See also Condorcet, Sieyès, Duhamel, *Journal d'Instruction Sociale*, Paris, 1793.

44. The most important works dealing with education are: E. J. Sieyès, *Essai sur les privilèges*, op. cit. and *Qu'est-ce que le Tiers Etat?* , 3rd ed., Paris, 1789. Cf. P. Bastid, *Sieyès et sa pensée*, Paris, 1939.

45. 'Political economy, though its object be to ascertain the means of increasing the wealth of nations, cannot accomplish its design, without at the same time regarding their happiness, and as its largest ingredient the cultivation of religion and morality'. Thus Kay-Shuttleworth signalled the reincorporation of religion as a form of social control into middle class thought. J. Kay-Shuttleworth, 'The Moral and Physical Condition of the Working Classes in Manchester in 1832', in *Four Periods of English Education*, London, 1862, p. 39.

46. B. Simon, *Studies in the History of Education, 1780-1870* op. cit. See also E. Dolléans, *Le Chartisme (1830-1848)*, Paris, 1912; A. R. Schoyen, *The Chartist Challenge: a Portrait of George Julien Harney*, London 1958; R. H. Tawney, *The Radical Tradition*, London, 1964; and *The Life and Struggles of W. Lovett* (Tawney ed.), London, 1920.

47. B. H. Sumner, *Peter the Great and the Emergence of Russia*, op. cit., p. 152.

48. William H. E. Johnson, *Russia's Educational Heritage*, op. cit., p. 81.

49. P. L. Alston, *Education and the State in Tsarist Russia*, op. cit., p. 31.

50. Quoted by Willis Dixon, *Education in Denmark*, op. cit., p. 28. That pietist classicism was depriving the Monarchy of useful servants of state was the message transmitted at Holberg's College at Sdro, and this was to prove influential with the Professoriat until the end of the century.

51. Ibid., p. 41.

52. Lucien Trichaud, *L'education populaire en Europe*, Paris, 1969, Vol. II.

53. K. B. Andersen, 'Political and Cultural Development in 19th century Denmark', in J. A. Lauwerys (ed.), *Scandinavian Democracy*, Copenhagen, 1958, p. 157.

54. Erica Simon, *Reveil national et culture populaire en Scandinavie*, Uppsala, 1960, p. 591.

55. The monitorial system was devised by A. Bell and described by him in *An Experiment in Education made at the Male (Orphan) Asylum in Madras, suggesting a System by which a school or family may teach itself under the superintendence of the Master or Parent*, 2nd ed., London, 1809. This system was used extensively during the early years of the British and Foreign School Society and thus played a part in middle class substitution. It was used in France, experimentally towards the end of the Empire and more extensively during the Restoration. There it represented bourgeois anti-clericism and the attempt to replace the Teaching Orders by the State as controller and supplier of elementary instruction. In Denmark after the Great Commission in 1814 the King introduced the Lancastrian system in an attempt to break the clerical monopoly of teaching staff and simultaneously to 'diminish the burdens that are necessary otherwise for

the organisation of the common-school system' (Willis Dixon, *Education in Denmark*, op. cit., p. 56).

56. Cf. Michalina Vaughan and Margaret Scotford Archer, *Social Conflict and Educational Change in England and France 1789-1848*, op. cit., p. 89-92.

57. Willis Dixon, *Education in Denmark*, op. cit., p. 29.

58. P. Manniche, *Denmark: A Social Laboratory*, Oxford, 1939, p. 41.

59. D. B. Leary, *Education and Autocracy in Russia*, Buffalo, 1919. Aristocratic substitution began early . . . 'the desire was growing on the part of the nobility for a higher education. New interest in foreign countries resulted in the sending of children abroad and the importation of foreign tutors, as well as the establishment and growth of private boarding schools, established by foreigners, which sprung up in large numbers during the reign of Elizabeth (1741-61) . . . By 1746 there were some 27 such institutions giving higher education to some 6000 pupils', p. 42.

60. 'The Empress Catherine herself unwittingly added to the prestige of this imported instruction when, in preparing the ground for the advent of her system of free indigenous schools, she ordered the Commission on the Establishment of Schools to make a thorough investigation of all foreign teachers in the Empire in 1784. The Commission's Report revealed those schools operated by foreigners to be far superior to those run by Russians', W. H. E. Johnson, *Russia's Educational Heritage*, op. cit., p. 57.

61. The main educational plans to come before the three revolutionary assemblies were those of Mirabeau, Talleyrand, Condorcet, Romme and Lanthenas, Lakanal, Sieyès, Daunou and finally that of Lepelletier. They differ considerably in their underlying principles and in the programmes of educational change advocated. Cf. R. Sevrin, *Histoire de l'enseignement primaire en France sous la Révolution, le Consulat et l'Empire*, Paris, 1932; Also see H. C. Barnard, *Education and the French Revolution*, Cambridge, 1969.

62. One of the main reasons why the Tsarist Bureaucracy's attempt to get state education underway petered out at the end of the eighteenth century was 'lack of students. It was very hard to find students for the two higher classes . . . of the main schools, due largely to the competition of the private schools – usually run by foreigners – and the practice of employing foreign tutors in wealthy homes'. V. G. Simkhovitch, 'History of the School in Russia', *The Education Review*, May, 1907, pp. 502-03.

63. Quoted by P. L. Alston, *Education and the State in Tsarist Russia*, op. cit., p. 25.

64. Ibid., p. 26.

65. Ibid., p. 37.

66. The brother of Alexander II argued that after the Crimean defeat the government accepted that 'we are weaker and poorer than the first class powers. We are poorer not only in material means but in intellectual capacity; and we are especially short of trained administrators', quoted by P. L. Alston, *Education and the State in Tsarist Russia*, op. cit., p. 44.

67. Agricultural resources were divided roughly equally between 30,000 nobles and 20 million peasants.

68. This view was clearly expressed by Thomas Arnold and acted upon by his influential pupils. Cf. T. W. Bamford, *Thomas Arnold*, London, 1960; J. Fitch,

Thomas and Matthew Arnold and Their Influence upon English Education, London, 1897; J. J. Findlay, *Arnold of Rugby*, Cambridge, 1898; and A. P. Stanley, *Life and Correspondence of Thomas Arnold*, London, 1846.

69. Willis Dixon, *Education in Denmark*, op. cit., p. 38.

70. Ibid., p. 41.

71. Loc. cit.

72. E. J. Borkup, 'Free Schools for Children', in A. Boje, E. J. Borkup and H. Rutzebeck (eds.), *Education in Denmark*, Oxford, n.d. pp. 69-90.

73. Holger Begtrup, 'The Folk High School and Other Institutions for Adult Education in Connection with the Folk High School', in A. Boje, E. J. Borkup and H. Rutzebeck, *Education in Denmark*, op. cit.

74. Erica Simon, *Reveil national et culture populaire en Scandinavie*, op. cit., p. 594.

75. Lucien Trichaud, *L'education populaire en Europe*, Vol. II., op. cit. Sørensen founded Uldum to give such a political and practical education that 'Les paysans pussent jouer leur rôle politique dans le cadre des communes, des provinces ou de la nation, au même titre que les autres catégories sociales', p. 42.

76. In the aftermath of the 1848 revolutions, it was constitutional government rather than Parliamentary democracy which was introduced in Denmark. The new constitution and its subsequent revision had the effect of isolating the lower house, the folketing, based on general suffrage, from the landsting in which landowners had overwhelming representation and the prerogative of decision-making. The King retained the privilege of selecting Ministers from the landsting regardless of who had the majority in the folketing. Thus the eighteenth century politico-economic alliance had transformed itself into a constitutional ruling class. Other sections of society may have acquired a political platform, but they were still without political power.

77. P. Manniche, *Denmark: A Social Laboratory*, op. cit. 'From about 1880 the agriculture, however, again had to cover its capital requirements from other resources, both inland and foreign, in order to be able to undertake the change from grain growing and to undertake a large-scale, far-reaching extension and rationalisation of the industry', p. 41.

78. Willis Dixon, *Education in Denmark*, op. cit., p. 83.

79. Erica Simon, *Reveil national et culture populaire en Scandinavie*, op. cit., 'Tout ce que l'Intelligence défendait: son éxistence matérielle, son prestige culturel et son influence politique, ne fut menacé que lorsque la culture populaire, de la *højskole*, qui jusqu'alors avait été son seul siège, tenta de s'introduire dans les institutions reservées à l'intelligence. En effet les projets de Grundtwig ne s'étaient pas réalisés: le système grundtvigien ne pouvait s'appuyer ni sur l'Academia Sorana, ni sur l'Université du Nord. Seul existait la *højskole*, et de celle-ci, les circonstances pédagogiques avaient imposé un niveau de culture peu élevé et que les paysans seuls fréquentaient', p. 599.

80. Ibid., p. 607.

81. In 1872 the Left Alliance gained a majority in the folketing and insisted on a Parliamentary system with Ministers selected from the Party holding the majority in that house. The struggle persisted until 1901 but throughout the period the Left Alliance had a growing majority in the folketing. For example in 1884 they had 81 seats out of 102. Cf. K. B. Andersen, 'Political and Cultural

Development in 19th century Denmark', in J. A. Lauwerys (ed.), *Scandinavian Democracy*, op. cit.

82. Quoted by Erica Simon, *Reveil national et culture populaire en Scandinavie*, op. cit., p. 596.

4 STRUCTURAL ELABORATION: The Emergence of State Educational Systems

This chapter is concerned with the final phase of the cycle, which is also of course the first phase of the next cycle. It deals then with educational changes which result from the social interaction just discussed — with structural elaborations which will in their turn condition future interaction and further educational change. The aim here is to link a specific mechanism of change (the interaction of educationally dominant and assertive groups) with its effects on the structure of education and the relations between education and society. It should be underlined, however, that none of the macroscopic changes which will be discussed are presumed to be more adaptive, efficient, stable or legitimate than the preceding forms of education with their different relationship to the wider social structure. Such concepts can be used to describe or assess the *consequences* of social change (which may or may not reveal greater adaptation, efficiency, stability or legitimacy), but they cannot be used as a substitute for analyzing the processes which produce change or examining the characteristics which are transformed.

The forms of structural elaboration to be discussed can be summarized in two propositions, which will be advanced and defended throughout this chapter.

(i) The integration of education with the State and with a plurality of other social institutions emerges from the interaction of dominant and assertive groups. Thus distinctive changes in the structural relations between education and society derive from this specific process of interaction.

(ii) These changes in external structural relations are accompanied by various structural changes taking place *within* the educational field itself. The most important of these are the development of 'unification', 'systematization', 'differentiation' and 'specialization'. Each is regarded as a specific type of change; together they summarize the internal changes stemming from the interaction of dominant and assertive groups in the past.

It is important at this point to be clear about the scope of the explanation which is presented here. Firstly this part of the book attempts to delineate the sufficient conditions for the emergence of state educational systems possessing the structural characteristics listed in the above propositions. It seeks to explain the *autonomous* emergence of these macroscopic changes as the result of group interaction in countries where they cannot be attributed to external intervention, via conquest, colonization or territorial redistribution. Obviously this reduces the applicability of the theory to a particular group of countries and probably even to a minority of cases when world educational development is considered. Nevertheless, a theory which limits itself to endogenous processes of educational change is important, both in its own right, and also because it helps to account for the nature of instruction imposed abroad.[1] The origins of the particular system which is exported must thus be understood in order to account for educational change in conquered or colonized countries. In itself, our kind of theory will not fully account for educational development in such countries, but it is indispensable to a full account.[2]

Secondly, unlike general or unified sociological theory, this type of explanation relates to specific structures and is not atemporal. It only refers to the cycle of interaction immediately preceding the emergence of State systems, and not to the whole history of educational change. Hence it predicates certain developmental features of both systems and social integration. The key concept underlying the earlier discussion of ownership and subordination, of obstruction and complementarity, was that of differentiated institutional orders. Without it the notion of systems integration is meaningless,[3] for this refers to the relations between differentiated units with relative degrees of autonomy. Similarly, the discussion of domination and assertion presupposed not only the existence of a differentiated institutional order (to which different groups were associated), but also an analogous situation at the level of social integration[4] – the relative autonomy of differentiated interest groups. This means that the theory advanced here is not applicable to earlier social formations, such as the historic Empires or the ancient Eastern civilizations, which displayed relatively low levels of institutional differentiation (monolithic social structures) and social autonomy (elite superimposition and mass subordination).[5]

Thus to analyse interaction prior to the emergence of State systems is to take the context in which they develop as given. Obviously this context itself emerged from previous interaction[6] and can only be explained by reference to it. Our theory then is tied to these contextual features (which it does not itself explain) and it *must not* be detached from them in any unwarranted attempt to increase the historical scope of explanations.

1. UNIVERSAL CHARACTERISTICS OF STRUCTURAL ELABORATION: MULTIPLE INTEGRATION AND STATE SYSTEMS

This section will concentrate on the emergence of the universal changes already listed in the first proposition. These concern two major changes in structural relations which gradually develop from the interaction between dominant and assertive groups – *the integration of education to the political centre and also to a plurality of other social institutions.* Thus the process of interaction which accounts for education losing its mono-integrated status is also responsible for linking instruction to the central decision-making agency of a society. In other words, these two changes are themselves linked because they are the joint-products of interaction: for various reasons which will be amplified later it is unlikely that there will be a long time-lag between the emergence of one and the appearance of the other. Both changes are the products of a competitive process of interaction, but this does not mean that they follow from a uniform sequence of events. As has been seen there are two different kinds of strategies which Assertive groups can employ to devalue the monopoly of the educational ownership group – those of *Restriction and Substitution.* The precise way in which these universal changes developed varies according to which of the strategies was pursued in each country. The use of either restrictive or substitutive strategies also affects the order in which the two major structural changes occur and the extent to which they are a direct and intended consequence of interaction. Because of these differences the emergence of multiply-integrated State educational systems will be traced from the two assertive strategies in turn.

1(a) From Restrictive Strategies

As a method of assertion, restrictive strategies depend upon using the state legislative machinery to devalue the monopoly of the dominant group. So far, in concentrating on this process of devaluation, we have been concerned with how the subordination of education to another social institution was destroyed, not with its reintegration with other parts of society. Yet this destructive phase is not in itself successful assertion. Although the antecedent structural relations have been dissolved, the old dominant group has merely been deposed but not replaced. Even if an assertive group succeeds in carrying out *restriction, it may not be able to bring about replacement* of the facilities supplied by the old dominant group. In this case new structural relations do not emerge between education and any other social institution. For restriction simply anihilates existing educational provisions, unless replacement takes place immediately. Until new resources, buildings, textbooks, trained teachers, etc. are supplied, it is logically impossible for relations of interdependence to be established between education and any part of the social structure. This means that state intervention (for purposes of restriction) does not of itself lead directly to the integration of education to the polity. Such was clear in the case of France where successive Revolutionary Assemblies failed to move from the destructive phase of restriction to the constructive stage of replacement: it was under Consular not Revolutionary government that new educational facilities began to be consolidated.[7] It was even clearer in Russia where we have seen that the delay between restriction and replacement was considerably prolonged by the intervention of counter-assertive groups.

It is in this need to replace as well as to restrict, if a new group is to accede to educational control, that the mechanism is found which accounts for the emergence of State educational systems. The mechanism itself entails nothing superordinate to the actors involved, it is simply the result of an assertive group continuing to seek educational control. As such its effects are obviously contingent upon the consistent pursuit of this goal. Were an assertive group to falter in the face of difficulties with replacement, and to renounce its desire to define instruction, the predicted consequences would not follow. As in any sociological theory which focuses upon goal-oriented behaviour, it must be recognized that actors and groups of actors can change the goals they seek to attain, for to reject determinism is to admit that ultimately circumstances force no-one to do anything. Nevertheless for a theory of this kind to have explanatory power there must be good reasons why a particular goal is highly likely to be sustained by a group and thus lead to the predicted consequences. Unless a theory gives such reasons, (or clearly specifies the conditions under which goal-orientations change), it is no theory at all and social change remains the unexplained effect of random shifts in actors' aims.

Here the goals contained in the assertive group's ideology are seen as conditioned by the institutional operations with which it is associated. Initially the group sought educational control because these operations were being seriously obstructed, and it wished to have the power to redefine educational services. Its activities continue to be impeded in the absence of educational provisions (for if its operations could dispense with such services, this group would originally have fallen in the neutral category) and may again be obstructed by the resurgence of the old dominant group if replacement does not occur. Thus continuity in conditioning, represented by the endurance of obstructions, accounts for the assertive group's pertinacity in seeking educational control. It is the reason why groups which have accomplished the negative restrictive phase will struggle to achieve educational replacement.

To call this a struggle is not simply to reflect upon the historical course of events in various countries; it derives instead from the reasons which lead an assertive group to employ a restrictive strategy in the first place. It was argued earlier that there were negative constraints which predisposed towards the adoption of restrictive strategies, the significance of which now becomes clear. The alternative assertive policy — substitution — consists in devaluing the dominant group's monopoly by providing a competitive supply of educational facilities. If it is to be successful, the wealth required is considerable and this presupposes an access to financial resources which parallels the access to legislative influence needed for restriction. Now it was argued that few assertive groups had a choice of strategy because the distributions of the two major social resources – power and wealth – are not fully super-imposed. Most such groups were thus better placed for conducting one or the other strategy, and those which endorsed restriction did not usually have financial resources commensurate with their political power. This was the case in both of our examples of successful restric-tion, since economic wealth was concentrated outside the assertive groups – in the hands of the French landed aristocracy not the Third Estate, and of the Russian nobility not the Tsarist Bureaucracy. Because of this the assertive group which had waged a successful policy of restriction was completely unable to replace educational facilities out of its own resources. It thus had the motive but not the means to complete the process of assertion, unless further recourse was made to the state machinery.

However, when the assertive group and the political elite are co-terminus, the lack of resources does not preclude replacement. For the advantage such an assertive group possesses over any other is that it can use the central legal machinery to organize *public* educational financing rather than having to provide such facilities itself. To do this is not an easy or automatic procedure, if only because it is an innovatory one which involves withdrawing central resources from existing priorities and/or increasing the burden on the public. It is one, however, that presents the doubly irresistible attraction of allowing the assertive group to control educational output in conformity with its goals and to do so at national level. Just as central legislation enabled the restrictive phase to be thorough-going and nationwide (in contrast to the patchy results of even the most effective substitutive strategy), so too centrally organized public financing means that the same kind of scope can be envisaged for reconstruction.

However, what takes place in this situation is not merely the integration of education to the polity, but the emergence of national State education. The assertive group does not simply replace the old dominant group, for it cannot subordinate education by making it dependent on resources it owns and supplies. These are public resources, and with their mobilization for purposes of instruction, *educational ownership and educational control become separated for the first time.* There was never any question of the assertive political elite being able to appropriate public funds and thus to constitute itself as an ownership group, for such wealth was not centrally located. In both cases the amounts which could be diverted from the national budget were totally inadequate to the task of replacement. Each of the assertive groups accepted sooner or later (after students moved into the countryside in Russia and after the political loyalty of teaching orders was questioned in France towards the end of the Empire) that educational control would remain imperfect while ever replacement remained incomplete. Here the financial positions in which they found themselves had much in common: the solutions they worked out are striking in their similarity. Both of them involved supplementing central funding by mobilizing local resources for replacement.

These solutions were similar in the sense that in the two countries the limited amount of direct financing by Government was devoted to replacing the upper levels of instruction. The budget of Imperial France contained no allocation to elementary instruction,[8] while State expenditure on secondary and higher education in Russia during 1879 was six times higher than outlays on lower levels.[9] In both the basic device for ensuring replacement was firmly to place financial responsibility for elementary and higher grade instruction on the local areas. Thus the Russian Public School Statute passed in 1864 made the district and provincial *Zemstvos*, (representative assemblies created to bridge the gap between Government and village created by the abolition of gentry command over serfs), responsible for the establishment and maintenance of local elementary schools. Similarly, in 1872, the municipal *dumas* were to provide the financial support for urban higher grade schools.

Perhaps the budget of the Imperial University gives the clearest picture of the importance of central mobilization compared with direct central financing. Despite considerable complications surrounding payment of State contributions,[10] the receipts of the *Université* as a whole can be broken down under several headings. Firstly, the resources (physical and financial) of older educational establishments were made over to it; secondly, the Université was given a million francs credit to cover initial expenses, but this carried an interest rate of 5 percent; thirdly, a recurrent grant was made of revenue from certain public investments. However, much that the Université treasury received came from local contributions – Faculty examination fees were paid into it and one twentieth of both private and public school fees were commandeered for it. Furthermore, by 1811 the Municipalities were charged with the upkeep of *Faculté, Lycée* and *Collège* buildings and the principal Communes were compelled to create grants for secondary school pupils or pay a contribution into the treasury which was earmarked for this purpose. In sum, the elementary schools, Lycées and some Facultés being self-supporting, the Université treasury had only to maintain in full the central educational administration and the national network of academic administration.

Thus the assertive group succeeds in bringing about replacement not through the supplies it provides itself but by use of its political authority to mobilize the necessary resources. It has gained educational control, not on the old basis of monopoly ownership of facilities but by virtue of its legislative power. Control ceases to be entrepreneurial and becomes managerial, for although education remains subordinate, it is dependent upon resources owned and supplied by the State, not by a dominant group. The capacity to define instruction becomes firmly linked to political position, and, what is completely novel, can be lost with the declining political fortunes of a group. Thus the emergence of national State education is the result of a group attempting to complete a restrictive strategy, but the control it gains over it is of a different and weaker kind than that previously enjoyed by dominant ownership groups.

So far it has been the development of the integration between education and the State which has been accentuated as the end result of the replacement phase. However, the same two factors — the assertive group's desire to gain educational control and its use of public resources to do so — also account for the simultaneous emergence of multiple integration. Firstly, all assertive political elites face considerable problems in arranging the public financing of education for the first time. This is necessarily the case since such resources must either be redeployed away from existing recipients or new revenues must be raised. The former may be resisted by other elites or sub-elites, the latter by the newly levied or more heavily taxed sections of the population. The scale of resources required involved *both* the raising and the redeployment of revenues in the countries considered, and it is difficult to see how this could have been otherwise when the emergence of state education predated the advanced industrial society. Its major implication was that the assertive group had to seek political support for large-scale public spending on education — support within the political elite for giving educational spending a high priority and outside it for supplementing central educational expenditure. In turn the latter groups made their support conditional upon their own educational demands being met by government.

If previous forms of education had been unhelpful, or if the new educational ideology led groups to think that the new outputs would be incompatible with their aims, support could be withheld unless certain conditions were met. The assertive group is now in the difficult position that it cannot gain control (by completing replacement) without support. Yet support is conditional upon a diversification of educational outputs beyond the goals of the polity. This is one of the main sources of multiple integration and one which is as important for authoritarian regimes as for those based on authority. *It is however an unintended consequence, for the diversification of educational outputs in order to service a multiplicity of operations is the price the assertive group pays for the mobilization of resources. It is the cost of control without ownership.*

In addition, however, some of the new structural relations which develop between education and other social institutions are intended ones which stem from the goals of the assertive group. By definition all political elites have a plurality of aims which impinge upon the operations of various institutional spheres — economic, administrative, judicial, military, etc. as the case may be. Specific changes in educational output will help in the attainment of these aims. In other words, a certain amount of diversification of educational services is envisaged by an assertive political elite — but only to help those activities which the elite itself designates. Furthermore, although a certain unity of educational aims may have characterized the restrictive phase of assertion, political elites are not homogeneous, and when it comes to replacement, sectional and factional interests (derived from differences in political role position and in ideological conviction) may mean different priorities about the new kind of educational services to be developed. No political elite is truly monolithic, and sub-groups like the military may want educational outputs rather different from those sought, for example, by heads of civil administration. This makes an important contribution to multiple integration for it introduces problems of elite cohesion, whose solution generally involves concessions. *Ideally the assertive group would like to establish interdependence imperatively between education and those operations designated in its blueprint; in practice this is modified because of the need for support from sectional interests within the elite and for public support outside it.* Thus the two sources of multiple integration, the intended and the unintended, intermingle and determine the exact nature of the structural relations which emerge. Their relative importance, however, can be very different as the cases of France and Russia indicate.

In France replacement was inhibited during the three Revolutionary Assemblies since the need for popular support precluded the high levels of public taxation required. This also accounted for the assertive group accepting considerable modifications in its goals during this period. The various blueprints discussed[11] show progressive concessions being made to social levelling through education, and their fates witness to the impossibility of passing legislation consistent with bourgeois interests. Under the *Convention*, with the Assembly divided into competing factions and the Republic threatened on its frontiers, educational planners dared not be socially divisive – elementary schooling was to inform and enlighten citizens not to indoctrinate or train inferiors and secondary instruction in the few *Ecoles Centrales* of 1795 was to be non-elitist and non-vocational. Only in the *Grandes Ecoles*, especially *Polytechnique* and *Ecole Normale*, were specialist skills developed. Maintaining the unity of the Third Estate was necessary for the defence of the Republic but it militated against financial mobilization for replacement of educational facilities.

Under the Consulate and Empire, strong government was less reliant on popular allegiance; national unity and state utility became more prominent political goals. But the financial problem remained and despite ingenious means of raising revenues they would not stretch to match the scale of Napoleon's educational designs. The choice was made to develop those forms of instruction from which central government would gain most . . . 'to instruct is secondary, the main thing is to train and to do according to the pattern which suits the State'.[12] Accordingly a national network of Lycées was developed whose *baccalauréat* gave entry to state-employment or specialized further training in reorganized Grandes Ecoles.[13] Thus the Consulate 'destroyed that which the Revolution would have probably retained, the Ecoles Centrales and maintained and developed those which it certainly intended to replace, the great special schools'.[14]

The Grandes Ecoles bear very clear witness to the precise services that education was to provide at the highest level for other institutional operations: for example, St-Cyr supplied the officer corps for the army, Polytechnique, a flow of scientists and mathematicians for the Civil Service, and Ecole Normale stocked the highest reaches of the teaching profession.[15] Selection by merit to the Lycées, military discipline within them, and occupational rewards on graduation, harnessed ability to state service, and, by creating a diploma elite from among the bourgeoisie, distributed vested interests in political maintenance. As the State only needed a limited number of trained cadres, extension of education to the masses would be financially wasteful, for the individual had no right to instruction if the State had no need of it. Nevertheless the wish 'to use the masses for manual labour and above all . . . to obey and to die beneath the flag'[16] required a political socialization which would cost money. To provide this at State expense would have subtracted from secondary and higher provisions, but to concede to Catholic pressures for readmission to the educational field had the double advantage of securing Church support for the new policy whilst passing it the bill for elementary instruction. This compromise was prompted not only by financial expediency but also by the desire to use religion for political control: theology itself would promote social quietism and, when linked to the Imperial Catechism,[17] would reinforce political loyalty and nationalism. State inspection (decreed in 1811) would prevent the Church from exceeding its brief and pursuing autonomous religious goals.

During his Hundred Days Napoleon was to regret clerical entrenchment at this level, for under the Empire 'the Brothers remained what they had been before and their subordination was nothing but nominal . . . it appeared that the main goal of primary instruction was as before to instruct the people in the Catholic religion'.[18] Thus the forms of multiple integration developed under the Empire linked post-elementary outputs as closely as possible to the military, bureaucratic and political operations of State, whilst the traditional interdependence between the Church and elementary schooling remained basically undisturbed.

In many ways Napoleon had rightly forecast that 'public education is the future and the duration of my work after me', at least as far as the secondary and higher levels were concerned. For the structural relations he had established were simply too advantageous to Government for subsequent political elites to dispense with them, during the Restoration and July Monarchy. Increasingly, however, various political groups felt their goals blocked by the exclusive integration of elementary education to the Church. Thus to the Liberals the State should take over responsibility for this form of instruction which would reinforce constitutionalism, whilst to the Monarchists it would inculcate dynastic loyalty; to both, on the eve of the July Revolution, government should compel local authorities to maintain elementary instruction. It was not these pressures which prevailed but bourgeois interest in establishing a form of integration which Napoleon had completely neglected – between education and economy.

Temporary revival of popular support had been essential for the proclamation of the July Monarchy and was sufficient for the new bourgeois political elite to transform educational services to meet economic ends. Rejecting the diversification of secondary education, where broadening of the curriculum might have democratized its intake, the social composition of the political elite led them to prefer to introduce this new form of integration at elementary level. The establishment of higher grade schools (primaires supérieures) in 1833, as vocational schools, provided the skills increasingly sought in commerce, industry and business administration. According to Guizot's aim it 'enabled the lower classes of society to increase their output, to improve their living standards and thus to create new sources of wealth for the State'.[19] Thus the previous integration between religion and elementary education was destroyed to be replaced by a new structural relationship with the economy. And this occurred without disturbing the connections previously established between secondary education and the State or between social class and educational opportunity. For the changes involved in this new aspect of multiple-integration were specifically designed by the political elite to introduce 'the degree of expansion in popular education which the evolution of the occupational structure demanded and a stable society could accommodate'.[20]

The Tsarist Bureaucracy had, as an assertive group, sought educational changes of a kind which would have serviced a number of institutional operations, important to the political elite – instruction relevant to bureaucratic efficiency, to political loyalty, to military strength and to economic development. However, at the precise point when replacement became a practical possibility, in the 1860s, the combination of student nihilism and Polish nationalism – the one threatening the life of the Tsar the other the revolt of the Western borderlands – reduced the immediate educational aims of the Minister of Education, Dimitri Tolstoy, to that of using instruction to buttress the régime. In this context 'Tsardom's search for an educational solution to the problem of control of social change'[21] resulted in the bald etatist formula that schooling should promote the political trinity – socialization, integration and recruitment. In other words, it was not from Tolstoy, as 'mouthpiece of the State',[22] that a strong impulse towards multiple integration originated. Only at the very uppermost

level, after intensive pupil selection and socialization, was some diversification envisaged in order to serve specialist bureaucratic requirements.
Much more important in the Russian case was the need for political
support to pass the legislation and gain acceptance of the ministerial
regulations which brought publicly financed education into being. Here
pressures from outside the political elite and from sectional interests
within it, brought about multiple integration. At the broadest level of
generalization, struggles amongst the elite were the crucial factor in
extracting diversified outputs from secondary and university establishments in return for supporting central funding of these institutions,
whilst the need for local contributions towards urban and rural schooling made presures from the non-elite more significant for elementary
instruction. However, what this dichotomy misses is the way in which
ministerial needs for both elite and popular support interacted to
determine the operations that state education came to serve.

Tolstoy's intention was to concentrate governmental resources on
secondary education and to divide it into separate *realschule* (preparing
for local affairs), and classical gymnasia (the channel to State service) in
which the study of dead languages was to deaden the political passions.
This was denounced as expected by the student intelligentsia, but more
significant was public opposition to the standardized classical curriculum on grounds of its irrelevance to important social activities. The
protest raised by Ushinsky[23] that 'at the present time we do not need
Hellenists and Latinists. We need people active in the State and public
service, *factory workers, machinists, industrial managers, agricultural
specialists, and other real people*',[24] was taken up by the liberal press
and found sufficient resonance within the political elite itself to force
the formation of a Council of State committee to examine the education Bill.

At committee meetings demands for further differentiation of educational services were strongly voiced by General Miliutin, Minister of
War. Within the Defence Ministry he had already remodelled the five
military academies, linking them to recruitment. This was a useful
initiative but did not in his view go far enough. The Military Statute
was under debate at the same time and in the interests of substantially
increasing army efficiency Miliutin counterproposed a single general
high school with different branches which would mean that natural
scientists could enter the universities as well as classicists. His proposals
for elementary instruction would also have had the same effect of
serving military as well as civil requirements. Although the full meeting

of the Council of State supported Miliutin's diversified plan against official standardization, the political trial of students held responsible for the University riots of 1869 led the Tsar to override this decision and to ratify the statute for Tolstoy's gymnasium. Nevertheless, the force of demands for more specialized education had been felt, and having secured the services of the gymnasia for governmental bureaucracy, Tolstoy had to concede much on the seven-year realschule.

Specialization would characterize the final three years with terminal courses in business and accounting, mechanics and chemistry and a general course leading to agricultural, engineering, mining and veterinary colleges. Again able to address themselves to secondary education, the committee of the Council of State took this opportunity to reassert its preference for the general but differentiated gymnasia and thus rejected these proposals. Denied backing from important sections of the political elite, Tolstoy courted public support by extending the right to adapt (Real) educational services to local needs.

> Zemstvos, estates of the realm, public organizations and private persons contributing substantial financial support to an institution were given the right to elect an honorary curator with a seat on the pedagogical council. The Council, in turn, was free to organize the last three years of the course of studies to meet local needs. For its part the Ministry of Education undertook to open 50 new schools and make stipends available to train the necessary teachers of chemistry, mechanics and accounting.[25]

With the public support this elicited, and against the wishes of important sections of offical opinion, the Tsar ratified the realschule statute of 1872.

This bifurcated plan delineated the form of multiple integration which was to last until 1917: with elitist gymnasia servicing the civil state, and public realschule defined as the limited area in which other institutional operations — commercial, industrial, technical and professional — might gain some of the specialized outputs required. The same formula was applied to the earliest forms of schooling. A preparatory class was added to the gymnasium, for children between eight and ten, and its curriculum anticipated later concentration on classics. On the other hand, the Urban schools of 1872, financed by the bourgeois town councils, offered a more diversified course of advanced primary instruction, as did the rural schools maintained by the Zemstvo School Boards, though at a much more basic level. The need for political and financial support prevented the Tsarist bureaucracy from simply replacing one form of mono-integration by another, but Tsarist autocracy succeeded in confining its concessions to inferior institutions, running in parallel to those which furnished the political requirements of state.

1(b) From Substitutive Strategies

Since these two major changes in structural relations are held to be universal consequences of the interaction between dominant and assertive groups, we must now turn to their derivation from substitutive strategies. As a method of assertion, substitution is an attempt to displace an existing dominant group by devaluing its monopoly of educational supplies through market competition. Here the assertive group develops and provides new schools and teachers, hoping gradually to corner the educational market and thus impose its own definition of instruction. Unlike cases where restrictive strategies were employed, the integration of education to the central polity is an indirect consequence of interaction and certainly not one which groups embarking on substitution intended to occur.

The aim of those employing substitutive strategies is to assume the position of exclusive control enjoyed by the dominant group. In other words, they seek to change the part of society which education serves, but to retain its mono-integrated status. However, the immediate effect of this type of assertion is to introduce a rudimentary form of multiple integration which becomes more complex and extensive as conflict continues. When an assertive group enters the educational market for the first time it does so because it seeks a very different kind of instruction from that defined and provided by the dominant group. Consequently the output from assertive schools is designed to serve operations and activities which had previously gained nothing from the only form of instruction available. Now two different parts of the social structure are benefiting from two very different types of instruction and there is every reason why this preliminary form of multiple-integration should continue.

Even supposing that an assertive group was so successful in its policy of substitution that it reached a point where the monopoly of the dominant group was severely damaged, (i.e. the latter now has less schools and teachers than the former), this does not mean that it assumes supreme educational control. For the crucial thing about substitutive strategies, as this limiting case shows, is that they are incapable of completely excluding the old dominant group from the educational market. A variety of means, (ideological, financial etc.) can be used to increase the appeal of the new substituted schools and to decrease the attractiveness of establishments still operated by the old dominant group. Ultimately, however, competition can only reduce school enrolment and increase costs for the dominant group; it cannot deprive them of the facilities they own or the right to keep on supplying them.

It is here that we see the significance of factors leading to the adoption of a substitutive strategy in the first place. In this case the predisposition towards using this kind of strategy was the opposite of that conducive to using a restrictive strategy. In other words, few assertive groups are equally well placed for conducting either strategy, and those which adopt substitution are groups whose economic surplus outweighs their political influence. They lack the degree of access to central legislative machinery necessary for successful restriction. This being the case, and no major change in the distribution of political power having occurred, the assertive group lacks the legal constraints necessary to exclude the old dominant group completely from the market. Actually in neither Denmark nor England did middle class substitution prove so damaging that it only required legal leverage to consolidate control. In the former this probably went further than in the latter, for by 1845 the majority of children in Copenhagen attended private schools and these were largely the *Fri* schools of the commercial classes. However, not only was the capital atypical of a rural country, but this assertive group lacked political power under the absolute monarchy. Furthermore, it had no chance of exerting political influence to consolidate its educational control since the governing elite was busy furthering the restrictive designs of the large landowners.

This characteristic lack of legal constraints has further implications for the extension of multiple integration in its rudimentary form. The lack of such constraints not only prevents the substitutive group from fully excluding the old dominant group from educational activities, but it also means that *other* assertive groups cannot be stopped from entering the educational market. As and when operational exigencies lead groups from other institutional orders to contemplate substitution on their own behalf, nothing but their own limited resources can prevent them. This may well occur, for there is no reason to suppose that over long periods of time the dominant definition of instruction will only prove obstructive in one quarter. It is possible that incipient forms of substitution can be contained by the leading assertive group. Its ideology may provide a broad enough umbrella to shelter or appear to shelter the new educational changes pursued. This was certainly the case with English middle class assertion, which retained working class support until 1832. But whenever and wherever a second assertive group engages in independent substitution — as the Chartists did when convinced that their educational aims were diametrically opposed to entrepreneurial interests, and as the Danish Peasant Proprietors did in the belief that rural activities required a form of schooling geared closely to them — multiple integration increases in scope.

This is necessarily the case for no new group will launch a substitutive strategy unless it is profoundly dissatisfied with the services provided in the schools of both the dominant and the leading assertive[26] groups. It enters the market because it wants something different from what exists, and this is what it provides. Thus the Danish Folk High Schools and the Mechanics Institutes, Halls of Science and Academies[27] of the English working class alike developed a non-vocational definition of instruction, geared to popular enlightenment, and serving the political advancement of a group which all other forms of schooling neglected or tried to contain. Through these independent efforts new parts of society received educational services for the first time. This form of multiple integration is rudimentary because, although 'education' as a whole has plural dependencies on the supply of resources from different groups, the various independent networks of establishments are completely separate from one another. There is in fact no 'education as a whole' except in the sense of it being the sum of these various parts, owned by different groups, serving diverse institutional operations, and operating in isolation from one another. The networks are totally segregated in terms of roles, personnel, administration, financing, intake, examination, and above all, definition of instruction.

Thus in England, by the mid nineteenth century, competitive conflict had produced three main independent networks. The catechistic nature of elementary schooling and the classical character of secondary curricula meant that Anglican education served predominantly religious goals. Schools developed by members of the middle class tended to be linked to the occupational structure of industrial society and to transmit highly compatible values, whether secular or dissenting in form. The working class educational movement remained concerned with the practical skills and political knowledge which contributed to group advancement. At the same date the Danish picture was equally complex with four different networks, but in contrast to England, each of these concentrated on a particular level of instruction to a much greater extent.

Thus the residual Lutheran network, especially strong at elementary level in the countryside, continued to serve religious goals; the private proprietary schools run by the commercial classes prepared for business careers and represented the only higher grade instruction available in urban areas; the landowning political elite came closest to embracing the three levels, but concentrated its resources on the Learned Schools and Universities whose classical and academic curricula served to confirm the status of landed gentry and to form traditional servants of State; the peasant proprietors, like the English working class movement, began with adult education and controlled a network of Folk High Schools devoted to national culture and rural awakening, although the Agricultural Schools it later developed were very closely geared to practical farming.

However, this rudimentary form of multiple integration, where each different kind of educational output was provided independently by and for the owner of that particular network, is of enduring importance. For the origins of multiple integration proper are found in these vigorous independent networks, each one embodying a different definition of instruction. Basically this comes about through a process of *incorporation*, as these segregated networks become connected together to form a system. But this is not a simple additive process: the type of national education which emerges is not just the sum of these various sets of establishments. It is the product of negotiation, conciliation, concession and coercion, all of which result in modifying the original networks – accentuating some, altering others and partially suppressing certain institutions. Nevertheless, diversity in national education stems from the incorporated networks retaining much of their early distinctiveness. Hence multiple integration derives from their continuing to supply the kinds of services for which they were initially established.

Incorporation is an unintended consequence of educational conflict, for each of the groups engaging in substitution does so in the hope of attaining domination. It is the result of interaction between dominant and assertive groups taking the form of market competition. This, as we have seen, cannot give any group supreme educational control and prospects of it decline as new forms of substitution develop. From the continuing conflict between private ownership groups, (and their quest for support) integration to the polity gradually occurs. Because substitutive strategies mean that various groups come to own and control independent networks, of differing size and importance, the types of action and interaction which link education to the polity are quite different from those which characterize systems with restrictive origins. There, a political elite sought financial support to develop national education; here, educational entrepreneurs seek political support to consolidate their control. There, educational systems developed centrifugally, by governmental initiative spreading outwards; here, they emerge centripetally, from peripheric innovations which converge on government. The difference between these processes is, metaphorically, the difference between imperialism and confederation. In the former, *a powerful elite founds a national educational system in order to serve its various goals: in the latter, educational networks already serving different goals become incorporated to form a national educational system.*

Once again the mechanism which produces these changes is nothing other than the consistent pursuit of their educational goals by the conflicting parties. To trace the emergence of change from interaction is to focus on what competition does to the groups involved and to their prospects of attaining educational control. We have already argued that where only two groups are involved they eventually reach a stalemate position — each may commit more and more resources to substitution or to buttressing domination, but because both lack legal sanctions, neither can ultimately exclude the other and assume supreme control. This was discussed as a limiting case because in practice competition generally ceases to be bipartite. When 'new' assertive groups enter the market, even if they concentrate upon different kinds or levels of education, their substitution creates difficulties for both the dominant and the 'leading' assertive group. It makes educational conflict increasingly complicated and advances the date at which deadlock is reached by the different parties.

When first challenged the dominant group reformulated its ideology, strengthening its source of legitimation to repulse the ideas of the initial assertive group, and directed its available constraints against this group. It is now faced with opposition from several quarters, and to defend its position, constraints and ideology must be directed simultaneously against all forms of assertion. To do this requires additional resources, but they are needed at precisely the time they are least available. For the extra funds it mobilizes must be committed to market competition – to founding and maintaining more schools, and to supplying and paying their teachers. It must compete directly or its monopoly will be undermined: since its constraints and ideology have proved inadequate to restrain substitution, the dominant group must now fight it in the market place. It must match school for school if its position is not to deteriorate further, and greatly improve on this ratio if control is to be protected. Yet when pluralistic assertion is involved, it becomes increasingly expensive to do this on several fronts.

The 'leading' assertive group is faced with the same kind of problem. If it concentrates its resources on challenging the dominant group it leaves other forms of substitution to corner part of the market: if it diversifies its activities to repulse other assertive groups it inflicts less damage on domination. Whichever alternative is adopted more resources are required. For competition itself has stimulated the dominant group to increase the facilities it owns and hence substitution must occur at an even faster rate if assertion is to make progress, or merely to stand still while opening up a second front.

The initial effect of competitive interaction is considerable educational expansion as the various groups seek to move forward against each other. The final result is that deadlock arises between them. The resources which can be mobilized by any group for educational purposes are not limitless and as conflict becomes protracted each party is trying to run faster in order to stay put. Not only does no group make headway against the others but each becomes depressingly aware that the enthusiasm it can generate among its supporters to found schools is not backed up by a lasting determination to maintain them. The situation in mid-century England was typical – rivalry 'did not produce a surplus of schools and cheap education, as some educational 'free-traders' expected, but tended to paralyse the activities of all parties, so that schools were built that could not be maintained and children were taught for such short periods that they could benefit very little from the instruction given'.[28] Increasingly then the independent networks locked in conflict, and prospects of retaining or attaining educational control through further market efforts diminished accordingly.

From this situation of stalemate pressures develop which culminate in the integration of education to the State. Each of the competitive parties seeks to break out of the deadlock and this can only be done in one of two ways – by obtaining considerable new resources or by acquiring legal constraints to use against competitors. It is obvious that the central government is the only source of the latter, but less self-evident perhaps that it is also the greatest untapped supply of wealth for educational purposes. For when deadlock occurs it means not only that active supporters of the competing groups have dug as far as they can or will into their own pockets, but also that the rest of the population has been bombarded by appeals for subscriptions by all parties. It is for these reasons that the reactions of the conflicting groups are identical and involve the quest for State support.

It matters little if the first move towards State intervention is made by a dominant group in search of legal constraints (like the Anglican Church turning to its old adventitious beneficiary the Tory Party), or an assertive group in pursuit of financial resources (like the Danish Fri School movement after decline in agricultural and commercial profits in the 1880s). Education is irresistibly dragged into the political arena, for all competing groups are threatened if one alone begins to make headway with central government. Thus profound educational conflict produces a strain towards state intervention as a means to protect or advance the various networks, not the integration of education to the polity as an end in itself. At this stage each party seeks political intervention on its own behalf, to strengthen its independent network against the others. As might be expected, assertive groups with the most limited resources at their disposal are the first to accept this as a necessary adjunct to their strategy. Equally, competing groups which enjoy links with members of the political elite are the earliest to hope for legal protection. Thus the development of a national state educational system does not originate from the goals of either dominant or assertive groups. It is the unintended product of all of them seeking State intervention for their own ends *simultaneously*.

Because all competing groups do this simultaneously, the conflicting parties in education have to accommodate themselves to the structure of political conflict. Unless they can insert their aims prominently in the programme of some influential political grouping they have little chance of extracting governmental support and recognition. Thus a period of alliance formation follows in which political opponents (organized in parties so far as England and Denmark were concerned) meet the educational competitors (the independent ownership groups). The alliances formed may represent a two-way accommodation. On the one hand, several educational groups may have to work through a single political party, one doing so through elective affinity, another perhaps through lack of alternative, its social base and educational aims being

least *in*compatible with that party. On the other hand, political alignment itself may be somewhat modified by the structure of educational
competition. These alliances transmit educational conflict from the
market-place to the centre of the political arena. However, political
struggles *over* education take place in the context of established market
positions. The independent ownership networks exist and their political
advocates seek central financial support and legal recognition for them
and for the definition of instruction they embody, albeit with modifications that the parties themselves may impose.

Political conflict itself has the effect of preserving the networks,
sometimes through successive parties giving financial aid and legal
backing when in Government to different ownership groups (thus
positively strengthening them), sometimes through opposition preventing government from undermining a network through financial or
legal sanctions which would lead to its repression or nationalization
(thus defending them negatively). Typical of this process was the
Newcastle Commission's recommendation that the English voluntary
system should continue: equally revealing are the reasons Robert Lowe
gave for this decision in 1861.

> In making that recommendation, the commissioners, so far as I can understand
> the case, express, I will not say the opinion of the whole country, or of
> philosophers, or of persons of great powers of abstract thought, *but they
> express the opinion of those to whom education in this country owes almost
> its existence – of those who gave both time and money to promote education*
> before the present system was called into being. If we have spent £4,800,000
> in educating the people, private liberality has spent double that sum ... *So
> long as it is the opinion of those who contribute to the maintenance of the
> schools that the present system is the right and the best one, so long will the
> present system continue* ... it is not the intention of Government to infringe
> on the organic principles of the present system.[29]

In the process the independent networks become increasingly public:
they receive public funding and in return have to yield some autonomy
to accountability; they receive legal recognition but have to cede
independence to incorporation. For central agencies are developed by
the polity to control the public financing of instruction and to ensure
adherence to the rules governing legal recognition. Thus a national
educational system gradually emerges from increased governmental
expenditure and legal authorization, since the concomitant of both is
the development of central control. Such systems are literally made up
from the old independent networks. Their incorporation and co-ordina-

tion is the product of relations between educational ownership groups and political parties and the final form of system to emerge is shaped by the interaction between government and opposition. Thus systems with substitutive origins are bred out of the private competitive networks by institutionalized political conflict.

It is the self-same process which simultaneously defines the nature and degree of multiple integration characterizing the new system. For it is political conflict which modifies the rudimentary form of multiple integration by determining how the independent networks are incorporated into the system and how these constituent parts are linked to one another. For all competitive ownership groups there is a tension between their need for central support and recognition, and their desire to maintain the distinctiveness of their educational outputs. The former cannot be gained without political sponsorship, but obtaining it will cost different amounts to the groups involved, if prices are calculated in terms of departures from their independent definitions of instruction. Furthermore, of course, the political parties themselves may not be well balanced — an educational group allied to a strong governing party will tend to see its own network attain a prominent place in the educational system and will not be forced to make great concessions over its outputs and the parts of society these serve; one which has to work through a weak form of opposition will tend to see its network relegated, subject to governmental modification, and loss of distinctiveness. What in fact occurs, however, is not this static picture in which incorporation is determined by initial differences in the strength of their political sponsors. The form of multiple integration which characterizes the new system is the result of protracted political interaction — it is the effect not only of the factors highlighted but also of intervening social and political changes.

Thus to account for the nature of multiple integration to develop in any substitutive system involves a very detailed analysis of prior political relations. Such a task cannot be accomplished here; instead I will simply accentuate those aspects which were crucial in establishing the structural relations of English and Danish educational systems and refer to a number of histories of these processes.

After deadlock had been reached in Denmark just before 1870, educational conflict became associated with national politics. In turn its influence was so strong that it modified political organization, as witnessed by the emergence of the Union of the Right and the Union of the Left that year. The political alliances formed had two characteristics which were to have a crucial effect on multiple integration. Firstly, each political party was a firm partisan of the independent networks in question. The Folk High Schools and Urban Real Schools were supported by the Union of the Left, and the Learned Schools and Universities had the support of the Union of the Right. In other words, the quest for political sponsorship did not involve renunciation or dilution of the educational goals of the ownership groups. The peasant proprietors' Folk School and the urban Fri School movements, which both operated through the Union of the Left, had accepted for some time that they represented the rural and urban equivalents of the same ideals and were complementary rather than contradictory. Secondly, these politico-educational alliances divided cleanly on class lines and were strongly reinforced by a parallel bifurcation in political culture — stimulated by the development of the Kulturkamp movement and its virulent attack on conservative intellectual elitism.[30] If one adds to this the fact that the various independent networks concentrated on different levels of education, one has the three factors which in conjunction exerted the strongest influence to preserve intact the type of multiple integration which already existed in rudimentary form.

Until the turn of the century the political struggle remained unequal. In the absence of parliamentary government the Right alliance leaned on the *Landsting* and maintained the king's privilege of selecting ministers from it, regardless of who had the majority in the *Folketing*.[31] From 1875 onwards, the Left had a growing majority in the Folketing and insisted on a shift to a parliamentary system.[32] The effect of this situation was to strengthen the independent networks. The Right could continue to maintain the Learned Schools and Universities, defending their classical definition of instruction and successfully repulsing projects submitted from the Folketing to introduce national culture into secondary education.[33] It could not, however, undermine the assertive networks which had earlier gained legal recognition nor make any advance in central control beyond enforcing government inspection. On the other hand the Venstre party could make no inroad in secondary and higher education, but reinforced the rural and urban networks by obtaining financial grants for them. Government grants towards the Folk High Schools increased steadily after 1892 without great loss of autonomy,[34] inspection was conceded but not control of examinations. At the same time an annual subsidy was made to urban Fri schools which had increasingly found that 'school-pence are too low for the school but too high for the home'.[35] Independent Technical

Schools formed their own union after 1891 and private schools in Copenhagen founded the United Schools Association: they were granted a state loan and were successful in preventing this from being conditional on no new private establishments being founded for ten years. Thus by 1901 when the Venstre Party came to power for the first time with parliamentary democracy, it confronted networks which had been strengthened by thirty years of political checks and balances,[36] and whose divergent definitions of instruction remained largely intact despite the gradual development of a state administrative framework.

Since 1870 Venstre's aim had been an attack on every level of instruction in order to insert national culture in all forms of education. Once in power it sought to promote this new definition of knowledge by according the Folk and Real school networks a prominent place in national education, thus reducing the cultural hegemony of the Learned Schools and simultaneously diluting their classical definition of secondary instruction. The aim of the Left was to accentuate these two assertive networks and to move the Folk School movement to the middle of the educational stage – until the age of eleven Folk School attendance should be the common starting point for all, and the natural form of further education would be gained at the Folk High School, with Real Schools as an alternative. The immediate response of the University, Heads of Learned Schools and the Union of the Right was to defend the supremacy of Learned Schools at secondary level and as the gatekeepers to higher education. This defence involved concessions and some dilution of distinctiveness, the Headmasters agreeing to curricula modernization (in 1901) in order to 'make it possible to go over from the Folk School to the Higher School'.[37] This concession of course also involved accepting the Folk School rather than the private preparatory school as the avenue to secondary instruction. It was thus really a proposal for educational partition along the lines traced out by the independent networks, in which the Learned Schools would continue to dominate the secondary level and the Folk School movement would have an equivalent position at primary level. Grundtvigian teachers objected that this formula would result in creaming off the best pupils and would leave the Folk High Schools with the residue. Their parliamentary representatives argued that a new link with Learned Schools should only occur if they were drastically remodelled, ceased to be anterooms to University, and were provided by the State for all who were able to profit from them.

In this context Venstre was forced to compromise, it lacked the parliamentary strength to advance the Folk School dramatically, imposing its definition of instruction on all levels. At the same time, as the governing party, it could impose greater changes on the Learned Schools than those voluntarily conceded by their Heads. Compromise consisted in acknowledging the 'established rights' of the independent networks, in accepting that rather than an integrated system, Danish education would be made up of different types of schools in 'organic connection', and in attempting to incorporate them in a form which advanced the aims of the Left but remained within the bounds of political feasibility. Venstre's basic device was to co-ordinate the networks in such a way that the Folk and Real Schools moved into secondary education proper, whilst the modified Learned Schools retained the commanding heights but lost cultural hegemony over the definition of all post-primary instruction. The novelty of this solution was that it proposed clearing a middle zone between Folk and Learned Schools. Practically, this involved the universalization of Grundtvigian ideas at primary level as the curriculum of the Folk Schools (which were now to be established in all areas with the aid of State building grants) concentrated on Danish culture and knowledge relevant to life. End on to the Folk schools at the age of eleven were Middle schools; either self-standing institutions giving a three year Real education (thus recognizing and incorporating the urban commercial and industrial network), or attached to Folk School or Gymnasium. The latter types of Middle schools extended the general grundtvigian curriculum until the age of fifteen, then by examination pupils could proceed to a one year Real class or enter a Gymnasium for a further three years. The Gymnasia were the modified Learned Schools whose classicism had been eroded by the addition of parallel courses in modern languages and mathematics/science. It was further undermined by the method of co-ordination with the Real classes and Real Schools, for pupils could enter from the latter and proceed directly to the maths/science course. Nevertheless, the traditional link between the Learned Schools and University was recognized, the terminal *Studentersksamen* in the Gymnasium alone qualified for entrance. Social elitism was somewhat modified as entrance fees were abolished, (though course fees remained), and a sixth of places were free for children of poorer parents, though only after the pupil had attended the school for a year.

Because the 'organic connection' which welded the independent networks into an educational system was politically negotiated by strong Party defenders of their respective definitions of instruction, and because they had focused on different levels of education anyway, the type of multiple integration which emerged was not too different from its original rudimentary form. The Folk Schools and Middle Schools provided a general education for practical life in rural and urban areas: the Real School and classes served the technical, scientific and commercial requirements of business, industry and agriculture: the Gymnasium and University continued their status confirming functions for the landed elite but had added advanced level scientific and linguistic services for industry, administration, commerce and diplomacy. The political conflict shaping incorporation had preserved and augmented the diversity of services to different parts of society which educational competition had initiated. The only institution whose operations were progressively deprived of services during the political phase of conflict was the Lutheran Church. Any element of clerical supervision at local level was virtually eliminated by 1909. Although integration was not completely destroyed since schools still prepared for Confirmation, the weakening of the link was highlighted by an official circular of 1906 stressing that this 'should make as little disturbance as possible in ordinary schooling'.[38]

The three factors which were responsible for transmitting the rudimentary form of multiple integration to the Danish State system, in modified but easily recognized form, were almost completely lacking in the English case. There the situation was considerably more complex, and, at elementary level especially, the form of national education which emerged bore only a faint resemblance to the original networks. The aim of certain groups to use state intervention for consolidating their own position and undermining that of others was a complete failure in some cases. Only at secondary and higher levels did political interaction preserve initial diversity and incorporation protect multiple integration in something resembling its original rudimentary form.

The Liberal majority of 1868 made the political displacement of the voluntary system of elementary education (which had proved favourable to the Anglican Church) a parliamentary possibility. The Educational League, formed to 'make the government "go faster" '[39], was mainly an alliance of members of Nonconformist, radical, and entrepreneurial groups, together with the Trades Union Congress, in pursuit of national and unsectarian education, maintained from local rates and managed by local authorities. The very fact of entering this alliance spelt a modification of their earlier goals for certain groups. To Nonconformists, joining the League meant abandoning a denominational definition of instruction: to working class supporters it meant renouncing the political aspect of schooling, for this was the price of putting effective pressure on parliament. In other words, this coalition represented a reduction in the diversity of educational goals which had previously characterized the assertive networks. Furthermore, the League did not enjoy the whole-hearted sponsorship of the Liberal Party, for the clear superimposition of educational assertion, social class, and political party, which occurred in Denmark, was lacking here. The League was a pressure group within Liberal politics and its effectiveness was muted by other party considerations.

At this level of instruction the Anglican Church remained the largest proprietor.[40] There was no chance then of a neat party political partition of the educational field according to level, but instead an intense parliamentary conflict over elementary instruction. The counterpart of the League was the defensive National Educational Union, through which the Church sought to consolidate its position by 'judiciously supplementing the present denominational system of national education'.[41] Undoubtedly it gained more clear-cut support from the Tory party than the other networks received from the Liberals, and, initially at least, this sponsorship did not involve a substantial dilution of Anglican educational goals.

The settlement of 1870 reflected the balance of power between the two coalitions: rate aided School Boards could be elected where the Education Department was satisfied that a shortage existed; voluntary denominational schools were to continue receiving government grants but not to be rate aided. The Liberal cabinet had steered a course between conciliating the forty Members of Parliament affiliated to the League and not alienating its Anglican members by depriving the Church of the right to control what it owned. 'There was of course no question of establishing in England a system of "common" schools. Denominational schools existed and the State could not dispense with them'.[42] But this was the balance of power with the Liberals in Office;[43] the assertive alliance was to fare much worse when they were in opposition, and especially after the defection of the Unionists, among whom had numbered some active supporters of the League.

The 1870 Act had the short-term effect of incorporating those definitions of instruction current in the assertive alliance, since the democratic method of election[44] enabled many interests to be represented on different Boards. Sometimes, as was the case with the

London School Board, a socialist majority gained control and worked 'on a practical plane to realize . . . the aims summarized in their programme as "state maintenance" ';[45] sometimes, as in Bradford, schooling was geared to the requirements of local industry. In addition more complex commercial and industrial demands were met, mainly in northern manufacturing towns, by founding Higher Grade Schools which received working class support as they opened the door to advanced instruction. Although certain Boards (like Manchester) were captured by Churchmen 'to see that the schools they had to manage did as little damage as possible to their own schools',[46] it appeared by the mid-eighties that rate aid plus local democracy was a formula favouring the assertive alliance. After 1875 the Anglican National Society complained increasingly of falling subscriptions, rising costs, and competition from Board Schools.

The Salisbury Government (1885-86) appointed the personnel of the Cross Commission, to examine the working of the 1870 act, and its majority report signalled active Tory support for the Anglican cause. The established rights of the Church, still enrolling 64 percent of pupils at this level, were recognized[47] and should be rewarded by state aid: its even deeper entrenchment in secondary education should be protected by dismantling the Higher Grade Schools. By a series of legal and administrative steps, taken from 1895 onwards, and a tightening of the unseen grip of the Treasury,[48] the type of instruction developed by the School Boards was undermined. Standardization was introduced by a pincer movement of audit and code. With their massive parliamentary majority in 1900, yet despite considerable opposition from the Liberals, the Labour movement and the Free Churches, the Act of 1902 was passed. School Boards were abolished and replaced by less radical county and county borough councils and voluntary schools became rate aided.

In becoming part of a national system, elementary education had lost much of its earlier diversity. Variety declined as the innovations of the School Boards were eliminated and as Anglican schools finally had to concede some substantial surveillance in return for public subsidies. (The local authority became responsible for their secular teaching and made up one third of the managerial body of each school). Here incorporation had increased standardization: the compromise between the two alliances, both involved in protecting their interests at this level, had favoured the Anglican network but had massively reduced the diversity of outputs from elementary schools. Undoubtedly the definition of instruction supported by the working class organizations lost out most. It was virtually eliminated from national education because they had only contested this level and had seen 'further' education as extending out of it in the Higher Grade Schools which were now suppressed.

On the other hand, the interests of middle and upper class owner-ship groups were much better protected through political interaction. Their networks were directly incorporated at post-elementary level and without great loss of distinctiveness. The crucial aspect distinguishing these political negotiations from those concerning elementary educa-tion was the absence of a class threat overshadowing the actions of both parties. To the Tories the 1902 Act had contained the working class educationally, so the established rights of other groups need not be severely undermined, especially as their respective networks concen-trated on different types of instruction. Indeed this appeared to be the Tory strategy throughout the last decade of the century when it furthered the aims of the National Association for the promotion of Technical Education (largely inspired by industrialists) as a weapon against the School Boards. The Technical Instruction Act of 1889 and the Whisky money encouraged this network at post-elementary level, that is outside the aegis of the Boards. The technical definition of instruction was thus incorporated into the system and came under the control of the local authorities in 1902. Consistent with this strategy was financial support for the University Colleges, again a predominantly middle class network. This policy of Tory divide and rule, coupled with Liberal defence of entrepreneurial and dissenting networks at secondary and higher levels, protected their distinctiveness. On the other hand, the Headmasters' Conference with its 'extensive connections which could gain the ear of any government',[49] played an equally significant role in preserving the Public Schools intact. Compared with the ferocity of elementary school politics, incorporation at higher levels was settled by give and take among the party elites.

The terms of reference of the Bryce Commission indicated that the Liberals also accepted the importance of ownership. It was 'to consider what are the best methods of establishing a well organized system of secondary education in England, taking into account existing defi-ciencies, and having regard to such local sources of revenue from endowment or otherwise as are available'. In their report they indeed concentrated on deficiencies and 'sketched out a plan whereby private and   proprietary   schools   may   be   turned   to   good   account, and . . . discountenanced any idea of driving them out of the field and thereby making secondary education purely a matter of State concern'.[50] Strong Liberal pressure during the passage of the 1902 Act obliged the Tories to widen the powers of the local authorities to 'consider the educational needs of their area', the opposition thus promoting diversity rather than uniformity at secondary level. Subsequent administrative measures made it clear that the government intended to build upon the tenuous basis of the endowed grammar schools, but to incorporate, not interfere with existing networks. Thus the Public Schools and ancient universities remained 'a more or less closed system of education which played a vital part in formulating and disseminating the values and upholding the status of the upper class'.[51] Just as these Anglican strongholds retained their traditional definition of instruction, so too did the most ambitious of the middle class institutions – the newer universities. The University of London had vastly expanded its influence on scientific, technical and professional training through concentrating on examining and by affiliating a dozen extension colleges.[52] Receipt of grants and Charters represented governmental recognition, but not loss of autonomy or change in the services provided to business and commerce. The Catholic[53] and dissenting secondary schools also maintained their flow of special kinds of outputs. Thus, although the endowed grammar schools increasingly served the growing bureaucratic requirements of government, other parts of post-elementary education could preserve their distinctive definitions of instruction.

STRUCTURAL ELABORATION WITHIN EDUCATIONAL SYSTEMS

To turn now to the internal changes taking place in national education is partly to engage in an exercise of analytic convenience, in the sense that the transformations to be examined are not separate from those already discussed. Indeed they result indirectly from the same processes of interaction and thus take place almost simultaneously. There appear to be four types of internal change which are universally related to the emergence of educational systems: unification, systematization, differentiation and specialization. The first pair are associated with the attachment of national education to the State and the second pair with its multiple integration to different social institutions. These changes will be examined first to show how they too stem from the educational competition and political interaction just discussed. Much more detailed attention will then be given to the development of these characteristics in systems with restrictive and substitutive origins.

Unification

The first universal characteristic of state systems refers to the scope and nature of educational administration. Unification involves the incorporation or development of diverse establishments, activities and personnel under a central, national, and specifically educational framework of administration. In turn this spells certain uniform controls emanating from the centre, and the standardization of certain educational inputs, processes and outputs on a nationwide basis. Such unification may be partial, as some kinds of educational institutions, some forms of instruction, and some types of teachers may remain outside the central administrative framework. However, as we shall see later, the degree of unification is not simply a function of the size of the free or private sector in education. To talk about degrees of unification is to refer not only to the extensiveness but also to the intensity of administrative control. In other words, unification has a quantitative and a qualitative dimension, and both must be taken into account when making cross-cultural comparisons and assessing differences

It is not suggested that every aspect of unification mentioned in the definition has its origins in the advent of state systems. Certain elements may have been present in the antecedent period — three of the churches discussed, the Danish Lutheran, French Catholic and English Anglican could perhaps claim to have administered a national educational network, but their administrative agencies were neither linked to the political centre nor were they specifically educational in character. Thus the significance of state systems for this type of internal change is twofold: only with them are all aspects of unification found in conjunction and only with them is unification universally developed and maintained.

As the definition makes clear, unification is equally characteristic of systems with substitutive origins, which emerge through incorporation and of systems with restrictive roots, which develop through replacement. In the former the development of a central authority for education is a slow and cumulative process which is not completed until incorporation has taken place. The administrative framework is gradually elaborated, its controls are accepted and its standardizing influence becomes felt, as the independent networks seek central financial support and legal recognition. As educational competition reaches deadlock and passes into political interaction, central administrative agencies become more specifically educational. They are slowly dissociated from other bodies, Charity Commissions, the Church, Poor Law agencies, etc., as a direct product of the ongoing educational conflict.

Partly, of course, the demand for increased state intervention simply expands the educational work of government to a point at which its volume, complexity and above all, range, cannot be accommodated by traditional agencies. More importantly, the political sponsors of the independent networks recognize the impossibility and undesirability of dealing with these relatively undifferentiated bodies and themselves propose innovations in central educational administration. The precise form which develops is a product of political conflict, but in all cases it is specifically educational and only becomes fully national when the process of incorporation is completed. In the case of systems with restrictive origins, unification is generally quicker and more dramatic. Once the restrictive phase has been accomplished, replacement immediately takes a unified form — it is centrally directed, national in scope and controlled and orchestrated by specialized administrative agencies, which are often (as in France) new organs designed for the purpose.

It is important, however, to distinguish the emergence of unification from the development of centralization, to which it may or may not be related. Unification is not synonymous with the centralization of education, although the former is clearly a precondition of the latter. The concept of centralization denotes specific relations between the unified parts. 'A centralized system is one in which one element or sub-system plays a major or dominant role in the operation of the system. We may call this the *leading-part*, or say that the system is *centred* around this part. A small change in the leading-part will then be reflected throughout the system, causing considerable change'.[54] A centralized system is thus a special type of unified system, but not all unified systems are centralized; to argue otherwise is to assume that in all forms of state education the largest educational changes follow from the smallest initiatives of the political elite. On this point one can fully concur with Cohen that it is simply not the case that state institutions always influence others more than the state is influenced by them.[55] The existence of a central administrative framework does not automatically make it the leading part and it is interesting in this connection to note how various educational philosophers, writing before the emergence of state systems, produced blue-prints specifying how the advantages of unification could be obtained without the dangers of centralization. The most famous of these perhaps is Condorcet's, with his notion of 'L'Etat comme caissier'.[56] Centralization, as previously defined, is regarded as a variable elaborative characteristic, whereas unification is a change which is universal upon the emergence of state systems.

Systematization

Accompanying unification, through which new educational boundaries are defined, are further internal changes which represent a transition from summativity to wholeness as the new systems become consolidated. Instead of national education being the sum of disparate and unrelated sets of establishments or independent networks, it now refers to a series of interconnected elements within the unified whole. Systematization consists in the 'strengthening of pre-existing relations among the parts, the development of relations among parts previously unrelated, the gradual addition of parts and relations to a system, or some combination of these changes'.[57] This progressive systematization is analytically distinct from unification, since the latter is equally compatible with summativity. Empirically, however, these two changes go hand in hand for both appear to be universal upon the emergence of state systems.

One of the most important aspects of this change is the development of hierarchical organization. This refers to the gradual articulation of the different educational levels — levels which may previously have been unrelated, could have been controlled by different ownership groups, and might well have been completely uncoordinated. Hierarchical organization develops because educational goals, even if focused intently on a given level of instruction, are hampered by a lack of complementarity with inputs, processes and outputs at other levels. The impetus towards this form of change is not provided by some abstract 'strain towards efficiency', but reflects *the increased co-ordination required if a multiplicity of educational goals are to be attained and the pressure exerted by their advocates to see that they are met.*

This has already been examined when discussing the sources of multiple integration in emergent educational systems. In the case of restriction, we saw how interaction between factions of the political elite and its quest for public support determined the services education provided and defined the structure to do this (pages 151-57). The structures which developed were internally co-ordinated and hierarchically organized — *but* in accordance with the prevailing balance of power and not as an abstract process of optimization. Thus, for example, the Tsarist Bureaucracy attached preparatory classes to the gymnasia, which in turn linked upwards to the universities and state service. They were deliberately separated from parallel institutions, the Urban and Zemstvo schools which linked with Real schools and active life, and hence the former was protected from interference by the inputs, processes and outputs of the latter. Equally evident was the way in which shortage of resources could delay full co-ordination of all levels for some considerable time. In this case hierarchical organization only initially characterized those levels which were of most concern to the political elite, provided it was in a position to concentrate public finance there. Thus, for example, Napoleon's Imperial University established close links between the lycée and higher institutions, but both remained uncoordinated with elementary education until the July Monarchy. Similarly where systems had substitutive origins, the whole process of incorporation was analyzed as the co-ordination of the independent networks through political negotiation (pages 165-73). Certain unique features in the case of Denmark meant that the 'organic connection' established between the networks in fact spelt hierarchical organization, since each network had concentrated on a particular level of instruction.

To avoid confusion it should be stressed that the concept of hierarchical organization does not imply the existence of an educational ladder. While the former is a pre-condition of the latter, it does not constitute the sufficient conditions for its development. The co-ordination of inputs, processes and outputs at different levels of instruction does not necessarily imply that pupils can or do pass from the lowest to the highest level. Indeed, with reference to certain goals, it involves organizing processes at the lowest level in such a way that its pupils *cannot* enter the next level and do not have the qualifications to do so. Hierarchical organization can thus operate positively to encourage movement between levels, by dovetailing inputs, processes and outputs, or negatively to discourage them by placing barriers between the parts. Both the positive and negative aspects will be found in most systems, but the particular levels at which they operate depends on the goals pursued and the outcomes of political interaction. In the case of England, for example, the 1902 Act enforced disjunction between elementary education and other levels, but at the same time linkages between secondary and higher levels were reinforced and they became better co-ordinated.

Other important aspects of progressive systematization include the following changes, not all of which immediately characterize new educational systems, and most of which continue to be refined during the following decades. First is a series of national examinations (or ones whose validity is nationwide), corresponding to the boundaries delineated by the administrative framework and graded in relation to the various levels. These serve to co-ordinate entry or transition, to standardize teaching and learning processes and to provide the outputs with different sets of qualifications. Second are regular forms of teacher recruitment, training and certification, valid throughout the system and appropriate to the various levels. Third is the development of a variety of roles, services, establishments, trained personnel, where and when required as link-units to complete the co-ordination process. Again all such changes derive from the pursuit of a plurality of educational goals within a unified framework; they are the joint product of multiple integration and the emergence of state systems.

Differentiation

The fact that education comes to serve several different parts of society has far reaching effects upon its organization. The first concerns the increased differentiation of education from other parts of society, the second involves the development of internal educational specialization. Both effects derive from educational competition and political conflict, although the former characterizes the new system from the start whilst the latter continues to develop during subsequent decades.

In the antecedent period one consequence of ownership was a relatively low degree of differentiation between education and the institution whose elite subordinated it — low in terms of the definition of instruction itself (usually confounded with the operations of the subordinator — education for example being considered as the formation of the Christian); in terms of the educational role structure (often completely overlapping that of its subordinator and illustrated most clearly by the religious 'teaching orders'); and finally, of course in terms of its administrative framework. Multiple integration, on the other hand, is associated with the development of a specialized educational collectivity, occupying a distinctively educational role structure, and transmitting definitions of instruction which are not co-terminus with the knowledge or beliefs of any single social institution. For the pursuit of diverse educational goals and the effective pressure of a plurality of groups together prevent the new educational system from being organized at the same low level of differentiation.

The basic reason for this is that if education is to serve a variety of purposes (requirements of the institutions to which it becomes integrated), it cannot do so unless a higher degree of differentiation takes place. Quite simply a form of education which remained confounded with, for example, religious practices and personnel, would hardly satisfy military training requirements. If education is to service several operations simultaneously, it can only do so if it stands somewhat apart from all — for proximity to one will be prejudicial to the others. In other words, the re-establishment of exclusive links with any given institution would militate against the receipt of desired educational services on the part of others. There are strong reasons in systems with both types of origins why this does not happen and which protect against it happening.

Where restriction is concerned the very plurality of political goals vis à vis education is itself a reason for educational differentiation. The position of the political elite is totally different from that of dominant ownership groups, for the very extensiveness of political goals precludes the uniform and unifunctional type of education which is associated with its lack of differentiation. Certainly there may be sections of this elite who preferred a low level of differentiation, with an intermingling of political and educational roles and activities, such that trained teachers represented loyal cadres and political ideology dictated the definition of instruction. In both countries, however, the multiplicity of services sought from education by the various sections of the elite meant that the pressures they exerted did engender and sustain a higher overall degree of differentiation than was the case in the antecedent period. At the very least such interests succeeded in protecting parts of the new system, and the need for public support also reinforced this.

The same factors are responsible in systems with substitutive origins, although they operate in a very different way. The political negotiations surrounding the incorporation of the independent networks fundamentally preclude a low differentiation of education. Since each assertive group works through its political alliance to defend the distinctiveness of its network while gaining state support, their interaction necessarily has the effect of opposing a tight relationship between education and one institution alone. Indeed, incorporation could not be negotiated were this the case, for all networks but one would have everything to lose and nothing to gain. Instead the terms negotiated are essentially ones which deny any assertive group exclusive powers to define instruction, supply its personnel or control administration. All to varying degrees lose something of their distinctiveness and autonomy upon incorporation. At the very least they have to concede things like school inspection, financial accountability and teacher certification. But the development of central agencies to undertake such tasks is jealously monitored by the networks and their political sponsors to ensure that their composition is as favourable as possible. The conjunction of these different interests, and the endless wranglings about seats on Boards and membership of Committees to which they give rise, produces and maintains a high level of differentiation of education. Each interest group acts as a watch-dog to prevent the re-establishment of exclusive links between education and another party.

Thus the source of educational differentiation in state systems is located in the multiplicity of goals imposed on education by various influential parties. It thus derives from the cross-cutting pressures of powerful interest groups associated with different social institutions — whether these are sections of the central political elite or independent assertive groups. It is the same factors which are also responsible for introducing internal differentiation into the new educational systems — a characteristic which for purposes of clarity has been termed specialization.

Specialization

So far we have seen how a change towards hierarchical organization helps to avoid the various educational goals from being mutually exclusive. However, the co-ordination of parts and levels only helps in the negative sense of removing obstacles to multiple goal attainment. In itself it does nothing to ensure that education does serve a variety of demands and service a plurality of institutional operations. Indeed logically a hierarchically organized system could be a unifunctional one; it could mean co-ordination of parts and levels for a single purpose. However, a further effect of multiple integration *is* to promote the emergence of educational systems which are internally differentiated. In other words they are characterized by a certain degree of specialization in intake, processes and outputs to meet demands whose diversity is incompatible with unitary procedures. How much specialization develops depends partly upon the range, variety and complementarity of the services demanded from it, and partly on the relative power of those voicing the demands.

In systems with restrictive origins we have already seen that some diversification of educational services is the price of elite cohesion and public support. In both countries these pressures had the effect of increasing specialization during the replacement phase. Thus in Russia opposition from the military section of the elite in conjunction with local interests in applied instruction prevented Tolstoy, as Tsarist spokesman, from legislating simply for the academic gymnasium, leading via the university, to various forms of bureaucratic service. Their opposition was not strong enough to impose the form of specialization they sought (the gymnasium with branching courses which Tolstoy thought incompatible with political security), but the foundation of the Real Schools imposed a diversification of services which exceeded original proposals. Similarly, in France the establishment of the écoles primaires supérieures, useful to business, commerce and finance, introduced further specialization to meet the economic demands which the Imperial University had neglected.

Where substitution is concerned specialization is transmitted to the new system through the incorporation of the independent networks. Since each network was founded to provide a particular service and developed a distinct definition of instruction in relation to this end, they were very different. Thus the more such networks were incorporated intact, the greater the initial specialization of the educational system. In Denmark we saw that political interaction had the effect of preserving the distinctiveness of the networks (although confining their specialist services to particular levels), whilst in England elementary instruction became rather uniform and diversity was only incorporated at secondary and higher levels. As in the case of restrictive systems, it is the possession of power that determines which demands are given most specialized attention in the new system.

The concept of specialization refers to a range of internal changes rather than to any single one. To serve a particular demand may involve the development of new types of establishments or the pursuit of new activities in existing ones; the delineation of new roles, forms of recruitment and training; the increased complexity of intake policies and the development of branching paths of pupil allocation, within or between levels and types of establishment; additional variety in curricula, examinations and qualifications throughout the educational system; the development of special facilities, teaching materials and equipment.

The Problem of Integration

So far the term 'integration' has not been mentioned in this discussion of structural elaboration within educational systems. The reason for this is that since integration between parts of a system can only properly be considered as an unintended product of social interaction, it is therefore the variable outcome of the changes already discussed. In other words the degree of integration prevailing in any new educational system depends upon the extent to which its specific forms of unification, systematization, differentiation and specialization are complementary or contradictory. No assumption can be made in advance about a universal trend towards structural integration.

These four changes take place within the same system, they may occur simultaneously or sequentially and are forms of growth which can go on indefinitely. Since each aspect of this internal elaboration derives from social interaction, the specific changes which result are not necessarily complementary. They are not synonymous with a better adaptation of the educational system to its environment or with an optimal arrangement of activities for giving maximum services to a variety of social groups. They do not eliminate educational conflict and indeed may stimulate it, for a change which improves services to one group may have the opposite effect for those with different requirements.

Furthermore, these processes in conjunction usually themselves generate conflict. In *general* simultaneous specialization and systematization produce strains because they 'pull' in different directions. The latter draws all parts together and in rationalizing the relationship between them is unfavourable to divergent developments: the former enhances the diversity of the parts and thus makes it harder to link them together coherently. These strains will be experienced as practical exigencies by specific groups involved – for example, a specialized type of school might find that it cannot insist on appropriate entry qualifications but must recruit its intake from those whose prior studies are quite irrelevant. Alternatively, a particular kind of employer of school leavers might find extensive in-service training necessary, because of the generalist background of the new employees. Obviously such exigencies may be relatively trivial or of crucial importance to the groups involved. Their consequences, in so far as they condition further educational conflict, are just as likely to result in the intensification of existing contradictions as in the development of a higher degree of structural integration which transcends them.

However, this does not mean that any discussion of internal changes immediately reduces to investigating the empirical characteristics of individual educational systems. If our theoretical approach can account not only for general types of elaboration, but also for variations in these changes, then comparative analysis of the new educational systems will not be purely empirical. Instead it should be possible to state additional and more detailed propositions about the relationships between the four main internal changes in different systems – and therefore about structural integration and further educational conflict.

Turning now to this analysis of variations in the elaborated characteristics, it appears that they are closely related to the way in which the educational system developed – by incorporation or replacement. As we have seen when systems have substitutive origins they are consolidated from independent parts which are already highly differentiated. Where restrictive origins are concerned, replacement occurs from the centre at the initiative of the political elite. It is now suggested that these different social origins of educational systems profoundly affect the internal changes taking place. In particular they produce differences in the strength of the two pairs of characteristics (unification/systematization and differentiation/specialization) relative to one another. This in turn influences the relationships between these pairs and the problems of integration experienced within new educational systems. In other words, systems developing from replacement or incorporation have different problems, generate different kinds of strains, and confront their clients and participants with different kinds of exigencies. If these theoretical links can be established then the cycle will be complete – we will have shown how structural change emerges from interaction and have begun to indicate how the elaborated structure exerts new influences upon future interaction.

2(a) From Substitutive Origins

Substitution means that the various independent networks established by assertive groups are by definition specialized. The raison d'être of each one is the pursuit of a different definition of instruction, a new kind of output designed to serve specific institutional operations. Although in any particular network the educational role structure and processes may not be clearly distinguished from those of their ownership groups, when considered collectively their existence clearly differentiates education from the activities of one social institution alone. In other words, this pair of characteristics, differentiation and specialization, but especially the latter, are clearly accentuated before deadlock is reached between the competing parties and gives rise to pleas for state intervention. As has been seen, unification is an unintended product of these quests for state finance and legal recognition. At the same time, the development of state educational systems represents a transition from summativity to wholeness. Indeed the process of incorporation can be seen as the negotiation of systematization. Through political interaction the place of each network in the system is determined and relations between them established. *Thus the crucial point about substitutive systems is that the second pair of characteristics to emerge from educational competition, namely unification and systematization, are superimposed on the networks which are already specialized and differentiated.*

What this means in practical terms is that the degree of unification brought about over the whole range of educational establishments is relatively low. In the same way systematization is imperfect and various discontinuities in inputs, processes and outputs between different parts and levels witness to its incompleteness. The weakness of these two characteristics is a direct product of the interaction which leads to incorporation. It arises from defence of the independent networks in which specialization and differentiation are already entrenched. In defending the distinctiveness of their own definitions of instruction and their autonomy of control, the assertive groups, or rather their political sponsors, work to minimize the extent of central control and to resist the standardization, which accompanies the growth of systematization, as far as possible.

Where unification is concerned each assertive group has a vested interest in retaining managerial autonomy over its network. Without this it cannot guarantee the continued flow of those services for which the network was founded in the first place. As we have seen the receipt of legal recognition and financial support does entail some loss of autonomy, which is most severe when the political sponsorship of a network is very weak. Nevertheless, pressures stemming from the assertive groups combine to ensure that unification will not be intense or extensive. Ultimately, the conditions under which a high degree of central administrative control could be introduced, would involve the dispossession of the assertive groups and nationalization of the networks. The political balance of power prevents this as each Party sponsor protects educational property rights. The networks thus remain in their original hands, and further political action seeks to prevent a divorce between ownership and control. Initially it appears to be very successful, as the voluntary system and the 1870 settlement in England illustrate — the role of state is still principally that of central paymaster. With incorporation there is reduction in, rather than loss of, managerial autonomy.

What is even more important as incorporation advances is that political action continues to repulse the emergence of a strong central authority with extensive powers. This is largely an effect of the politico-educational alliances themselves. To a significant degree party hands are tied. However much a strengthened form of central educational administration might make political good sense, there is the support of the educational interest groups to consider. The latter, as highly organized bodies for exerting party influence, constantly use it to minimize such tendencies. The crucial point here is that such pressures are being put on both or all parties simultaneously. In sum then, *forceful* political initiatives in favour of a *strongly unified* system are lacking in such countries. This situation cannot be compared with the total commitment of political elites to central unified control in systems with restrictive origins. Finally, party conflict itself defines the limited degree of unification possible. Political suspicion (of the other party developing a control structure biased in its favour) results in parliamentary opposition to proposals for strengthening central educational administration and means that legislation generally embodies the lowest common denominator of unification – all that compromise will allow.

Furthermore, unification is not fully extensive and does not cover all types of establishments. Important parts remain substantially outside the central administrative framework. Certain potential participants in state education simply withdraw, retaining their private status, if it appears to them that their position in the unified system would be disadvantageous, and if they have adequate resources to support themselves independently. The private sector in education develops from such cases (they are rather like companies whose Directors find the terms of a proposed merger unacceptable). Probably in no educational system is unification total; perhaps in none has any State completely monopolized instruction so that no establishment evades central control. In other words, it is not the existence of a private sector *per se* which is the peculiar characteristic of systems with substitutive origins. It is the conjunction between *incomplete and weak unification* which is significant here. For it gives rise to a private sector which is the most independent in the world.

England between 1870 and 1902 presents a clear picture of political sponsors interacting to minimize the degree of administrative unification imposed on the independent networks at central or local levels. As has been seen, the 1870 Act represented a partition of control because Radicals and the League exerted sufficient Parliamentary pressure to introduce national elementary schooling, but not enough to undermine vested interests in the maintenance of existing voluntary institutions. The net result was that the Education Department of 1870 had the position 'more of a central paymaster than that of a Ministry',[58] and the next quarter of a century did not fundamentally alter this situation. Throughout the period a high level of local managerial autonomy was retained by both networks. On the one hand, although the Liberals endorsed the popular management of the voluntary schools in order to gain further support among the people, the Salisbury government succeeded in preventing this. It conceded free education in 1891, to prevent defection of its popular vote, but defended management of voluntary schools from local control, thus retaining Anglican allegiance. On the other hand, the School Boards continued to be elected by the local ratepayers, on a cumulative voting system, and their managerial autonomy was not seriously affected by district audit or central Code until the late 1890s. The Boards were not 'in any sense the partner, or the agent, of the central body in a joint enterprise; the central Body was mainly a watchdog over its expenditure'.[59]

At secondary and higher levels independence was even more pronounced. As the Taunton Commission witnessed, 'innumerable bodies of trustees continued in perpetuity, whose schools were submitted to no public test of an official kind, whose actions were virtually uncontrolled save by the terms of statutes'.[60] Liberal attempts to undermine these predominately Anglican strongholds, to rationalize their statutes and financing, and to exchange public support for central inspection and examination, met with severe opposition. The Headmasters' Conference was established in 1869, to oppose Forster's earlier version of the Endowed Schools Bill, and ensure that the public schools 'should be free from any form of external guidance and control'.[61] Their political influence was sufficient to have this draft withdrawn and replaced by a makeshift expedient which appointed three commissioners to deal with the Endowed Schools alone — a far cry from the central authority envisaged by Taunton. Yet even this compromise, negotiated by a Liberal government, was reversed when the Conservatives returned to office. Although the Commissioners had not made great progress in elaborating new schemes for the improved use of individual endowments, their approach had not been timid or constrained by the Court of Chancery doctrine that an educational foundation must be regarded as belonging to the Church of England in the absence of evidence to the contrary. The Act was opposed by Anglicans who held that it secularized endowments, by the public schools who feared for their own independence, and by popular spokesmen, who viewed it as expropriating endowments intended for the poor, in the interests of the middle class. In 1874 Disraeli introduced a Bill to destroy the Commission and bring about 'the denationalization of schemes made under its authority'.[62] In other words, this was a clear piece of political sponsorship 'proposing the wholesale redelivery to one religious body, of schools which, founded for national purposes and endowed with national property, have been set free'.[63] The new Bill transferred the duties and powers of the Commissioners back to the more conservative Charity Commission — a better safeguard for independence since it lacked an organized system of inspection, examination or supervision.

Thus by the mid-nineties a complex administrative picture had developed from the conflict between the political sponsors. Some reduction in autonomy had been the price of state aid and recognition, but it had been lost to a chaotic array of bodies, whose nature was the outcome of struggle not the product of design. Together they represented a low degree of administrative unification and one whose increase was strongly resisted. The only titular *local* authorities for 'education' were the School Boards which had partial control over elementary instruction, but no jurisdiction at all in secondary or technical instruction, though many of their schools gave both. A similar lack of co-ordination characterized the *central* authorities responsible for the three main sectors of instruction (elementary, technical and secondary). A patchwork of statutory instruments, financial regulations and governmental agencies made up the central machinery for educational administration. The central authority for secondary education, in so far as one existed, was the Charity Commission, although certain endowed elementary schools also came under its jurisdiction for the management of their Trusts. Here Disraeli's defence of the old Commission (to protect the Anglican network) meant retaining an administrative organ unresponsive to government. As Forster, when Liberal Minister, was to report about his official membership of the Charity Commission 'I found no ministerial power there . . . my vote went for no more than those of anyone else'.[64]

The Science and Art Department, the central authority for Technical education, was not originally intended to be a Department of Education, but to encourage the study of subjects which traditional curricula did not recognize. Although to all intents and purposes it remained independent from the authority responsible for elementary education, its influence extended to the higher grade as well as to secondary schools proper, since its grants were given in return for inspection on the payment by results model. Such an exchange was opposed by the Technical Schools, who wanted the greater autonomy associated with block-grants, and by the School Boards whose independence was limited by having to receive two kinds of inspectors and comply with two sets of regulations – those of the Science and Art and Education Departments.

The Education Department itself had no statutory association with secondary education, although in practice it dealt with the higher grade schools and training colleges, and was chiefly concerned with the assessment of results for allocation of payments to schools. The opposition excited by Tory manipulation of audit and Code to constrain the activities of the School Boards, together with 'the narrowness of the Department's outlook and the illiberal character of its policies, damaged its reputation to such a degree that, on the one hand, the politicans declined to place secondary education under a central authority of which it would form a part, and, on the other, the public schools refused to have anything to do with it'.[65] Finally, to complete the picture, the Universities had succeeded in remaining substantially independent of State control.

The Bryce Commission, reporting in 1895, represented a Liberal attempt to press forward with administrative unification, since it considered managerial independence responsible for the deficiencies of secondary education. It advocated one comprehensive central authority to formulate policy which 'ought to consist of a Department of Executive Government, presided over by a Minister responsible to Parliament, who would obviously be the same Minister to whom the charge of elementary instruction is entrusted',[66] together with local authorities with substantial executive powers. Perhaps because it appeared after the Liberals' defeat, the report implied a cautious administrative encroachment rather than an assault on Anglican strongholds of independence. It stressed that the aim was not to make 'secondary education purely a matter of state concern':[67] it accepted the existence of a large and important private sector which could not be highly controlled. It sought to make public recognition dependent on satisfying the central authority about the adequacy of buildings, staff, curricula and examinations, but accepted that such a code of regulations and system of inspection would bear no resemblance to those used by the Education Department for elementary schools. It did not propose certification of teachers, only the keeping of a central register; it did not advocate central examination, merely the regulation and co-ordination of those held by the differing examining bodies already at work. Its careful insistence on guidance, not control, and on co-ordination rather than nationalization indicates the low degree of unification the Liberals thought politically feasible. Yet it was to be an even lower degree which was introduced by the Tories in the next seven years.

In the interests of Church schools, Salisbury's third administration decided to implement only those Bryce proposals relating to local administration. Here the aim was to shore up the voluntary schools against popular control by dissolving the School Boards in local areas and transferring their powers to the new County Councils. Were they to become the local bodies responsible for administering secondary education, the Tory dominated County Councils could be relied upon to favour the Grammar schools and popular control of School Boards would have been overcome. Although this Bill was defeated in 1896, the Government in fact implemented its provisions by administrative means. As far as a central authority was concerned, the lowest common denominator acceptable to the Tories was a Board with three Departments under it. The duties and powers of the Education Department, the Science and Art Department and the Charity Commission should be brought together, although a guarantee was given that there would be a separate organizational method of dealing with secondary as distinct from elementary and technical education. The 1899 Act instituting the Board of Education, presided over by the Minister in charge, represented a weak form of unification. Its weakness was underlined by the fact that it was not opposed by the Grammar and Public School organizations . . . 'a phenomenon that might legitimately, if uncharitably, be ascribed to the fact that the Bill was agreeably innocuous. It afforded such benefits as might be derived from association with a Department of State, without their being obliged to surrender any fundamental liberties they enjoyed'.[68] It was unopposed precisely because it was, in the words of the Chairman of the London School Board, nothing but 'a miserable little piece of Departmental machinery'.[69] Nevertheless for the first time 'the existence of the central authority implied that the administration of all public instruction was essentially a unity'.[70] However, when compared with countries of restrictive origins there is no denying that 'the rise of a central authority for English education had been a slow, tortuous, makeshift, muddled, unplanned, disjointed and ignoble process',[71] and that the unification resulting was both less intense and extensive.

The large majority with which the Tories were returned in 1900 enabled them to settle the local authority issue in the 1902 Act, which transferred elementary education to the County Councils as the local authorities for all education. In this way the School Boards and their popular control were suppressed, and the Church succeeded in its aim of gaining the maximum public subsidy while conceding the least possible control.[72] Loss of autonomy by particular networks had indeed been in proportion to the strength of political sponsorship, but the low general level of unification which emerged was the product of the alliances seeking unified authority, not for its own sake but only to limit others.

To turn to Denmark is to reverse the picture just examined. For unlike England, unification took place under the aegis of the assertive group. It was not therefore shaped by rear-guard action to protect traditional rights and practices or to undermine the local control of new institutions. On the contrary, when Venstre came to power, its aim was to give as prominent a place as politically feasible to the Grundtvigian network and principles. Since the Folk High Schools and Urban Fri Schools were also private schools based on communal control it was not government policy to nationalize them or to undermine community management. Instead Venstre was responsive to popular 'requests for more financial support from the State for private schools and a demand that parents should exercise rights within the direction of the public school system'.[73] Because of the latter, the Government itself was averse to the development of a strong central authority for national education. The unification it sought was one which drew the independent networks under the State umbrella for recognition and funding, which allowed for local governance of public schools, and which yet had enough administrative bite to gain purchase on the Learned Schools so as to redirect their operations. As in England, the unification which emerged was rather weak because no one wanted it to be strong, but unlike England, this was more a matter of principle than the result of self-defence.

The private schools had been founded by relatively poor groups; they were unendowed, and their maintenance was increasingly difficult towards the end of the century. For the last decade the Folk High Schools, independent Technical Schools, Real Schools and private urban schools in Copenhagen, had negotiated Government grants, in the face of political opposition, and without great loss of managerial autonomy. Yet the sums involved fell short of requirements, and on its advent to power, Venstre sought to remedy the situation despite resistance from the Upper House. A yearly subsidy was increased to private schools but distributed only to those recommended by School Commissions as giving an instruction equal to that of public schools. Private training colleges were also to benefit from the same arrangement. The immediate effect of these changes was that by 1905 about one tenth of public educational expenditure was flowing to the private schools.[74] Previously, private and communal schools were not clearly linked to the ordinary school system; now they became attached financially and in return had to meet certain academic standards. Undoubtedly the supervision of private schools was 'gentle and broadminded',[75] for it involved neither dispossession, standardization nor subordination by the State. Venstre's action was not of marginal significance for it protected a situation in which one fifth of pupils were educated outside the public sector. In this sense the private sector remained strong, although in comparison with England, its independence was less financially secure.

Just as academic standards were the main aspect of central administrative control for the private networks, so the same device was employed to unify the new public *Forskole* at elementary level. Management agencies themselves remained locally based and accentuated the principles of communal control and parental involvement. At the lowest level was the school Council, formed at each individual school from all teachers, under the chairmanship of the Headmaster. Under the 1904 Law its powers appertained to instruction within a particular school, thus giving some autonomy of decision-making and conferring the right to be consulted on all matters concerning that school. Above the School Councils was the School Commission, whose administrative area was that of the Parish. Here pressures for direct communal control were not fully successful even in rural areas, as members were chosen by the Parish Council, although it was stipulated that at least two should be parents with school-aged children and two should not be Councillors. At the next level the Communal Council in urban areas and the School Directorate in rural ones, linked upwards to the central Ministry. Economic power and the authority to nominate teachers or propose their dismissal were located at sub-ministerial level. Within this decentralized framework only three elements were placed in governmental hands — development, curricula and examination — yet even here consultative rights were widely dispersed. The two main instruments concerned were the School Plan and the Instruction Plan. The School Plan specified number of schools and catchment areas, the number of teachers and their salaries, together with other points about the local authority provisions made to meet legal obligations. The Communal Council was responsible for the School Plan, based on proposals by the School Commission, but it was then forwarded for final Ministerial approval. The same agencies elaborated the Instruction Plan, which dealt with the curriculum of each class, the material covered in each subject, the timetable and teaching arrangements. Here not only did Ministerial veto prevail but also a series of governmental circulars regulated in great detail the content of syllabuses, purposes of teaching different subjects and methods of examination. Thus although administrative unification was weak, and intentionally so, the Government drove with long reins and guided the system by the central management of knowledge.

As we have seen, the 1903 Law on Higher Public Schools was mainly concerned with opening up secondary education and reducing the cultural hegmony of the Learned Schools. The resulting legislation was a compromise, but one which brought about unification at this level. It did so by bringing all the institutions engaging in this kind of instruction together and submitting them to the same kind of administrative controls — again mainly those of curricula and examination. Perhaps this is clearest in the case of the Middle School which was not a self-standing institution but a 'legalized' four year course taking place in different establishments.

Significantly, Middle School examination rights could be given to private, communal or real schools, although here the administrative net tightened, for they were expected to prepare pupils in the same way as State Schools. On the other hand, since Gymnasia could not exist by themselves but must always be linked to a Middle School (public or private) their classical monopoly was reduced by administrative means. Timetables and curricula were published for the Middle School in 1904 and for the Gymnasium in 1906. Thus unification was no more extensive at secondary than elementary level, for in both the existence of an important private sector was acknowledged. Unlike England any loss of autonomy by independent schools was well compensated by the rights acquired relative to public schools. Unification was, however, rather more intense at secondary level, for in Denmark the aim of the new Government was to capture, tame and integrate the traditional Learned institutions, whereas in England the aim of the old political elite had been to protect the independence, elitism and separateness of the traditional endowed schools.

Turning to systematization, here again attempts to preserve the autonomy of the networks limited the extent to which it could develop, just as they had reduced the degree of unification which could take place. The two issues of course are closely related, for without strong unification it is unlikely that a high level of systematization can be maintained, and, on the other hand, the defence of specialist activities involves repulsing pressures towards standardization. There are, however, several important points to add to bring out the nature of resistance to systematization. Each politico-educational alliance was basically concerned to defend the integrity of its network and to ensure a prominent place for it after incorporation. Again, (in exact parallel to the argument about unification), if prominence of individual parts is the political concern of all, then a rational relationship between them is the priority of none. As we have seen co-ordination of the various parts is determined by political power not educational plan. Because of the collective concern to evade standardization, those changes which facilitate a dovetailing of parts are not strongly developed in the new systems, if they are present at all. For example, instead of a teaching profession, recruited and trained in a uniform fashion (according to level and discipline) and subject to stringent legal statutes, it is more likely that there will be diverse bodies, differently recruited and responsible to various authorities. Instead of uniform methods, curricula and examinations, these may vary from area to area and from one type of school to another. Instead of an integrated policy of pupil intake for the whole system there may be divergent sets of practices. Not all of these will be found in every system with substitutive origins; they are simply illustrative of factors which can inhibit co-ordination. Not only is systematization weak overall, it is peculiarly weak at certain points. There are establishments which, although part of the unified system, succeed in retaining a relatively segregated status and in repulsing pressures to dovetail them with others. These are cases whose political sponsors have defended them well, but also where a continuous flow of resources is maintained towards such establishments and their management groups. Resources need not be strictly monetary, but may include an element of prestige although the former appears essential for the long-term retention of this status. Such parts may or may not enjoy a prominent position in the system as a whole. In all these ways the characteristics of specialization and differentiation, which were entrenched before the development of state education, remain predominant and limit the degree of unification and systematization achieved.

In Denmark, the concern of each alliance to defend its network clearly militated against a high degree of systematization, despite Venstre's attempt firmly to implement the positive principle of hierarchical organization. The invention of the Middle School had been their main device for linking the Folkschool to the Gymnasium. However, as it was not a self-standing institution and did not have the support of either the protagonists of the Grundtvigian network or the defenders of the traditional learned network, it could not play the role of co-ordinating the two. Instead it was pulled in different directions at once by these historical antagonists. The forces of the right, attempting to preserve classical elitism, sought either the downfall of the Middle School or its redefinition as an antechamber to traditional secondary education. In no way were they willing to see these schools as meeting grounds which would integrate primary and secondary curricula, as this could only lower their own standards. In other words, they worked to repulse co-ordination and to retain the negative principle of hierarchical organization. In this they were supported by the autonomous University which used its freedom to defend the same traditional kind of instruction. On the other hand, the forces of the left were not satisfied with the Middle Schools as a compromise formula. To them the natural form of further education was at the Folk High School, which would only suffer if the best pupils were creamed off to the Middle School. In any case to them a link should only be forged with the Gymnasia if these were drastically remodelled. Otherwise, if the old Learned curriculum continued, the Middle Schools, as link institutions, would provide instruction completely unrelated to active life. Consequently they continued to support the separate Real Schools, which had been left in an ill-defined relationship to the Middle School and to extend alternative forms of practical post-elementary instruction (agricultural, technical and later commercial) which ran in parallel to the mainstream of public education, but were uncoordinated with it. Since these institutions proved extremely popular, and eventually thrust upwards into higher education, they represented further parts which were not dovetailed into the overall system.

In sum, the major co-ordinating agency — the Middle School — had no strong supporters: the systematization introduced by this compromise formula had no defenders, for it did not go far enough in implementing the educational ladder sought by the Grundtvigian alliance whilst it departed too much from the negative principle advocated by the right alliance. Even so Venstre had tried to link the main parts of education in a positive manner when it orchestrated the 'organic connection': the opposite was true of the Tory Party which sought to defend what it could of the bifurcation between elementary and secondary education in England.

The level of systematization achieved by the English 1902 Act was by far the lowest recorded in any of the four new systems examined. Indeed the Act itself said *nothing* about the relations between secondary education and elementary schooling. In practice the various institutions operating at these two levels showed the greatest discontinuities between one another: they were not dovetailed in terms of pupils' ages, their curricula or their examinations, but overlapped and contradicted each other at every point. This situation had arisen because the two major political sponsors had consistently pursued incompatible principles of hierarchical organization. The Tory party, to defend the Anglican network and to repulse popular control in education, advocated the negative principle. Elementary education should be confined within clear limits and separated from a co-ordinated network of secondary schools with which it was in no way linked. The Liberals, on the contrary, in sponsoring the School Boards, Technical schools and new universities, endorsed the positive principle of hierarchical organization — the educational ladder. However, it was not merely that they sought different kinds of systematization, it was that the *parts* they respectively thought should be related in these two ways were *themselves* different. Neither of the political antagonists struggled for a rational relationship between *all* current types of institutions — their aim was to suppress, limit or transform their opponents' institutions and *then* to systematize relations between the remaining parts. It was precisely because neither part was fully successful in the preliminary ground clearing operation that systematization could not be far-reaching. Hence the 1902 situation of overall discontinuity, with occasional linkages between pairs of institutions bearing witness to the partial success of various sponsors in imposing their principles.

The Taunton Commission report (1867) provided a clear and early statement of the Liberal principle, for it recommended attaching certain (third grade) secondary schools to elementary schools, treating the latter as lower divisions of the former and allowing passage from one to the other by examination. Simultaneously a series of devices, such as central instruction plans, inspection, examination and teacher training would ensure dovetailing. The implementation of this principle did, however, imply a really fundamental assault on Anglican foundations at secondary level, since it was to be financed by pooling their endowments. We have already seen how strongly the Headmasters' Conference fought back to prevent such legislation and that under Tory sponsorship the public schools contracted out and established their independent status.[76] Categorically severed from the lower levels, upward linkages were reinforced, and of a kind which no nineteenth century legislation could break ... 'As the public schools expanded, connections with Oxford and Cambridge Colleges were strengthened; in the half century 1850-99 over four fifths of students came from these schools ... Tightly integrated institutions, the public schools and ancient universities now constituted a more or less closed system of education'.[77]

If the major secondary establishments had thus been cut off, in practice and in principle, from elementary instruction, the reverse was not the case. For the School Boards, by initiating changes in the Education Department's Code,[78] and profiting from Science and Art Department grants, were developing higher grade schools and moving into secondary territory.[79] This redefinition of 'elementary' instruction had the support of Mundella, during the Liberal Ministry of 1882-5, but the majority of the Tory appointed Cross Commission (1888) reproved the School Boards for underselling the endowed secondary schools and giving an instruction 'unsuitable for labouring poor'. Instead they favoured the redelineation of a truly elementary curriculum to discourage this upward development. In subsequent years, Tory governments sought to impose this demarcation and manipulated technical instruction to this effect. The Royal Commission on Technical education (1881) established by the Liberals had advocated co-ordination between the different levels of Technical Schools and other elementary and secondary schools. Salisbury's government, on the contrary, was willing to encourage its expansion by granting rate aid, provided it was firmly defined as secondary.[80] A final Liberal attempt to rescue the potential linkage between School Boards, Technical Schools and Extension Colleges failed when Roscoe's bill to enable the Higher Grade Schools to receive this aid was unsuccessful.

In this context the recommendations of the Bryce Commission represented a recognition of Tory intransigence about the divide between elementary and secondary instruction (negative hierarchical organization), and also the practical independence already achieved by important secondary institutions. On the other hand, its proposals were an attempt to salvage something of the positive principle of systematization despite these constraints. On the negative side it acknowledged the existence of an important private sector which could not be dovetailed with the rest of education if it did not depend on public support. Furthermore, it accepted the impossibility of co-ordinating educational processes by integrating the curricula of elementary and secondary schools. Such curricular rules would impose uniformity and thus be unacceptable to the latter.[81] Instead the Bryce proposals sought to co-ordinate inputs and outputs and to fill gaps. All secondary schools in receipt of public money should provide a number of free places and there should be a liberal provision of scholarships from elementary schools. To make this national practice, some endowed schools should be moved from depopulated rural areas, new secondary schools built where provision was inadequate, and 'secondary tops' added to elementary schools in isolated regions. If the central register of teachers and the co-ordination of examining bodies are added to these recommendations, this represents the amount of systematization that the Liberals thought could be achieved within the context of weak administrative unification.

However, the Tories, when back in office, were determined to enforce the negative principle and to do so by killing the Higher Grade Schools and drawing a firm line between elementary and secondary instruction. This two-pronged attack firstly involved protecting the grammar schools by placing them under the wing of the County Councils: secondly, it meant limiting elementary instruction to the age of 15, to be given in establishments without any pretensions to secondary level work, of which the Higher Grade Schools had been guilty. Since, for example, only four of the seventy-nine Higher Grade Schools run by the London School Board were recognized as Higher Elementary Schools,[82] the intention was clearly to destroy the former. These actions signalled 'getting up steam'[83] for an Act which would finally halt the upthrust of elementary schools and separate off the secondary level. United opposition from Liberals, Non-conformists and the Labour movement, in defence of the Bryce programme, could neither win reprieve for the School Boards nor enforce linkage between levels. From the Tory point of view the 1902 Act had successfully precluded competition from a parallel network which would have threatened social stability — for the Labour movement had sought post elementary instruction through different establishments, the Higher Grade Schools, not through the Grammar Schools which were alien class institutions. Yet the Act itself had not been able to adjudicate between the two principles of systematization. Oppositional pressures had forced the inclusion of clauses making it obligatory for the LEAs to promote post-elementary education in relation to the needs of their areas. The government had only managed to leave the relations between the two levels vague, not to impose its principle of complete separation.[84] 'The solution of the key problem of the relation between elementary and secondary education — a solution that determined the basic structure of the education system for the next half century and more ... was carried through by the Board of Education in the months and years immediately following the passage of the Act'.[85]

In the next few years, by attempting to close schools which crossed the divide, or damage them by discriminating in grants awarded, the

Board sought to clear the middle ground and to organize secondary education as something different and apart. 'Yet to plan secondary education as something quite different from elementary education, different in particular, from what had been provided in the higher grade or science schools, inevitably meant recourse to the academic tradition perpetrated in grammar and public schools'.[86] Progress in this direction was such that when the Liberals finally returned to office all they could accomplish was the introduction of 25 percent of free places in secondary schools, thus linking the two levels by competitive scholarships. At elementary level their own network and definition of instruction had lost out — all they could do was to partially impose their principle of hierarchical organization on their opponents' institutions. Nevertheless, Tory single-mindedness about establishing this separation had tended to deflect the thrust of negative systematization away from the Technical Schools and Extension Colleges. These survived, they remained linked to one another, but uncoordinated with their opposite numbers, the Public Schools and older Universities.

In other words, educational systems originating from substitution retain specialization and differentiation as their dominant pair of characteristics and these constantly create strains and problems which as we shall see are barely contained by simultaneous but weaker pressures towards unification and systematization. Such systems are frequently and properly referred to as decentralized — they indeed have no leading-part. Finally, although such systems have a marked tendency towards low internal integration, no assumption can be drawn from this about their lesser 'survival value'. Indeed it may be that this 'looser' internal structure has advantages for durability since it allows of experimentation, diversification and further incorporation. In view of the dubiousness of seeking social referents for these organic terms, it seems preferable simply to distinguish between types and rates of change. Later, it will indeed be argued that the loosely integrated internal structure is associated with distinctive processes of change.

2(b) From Restrictive Origins

Where restrictive strategies prevailed the picture of internal structural elaboration is almost the reverse of the pattern common to educational systems which emerged from substitutive competition. Here, as we have seen, no element of multiple integration precedes the development of state systems. This is negotiated during the replacement phase but within the context of strong pressures towards unification and system-atization. This pair of characteristics emerge first and are inextricably bound together for there is no intervening period in which a gradual transition is made from summativity to wholeness. Once restriction is completed and replacement begins, it takes place within a unified administrative framework. From the start all new educational pro-visions are made and co-ordinated by this central authority.

Restriction itself involved manipulation of the state legislative machinery in order to terminate educational activities which were harmful to the operations of the political elite. Through replacement this group seeks to institutionalize a new definition of instruction which is highly compatible with its requirements. Yet if it is to ensure that the new establishments and personnel provide the services needed, then it must control them closely. Hence one of the first innovations made during the replacement phase is the development of an admin-istrative structure tailored to this task. This must simultaneously guarantee the responsiveness of educational institutions to the direc-tions of the political elite and seek to eliminate countervailing or disruptive tendencies. In other words, if the aims of the political elite are to be satisfied, unification must be intense and extensive. What is significant about such systems is that this group is in a position to *design* the unified administrative framework in accordance with its goals.

The central administrative agencies formed are not identical, but they have much in common. They have a strong, hierarchical distribu-tion of authority in which each lower administrative level is subject to a higher one and ultimate control is exercised at the apex by a political officer. In turn this means a very low degree of autonomy of decision-making in the various regions or in individual schools. It is not uncom-mon for every decision concerning expenditure, appointments, examination, curriculum and recruitment to be referred to a higher authority. Similarly, the autonomy of educational personnel is not great and it is common in such systems to find that teachers are civil servants and thus subject to more limiting legal statutes than other professions.

Equally important is the fact that unification is very extensive. The restrictive phase had prevented many institutions from operating and had eliminated some altogether. During the replacement phase the political elite seeks to possess a monopoly in the field: freedom of instruction could only interfere with the attainment of its own goals. Usually, however, this group cannot mobilize the resources required for immediate replacement and has to rely on establishments and personnel inherited from the antecedent period. Through procedures like authorization, licensing and certification, old facilities are harnessed to new purposes to solve short-term problems of building and staffing. This was the case in both the countries considered – provided the unified controls were accepted, older activities could continue if the political elite required them.

In neither country did the boundaries of the state system become co-terminus with those of national education. Indeed sometimes the very dependence on resources retained from the earlier period led to the old dominant group demanding freedom of instruction and independent status for its establishments. Nevertheless, even if these demands met with some success, as in France for example after the loi Falloux, the private sector does not achieve much autonomy as it does not escape from the controls and common practices imposed by the unified framework. For instance, the existence of a single series of state organized examinations limits the definitions of instruction which can be pursued within the private sector. Because of these factors unification is more marked in systems with restrictive origins, and the private sector is less able to create exigencies for the public sector because it is more closely controlled. Quite simply it is less problematic because it is less different. At the same time, however, the fact that the private sector is unified also prevents it from functioning as a shock absorber for the state system by serving unsatisfied demands and thus chanelling a potential source of conflict away from public education.

In founding the Imperial University Napoleon could not have been more explicit that he was creating an instrument of government.

> Teaching is a function of the State, because this is a need of the nation. In consequence, schools should be state establishments and not establishments in the state. They depend on the state and have no resort but it; they exist by it and for it. They hold their right to exist and their very substance from it; they ought to receive from it their task and their rule. Then again, as the state is one, its schools ought to be the same everywhere.[87]

Given this charter for unification it is unsurprising that the administrative structure should be designed to maximize responsiveness to political direction and minimize countervailing influences bending education to other ends. Thus the decree of 1808 establishing the framework of the Imperial University embodied two basic principles — that of supreme central control and of a state monopoly of instruction. The former thus refers to the intensity of unification and the latter to its extensiveness.

To ensure central control, a rigidly hierarchical administrative structure was erected which subordinated regional *académies* to the authority of a *Grand-Maître* who in turn was directly responsible to the head of State. Such a policy embodied Napoleon's determination to consolidate his Université as the ultimate authority in education, and loyalty to his régime as the ultimate goal of instruction within a single state system. The Imperial University was the name given to this system as a whole, not to a specific establishment. It proclaimed uniformity in instruction throughout the country and the government's right to enforce this. While this legislation did not make every school government property, it placed them all under official control, thus ensuring both ideological orthodoxy and geographical uniformity. The latter aim was achieved by standardizing curricula throughout the country and making all qualifications (*Baccalauréat, licence, doctorat*) national ones. All schools were to impart the same instruction at the appropriate level and to each level corresponded a specific type of school organization. The uniformity of equivalent establishments throughout the nation was thus guaranteed.[88] It is in a direct line of administrative succession that the legendary minister of the Second Empire was supposed to have remarked that 'à cette heure, dans telle classe, tous les élèves de l'Empire explique telle page de Virgile'.[89] But central control did not end with administrative personnel and school regulations; it also embraced the teaching profession as civil servants and sought to ally them to the state by more than statutory bonds. To Napoleon 'il n'y aura pas d'état politique fixe, s'il n'y a pas un corps enseignant avec des principes fixe. . . . Mon but principal dans l'éstablissement d'un corps enseignant est d'avoir un moyen de diriger les opinions politiques et morales'.[90] The loyalty of the teaching profession, modelled jointly on the Jesuit corporation and the military hierarchy, was to be ensured by a judicious mixture of training, incentives and surveillance.

The decree creating the Imperial University also attempted to give the state educational system an absolute monopoly over all instruction. State controls over private education were elaborated and reinforced in 1811, thus greatly increasing the extensiveness of unification. The most important restrictions, which virtually made these establishments part of the public system, included governmental authorization before any school could be opened, subordination to Université regulations and inability to confer their own diplomas. In addition, to prevent competititon with public education, private schools were weakened financially by a per capita contribution to the Université paid on each pupil, and academically by a requirement that all private pupils entering for the Baccalauréat had to present a *certificat d'études* attesting that their last two years of study had been in a public *lycée* or *collège*. Fearing above all resurgence of the Catholic church, their schools were limited to one per *Département* and prohibited altogether in towns where lycées existed. Certainly at elementary level the religious orders were allowed to continue teaching but as part of a dual policy to control the church in the state and the people in society. By enforcing their registration with the University and compelling them to swear an oath of allegiance they were less of a danger as civil servants inside the system than as independent groups outside it who were loyal to a foreign power.[91]

In terms of the exclusive etatist ideal of its founder, the unification of the Imperial University was imperfect in two respects. On the one hand, shortage of resources precluded the formation of State elementary education. The *Frères des écoles Chrétiennes* continued much as before and their schools were unified only to the extent of state inspection and control of syllabus — thus perpetuating a clerical entrenchment which Napoleon was subsequently to regret. On the other hand, the state did not achieve its monopoly in the sense of eliminating the private sector altogether. Largely because the administrative head of the Université condoned Catholic infringements, private schools lost only about half their pupils after the 1811 legislation which had sought to transform the monopoly into reality.[92] But what to the state was a partial failure in its public education policy was a crushing blow to the autonomy of private instruction. 'Pour ce qui est de l'enseignement, le monopole ne fût d'abord qu'une surveillance plus reglée, par l'introduction de toutes les écoles privées dans le cadre de l'Université'.[93] The principle of strong unification had been established, it had been implemented in practice at secondary and higher levels, a national administrative structure had been created to enforce it and a series of central examination and certification procedures developed to protect it. These legacies of the original Imperial University were a political heritage which subsequent regimes respected in their own interests. Although modifications were introduced, unification remained both intensive and extensive.

Before the consolidation of the Russian educational system, the

Tsarist bureaucracy was clear about the form it should take and the purposes it should serve. Strong unification was one of the first priorities, and in the 1860ties, 'despite the argument that decentralization would allow experimentation and attract public support, the commission was loath to subsidise cultural self-determination, racial nationalism, religious separatism, political federalism, or geographical secession in the schools'.[94] At that time, however, government failed to eliminate these educational characteristics — the Universities had just achieved a measure of self-government, the parish schools of the Holy Synod remained outside the Ministry of education and all elementary schools were not under the control of school boards and hence insulated from subversive influences. Dimitri Tolstoy was thus appointed to introduce a unified system, in the hope that he would seize the initiative in the schools as part of a positive, long-range programme to strengthen the unity of the Empire. By the end of his tenure at the Ministry there is no doubt that he had succeeded in fashioning an instrument whose unique responsiveness to central political directives allowed schooling to be employed 'as both an inflationary and a deflationary device, now expanding, now contracting the conduits of upward mobility for different segments of the population, deliberately fitting the level and direction of national enlightenment to the demands of international security and domestic stability'.[95]

Convinced that the key to overall educational control was found at secondary level, the Gymnasium was made a special property of state and it alone unlocked the door to the universities and social privilege. Here stringent unification had three aspects. Firstly, there was central standardization of lesson plans, hourly time-tables and sequence of topics taught. Because its role was national, its processes must be uniform and 'every phase of its operation must be protected against the accidents of place and the erosion of time'.[96] Secondly, the public Maturity Certificate, like the Baccalauréat, guarded the exit from secondary to higher instruction. Since satisfactory reports from political class counsellors were a precondition of passing, the certificate contained a fine inner mesh which increased its effectiveness as a filter. Finally, central rules for entering the gymnasium were published in 1872 and were coupled with the creation of preparatory classes which guaranteed a uniform instruction under state control. Initially this stringent unification was only possible at secondary level, it had been exploited 'to the full in order to convert the college preparatory school into a bulwark of administrative absolutism',[97] but in the decade that followed it was extended to other types of schools.

Because of the need for their support and resources the Tsarist bureaucracy had been forced to share responsibility for socializing the peasantry with the Church and the gentry at elementary level. Similarly, the price for consolidating the state gymnasium had been a certain amount of local control and autonomy for the Realschool. Subsequent legislation was designed to curtail the influence of other institutions and to eliminate internal initiative. To this end provincial and district school boards were reorganized and church schools were placed under them. The office of state inspector of primary schools was created and his presence on the school board was intended to give the Ministry of Education firm control over policy. As student unrest spread to the countryside and terrorist cadres threatened the towns, Tolstoy passed his 1875 directives to tighten the offical grasp on the lower levels. The rigid rules for operating gymnasia were now applied to Realschools, the administrative distinction between the highly controlled state preparatory schools and the rather more flexible public terminal establishments disappeared, and a network of public colleges was opened for the politico-pedagogical training of the rural school master. In combination these laws and directives of the 1870s severely reduced any regional or institutional participation in educational decision-making and any freedom of action on the part of educational personnel. Only higher education still escaped complete unification because its statute of self-government remained in force.

Only after the assassination of Alexander II in 1881 did the political elite complete the process of unification in a climate welcoming law and order. University autonomy was reduced in several ways simultaneously; its administrative officers became public officials not elected professors, Rectors were nominated directly by the ministry, and the policing of the student body increased. In the following years intake policy was closely monitored by government, to ensure that education played its part in political integration. Exactly the same motive accounted for the policy of russification which was imposed on the schools of all national minorities at this time. After the lesson of 1881 'the nationalist party was more convinced than ever that as long as the Romanov realm remained a loose assembly of different languages, disparate cultures, and conflicting creeds, held to the Muscovite core by physical compulsion', it would be insecure'.[98] Thus the Tsarist definition of instruction, presented in the Russian language, was imposed through uniform state schools on Armenian, Polish, German, Finnish and Baltic minorities.

As in France, the intensity of unified control was matched by its extensiveness. Offical repression of the private sector in fact pre-dated the establishment of the educational system, for the Tsarist bureaucracy had to restrict the operation of aristocratic boarding schools before it could achieve educational hegemony. As it had long proved impossible to suppress them completely, a policy had been elaborated in the 1820s which was found to be successful during the rest of the century. Private schools were required to observe the same rules as state schools in terms of courses, examinations and personnel. Each establishment was subordinated to the local public school director or inspector and even private family tutors had to abide by the general regulations for all teachers.[99] They could only differ to the extent of adding to the minimum course of study and even then permission was required to use special texts. Although legislative details changed, the principle remained unaltered — heavy state control protected public education from exigencies created by deviations in the private sector. Just as the French republicans were often slow to acknowledge their enduring debt to the centralized Imperial University structure, so too 'a century after Dimitri Tolstoy established his system, the Soviet bureaucracy was not yet ready to acknowledge the hated minister as a native pioneer of central academic mechanisms for the control of nationwide social stimulation'.[100]

In both cases the centralized administrative structure was designed and in place before the replacement phase was fully underway. New developments took place under their aegis and guidance. It is this which accounts for the second major characteristic they share in common, namely that the form of national education which comes into existence is a system from the start. Because restrictive strategies, unlike substitutive ones, present the opportunity for beginning largely from scratch, any successful political elite will avoid internal bottlenecks, contradictions and inconsistencies by dovetailing inputs, processes and outputs in its own interests. At first such systematization will only involve those parts and levels to which the political elite has given priority in its replacement policy, although others are added later. The principles guiding co-ordination are the operational requirements of the political elite. As we have seen the educational services sought by such elites are more varied than those for which the dominant group provided, but they are still limited. This means that in themselves political interests lead to a higher, though not vastly higher, degree of specialization and differentiation than in the antecedent period.

Pressures towards further specialization and differentiation arise as has been seen from multiple integration which is an unavoidable consequence of the quest for resources and support during the replacement phase. Their importance is directly proportional to the dependence of the political elite upon the mobilization of these additional resources. Ideally the political elite would like to construct a tightly controlled educational system with just that degree and kind of specialization needed to meet the various etatist goals. Further differentiation threatens the responsiveness of teaching personnel to political directives, it risks the creation of an independent corporation. Further specialization involves expenditure on forms of instruction irrelevant to the State and also disrupts the co-ordination of those parts which are vital to its operations. Hence the political elite seeks the maximum contribution and support from other parts of society in return for conceding the minimum amount of diversification. In the cases examined it was never entirely successful in this and broader concessions had to be granted. Nevertheless, their introduction was orchestrated by the political elite so as to ensure least disturbance to its own priorities. Sometimes, as in Russia, this meant relegating the practical sector of education to an inferior position running in parallel to, though unconnected with, academic institutions which directly served the State. In France the same aim was achieved by confining to the primary level those forms of specialization which were of little interest to the State. Thus because demands for increased diversity are minimized and modified by the political elite the concessions made to them do not reduce the high level of systematization. Because they are introduced by government the new specialized institutions do not escape central administrative control and thus lower the high degree of unification. In other words, systematization and unification remain the predominant pair of characteristics as specialization and differentiation are accommodated to them.

Such systems may properly be termed centralized — they have a distinct leading part in their respective administrative frameworks and small changes initiated through them have ramifications for all the other component parts of education. Since changes in the various elements are carefully monitored by the centre, their reciprocal influence is not of equivalent strength. They are also systems with a tightly integrated internal structure. This is partly because they are planned to a much greater extent than those with substitutive origins. Also the fact that the political elite curtails specialization in turn reduces the diversity of parts and hence the problems of dovetailing them. Partly too the fact that this group contains and directs the specialized parts to emerge means that it actively co-ordinates them with others to prevent bottlenecks and contradictions from threatening state-oriented educational activities. This as we have seen may be a purely negative operation of stopping the former from creating problems for the latter – it does not necessarily imply the forging of positive links between them. There is no reason to think that the existence of an educational ladder is more likely to be found in the centralized than in the decentralized system, anymore than that negative hierarchical organization will preponderate there. The appearance of either depends on the goals and nature of the political elite in the centralized system: what distinguishes it from those with substitutive origins is that systematization will be more pronounced *whichever* principle of co-ordination is adopted.

NOTES

1. For example, the exporting of the Imperial University structure after Napoleon's conquests or the establishment of metropolitan educational practices in colonial territories. Cf. A. Moumouni, *L'éducation en Afrique*, Paris, 1964. Michel de Beauvais, 'Education in Former French Africa', in J. S. Coleman (ed.), *Education and Political Development*, Princeton, 1965. A. Mayhew, *The Education of India*, London, 1928.

2. A full account would have to deal with interaction between the imposed system, local culture and social organization. It is this interplay which governs the retention, rejection or adaptation of the metropolitan model. Our type of theory only helps to account for the nature of this model itself – not its reception or fate abroad.

3. Systems analysis of necessity depends on the existence of differentiated parts. While there is no need for such parts to be represented by social institutions, only three other possibilities remain. Firstly, the parts referred to may be conceptualized as social groups – in which case the analysis of systems integration is collapsed into the analysis of social integration. This procedure was rejected in Chapter 1 on theoretical grounds. Secondly, the parts may be conceptualized as smaller scale differentiated units. In this case analysis focusses on systems *in* Society and not on the social system. This is clearly inappropriate when the problem in hand is not a restricted one but involves examining how education is

related to the rest of society. Finally, society as a whole may be regarded as engaging in exchange with its external environment (a broader system of which it is a part). This latter method of conceptualizing parts is inappropriate for the present study since it means that system change is necessarily viewed as exogeneous in origin.

4. Here the distinction drawn between 'systems' and 'social' integration is the same as that outlined by D. Lockwood, 'Social Integration and System Integration', in G. K. Zollschan and H. W. Hirsch, *Explorations in Social Change*, London, 1964.

5. 'Differentiation' is used by Eisenstadt as a classificatory concept which refers to the ways in which the main social functions of the major institutional spheres of society become dissociated from one another, attached to a specialized collectivity and roles, and organized in relatively specific and autonomous symbolic and organizational frameworks within the confines of the same institutionalized system. Cf. S. N. Eisenstadt, 'Social Change Differentiation and Evolution', in N. J. Demerath and R. A. Peterson, *System, Change and Conflict*, New York, 1967. As far as education was concerned it was not dissociated organizationally, symbolically or in terms or roles and personnel from various other parts of the historical empires or imperial civilizations. Educational activities intermingled with others which were themselves relatively indistinct – for example, the position of the litterati in China and to a lesser extent the Brahmin in India witnesses to the intermingling of religious, political, educational and stratificational spheres.

6. What is of particular interest about the transformation of the historic empires and ancient civilizations, analyzed by Weber and Eisenstadt, is that the characteristics which Eisenstadt saw as *emerging* from them (societies with increased differentiation and higher levels of mobilization) are exactly those which make up the *initial* context at the time this study starts. In other words the end of their cycle is the beginning of ours.

Eisenstadt in fact analyzes the preceding cycle in very similar terms to the ones used here – the interplay of structural aspects with processes of elite formation. To him transformation of traditional social structures arises from the activities of relatively autonomous elites. Some degree of cultural autonomy facilitates the development of a symbolic system supporting social change, and similarly the partial autonomy of groups allows challenge of the dominant centre, whilst the relative differentiation of any institutional sphere favours the development of organized nuclei within the periphery. In other words, some degree of autonomy is a necessary condition of modernization, which itself represents an intensification of social differentiation. 'Transformation of Social, Political and Cultural Orders in Modernization', in his *Comparative Perspectives on Social Change*, Boston, 1968.

7. C.f. E. Despois, *Le vandalisme révolutionnaire*, Paris, 1868; R. Sevrin, *Histoire de l'enseignement primaire en France sous la Révolution, le Consulat et l'Empire*, Paris, 1932; C. Hippeau, *La Revolution et l'éducation nationale*, Paris, 1883; O. Gréard, *La Législation de l'instruction en France depuis 1789*, Vol. 1, 1789-1833, Paris, 1887; and A. Duruy, *L'instruction publique et la Révolution*, Paris, 1882.

8. C. Jourdain, *Le budget de l'instruction publique et des établissements scientifiques et littéraires depuis la fondation de l'université impériale jusqu'à nos jours*, Paris, 1857.

9. P. L. Alston, *Education and the State in Tsarist Russia*, Stanford, 1969, p. 273, note 28.

10. C. Jourdain, *Le budget de l'instruction publique*, op. cit.

11. J. Guillaume, *Procès-verbaux du comité d'instruction publique de l'Assemblée Législative*, Paris, 1889; and *Procès-verbaux du comité d'instruction publique de la Convention Nationale*, (6 Vols.), Paris, 1890-1907.

12. Quoted by L. Liard, *L'enseignement supérieur en France*, (2 Vols.), Paris, 1888, p. 69.

13. Cf. Michalina Vaughan, 'The Grandes Ecoles' in R. Wilkinson (ed.), *Governing Elites: Studies in Training and Selection*, Oxford, 1969.

14. L. Liard, *L'enseignement supérieur en France*, op. cit. Vol. 2, p. 1.

15. Cf. M. d'Ocagne, *Les grandes écoles de France*, Paris, 1873.

16. Napoleon quoted by J. Simon, *Réforme de l'enseignement populaire*, Paris, 1874.

17. Cf. A. Delfau, *Napoléon Ier et l'instruction publique*, Paris, 1902.

18. A. Aulard, *Napoléon Ier et le monopole universitaire*, Paris, 1911, p. 242.

19. F. Guizot, *Essais sur l'histoire et sur l'état actuel de l'instruction publique en France*, Paris, 1816, p. 4.

20. J. Simon, *Victor Cousin*, Paris, 1910, p. 107.

21. Ibid., p. 79.

23. Konstantin Ushinsky, the most effective opponent of the reforms leading up to the Tolstoy system, published his *Man as Educable Subject: An outline of Pedagogical Anthropology*, in 1870. C.f. N. Hans, *The Russian Tradition in Education*, London, 1963, Ch. 4. and *History of Russian Educational Policy*, London, 1931.

24. P. L. Alston, op. cit. p. 90.

25. Ibid., p. 96.

26. A 'leading assertive group' simply refers to the group which has made most progress at a particular time in devaluing the monopoly of the dominant group. It is identified by the number of schools and teachers it provides or alternatively by the number of pupils it enrols relative to the dominant group.

27. Cf. M. T. Hodgen, *Workers' Education in England and the United States*, London, 1925. M. Tylecote, *The Mechanics Institutes of Lancashire and Yorkshire, before 1851*, Manchester, 1957.

28. Eric E. Rich, *The Education Act 1870*, London, 1970, p. 63.

29. Quoted by D. W. Sylvester, *Robert Lowe and Education*, Cambridge, 1974, p. 59. Emphasis added.

30. For example, in 1871 a spokesman for the Union of the Left declared that, 'Le parti national-libéral (which entered the Union of the Right) qui s'appuie d'abord sur les fonctionnaires formés par le collège latin et l'Université, lutte, à n'en pas douter, pour défendre ses foyers et ses positions'. E. Simon, *Reveil national et culture populaire en Scandinavie*, Uppsala, 1960, p. 598.

31. C.f. K. B. Andersen, 'Political and Cultural Development in Nineteenth Century Denmark', in J. A. Lauwerys, *Scandinavian Democracy*, Copenhagen, 1958.

32. Op. cit. For example in 1884 the Union of the Left had 81 seats out of the 102 seats in the *Folketing*.

33. For example in 1871 Høgsbro submitted to Government, as a project of the *Folketing*, a plan to introduce national culture alongside classical culture in secondary education. This plan was rejected.

34. Cf. Thomas Rørdam, *The Danish Folk High Schools*, Copenhagen, 1965.

35. Quoted by Willis Dixon, *Education in Denmark*, Copenhagen, 1958, p. 97.

36. One illustration of this point is the fact that Real Schools had twice as many pupils in 1901 as in 1891.

37. Cf. Willis Dixon, *Education in Denmark*, op. cit., p. 103 ff.

38. Ibid., p. 114.

39. The chairman of the founding meeting of the League declared in 1869 that 'what we are going to do is this; by means of this League and its branches, we are going to rouse the people – in whom now, happily is placed political power – in order that we may say to Mr. Forster, "Be our leader and give us what we want; we'll support you' ". Quoted by J. W. Adamson, *English Education 1789-1902*, Cambridge, 1964, pp. 350-51.

40. The Report of the Newcastle Commission (1861) had shown that 76 percent of children in schools attended Church of England schools. *Report of the Royal Commission on the State of Popular Education in England and Wales.* See also, M. Cruikshank, *Church and State in English Education, 1870 to the present day*, London, 1963.

41. Cf. E. E. Rich, *The Education Act 1870*, op. cit., K. M. Hughes, 'A Political Party and Education: Reflections on the Liberal Party's Educational Policy, 1870-1902', *British Journal of Educational Studies*, Vol. VIII, No. 2.

42. D. W. Sylvester, *Robert Lowe and Education*, op. cit., p. 123.

43. Even then radicals like John Bright argued of the 1870 Act, 'The fault of the Bill, in my mind, is that it has extended and confirmed the system which it ought in point of fact to have superseded . . . it was a Bill to encourage Denominational education, and where that was impossible, to establish Board Schools. It ought, in my opinion, to have been a Bill to establish Board Schools, and to offer inducements to those who were connected with Denominational Schools to bring them under the control of that Privy Council'. John Bright, *Public Addresses*, London, 1879, pp. 201-02.

44. 'The role of the 1870 Education Department was to be more that of a central paymaster than that of a Ministry'. 'The School Board was not to be in any sense the partner, or the agent of the central body in a joint enterprise; the central body was mainly a watchdog over its expenditure'. E. Eaglesham, *From School Board to Local Authority*, London, 1956, p. 12 and p. 16.

45. Brian Simon, *Education and the Labour Movement 1870-1920*, London, 1965, p. 158.

46. S. D. Simon, *A Century of City Government; Manchester 1838-1938*, London, 1938.

47. Royal Commission on the Elementary Education Acts. (Cross Commission) Final Report, p. 195.

48. 'The Minute of April, 1900, was to be used in a pincer movement against the higher education given in school board day schools. The "elementary" claw of the pincers would ensure that elementary schools were restricted in scope; in length of school life; and in subject matter; the "higher" claw would keep them few in number, and limited to a narrowly selected range of pupils and specially equipped buildings. And the powerful arms of the pincers would rest in the unseen grip of the Treasury'. Eric Eaglesham, *From School Board to Local Authority*, op. cit., p. 52.

49. Brian Simon, *Education and the Labour Movement*, op. cit., pp. 107-08. See also E. C. Mack, *Public Schools and Political Opinion since 1860*, New York, 1941.

50. Royal Commission on Secondary Education (Bryce Commission), Report, Vol. I, p. 324.

51. Brian Simon, *Education and the Labour Movement*, op. cit., p. 112.

52. Cf. R. D. Roberts, *Eighteen Years of University Extension*, Cambridge, 1891.

53. V. A. McClelland, *English Roman Catholics and Higher Education, 1830-1903*, Oxford, 1973.

54. A. D. Hall and R. E. Hagen, 'Definition of System', in Joseph A. Litterer, *Organisations, Systems, Control and Adaptation*, New York, 1969, Vol. II, p. 36.

55. Percy S. Cohen, *Modern Social Theory*, op. cit., p. 229.

56. Cf. M. J. A. de Condorcet, *Sur l'instruction publique*, Paris, 1792. See also F. Vial, *Condorcet et l'éducation démocratique*, Paris, n.d. F. Alengry, *Condorcet – guide de la Révolution française*, Paris, 1904. J. Bouissounouse, *Condorcet, le philosophe dans la Révolution*, Paris, 1962.

57. A. D. Hall and R. E. Hagen, 'Definition of System', loc. cit.

58. Eric Eaglesham, *From School Board to Local Authority*, op. cit., p. 12.

59. Ibid., p. 16.

60. J. W. Adamson, *English Education 1789-1902*, op. cit., p. 267.

61. Brian Simon, *Education and the Labour Movement, 1870-1920*, op. cit., p. 103.

62. A. S. Bishop, *The Rise of a Central Authority for English Education*, Cambridge, 1971, p. 234.

63. Idem, quoted from *The Times*, 22 July 1874.

64. *Report from the Select Committee on Education, Science and Art (Administration)*, 1884, p. 399.

65. A. S. Bishop, *The Rise of a Central Authority for English Education*, op. cit., p. 273.

66. *Report of the Royal Commission on Secondary Education*, 1895, Vol. I, p. 257.

67. Ibid., p. 324.

68. A. S. Bishop, *The Rise of a Central Authority for English Education*, op. cit., p. 262.

69. Ibid., p. 263, quoted from *The Times*, 16 February 1899.

70. J. W. Adamson, *English Education 1789-1902*, op. cit., p. 469.

71. A. S. Bishop, *The Rise of a Central Authority for English Education*, op. cit., p. 276.

72. Cf. George Baron and D. A. Howell, *The Government and Management of Schools*, London, 1974. Not only were County Councils dominated by parson and squire but they were to provide support from the local rates and did not exact a great loss of managerial autonomy in exchange. Governing bodies of schools had a two-third majority for their owners and representatives of the Local Education Authorities made up the remaining third. The main losses were the LEA acquiring responsibility for secular education and gaining powers of veto over appointment and dismissal of teachers.

73. Willis Dixon, *Education in Denmark*, op. cit., p. 97.

74. Ibid., Ch. 4 and especially p. 115.

75. Ibid., p. 117.

76. Brian Simon, *Education and the Labour Movement, 1870-1920*, op. cit., p. 103 ff.

77. Ibid., p. 112.

78. Eric Eaglesham, *From School Board to Local Authority*, op. cit.

79. Cf. A. S. Bishop, *The Rise of a Central Authority for English Education*, op. cit., Chapters 7 and 8.

80. J. W. Adamson, *English Education, 1789-1902*, op. cit., p. 409.

81. Opposing curricular standardization the Report argues that 'we should deplore as certain to be hurtful to educational progress the uniformity of system which such rules would tend to produce', quoted ibid., p. 458.

82. Brian Simon, *Education and the Labour Movement, 1870-1920*, op. cit., p. 198.

83. B. M. Allen, *Sir Robert Morant*, London, 1934, p. 153.

84. In practice the overlap and disjuncture continued. In terms of inputs, the secondary schools took pupils from the age of seven or eight, thus overlapping with elementary schools; in terms of processes a number of establishments occupied a confused middle ground, including the Higher Elementary Schools, the few surviving Higher Grade Schools, and some lower secondary schools; and in terms of outputs elementary school leaving was not necessarily terminal, especially as far as the Pupil-Teacher centres, which lay end-on to the elementary schools, were concerned. All of these challenged the Tory idea of a separate, class based secondary level and testified to its inability fully to eliminate oppositional institutions.

85. Brian Simon, *Education and the Labour Movement, 1870-1920*, op. cit., p. 237.

86. Ibid., p. 242.

87. L. Liard, *L'enseignement supérieur en France 1789-1889*, op. cit., Vol. II, p. 35.

88. Cf. M. Vaughan and M. S. Archer, *Social Conflict and Educational Change in England and France, 1789-1848*, Cambridge, 1971, see Chapters 8 and 10.

89. Quoted in Antoine Prost, *L'enseignement en France, 1800-1967*, Paris, 1968, p. 338.

90. A. Delfau, *Napoléon Ier et l'instruction publique*, op. cit., p. 16.

91. Ibid. 'C'est en les comprenant dans l'Université, dit il (Napoleon), qu'on les rattachera à l'ordre civil et qu'on préviendra le danger de leur indépendance', p. 19.

92. A. Aulard, *Napoléon Ier et le monopole universitaire*, op. cit. Aulard calculates that before the 1811 legislation the numbers of pupils in religious and private schools was roughly equivalent to those in public schools. By 1913 the total number of pupils in State schools was 44,051 and the total number in private schools had diminished to 27,121, p. 307 f.

93. Ibid., p. 369.

94. Patrick L. Alston, *Education and the State in Tsarist Russia*, op. cit., p. 54.

95. Ibid., p. 247.

96. Ibid., p. 97.

97. Ibid., p. 110.

98. Ibid., p. 120.

99. William H. E. Johnson, *Russia's Educational Heritage*, Pittsburg, 1950, pp. 94-95.

100. Patrick L. Alston, *Education and the State in Tsarist Russia*, op. cit., p. 249. A similar stress is placed on the continuity of the Tsarist educational system after the Revolution by N. Hans, *The Russian Tradition in Education*, op. cit.

Part II

EDUCATIONAL SYSTEMS IN ACTION

5 STRUCTURE: State Systems and Educational Negotiations

The preceding chapters have sought to explain the emergence of State educational systems. In tracing their development, the interaction of dominant and assertive groups was held to be the 'guidance mechanism'[1] responsible for repatterning the relationship between education and society and transforming the internal structure of education itself. These changes were then examined in detail and the characteristics common to all new educational systems were distinguished from their variable features which originated from different types of educational conflict. It is now time then to turn to the *consequences* of the new State educational systems for subsequent interaction and further educational change.

If the argument advanced earlier is correct, that particular structural relations (i.e. ownership, mono-integration, subordination) influence the nature of social interaction and the processes leading to educational change — then an extremely important implication follows. Once the original relations of mono-integration are replaced by multiply integrated state systems, the latter begin to exert a new and different influence upon educational interaction. In other words, the educational context in which people now find themselves, the problems they experience, the things they can do about them, and the ways in which they may go about it, are all conditioned in a very different way from in the past. They react and interact differently and their collective action gives rise to educational change through processes other than the competitive conflict of earlier times. Ultimately what this means is that *once State systems have developed the domination and assertion approach ceases to be appropriate for the analysis of educational change, since the structural relations which made it so have now disappeared.*

In the antecedent period a whole series of effects stemmed from education only being linked to one part of the social structure and being subordinate because of its complete dependence on the flow of resources from the ownership group. This determined educational control, the prevailing definition of instruction, and the nature of educational services available to the rest of society. It conditioned a very distinctive form of competitive interaction which eventually destroyed the structural relations that had helped to engender it. Instead education began to serve a plurality of social institutions and its control largely ceased to rest on the ownership and provision of physical and human resources. Education remained highly dependent on the *receipt* of these resources, but the majority of them were now provided from public finance not private means. Correspondingly, educational control became more indirect and more concerned with the legitimate right to deploy public finance for particular educational ends. The resources themselves continue to give a very considerable leverage on education, but it is their command which is now at issue. And, as we have already seen, this means that no single group can impose its definition of instruction in pure form and thus direct educational services towards its operations alone.

The new more complex State systems, linked to and serving various different social institutions, continue to produce strains in the wider society, but condition very different types of interaction vis-à-vis education, and do so universally. One point of importance should however be noted in advance. It has been argued that the emergence of state systems and of multiple integration were the general consequence of the competition between dominant and assertive groups; this self-same interaction process has also been held responsible for variations in the elaborated characteristics which were generated simultaneously. In particular differences in these respects between systems with restrictive origins and those emerging from substitution were underlined at the end of the last chapter. Because of this it should not be expected that the subsequent structural conditioning of educational interaction will be identical in countries whose systems have dissimilar origins and which are now centralized or decentralized in structure. For the different kinds of structural elaboration which developed in the past in turn condition diverse forms of interaction in the present, and thus may influence divergent patterns of change in the future. An understanding of these differences as well as the similarities in conditional influences which stem from the new systems are vital in the explanation of educational conflict and change in the modern period. Firstly, however, we will examine the general consequences of State systems and multiple integration for education and for other social institutions, before proceeding to the variable effects exerted by particular structural characteristics. The significance of unification and systematization or differentiation and specialization as the dominant pair of characteristics will thus be explored later, when centralized and decentralized systems are examined in turn.

EFFECTS ON EDUCATION

The first and most obvious consequence of the new linkages established between education and society is the loss of its previous mono-integrated status. In turn, of course, many of its implications for education also disappear. However, the fact that education ceases to be mono-integrated does not automatically imply that it loses its earlier position of subordination. Indeed it is quite possible for the elites of two or more institutional spheres to subordinate another and to define its outputs in accordance with their own operations. For this to occur (i.e. for subordination to continue) education would have to remain dependent on the supply of resources from these parties. In other words dependency rather than reciprocity would still characterize the relations between education and society: the service provided by instruction would not outweigh its very high resource requirements. The price of their supply would be the continued loss of educational self-determination, for provision of resources would be made conditional on receiving the relevant kind of educational services. Thus the definition of instruction would continue to be imposed from outside rather than being internally determined by those actively engaged in teaching and learning. Under these circumstances education would still have very low autonomy vis-à-vis the other parts of society on which it depended.

However it was argued earlier that subordination never involves a greater loss of autonomy than when it occurs in a relationship of mono-integration. Indeed it appears that with the development of State systems several factors come into play which alter the picture sketched in above. The fact that these systems are multiply integrated has the gradual effect of lifting education from its earlier position of *total* subordination. It certainly does not transform this situation completely, for instuction remains more dependent on financial resources than are other parties upon educational services. Ultimately few schools or colleges could continue to function for more than a fortnight after resources were cut off, but businesses and bureaucracies are more resilient to the interruption of educational outputs. Nevertheless, with the end of mono-integration four interrelated factors begin to inject a greater reciprocity into the relations between education and the social institutions it serves. All of these stem from the fact that the resources used by education are no longer owned and monopolized by one party. Together they do not introduce a balanced exchange, but *although reciprocity remains imperfect, a significant amount of educational autonomy develops for the first time.*

(i) To begin with, the fact that it is public resources rather than private means which now finance education does something to correct what we called the 'fundamental asymmetry of dependence'. In the period before the emergence of State systems we saw that education was totally reliant on financing from the ownership group and that it had no chance of bidding up supplies against services for two reasons. On the one hand the dominant group could do without services longer than education could do without supplies; on the other hand, alternative resources would not be forthcoming from other parts of society. If one imagined such a conflict taking place, and historically this is very unlikely because of the dominant groups' tight control over educational personnel, several stark contrasts appear between this earlier period and the time at which State systems begin. Then education was small in scale and only a very limited part of the social structure sought to maintain educational outputs of a type it had itself defined. Thus had a conflict taken place it would have been a very sectional affair, restricted to the two parties involved with perhaps at most some intervention by adventitious beneficiaries, but one which did not involve the vast majority of the population in any way. Because of the asymmetry and lack of alternative suppliers, it would necessarily have been resolved in favour of the dominant group. Each element in this hypothetical scenario changes with the emergence of State systems. One consequence of the interaction which gave rise to such systems was, as we have seen, very considerable educational expansion – in both strategies this gradually meant that more and more children were being enrolled and thus that an increasing proportion of the population had a practical involvement in education if only as parents. This, *in conjunction* with public financing, reduces the 'asymmetry of dependence'. It remained (and still remains) in the sense that business and bureaucracy retain their resilience to short-term interruptions of educational services, but they have lost their capacity to put this to the test. For the parental outcry which would result from closure of schools and the student action from shutting of universities would be strong enough to restore the flow of *public* resources to these institutions. From being completely without influence over formal education in the antecedent period, the position of the mass of the population has improved because of the pressures they can exert over public spending. Generally, these pressures operate through an awareness of them on the part of those elite groups directly concerned with transmitting public funds to education who know that a show-down is to be avoided. Because of this new factor, any desire for additional or improved services on the part of interest groups will tend to be expressed, not by increased coercion as in the past, but by the offer of further resources. Business and bureaucracy have simply been taken as illustrations of the ways in which the parties integrated with education react, in order to show how the *fundamental* asymmetry is overcome and an improvement in reciprocity takes place. Initially at least this does not approximate to 'fair' exchange – educational services are at best imperfectly reciprocated because the control of resources remains in the hands of a limited number of groups who retain something of their earlier resilience.

(ii) However what we have been discussing is simply one aspect of a much broader process. So far the argument has focused on what happens to education once monopoly ownership is superseded, but multiple integration strongly reinforces this movement towards greater reciprocity. It does so because of the relationship between the various parties now linked to and served by education. Such groups are associated with different institutional spheres, their operations are distinct, and their optimal service requirements may show considerable divergence, as has already been seen. This means that the outputs these groups seek from education will not be identical, however strong the alliance between them, and whatever the mutual interdependence of their own operations. Indeed it matters little in this connection whether such groups are sub-sections of a governing elite or are competing elements in a pluralistic social and political structure. The fact that the services sought by these parties are different is of crucial importance once no single institutional sphere can hold education in 'fief' because of its monopoly.

The very plurality of the institutional orders with which education is integrated in itself fosters increased reciprocity because joint reliance on educational services represents a counterpressure against any particular party subordinating it to its own ends alone. On the contrary, as Gouldner has argued,[2] the existence of third parties, (that is mutually interdependent institutions), encourages reciprocity through fear of the harm which would result for their own activities were educational services to be defined and commandeered exclusively by one party. In other words, each of the groups involved has a vested interest in preventing instruction from again becoming supremely dependent upon one among them. Thus pressures operate against the re-emergence of the old mono-integrated and subordinate pattern for education. In the context of State systems, the policing function of third parties consists in preventing any one group from being able to make the flow of public funds to education conditional on instruction meeting its requirements alone. Since all integrated parties want different educational services and since all play the policing role towards each other, the overall effect is an increase in funds for education. This growth in reciprocity is the only possible compromise if no party is allowed to monopolize it and all groups press simultaneously for their requirements to be met in full.

Additional resources gained in this way constitute a move toward greater reciprocity and, if they result in a surplus over the costs involved in producing the agreed outputs, this can be devoted to the pursuit of internal goals. Furthermore, educational personnel can profit from this situation to increase their surplus by playing off the external demands against one another to their own advantage. For example, they may succeed in arguing that to meet two increased demands, let us say for more science teaching and more military training, they need two increments in staffing and physical facilities, when in fact some of the same staff and space are used for both. The spare resources acquired in this way can be used, within certain limits, to accomplish the goals of the educational personnel themselves, whatever these may be — developing new courses, lowering the pupil-teacher ratio, devoting more time to research and travel, improving library and leisure facilities, etc. *Thus the net consequence of multiple integration for education is an increase in autonomy, defined as the capacity for internal determination of its operations.* This may not be extensive in certain cases, but its existence to some degree in every State system is a complete contrast with the total lack of autonomy which characterized education in the state of mono-integration.

(iii) It should be clear, however, that neither of the changes just discussed would be of much significance if educational personnel remained as tightly controlled and unable to articulate their own demands as in the past. Were this the case, then no amount of increase in resources would enable them to be used for achieving internal goals. Because of sanctions used against them teachers and academics would simply not be in a position to profit as a group from the new flexibility in resources. In fact, on the contrary, the changes just discussed go hand in hand with a third — the transformation of the teaching role itself. Indeed these changes are important precisely because they do occur simultaneously. It is because educational personnel become more independent of external controls at the same time as the resource flow becomes more flexible that a new process of educational change is set in train.

As we have already seen, when education begins to serve a plurality of operations because of multiple integration, the definition of instruction becomes more complex and an internal differentiation of educational processes develops. As outputs lose the unitary nature which characterized them when they were designed to serve one part of society alone, then specialization is the method by which a diversity of teaching processes are accommodated with one another. Simultaneously a parallel differentiation among teaching personnel takes place which involves both growth in numbers and increase in occupational specialization. Educational personnel become clearly distinguished from the professional role structure of other social institutions — the mixed roles of priest-teacher or warrior-teacher disappear and together with them the stringent sanctions that the Church or the military had exercised over their teaching activities. As the role of the teacher develops this has the important effect of creating professional educational interest groups for the first time — that is people whose vested interests lie in the improvement of their educational positions because of their exclusive and full-time employment in them.

A major consequence results from these developments which is of considerable importance in relation to subsequent interaction and change. For the net effect of differentiation and specialization in the new systems is to facilitate the emergence of professionalization. The independence of educational personnel, coupled with the specialized activities in which they now have to engage, gradually enables them to sustain the claim for having special competence to pronounce on educational matters. These two factors mean that for the first time educationalists become the curricular experts. Although the definition of instruction is still largely formulated elsewhere, there is no longer a body (such as theologians) with an expertise in the management and transmission of knowledge superior to that of academics. Its most important initial effect is the transformation of a loose collection of teaching personnel into a self-conscious teaching profession. In other words, as in the early stages of any kind of collective organization, its first effects are registered inside the group itself, which becomes organized and consolidates common goals. Thus educational interest groups articulating internal demands for change develop throughout the new educational systems and seek to acquire the same rights as other professional associations. Although this may take time, their increase in autonomy together with the greater flexibility in resources available can immediately be used for internal goal attainment. Thus almost from the start interest groups can begin to cumulate surplus resources and to use these to introduce some of the changes they see fit.

(iv) So far we have discussed the ways in which educational interest groups can take advantage of changes which are occurring simultaneously in the new educational systems. Finally, however, reference must be made to certain actions which can be taken by the educational personnel once they have become organized, and whose effect is to augment the attainment of internal goals. It is only when such a body exists that any kind of direct transactions can be conducted between external interest groups and education itself. During the earlier period any such transaction, whether involving negotiation or competition, was necessarily indirect. It was carried out perforce with the dominant group, by-passing education which did not enjoy the requisite autonomy for direct negotiation. Now professional educational interest groups may themselves initiate transactions with the exterior or be approached by outside parties. Such relations can take a strong or a weak form, although the latter is undoubtedly the more universal.

The weak form consists in the use of influence and usually operates at the level of ideas. Thus for example, the profession may succeed in getting one external group to represent to others that it cannot perform a particular task without additional facilities. Alternatively it may convince others that present procedures are inefficient, that the staff-pupil ratio is undesirable, that injunctions to teach particular things to given people in set ways are impossible. Ultimately, with full professionalization, forms of collective action can be developed which give force to these views. Influence also works the other way round, with external groups trying to convince the profession directly that certain courses of action are in both their interests. (For example, they might argue that there is demand for a new applied course and that to start it would generate new posts for teachers, protect against redundancy in undersubscribed areas, yield new facilities in the long run, etc.) Here the external agency is itself seeking to benefit from the autonomy of education by getting the profession to invest its surplus resources and use its new freedom of initiative in ways which are advantageous to it. In the former case the profession tries to gain outside support for policies which are in its interests. Although neither tactic is likely to be successful unless some mutual advantage is perceived, this does not prevent such direct transactions from being an important and novel source of change.

Secondly, there is a stronger form of direct negotiation which actually involves the exchange of resources for services. In certain systems the degree of autonomy acquired by the profession may enable them to deal with outside parties, to accept resources in terms of research grants, buildings, equipment, or additional staffing in return for increased intake, for receiving pupils/students from particular parts of society on particular terms, for laying on new courses, for making special forms of training available, and for undertaking applied research projects. Again this type of transaction may be initiated by either party and will not be concluded unless it is felt to be mutually advantageous. In both cases however the effect is similar, for relations with the exterior are manipulated by the professional interest group in an attempt to further its own goals. This is simply more blatant in these stronger cases because money actually changes hands, rather than support which is a less tangible commodity. However, to negotiate either places the profession in a better position to accomplish more of its goals.

These four factors which come into play with the end of mono-integration represent different aspects of the changes taking place in education itself. Thus increased autonomy is the main repercussion of multiple integration upon the internal organization of education. In turn this new autonomy means that professional interest groups can pursue and attain some of their own goals: for the first time educational operations are not determined exclusively by groups from other social institutions. Thus an extremely important implication of the emergent state systems is that *much more endogenous change must be anticipated now that education is multiply integrated.* The teaching profession will collectively formulate its goals, will play a more significant part in interaction and the negotiation of educational change. Because of this their activities cannot be ignored as in the antecedent period. *In other words, the form of explanation offered for change in state educational systems must be altered now that their personnel have ceased to be passively controlled and started to be professionally active.* Explanation must now include reference to changes which are initiated autonomously within the educational system, whether this is due to the internal cumulation of resources or to transactions with external groups.

EFFECTS ON OTHER
SOCIAL INSTITUTIONS

The educational changes which have taken place affect other institutions in two main areas – in terms of the services their members receive and in terms of the control that their members can exert. Change in the former is largely due to the development of multiple integration, change in the latter must also be attributed to the linkage of national education to the political centre. In discussing their effects in this section, attention will again focus on *general* implications for *all* state systems. A little later on the relative importance of the universal and the variable changes, vis-à-vis one another, will be considered in relation to the distribution of services received and to the accessibility of educational control. The new relationship between education and society, consequent upon the emergence of State systems, has the same general effect on the pervasiveness of control and the availability of services. For either the major effect is a shift away from the near zero-sum situation which prevailed in the past. In the antecedent period, if a group was the dominant group then it enjoyed the most extensive powers over education, if it were not, then it was powerless to institute anything but the most minor changes in instruction. With integration to the political centre, the dissociation of control from ownership spells the end of this situation. As a basis of educational control, monopoly ownership necessarily implied the zero-sum formula. When private ownership largely gave way to public funding, educational control increasingly resided in the capacity to influence public spending. Here the possession of considerable influential power by one party does not mean that another is proportionately deprived of influence. In other words, the fact that the military elite exerts an importance influence on educational spending does not imply a corresponding lack of control on behalf of the economic elite. This example should also serve to indicate that the spreading of educational control is not necessarily synonymous with a more democratic distribution of it. What is being accentuated then is simply a constrast between the two periods — control being restricted to a single ownership group before the development of State systems, but becoming more pervasive after their emergence. The significance of this change will be discussed slightly later.

Multiple integration obviously has a very similar effect on the services received from instruction. In the past the distribution of services approximated rather less closely to the zero-sum position than was the case for educational control. Although outputs were designed to serve the requirements of one group alone, certain other parts of society could sometimes make use of them and thus became adventitious beneficiaries. However, with the advent of the new system the fact that various institutional spheres are served by education ceases to be a matter of happy accidents, enjoyed without any security about their continuation. Instead the more specialized outputs are intended to service different operational requirements simultaneously. This is not to argue that unintended spin-offs cease altogether — a course which is designed to serve X may turn out to be equally acceptable to Y, without the latter having pressed to obtain it. It is merely to say that with the advent of multiple integration, services are spread so that the fact that one party receives them does not mean that any other doing so must automatically be an accidental recipient. Hence change in the distribution of services is of the same kind and in the same direction as change in the distribution of control. The effects of both will now be considered in greater detail, beginning with educational services.

The more widespread distribution of educational services has the immediate effect of abolishing the tripartite division between other social institutions vis-à-vis education. In the past the relations of the three different categories were *different in kind.* They could easily be classified as adventitious beneficiaries, as neutral, or as obstructed institutions according to the goodness of fit between their operational requirements and the education available. With multiple integration these stark contrasts fade. The sharp differences in kind are partly transmuted into *differences of degree.* For some parts of society at least, the receipt of educational services ceases to be an all or nothing affair, but becomes a less clear-cut matter in which some of their requirements are met by existing outputs whilst other needs are neglected. The blurring of the tripartite division has the important consequence that it can no longer be used as a simple guide to identifying loci of support for and opposition to the educational status quo. This perhaps is best clarified if the changes introduced by multiple integration are considered in relation to the three old categories.

Instead of adventitious beneficiaries being the only parties (apart from the dominant group) to receive educational services as in the past, these are now much more numerous. Certainly not all parts of society are in receipt of such services, but only those sectors which moved into an integrative relationship with education during the interaction sequence which established the new system. Certainly too it was seen that even those groups which did so were often compelled to accept a level or type of output which was far from optimal for their activities. For example, the resolution of competing claims and pressures meant that some groups which secured services had to take them from inferior parts of the system; others had to see the precise outputs they required modified, diluted, and reduced in scope or scale. Few of the new parties establishing structural relations with education, even the powerful political elites spearheading restrictive strategies, gained precisely what they wanted, and none gained what they did without concessions to other groups. But they did gain something and it came with a bonus never enjoyed by adventitious beneficiaries — security, or at least a certain measure of it.

The adventitious beneficiary had received something for nothing because of the harmony between its requirements and the definition of instruction imposed by the dominant group, a tenuous situation since either element could change and destroy this compatibility. The new services received are not accidental but neither are they free, they cost something in terms of resources or support, but in return they cannot be interrupted by unexpected shifts in the definition of instruction which are totally outside the control of their recipients. In conclusion then, more parts of society gain some of the services they require on the advent of State educational systems. Furthermore they simultaneously acquire a vested interest in the continuation of these services, even if they want to see their scale extended or their relevance increased. *For the first time a plurality of institutional spheres have a lasting stake in the existing form of education.*

The main change which takes place as far as the old category of neutral institutions is concerned is its drastic curtailment. Compared with the antecedent period there are fewer and fewer parts of society whose operations are neither helped nor hindered by the prevailing definition of instruction. This is partly due to the transformation of education itself, but partly too to general social changes proceeding apace.

On the one hand, the expansion of instruction, which has been seen to accompany the development of State systems, affects *all* institutions in important ways.[3] In the old days, when education was a minority affair, neutrality consisted in a group getting on independently with its own activities, inducting the young, and informally preparing them to assume particular roles. Such neutral parties were not exclusively engaged in traditional operations like agriculture, the category also embraced modern commercial, mercantile, and craft groups at certain times and places, for it was delineated in terms of independence of and indifference to the prevailing type of education. However, as school enrolment increased spectacularly, fewer parties could remain in this position. Instead of being able to go their own way, inducting and initiating the next generation, they were increasingly forced to recruit school leavers and eventually could recruit nothing but them. In this situation complete indifference to the skills and values they had acquired was difficult to sustain. The new 'educated' recruits were either better or worse for the job than their predecessors — the only thing they were not was just the same as before, and one difference they shared in common was that of being significantly older. Furthermore at approximately the same time that such parties were being jogged out of their neutrality by educational expansion, the State systems were taking root. As the new systems were funded indirectly by these groups, like all others, it is unsurprising that the majority began to want value for money — a form of education better adapted to their operations.

On the other hand they were not simply pushed to seek inter-dependence because independence was no longer possible. There was also the pull exerted by the changed nature of their own operations themselves. Perhaps some of these changes too were the indirect effects of educational transformation, but on the whole it was broader social processes which progressively increased the salience of instruction — bureaucratization, the application of science to production, the com-mercialization of agriculture, the opening of world-markets, and colonialism. Few institutional spheres remained immune from all of these influences, whose general implication was the need for a higher level of skill to cope with the increased complexity of operations. Obviously formal instruction had no monopoly in the transmission of skills, for successful forms of in-service training had developed in many areas. Nevertheless, with the establishment of State systems it is again not surprising that many parties should cease to want to pay for them twice over. In sum the old category disperses; not all parties seek or attain integration, some merely become impeded by State education, but in either case the possibility of neutrality has been severely under-mined.

In the previous era considerable importance was attached to the class of institutions whose respective operations were obstructed by the nature of education. The emergence of multiply integrated State systems has implications for this category which closely parallel those affecting adventitious beneficiaries. The main consequence of the greater spread and diversification of educational services is that in general fewer groups are totally obstructed *relative to* the previous period. This, however, is a *strictly comparative* statement and 'totally' is the most important word in it. The basis of this change is of course the new differentiation and specialization of education. The former, as we have seen, prevents an exclusive identification between education and any one institutional sphere, thus giving instruction a certain degree of autonomy: the latter means that the inputs, processes and outputs become less uniform and more diverse. Thus this new diversity softens the impediments experienced by some parties — if one kind of educa-tional activity is still uphelpful or irrelevant, another may be more useful. None of this is to argue that the obstacles experienced by *some* groups will be felt less keenly or will be less serious for their respective activities.

However, perhaps the most crucial change stemming from the new systems lies in *whom* they hinder rather than *how much* hindrance they create. For this latter question is impossible to answer in quantitative terms, and our reply of 'less rather than more' overall obstruction is a blanket statement of little practical utility. It does, however, have considerable relevance when considered in relation to the former question about who is hindered. This can be clarified by referring back to which parties successfully imposed (some of) their service requirements on the new educational systems at their foundation.

As far as systems with restrictive origins are concerned, the basic definition of instruction was designed by the governing elite, was modified, often substantially, by pressures from different sections within it, and was finally qualified by the need for political and financial support from various parts of the population. The definition of instruction determines what educational services are available in society; what is obvious in such countries is that the more closely groups were clustered around the governing elite the more say they had in the defining. With some oversimplification, the receipt of educational services can be pictured as a series of gradients: firstly, the governmental bureaucracy at the centre receiving most of its service requirements; secondly, sub-sections of the political elite in receipt of many of the outputs needed for the institutional operations with which they are identified; thirdly, a partial satisfaction of educational demands among explicit supporters of government; finally, a severe tailing off of educational services to other sections of the population. This is oversimplified because, as has been seen, certain sections of the elite may get far less than they require, institutions not closely integrated with the polity probably receive nothing at all, and the partial satisfaction of governmental supporters may fluctuate considerably with the strength and wealth of the regime. Nevertheless this picture serves to highlight an important contrast with the antecedent period, namely that *total obstruction will now be experienced by non-elite groups in the main.* Instead of education representing a similar hindrance to leaders of major institutions (the military, economy, judiciary, etc.) and to popular groups alike, severe obstruction now becomes concentrated among the people.

Exactly the same occurs in systems with substitutive origins. Here the definition of instruction derives from the independent networks run by those who had been able to mobilize resources to found and operate them. During the consolidation of the system certain networks attain a prominent place, thus guaranteeing continuity of services to their sponsors whilst others are relegated, their outputs modified and their utility to those who had started them is correspondingly reduced. Again one can picture gradients in educational services received, with these tailing away for groups which had not been able to protect their definition of instruction from erosion during incorporation, and petering out altogether for parts of society which had never developed a competitive network. Thus in these systems too the experience of total obstruction will be concentrated among non-elite groups (who lacked the resources to develop strong networks and the power to defend them) to a much greater extent than in the earlier period.

Hence in the new educational systems, maximal educational obstruction will, for the first time, show a strong tendency to be concentrated among the less privileged sections of the population. It is not that their position vis-à-vis education has necessarily worsened, although in fact some of these groups did enjoy the independence and indifference of neutrals in the antecedent period. What has changed is that the experience of grave impediments to their operations is no longer shared with a number of important institutional elites. And this will be seen to have important implications for subsequent interaction. It is not however being suggested that all underprivileged groups in all societies find themselves in precisely the same relationship to national education. On the contrary, the ways in which certain popular groups acquired partial satisfaction of their demands either through threatening to withhold their support or by gaining a toehold for their small network in the new system, have already been analyzed in the last chapter. What is being stressed is simply a contrast between the two periods.

Obviously this tendential change takes place because multiple integration means that many more institutional operations are being serviced by education to some degree. There are exceptions to this. Firstly, and very importantly, in systems with restrictive origins, the radical redefinition of instruction, if coupled with their complete loss of control, will seriously hinder the old dominant group. Secondly, it is possible that certain peripheric elites, whose operations remain independent of government, also find themselves in this position. It is for this reason that extreme impediments are not *exclusively* concentrated on the activities of the underprivileged, although this is the group which is *universally* penalized.

However, for those parties which are now integrated with education, any frustrations they experience will be a matter of degree. This is not to say that educational services will not be grossly inadequate for some and a source of great concern to other groups involved. But it will now be a question of wanting more and better services and rarely one of overcoming an unmitigated hindrance – however high feelings may run about educational inadequacies. Since such frustrations are a matter of degree, then certain groups will experience them more than others: the category of those now suffering from a lack of fit between the prevailing definition of instruction and their operational requirements becomes increasingly heterogeneous with the advent of the educational system – it includes the completely, the severely, and the partially obstructed. Apart from the previous discussion of the underprivileged, it is impossible to determine analytically which social institutions will suffer these partial impediments. For this of course depends on which parties become integrated with education, and upon the nature of this relationship in any country.

However, a final negative point of considerable importance can be made in this connection. Since it is universally the case that the new forms of national instruction are *State* educational systems, then it follows that the governing elite will rarely be found in this category. It will not gain precisely the services required because, *inter alia* of inefficient planning, unintended consequences, a backwash from the private sector, the interference of other objectives pursued in the system, and independent activities initiated by teaching staff. Nor will it alone define the nature of instruction, for other groups play an important and often crucial role here. But the fact that it is always *im*perfectly served does not mean that it is ever severely obstructed. Its legitimate control of resources is proof against this. Thus the final contrast with the antecedent period is that *nowhere will the State appear as an obstructed party in any serious sense of the term.* The far reaching implications of this for interaction and change will be introduced later on.

Thus the inception of State systems alters the relationship between education and different parts of society. The loci of support for and opposition to the new definitions of instruction are still conditioned by benefits received from it and frustrations induced by it. However, it has been seen how the distribution of these rewarding and frustrating situations among different social institutions changes because of multiple integration. It alters both quantitatively (in terms of the number of institutional spheres assured of services) and qualitatively (in terms of the degree of service or obstruction experienced). It remains to link these alterations in the social distribution of educational services and the parallel transformation of educational control to the question of interaction and change.

EFFECTS ON THE PROCESSES OF
EDUCATIONAL CHANGE

Turning now to consider how change is brought about within the State educational system, this too is found to differ considerably from the earlier period. There is a fundamental move away from competitive conflict as the only process by which large-scale educational change can be introduced. In the past the importance of competitive conflict was due to the nature of the structural relations between education and society — to the fact that only by displacing the dominant ownership group could macroscopic change take place. The transformation of these structural relations, the emergence of multiple integration and of linkage to the political centre, which are intrinsic to the new educational systems, mean that other processes of change become more important.

As has just been seen, more institutional orders now receive educational services, although this is not synonymous with all external demands for education being met. Not all spheres become closely integrated with education and its definition may present severe problems for their operations. Secondly, for other parties, the services received may fall very short of operative requirements. Although such groups will interact to stabilize the multi-functionality of instruction, any one of them may seek considerable improvement in the fit between educational outputs and its own activities. In other words, they will attempt to modify the prevailing definition of instruction substantially. However, in both cases the new structural relations exert a similar and powerful influence on the processes of interaction through which these operational impediments can be overcome by giving rise to the kind of educational change desired.

Where existing educational outputs constitute a severe obstacle to a particular group or fall short of its perceived needs, then direct competition is no longer the readiest means of overcoming it in the new State system. Indeed it is extremely unlikely that any group could gain educational control by either of the old competitive strategies. On the one hand, the resources upon which educational control now rests are no longer concentrated in the pockets of a single group and their supply has ceased to be based on the private ownership of indispensable facilities. This implies that strategies based on substitution are extremely unlikely to succeed because of the volume of resources now absorbed by education. (This is a corollary of multiple integration: more resources are needed if different kinds of services are to be provided simultaneously, more and more are forthcoming for this to be done because of the conjunction of pressures exerted by powerful interested parties). Thus it is practically unimaginable that any institutional sphere could command the volume and type of resources necessary to mount a successful substitutive campaign. Indeed as time goes on and the resource flow to education increases in all countries, for the reasons just mentioned, the chance of private supplies being able to compete with public ones soon becomes inconceivable. Since substitution is effectively precluded on financial grounds there is no need to dwell on the legal and coercive measures which could be used to prevent it, in defense of the State system.

On the other hand, the educational status quo will receive considerable support from those parts of society whose operations are adequately if not ideally served by it. Indeed one of the main results of multiple integration is the development of a *plurality* of groups with vested interests in the prevailing form of education, and this support will be of greater durability and strength than that provided by adventitious beneficiaries in the antecedent period. Thus a restrictive strategy launched by a dissatisfied group would be most unlikely to succeed. To do so it would have to overcome the governing elite (for it is now inconceivable that the latter could be convinced that State education was not in its own best interests) as well as undermining the other parties exerting varying degrees of educational control. Because it would have to contend with a defence of the educational status quo which is now centrally directed and socially extensive, restrictive competition ceases to be a possibility for those who receive no services at all or ones which are grossly inadequate. Thus restriction becomes impossible unless it is coupled with a complete social transformation in which the State itself is overthrown and educational grievances merge with other, more important causes of revolution. With this exception, those who gain very little from the system will not be able to change it fundamentally, by either of the old strategies, because of the defensive action of those who profit from its maintenance.

Furthermore dissatisfied groups are themselves less likely to consider engaging in direct competitition, despite severe imperfections of fit between educational outputs and their own operations. Several factors account for this and explain the strong tendency for processes of educational change to be diverted into other channels. Firstly, the position of many institutions has changed such that they do receive *some* services (hence the definition of instruction is not a *complete* impediment to their operations) and their members do possess *some* element of educational influence. However inadequate educational services are, this new interdependence means that for the first time the obstructed party has something to lose by an all-out attack on them. In the past such a challenge could only be advantageous. Even if it stopped education from functioning altogether (as for instance when restriction was not immediately followed by replacement) this was no more prejudicial to the assertive party than its continuation in obstructive form. With State systems the situation changes, for a group could lose the services it does get if by any chance it sparked off competitive conflict which seriously damaged the day to day functioning of education.

However it is the two aspects of interdependence which in conjunction make this course of action unlikely. It is not only that many parties get something out of education, for after all it could still be argued that they have more to gain from change than to lose from the status quo. It is also that their newly acquired influence over educational decision-making now provides an alternative means for modifying the definition of instruction. This influence can be used to negotiate the changes required. The possession of resources, which in the past could only produce change through competitive substitution, can now be employed to transact modifications. Similarly political influence can now be used to negotiate changes in the State system, via the central government to which it is attached.

The point is not that competitive conflict gives way to negotiation because satisfaction can always be gained through the latter. *It is simply that the possibility of obtaining substantial changes through negotiation opens up at exactly the same time that the chances of successful competition are drastically reduced.* In the past competition introduced sweeping educational changes in many countries whereas negotiation only produced the minor modifications, acceptable to dominant ownership groups. With the advent of State systems this is no longer the case: *the conditions for successful competition become vastly more stringent whilst the scope of changes which can be negotiated increases enormously.* These two factors will be considered in turn to account for negotiation now prevailing as the most important process of educational change.

After the emergence of State systems it is doubtful if interaction can take a competitive form except under rather special circumstances. For this to occur it would first be necessary for the nature of instruction to generate strains in more than one of the institutional orders it was supposed to serve: otherwise groups with vested interests in the status quo would easily restrain competitiveness by means of law. In the second place it is not enough for several parties to be severely obstructed; in addition the educational requirements of these groups must also be sufficiently complementary for them to combine in opposition. This too is now more difficult because the greater diversity of services offered by State education itself means that the demands of obstructed groups will be for further kinds of diversification which may well lack a common denominator. Thirdly, other kinds of allegiances and interdependencies must not cut across to preclude consolidation of the competitive alliance. Yet because of general changes, the societies which have generated educational systems tend to be more complex than the earlier less integrated social structures. This increased structural complexity engenders a broad network of strains and dependencies between various parts of society whose patterning affects educational interaction. Thus unless tensions arising from the malintegration between education and other social institutions condition the emergence of interest groups whose alliance is reinforced by wider structural and social relations, competitive strategies for educational change are most unlikely to be successful.

In consequence, large-scale educational change will not be brought about by competitive conflict unless social disintegration is extremely far reaching. In other words, it is only likely to occur as part of a general social upheaval in which the ruling class is overthrown and the State apparatus changes hands. Without these conditions the support for the educational status quo would be too strong, and the competitive alliance too weak and divided. This is what was meant by saying that the conditions for competitive conflict become more stringent, for it will be recalled that in three of the four cases examined (Russia,

England and Denmark) education was transformed without the overthrow of the State in the antecedent period. Thus substitution ceases to be a feasible strategy once educational resources are publicly funded. Similarly restriction, as a strategy conducted by the political elite, becomes impossible by definition once its members are themselves a major controlling group in education. Hence there is now only one way in which competitive conflict can succeed and, although it will happen, the necessary conditions are severe enough to make it a very rare occurrence. The Russian Revolution is our sole example of it.

Thus it is that more attention must be paid to negotiation and non-competitive transactions in accounting for change in State educational systems. It will be remembered that the main reason why such processes were held irrelevant to large-scale change whilst education remained in private ownership was that their effects would systematically be limited to those acceptable to the group subordinating education. In other words, negotiation presupposed acquiescence to the prevailing form of structural relations: it involved acknowledgement of the dominant group. However, with multiple integration the spread of educational control means that no single party can impose its limits on what may be negotiated. Just as the definition of instruction is no longer designed to serve one party alone so too no group by itself can veto the introduction of far reaching changes if these are sought by other groups. The only limit to what is negotiable are those imposed via the interaction of the influential parties themselves — the way in which they block one another, the compromises they mutually enforce, and their collective concern that changes should be compatible with present services which are still required.

Hence these mutual checks and balances are the only possible barrier to large-scale change, and they do not always operate to prevent it. Firstly, there are no logical grounds for assuming that radical change will never be jointly sought by all influential parties or by a group of them who together are powerful enough to transact it. General social change can alter the operational requirements of several institutional sectors simultaneously and lead their members to press for similar (or compatible) forms of educational change. Perhaps the commonest circumstance in which this has occurred in most educational systems is the aftermath of war. Secondly, there is no reason to suppose that smaller changes negotiated from month to month will not accumulate until they represent a considerable departure from their starting point. The checks, balances, and compromises are no homeostatic mechanism guaranteeing the maintenance of the educational status quo. On the contrary the pursuit of their own interests by all parties gives rise to transactions which alter the educational context in which they act. As each transaction is accomplished, groups realign according to how it has affected them, and further interaction produces new departures. Change which is gradually accumulated in this way may be no less far reaching in its consequences than the radical legislation which was mentioned first.

Thus there are no grounds for expecting that less change will occur after the emergence of State systems or that it will be of a less radical nature than in earlier times. All that alters is the process predominantly responsible for bringing it about. Instead of negotiation being of limited importance it becomes the process which accounts for most of the change most of the time in most countries. On the whole it is less dramatic: sweeping changes are introduced less precipitously, important modifications may be transacted without polemic, and innovations can be initiated unobtrusively. As a process it is also vastly more complex: with competitive conflict one set of relations were crucial for change (those between the dominant ownership group and others), whereas in negotiation several sets of relationships between education and society account for the changes taking place. These must be examined because together they specify the range of interaction which has now to be taken into account in order to explain educational change. In other words, as the process leading to change becomes more complex, so too must the nature of analysis.

The general process of negotiation can be broken down into three different kinds, all of which come into play with the development of State educational systems. They are different in the sense that each pinpoints a particular source of change which must be analyzed for all systems. As will be seen the three kinds of negotiation are not equally accessible to all social groups, so that to examine them is to investigate three different sets of relations between education and society. The changes which are observed to take place will stem from the three in conjunction.

The first type of negotiation, INTERNAL INITIATION, has already been touched upon in the previous section. It was seen that their increased autonomy enables professional educators to play a part in determining the rate of exchange between resources received and services supplied. Surplus resources could then be devoted to accomplishing professional goals within the educational system. In other words, this source of change is the school, the college, and the university. It can be brought about on a small scale by independent initiative in a particular establishment, and on a much larger scale by collective professional action. The relations which are significant here are those taking place between professional educators on the one hand and the suppliers of resources on the other. Obviously since the majority of resources are public ones supplied by the State, interaction between the profession and the governing elite will be most important. However, the State is often not the sole supplier, the ownership of buildings, the administration of endowments, and the management of financial assets can remain in other hands. In such cases interaction between the profession and these other groups must also be taken into consideration. Certain educational changes will flow directly from these relations in all State systems.

The second form of negotiation, EXTERNAL TRANSACTION, involves relations between internal and external interest groups. It is usually instigated from outside educational boundaries by groups seeking new or additional services. As before, the profession is one of the groups involved in these negotiations, but the other party opts into the transaction of its own accord. It is this which distinguishes EXTERNAL TRANSACTIONS from INTERNAL INITIATION: in the latter the parties engaging in negotiation are given, and their interaction is inescapable; in the former the external parties vary and their inter-action with professional groups is voluntaristic. In the antecedent period groups seeking educational change could only pursue this indirectly by dealing with the dominant group, they could not nego-tiate directly with education itself. The increase in autonomy, accompanying the emergence of educational systems, now means that educational personnel can begin to deal with the outside world. It is not suggested that these direct transactions will predominate over indirect ones (conducted via the political centre), indeed in certain countries they will be of very limited scope. In others, however, they make an extremely important contribution to educational change.

It has been seen that certain parties do not receive all the educa-tional services they require. Some among them will be keen to rectify this situation and may attempt to do so by entering into negotiations with the profession, offering more resources in exchange for better services. Basically then the external agency will try to buy the educa-tional changes it wants, although the currency need not necessarily be monetary. External transactions can take place at all levels. For example, a particular local firm may offer equipment and facilities for a college to lay on a specialized form of training, the armed services may provide scholarships and a subvention in return for the enrolment of their cadets, the police, farmers and various professional groups may sponsor or support specialized establishments and industry may negotiate applied research in return for grants, professorships, laboratories etc. This list is illustrative of the variety of transactions which have taken place in various countries. That fact that it is greatly more varied than the examples given should not, however, be taken to mean that any outside party can negotiate anything it wants provided it has the necessary resources. There are two major obstacles to unlimited negotiation.

On the one hand the profession itself has the power of veto. It need not accept all propositions put to it. Like other groups it is motivated by vested interests and will refuse transactions which compromise these. If, for instance, the services sought by outside agencies involve work held to be professionally degrading (such as being asked to train rather than to educate, to purvey some brand of irrationalism like quack-medicine or pseudo-science, or to disseminate unacceptable values such as racism) the terms will be rejected. If they imply a less attractive work-situation, worse conditions, longer hours, more pupils, lower standards, they will probably suffer the same fate. Similarly, terms which are advantageous in their own right will not be accepted if they are likely to damage other desirable negotiations, or to disrupt the smooth functioning of instruction. For example, a university may turn down a military research contract, however attractive its terms, in order to avoid student outcry. Thus in seeking to advance and project itself professionally, the educators filter external demands and conclude transactions only where these are held to be reputable, profitable, and compatible.

On the other hand, as the major supplier of resources, the governing elite also enjoys the power of veto in certain circumstances. It will try to prevent transactions taking place which are contrary to its current policies, at least as far as public education is concerned. However, not all external transactions will meet with political censure and some indeed will be welcomed — if services are provided in exchange for private resources they take the strain off the system both financially and in the sense of removing pressure from government. Furthermore the composition of governments varies and what might once have been vetoed, may become acceptable, pass into established practice, and survive future political change. Finally, the private sector of education, in certain countries, can enable external transactions to take place even if they have been politically vetoed for public instruction. Changes introduced in this manner may well have important repercussions for the State system itself.

It is probably clear from the foregoing that EXTERNAL TRANS-ACTION is a form of negotiation which is open only to those groups which have substantial resources at their disposal. Thus both processes of change discussed so far involve relations between education and rather restricted parts of the social structure. The same is not true of the third kind of negotiation, POLITICAL MANIPULATION. On the contrary, this is the principal resort of those who have no other means of gaining satisfaction for their educational demands — despite the fact that they may also be the least successful at manipulating the political machine. This form of negotiation arises because education now receives most of its funds from public sources. In turn a whole series of groups (depending on the nature of the regime) acquire formal influence over the shaping of public educational policy. It is this of course which encourages popular groups of various kinds to use the political channel in the absence of alternatives. In the endless quest for support and party votes, it is this too which focuses much of the public dialogue about instruction on popular or democratic themes. While this is of considerable importance it would be deceptive to assume that the intensity of educational debate is met by a commensurate degree of political action on these lines.

However this does highlight an important change which accompanies the development of State systems, namely that educational influence is not tightly restricted to those parties which are already closely integrated with it. Instead *all groups* can attempt to work through the polity, wielding whatever political influence they possess, to modify national educational policy in their favour. This in turn points to some more general implications of the emergence of national educational systems which represent a distinct break with the past. In the antecedent period the distribution of educational control remained relatively static while ever the monopoly of vital resources was maintained by the dominant group. Now that ownership and control have largely been dissociated, educational influence becomes much less stable over time since it varies with the balance of political power. Thus the question of which groups receive educational services, and to what degree these coincide with operational requirements, may receive different answers as time passes and the composition of the governing elite alters. In other words to understand educational changes stemming from governmental directives we need to analyze the political inter-action through which various groups negotiated their introduction. Obviously the groups which enjoy the greatest continuity of political power will receive a complementary and uninterrupted flow of educa-tional services, and vice versa. Nevertheless since this is not a zero-sum situation, there will be a whole series of political pressures, alliances, and concessions whose result is the continuous modification of the definition of instruction.

Thus the fact that the State everywhere plays a major role in the regulation of resources flowing to public education means that attempts to manipulate the political centre will often replace past policies of manipulating resources in order to implement change. The extent to which the State performs this regulatory role determines the import-ance of the political structure and interaction in producing educational change. In contrast to the earlier period, the State will always be a party to the process of structural elaboration in education, although political manipulation will not be the only process involved.

In sum the three new forms of negotiation add up to a much more complicated process of change than the old style of competition. To analyze it involves examining group interaction at the levels of the school, the community, and the nation, and the interrelations between them. For these different types of negotiation do not take place in isolation from one another. POLITICAL MANIPULATION influences negotiations between government and the profession, thus affecting the amount and type of INTERNAL INITIATION which can occur. It also helps to determine the nature of EXTERNAL TRANSACTIONS, partly because of the power of veto and partly too because it helps to define which groups engage in such negotiations, i.e. those whose demands are not well served by public policy. In turn EXTERNAL TRANS-ACTIONS, conducted with the profession, increase the surplus re-sources of the latter and thus influence the scope and sometimes the character of changes brought about by INTERNAL INITIATION. Together the changes introduced in these two ways modify the defini-tion of instruction independently of the political centre. This alters the services available in ways which will be favourable to some groups and detrimental to others, thus affecting their policy orientations and the goals they subsequently pursue through POLITICAL MANIPULA-TION. Thus each form of negotiation and the changes to which it gives rise has repercussions on the others. This then is the complex network of interaction and change which must be unravelled in order to explain the transformation of educational systems. If our explanations are to do justice to this complexity, then the relative simplicity of the domination and assertation approach must be left behind, where it belongs, with the period antecedent to the emergence of educational systems.

STRUCTURAL RELATIONS CONDITIONING EDUCATIONAL INTERACTION

The preceding analysis of universal modifications in processes of educational interaction and change, which take place as State systems develop, lends itself to few predictions and allows for an enormous range of variation between different national systems of education. All that has been accentuated is the way in which replacement of one set of structural relations (ownership and mono-integration) by another (multiple integration and attachment to the political centre) involves the analysis of a different process of interaction for the explanation of macroscopic changes. Thus in discussing the implications of the emergence of State systems I have only highlighted certain universals in educational development up to this point. Yet, as Eisenstadt has argued, different societies may arrive at broadly similar stages in terms of differentiation and integration of institutional spheres, but 'the concrete institutional contours developed at each such step, as well as the possible outcomes of such institutionalization in terms of further development, breakdown, regression or stagnation, may differ greatly among them'.[4] In other words, the specific structural changes shaped by the past interaction of competing groups, and not just the general modifications in structural relations, are essential to an understanding of subsequent developments.

Chapter 4 outlined differences in the structure of the new educational systems which co-existed with the universal changes in structural relations. In particular, restrictive competition was seen to have shaped a centralized educational system whereas substitutive competition fostered the emergence of a decentralized one. The two types of systems were shown to have considerable differences in terms of their administration (unification), internal organization (systematization), diversity of activities (specialization) and separation from other parts of society (differentiation). These differences between the systems are just as important as their similarities where subsequent interaction is concerned.

It must not be forgotten that structural factors only influence interaction because they shape the action-contexts in which people find themselves. These contexts are very specific — they only occur in a particular part of society at a given time in a particular country. In other words, what affects people is their own educational system and their place in it. Their actions are not conditioned by universal changes in structural relations as such; these are only influential because their own national system shares them and moulds action-contexts in a new way because of this. But their national system may be a centralized or a decentralized one and this will also affect the real-life situations in which people find themselves. Thus the *actual* situations to which people react, and which predispose them to act in particular ways, are moulded by their national system: this system will reflect universal changes but it will present them to people as part and parcel of its own particular structure. Thus if we are to explain interaction we must leave the general discussion of universal changes behind and get down to the question of how these are mediated and modified by differences in the structure of particular educational systems.

In considering structural influences on interaction, it is the same two factors — the distribution of educational services and control — which will be examined in greater detail. The former of course helps to determine which groups will be actively pursuing change whilst the latter helps to account for the ways in which they go about it. Here it will be shown that centralized and decentralized systems exert dissimilar influences upon interaction because of differences in their distributions of services and control. It must be stressed, however, that the structures to be examined below are those which characterized educational systems at the time of their emergence. The conditional influences on action are those exerted by the systems just after they had developed. In other words, the period involved is still a historical one and some of the structural characteristics described are ones which no longer pertain to contemporary educational systems. They will have been changed as a result of the interaction which we are now discussing.

In Decentralized Educational Systems

Earlier it was seen that systems originating from substitution are much more loosely structured. Because specialization and differentiation were entrenched in the independent networks before the development of State education, they remained the predominant characteristics. The interaction surrounding incorporation defended much of the autonomy and integrity of the networks and thus limited the degree of unification and systematization taking place. Hence such systems are decentralized, they have no leading part, and are loosely integrated because of the relative segregation of their component elements. The predominance of differentiation and specialization leads to a distinctive set of strains which develop between education and society in countries with this kind of system. These strains, which are experienced by actors as deficiencies in educational services, derive from weak unification and systematization. In particularly they result from the latter not being able to contain certain tendencies implicit in the predominant characteristics.

Basically strains arise because various parts evade the unified controls and create problems for the rest of the system, and because the various elements are insufficiently co-ordinated to avoid exigencies arising at various points. For example the continued existence of a strong private sector means that its activities can disrupt those of public education (through socially biased intake policies, more attractive processes of instruction, and preferential placement of outputs). The echo of this problem is heard at a much later date in comments like 'what is the point of going comprehensive if the public schools remain?' Similarly, each element which continues its specialized activities may inhibit the attainment of other goals in different parts of the system. (For example, concentration on technical subjects in a realschool can prevent its pupils from being qualified for higher education; early confessional schooling can lead to clashes in the definition of knowledge if pupils later transfer to secular establishments; and all higher levels of activities may be impeded by the pupils' preparation at lower ones).

Strains develop then because unification and systematization are too weak to provide the co-ordination which would prevent them. On the one hand, the system is sluggish and unresponsive to administrative control, its parts going their own way, often contradicting and obstructing central policy through their activities. Yet its component parts are highly resistant to any attempt to infringe their autonomy, and thus continue to evade such controls. On the other hand, this same autonomy threatens the internal integration of the system, leading to bottlenecks, barriers, and blockages which persist because each element defends its own specialized practices and none is strong enough to make order among them.

These strains, represented by unresponsiveness to central control and internal disjunctures, are experienced by various groups as deficiencies in educational services. To some groups this means that they will find they have access to certain levels of instruction but are debarred from entering higher establishments or elite enclaves. The disjuncture between elementary and secondary instruction, frequently inherited from the networks (together with the independence of the private sector), means that some groups only receive services from the lower levels. Their experience is thus one of frustration, and ironically it is more intense the more useful the elementary instruction which *is* received is felt to be. To other groups frustrations will consist in certain studies not continuing beyond a given level (for example, it may be impossible to gain a degree in technical or applied disciplines); in lengthier and thus more expensive training because a lower level did not prepare properly for a higher one; in substantial discontinuities between supply of and demand for places in various parts of the system. Each of these will be experienced as personal frustrations by different sets of pupils (and their families), and as recruitment problems (in a broader sense than the strictly occupational) by those concerned with other institutional operations. In addition, the latter often find that the types of specialization they require run counter to those carried over from the competitive stage of educational conflict.

Thus it is the underlying lack of co-ordination of the system which creates exigencies in different parts of society. These in turn condition pressures for change from the various groups involved. However, it should be clear from the above examples that different problems are experienced by different groups — those debarred from secondary instruction are not the same people, by and large, as those whose recruits have not undergone the specialized training required, and these in turn may be quite different from the people suffering from shortages in numerical output of a particular type. Furthermore, some of these exigencies could be overcome without substantial change in the system. The problems of certain groups could be solved by modifying course composition, entry qualifications, admission quotas, etc. In conjunction these two points indicate that the emergence of a single solidary oppositional group committed to far-reaching educational change is unlikely in this type of system. Generally the dissatisfied will not have enough grievances in common to establish a joint cause and they will not share enough in terms of social position to unite despite other allegiances and antagonisms.

So far it has been argued that the distribution of services in systems with substitutive origins is such that various types of changes, some of them not very profound, will be sought by different kinds of social groups. Turning now to the distribution of control in the decentralized system it will be seen that change can be initiated in a number of ways. Not all of these are open to every discontented group: their position in the social structure largely determines which ones they can use success- fully. The fact that different groups can pursue change in different ways is a further reason for not expecting the development of a united opposition movement. Instead it is anticipated that fragmentary interest groups will initiate change through different forms of negotia- tion in the decentralized system.

Firstly, *internal initiation* will be an extremely important process of change in systems with substitutive origins. This form of negotiation helps to satisfy professional demands but also makes a significant contribution to meeting demands which are accumulated in the outside community. The importance of this process derives directly from the high autonomy enjoyed by professional educators. Because of the strongly differentiated nature of the system, they avoid heavy tutelage by any group and have considerable freedom of action. Because of the decentralized nature of the system, not all the resources they absorb flow exclusively through the central administrative framework. The two factors are of course inter-related but they operate in a mutually reinforcing fashion: freedom from constant interference enables the profession to add to its resources which strengthens its autonomy. This in turn has three important consquences for the initiation of change.

(i) In decentralized systems the profession rapidly becomes an active participant in the formation of educational policy. Because of their greater initial autonomy and their access to independent resources in terms of endowments, bequests, subscriptions, fees, and earnings, the process of professionalization occurs early. They are not so subject to legal control as to preclude the formation of professional associations, nor so financially dependent on one party as to tie their hands in any negotiations. Thus professional organizations with a tough insistence on unionist rights develop in these countries. There is a strong tendency for them to emerge first from the richer networks where their favourable resource balance gives them special interests to protect and of course the means of putting up a good defense, (for example the Headmasters' Conference in late nineteenth century England). It merely takes longer for them to develop in other parts of the system, for in none is control or dependencey stringent enough to prevent it. Their consolidation means that the profession can begin to negotiate directly with the polity on an organized basis.

The establishment of professional status coupled with the development of collective bargaining prevent government from subordinating the educators in such negotiations. Instead the professional bodies begin to affect policy formation in a variety of ways. They press for and gain representation on advisory committees to government; they independently initiate changes which are then submitted as 'evidence' or 'precedent' to support their case in political bargaining; they refuse to implement central policies or subject them to considerable modification at the local level; they negotiate continuously for better conditions, facilities, and pay. The relationship thus becomes a two-way one and the educators no longer passively receive directives but collectively help to frame legislation and mould practice.

(ii) In addition their relative autonomy enables them to negotiate directly with external agencies and often to earn extra resources in the process. The latter are important because among other things they strengthen independence from central government and thus facilitate evasion or circumvention of its controls. In this way they can satisfy a series of external demands and have the power to adapt their establishments to local conditions and requirements. However, the significance of this for the introduction of change is not limited to the exchange of services for financial resources. The decentralized system allows a variety of external pressures to be filtered into local education at the discretion of the educators. Pressures may be exerted by groups of parents, by local associations devoted to cultural, linguistic, rural, or welfare goals etc., and by special interest groups of all kinds — in the knowledge that the schools, colleges, and regional authorities have considerable discretionary powers. Their aim is to press the professionals into using their autonomy to innovate, experiment, and diversify in the desired direction. In this way changes are introduced which satisfy a wider range of external demands. Obviously all do not obtain satisfaction, but often the reason for this is not lack of power to introduce the change in question, but because it is contrary to the interests of the profession. Those best placed to instigate change by this method are those who propose modifying educational services in such a way as to enrich the profession or enhance its status in the community.

(iii) Finally their independence enables the profession to make substantial internal innovations on the basis of its own experience, the teaching situation it faces, and the collective goals formulated by its associations. In decentralized systems the range of changes which can be introduced in this way is broad and often includes the capacity to alter curricula, texts, examinations, teaching methods and disciplinary processes as well as to improve the professional work situation. Included in this is a considerable ability to accept or reject *in situ* the demands voiced by pupils and students — whether these concern the above areas or relate to greater participation in decision-making. In this type of system the profession is indeed in a privileged position to determine educational change, but this is not to say that internal initiation does not benefit other parts of society by rectifying certain deficiencies in services.

Secondly *external transactions* represent a process whereby certain groups negotiate substantial changes in decentralized systems. Those parties who dispose of considerable resources and have aims acceptable to the profession can often gain satisfaction from the public sector. They are most successful here in arranging transactions with those parts of the State system which are more independent than others. In other words, there will be levels of instruction or types of establishment whose lower autonomy severely limits this kind of negotiation. For example it was seen that in England elementary instruction emerged as the least independent of all levels. Accordingly it has been the technical schools, colleges, and universities which have been involved in the majority of external transactions. Nevertheless even here certain groups with adequate resources fail to obtain the changes in inputs, processes, or outputs that they require. This may be because their requirements lack 'respectability' in the eyes of the profession, or simply because their demands are too specialized, or different, to be integrated with current educational activities in these establishments.

However, for groups in this position or for those whose demands focus on levels which are virtually closed to external transactions, another possibility exists in the decentralized system. We have already seen that in such countries strong private sectors of education flourish with relatively little interference from the administrative framework.

Here, then, many groups with sufficient resources can gain the services they require, either by negotiating with existing institutions or by founding new ones. Certainly for some groups, including some very wealthy ones, working through the private sector is only a partial solution and this will be especially true if the change sought is the universalization of particular values or beliefs through education. For others, however, the possibility of buying the special services they seek is an adequate and important method of introducing educational change.

Indeed the changes brought about in this way are very varied and embrace all levels of instruction. They can include the development of pre-school education, of preparatory establishments, of experimental or specialized secondary schools devoted to music, the arts, religion, foreign or minority languages and culture, commercial and industrial training; of technical, theological and trade colleges; of business schools and even of independent universities. The variety is as great as the list of buyers, for there are few barriers to entering the private market in education, especially where the older age groups of pupils are concerned. Obviously this openness means that a number of disreputable institutes devoted to strange or sordid ends will be found in their midst, but the significant point about the private sector in a decentralized system is that its component establishments are not *condemned* to be second rate.

Because they are not compelled to enter pupils for state examinations or to follow standard curricula, they are not forced to ape the public sector and thus to dilute their own activities. Instead they can develop clear and distinctive courses which establish their own prestige, and can award qualifications which are recognized for their relevance in appropriate areas. Because of this they can recruit good pupils and charge high fees. In turn they can pay staff well, have good teacher-pupil ratios and superior facilities. The quality of the output improves and the process becomes self-reinforcing. Obviously, this felicitous cycle is not shared by all parts of the private sector — many fail through misconstruing market-demand for their educational products, through offering them at unrealistic prices, or simply through bad organization. But success is not uncommon and can be attained equally by a short trade course, a hairdressing institute, an elite business school, or a trade union college. Because of this, a number of groups can introduce educational changes which satisfy their requirements and at the same time do not compare unfavourably with the standards of the public sector. This form of external transaction is, however, only available to groups who have considerable resources at their disposal. In the decentralized system it is not difficult to buy educational change but neither is it cheap.

The third form of negotiation, *political manipulation*, tends to be most important where external transactions are least possible, and for those who are least able to engage in them. While government has certain powers of control over educational institutions, their greater autonomy prevents political manipulation from being *the* distinctive form of change in decentralized systems. However, although unification is weak when national education has substitutive origins, certain parts and levels emerge with less autonomy from the political centre than others. Because they are more controlled they have less scope for increasing their autonomy by earning resources in exchange for services. Because other groups cannot transact services directly, they are forced to do this indirectly by political manipulation if they want their requirements met by changes in those particular public institutions. In other words, they have to influence governmental policy and to counteract the political pressures of other groups to shape it in conformity with their needs. It is not that interest groups fail to pressurize government about other parts of the system, naturally they do because any concessions they gain cost them nothing. The point is merely that political manipulation will be most intense, and most important in accounting for change, when alternative courses of action are most limited.

However, the majority of the population is not in a position to use the other forms of negotiation even when they are available. The lower classes, immigrant groups, and ethnic minorities, cannot engage in external transactions on a significant scale because they lack the resources. Generally too the nature of their subcultures is so different from prevailing academic values that they do not harmonize spontaneously with the teaching profession. Perhaps the greatest effect of this cultural divide is to prevent them from trying. It is not the only one, for on the whole many of the things they would want teachers to do — keeping playgrounds open after school, running holiday activities, opening canteens for an after-school meal, actively respecting foreign cultures, organizing bilingual instruction, coping with handicapped children within the local schools, to name but a few of the most practical demands — are not those that improve the work situation or enhance professional status. For these groups, or more specifically the organizations representing them, political manipulation is the major method used in the attempt to gain *any* kind of educational change. It is significant that even the powerful Trade Union movements make most use of this form of negotiation and tend only to dabble in external transactions to meet their own bureaucratic needs.

In other words, political manipulation is used intensively by those whose demands have little chance of satisfaction through other methods. Thus it is via the political party, organization, and pressure group, that non-elite groups seek educational change. They are not of course the only ones to use this channel nor the most successful by any means, but because their pressures are continuous and intense they colour the nature of public educational debate in decentralized systems. In dragging class, ethnic, and minority claims to the centre of the political arena, other groups are irresistibly drawn to debate in these terms when defending their own interests. For this reason most of the central legislation passed will be found to concentrate on such issues. However, the parliamentary or political prominence accorded to the educational problems of the underprivileged should not mislead us about the character of educational change in general. As we have seen, in the decentralized system other kinds of changes can be introduced unobtrusively through different forms of negotiation, without visible political struggle or social polarization.

Thus, in conclusion, the most outstanding feature of interaction in these systems with substitutive origins is its complexity. We have seen that there is a rough parity of importance between the three forms of negotiation for educational change. If change is to be explained satisfactorily then all three kinds of interaction must be examined, together with the interrelations between them. Analysis will have to concentrate on the distribution of educational deficiencies, on the differential availability of the three sources of changes according to the position of the groups affected, and on the different forms of negotiation themselves. It is obvious that this interaction will be far too complex to be conceptualized as the interplay of dominant and assertive groups, or any equally simple formulation. Indeed the very structure of the decentralized system works against polarization in educational conflict. Instead it encourages fragmented pressures for change because of the way in which services and control are distributed in systems originating from substitution.

In Centralized Educational Systems

In the last chapter it was seen that systems with restrictive origins have a tightly integrated internal structure. Because their emergence was orchestrated by the political elite, the various parts were co-ordinated from the start to protect its own educational requirements from interference by other services which had to be provided simultaneously. Because such elites sought a system which would be uniquely responsive to their changing needs, the administrative frameworks were expressly designed as the leading part of each such system. Through them educational change could be filtered and monitored so that it never escaped the control of the governing elite.

However, to argue that such systems are centralized in structure and streamlined in organization is far from saying that they experience no problems of integration. On the contrary, the very predominance of unification and systematization generates severe exigencies for the system as a whole. Specialization and differentiation, which are essential for meeting a plurality of demands, are not easily built-in to a system whose leading part resists diversification (because it disrupts existing dovetailed arrangements) and rejects the alternative solution, the development of highly autonomous and specialized institutions (because these bid to escape its control). In other words, the dominant pair of characteristics limit the degree to which public or private education can become diverse enough to meet external demands.

Thus specialization can only develop in so far as it 'meets' strict criteria of compatibility with other inputs, processes and outputs within the system. In a system whose interrelatedness is high, to accede to new demands will generate more exigencies than in one whose parts are loosely knit — except in the unusual case where new patterns dovetail perfectly with pre-existing ones. Change at one level will have immediate repercussions on others, and those who have vested interests in the latter may place a brake on innovation through their defence of the status quo. Similarly, segmentation can only develop as long as administrative controls are not evaded. In practice this means that few institutions gain enough autonomy to specialize intensively. The standardizing influence of strong unification is witnessed by the private sector in such countries. Because of tight central control over matters like appointments, curricula, and examination it can never represent a clear and distinct alternative to public education. Because of this, the centralized system has little internal elasticity and few external shock-absorbers.

In turn, the problems of integration faced here are of a very different type from those common to systems with substitutive origins. Instead of the strains which develop representing a constant threat to the internal co-ordination of the system and a danger to governmental control, here the exigencies generated by a tightly articulated and centralized system create problems for groups in other institutions. Internal rigidity and central control are prejudicial to the satisfaction of their interests. Thus in the centralized system tensions will be manifest between the system as a whole and other parts of society whose demands have inadequate educational expression.

Weak differentiation and specialization will be experienced as major deficiencies in the services received by a number of social groups. The uniform and standardized nature of schooling means that many do not get the type of service they require. Despite differences in aspirations and aptitudes, parents and pupils confront a system which provides them with relatively little choice or a forced selection between a prestige mainstream and inferior branching alternatives. Other groups will suffer because specialization hardly begins to meet their needs. They will find themselves compelled to develop various forms of in-service training in the broadest sense of the term; they will experience recruitment problems because of the prestige attaching to mainstream education and its outlets into State service; they will suffer from the implicit or explicit denigration of their activities and values by the official definition of instruction. Many groups in different parts of the social structure will find themselves experiencing severe deficiencies and among them may number the elites of certain institutions. For example, a public system which is completely secular will be a major impediment to religious leaders, and one which is geared to a predominantly industrial economy will obstruct rural activities. Which particular parties receive least from the system depends of course on the precise form of multiple integration to emerge with the new system. The only generalization which can be made is that groups in opposition to the prevailing political elite are almost certain to want substantial educational changes.

If it is these deficiencies which condition pressures for change then it is clear that they structure educational opposition very differently in the centralized system. To begin with, the uniformity of public education means that there are more groups who gain very little in terms of services from it. In turn this means that there is less chance that each deficiency will be experienced discretely by isolated groups. Some of the problems will be faced by the same people or by related individuals. Added to this, the severity of educational grievances provides more opportunity for various groups to discover common ground. The obstruction of certain elites has the consequence that those who seek the largest educational changes are not necessarily those who have the least power and resources in society. Taken in conjunction these factors imply that the development of a united opposition group or groups is less unlikely in systems with restrictive rather than substitutive origins. This is certainly not to argue that the formation of a single opposition group is a frequent occurrence — on the contrary social disintegration would have to be extremely wide-reaching for that to occur. It is simply to point out that in contrast to the decentralized system, the centralized one does not condition the emergence of fragmentary interest groups whose main concern is the introduction of very specific changes. Here the service deficiencies are often too gross to be overcome without substantial change and, as we shall see, the distribution of control is such that it is difficult to remove them gradually by a series of transactions. The spread of control in the decentralized system allowed a variety of demands to be negotiated separately through different forms of interaction. Thus dissatisfaction did not build up outside the system because particular groups at different times and places could introduce modifications in one of several ways. The contrary is true of the centralized system. The spread of control is narrower, the opportunities for negotiation are reduced, and in consequence the pattern of action leading to educational change is quite unlike the one just discussed.

Firstly *internal initiation* will be a less important process of change than in decentralized systems. This form of negotiation is narrower where systems have restrictive origins, both in terms of who can use it and what can be accomplished through it. The most important difference is that, by and large, it is not a channel through which external and consumer demands can be filtered and satisfied in the centralized system. Instead this process tends to be the exclusive prerogative of the profession itself, although the range of changes which it can introduce are also more limited. These differences derive from the fact that professional educators enjoy a lower degree of autonomy in this kind of system. Although teachers are a highly differentiated body, compared with the antecedent period, they have less independence from governmental control than in the decentralized system. The financial resources used in educational activities flow almost exclusively via the administrative framework. Tight control coupled with supreme dependence on public finance means that the scope of negotiation narrows to trans-actions between goverment and the profession. This in turn limits the scale of changes which can be introduced internally.

To begin with, the whole process of professionalization takes place with greater difficulty over a longer period in the centralized system. The teaching body starts off with relatively little autonomy from the administrative framework. It is the latter which initially defines the teacher training programme, which supervises the recruitment and certification procedures, and organizes placements. Usually, to ensure continued control, teachers are made civil servants and are subject to the same restrictive statutes. Thus the teaching body is less dif-ferentiated — it is still, in one way, attached to the role structure of another institution. This limited autonomy makes professional organi-zation difficult, for civil service statutes generally deprive them of the right to combine or to engage in political action. Teachers' associations thus emerge late, after a hard battle for recognition of professional expertise and the eventual lifting of the most repressive statutes.

The associations which do develop are usually official ones because the political elite ultimately determines the bodies with which it is prepared to deal. Educators lack both the freedom or the resources to establish alternative forms of organization. As a result, the price of recognition for any professional association is heavy central control and it is paid because of the lack of an alternative option, on the principle that some form of organization is preferable to none. On occasion the professional body may be little more than a government agency whose representatives are selected on grounds of political orthodoxy. This is certainly not always the case, but in general these associations will enjoy very limited 'unionist' rights. They can engage in collective bargaining but often are prevented from employing 'legitimate' restric-tive practices. Obviously this affects their capacity to influence educa-tional policy. They have less power to resist government directives and less resources to experiment on a significant scale. They can only seek to use their professional expertise as a lever on government in order to raise additional resources which can be devoted to their own ends. Here they can use their special status as educational experts to insist, for example, that a particular level of finance and facilities are essential for implementing governmental policy. If one adds in a general advisory role, through which the associations can pronounce on the feasibility and desirability of certain changes, this represents the sum total of

professional influence over policy formation. It is not a one-way relationship, but the profession is far from being an equal party in negotiations with government. *Compared with their counterparts in decentralized systems the professional body receives more directives from the
centre and is able to initiate fewer in return.*

This lack of autonomy also means that teachers and academics
cannot negotiate directly with external agencies or earn extra resources
from them. They themselves are too closely controlled to be able to
offer the kinds of modifications sought by various groups in the
community. They cannot alter courses, curricula, assessment, examination or selection procedures, for these are established centrally and are
not susceptible of local variation. Thus the most important issues are
removed from the negotiating table. Local groups cannot hope to
influence the profession to make good the deficiencies that the former
experience in educational services. The teachers bear the brunt of local
grievances but are impotent to do anything about the most serious
ones. Only in the most limited ways can the profession be of service to
the community. It can only satisfy those kinds of demands which do
not contravene the letter, or contradict the spirit, of central policy.

It is for this reason that formal contact between the profession and
influential interest groups will not be great at local level. The latter are
well aware that the teachers' hands are tied and that their own efforts
are better directed elsewhere. Similarly, and in contrast to decentralized
systems, a strong network of parent-teacher associations will not
develop. Those that do will concentrate their school-based activities on
peripheric issues with which central government does not interfere –
extra-curricula recreation, school trips, use of local facilities, and some
aspects of pupil health and welfare. The only other activity open to
such associations is the framing of pious proposals for reform. Thus the
profession, if it wishes, can make minor concessions to public demand
or lend its name to abstract documents proposing revision of the
system. What is missing here is the hard, practical, and productive
dealing, which characterizes' systems with substitutive origins.

Finally, the profession has a limited capacity to introduce internal
changes in conformity with its own ends, using the surplus resources
extracted from government for this purpose. Usually it can only initiate
changes which are acceptable to the political elite and compatible with
the existing organization of the system. On the whole these are modifications which are of concern to the profession but a matter of
indifference to government – enhancing the status of academics by

internal subdivisions of power, creating new Chairs, employing assistants, technicians and teaching auxiliaries; improving working conditions, library, technical, and research facilities; accentuating the pure over the applied and initiation over training; providing lighter teaching loads for those pursuing higher qualifications, subventions for research, and subsidies for publications, thus aiding professional advancement. Hence the changes it can and does initiate internally are those which benefit itself alone. In the centralized system the profession can only function as a vested interest group. It cannot filter in the far reaching demands of students, parents or employers, *but* in introducing its own small-scale modifications it can increase the deficiencies experienced by others. The cumulative tendency of these minor changes is to make knowledge more academic, learning progressively divorced from practical life, and teaching an intellectual adventure and an end in itself.

Secondly *external transactions* are also of limited importance as a process by which major changes are negotiated in the centralized system. As has been seen the profession itself has insufficient autonomy to deal directly with external groups. No part of the public sector is independent enough to introduce new services in exchange for resources. Because it cannot earn, its autonomy remains low and State education stays closed to transactions, however great the resources offered by the external groups and however acceptable their proposals might be to the teaching profession. It may seem to follow that negotiations with the private sector will therefore be a more important source of change in the centralized system, precisely because of the closed nature of State education. The opposite is in fact the case.

Certainly groups with adequate resources can found new establishments or negotiate changes with existing private institutions, but the services acquired in this way are rarely sufficient to meet their demands. They are nearly always inadequate because the private sector is not free from State interference and finds it difficult to offer a proper alternative to public instruction. To begin with, the effect of strong unification is that private establishments are more closely controlled in terms of their inputs, processes, and outputs. They are subject to State inspection, certification, and often examination. They usually have to maintain certain standards of building, qualification of teachers, and facilities for pupil welfare, all of which are difficult for a new venture to achieve immediately and are sufficiently expensive to discourage some from starting. More important, however, is the fact that such establishments are irresistibly drawn to imitate public education. For instance if their pupils or students are to sit for national examinations, then they must follow public curricula, use the set texts, and appoint teachers adept in the appropriate methods, otherwise their failure rate will exceed that of the public sector. Here the problem for these institutions is that their external sponsors and parental feepayers are not going to invest in something which they can all get free of charge anyway.

Yet even if the private sector, for example, awarded its own qualifications, these have little chance of establishing their value on the educational market. This is by no means a free market since only State qualifications are recognized for a whole range of purposes which are of vital concern to those taking private diplomas — university entry, deferment of military service, public appointments, possession of a degree, title or letters, eligibility for certain offices etc. Private institutions are in a cleft stick, for they go it alone in the knowledge that what they have to offer cannot compete with the advantages and prestige attaching to public certificates, and that therefore they will tend to enrol worse students and be unable to charge high fees. They thus enter a vicious circle and have little chance of breaking out, because without high fees and good students they cannot teach sufficiently well to produce graduates whose quality raises the standing of their diplomas. By following this alternative, they by and large condemn themselves to being second-rate and to giving a corresponding lack of satisfaction to those they serve.

External interest groups seek neither the second-rate nor a carbon-copy of public instruction; they want a different kind of service from private education, but this difference is precisely what State interference militates against. For instance, schools set up for religious purposes constantly find that their religious instruction, far from dominating the timetable, is being squeezed out by examinable subjects. Whatever the purpose of a particular institution, it finds itself torn between the need to offer special services involving specialized teaching, courses, and activities, and the remorseless pressure towards standardization emanating from the State. Here we have concentrated on the effects of examinations for purposes of illustration, but the pressures operate in exactly the same way where State inspection and certification of schools are concerned.

This attempt to serve two masters, to match up to the standards imposed by government and to meet the requirements of private investors, is less than successful as far as the latter are concerned. Their demands are not satisfied in full because the private sector cannot specialize or diversify enough to meet them. Some will nevertheless consider it worthwhile, but it is certainly not every group which thinks, for example, that it is more important for its children to have a religious training than for them to achieve the highest academic standards. Yet these are the kinds of priorities which determine whether private instruction is a satisfactory alternative for a particular group, since in the centralized system such establishments are not elitist ones. Too much prestige attaches to the public sector, because of its official connection with elite positions in society, for this to be otherwise. The private sector thus remains weak, for too many groups seeking substantial educational change know that they can only get a modicum of satisfaction from it. Among them may be rich elites who could buy the services they require in a different kind of system. Here their demands are scarcely met by external transactions so they are forced to (re)present them through other forms of negotiation.

Thus *political manipulation* is by far the most important form of negotiation in centralized systems. Because education as a whole has so little autonomy from the government and because groups seeking change have few alternative means of obtaining them, most pressures converge on the political centre. The provisions which do exist for serving other parts of society are those which the political elite had to concede historically because of its need for support and resources. This remains the case for future changes in the definition of instruction — these stem predominantly from processes of political interaction. In other words, the parties seeking new services must cumulate their demands, form alliances, and organize themselves to work though the political machinery.

This is the case for most groups, including the professional educators who might be thought to occupy a somewhat privileged position for the initiation of change. The latter is true in one sense, but when their demands exceed the bounds of professional self-advancement and involve broader educational issues they cannot introduce these directly. Instead they must, as it were, go outside the system in order to influence it, by joining a political faction or external pressure group. Indeed it is characteristic of the centralized system that teachers and academics tend themselves to be members of outside organizations devoted to national educational aims, rather then local groups converging on the school or local authority to thrash out changes on a community basis. The same applies to the majority of affluent groups who cannot transact changes directly; they too must seek to transform public policy through political manipulation. This represents a major contrast with the decentralized system, for instead of political inter-action being the resort of the underprivileged, it is the main channel through which *all* social groups work to bring about educational change. Thus political manipulation is the distinctive process of change in centralized systems and is considerably more important than the other two forms of negotiation.

Consequently, although internal initiation and external transactions cannot be ignored, explanations of educational change must con-centrate on political interaction. In other words, a more restricted area of social conflict needs to be examined to account for change in the centralized system, compared with the decentralized system. Analysis will have to concentrate on the distribution of educational deficiencies, the differential ability of groups to exert political influence, and the nature of political interaction itself. Again the struggle for educational change cannot be captured by the domination and assertion approach. Control may be restricted in the centralized system, but it is not the exclusive prerogative of one group: the ways in which opposition can be effective may be limited, but they are different from the strategies used before the development of State educational systems. Instead we can look towards political science for help in conceptualizing the process of educational change in these countries.

DETERMINANTS OF
EDUCATIONAL INTERACTION

As in the preceding period due allowance has to be made for the influence of other structural and cultural factors, which are non-educational in origin, upon the processes of interaction and the resulting patterns of change. Equally the intervention of independent sources of ideas and action must not be minimized. In the most general terms these factors exert the same kind of influence as in the past, that is they serve to reinforce or to dilute the conditional influences on educational interaction which have just been discussed. Rather than retracing the ground covered in Chapter 2, in the section dealing with determinants of educational interaction, only new aspects of this rela-tionship will be mentioned now.

Firstly, since the network of influences conditioning educational interaction has been reshaped between the two cycles, there will be new points at which the intervention of other structural and independent factors become important, and these may themselves differ from centralized to decentralized systems. Secondly, the transition from the first to the second cycle is a historical process of quite lengthy duration in the four countries examined, and thus considerable social change will have been unfolding alongside the educational changes already analyzed. In starting to discuss the second cycle we must now insert those alterations in the social context of educational interaction which distinguish it from the social environment of domination and assertion in the past.

It was possible in Chapter 2 to examine non-educational influences simply in terms of how far they fostered or discouraged the actualization of assertive groups or of groups supporting domination. In general we are concerned with the same phenomenon, and the same generalization holds good — that the closer the social and cultural ties between those sharing educational control, the more they will present a solid front in defence of the educational status quo. However, it has also been seen that educational control is spread more widely with the transfer from private ownership to public systems. In turn this will increase the salience of other social influences, for it means that a much larger category of influential parties has to hold and work together, if the definition of instruction is to remain unchanged. This has different consequences for the decentralized system, where the three processes of change are of roughly equal importance, than for the centralized system, where political manipulation is the pre-eminent process.

Although it is still true in the decentralized system that the more the influential parties are linked by kinship, class, or overlapping membership (e.g. businessmen in Parliament, politicians as churchgoers and shareholders, teachers as members of political parties), the more they will defend common interests at all three strategic points — the school, the community and the central political arena — nevertheless, the spread of groups involved increases the likelihood of significant social differences between them and cultural pluralism amongst them. The nature of the system is such that vested interests, structured elsewhere in society, do not have difficulty in finding educational expression. Given three different outlets for change, there is a high probability that different interests and values will be pursued through them. In other words, there is no longer the need to cumulate, articulate, and thus dilute demands, as in the old alliances of the past: instead particular social interests can and will attempt to negotiate their requirements in all their detailed specificity.

On the other hand, in the centralized system, the supreme importance of political manipulation still places a considerable premium on the ability of both government and opposition respectively, to hold together if they are to be successful in the maintenance of the status quo or the transaction of change. Thus if the spread of control has increased the social and cultural diversity of the controllers, mutual accommodation is still needed for them to arrive at a common programme. Yet this will be harder to obtain and its absence may lead to a political immobilism which is detrimental to all their interests.

So far it is the effects of multiple integration which have been examined in relation to other social factors. Equally significant is the attachment of all new systems to the political centre, for this implies that the structuration of political power becomes of universal importance. Thus the relative closure or accessibility of State power will have far reaching consequences for educational interaction in every system. This is absolutely crucial in the centralized system since political manipulation is the main process for negotiating change. It is still very important in the decentralized system, although the effects of political closure can be offset, to some extent, by the intensive use of the other two processes. Thus, in contrast to the antecedent period, there is now an interface between education and the polity in all countries where educational systems have emerged.

The growing complexity of social structures, which develops as societies move towards full industrial status, involves the mobilization of broader sections of society, the differentiation of a larger number of corporate interests, and the interpenetration of diverse collectivities. The social environment of education enlarges correspondingly (practically no-one remains disinterested in the definition of instruction) and becomes more complicated as the nature of educational demands undergoes a parallel diversification (matching the differentiation of interests). In all new systems this spells greater educational activity, and more pressures for the modification of outputs, although the growing interconnectedness of modern social structures will also encourage the negotiation of change rather than the exchange of injurious acts in competitive conflict.

The concomitant cultural changes which have taken place will have the same effect of intensifying educational activity. The increasingly international nature of value systems, consequent upon mass communications, mass literacy and mass mobility means that limited access to alternative legitimatory values no longer operates as a barrier to the organization of opposition, except perhaps in countries with very efficient forms of censorship. On the contrary there is a growing fund of cosmopolitan, or even inter-continental movements, ideologies, or schools of thought in education. Educationalists, propagandists by nature, ensure that no lack of knowledge about alternatives or of justifications for them will hold back the potential forces for change.

Again in the decentralized system this heightened level of activity and debate has three outlets through which it can be expressed, and the fissiparous influence of intense value conflict need not be negative because minority movements can often make use of external transactions or internal initiation. However, in the centralized system intense value conflict will be more destructive because the supremacy of political manipulation still makes it imperative for opposition to remain united if macroscopic change is to be introduced. Thus in so far as politico-educational factionalism is encouraged by the wide diffusion of very different political ideologies and educational philosophies it will impede the practical introduction of change. If this happens, then given that the level of educational activity will be just as high in countries with centralized systems, the pool of discontent will grow over time and may reach serious proportions because it lacks the safety-valves which the decentralized system possesses in the processes of external transaction and internal initiation.

Taking the whole of the foregoing discussion together, the different patterns of interaction which are conditioned by the two different kinds of educational system, can be summarized in the following basic diagrams. These stand in the same relation to the second cycle as did Figure I (Chapter 2) to the first cycle, when educational change was heavily conditioned by ownership, mono-integration, and subordination. The fact that there are now two diagrams for the second cycle reflects the importance attached to centralization and decentralization as conditional influences on subsequent interaction. Both diagrams have been deliberately simplified at this stage in order to accentuate the different patterns of educational interaction to which the two systems give rise.

Figure II shows the typical convection currents of action conditioned by the centralized system, where demands originating in the
school or community have to be aggregated, passed upwards to the
central decision-making arena, and negotiated there before being transmitted down to education in the form of polity-directed changes. In
contrast Figure III presents the more complex cross-currents of interaction conditioned by the decentralized system. Due to the fact that
there are three different outlets for the negotiation of change there is
no necessity for demands to be cumulated or passed upwards, since
changes can be introduced locally or internally. However, because
groups can and do make use of all three processes, the more complicated cross-currents are produced as the typical action pattern.

FIGURE II

The Structural Conditioning of Educational Interaction
in the Centralized System

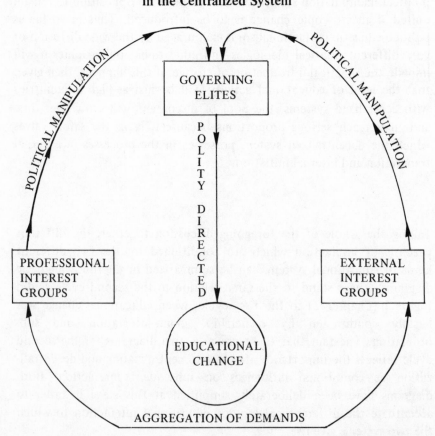

FIGURE III

The Structural Conditioning of Educational
Interaction in the Decentralized System

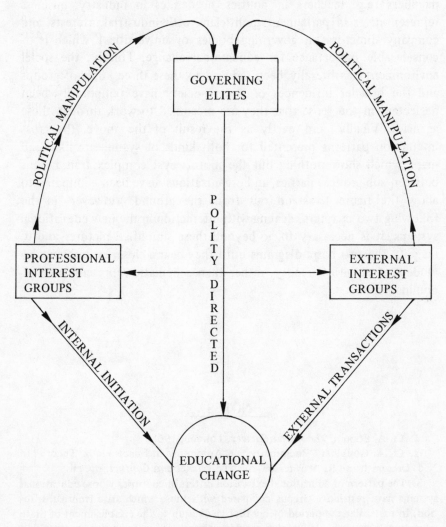

These two basic diagrams involve considerable oversimplification. In particular they treat all three groups — governing elites, external interest groups, and professional interest groups — as *undifferentiated* entities, when in reality each always displays a high level of sub-division (into parties, factions, associations, unions, confederations, institutes etc.) and a good deal of internal conflict between them which is also ignored here, although it is taken up in detail in the next two chapters. Secondly, the three types of groups have been presented as *distinct*, whereas in fact there is usually a substantial overlap between their members (e.g. teachers in politics, academics in industry, business representatives in parliament, politicians with industrial interests, and company directors on governing bodies of universities) which is of considerable importance for educational change. Thirdly, the social environment has literally been reduced to these three kinds of groups and the broader influences of wider society have temporarily been neglected, in the sense that they are presumed to work through these agencies. Finally, and partly as the result of the above, the gross interaction patterns presented for both kinds of system are like road maps which show nothing but the motorways: complex transactions between sub-groups, parties, and organizations have been eliminated to allow the figure to stand out from the ground. However, in the following two chapters, dealing with interaction in the new educational systems, it is necessary to go beyond these simplified pictures and to magnify the two basic diagrams until they bear a closer resemblance to models of empirical reality, rather than schematic representations of dominant traits.

NOTES

1. Cf. A. Etzioni, *The Active Society*, London, 1968.

2. Cf. A. Gouldner, 'Reciprocity and Autonomy in Functionalist Theory', in N. J. Demerath and R. A. Peterson, *System, Change and Conflict*, op. cit.

3. The pattern of educational expansion differs in countries whose educational systems have restrictive origins compared with those which arise from substitution. In particular the period of conflict leading up to the establishment of State educational systems shows the greatest divergence: substitutive competition results in substantial numerical expansion as the networks vie with one another to found schools, provide teachers, and enroll pupils — the restrictive phase leads initially to a reduction of provisions which can be very sharp indeed as schools are closed down, property confiscated and teachers proscribed. Only with the replacement phase does the curve begin to rise again, although it may take decades before the rate of expansion equals and overtakes the previous level of provision maintained by the old dominant group. On the other hand, the curve produced by substitution flattens out during the incorporation phase, from which the de-

**The typical pattern of educational expansion in countries
whose systems have restrictive origins and those
which have substitutive origins**

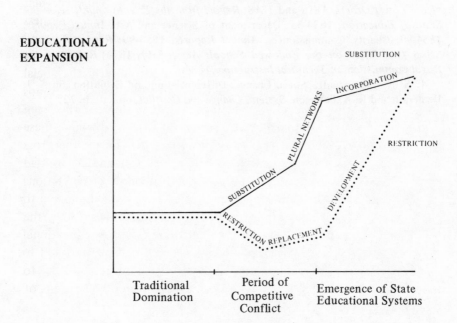

EDUCATIONAL
EXPANSION

SUBSTITUTION

INCORPORATION

PLURAL NETWORKS

RESTRICTION

SUBSTITUTION

DEVELOPMENT

RESTRICTION REPLACEMENT

| Traditional Domination | Period of Competitive Conflict | Emergence of State Educational Systems |

EDUCATIONAL CONFLICT

centralized system emerges, as competition yields to rationalization. The following diagram shows the contrasting shape of curves in ideal-typical form.

For convenience of presentation a number of assumptions have been incorporated which will not be borne out in reality. Firstly, it is assumed that the level of traditional provision is the same for all countries; secondly, the diagram implies that whichever strategy is used, the emergent systems expand to the same point within a few decades — both these assumptions are counter-factual. Thirdly, the steepness of the rises and falls of the curves are purely notional and numerical provisions cannot be read-off them. Finally, it is also assumed that only one kind of strategy, *either* restriction *or* substitution, is being pursued in a particular country prior to the emergence of a State educational system. Thus the numerical data on educational expansion in Russia or Denmark (where both strategies were used by different groups) would not coincide with either of the ideal-typical curves. None of these problems could be overcome given the non-comparability of the national data-bases, which in themselves are often inadequate and incomplete. Available statistics for France and England appear to accord with the *patterns* of expansion expected from a clear case of restriction and one of substitution. For France Cf. E. Kilian, *Tableau historique de l'instruction secondaire en France*, Paris, 1841; A. F. Villemain, *Rapport au Roi sur l'instruction secondaire*, Paris,

1843; M. Gontard, *L'Enseignement primaire en France de la Révolution à la loi Guizot*, Paris, 1959. A composite picture for England can be gained from the following official reports: *Reports from the Select Committee on the Education of the Lower Orders*, 1816 and 1818; *Report from the Select Committee on the State of Education*, 1834-35; Department of Science and Art, *Annual Reports*, 1854-99; Charity Commissioners, *Annual Reports*, 1858-99; *Report from the Select Committee on the Endowed Schools Act (1869)*, 1873; *Report of the Royal Commission on Technical Instruction*, 1884.

4. S. N. Einsenstadt, 'Social Change, Differentiation and Evolution', in N. J. Demerath and R. A. Peterson, *System, Change and Conflict*, op. cit., p. 229.

6 INTERACTION: In the Centralized System

Political manipulation is the main process through which educational change is pursued and produced in the centralized system. The study of interaction is therefore the study of educational politics *stricto sensu*. Thus the basic diagram (Figure II) at the end of Chapter 5 accentuated the upward flow of educational demands to the political centre and the reverse flow of policy-directives, from the top down to the component educational institutions. Interaction in centralized systems is centripetal in nature, for the negotiation of change depends upon the aggregation of grievances, the acquisition of political sponsorship, and the percolation of these demands into the central decision-making arena.

However, the basic diagram must now be expanded and its oversimplifications left behind. In order to gain explanatory purchase on the complexities of educational interaction in the real world, we can no longer treat governing elites, professional, and external interest groups as distinct, undifferentiated entities, nor can the social environment of education be reduced to, and subsumed under, these three types of groupings. Instead it is vital to allow for overlapping membership between the three — for the commitment of certain parts of the teaching profession to different political parties, for closer contacts between some institutional elites and academia than others, for the greater governmental or administrative involvement of certain corporate interests compared with others. Equally the scale must be magnified to reveal the internal differentiation of political elites (into governments, oppositions, parties, alliances and factions), of the profession (by qualifications, titles, level, workplace, union, syndicate and association), and of external interest groups by any number of criteria, amongst which some of the most important are resource-holdings, political involvement, social status, and cultural orientation. Finally, the different ways in which the social environment impinges on different parts of the polity, of the profession, and of the institutional spheres, also needs to be introduced.

The expanded diagram (Figure IV) gives a stylized representation of these more detailed characteristics and relationships. It breaks up each of the three old categories (governing elites, professional and external interest groups) into sub-divisions and shows the kind of interplay which can take place between them in the course of educational interaction. Each such relationship is illustrated only once, for clarity of presentation, and only then if it is a fairly common occurrence. Thus Figure IV, and its counterpart in the next Chapter (Figure V), do not approximate to models of empirical reality. The sub-units (I i, I 2, I $3'$/P i$'$/E i$'$) which figure in them do not represent specific social institutions, actual political parties, or particular professional associations. Similarly, the relationships depicted do not portray current events in any given society. They are illustrations of common occurrences, but in any society at a certain point in time, some may be found in greater profusion than shown here, whilst others might be lacking altogether. In other words, models of empirical reality would be numerous and varied, for they would have to change over time and with events, and would picture these changes by patternings of lines which might convey very different overall impressions.

Instead of modelling empirical reality, Figure IV is intended to be of heuristic and theoretical utility in understanding patterns of interaction common to all instances of a centralized system of education. Without stylization and abstraction there would be little possibility of generalization and thus of theory formation. However, a few practical examples of the relations denoted have been added at the end in order to show the kind of flesh which covers its bones. The rest of the chapter will in fact be devoted to fleshing out this skeleton for Russia and France in turn.

FIGURE IV

Educational Interaction in a Centralized System

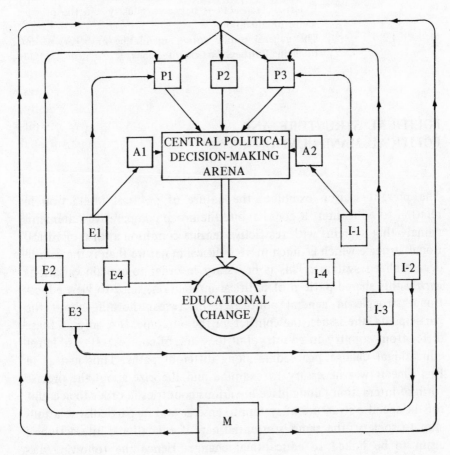

KEY

P	=	Political Party or Faction	A =	Advisory Committee or Council
I	=	External Interest Group	E =	Professional Interest Group

M = General Public

Patterns of Interaction — Illustration

E1 – P1	A teachers' union affiliated to a political party.
E1 – A1	Educational advisory committees to government with strong professional representation.
E3 – I3 – P3	The alliance between denominational teachers, their church and a sectarian Political Party.
E4	Internal Initiation to advance professional interests.
I1 – P3	A trade union or business federation affiliated to a political party.

I2 – M – E2 – P1	A pressure group of an agricultural organization, farming parents, rural schoolteachers, and a political party sponsoring agricultural interests.
I4	External Transactions between industry and the private sector of education.
M – P1, P2, P3	The general public voting, mandating or otherwise influencing Political Parties or factions.

POLITICAL STRUCTURE AND POLITICAL MANIPULATION

The present section examines the nature of political interaction in relation to education. It goes beyond the broad comparative statement, namely that systems with restrictive origins condition a form of educational struggle which is much more political in nature than is the case in decentralized systems. This is necessary in order to explain variations *within* this shared pattern of political interaction, since to view educational struggle in general political terms reveals nothing about the participants, the issues, the conflict, or the outcome. Not only do these differ from country to country, but they are, of course, responsible for educational change proceeding along different paths. Thus just as in Part One it was necessary to examine and theorize about the precise form of interaction taking place in various countries in order to account for the specific structure of system to emerge and its particular relationship to society, the same is essential here if educational interaction is again to be linked to educational change. Hence the following discussion explores the nature of political manipulation, or to put it another way, the contours and contents of educational politics.

In centralized systems two variables exert a crucial influence on the course of educational politics: *firstly, the structure of political decision-making* (an aspect of the political structure), and *secondly, the structure of educational interest groups* (an aspect of the social structure). Both of these can and do change over time in different countries, and their transformation does not necessarily take place simultaneously. It is, for example, quite possible for major political modifications (perhaps in enfranchisement, in Constitution, or scope of government intervention), to occur independently of any alteration in educational interest groups. Similarly the latter can alter (perhaps in composition or organization) without this entailing any concomitant variation in political structure. Obviously change in either will affect their inter-relationship, and this will be of the utmost importance for educational interaction, but changes in each can be brought about by factors extraneous to the other — e.g. international relations influencing political structure or technological development affecting educational interests. Before going on to examine the relationship between them, some conceptual clarification is a necessary preliminary, because the political variable has become entangled in recent controversies about power and pluralism.

The Structure of Political Decision-Making

For the purposes of the present study the vital aspect of political systems is how broad or narrow, open or closed, accessible or inaccessible are their structures in nature. This will exert a direct effect on political manipulation, for, as will be shown, it helps to determine how much educational change is negotiated, what kinds of changes are negotiable, and who can engage in negotiations. Hence the need to conceptualize different national political structures in these terms in order to make comparisons between countries and between different historical periods. In attempting to do this a distinction is made and maintained between:

(i) the framework of the State (within which elites are recruited, and within which they work, shaping policy and making decisions)
(ii) elite relations (of solidarity or disunity)

There are four reasons why it is important to maintain this distinction.[1] Firstly, a great deal of conceptual confusion arises when the two are treated interchangeably, or as indistinguishable from one another. This is clearly illustrated by the muddled American debate over pluralism.[2] Secondly, the two elements are logically and often empirically distinct. The constitutional framework of government can remain constant, whilst the unity among elites varies. Indeed Rex has recently opened up an interesting line of thought about the conditions under which elites share the same loyalties and have a sense of belonging together,[3] and of the issues whose salience at a particular moment can increase elite integration or fragment its unity. Similarly, solidarity between elites can remain unchanged whilst constitutional arrangements are transformed: indeed their very unity might enable this group to introduce closure and centralization of government.

Thirdly, to fail to make this distinction or to use the two terms interchangeably usually involves the assumption that all statements about political structures can be reduced to statements about elites. Although this was most obvious in the overt behaviourism of early pluralists like A. F. Bentley, who argued that where politics are concerned 'when the groups are adequately stated, everything is stated',[4] Lukes rightly takes the contemporary 'decision-making' and 'non-decision-making' approaches to task[5] for also concentrating on acts which are individually chosen or on individual inaction.[6] To concentrate exclusively on relations between elite groups leads to a complementary neglect of the structural bias exerted by the political system itself. Many of its characteristics, such as its extensiveness (whether its responsibilities extend to education, health, colonial administration, or sport), its openness, or its hierarchical nature are necessary to fully account for why 'some issues are organized into politics, while others are organized out'.[7] Thus to conflate the two elements is to weaken explanatory power.

This leads directly to the final point, namely that the two must be kept separate because elite relations themselves cannot be explained without reference to the framework of government. As Nicholls has argued, 'group structure and activity in a particular State can be understood only in the context of the whole "political system". The manner in which groups operate, it is suggested, will depend upon the way in which power is distributed in a country, and upon the way in which decisions are made'.[8] In other words, factors like the method of attaining elite positions, the range of elite action, and the machinery at their disposal, as well as countervailing checks limiting their freedom of decision-making, all depend on the prior existence of a State framework which cannot itself be explained in terms of interaction among *contemporary* elites. The emergence of a political system can only be explained historically, with reference to *other* groups in the past, themselves conditioned by an even earlier political context. Even in a revolutionary situation, its leaders are constrained by the pre-existing political structure and subsequent elite relations are conditioned by the new constitutional arrangements which are designed.

Hence in the following discussion which moves on towards a practical examination of relations between political structure and political manipulation, this distinction between governmental framework and elite relations is consistently maintained and can be expressed as follows in formal terms.

TABLE I
Schematization of Political Structures

State Framework	Elite relations	Polity
X	a	Xa
X	b	Xb
X	c'	Xc'
Y	a	Ya
Y	b	Yb
Y	c'	Yc'

The Framework of the State

In fact underlying *any* discussion of power, of who exercises it, and how, is a recognition of the existence of some kind of political framework. Thus Dahl[9] refers directly to the 'openness' and 'diversity' of pluralist government: Bachrach and Baratz[10] talk variously of a 'decision-making arena', of covert conflict being 'outside the political arena', and of certain grievances being denied 'access to political processes': Lukes discusses how 'political systems' prevent demands from becoming 'political issues', or even being made.[11] In other words, despite their completely different theoretical perspectives on power all acknowledge the existence of an *area which is distinctly 'political'* (where issues, decisions, processes occur), and *which has distinctive characteristics* (like being open, or of restricted access, or organized so as to repulse demands). What is needed for the present purpose is a delineation of this area and its characteristics, before going on to discuss what kinds of interaction take place inside it, outside it, and above all across its boundaries.

There are various ways of going about this, but here I shall proceed formally (to facilitate the comparison of very different national polities), focussing upon the main organs of the State (for it is in relation to these that political manipulation has been defined), and doing so with special reference to governmental characteristics which seem important in relation to education. Obviously power itself is a much broader phenomenon than this — it is exercised throughout society, in areas other than the strictly political, and without special regard to stability or change in any particular sphere. Furthermore power is a different kind of phenomenon. Power is a matter of responsibility – it involves the capacity on the part of those who exercise it (whether individuals or collectivities) to have acted differently. What will be delineated here is *not* 'who governs' (in its broadest sense, meaning who takes decisions, makes non-decisions, or manipulates), but rather the structure of governments, which is not a matter of responsibility but of past historical determination.

A simple formal classification in terms of degrees of governmental closure seems adequate here for differentiating between different political structures at different times. Closure is defined and identified by the accessibility of the main organs of government. Such organs are considered inaccessible if socially significant parties can make no use of them and are systematically turned down by them, if such organs give no hearing to issues held important by these groups, or if such organs operate coercively or manipulatively to exclude these parties, their issues, or their interests. Sometimes it is relatively easy to establish accessibility, sometimes the empirical problems are exceedingly difficult, but these practical questions will be taken up later in relation to the countries examined. The main organs of national government are thus taken to delineate the central political arena and its degree of closure is the main structural characteristic to be accentuated: because our interest is centred on the manipulation of the former it is their manipulability which is stressed. Clearly the main organs of government will be very different in various countries, and even if they share a similar degree of closure they may vary in terms of other structural characteristics (extensiveness, hierarchy, differentiation etc.). To this one must be constantly alert and ready to advance supplementary grounded hypotheses for future testing. Nevertheless, it seemed preferable to begin with a simple form of classification which is comparative, minimalistic, and problem oriented (as well as being susceptible of later refinement), rather than putting forward or reproducing complex, abstract political typologies.

In these broad terms three types of State frameworks are distinguished:

A. The impenetrable political centre
B. The semi-permeable political centre
C. The accessible political centre

The three different degrees of accessibility are expected to affect the volume and kinds of educational demands which are successfully negotiated through political manipulation. In other words, the higher the penetrability of the political structure the greater the number of parties to gain redress for their educational grievances and the broader the range of changes introduced in centralized systems. For *in practice* Dahl is right in asserting that where *change* is concerned 'a political issue can hardly be said to exist unless it commands the attention of a significant segment of the political stratum'.[1 2] Where he is wrong is in assuming that this capacity to command attention is universal (that nearly any group can make itself heard in decision-making) rather than being problematic. Change does depend on accessibility, but access varies with political structure and only from an ideological position can it be taken as given. The social distribution of this capacity to command political attention differs from time to time and from country to country, according to degrees of governmental closure. Here it is anticipated that:

A. With an impenetrable political centre, only sub-sections of the governing elite will be able to *negotiate* educational demands by political manipulation.
B. With a semi-permeable political centre, sub-sections of the governing elite together with government supporters will be able to *negotiate* educational demands by political manipulation.
C. With an accessible political centre, governmental opponents too will be able to *negotiate* educational demands by political manipulation.

Elite Relations

The structure of governing elites is something which, it has been argued, should not be conflated with the type of State framework with which it co-exists. Relations among such elites are variable: at one extreme they may display unity, homogeneity and superimposition (sharing the same background, similar or compatible interests and consciousness of belonging and working together), at the other extreme they may be heterogeneous in origin, have cross-cutting affiliations and pursue disparate goals. Potentially both kinds of elite relations can be found in conjunction with *each type* of political centre outlined above. However, there are at least two reasons why it is important *to examine* governing elites and the State framework in which they operate, in association with one another.

Firstly, governing elites always have the capacity to command political attention (they merely differ in the extent to which this is exclusive to them alone). Because of this, elite relations everywhere exert an influence on the kinds of educational changes which are introduced or blocked. Obviously this influence is most crucial where the political centre is impenetrable, because then the governing elite alone constitutes the restricted circle of those with direct access to decision-making organs. Under these circumstances the type and diversity of educational change sought (or the extent to which existing educational practice is defended) will be highly dependent on the relations between sub-elites, their relative independence from one another, and the extent of their unanimity about educational goals. It seems likely that the greater the homogeneity of the governing elite, the more standardized and undifferentiated will be any educational reforms introduced. Lack of unity, homogeneity and superimposition between sub-elites, on the other hand, encourages a more diversified educational policy. However, it also seems to be the case that often the effects of their divergent educational interests can be to block change, especially where the different sections are evenly balanced. Finally, it must not be forgotten that governing elites who are divided on decision-making may be united on non-decision-making. For example, military and civil service heads can seek very dissimilar types of curriculum without any disagreement about which class of people should receive either kind of instruction. Empirically one of the greatest problems of analyzing elite relations is thus to tease out and stress the quiet areas of educational accord as well as accentuating the blatant conflicts over policy.

Secondly, relations among the governing elite are important because of their repercussions on the political structure itself. Political scientists have often drawn attention to the role of united elites in maintaining (or trying to maintain) closed political centres, whereas disunited elites, seeking external support to further their designs against other sections of government, may broaden the arena of decision-making by devices like franchise reform. Over time the effect of such struggles can reduce the closure of the political centre from A to B and even to C. Equally a movement towards increasing closure (C –> B –> A) can result from growing solidarity amongst the governing elite, the most dramatic example of which being when it grants itself emergency powers. All of this represents the dynamic aspect of the relationship between governing elites and political structures. Its main implication is that the classification presented here is a static device which only captures the political state of affairs at one moment in time. If the same countries are compared at different periods, they are very likely to change category with regard to closure. It will not be possible to explore the complex interaction which produced these transformations, for this would involve a full-scale political analysis which is outside the scope of this study. All that can be done is to take account of these changes in the political centres over time (rather than explaining them), and to do so by using the classificatory scheme as a template which is moved longitudinally through the political histories of the four countries. This has the effect of dividing a nation's past into periods when its political centre was of the A, B or C variety. In this way it becomes possible to compare countries *at the same date*, and also to ask important questions about patterns of educational interaction and change when different countries displayed similar degrees of closure *at different times*.

The Structure of Educational Interest Groups

Already in discussing elite relations one relevant aspect of social structure has been touched upon, but where interaction patterns are concerned the other side of the coin is equally crucial — namely, the nature and relationships of educationally discontented parties outside the political arena. As in Part 1, dissatisfaction is not interpreted in a narrow behavioural sense (those who voice grievances and advocate alternative policies): it can remain latent and covert, rooted in objective contradictions of educational interest. However, just as then our concern was with the oppositional groups to which it gave rise, so now it is with the manipulative political action that it engenders. Of particular importance is the nature and intensity of attempts to engage in political manipulation and the conditions under which it will be successful in producing educational change. Once again it is a combination of structurally conditioned and independent factors which govern the emergence of strong interest groups, committed to reform.

The intensity of manipulative action, that is the extent to which groups pursuing educational change (or defending the status quo) exert pressure on the political centre, appears to depend on two major characteristics: the relative superimposition of dissatisfied parties and the degree of organization attained by them. For manipulative action to be effective, dissatisfaction must be shared and organized. These two elements of course interact with one another. Even a small pressure group organization can, through propaganda and publicity, heighten the significance of superimposition by making (congruent) latent grievances manifest. Analogous processes of consciousness-raising have been witnessed recently in the black movement and the women's movement, and in both cases its effectiveness derived from stressing that racial/sexual discrimination was superimposed on power, status and economic disadvantages. Thus groups which cumulate a series of grievances (or advantages) among their members seem more likely to generate and sustain effective organizations than others where cross-cutting interests and allegiances can vitiate concerted educational action. In the latter case the divergence of non-educational interests can weaken or even destroy the educational organization itself, through in-fighting, conflict over priorities and through schism, all of which distract and detract from the application of political pressure.

At this point, the discussion of the structuration of support and opposition meets and merges with the general sociological debate about the social structure of developing societies, for in France and Russia we are now dealing with industrializing nations. As I have detailed elsewhere,[13] this debate is basically polarized between those stressing convergence towards a unidimensional pattern of stratification and those accentuating divergence and multi-dimensionality. The former describe or anticipate a general growth in superimposition of interests (class, status, and power) throughout society, and usually see in this an increased potential for profound social conflict: the latter stress the development of cross-cutting interests and allegiances which to them makes a polarized confrontation increasingly unlikely.

The intention here, in advancing a series of propositions about *educational* interaction, has been to remain neutral in this debate. On the one hand, neutrality is maintained because none of the propositions are themselves predicated on either of the above sets of assumptions about social stratification. Once again, as in our analysis of the first cycle, if either position is correct, whether in general or for a particular country at a given time, this will show up and can then supplement the present analytical framework. Thus, for example, if class analysis alone is sufficient to account for the pattern of interaction in all parts of the superstructure, this will become apparent in the educational sphere since the line-up for political manipulation will reflect class divisions. Were this to prove the case for class analysis or any other kind of stratification theory, then links could be forged between it and this more modest attempt to theorize about interaction and change in one particular institution. As in Part 1, this is seen as a reciprocal relationship between the two types of theory. To pursue the case of class analysis, Rex has perceptively stated that the real problem about elites is 'the problem of those who actually exercise power of command, *given* the existence of class interests of one kind or another which are being defended'.[14] The same, of course, can be said about the organization of opposition – 'nowhere in Europe can party politics be read as a straightforward translation of class issues on to the political state'.[15] And this point about *who* really exercises or contests control is pertinent in each institutional sphere. Without this specification, class or any other form of stratification analysis remain at too high a level of generality to give significant purchase on the intricacies of institutional stability and change. It is for these reasons that the present theory is stated in the guarded language of neutrality. The vocabulary of elites, groups, and parties allows for the discovery that they are undergirded by broader social relationships and thus for subsequent interchange between the two levels of theorizing.

At this point too the discussion of the structure of educational interest groups now links back to the earlier considerations about the nature of the political centre, at the start of this chapter. For whilst superimposition and organization are vital to the exertion of strong political pressure, the characteristics of oppositional (and supportive groups) are only half the story. Now that we are dealing with political manipulation, the relationship between external opposition and the penetrability of the political centre becomes equally crucial. Since interaction is necessarily across the boundaries of governmental organs (even if this consists in the overt rejection or covert manipulation of oppositional groups), any statement about the preconditions for introducing change must make reference to both factors – the pressure exerted on government and the degree of political closure.

EDUCATIONAL POLITICS

To concentrate upon political manipulation is itself to stress the common form of interaction which is supremely characteristic of centralized educational systems. However, the aim is to go further than this and move on to a more detailed discussion of *interaction within such systems* – in other words, to an exploration of variations on the common theme. This discussion however will not remain at the descriptive level but will attempt to go some way towards explaining actual events and changes in the two countries concerned. Specific patterns of interaction (i.e. observed in a particular country during a given period) are held to derive from the *combination* of the two factors already outlined – the penetrability of the political centre and elite relations within it, and the superimposition and organization of supportive and oppositional interest groups in education.

It is possible to state a number of broad hypotheses about such combinations in relation to educational interaction, but it appears more revealing to ground these in discussion of actual cases rather than to present them in a highly abstract form. They will, however, be summarized in this way at the end of the following three sections.

I. PATTERNS OF INTERACTION IN IMPENETRABLE POLITIES

CASE 1 RUSSIA: The Twentieth Century

From the foundation of the Tolstoy system onwards developments in Russian education have taken place in the context of an impenetrable polity – a structural continuity which has survived major political upheaval. The 1917 Revolution itself represented one of the rare instances in which the stringent conditions for a resurgence of competitive educational conflict were met in full. Social disintegration was wide-reaching, educational discontent merged with other more important socio-economic grievances, and the overthrowal of Tsarist autocracy also meant the transfer of educational control to the new political regime. However great the differences in social philosophy and political goals between Tsardom and Bolshevism, in terms of closed government they crowd together at the extreme end of the continuum. Furthermore the adoption of 'democratic centralism', as the doctrine underlying Party organization and action, in turn protected, confirmed, and reinforced the centralization of educational control. A supremely responsive system of education was as valuable to the new regime as it had been to the Tsarist bureaucracy, precisely because it was to be used for such different political ends. Thus the move from one impenetrable polity to another protected centralization in education, ensured that political manipulation would remain the principal source of change, and perpetuated a situation in which Internal Initiation and External Transactions would be of subsidiary importance as processes of negotiation. This latter point will be examined immediately, before analyzing the history of political manipulation in the post-revolutionary period.

Limitations on Internal Initiation

The history of Russia provides a clear illustration of the fact that a centralized system allows little autonomy for its educators, that this in turn delays the emergence of professional associations, and that when such organizations do eventually seek large-scale change they must pursue it through political manipulation because the scope for internal initiation is so limited. Thus it is worth following through the sequence of events which starts with teachers suffering the lowest autonomy under the Tolstoy system and ends with them in the same position under the Soviet educational system. By 1930 the professional interest groups were again tightly muzzled, after Russian teachers had mounted strong resistance to central control, thus highlighting the ways in which professional action is constrained when educators pursue goals and endorse values which are diametrically opposed to those of the central authorities.

At the start of the Tolstoy system the gymnasium was the special property of the State and functioned as the main bulwark of administrative absolutism. In it, the now familiar central controls regulated every aspect of inputs, processes and outputs, with the State Maturity certificate giving the bureaucracy overall leverage, for 'the government guarded the final rites of acquisition with minute attention'.[16] The appointment of class counsellors in schools subjected pupils to political screening, and placed teachers under political surveillance, unless shared orthodoxy made them natural allies. However, the gymnasium was only a model and a base from which to expand the sway of the Ministry of Education 'outward over the realschulen at the expense of local initiative, downward over the village schools in competition with the church, and upward to the seats of scientific learning against the wishes of academic liberals'.[17] By reducing educational autonomy, Tolstoy aimed to eradicate the 'curricular anarchy and abdication to "local needs"',[18] which had deprived the Empire of a disciplined educated class — in other words, to eliminate internal initiation and external transactions. Despite opposition, restrictive directives were passed regulating realschulen on the same lines as gymnasia, controlling the training of rural schoolmasters, and finally undermining the traditional autonomy of the university in 1884. Members of the professoriat were already civil servants, but in addition administrative officers became appointed officials, University rectors were named by the Ministry, District Curators were given broader powers to police students and special commissioners began to supervise the civil service examinations — the university's main claim to independent status in the past. Yet from the beginning such moves provoked resistance from amongst the educated class, firstly from academics anxious to emancipate the university, secondly from those students whose social origins and political values gave them an enduring antipathy to State cadres, and finally from classroom teachers as Ushinsky's pedagogy[19] weaned them from bureaucratic formalism and 'prepared them for acceptance of a professional educational ideal'.[20]

Since the freedom of assembly was narrowly circumscribed, political associations were illegal, and professional groupings were closely monitored, 'the tightly controlled pedagogical estate lacked an organizational arena'.[21] Gradually, however, working through learned bodies, educational societies and mutual aid fraternities, the profession made headway in organizing itself despite official repression. The All Russian Congress on Technical Education (1896), represented the teachers' first national platform. The Moscow Pedagogical Association, formed two years later, 'became a meeting place for professors, secondary school teachers, school physicians and educational writers. It thus enabled one of the most tightly controlled segments of the civil service, the teachers, to share in the movement towards public organisation'.[22] In the next few years a variety of illegal teachers' unions based on lines of specialization, nationality and political belief were founded.[23] These associations marked the emergence of a self-aware professional class which challenged both the control and content of the centralized system. In sum they attacked the authority of the school director, who as a state official implemented the ministerial directives and ensured that staff complied with them. Instead the profession advocated the revival of the school pedagogical council as the decision-making body at this level. In terms of content they denounced the academic formalism which, enshrined in a network of central rules and regulations, dominated the gymnasium and, via the maturity Certificate, the whole educational system. Instead the profession sought a pluralist rather than an autocratic definition of instruction, a unified secondary school rather than parallel but unequal institutions, and the primacy of teaching and learning over examination and assessment for the State. Control and content were obviously related, for to attack the Maturity Certificate was to attack bureaucratic centralism itself.[24] From their earliest beginnings, however, the professional associations recognized that political manipulation was their only possible strategy, and soon realized that 'the liberation movement, of which anti-formalism was a part, would have to crack the political defenses of the regime and force upon the central authorities the decision to reform the schools'.[25]

For a brief period between 1899 and 1902 the internal negotiation of educational change seemed possible. Under the temporary political dominance of Witte and Bogolepov, both of whom were more concerned with economic growth than autocratic control *per se*, it appeared that they would concede some decentralization of control and diversification of content, and do so in consultation with the profession. But the loosening of the Tolstoy system proceeded too slowly for many of the educated class and the outbreak of violence in universities and gymnasia reinstated repressive policies. Its effect, however, was to reinforce the drive towards effective professional organization. For the first time this was supported by parental pressure groups, as fears for their children's safety prompted solidarity with the teachers after the Kursk gymnasium killings. The 1905 Manifesto of the Moscow Pedagogical Society, demanding freedom of the school from the police-bureaucracy, signalled the most important change in strategy – if the existing political structure made negotiation impossible, then representative government must be sought as the prerequisite of educational reform. Although the Ministry of Education suspended the Society's operations, claiming it had violated its constitution by abandoning pedagogical discussion for political agitation, unionization was not crushed by repression. The All Russian Teachers' Union, with representatives from 30 provinces, was now formed for the political pursuit of 'freedom, democratization and decentralization' of education. The demand for educational reform was now second only to, and inextricably linked with, the demand for government by Constituent Assembly.

In an attempt to divide the educated classes from the masses and to deflect them from the pursuit of constitutional reorganization, the government restored autonomy to the universities. This concession proved counterproductive as university quarters, now freed from policing, were used to rally political opposition which in turn helped to gain the October Manifesto conceding a State Duma and freedom of association. Although temporarily disuniting the supporters of educational reform, these changes strengthened the processes of professionalization and professional organization. Since the State had relied on orchestrating the teachers by manipulating certification procedures and backing these up by surveillance, its control had rested on selection and constraint rather than socialization and training. Taking advantage of this gap and of their hard-won rights, the professional associations developed teacher training courses which heightened awareness of special expertise at secondary level and increased solidarity between primary and secondary personnel. This ran counter to the State policy of selecting primary schoolmasters from primary schools, thus insulating the masses from the intellectual dissidents. Although the Ministry of Education clamped down on both kinds of activities, it could not stem analogous developments in unionization itself. For simultaneously the various teachers' unions moved to organize themselves at national level and to forge links between them. The Moscow and St. Petersburg Unions of teachers held a congress in 1906 to establish a nationwide organization of secondary personnel, in 1909 the first Empire-wide convention of town school teachers was held, and in 1911 the first All-Zemstvo Congress on public education. Co-operation between primary and secondary Unions dates from 1906, and despite the more radical political involvement of the former, agreement was reached on two common priorities — professional autonomy and structural decentralization.

The reforms passed between 1906 and the outbreak of war encouraged optimism among teachers about their prospects of influencing educational policy. It was in order to consolidate this achievement, which the profession had consistently held to be dependent on representative government, that many teachers supported the February Revolution of 1817,[26] and that the All Russian Teachers' Union sought the convocation of a Constituent Assembly to determine the future political regime. Firmly on the side of democracy, members of teachers' unions were hostile to the October Revolution and denounced it for being based 'not on the clean ballots of free citizens but on bayonets'.[27] As the Bolsheviks dispersed the Constituent Assembly, the All-Russian Teachers' Union proclaimed a stike which lasted months in major cities. When the resistance of teachers continued, despite a conciliatory pay award, the Bolshevik Party thought to end it by dismantling the professional organization itself.

Party support was given to the minority pro-Soviet group of teachers (called the internationalists), who were encouraged to secede from the All-Russian Teachers' Union. Lenin transformed the break-away faction into the State sponsored Union of Educational Workers (*Rabpros*), with which teachers had to register. The independent Teachers' Union was then dissolved by decree and the various pro-fessional associations in the national republics were disbanded by the new local authorities. Thus the profession lost the organizational means for defending its own interests less than a decade after having developed them. And this was only the start of a downward spiral of changes which wound their way through the universities, the higher schools, and primary establishments, undoing what had been achieved, replacing Party hegemony for academic autonomy, and re-instating political direction instead of self-determination.[28] The profession's capacity to engage in internal initiation and external transactions, which had just tentatively begun to take place, disappeared along with educational autonomy. Once again teachers were forced back onto political manipu-lation as the only process through which change could be introduced, only now they were doubly disadvantaged in having to operate through officially appointed organizational channels as well.

Limitations on External Transactions

In arguing that the stringency of central control reduces the scope of internal initiation to the defense of professional vested interests, it will also have become clear that teachers lack the autonomy necessary for responding to external demands. However much they may agree in principle about the desirability of changes sought by local groups there is little they can do except add them to the political agenda of their national professional association. Thus for all serious intents and pur-poses, external transactions with public educational establishments are precluded. Yet the very uniformity which central control imposes on its schools means that there will be a pool of people dissatisfied with the contents of the standardized curricula, selection criteria, and qualifications. For them, always assuming they have the resources, the private sector might provide acceptable alternatives. However, it has already been suggested in earlier chapters that there are good reasons to believe that transactions with private education are not able to offset the deficiencies of public instruction for most dissatisfied groups. The changes they require cannot be met, or cannot be met adequately, by the private sector which does not, therefore, deflect serious discontent away from State education. Frustrated by the impossibility of transactions with public instruction and the inadequacy of negotiations with private instruction, external interest groups turn to political manipulation as their only resort and main hope of obtaining the changes they seek.

The major reason why external transactions with the private sector are not expected to be very satisfactory is because private education is too controlled to present a real alternative to public instruction. Because it cannot become too different, neither can it provide the diversity of services necessary to satisfy demands frustrated by the rigid public sector. The constraints preventing diversification are of two kinds. Firstly, the direct controls that the State exercises over all educational establishments place considerable limitations on the freedom of the private sector in centralized systems. Secondly, indirect constraints deriving from the privileged position of public institutions make it hard for private ones to compete on equal terms. In systems with restrictive origins such constraints are mutually reinforcing, although the influence of one may prove more debilitating for the private sector than that of the other.

Tsarist Russia perhaps presents the clearest example of the ways in which central control prevented private institutions from becoming too different from public ones and penalised them for departing from the State definition of instruction. We have already seen (Chapter 4) how the principle was established early-on that the private school should be subject to the same curricular controls and governmental regulations as the public school, that it was placed under the same authorities and its personnel restricted in the same ways. Deviations from the uniform pattern required special permission and the standardized definition of instruction was closely guarded. Thus, for example, the authorities closed down the Armenian schools, and the russification drive among the German, Polish, Finnish and Baltic minorities restricted local language instruction not only in public establishments but private ones too.[29]

The second way in which private schooling was penalised hinged on its relationship to State schools and especially to the gymnasium. The Tsarist-bureaucracy kept the closest grip on this 'centrally standardized filter of the 14 class governing society'.[30] Preparatory classes were added in 1871, to give pupils a more uniform and controlled preparation than was received from private tutors, and central rules were laid down for entrance and exit examinations. The State thus stood as gatekeeper, commanding the passes into and out of the gymnasium and ensuring that this was the only route to elite positions in government and society. In particular the maturity certificate conferred certain rights on its holders which ensured the pre-eminence of the official prestige school. Until the end of Tsardom only this diploma gave access to higher education and privileges for civil service entry. Other public institutions could not attract parental support because they were denied these rights and even at the end of the century there were more pupils enrolled in gymnasia and pro-gymnasia than in realschulen, district, and urban schools combined. If this was the case for them, then the private school was hit even harder, for it conferred no privileges but had to charge a higher price since it was maintained exclusively from fees.

The private sector was thus caught in a nutcracker movement between the direct State controls, which precluded diversification, and the indirect constraints, which prevented competition. Whichever way private schools moved they were trapped. If they prostrated themselves before government and requested the right to grant the maturity certificate, they were condemned to ape the public gymnasium in every detail. In fact before 1905 only seven schools were given this right anyway, but having achieved it they became indistinguishable from the State school, except that they were a good deal more expensive. When this 'solution' was adopted the private establishment offered no alternative to the public institution, and could satisfy no demand frustrated by the officially standardized definition of instruction. It had been forced into the identical mould itself and the only demand it thus met was one for more of the same. Its sole function was to provide a second chance for privileged pupils who had been rejected by the prestige gymnasia. Yet if, on the other hand, the private school remained without State rights and attempted to provide something different, then it was condemned to inferior status. It could neither offer its pupils the official advantages of public instruction nor could it give them a complete alternative which might justify itself in its own terms. Thus for example the independent schools run by national minorities were not free to develop ethnic definitions of instruction. The use of regional languages in private establishments was only allowed providing Russian language and literature were also taught and that lessons were given on national (i.e. all-Russian) history and geography.[31] These schools could meet a certain demand, but only from those parents who put defense of local culture before their children's educational advancement and also thought half a loaf preferable to no bread. Thus, to derive any satisfaction at all from the private sector, a group had to care very deeply about something like language and to be willing to sacrifice the prospects of higher education and higher qualifications in return for it. Whether it moved one way or the other, the private school remained second-rate and could never aspire to the status of the prestige public sector.

This situation was only modified, not changed, under the pressure of revolution and war in 1905. Although more private gymnasia gained the right to grant the maturity certificate, they still had to follow public practice and although more private schools were permitted to use minority languages, they still could not issue valid diplomas.[32] At the lower educational levels private agencies together with municipalities were allowed to open schools, but unless they conceded public control 'their graduates were deprived of an official certificate of completion which carried with it privileges on entering military and civilian service'.[33] On the other hand when externs, who might well have attended a private school, were given the same legal privileges as interns at state examinations in 1912, the central authority merely sanctioned the widespread imitation of its own programmes and processes. Thus control of educational qualifications remained in State hands and was consistently used to enfeeble the private sector either by maximizing its inferiority or by minimizing the differences between it and the public sector.

Thus private education could not work as a shock absorber by satisfying and thus deflecting grievances about the official definition of instruction. Discontented parties who wanted a different kind of education, but one which they could afford and one which was of the highest quality had no resort but political manipulation. At the turn of the century conferences organized by all kinds of interest groups invariably turned political because so little could be accomplished without the permission of the central bureaucracy.

POLITICAL MANIPULATION IN AN IMPENETRABLE POLITY

A. The Framework of the State

A(i) Accessibility of the Political Centre

The impenetrable political structure established after the revolution was a product of the attempt to build a new socialist order in the absence of the democratic and capitalist foundations which Marxist theory had held to be indispensible. Although Lenin had made it clear in advance that he identified parliamentarianism with bourgeois democracy, the soviet version of dictatorship of the proletariat was also shaped by the predominance of primitive peasant agriculture, the exhaustion of industry after meeting wartime requirements and the threats posed by national recession and international hostility. The 'fundamental difficulty of the attempt to run in double harness the anti-feudal revolution of the peasantry with petty bourgeois aspirations and the anti-bourgeois, anti-capitalist revolution of a factory proletariat'[34] accounted for the disastrous early years of 'war communism'. Again from the beginning Lenin had accepted that a revolution would only be made by a centralized, disciplined, and therefore 'closed' Party, but it was only after the country reached economic prostration in 1920 that the soviets were relegated to a backseat and the Party assumed greater political and economic control.

The practical rather than ideological origins of impenetrability thus date from the elaboration of 'democratic centralism' as the basis of Party organization which was embodied in the Statutes of 1924 and the Constitution of 1928. According to this principle, lower Party organs were subordinated to higher ones and opposition of the former to the latter was condemned as 'fractionalism'. As a whole it was to be the leading part of society. To Lenin, dictatorship was exercised by the proletariat, organized into soviets and led by the Party. Only a change of emphasis was required for Stalin to maintain that in essence this meant dictatorship by the Party as vanguard. However, it was not the hierarchical nature of political decision-making or the extensive powers of State control over society which alone added up to an impenetrable political centre — indeed some would argue that these are almost universal characteristics of modern polities. It is because of three additional factors that it can be considered as such: the fact that access to governmental organs was closed to large sections of the population, the fact that organized opposition was repressed, and the fact that coercive and manipulative controls were used to exclude certain parties, interests, and issues from the political arena.

The first point hinges on the growth of Party elitism in parallel with the growing importance of the Party in the State. Already by 1925 the 14th Congress had turned down the proposal to co-opt 90 percent of industrial workers to membership in order to check bolshevik embourgeoisement. At that time, 56 percent of delegates were classed as 'workers from production' but by 1934 these had fallen to 9 percent, as distinct from those now categorized as 'former workers'.[35] Furthermore, the Party became more hierarchical and weakened the powers of rank and file, its leadership more permanent and professional and its proceedings less open, as annual conferences were dropped and triennial Congresses became irregular. 'The result has been to give unlimited power to the central party organs . . . thus the tendency, at least from the thirties, has been to make the party less proletarian and less democratic and to convert it into a centralised bureaucracy'.[36] Simultaneously, the growing powers of State were embodied in a new Constitution of 1936 whose effect was also to deprive the soviets of their original constitutional position, in favour ultimately of Party influence. Restricted membership and extensive powers are the two features whose conjunction led Djilas to talk of a 'new class' in this connection.

Secondly, the repression of opposition operated at two levels and was doubly effective because of it. Not only was there the overt and well known embargo on independent political organizations but also a less obvious process of depriving potential opposition of any organizational base, whether national or institutional. Although the secession of national minorities, after the fall of the Tsarist Empire, forced Moscow to recognize the separatist governments as separate states, the populist or nationalist aims of these movements were subordinated to the dictates of the class struggle.[37] In practice this meant the intervention of the Red Army, the formation of the USSR as a federation of officially independent Soviet Republics, but also the careful preservation of the unity of State and centralized decision-making. If this protected the centre from challenges from the geographical periphery, tight political control over the major social institutions also precluded their use as sectoral bases of opposition.

Thirdly, the use of a series of coercive and manipulative techniques both repressed opposition and encouraged compliance. The role played by Beria's security police is notorious, but the control of information, ideological indoctrination, and manipulation of scarce resources were equally important. Indeed, the 'new course' on which the Presidium embarked in the mid-fifties, as a reaction against Stalinism, was more concerned with reducing terrorism, which anyway had proved counter-productive, than with lifting manipulative social controls, which were indispensable to State planning and therefore considered as legitimate instruments for social guidance.

The broad outlines of Soviet political development are too well known to need repeating and the details are too complex for discussion here. The above is only intended as the roughest sketch of the arrangements and activities making for an impenetrable polity in the post-revolutionary period. Attention must now be turned to its co-existence with a high degree of elite superimposition, for it is this conjunction which distinguishes the Soviet Union from the Second French Empire in terms of our classification of political structures.

A(ii) Elite Relations

Although the Soviet elites were to become highly superimposed and homogeneous as well as attaining a considerable unity of purpose, this did not really happen during the first decade of the regime. Certainly the construction of socialist society was seen to imply a close articulation of political, military, cultural and economic activities and hence an equally close co-operation among these institutional elites, but progress towards it was not equally fast in all spheres.

The problems of economic co-ordination were especially intractable. Although the 'economic backwardness of Russia had smoothed the path for the political triumph of the revolutionaries, since they had been opposed only by the survivals of an obsolete feudalism and by an undeveloped and still inefficient capitalism',[38] the fact remained that the peasantry formed 80 percent of the population and the country was starving. The three years of war communism saw the concentration and centralization of industrial control, which placed its direction in the hands of the Party. Simultaneously, however, an intensification of peasant unrest took place with the abolition of the market economy in agriculture and the requisitioning of grain.

The need to retain peasant allegiance, essential to the continuation of 'proletarian' rule and to capital accumulation for industrial take-off, prompted the tactical retreat into the 'new economic policy'. This return to limited private enterprise was a concession to the peasantry in order to increase agricultural output, which in turn would boost industrial production. It was this major discontinuity between the type of political and economic control which prompted Lenin's sarcastic comment that the socialist revolution had already been achieved – the political half in Russia and the material half in Germany, as state monopoly capitalism. The problem of how to end this retreat, to transcend the age old urban-rural divide and to introduce a new economic structure, was complicated by political divisions about whether this was an indigenous problem at all, or whether its solution was not contingent upon world revolution. It was only after Lenin's death and the termination of a series of inter-Party controversies (against Trotsky, Zinoviev and Bukharin), that Stalin ended the retreat and initiated a new strategy of economic planning including the imperative co-ordination of agriculture.

The policies adopted from 1928 onwards all stemmed from the doctrine of 'socialism in one country' (adopted by the 14th Party Conference in 1925), and together they spelt a tightening of links between institutional elites. This doctrine asserted that the Soviet Union could accomplish socialist reconstruction 'given a long-term policy of building up the resources of Russia so that she would eventually be strong enough to direct world revolution instead of being dependent upon it. But to carry out such a policy it would be necessary greatly to accentuate the pace at which industrialization was proceeding; and this, in turn, would call for a tightening of government control'.[39] Essentially this consisted in the extension of State control over all those institutional operations required to make the command economy work. In turn this meant that their respective elites must not function independently in pursuit of discrete sectoral aims and interests.

The crucial variable in Soviet planning was the percentage of investment goods then reinvested in the production of the means of production. Ploughing resources back into heavy industry[40] meant counteracting market forces (favouring consumption) in order to (a) increase independence from capitalist markets, (b) strengthen military capacity, and (c) improve standards of living. But rapid industrial growth created an urban workforce which trebled in three decades and had to be fed. Yet low factory wages, (set low to reduce consumption and favour re-investment), did not give enough purchasing power to encourage agricultural production. Instead it led wealthy peasants to restrict the produce marketed in order to bid up urban prices. The policy of collectivization of agriculture, on which Stalin embarked in 1929, ended in the expropriation of the Kulacks – in other words the dispossession and replacement of the surviving, independent, agricultural elite. Furthermore, effective planning required a responsive factory system, whose component units were reliable in meeting the targets set. A managerial incentive scheme, primarily rewarding the fulfilment of planned norms, was introduced to this end, but it involved enlarged wage differentials, the abandoning of equal pay as a policy now 'alien and detrimental to socialist production' and the formation of a new State industrial elite. Finally, the operation of a command economy under conditions of material scarcity involved a high degree of labour discipline, in order that production norms should be met without providing the incentive of corresponding improvements in the standard of living. Partly this was to depend on cultural agencies spreading an ideological commitment strong enough to induce deferred material gratification. It accounts therefore for the interpenetration of political and cultural elites and the strict curtailing of independent religious or educational activities.

Leadership in the military, industrial, agricultural, cultural and political spheres did not add up to a completely monolithic elite even in the Stalinist era, but it approximated to it. For party membership and tenure of high positions in the various institutional spheres were superimposed, common training and interests increased homogeneity especially as the elite distanced itself from the mass, and the sticks like the carrots reinforced a unity of purpose, if only by the purge of dissident elements. If elite relations did not change greatly during the post-Stalinist 'new course' it was because the recruitment, interests, and mutual dependence of elites did not alter substantially.

Despite initial pronouncements about increased availability of consumer goods, the greater concessions made to collective farmers, and admissions of paralyzing over-centralization, the structure of decision-making was modified rather than transformed. To begin with international political considerations meant a continued concentration on heavy industry, to allow for technical aid to the third world, the arms race, and Chinese modernization. Transition to light industry and an ending of the anti-consumer bias in the economy as a whole was condemned as a right wing deviation. As before imperative planning remained in political hands and no resurgence of market forces was allowed to undermine this. The limited decentralization whereby factory managers were given wider powers to adapt enterprises to local conditions, under the slogan 'planning from below', hardly created a sub-elite which could conduct economic policies at variance with political directives. Similarly in agriculture, the interpenetration of managerial and political elites continued, and if anything was increased in the hope of remedying the deficiencies of collective farming. Management was transferred to the local Machine Tractor Station and became the joint responsibility of its head and the district Party secretary. Although in 1955 each collective was given the right to plan its own production, devolution of decision-making was more apparent than real as local plans had to be approved by the MTS. Thus 'their members gained materially from higher prices and other concessions, but were more closely integrated into the party machinery of control'.[41] Hence the effect of the 'new course' on the major social institutions was to encourage initiative rather than to foster independence. Elite relations have remained close and are under-girded by common party membership. Not only does this continue to represent a considerable superimposition of sub-elite members, but also a shared discipline and a common, authoritative articulation of social goals and institutional activities.

A(iii) Structure of Educational Interest Groups

Throughout the post revolutionary era the emergence of strong educational interest groups has been inhibited by lack of superimposition among those seeking alternative definitions of instruction and by the restrictions imposed on any form of oppositional organization. Although the latter was a direct result of official repression, the former was only an indirect and a partial consequence of the political regime.

Superimposition was impeded by the co-existence of several unrelated divisions in society. The enduring importance of the urban-rural divide has already been discussed, but what was equally significant was the fact that this did not map neatly on to the cleavage between the old and new ruling classes. In addition, ethnic nationalism, highly salient after the civil war, was a dimension which effectively bisected the previous two. Here the limited superimposition which did exist favoured the governing elite rather than opposition, for in territories like the Ukraine, Azerbaidzhan and White Russia, the proletarians tended to be urban groups of great Russian origin. These were the groups which had opposed secession and benefited under federation. The nationalist movements, on the other hand, were sometimes bourgeois and sometimes populist, recruiting both from old ruling class and indigenous peasantry and frequently from town and country alike. Obviously the principle of *narodnost* (nationality) made for separate oppositional groupings and these were as important in educational conflict as in political struggle, for each generally involved a mixture of linguistic, religious and ethnic factors whose distinctiveness the movements sought to protect in separate, territorial systems of schools. Finally, adding further complexity to this picture were subdivisions following lines of religious allegiance, which sometimes coincided with the national minority movements (as in the Moslem case) or with urbanism (as with the Jews), but frequently varied independently.

Already the difficulties of organizing opposition have been touched upon, but in the educational field particular importance should be attached to the use of official instruction to discourage its formation. In the absence of freedom of association, educational interest groups could only be effective if they could use some existing organization as a 'carrier'. Given State domination of the major institutional bases, religious organizations were the only possibility. Although these had been repudiated by the regime they still remained in existence. However, the Orthodox Church which had most to offer in terms of a strong national organization was also the least acceptable to opposition because it had been compromised by its relations with Tsardom. Indeed its capacities for serving the new Caesar were exploited by government during the second world war.[42] That left the Protestant Churches which initially had been 'less curtailed in both educational work and civic activities because their memberships have not been large and because, also, they have been persecuted under the old regime'.[43] To a limited extent they have functioned as a focus for opposition, but in proportion have attracted repressive measures. However, their impact in the educational field has been particularly weak, partly because membership has remained low and partly because of the enduring ban on formal religious instruction. When there are difficulties in organizing opposition, this frequently means that grievances are given institutional rather than associational expression. Here this is not the case to any significant degree, in view of the tight relations between institutional elites already discussed.

B. Educational Interaction

B(i) At the Political Centre

When elites are closely related it seems improbable that their inter-action will block educational change: instead the more likely pattern is the introduction of packages of changes intended to serve the common interests of the elite at any time. What is contained in the packages will depend upon shifting elite priorities at various times. Ultimately their definition will depend on 'judgements of appropriateness', made in the light of general ideological convictions and assessments of the prevailing situation. However, in this type of polity the high-level elite inter-actions which produce policy changes tend to remain obscure because they rarely take place publicly. In the Soviet Union it is clear that educational change follows changes in elite leadership at the highest level. However, the interpersonal relations behind struggles for leader-ship remain matters of speculation — the key to high politics blocks the keyhold in impenetrable political structures. What can be done is to follow through the educational consequences of changes in leadership and the processes through which they are implemented. On this basis three major phases can be distinguished after the Provisional govern-ment had placed all schools under the control of the Ministry of Public Instruction.

The first phase, covering the initial decade of the new regime, saw the party acquiring the power to initiate educational policy and founding a series of organs, including the Komsomol, to ensure its execution. The Eighth Congress (1919) formulated the programme for a united labour school for all, with formal teaching linked to productive labour. Lenin himself signed the RSFSR regulations throwing open higher education in order to promote the 'proletarianization of the universities'. This progressive policy was dominated by the political need for mass literacy,[44] the social commitment to egalitarianism, and the conviction that economic and administrative skills could be 'per-formed by every literate person'.[45]

The second phase opens with a series of Party purges and the growing dissatisfaction of the new leadership with education, which Stalin viewed as violating the interests of State. Reforms concentrated on linking educational outputs to the planned economy. They were marked by their concentration upon vocational rather than poly-technical instruction, on specialist training of elite cadres not universal instruction, and on Makarenko's military discipline not Krupskaya's more child-centred 'pedology'. Because of its importance to economic policy, the aim was to subordinate all higher education to the Moscow centre and all vocational and Technical instruction to the Federal Ministry of Labour Reserves. Few attempts were made to maintain a facade of Ministerial independence in the constituent Republics, and party leaders were equally unapologetic about the restoration of examinations, offical textbooks, and degrees.

The third phase begins under Khruschev's direction in 1956. The dominant objective of the new leadership was 'to keep the Soviet school system on a balanced track and to reconcile as much as they can the conflicting demands of 'education for all' and 'education for the elite'.[46] Their general concern was to re-establish the connection between school and work at all levels and to improve the specialized skills available to the State, whilst preventing the crystallization of a privileged new class. Once again it is important to note 'that Party leadership, not the Ministries of Education and Culture or the educational profession made these decisions'.[47]

However, in the destalinization era some of the manoeuvrings which shaped legislation became more visible, and perhaps too tensions within the elite became more pronounced during the thaw. Debate and disagreement in the *Teacher's Gazette* and *Pravda* surrounded the reforms, and especially the controversial notion of special schools for those possessing scientific talent, with 'politicians' condemning its undemocratic and contradictory nature in a plan intended to instill a love of physical labour in all Soviet youth. On the other hand, as far as the general aim was concerned, 'the reform, with implications for lowering standards and cutting off the flow of elite education, was alarming to those who felt that industrial production must continue to enjoy priority or that the interests of their class were threatened by denying their children special educational opportunity. As a result of the opposition by what could be termed loosely the intellectual classes, the very outcome of the reform was modified'.[48] The practical effects of reaction and counter-reaction will be traced in the next section.

What remains to be assessed here is how far professional groups or external interest groups could play a part in shaping policy or whether this was exclusively an elite concern, even in the last phase. Here most commentators appear agreed that the hierarchical structure of educational administration ensured the transmission of élite decisions throughout the system, and the following is a fairly representative statement of this general view.

Educational policy in the Soviet Union is determined by a relatively small group and is filtered down through succeedingly larger administrative units until it is finally put into practice at the local school level. Modifications of existing policy or innovations begin in the Central Committee of the Communist Party and are transmitted to the Council of Ministers of the Supreme Soviet of the USSR for legal action. The Council of Ministers then issues instructions to the ministeries of education in the 15 republics of the Soviet Union ... The RSFSR, the largest of the republics, usually works out the details for implementing the decrees in co-operation with its Academy of Pedagogical Sciences and the Academy's related research institutes. When the details have been developed satisfactorily, each of the other ministries puts into effect, with a few local modifications, the educational policy of the Central Committee of the Communist Party. In due time the Ministries of Education of the other republics receive the policy and plans for its implementation and transmit them, in turn, to regional, territorial, city and district boards of education. They are then given to directors of local schools, who are responsible for working with their assistants and teachers to see that the policy is finally put into operation.[49]

Central policy is protected against substantial erosion or modification, because the Party which is the initiator, operates in many ways as the executor too. Thus, for example, in 1956 ten Ministers of Education in the Republics were also members of Party central committees.[50] In addition the Party 'operates in parallel to the machinery of government. This ensures a further degree of vertical control, from the Central Committee's Department of Education, Higher Schools and Science right down to the powerful Party and Komsomol (youth league) branches in the institutions themselves. Horizontally, the party maintains links with branches in the locality outside the institution'.[51] Although these views on the downward flow of directives appear to be substantially correct, a complete discussion of political manipulation as a process of educational change involves asking two further questions about the role of professional and external interest groups. The first concerns whether they can exert a negative, obstructive influence on policy, even if a more positive role is denied them. The second asks whether the Party machinery itself cannot accommodate an upward flow of professional and local pressures, which thus become influential in shaping policy?

B(ii) Professional Interest Groups

Descriptions of individual educational institutions, especially during the second two phases, invariably stress that teaching personnel 'have only limited autonomy in reaching day to day operational decisions. Such decisions are merely tools in the implementation of certain aspects of educational policy, and the overall educational effort remains centrally co-ordinated and centrally supervised'.[52] In terms of vertical controls, inspection and supervision appear to have been stringent throughout the period, and the position of the School Director in the administrative hierarchy 'is as pure a concept of staff-line connections as can be found anywhere'.[53] The staff Pedagogical Council in each school has nothing to do with legislative matters and its activities are limited to discussing the ways in which new Ministerial decisions may be put into effect. Furthermore, when working out curricular plans in conformity with central and District instructions, teachers also find themselves forced to co-operate with a series of agencies which represent horizontal constraints — in particular the Trade Union, Pioneer, and Komsomol organizations. Participation of the Komsomol in matters like student selection and assessment represents a direct infringement of professional expertise in favour of political orthodoxy.

Enmeshed in this grid of central and lateral controls, it is not surprising that schools and institutes show little capacity to block the implementation of policy. Individual establishments lack enough autonomy for their staff to use them to play a negative part in political manipulation. In so far as obstruction does occur, for 'even in a highly centralized system it seems that the size and complexity of the country, plus a fair amount of bureaucratic muddle, impose practical limitations on the exercise of power',[54] it is random, uncoordinated and ineffectual. The fact that some teachers fail to take up their appointed posts, that practical instruction has sometimes been interpreted as potato-picking, or that many school-leavers are ideologically apathetic, hardly represents a systematic and negative influence on inputs, processes or outputs. It is more a matter of the evasion of regulations by individuals for personal reasons than the principled obstruction of authority by professional groups.

Does this then mean that the profession never overcomes its subordination at the start of the regime and begins to play an active part in political manipulation? In the sense of an organized group able to pursue and protect its own particular interests during policy negotiations, this seems largely to be the case. The profession is constrained to work through officially appointed channels, and the Educational, Cultural and Research Workers' Trade Union to which about 98 percent of teachers belong, is a governmental instrument rather than an independent organization putting pressure on government. It functions partly as a control agency to 'transmit the demands of state for increased production, assure the satisfaction of minimum welfare needs, absorb and deflect dissatisfactions, and rally, insofar as possible, the workers to the support of the regime'.[55] This is underlined by the fact that its main organ, the *Teachers' Gazette*, is a joint publication of the Union and the RSFSR Ministry of Education. Furthermore since the Union covers all personnel working in schools, and not just teachers, its membership is not that of a professional association. Taken together these factors mean that the Union is only really free to protect the interests of its members in individual terms (defending particular teachers against administrative abuses) but cannot play an independent role in advancing collective professional interests except in the area of welfare provisions, working conditions and salary negotiations.

However, provided it remains within the confines of orthodoxy, professional expertise is recognized and its bearers can participate in policy formation. For the control mechanisms discussed are not purely repressive, they are selective and they reward satisfactory performance by promotion to posts in the inspectorate. A cyclical mechanism of administrative reproduction is at work and this means that 'successful' teachers make the transition from being controlled to doing the controlling. Secondly, there is another category of teacher whose participation does not have to await their promotion, (though it makes it more likely), namely those who are also Party members. In the 1950s between a quarter and a third of the profession were estimated to belong to this category,[56] and 200 of them participated directly in government as members of the Supreme Soviet. Since education is a national process of ideological reproduction, and teachers are the means of intellectual production, as well as its past products, it is not surprising that the profession includes a disproportionate number of Party members. This being the case it is equally unsurprising that professional leadership itself helps to contain oppositional elements among its own ranks, thus functioning as the politico-educational elite it is. The positive side of the same coin is that as a sub-elite it can bring educational considerations to bear when political 'judgments of appropriateness' are being made in the field of instruction.

Thus, in so far as these sections of the teaching body engage in political manipulation, they do so by virtue of their dual role positions in the educational and political structures. It is as part of the elite itself and not as an independent and organized collectivity that professional interest groups are influential.

B(iii) External Interest Groups

The factors which preclude the emergence of strong, organized oppositional groups in society are equally important in discouraging the crystallization of powerful external interest groups. However, a series of specifically educational constraints were directed towards the control and fragmentation of potential groups of this kind and these appear to have been consistently successful. By their very nature such constraints concentrate on parents and pupils; the more general forms of social control function to depress the amount of political manipulation engaged in by those less proximately involved in instruction.

The Parents' Committees which exist in each school (RSFSR decree of 1947), have a well defined role which is limited to planning extra-curricular activities, improving school facilities and other rather peripheric concerns. No overall city-wide organization is permitted so parental groups are fragmented school by school, town by town and republic by republic: since they are not allowed to levy dues among members they have no resources. As a whole they are thus kept weak and dispersed, with activities limited to those which reinforce the school or are not of great central concern. Pupils are subjected to a complementary system of socialization and are enmeshed in a network of youth organizations which influence career prospects. The maintenance of this tight official connection between educational performance and occupational placement probably has a more salutary effect than does the ideological programme, whose effectiveness has been found wanting throughout the period. Paradoxically perhaps, the very efficiency with which this mechanism contains expressions of discontent also carries its own backlash, for it encourages more and more pupils and students to seek longer and higher education because of the rewards it brings.

This build up of a dumb numerical force for mass education is the way in which parental and pupil demands prove most influential, because unlike collective associations, aggregate effects cannot be sanctioned or proscribed, they have to be taken into account. Nevertheless, the way in which educational constraints muzzle parents and pupils seriously undermines the foundations of *any* potential external interest group. Indeed their main significance is that they affect the majority of the population at any one time, and that over time most people simply shift from the category of pupil to the parental category. This under-cutting, together with other types of repression and a general lack of superimposition among the dissaffected groups, accounts for the small impact of national, religious, rural etc., interests on the politics of educational change. It is with some precision that the vocal educational protest of a few free floating intellectuals is termed 'dissidence', for this highlights its fundamentally individualistic character.

CASE 2 FRANCE: The Second Empire 1852-1870

The impenetrable polity which was a continuous feature of twentieth century Russia also characterized France during the last two decades of Bonapartist government. The Presidency of Louis-Napoléon involved a similar degree of political closure despite the complete contrast between constitutional arrangements and ruling ideology of the Im-perial and Soviet regimes. More important for our present purposes than formal differences in the nature of the two regimes are the sociological differences in elite relationships which distinguished between them. Instead of the strong unity, homogeneity, and super-imposition of Soviet elites, the Second Empire was a period of cleavage, animosity, and factionalism within the governing elite. This, as will be seen, prevented the coherent pursuit of a clear-cut educational policy during these years. It did not, however, preclude considerable consensus in relation to non-decision-making. A brief examination of Internal Initiation and External Transactions will reveal general agreement that the profession should not increase its autonomy by one iota and that the State must not abdicate any of its powers to direct public instruc-tion, thus allowing the special interest groups warring its boundaries to participate in its control.

Limitations on Internal Initiation

Events in Russia illustrate the fact that there is nothing inevitable about professionalization in centralized educational systems. On the contrary it is a halting process whose hard-won victories may suffer political reversal. In France the teachers eventually became more of a force in determining educational policy than was the case with their twentieth century counterparts in Russia, but this development of professionalism only began with the Third Republic. During the Second Empire the same official attitude of suspicion, coupled with surveillance, served to delay the emergence of professional organizations. Although the French teaching body has borne the imprint of centralization throughout its history, this has never revealed itself more clearly than during the Second Empire — in the teachers inability to engage in external transactions with the community, in the constraints curtailing the internal initiation of change, and in their pursuit of educational reform exclusively through national politics.

Napoléon's *Université*, created in 1808, was both an administrative structure and a secular corporation of teachers at secondary and higher levels. While the careers of its members were closely regulated from recruitment to retirement, as a body the *universitaires* exerted some influence within the Université. This distinction between corporate influence at the national level and lack of personal independence in the classroom is one of the most significant and enduring characteristics of the *corps enseignant*. On the one hand, the original head of the *Université*, the *Grand Maître*, shared his powers with a *Conseil de l'Université*,[57] which under the July Monarchy was made up of ten faculty professors with considerable powers over budgetary allocation, award of qualifications (*baccalauréat, licence, doctorat*), supervision of personnel, and the work of the inspectorate. On the other hand, the ordinary teacher in the lycée or communal collège, holding an insecure post with few prospects and living-in for the most part,[58] his activities dictated by the Baccalauréat,[59] circumscribed by the standardized curriculum, and supervised by the inspectorate, was thus left with no freedom to manoeuvre.

If the *instituteurs* in primary schools escaped central control until the July Monarchy began to prescribe curricula, supply manuals, institute inspection and begin teacher training, they were completely at the mercy of local mayor and *curé*. To work as secretary to the one and sacristan for the other was often necessary to supplement a derisory salary, but it increased subordination to these two types of village *notables*. The instituteurs were merely peasants who could read and write: until the mid-century they were still slowly acquiring the minimal characteristics on which claims to professional status are generally based — reasonable remuneration, qualifications, training, specialized roles and professional values. In these circumstances collective action was inconceivable, whilst individual behaviour was also closely supervised. Like secondary teachers they were subject to stringent constraints; their own dependence on the local authorities being paralleled by the statutory limitations binding on the universitaires as civil servants. Furthermore, in their capacity as citizens neither could play much part in politics, their poverty placing both groups outside the *pays légal* until 1848.

For all teachers the Second Empire was a period of increased surveillance, mistrust, and an actual recession in influence.[60] The inspectorate had already been brought under direct ministerial control rather than that of the *Conseil de l'Université*. In turn this body had been reduced to administrative status and its professional members virtually eliminated in favour of political, religious, and bureaucratic representatives. Ministerial power grew as academic influence was reduced and effective administration now stemmed directly from the rue de Grenelle offices, via the inspectorate to the lyceé classrooms and faculties. There central tutelage regulated the smallest details and teachers had, for example, to keep notebooks about the topics taught and exercises given so that inspectors could verify that the new restricted programmes had been observed.[61] At primary level Guizot's Departmental Normal Schools narrowly avoided supression on the charge of endangering social order, over 800 instituteurs were dismissed for suspected socialist opinions and administrative surveillance increased in rigour as general responsibility for primary schools was taken over by the Prefecture.

Standards rose among instituteurs in the 1860s; they acquired a modest competence as a body and shed their additional extra-mural occupations, but dissatisfaction with their position increased proportionately. In particular they resented their material situation (pay was roughly equivalent to that of Paris laundrywomen) and their moral subordination to mayor and *curé*, whose equals they now considered themselves to be.[62] They were becoming conscious of belonging to the same body, sharing common interests, and were starting to weld an ideology which was expressed through reviews like *Le Journal des Instituteurs*. Their desire for professional advancement led them to revalue the role of instruction in society, thus adopting a profoundly republican outlook which went hand in hand with their growing rationalism and opposition to the clergy. It was this desire to be freed from the incompetent tutelage of local notables which led them to look to the central administration to save them by introducing uniform payments, rules about lodgings and delineation of duties. Thus on the eve of the Republic, the instituteurs were beginning to push their profession towards the public service, believing that to become civil servants would guarantee their independence from local notables.

During the Second Empire the situation of secondary teachers had deteriorated in terms of qualifications[63] and recruitment, whilst pay compared unfavourably with that of other professions. They lived on the margins of society – as a socially mobile group[64] they no longer belonged to the people, but through lack of money, influence, and connections were not assimilated into the bourgeoisie. Napoléon's monasticism endured: until 1880 over a half were unmarried, one quarter still lived-in, those who did marry usually chose other teachers, and increasingly the new entrants to the profession tended to be the children of teachers.[65] It is this perhaps which explains their passionate attachment to academic culture – the classicism they had learned and now taught was their sole claim to esteem, it alone distinguished them from the masses and identified them with the elite. Perhaps too this marginal position in society accounted for the political reserve displayed by teachers at this time. They were united in seeking independence and self-administration for the université, but not ideologically prepared for corporate action at the national level. 'Entre la bourgeoisie et la peuple, le corps enseignant flotte encore, et son isolement dans la nation n'en est que plus profond'.[66]

Limitations on External Transactions

As in Russia, tight central control over public instruction repulsed external transactions and propelled external interest groups towards private education as the only place where they might satisfy their requirements by direct negotiation. However, the history of the private sector in France illustrates a similar inability to respond freely to external demands, but it involved a much longer and more complex struggle which was dominated throughout by a single party, the Catholic Church. Other types of private education, whether religious or secular, tended to be dragged in its wake, benefiting from or being penalized by, the legal and administrative provisions hammered out between Church and State. The details of their confrontation, which spans a century and a half and raises every important educational issue, are too intricate to be presented here. Instead attention will be focussed more narrowly on the Church spearheading the movement for freedom of instruction. Like the Tolstoy system in Russia, the Napoleonic Université was predicated on the idea of a State monopoly of instruction,[67] although such complete control was never approached in reality.[68] Nevertheless, the ideal of a strict monopoly did come to equal a severe monitoring of all educational activities. The attempt to throw off the central control over all schools was a struggle which advanced and retreated during the nineteenth century, making progress during the Second Empire, but suffering reversal at Republican hands. What the Church among others demanded, and at times nearly attained, was the withdrawal of direct and indirect constraints on the freedom of instruction. That it failed in this, as well as in its more grandiose ambition to dominate or destroy the Université,[69] accounts for the enduring weakness of the private sector in France.

The whole aim of the Restoration government was to gain the support of clergy without reducing the rights of the State in education. Direct controls confined the private sector to the lower levels of instruction, effectively compelled it to follow central curricula if its pupils were to pass public examinations, restricted its numerical and geographical expansion, and subordinated its directors to Université discipline. It was these unsubtle forms of constraint that the Church sought to overthrow, but although it made slight progress, the subsequent political regimes disappointed it by defending the Université. The principal bones of contention were the central authorization required by any private establishment and the *brevet de capacité* by which the State certified members of religious congregations to teach. This latter quarrel about qualifications, which was not finally resolved in favour of the State until 1880, involved the important question of whether private school teachers were members of a public service. The Restoration compromised on this issue; it safeguarded the principle of certification whilst avoiding an affront to religious authority by allowing the latter to authorize its own teachers. Whatever slight weakening in direct control this represented, it was more than compensated for by the reinforcement of indirect constraints. Above all the influence of State qualifications increased as the role of the Baccalauréat was strengthened in society. Its possession was a condition for entry to the liberal professions and enrollment in higher education, so that public secondary education became the vestibule to elite positions. It was this rather than the continuing obligation incumbent on their pupils to present a *certificat d'études* which cast private educational practice in the public mould. The only establishments unburdened by such constraints were the *petits seminaires* which prepared exclusively for the priesthood. Even here their intake was restricted in 1828 to 20,000, the precise number judged sufficient to ensure the future replacement of clergymen, without leaving a surplus of educated people who lacked the public imprint yet whose employment would be in secular society.

Forced to recognize the monolithic Université as a permanent structure the clergy under the July Monarchy increasingly sought to escape its influence rather than to impose their own upon it. Their new strategy, to demand freedom of instruction for private agencies, had a liberal appeal which recruited considerable non-Catholic support. Its violent campaign which exposed the oppressiveness of the Université temporarily concealed the fact that the Catholic aim was not a liberal pluralistic educational system, but rather the erection of a doctrinaire counter-Université. To do this it needed to lift central controls in order to consolidate a free sector based on a totally different definition of instruction. Headway was made at primary level, but with the return to power of the conservative coalition the Church was able to make its support of Louis Napoléon Bonaparte (for the Presidency of the Second Republic) conditional upon *liberté de l'enseignement.*

Freedom of secondary instruction was established by the *Loi Falloux* in 1850. Any Frenchman over 25 could now open a school, provided he had five years teaching experience and possessed the Baccalauréat or a Diploma given by a departmental jury on which the Bishop was influential. No qualifications were demanded of teachers, the certificat d'études disappeared and previous legal prohibitions on teaching orders were lifted. Nevertheless it was only the State monopoly which had been destroyed, not the Université system. The immediate aim of the clerical party was to weaken the latter by establishing a strong countervailing private system. Aided by legitimist notables who financed the opening of schools, the confessional network made considerable progress: religious colleges often damaged the communal college, in girls' education the Church gained a de facto monopoly, and the Catholic primary school competed fiercely with the municipal school. Only higher education remained, and the last victory of the clerical-legitimist party was to introduce liberty of instruction at this level in 1875. Freedom from direct control had thus allowed a private sector to be consolidated, one which was dominated by the Catholic church but legally accessible to any group wanting to establish schools outside the public system. But freedom had not been gained from the less direct, but equally important constraints. The Baccalauréat remained what it had been, the sole bridge to social and academic privilege, and even when higher education became free, the State retained control over tertiary qualifications. Thus 'si tout français capable et agé de 25 ans ou toute association peuvent ouvrir des cours ou des établissements d'enseignement supérieur . . . les étudiants des facultés libres passent des examens d'état devant les universitiés officielles'.[70] The standardizing influence of State examinations percolated downwards meaning that although there was now a substantial private sector, private education was not substantially different. In a century of political instability no government was willing to release its hold over qualifications and certification. The educational uniformity which stemmed from this central hegemony safeguarded political integration from the threat of *plusieurs jeunesses*. 'Précisement parce qu'en France aucun régime ne s'est jamais senti indiscutable, tous ont cherché à se faire consacrer par l'école'.[71] Thus the liberty of instruction was not synonymous with the freedom to diversify education.

A. Framework of the State

A(i) Accessibility of the Political Centre

The real beneficiary of the 1848 revolution was Louis-Napoléon: four years later the nephew was to restore the Imperial government of his uncle but to do so on the unlikely basis of universal male suffrage rather than pure military coup. The Interim Republic was over almost before it began. The conservative Assembly, panicking at an uprising of the Parisian unemployed, drafted a constitution providing for the direct election of a President by the new enfranchised voters. He in turn was to be counterbalanced by the rival power of a single Parliamentary body. Profiting from peasant illiteracy, Bonapartist loyalty and the split between Bourbon and Orléanist royalists, Louis-Napoléon won decisively and soon began to undermine the countervailing power of the Assembly and to manipulate extra-Parliamentary opinion by subsidizing newspapers, founding Bonapartist leagues, and organizing imperialist veterans. Ultimately it was the internal disunity of the Assembly (with the monarchists divided, the Republicans more afraid of these legitimists than of the President, and the Royalists themselves terrified by the 'red spectre' of the 1852 elections), which opened the door to Presidential government. The Assembly's final attempt to ensure conservative continuity, by cutting the electoral roll, allowed Louis-Napoléon to present himself as the friend of the people against the Assembly, to restore universal male suffrage, and with some military backing to gain plebiscitary ratification for personal autocracy. Significantly the new political organization was modelled on the Consulate, with all executive powers concentrated with the President (aided by Ministers, the Council of State and a Senate of notables), but clearly separated from the elected *Corps Legislatif* which was denied the right to initiate legislation or communicate directly with the public. 'Essentially the Empire was merely a subtraction from the powers of parliament and an addition to the powers of the executive.'[72]

Thus, like the first Empire which had profited from the deadlock between the Ancien Régime and the Revolution, this second round of Bonapartism was also based on the unlikely amalgam of 'plebiscitary and authoritarian institutions, whereby the dictator derived his powers directly from the electorate as a whole, over the heads of the warring factions of Left and Right. Hence universal suffrage was distorted to cancel out the forces of Left and Right and sanction the dictatorial rule of an individual'.[73] Thus, on the one hand, it was a government under *legal* but not *popular* control, because of the management of national elections and the deconcentration (not decentralization) of local administration. In Tocqueville's terms it represented an unstructured political organization with the masses standing in a direct relationship to the State: a situation inimical to democracy because of the absence, on the other hand, of secondary bodies cushioning the impact between elite and mass. Essentially the emasculation of the elected Assembly and the transfer of real political power to President and Council of State had the effect of introducing closure and preventing parliament from filtering popular demands. Effectively the separation of powers went further, for the frequent deadlock between government and assembly itself prevented sections of the parliamentary elite from translating its interests into policy. Given this degree of closure 'it became customary to think of democracy and government as two separate poles in politics, too far apart for the vital spark of democratic government to flash between them'.[74]

A(ii) Elite Relations

The effects of political closure were exacerbated by the heterogeneity of the governing elites and their mutual hostility. It is sometimes argued of nineteenth century parliaments that the absence of mass parties, of party discipline and even of meaningful party labels, did give members of such assemblies a unique freedom to control government and to contain political instability. This was only the case, however, if two conditions, both lacking under the Second Empire, were mutually reinforcing: namely, if the assembly itself was a legislative body and if its members had sufficient unity to exert consistent and consensual pressures. Instead a whole series of cross-cutting fissures fragmented the Corps Législatif, weakening rather than tightening its tenuous constitutional grasp on policy formation. It is true that the handpicked Deputies shared certain very broad class interests, common to the professional bourgeoisie, commercial bankers, and landed gentry, but these were more responsible for collective inaction on social issues than for concerted influence on government. Furthermore, these sectional interests were frequently at variance over particular policies, and more importantly still other structural and cultural factors cut across class solidarity. Culturally the two most significant were Catholicism and political tradition, and even these were imperfectly superimposed. At one extreme were the ultra-conservative legitimists, harking back to the ancien-régime, seeking monarchic restoration, but divided in their championship of the Comte de Chambord or the Comte de Paris though united in their Catholic orthodoxy. In the middle stood the counter-revolutionary forces of Liberalism, Bonapartism, and Liberal Catholicism, capable of alliance but very divided about the role of State in society and of Church in State. Thus, for example, Liberal Catholics repulsed both the Liberal conception of the 'omnicompetent' State which restricted freedom of instruction and also rejected Papal orthodoxy which limited freedom of conscience. At the other extreme the minority Republicans opposed monarchism, Bonapartism, any version of clericalism, and most forms of strong executive government. To this complexity must be added further structural cleavages which were not closely correlated with the above. The urban-rural divide acquired renewed saliance as the government pressed ahead with city, railroad and port building. Some deputies could be bought off with a branch line, but many rural members took the view that they 'sent their sons to the Army, their money to the cities and we are up to our knees in mud'.[75] Similarly, the financial involvement of government in such projects forced a wedge between conservative financiers like Rothschild together with thrifty bourgeois deputies, as opposed to the many notables on Boards of Directors who rated railway securities second only to *rentes* in acceptability. Such heterogeneity among the elite rendered their collective pursuit of a *positive* educational policy extremely unlikely, but at the same time in an impenetrable system it meant that their shifting balance of alliances became crucial for understanding educational change.

A(iii) Structure of Educational Interest Groups

Like the governing elite itself, France was far from being a homogeneous society during this period. No particular variable had overriding political significance in the alignment of social forces and this was reflected in the fragmentary character of educational interest groups. The existence of a variety of cleavages, some identical with those responsible for elite fragmentation, produced strong sub-cultures whose divergent interests precluded unified educational expression. Furthermore, the repressive nature of the regime with its stringent controls over freedom of the press, of association, and of local initiative, deterred interest group formation in ways which have already been discussed in detail for the Université itself. Its effects were not confined, however, to simply delaying the organization of educational interests, although this was undoubtedly one consequence of the prevailing political structure. The fact that before 1880, 'L'état libéral n'a d'ailleurs jamais été défendu que par les oppositions successives, et ses partisans ont rarement respecté leurs principes lorsqu'ils furent au pouvoir'[76] meant two things. Firstly, it implied a steady negative manipulation which specifically discouraged the *consolidation* of educational interests among certain sections of the population; the peasantry being the most glaring example since the enforcement of illiteracy and use of religious sanctions virtually excluded it from the educational debate. Secondly, political refusal to recognize external interest groups as legitimate sources for the expression of educational opinion had the effect of discouraging their *formation*. Especially at the beginning of the Second Empire, the *associational* character of interest groups tended to be depressed in favour of their expression in an *institutional* setting, that is within the official structure of authority. Thus the inter-relationship between social and political factors meant that such interest groups as emerged did so tardily, separately, were weak in numerical and organizational terms, and failed to touch large sections of the population. Typically, they were loosely organized around specialist Journals – like *L'Univers* (orthodox Catholic), *L'Opinion Nationale* (anti-clerical), *Journal des Economistes* (progressive industrialists) and *L'Atelier/Bibliothèque Utile* (republican working class. These groups showed no signs of superimposition until the end of the regime when the political structure itself began to undergo some loosening.

B. Educational Interaction

B(i) At the Political Centre

Compared with foreign adventurism, international economics and domestic development, Napoléon III took little interest in educational matters and viewed them as the most incomprehensible of his uncle's preoccupations. On the one hand this meant that imperial educational policy was constantly swayed by the political concerns, alliances, and problems of the moment, rather than by any longer term governmental design for the place of education in society. On the other hand this lack of involvement allowed Ministers of education considerable freedom to elaborate specific policy changes, even if they were consistently starved of funds and tended not to be men of political weight. In other words, within this closed political arena, educational policy was at the mercy of the fundamental constitutional tension between government and assembly and the unresolved issue of Ministerial responsibility. Ministers were thus the channels through which governmental directives flowed downwards and the views of the Corps Législatif percolated upwards – they were the focal point of political negotiation precisely because of their indeterminate responsibilities, but in the to and frow of political manipulation they were often unable to reconcile their own plans with the demands of ministerial colleagues, imperial directives and recommendations from the Assembly.

The educational policy of the 1850s was shaped by the alliance between imperial government and Catholic Church. Although divided on whether they sought a total revindication of the Church's control or merely wanted participation in national education, both ultramontanists and moderates could combine under the banner of 'liberty of instruction',[77] and make it a condition of their support for Louis-Napoléon. He in turn was convinced of the contribution religion could make to social order and believed Catholicism acted as a counterweight to republican forces. Thus he promised support in advance and immediately appointed one of Montalembert's party, Armand de Falloux, as Minister of Education. Using the device of an extra-Parliamentary commission (since until the 1849 elections the assembly was more republican than the government), Falloux, with Orléanist and some liberal bourgeois support, elaborated the legislation which was to bear his name. Thanks chiefly to the counter-pressures of liberal universi-taires the eventual bill was a compromise which encouraged Catholic influence at primary level, granted freedom for private confessional secondary schools, gave the Church a greater place in educational administration, but left the Université weakened but still intact. Like most compromise legislation it evoked more criticism than approval. The attacks upon it were initially mounted from the two extremes of papal orthodoxy and left republicanism but they eventually came from the centrist block of liberals, Bonapartists and Liberal Catholics which had produced the law.

On the Catholic side, as gallicanism dwindled and the hierarchy strengthened, religious opinion moved closer to the orthodox views expressed by Veuillot in *L'Univers*. The Church set about founding a competing system of confessional education and intensified its efforts to dominate the Université and enforce its views, without a shadow of the liberalism which had justified the freedom of instruction campaign. Veuillot's outlook could justly be characterized as 'quand je suis le plus faible, je vous demande la liberté parce que c'est votre principe; quand je suis le plus fort, je vous l'ôte parce que c'est le mien'.[78] And the Church made rapid progress. Politically the hierarchy was represented in the Senate, and in the Departments the Bishop was on a par with the Prefect. Administratively Bishops sat on educational bodies from the *Conseil Impérial* downwards and in their dioceses and the villages they could count on the educational vigilance of the parish priests. As the defender of property and order the Church was backed up by the notables on departmental and municipal councils and received financial aid from wealthy Legitimists. The multiplication of religious colleges which followed damaged the *Collèges communaux* and achieved a near monopoly of girls' instruction. The Church had made the greatest strides at Primary level, either by persuading the municipalities to confide their schools to the teaching orders, or by opening one in competition which scored because in general Catholic instruction was cheap and effective.

As Catholic intransigence intensified it was met predictably by republican anti-clericalism but of a kind which quickly crystallized into a specifically educational ideology – *'laïcité'* – the ideal of secular instruction. Its significance was two-fold. Firstly, it had considerable appeal among those who suffered most from the clerical yoke – the teachers – who as we have seen underwent dismissal, surveillance, reduction in salaries and restriction of their classroom activities during this period. Admittedly the vast majority, the instituteurs, were politically powerless, but nevertheless their electoral influence in the community had to be considered. This was interlinked with the warning that *'laïcité'* gave to the State about the fundamental antipathy between militant Church and integrated society. The doctrine of secularism underlined the political importance of teaching 'l'union, la paix, la concorde civile, au milieu des dissentiments inexorables des croyances et des Eglises'.[79] The lesson to the governing elite was that the superordinate interests of political stability were being threatened by excessive partizanship towards the Catholic cause. It was slowly learned, but once he had been confirmed as Napoléon III, government policy moved away from any relaxation of educational control whilst the rights of State had been guarded even in the loi Falloux itself. However, as professional opposition grew and the rich clientèle began to desert the lycées, so gradually did officialdom acknowledge that it was losing as much as it gained from the alliance.

Nevertheless, it took France's involvement in the Italian war of liberation, which reduced Pius IX's rule to the 'patrimony of St. Peter' and earned Napoléon III Papal denunciation as a traitor, to complete the rupture. 1860 thus represented a major shift in elite relations and educational policy. The Church increasingly allied locally with the upper class legitimists and the Papal publication of the *Syllabus of Current Errors* (1864) endorsed Veuillot's views and securely tied Catholicism to the national forces of monarchic reaction. The State now sought to combat the Church's expansion at Primary level, for to the Minister of Education 'the Legitimist-Catholic party has been able to perpetrate among the younger generation that division of castes and ideas which the unity of the University's education might have caused to disappear'.[80] In 1861 the Christian Brothers were forced to charge fees in order to reduce their competitive edge, and political control of

Primary instruction was transferred to the Prefects who, together with Université officials, prevented municipal councils from handing over their schools to the Church. No new male teaching orders were authorized, legislation restricted bequests which tied public schools to religious orders, and a series of attempts were made to revitalize public secondary instruction. 'The Catholic educational campaign was part of a political machine which in the long run could not be allowed to develop unchallenged by a government which based its local influence on a system of managed elections and official candidates. When the machine was put at the service of legitimism, it became a force to be combated openly'.[81]

However, the Church-State alliance of the fifties had three important and enduring consequences which effectively vitiated any prospect of educational change in the latter decade of the Second Empire. To begin with, the conjunction of two authoritarian powers in education had minimized both the differentiation and the autonomy of the system. Already by the mid-fifties Fortoul (the first Minister of Education) concluded that the best defence of the University from its critics and competitors was to make it equally moral, Catholic and respectable, thus increasing its appeal to the conventional bourgeoisie. But the price of strengthening the Université as an instrument of State power was the political violation of teachers' liberty of conscience by imposing an oath of loyalty on them as public servants. Fortoul thus became the most unpopular minister the Université was to know that century: the second consequence was thus the total alienation of the universitaires as a body. And the effects of decreased differentiation and increased alienation proved not to be unrelated. Fortoul had also sought to modernize secondary curricula, concentrating on scientific instruction where the public sector was relatively strong (because of preparation for the *grandes écoles*) and the Catholic schools weaker, thus appealing to the new middle classes. His attempted policy of bifurcation (dividing the Baccalauréat course and examination into a classics and a science stream which would replace both the preparatory classes to the grandes écoles and the shorter practical courses the schools had developed since the 1830s), failed largely because of professional hostility. The universitaires defended their classical claim to social status, the collège teachers opposed it for fear of losing their lower middle class clientèle who would only stay for shorter courses, and ironically their opposition was backed by the Legitimist Assembly for religious as much as traditional reasons. Thus, paradoxically, an attempt at polity-directed specialization was foiled by its formal allies and its official servants. But the nature of this reform highlighted the third consequence of the powerful Church-State alliance – namely that it had effectively excluded other interests, even within the elite itself. Although the bifurcation plan acknowledged the connection between economic development and scientific instruction, nevertheless 'the Saint-Simonian bankers and economists who helped to form the Second Empire's commercial and industrial policy had little say in education'.[82] It was another compromise reform, geared to administrative symmetry and overall systematization not to social demands or a recognition of the requirements of other groups. This, like the non-decision making involved in neglecting primary instruction and rejecting local demands for specialized professional training, indicates that the combination of intended and unintended consequences of the Church-State alliance strengthened unification and systematization by the end of the 1850s.

Each of these factors was to play its part in producing educational deadlock when Victor Duruy took over the Ministry in 1865. As a *normalien*, a mild-democrat and anti-clerical his appointment signalled the end of the old alliance but hardly heralded a new workable phase of elite relations. Having repudiated its supporters on the right the government sought to build them up on the left, but without forfeiting étatist educational control, or conceding its democratization. To Duruy this was an unsolvable dilemma, for however willing he might have been to concede to democratic pressures for universal primary instruction, industrial demands for professional education, and université clamourings for more autonomy, he could only count on the minority of liberal anti-clerical industrialists in the Corps Législatif. 'But it was, of course, support from the small parliamentary opposition, and here lay the dilemma which confronted him throughout his period in office. It was not these men he had to persuade, but his colleagues in the government, the officials of the Conseil d'Etat, and the conservative majority in Parliament'.[83] Various attempts at liberalization and modernization lacked the political weight to be pushed through, and it was the lowest common denominator of entrenched political, social, and educational interests which prevailed by and large.

The attempt to universalize primary instruction finished in a modest bill (1867) making it possible for municipal councils to abolish fees if they chose and an offer of the Minister's resignation. Mainstream secondary education bowed to the combined force of academic conservatism and political elitism; the profession was left with its traditional classicism intact and the scientific component of general education which bifurcation had imposed, was actually reduced – public bureaucracy was granted the precise degree of scientific instruction necessary to meet the requirements of government grandes écoles, and both were given the assurance that the needs of industry, commerce and the new middle classes would be met in a novel 'special' education, which would in no way compromise their above interests. Yet because of their exclusion from decision-making in the fifties and the imposition of a scientific Baccalauréat rather than an intermediate level of professional training, industrial interests looked to the Ministry of Commerce rather than Education for reform. The latter was seen to stand for uniformity, centralization and a pedagogic approach which repulsed practicality, whereas the former rightly appeared open to decentralized technical instruction which welcomed independent initiative and local differentiation. Precisely because of this, and the left-wing backing the *l'Enseignement Professionnel* group gave to the Ministry of Commerce, its bill died in committee, while Duruy's proposals were passed unanimously (1865), but without any budgetary allocation which might have allowed 'special education' to differentiate itself from the old special courses. Initial reactions to the four year course introduced in lycées and collèges were that 'the industrialists, merchants and landed proprietors who sit on our municipal councils have no reason to encourage this education' for it was not specialized enough for their purposes.[84] The modified version which allowed for local variations in syllabus and for pupils to follow only part of the course, failed to increase its attractiveness, largely because the fees for special education were no lower than for secondary education proper and no efforts were made to encourage transfer from the primary schools. The logic of divisive elite relations under the Second Empire was such that any concession to social mobility, via some sort of scholarship system which could have made special education work, would have violated the only dimension of political unity – the negative bourgeois consensus.

B(ii) Professional Interest Groups

The extent to which the Université was reduced to a purely consultative capacity at the beginning of the Second Empire has already been discussed, together with its importance in precluding the internal initiation of change. Similarly the alienation of personnel at all levels under Fortoul's stringent surveillance and petty restrictions has been touched upon. Nevertheless, dependence was not completely one-sided, for the government required some degree of co-operation from its teachers in tasks ranging from the intangible process of political socialization, through the execution of central policies, to overt electioneering. Close policing by the inspectorate and curés could produce overt compliance, but it also intensified antagonism which was ultimately counter-productive for the regime. Rouland, who became Minister on Fortoul's death in 1856, although himself a catholic conservative, recognized the desirability of replacing coercion by compliance. This was before it became a necessity upon the break with the Church and the withdrawal of the reserve inspectorate of the parish priesthood. Although effectively he only established new channels of direct consultation – an essay competition for instituteurs on the needs of primary education in a rural commune and a survey undertaken in Paris Lycées on teachers' attitudes to bifurcation – those methods at least allowed grievances to be transmitted to the political centre. When coupled with salary increases they represented an attempt to woo back the *corps enseignant*, and involved the signal concession of recognizing pro-fessional expertise. But this was a double edged weapon: it was extremely favourable to government when political and educational views coincided, but highly obstructive to central policy when they diverged. Both Rouland and Duruy were to find that the price of reduced antagonism was an increased power of resistance on the part of the teaching body. Thus after Rouland's inquiry he decided to take the heat out of the secondary teachers' opposition by conceding that common instruction in classics and science should be phased out and the old requirement of the Baccalauréat ès Lettres should again give entry to the Medical Faculties. Equally Duruy's more extensive 1864 investigation of university opinion on bifurcation lead to its further weakening. The universitaires were firmly committed to their guardian-ship of *culture générale*, and while the growing presence of science teachers protected the existence of the science Baccalauréat, the preponderance and prestige of classical studies was not undermined. Ministerial attempts to modernize classics and minimize Greek merely prompted the successful formation (1867) of the Association for the encouragement of Greek studies. Thus successive Ministers increasingly 'found that the opposition of teachers could frustrate their designs. The University had a real autonomy which could make it a refuge from depotism and which mitigated the apparent omnipotence of the centralized State'.[85] However, the negative nature of this influence should be underlined. It is not merely that the limited autonomy enjoyed by the University *happened* to be harnessed to the defense of a traditional definition of instruction which was endorsed by teachers and parents alike – although this certainly was the case. It is an illustration of a much more general point – namely that *in a centralized educational system with an impenetrable polity the only influence the professional interest group can exert is to block or obstruct governmental policy.*

B(iii) External Interest Groups

Until the very end of the Second Empire the organized interest groups which emerged were too divided from one another to exert concerted educational pressure on the State. Here cleavages based on class and economic interest were particularly significant in precluding superimposition. Although not alone in their discontent with the prevailing definition of instruction, the most important groups to articulate their dissatisfaction were representatives of the new middle and working classes. Both essentially found the system wanting in its lack of an intermediate level of instruction, but differed significantly on the remedies sought and the socio-economic functions these would serve. On the one hand, liberal industrialists speaking through the *Journal des Economistes* and on Fortoul's commission were already stressing the need for teaching natural science, mechanics, and design in the 1850s: with economic stagnation, the free trade treaty, and the cotton crisis in the 1860s more businessmen became concerned about the intellectual forces of production, especially in Northern and Eastern France. The report prepared after the 1862 exhibition by the heads of the *Conservatoire des arts et métiers* probably represents the clearest and most ambitious statement of these rather diffuse demands. It called for the differentiation of a complete specialized system of technical instruction with three levels, adapted to local needs and responsive to practical demands. As a corollary it should be free from the dead hand of the Ministry of Education, and this repudiation was seconded by the principal non-entrepreneurial organization. For, on the other hand, the more radical *Atelier-Bibliothèque-Utile* group which sponsored a *Société pour l'Enseignement Professionel* in 1864 also thought the

'University fundamentally unfitted to deal with the new education, since its instincts were towards uniformity, centralization, and the fossilization of routine'.[86] But here their common cause ended, for whilst the latter stressed manual labour, a training useful to workers, the union of school and workshop, and cheap instruction in the primary tradition, the former were more concerned with the technical induction of the new middle classes at higher levels, with a disregard to cost typical of the old bourgeoisie. Both accepted the need to work through political manipulation and sought the sponsorship of the Ministry of Commerce whose laissez-faire principles might allow more local autonomy and whose practical concerns might encourage more applied studies, but the ends they pursued and the interests they represented remained distinct.[87]

Though distinct, two factors encouraged co-operation though not superimposition towards the end of the regime. Firstly the growing alienation of private business from political autocracy increased entrepreneurial support for parliamentary government[88] and reduced one barrier to concerted action. Secondly the vigorous development of anti-clericalism provided common ground and encouraged 'a polarization of political and religious attitudes which was to continue in the seventies and determine the treatment of educational questions'.[89] It is not without significance that the Alsace region, where the presence of industry, the influence of protestantism, and the example of Germany were strongest, led the way in demanding universal primary education together with specialized technical instruction. In this context the *Ligue de l'Enseignement* gained 17,000 adherents committed to pressing these demands in politics by 1878. It had a popular audience and the support of the working class elite, even if the majority of its members and leaders were of the bourgeoisie. Differences in class interests and educational ideals had not disappeared but they had been diluted, and the League was partly the product and partly the agent of this process. The pursuit of laïcité in education was secular evangelism to the urban classes: the pursuit of practical instruction reflected the fact that the industrial classes at all levels were tired of their sons returning from school to be of no use to family or business alike. On these two bases, educational opposition became organized and effective at national level only by the very end of the regime whose policies had provoked it.

GENERAL PROPOSITIONS

From the foregoing analysis of France and Russia certain propositions can tentatively be advanced about educational interaction in the impenetrable polity. Patterns of interaction are the resultants of a parallelogram of forces consisting of political accessibility, elite relations, oppositional organization and superimposition. Specific configurations of action derive from different combinations of these factors, and the following hypotheses summarize the connections between them. Not all permutations of these four factors were observed during the period of educational history delineated by the presence of impenetrable polities in the two countries. However, the complete *absence* of certain permutations seems significant in itself. In particular, the impenetrable polity was at no time confronted by an organized and united source of educational opposition, regardless of whether it enjoyed solidary elite relations or not. This absence was neither accidental, nor could it be attributed solely to the malintegrated nature of the social structures in question. It was also due to the ways in which the consolidation of opposition was prevented, the profession was carefully surveilled and sanctioned, and certain interests were organized-out of the central decision-making arena. This leads to the first proposition about educational interaction in the impenetrable polity. The subsequent hypotheses have been arrived at in the same way and require independent testing against cases other than the two periods of national history in which they are grounded.

- The social heterogeneity of those who are dissatisfied with current education discourages the development of strong opposition to official educational policy: simultaneously, the polity actively seeks to prevent the formation of organizations committed to educational reform.

- The co-existence of a united elite and an impenetrable polity facilitates the smooth downward flow of polity-directed changes in education which represent packages serving the common interests of the governing elites. These follow changing national requirements, shifting ideological goals, alterations in leadership, or simply the collective hunt on the part of the governing elites for the optimal educational formula: at all events they are instigated from the top down.

— The contribution of professional and external interest groups to shaping educational policy is at its lowest when an impenetrable polity coincides with united governing elites. The former cannot even play a systematic negative role by engaging in a concerted policy of obstruction. The controls surrounding them prevent effective, co-ordinated action: teachers and academics have the narrowest consultative role as experts whilst parental and community interests are restricted to the peripheric aspects of education.

— Disunity amongst elites precludes their pursuit of a positive and coherent educational policy. It can lead to collective inaction, because of mutual blocking, or to sectional legislation favouring a particular elite alliance but dissatisfying other elite groups who receive too few of the educational services they require. Both add fuel to the political instability already engendered by poor elite relations.

— Disunity amongst governing elites allows professional and external interest groups slightly more scope to influence educational policy. The latter are not repressed by a solidary body, they can even receive encouragement from certain parts of the elite, and national associations committed to educational change may begin to be formed by different interest groups. In practice the major influence is of a very negative kind and consists in the profession obstructing the implementation of central policy. Political concessions made to increase professional co-operation tend to be counterproductive: small increments in autonomy, prestige or influence are used to intensify obstructiveness since they fall far short of teachers' demands.

— The stringent control to which the profession is subject limits association with external interest groups and response to their demands. Any small freedom of action or power of influence possessed or acquired by teachers and academics will be used for the advancement of vested professional interests.

II. PATTERNS OF INTERACTION IN THE ACCESSIBLE POLITY
FRANCE: The Third and Fourth Republics

Between 1873-75 France entered the IIIrd Republic backwards as the political arrangements designed for restoration of the monarchy became instead the basis of a system of parliamentary sovereignty. Its inception was a compromise preferred by most moderates to the white flag of the Bourbons or the red flag of the Commune. Even so the majority which in 1875 voted that 'the President of the Republic is elected by a plurality of votes cast by the Senate and the Chamber of Deputies united in a National Assembly' clearly intended stronger executive powers to attach to the Presidency than to the Chamber. In fact the opposite was the case and the next two years provide an example of the interaction between disunited elites gradually broadening the arena of decision making . . . the 'clash of social and political forces led, in turn, to a compromise regime which was designed by Monarchists, adapted by Liberals, and made to work by Radicals'.[90] The democratic political structure which emerged and endured until 1958, interrupted only by the wartime Vichy regime, provides an extended example of a highly penetrable polity. However, as the only case of this kind that we will be examining here, it should be noted that both the IIIrd and IVth Republics were also characterized by a number of features which are neither logically nor empirically associated with accessible polities. The slow, weak and fragmented development of political parties, in particular, must be considered as variable rather than universal features of political openness. In other words this period of French history represents a specific combination of the accessible policy with elite disunity, for which, unfortunately, our case studies furnish no contrasting examples involving more cohesive governing elites.

Limitations on Internal Initiation

From the IIIrd Republic onwards teachers made steady gains in professionalization until they became more of a force in determining educational policy than was ever the case with their Russian counterparts. However, as professionalization increased, cleavages in the *corps enseignant* strengthened[91] and added to the complexity of interaction in ways that did not have a chance of coming into play in the Soviet Union. Until the turn of the century, teachers at all levels enjoyed some increase in autonomy without making significant progress in professional organization. The most important sign of this change was the reinstatement of the *Conseil Supérieur* in 1873, as a consultative committee made up of a section of universitaires together with other interested parties. This change in policy was confirmed in 1880 when Ferry restored it as an exclusively academic council whose representatives were elected by their peers. In other words control of the Université returned to its original pattern, with the corps enseignant participating in its administration and able to defend their own interests. Nevertheless what had been gained, or rather regained, was corporate autonomy not the autonomy of the master in his classroom. He remained constrained by the battery of central regulations, requirements and prohibitions which prevented him from responding to internal or external demands. Teacher participation in the Conseil Supérieur was inadequate to alter this situation against Ministerial wishes. Changes of any magnitude (e.g. alterations in the Baccalauréat, in the timetable, in courses available at different institutions, or in pupil intake from one level to the next), generally required Parliamentary sanction. Thus, if the profession wanted to act as more than a vested interest group, if it sought a real voice in the central determination of policy, it had to go outside the educational system to organize and acquire influence in national politics. Yet this was precisely what the government was unwilling to allow from its subordinates. Only pedagogical societies were countenanced and when dissolving the first association of *répétiteurs* (assistant-teachers) in 1867 Rambaud, as Minister, voiced the doctrine that teachers could not legally unite to wield political influence against Ministerial policies. 'Il n'est pas admissible que, alors qu'un ministre sumet un projet de loi au Parlement, en vertu du droit d'initiative qu'il tient de la Constitution, il soit loisible à ses propres subordonnés de tenir des réunions pour le critiquer, de provoquer d'une bout à l'autre du pays parmi les fonctionnaires de son Administration un movement, des groupements, une action des groupes ainsi formés sur les membres du Parlement, pour combattre le projet'.[92]

For instituteurs the Third Republic was a time of unparalleled prestige, as rural France accorded them a place among village notables and central government a place in the national educational system, replacing the hated religious authority of the curé with the progressive leadership of men like Ferry and Buisson. While they willingly became the infantrymen of the republic in its work of national enlightenment, few instituteurs resented the fact that local tutelage had merely been exchanged for central control. Yet instituteurs had become civil servants and, as the State surrounded the primary school with its familiar armory of regulations and examinations after 1880, their duties and obligations were closely proscribed and supervised. As strong supporters of the Republic, it was not resentment which prompted the formation of departmental friendly societies, but a concern to provide mutual aid. That these inoffensive bodies which deferentially accepted the Chairmanship of *Recteur* or *Prefet* should attract political suspicion is an indication of the protectiveness with which central control was guarded. The moment the co-ordination of departmental *Amicales* into a national organization was suggested, in 1887, Ministerial hostility was sharp: 'à ce niveau, une contestation est possible sur les questions critiques des traitments ou de la direction d'école, qu'une autorité départementale, parce qu'elle n'en est pas responsable, peut facilement éviter'.[93] Jules Ferry responded immediately and repressively with a circular (September 1887) which categorically proscribed any national union of instituteurs;[94] Péguy's 'hussars of the Republic' were thus confined to barracks.

Hence for the corps enseignant as a whole, professional organization and political influence are twentieth century phenomena. Yet as they began to acquire them, internal divides widened and hardened. For the universitaires it was the dawn of a golden age of bourgeois acceptance and political incorporation. They were still a highly mobile category, threequarters coming from families which had not themselves received secondary education, and as demi-bourgeois were tenaciously attached to the prevailing definition of instruction[95] which distinguished them from their social origins. These characteristics were deeply scored into their first successful organization, the *Fédération Nationale des Professeurs de L'Enseignement Secondaire Public* (1905), an apolitical body which deferred to the authorities, repulsed links with aggressive unionism and sought merely to advance the corporate well-being of the secondary teacher in the nation. Centralization had forced them out into national politics, but once there everything encouraged them to play a moderate radical role. As *boursiers* not *héritiers* it was rare to find them supporting parties of the right, but as a group which had arrived and now had interests to defend, socialism was equally unattractive. This centre-left orientation was already pronounced at the time of the Dreyfus affair and it became fully institutionalized with the victory of the *Cartel des Gauches* in the 1924 elections. With 30 universitaires in the Cartel and Herriot (the best known academic) heading the government, this republic of professors finally authorized professional organization. The *Syndicat National des Professeurs de Lycée*, formed that year, signalled no change of policy but provided secondary teachers with a permanent legal agency for exerting political pressure to obtain the changes which they could not effect internally. That this capacity to organize had itself depended on a prior change of government was a graphic illustration of the crucial importance of political manipulation in centralized educational systems.

For the instituteurs the path towards legitimate organization was considerably rougher. Continued attempts to unite the departmental Friendly Associations at national level finally gained official acceptance in 1903, but since the Amicales were dominated by school directors, they did not provide an organizational outlet for the expression of instituteurs' grievances. After all, the control exercised by directors over their subordinates was the most proximate aspect of the broader politico-administrative surveillance from which primary teachers sought to liberate themselves. Recruited from the people and enjoying few privileges in their posts, a revolutionary current developed as certain teachers became aware that rather than agents of progress the role of primary schools was to keep the people in their place. Young teachers in the Seine launched a movement for *L'emancipation de l'instituteur* and in the same vein a group of Amicales published the *Manifest des Instituteurs Syndicalistes*. Between 1905 and 1914 the transformation of Amicales into syndicates took place in several departments, despite local reprisals and dismissals when officials invoked the law of 1884, forbidding civil servants to join syndicates.

The more revolutionary orientation of the instituteurs encouraged a growing solidarity with working class unionism and it was their support for the *Confédération Générale du Travail*, including its anti-militarism, which prompted the government to dissolve the departmental syndicates on the eve of war. By 1919, however, the majority of the Amicales joined the (now reformist) CGT and transformed themselves into the *Syndicat Nationale des Instituteurs* which finally gained legal recognition in 1924. In the SNI the instituteurs too had acquired an instrument for confrontation at the national level. Furthermore they had gained a national organizational framework which enabled them to exert a systematic influence on educational administration at departmental level — for after 1925 the vast majority of teacher delegates elected to the departmental councils were candidates of the SNI. The instituteurs thus obtained a corporate influence within the educational structure, somewhat equivalent to that which the universitaires already enjoyed through the Conseil Supérieur. Yet in the same way this internal influence was restricted to the defense of vested professional interests: macroscopic reforms had to be pursued by the syndicate, in affiliation with other unions, through the major political parties. Thus both sections of the teaching profession had been projected into the political arena in their quest for organization, and the centralized structure of the system constrained them to stay there if they wanted to influence educational policy. But the divergent interests with which it endowed them by virtue of their position in the primary or secondary schools reduced the likelihood that they would always pull in the same political direction.

Limitations on External Transactions

Once again the private sector was the only part of the educational domain open to external transactions, and as before the fate of the private sector as a whole hinged on how the confessional schools fared with the new regime. Opposition to the educational concessions granted to Catholicism under the Second Empire was built into the political composition of Third Republic governments. The gradual and general reintroduction of direct State controls reached a climax with the separation of Church and State in 1905. However, the initial policy of Jules Ferry was more concerned with the complete secularization of public instruction than the containment of private religious education. But though his own policy was one of educational partition, left wing radicals and many republicans pressed for one with more teeth since to them the Church should not have the freedom to socialize youth when Catholicism was not just a religion but also a socio-political doctrine. But even Ferry's moderate appeasement policy carried increased penalties for private education, for the gratuity of public primary education was obviously detrimental to any form of fee-paying school. This became crucially significant for the Church since the 1886 law chased them from the public schools and forced them entirely into the private sector. Because of this the total number of pupils at private schools doubled before 1901, but the burden of maintaining them and continuing to attract parents increased. For the indirect constraints exerted by State examination and curricula raised the basic problem of how to get parents to pay for an education which in many respects did not differ from what the State provided. The *Loi Falloux* may not have been rescinded but the confessional colleges run by Jesuits busily prepared candidates for Polytechnique and St. Cyr! It is these barriers to diversification which account for the steady decline in *secular* private education since the mid-nineteenth century. It could not provide enough of an alternative to make schools viable at the price, by satisfying those discontented with public instruction. This too explains the easy preponderance of religious schools in the private sector from then on, because once again for a group to derive satisfaction from it their requirements had to be non-academic. Only devout parents highly concerned that their children received religious instruction *combined with* roughly the same secular teaching the State provided gratuitously, could consider the investment worthwhile. Those, for example, who sought to remedy the undoubted deficiencies in professional training often made some initial use of the private sector but rapidly turned to political manipulation instead.

The separation of Church and State in 1905, making religion a purely private affair, had immediate educational implications. Supplementary legislation reintroduced many of the old imperial controls since both teaching orders and their schools required State authorization. Closures of uncertified establishments followed, and when religious orders were forbidden to teach (1904) they lost about one third of their pupils. The remainder were retained but only by the device of transforming private congregational schools into private schools which were officially listed as secular institutions.[96] As such their difficulties were twofold during the interwar years when republican pressures consistently defended the educational status quo. On the one hand, their financial problems intensified . . . 'avec le passage à l'éducation de masse, l'école privée peut difficilement subsister sans aide de l'Etat, sauf à ne recruter que dans les minorités privilégiées'.[97] Yet neither State aid nor an affluent clientèle were available on the right terms. The lengthy political lobbying by Catholics for *répartition proportionelle scolaire*,[98] an unconditional public subvention in proportion to the percentage of all pupils enrolled in private schools, was consistently rebuffed. On the other hand, they had great difficulties in maintaining high standards (because of their poverty) and in providing a real alternative education (because of control and constraint), both of which were preconditions for attracting parental support, especially if fees were high. In this they were torn, for the index of high standards was the success rate in public examinations which involved concentrating on public curricula, but this in turn subtracted from the time available for the subjects or activities making private schooling distinctively different. Thus, whichever way it turned, the private sector was trapped, snared either by standardization or second-rateness.

POLITICAL MANIPULATION IN AN ACCESSIBLE POLITY

A. The Framework of the State

A(i) The Accessibility of the Political Centre

Originally it was intended that the Chamber of Deputies, elected on direct male suffrage, should be counterbalanced by a Senate whose membership was biased towards the conservative forces of the countryside and a President who was an effective head of State. This balance was destroyed for good when the monarchist majority in the Senate persuaded President MacMahon to dissolve the chamber in the hope that through an election a less republican Chamber could be engineered. The plan backfired on two levels; a large republican and radical majority was returned in 1877 and its victory shaped the working of the Constitution for the rest of its long duration. The Chamber henceforth was the fulcrum of political power and it asserted a detailed and incessant control over policy and executive action alike. Presidential powers decreased accordingly, and by convention the holder became a figurehead, an elderly gentleman whose main duty was to wear evening clothes in daytime. Republican reforms of 1884 altered the electoral basis of the Senate making it more democratic, and representative of the larger municipal councils, thus undercutting the countervailing power base of the rural notables. Complementary reform of council and mayoral election procedures intensified the republican character of these bodies, and since the local Commune now became the electoral basis of the Senate, the conservative nature and influence of the latter was greatly undermined. Henceforth the real arena of decision-making was the Chamber: the constitutional balance had shifted away from the President and Senate, even though Senators still shared legislative powers with the Deputies. Executive power was now concentrated exclusively in the cabinet whose own existence and survival depended on majority support from the Chamber.

The fact that a large number of Party groups emerged, as might have been expected from the complexity of political divisions during the Second Empire, meant that 'every cabinet had to be a coalition of several such groups in order to get its majority support. Great power therefore fell into the hands of the centre groups, virtually indispensable to all ministries, and the marginal groups, whose adherence or desertion made and unmade governments. The Chamber became the great arena wherein the groups shuffled, bargained and manoeuvred: and the lobbies of the Chamber became the Bourse of politics. The whole centre of gravity of power shifted downwards'.[99]

The accessibility of the political centre was thus considerable under the Third Republic. Not only did the possibility of changing governments enable minorities to establish relationships with political authority and power, but also this capacity could be exercised *between* general elections. In the absence of strong party organization, the Deputies, selected and elected on a local basis, functioned as agents of local interests. Thus 'bands of independents or free-lance Deputies abounded in every Chamber. Lacking any wider party discipline, they reshuffled, bargained and voted as they pleased, and owed allegiance only to the constituents who had returned them to parliament... In a regime where the Deputy was intended to be the contrôleur of Ministers, scores of Deputies were abundantly free to exercise their powers arbitrarily. It was often boasted that every nuance of public opinion, however subtle, could find expression in parliament. What mattered more was that every special interest, however local and exclusive, could encumber national politics with its demands'.[100] Constitutionally and in practice all groups had access to the decision-making arena and all could seek to work through the shifting system of coalitions to negotiate their demands. Through the device of *inter-pellation* Deputies had a regular method of control over ministers and government policy, for it compelled ministers or ministries to justify their actions and thus to retain (or lose) the support of a majority of the Chamber at every juncture.

Certainly this degree of political accessibility and ministerial accountability carried a heavy price, for governmental stability was sacrificed to parliamentary control over policy. However, the fact that over 80 distinct ministries succeeded one another during the 70 years of the republic cannot be blamed on 'open' government, nor attributed exclusively to Constitutional defects. Much more accountable was the multi-party system which emerged — a weak fragmentary form of political organization which mirrored the divisive nature of elite relations inherited from the Second Empire. The accessibility of government merely allowed all demands to be conveyed to the decision-making arena — it was largely the fault of the party structure that they were not accumulated, expressed, and negotiated there in a less destructive way.

The history of the IVth Republic can largely be treated as a continuation of the parliamentary democracy initiated under the IIIrd, the two regimes merely being punctuated by the Vichy and Provisional governments. The new Constitution which came into force in 1946 steered a course between a Presidential system, as practised by both interim regimes and advocated by the right, and the single chamber system sought by the Communist party on the left. The compromise accepted was the old formula of government by assembly, modified by a weakening of the second Chamber. Neither the introduction of proportional representation and female enfranchisement nor constant experimenting with changes in electoral laws had a significant effect on the way the formula worked in practice. This may have been partly because these innovations tended to neutralize one another: proportional representation is usually held to make it easier for small new parties to gain a foothold, but, on the other hand, many of the electoral laws favoured large and centre parties. Whatever the reasons responsible, practical experience of the new Constitution in operation led to the verdict that 'the Fourth Republic is already dead: it has given way to the Third'.

Parliament continued to reflect with accuracy every nuance of opinion in the country, and theoretically the range of possible governing coalitions was considerable. The party system remained diffuse with a relatively large number of parties, which represented different facets of social cohesion, each obtaining a substantial share of the vote. Thus the accessibility of the decision-making arena remained high and a wide range of demands could be expressed and negotiated there, beyond those introduced by the government of the day. Indeed the best indicator of oppositional influence on policy formation is the fact that 30 percent of legislation passed during the IVth Republic was not sponsored by its governments.[101] The growing importance of the Committee system did nothing to mitigate this since members merely pursued their own interests whether or not these were hostile to the wishes of Government.

In this context the fact that parliaments exercised more control over governments than vice versa, despite a general increase in executive powers as a whole, had the same consequences for instability as under the IIIrd Republic — twenty-two ministries were formed and collapsed between 1946 and 1958. But the fundamental reason for this reversion to type is again found not in deficiencies of the new constitution but in the growing fragmentation of the multi-party system. These kaleidoscopic subdivisions, which intensified despite the development of party organization, reflected a basic lack of cohesion among elites and among other sections of the population. It is to both of these that we must turn in order to explain why such a highly accessible political structure did not produce an equally high proportion of the educational changes sought by different groups in society.

A(ii) Elite Relations

The dominant feature of both Republics was the failure to develop a stable and organized party system capable of translating external demands into a coherent programme which would form the basis for subsequent legislation. Instead governing elites remained fragmented, their cross-cutting allegiances only permitting the loosest of electoral alliances and most temporary of parliamentary coalitions. In part this was due to the enduring salience of traditional issues — monarchism, clericalism and militarism — and to the fact that the political formations which mirrored them survived the introduction of mass suffrage. Equally important was their firm entrenchment *before* the divisions of industrial society emerged and crystallized as political forces. Since the 'traditional' and the 'modern' cleavages cut across one another, the result was a multiplicity of parties which could form clusters on the basis of several shared factors, but could not coalesce because they were divided by equally important issues. The openness of the political arena *fostered* fragmentation, for no important social group was excluded from the Assembly, but it did *not create* it. Until the First World War the forces of conservatism, republicanism and socialism were not organized in solid party frameworks on the English model and this was particularly true of the right. At its extreme the Monarchists and Imperialists remained intensely hostile to one another, their championship of different pretenders being reinforced by rather different economic interests: the Bourbon Legitimists still representing large landowning groups, the Orleanists the business bourgeoisie, and the Bonapartists a militaristic and adventurist section of the same class. The modern successor to all of them – the *Union Républicaine Démocratique*, formed in 1903 after final acceptance of a republican regime – represented their common Catholicism and the shared interests of the *haute bourgeoisie*. While the extreme right had remained absorbed with internal hostilities, the Republicans could permit themselves the luxury of division; but at the turn of the century the moderate conservatives formed two loose electoral alliances – the Republican Federation and the Democratic Alliance – united only in anticlericalism and defense of business interests. In the Centre the Radicals, the republican party par excellence, completed the task of dividing the middle classes (for its individualism attracted peasant proprietors, small businessmen, professionals and officials) and further dividing the anticlerical vote. From within the loose Radical framework, the Radical-Socialists split off in 1910, though they retained a Centre-Left orientation in contradistinction to the United Socialist Party which designated itself as a revolutionary class organization in 1905.

In a multi-party system the central position is the most advantageous since those in the middle can ally with either the extremists of their own 'tendence' or with other moderates. Above all they can vary these alliances – an option not available at the extremes. Before 1914 the Radicals and Radical Socialists occupied this position and were normally indispensable to any governing coalition. The balance tipped towards centre-left, because whilst the monarchists on the extreme right could not yet unite with republicans of the centre-right, the radicals could work with the socialists. This centrism,[102] which was the dominant aspect of relations between governing elites under both Republics, sprang originally from disunity on the right, but this in turn had consequences for the emerging left. 'Until the Church was reduced to submission or even reduced to complete impotence, the French peasant, the French worker, could be induced to vote for soundly "Republican" candidates, often Jews or Protestants. Had the rich been united in one conservative party, the poor might have united against them.'[103]

On the contrary, in the twentieth century the right proved rather more united than the left: just as the anti-parliamentarian vision of a Restoration was fading and allowing a degree of rapprochement on the right, the anti-parliamentarian force of communism resurrected the vision of the Commune to divide the left. Despite, or perhaps because of its tighter organization, the United Socialist Party had already spawned a dissident group — the Republican Socialists — before the Great War. In 1920 the split between the Second and Third Internationals permanently shattered the unity of the socialist movement and led to the emergence on the one hand of the modern socialist party (SFIO) under the leadership of Léon Blum, and on the other of the modern Communist Party (SFIC) headed by Maurice Thorez. When the Unions divided in the same way two years later (into the socialist CGT and the Communist CGTU), disunity was complete until the Popular Front experiment in the 1930s. The Socialists were driven increasingly but unwillingly to collaborate with the Radicals in parliament, the CGT strived not to link its fortunes to any particular party of the left, whilst the Communists were trapped and isolated in an extreme position which deprived their Deputies of office throughout the IIIrd Republic. Not only did this fragmentation weaken the political impact of the working class movement, but its lack of cohesion probably carried heavier penalties than did disunity on the right which at least had other forms of institutional protection in industry, banking, and the civil service. Such factionalism on both right and left had a powerful effect on political interaction and via it, on governmental policies.

Firstly, it imposed centrism on twentieth century politics. With the emergence of the Communist Party, the Radicals moved from centre-left to centre-right and the socialists slipped into the position they vacated. The two kinds of extremism (militaristic on the right and revolutionary on the left) precluded coalescence of left or right and any move towards a two party system. Instead only the regular collaboration of centre parties in various permutations allowed the continuation of a parliamentary regime. But in policy terms the price paid for making the system work was its restriction to the minimum programme which the governing coalition could endorse. 'Thus everything conspires to trap center governments in immobility. In this respect, the alternation of power between the two centers, based on their respective strengths within the coalition and on their ability to establish reversible alliances, is more apparent than real. . . Sometimes there are center governments distraught at their inability to effect reforms, which they

thus promise for the future, and sometimes there are center governments which are delighted by their immobility and show no desire to
escape it, but neither moves very much in fact'.[104]

Continuing *'immobilisme'* under the IVth Republic can again be
attributed to the nature of the party system and, underlying it, the
sectional character of French society. From 1946 to 1957 fragmentation of the parties intensified throughout the political spectrum.
On the right de Gaulle formed his *Rassemblement du Peuple Français*,
but the extreme right position was later usurped by Poujadism – the
inarticulate howl of the small shopkeeper. The Centre was made up of a
complex array of Independents, the Catholic MRP, the Radical Party
(which itself split three ways in the mid-fifties) and Socialists. On the
left were the Communists and splinter groups of differing revolutionary
tendencies. Once again government from the centre was the only kind
of ministry which such elite relations allowed. Between 1946-54 the
pendulum swung within the limited margins of centre right and left, the
drift towards the right being more pronounced after 1951, and that to
the left after 1956. Centrist politics which were partly caused by the
existence of significant anti-constitutional groups at both extremes, also
intensified the alienation of the moderate right and left because of their
inability to play a part in practical politics.

Lipset has attempted to show how the overlapping of three different
cleavages in IVth Republic politics produced such a complex configura-
tion of parties.[105]

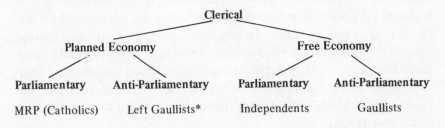

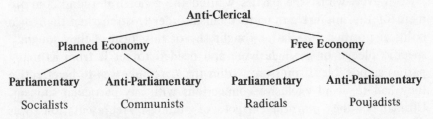

*Not an independent party.

Certainly party divisions were prompted by this mixture of historical, ideological and material considerations, rather than party structure being closely correlated with class structure alone. Given these lines of cleavage, the continued accessibility of the political centre ensured the continuing heterogeneity of the Chamber of Deputies and guaranteed that the work of government would still be immobilized by these cross-pressures in the Assembly. In this situation no party could seek to win power but only to share it, and no party could hope to implement a coherent programme but only to introduce its least controversial aspects. Educational interests, like most others, had no difficulty in gaining parliamentary expression, but in terms of execution of the policies sought few other groups could have been so paralysed by the cross-fire between members of the governing elites.

A(iii) The Structure of Educational Interest Groups

The political structure of the IIIrd and IV Republics encouraged interest group activity because of both its accessibility and its fragmentation. On the one hand, the relative weakness of each party led it to court every complementary interest. 'Under the IVth Republic the summit of party ambition was to win a share of power rather than to exercise it outright. One way to achieve this was to outbid one's rivals for the support of a clientele – Gaullists against Conservatives against MRP over the Catholic schools, Communists against Socialists against Radicals on behalf of secular education – and each against all for the favours of home-distillers, ex-servicemen, peasants or small shopkeepers'.[106] On the other hand, educational interest groups had to seek party sponsorship for effective manipulative action within the parliamentary arena. The dominance of the legislative branch of government made such contacts possible and this in turn spurred the mobilization of pressure groups.

However, whilst the parties wanted the general all-round commitment of the interest groups to them in order to strengthen their own political position, the latter fought shy of this. Instead they sought a specific pledge on a single issue and needed to get it from as many parties as possible; if pressure within the Assembly was to be effective they had to avoid exclusive connections with any particular sponsor. Ultimately the *political* effect of interest representation was destructive, since a different parliamentary majority was needed for almost every issue, whilst the *educational* effect was deadlock, since no sponsor(s) were strong enough for long enough to override others and legislate major reforms.

Most of the interest groups involved were of the associational type, but since educational personnel made up about a third of the Civil Service, professional groups were able to exert a certain amount of institutionalized pressure as well. A series of councils pertaining to various branches and levels of instruction, topped by the *Conseil Supérieur*, formally provided for the upward flow of suggestions from elected teacher representatives. However, although consulted on bills and decrees, their status remained strictly advisory and this prevented them from operating as effective professional beachheads within the administration. Indeed, from the teachers' point of view, the more mundane pre-war *Comités Consultatifs* and post-war *Commissions Paritaires* which were concerned with personnel rather than policy matters, were a good deal more effective. When less material considerations were involved, the profession like other groups was forced to organize outside the educational system.

The pressure groups at work could be divided into three broad categories. Firstly, professional associations, the most important being the SNI (primary personnel), SNES (secondary), SNET (technical), which banded together in the FGE (*Fédération Générale de l'Enseignement*) in 1926, giving way to the FEN *(Fédération de l'Education Nationale)* in 1946. To these must be added the SGEM *(Syndicat Général de l'Education Nationale)*, representing Catholic teachers, and special bodies like the elite *Société des Agrégés*. Secondly, there were the sectional interest groups which expressed the educational concerns of various organizations, including Churches, industrial bodies and labour federations. Finally, there were various associations founded for educational purposes like the *Ligue de l'Enseignement*, the *Compagnons de l'Université Nouvelle*, parental groups like the *Fédération des parents d'élèves de lycées et collèges*, as well as student organizations.

Despite their multitudinous differences these interest groups had one feature in common — they were all national bodies whose target was national politics. As Eckstein[107] has argued, pressure groups take on the same structure as the organizations they seek to influence: a centralized system spawns centralized interest groups because local organizations are pointless if negotiations cannot take place locally. Furthermore, to command the attention of national politics, interest groups must be as large as possible and thus a structural premium is placed on their ability to co-operate. Whenever this was possible it carried a political bonus, for example in the thirties, 'grâce à l'action conjointe des corporations enseignantes et des syndicats ouvriers, les problèmes se trouvent de plus en plus nettement posés à l'échelon national et gouvernemental'.[108] However a sectional society militates against successful co-operation (which requires a superimposition of grievances) and leads to organizational instability (as strong sub-cultures encourage fragmentation and schism). Much of the time firm alliances were impossible among clusters of groups sharing complementary educational objectives because of other divisive factors. They were of temporary duration and fragile in organization. Even when pressure groups sought the same educational goals their constant in-fighting and consequent breakdown were self-defeating: this often meant that they cancelled one another out, thus minimizing their political impact both jointly and severally.

Since throughout the period the articulation of interests was easy, then pressure groups spawned, but their aggregation was so difficult that they neutralized one another politically. This was equally true of the three categories of interest group distinguished above and also of the relations between them. Because of the kaleidoscopic complexity of these interactions, a single example must suffice as illustration. In terms of wasted potential the checkered relationship of the professional organizations, the labour federations and the parties of the Left, is the most striking for it severely undermined any attempt to press for the democratization of education. Shared anticlericalism, the poor economic condition of the elementary teachers, and their early acceptance of syndicalist and socialist ideas could not prevent communism from driving a parallel wedge through party, federation and association alike in the twenties. The lengthy and complex manoeuvring which subsequently united the majority of teachers in the FGE actually took place under the auspices of the CGT in 1928 and was a forerunner to the brief period of united action in the anti-fascist Popular Front. Rightwing demonstrations in 1934 prompted the CGT and CGTU to reunite, the Communist, Socialist and Radical-Socialist Parties to ally, and the revolutionary teachers' union, FMEL, to fuse with the FGE.[109] By 1937 the FGE had 100,000 members affiliated to the CGT,[110] but only three years later the Vichy régime had driven both underground.

Immediately after the war internal political divisions led to the disintegration of the six-million strong CGT, leaving the federation still bearing that name in Communist hands, and creating an important anti-communist breakaway association, the CGT-Force Ouvrière. The teachers' FGE had only just transformed itself into a more unitary organization, the FEN in 1946, which now incorporated 38 member unions. This association could not carry the majority of its members into *either* the CGT or the CGT-FO, without shattering its own new-found unity. Instead they opted reluctantly for the expedient of autonomy, insisting that none of their own component unions be affiliated to either labour federation. The simultaneous disintegration of political parties on the left had exactly the same consequence – in self-defence the FEN had to make itself and its fortunes independent of any particular political faction.[111] Henceforth, throughout the 40s and 50s, only the loosest relations maintained between professional association, labour federation and political party; guarded support was exchanged for temporary pledges on various occasions rather than a permanent unity of action exerting continuous educational pressure. There is no doubt that this disarray was damaging to the interests of all groups involved, and the critic of FEN policy who argued that 'autonomy has brought nothing to the teachers'[112] could just as well have addressed this to the labour federations and parties of the left.

This example has been used because of its importance which extends far beyond the educational sphere: indeed some have considered that it was this very division of the working world which made the 'progressive disaggregation' of the Fourth Republic inevitable. Examples could be multiplied, for the same lack of superimposition between material and ideal factors destroyed the internal unity of the profession itself (the primary teachers' SNI and the secondary teachers' SNES often pulling in different directions), of secularists or anti-clericals, (whose material differences even precluded the formation of a parliamentary inter-group to defend laïcité in schools), as well as of the labour federations and student associations.

The centralized structure of education predisposed towards the formation of large national organizations to exert pressure on parliament: the sectional structure of society ruined their cohesion and effectiveness. As Ehrmann argues, frequently 'the large confederation representing composite and diffuse interests is condemned to *immobilisme* in its own ranks and therefore proves a handicap against any measure involving a departure from the status quo'.[113] Thus the divisive relations which characterized the political elite were paralleled by those of the interest groups. The two exacerbated one another and proved mutually destructive: together they sacrificed the promise of negotiated educational change which was contained in the accessible polity.

B. Educational Interaction

Three main issues were the focal points of educational interaction throughout the IIIrd and IVth Republics — secularization, modernization and democratization. The interplay of political forces was complex, the influence of governmental opponents proving as important as the power of governing elites, and the effect of non-decisions was as significant as the legislation actually introduced. Three main phases can be distinguished: the initial period up to the First World War when the republican regime established itself, the inter-war years of shifting governing coalitions, and the post-war struggles of the IVth Republic. In all, however, the same three issues preoccupied politics, though in differing orders of priority, and much the same interests manoeuvred to resolve them in their favour, though with differing degrees of success.

Although the Republicans came to office committed to Gambetta's Belleville programme of 1869 (which specified free and compulsory public education, the separation of Church and State, and the legalization of unionism), the party had become more conservative by the time monarchism was subdued a decade later. The legislative election of 1881 consolidated the republican regime, the Republican Union with 200 seats being the strongest group in the Chamber. 'With the constitutional crisis settled, the chief area of strategic conflict between left and right now shifted to the field of education, in which political and social divisions were exacerbated by their identification with religious ones'.[114]

Jules Ferry as Minister in charge of education and a committed positivist,[115] sought to put education at the service of national unity and social order. This meant secular instruction, since religious influences were politically and socially divisive, a free compulsory system if State education were to unite the *deux jeunesses* and override class antagonism, but not an egalitarian system for the Republican ideal was the organic not the classless society. Ferry's was an anti-clericalism of moderation, explicitly not anti-catholic or monopolistic, and conciliatory about religious instruction outside school hours. It was a typical republican compromise which both the right and the left rejected in favour of confrontation. Catholic opposition was aroused by the introduction of free (1881) and compulsory (1882) instruction, not merely because of the economic threat to their schools but because the spectre of laïcité lurked behind both gratuity and obligation and was soon given flesh when teachers who belonged to unauthorized congregations were banned from teaching posts. The compromise which would have been acceptable to Premier and Papacy alike, whereby the government would renounce demands for authorization and the Orders their opposition to the Republic, was repudiated by the monarchist French hierarchy on the right and the anti-clericals on the left. President Freycinet, the architect of the policy, was also its chief victim; he was driven out of office in favour of Ferry himself, who in turn was forced to abandon moderation because of his need for support on the left – a fact which was confirmed when the 1885 elections returned more radical or 'intransigent' republicans than before.

The introduction of secular programmes in public schools, and the 1886 law excluding religious personnel from teaching in them, completed Catholic embitterment with republican educational policy. The Church was torn between total boycott of the new laws and attempts to modify their application. Its political position enforced prudence for no election gave a Catholic majority in the Chamber. Fear of the ultimate sanction of anti-clericalism – separation of Church and State which could rob the former of the resources it had held from the Concordat – resulted in a grudging acquiescence to Ferry's appeasement formula; namely laïcité in public schools and liberty outside them. Pope Leo XIII's attempt to reconcile the Church to the Republic, the *Ralliement* of the 1890s was a complete failure. The old Catholic legitimists preferred to ally themselves with the only other clericalist and anti-republican institution, the Army, to constitute a new revolutionary right. It was a fatal step, for the association of Catholicism with nationalism, militarism and anti-semitism led the more vociferous Orders to compromise the Church irretrievably in the Dreyfus affair. In educational terms, the seven year-long struggle for justice in the affair had united the republican forces with the growing socialist element in an anti-clericalism which sought retribution and temporarily muted other cleavages. The 1902 elections were waged and won by republican defenders on the clerical issue. Under the leadership of Combes a *Délégation des Gauches* was established to keep the parliamentary majority at heel in the Chamber and to persuade the socialists (rather than the orthodox Marxists) that to eliminate clerical influence was to dismantle the ideological apparatus of the old ruling class. Starting with the enforcement of authorization, then closure, the policy culminated in banning the religious Orders from teaching and proscribing their private congregational schools. In effect such laws went beyond the idea of separation (effected in practice a year later), which makes religion a purely private matter and thus implies that it cannot be a criterion for public discrimination. As a general political issue clericalism had driven a wedge between centre and right-wing conservatism: as an educational issue its net effect had been to postpone a split between the centre and the left on the question of modernizing and above all democratizing instruction. Once the passions whipped up and sustained by the Dreyfus affair had abated during the war, these items moved to the top of the agenda and became the main preoccupations underlying political manipulation for the next half century.

The interwar period and the *école unique* movement which dominated educational politics is a long drawn out example of political manipulation which failed. As a case of non-decision-making it is instructive because failure did not consist in an inability to gain sponsorship in parliament, or even in government, nor in the repressive powers of opponents, but ultimately in the inability of the left to hold together as a political force and steer through the legislation sought by those it represented. Other factors like disagreement between primary and secondary teachers played a part (though this was more important after the second world war) but on the whole the external interest groups sunk their differences and aggregated their demands with much greater efficiency than the parliamentary parties during the last two decades of the IIIrd Republic.

The movement was started well outside the political arena by a group of teachers calling themselves the 'Compagnons' and publishing *L'Université Nouvelle* immediately the war was over. They advanced a global critique of the system, condemning its rigid centralization and stultifying standardization, and advocated an equally thorough overhaul. They wanted neither a uniform school nor a State monopoly but an *école unique* in the sense of a single *type* of school with 2 cycles, 8-11 and 11-14, the latter being a period of observation and orientation used for guiding pupils into further education and professional training. Democratization would thus consist in breaking down the rigid isolation of primary from secondary instruction and the class differences they reflected and reproduced. Instead of the primary *degré* developing its own secondary tops (*primaires supérieures, cours complémentaires* etc.), and the lycées their own primary bases (the preparatory classes), all pupils would attend the same type of school until 14, and the positive principle of hierarchical organization would replace the negative one. Modernization would consist in technical education taking its place alongside the lycée and higher education, as well as instruction extending into professional training and research. 'En fait, les "Compagnons de l'Université nouvelle" ont, plusieurs dizaines d'années à l'avance, posé à peu près tous les problèmes de l'éducation moderne et prévu la plupart des solutions . . . Les Compagnons ont eu raison, mais ils ont eu raison trop tôt'.[116]

Although the Compagnons themselves were advocating a pedagogical not a political cause, the issue could not avoid politicization for without parliamentary action there could be no move towards reform. With the reshaping of party policies for the first post-war elections, école unique acquired the sponsorship of both the Radical and Socialist parties as well as the support of the CGT. However, the failure of the three to form an electoral alliance, together with the Right's successful anti-Bolshevik campaign, resulted in a Chamber of Deputies which was more right-wing than any since 1871 and a *Bloc National* government to whom egalitarian policy was an anathema. 'Educational reform was not the sort of issue that could swing an election even at the best of times. Reformers had to depend upon the election of a parliamentary majority sympathetic to their aims; but so long as the two large parties of the left were divided against each other, as they were in 1919, the outlook for reform was dismal . . . Unable to expect much action from the Bloc National, reformers had to continue and to expand their propaganda efforts outside Parliament'.[117]

In this attempt they met with almost immediate Catholic resistance, for free secondary instruction could only damage the confessional schools which were now finding the economic going hard enough (they had already mounted their own political campaign to obtain funding in proportion to their pupil intake). The hostility expressed by Catholic conservatives in *La Croix* led the Compagnons to drop their initial conciliatory proposal of subsidies to confessional schools. In turn this removed a barrier which had led passionate anti-clericals on the left to withhold their support, but it earned the école unique an irreconcilable political opponent. For many years Catholic manipulation of the parliamentary right was used to attack any move towards école unique as prejudicial to its own interests. Reform thus depended on the solidarity of the left and the conversion of the centre.

Already before the elections of 1924 the Radicals and Socialists had acquired the habit of working together in Parliament on educational questions, especially in opposition to the Minister's decree which re-introduced latin for all branches of the lycée and thus made transfer from the écoles primaires supérieures even more difficult, lengthy and expensive. Since the 1919 changes in electoral law favoured coalitions, the two parties allied to form the Cartel des Gauches and the école unique figured prominently in their minimum programme as an issue which both could freely endorse. With CGT support the Cartel won, but useful as educational reform had been for papering over differences during electioneering, it was a secondary question to the new govern-ment which was preoccupied with resolving the major difference between the parties about how to solve the economic crisis. The most that could be done was to abolish the latin decree, thus restoring the modern section to the lycée, to set up a commission of Cartelist representatives and Université experts to examine école unique, and to give some scholarships to enable transfer to the lycée preparatory classes. Preparations to place the latter under primary inspection stimu-lated opposition from secondary teachers and from the Catholic hier-archy which saw this encroachment into private education (for these classes were of course fee paying) as a move towards the monopoly of the atheist State. Coupled with socialist dissension and a worsening financial situation, the Radicals could no longer form a Ministry, and Poincaré took over with a government of National Union in 1926.

'Confronted with the meagre accomplishments of the Cartel des Gauches, reformers undertook to draw up a new blueprint for the école unique; the initiative briefly held by the government returned to private hands'.[118] Outside parliament various interest groups, the most prominent being the CGT and the teachers' FGE, worked to consolidate a joint organization for exerting pressure and a programme that they could all endorse which would serve as a legislative text. Thirty one associations joined the *Comité d'étude et d'action pour l'école unique* in 1925, including professional groups of teachers, trade unions, political parties and republican bodies like the *Ligue des Droits de l'homme*. Their divergent interests made the aggregation of demands difficult, but not impossible, although the final plan represented a considerable reduction in scope compared with the Compagnons policy – all reference to higher education was dropped, whilst the structure of secondary studies was hardly modified. The 'Organic Statute for Public

Education' was a compromise which advocated a common primary school, selection at 11, a year's orientation class, free secondary instruction, and raising of the leaving age to 15.

Of all the groups involved, its endorsement cost least to the Radical party: 'with hearts on the left, pocket books on the right, but a good share of their electorate in the centre, almost all they could promise workers was that their children could become members of the middle class – if they were clever enough'.[119] To the Socialists and the CGT, support meant abandoning any idea of imposing proletarian culture on public education in favour of broadening the access to existing institutions: to the SNI it meant relinquishing hopes for the nationalization of education and its control by an independent corporation of teachers, parents and State representatives. Nevertheless, with certain modifications and additions, all of them had endorsed it by the end of the twenties, including the broader federation of teachers, the FGE. This co-operation was furthered by the results of the 1928 elections which gave Poincaré a stable majority on the right and at last threw all the protagonists of école unique together in opposition.

In fact 'as a political device, the école unique could draw socialists and radicals together when they were in opposition, but it was too secondary an issue to keep them in agreement when they were in the majority. The cause of educational reform could therefore benefit more with the Left as a whole in opposition than when the Radicals assumed power with the Socialists' equivocal support'.[120] This was never better born out than in the years still to run before the war. In opposition they succeeded in beating Tardieu's government over the principle of free secondary education, for no Deputy from the Radical party leftwards could possibly have doubts about it. Their continued parliamentary pressures successfully extended gratuity to cover all classes of the lycée by 1933. Nothing in fact could provide a more tragic contrast with the forthcoming performance of the Popular Front in the educational field.

It is doubtful if the lycée became more accessible in becoming free, for it was still a lengthy and expensive undertaking and this change probably benefitted the lower middle class most. In other words, there was still a large and unsatisfied demand for democratization on the left which the Radicals, Socialists and Communists brought into their Popular Front government of 1936. With Léon Blum as the first socialist premier, a new educational deal was expected despite continuing economic depression. Jean Zay as Minister of National Education put forward a governmental project which owed much to the CGT plan of 1929, which in its turn was modelled on the earlier 'organic statute' of the action committee. It represented a complete endorsement of the positive principle of hierarchical integration but also sought to propitiate the conflicting interests of the two groups of teachers — primary instruction was to be unified and have the same programmes and teachers, an examination at 12 would signal the end of the primary cycle and, after a year's orientation class, pupils would then be allocated to classical, modern or technical secondary studies with provision for late entry and transfer between them. Thus 'pour la première fois, une volonté cohérente de réforme apparaît au niveau du pouvoir politique'.[121] In fact it never came before parliament for the Blum government was overturned in 1937, but the 'Zay project at least showed that under the third Republic there were still lines of communication open between thought and action, between the private sector of expert opinion and the government, between the seekers of change and those in a position to effect change'.[122]

Zay (as a Radical) retained his position and attempted to proceed by ministerial decree rather than parliamentary vote. Firstly, he placed the lycée preparatory classes under the same administrative section as primary instruction, whilst transferring the *écoles primaires supérieures* to secondary administration, thus preparing for the consolidation of a reformed modern section at that level. Secondly, he organized experimental orientation classes in 45 centres — an attempt at official experimentation, the only kind possible in such a unified system, in order to provide the kind of concrete information which tends to be freely available in decentralized systems. These measures were important, not just because they were the first practical steps towards reform, but because of the opposition they excited which was to dog each additional post war step. The mantle of unity which the FGE had worn as long as projects remained safely on paper could not cover divergent professional interests when they were confronted by concrete changes. The *Société des Agrégés* and association of lycée professors led the opposition to the *classes nouvelles* on the grounds that they were initiating the 'primarization' of traditional secondary studies which had a year whittled off them. This hostility was backed up by lycée parents fearing the beginning of the end where their educational privileges were concerned. 'The absence of high prestige private education meant that there would be no escape hatch for the children of middle class parents excluded from State secondary schools by a rigorous system of selection on academic grounds'.[123] Since the French system did not possess this kind of shock absorber, all demands focussed on public instruction and their confluence only inhibited change. On the other hand, to the instituteurs the orientation class meant they lost their best pupils earlier than before and that they themselves would be condemned to a lower level of activity. This opposition coupled with a halt on government spending, the CGT's preoccupation with the 40 hour week, and the approach of war were sufficient to bury Zay's project. Perpetual division of the Left had damned educational reform under the IIIrd Republic, for a Radical-Socialist alliance was the only combination which could have steered it through; it was to act in exactly the same way during the IVth Republic – with the same results.

Post-war attempts to democratize and diversify French education gave rise to a lengthy battle of projects which was merely a prolonged exercise in non-decision-making. The parties brought to power after liberation represented 'l'entente nécessaire mais provisoire au sein de la Résistance'.[124] The governing majority of christian democrats (MRP), Socialists and Communists appointed a study commission under Paul Langevin, with members from all levels of instruction. The Langevin Plan blended democratization with diversification: all would follow a common first cycle until 11, then proceed to four years observation and orientation in separate establishments, before going on to the final three years of theoretical, professional or practical secondary studies. The Report appeared in 1947, just as the tripartite majority dissolved, and it went no further. Since 'les gouvernements ultérieurs reposeront sur des majorités changeantes, souvent divisées, en tout cas plus conservatrices',[125] another political opportunity for reform had come and gone. Henceforth the intensification of professional divisions was to join political instability as a major cause of inaction.

The cleavages which had surfaced over Zay's experimental classes continued to be of importance in relation to the orientation period, and reflected the interests of different sections of teachers about where it should be held, how long it should last, and who should teach it. Within the FEN itself it was increasingly difficult to minimize hostility between the primary SNI, whose ideal was a system which educated the mass for as long as possible and thus delayed differentiation until as late as possible, and the secondary SNES, which would not risk debasing academic standards by delaying the start of the secondary studies proper or by broadening their intake. In its task of aggregating demands the FEN could therefore only pass the vaguest of resolutions: any attempt to be more specific foundered upon the SNI desire for a long period of orientation, incorporating the *cours complémentaires*, and SNES disdain for these higher grade courses and desire to keep orientation short. The FEN's organizational strategy of introducing horizontal geographical divisions of membership, to soften and counter-balance the vertical divisions among the component national unions, did not substantially improve cohesion. Disunity was particularly damaging to reform during this period for the IVth Republic had a good record of professional consultation, via the various advisory committees to government, and the FEN was officially recognized as representing the bulk of teachers.

The strength of professional divisions became clear when the abortive project of Delbos was submitted to the *Conseil Supérieur* in 1949. It intensified at the beginning of the fifties during discussions of Baccalauréat reform. The administrative director of the second degré drafted a reform project advising the creation of a shorter secondary education in lycées and collèges, running in parallel to the Baccalauréat, but preparing for positions in the *cadres moyens* rather than higher education. An orientation cycle would allocate pupils to the short or long courses, but the latter would not be truncated because the propedeutique year of higher education was tacked on to it. This plan gained the unanimous support of the advisory *Conseil de l'enseignement du second degré*, but met with immediate hostility from the instituteurs on the Conseil Supérieur, because it gave the monopoly of orientation to secondary establishments, to secondary teachers, and to pupils who had *already* been able to get into lycées and collèges.[126]

Instead a counter-project was advanced from the Directorate of the *premier degré* which involved a fusion of the higher forms of primary instruction and the first two classes of secondary, and a corresponding overlap of programmes, pupils and personnel. When discussed in the National Assembly these conflicts were simply transferred to the political arena and provided ample grounds for inaction: it was decided that overall reform was needed and the Minister of Education was charged with producing a legislative project. 'En fait, tandis que beaucoup souhaitent véritablement une réoganization générale de l'enseignement public, il s'agit, une fois de plus, pour certains, de gagner du temps et de repousser à plus tard une réforme qu'ils souhaitent ne jamais voir réaliser'.[127] After all inaction was a decision to perpetuate educational privileges.

André Marie's project was a compromise package made up from

parts of its predecessors: essentially it retained the idea of a short and a long secondary course, reduced the orientation cycle to two years in deference to the *professeurs*, but proposed that it be held in schools of the premier degré (not only in lycées and collèges), as a concession to the instituteurs. It was received unenthusiastically by the various consultative councils but the ministerial crisis of June 1954 intervened to prevent its consideration by the Assembly. Angered by political immobilism, the socialists in parliament drafted a law (the Depreux project), in the Langevin tradition, which was presented to the National Assembly in March 1955, referred to the *Commission de l'Education Nationale*, and quietly buried as Edgar Faure's government affirmed its intention of elaborating a general reform.

Once again the new Minister of Education, Berthoin, set up a commission (for the first time including representatives of private employers), once again a report was produced endorsing an orientation cycle and stressing subsequent differentiation of courses to meet practical needs, and once again it was killed in the cross-fire between interests and interred by the fall of government. As usual opposition came from the SNES, despite overall FEN support, but it was particularly well organized with about a third of secondary teachers joining *Franco-ancienne*, an action committee for the defense of the traditional curriculum, which was backed by the *Fédération des Associations de parents d'élèves des Lycées et Collèges*. Paradoxically they were joined by the UNEF, the national students' union, which objected to the capitalist implications of a clause linking grants to particular courses of technical study. But the decisive factor was the reanimation of the clerical issue, for many of those who might have been expected to give the bill parliamentary support refused all discussion of the project until a recent law, voted by the same parliamentary majority and giving aid to private education, was repealed. Once more anti-clericalism had deflected interest from democratization with the unintended consequence of helping the conservatives in their policy of educational inaction.

The 1956 elections returned a centre-left majority committed to moving fast and radically towards educational reform: under its auspices the last non-act of the Republic was played out in this field. By August the Minister of Education, René Billères, presented a legislative project to the Chamber – only the third after that of Zay (1937) and Berthoin (1955) to be of governmental inspiration. The key themes remained constant, social equality and national efficiency to be achieved through democratization and diversification – but the project clearly specified that structural change must precede change in educational functions. Separate Middle schools would undertake the orientation phase between 11-13, from there pupils would proceed to terminal vocational instruction, or to short secondary courses in collèges (replacing cours complémentaires, technical, commercial and industrial sections of existing collèges and apprenticeship centres), or finally to long secondary courses in general or technical lycées. The profession showed its familiar line up, with the instituteurs welcoming the idea of middle schools, the interpenetration of the different degrés and the increased value attached to technical studies, whilst the professeurs remained reticent and Franco-ancienne continued to be hostile. Nevertheless, the project gained the majority backing of the advisory councils and of the Conseil Supérieur (37 votes to 13). Encouraged by this, the project was adopted by Government and deposited for parliamentary discussion and vote. It incited strong opposition inside and outside the Assembly, most vociferously from the usual parental interest groups and from catholic defenders of the private schools. Added to this the government's difficulties with the Algerian war, Suez and the economic situation all favoured the adversaries of reform, for it gained them time. By May 1958 still no vote had been taken: on the 13th the IVth Republic fell and the new regime abandoned the Billères project. Like its predecessors this centre-left government had proved incapable of holding together a parliamentary majority whilst giving educational reform political priority. The cross-cutting character of educational interest groups coupled with divisive elite relations had consistently favoured the politics of inaction. Given that political manipulation is the main process of educational change in a centralized system it is unsurprising that the general physionomy of the Napoleonic Université remained largely unmodified.

GENERAL PROPOSITIONS

Patterns of educational interaction are held to derive from different combinations of four factors: political accessibility, elite relations, superimposition and organization among interest groups. However, the foregoing analysis of the IIIrd and IVth Republics in France shows that we have been dealing throughout with only one of the four permutations of these factors which can coexist with an accessible political centre. In other words this single case study has analysed one prolonged example where political openness coincided with pronounced disunity amongst governing elites and considerable fragmentation and disorganization amongst educational interest groups. Moreover this particular conjuncture manifested itself in an especially extreme form as was witnessed by the almost crippling degree of political instability which dogged it from decade to decade. Consequently, one must be acutely aware that any general hypotheses grounded in a context of such historical specificity will necessarily be very partial. Further examples of open polities which were accompanied by closer elite relations and greater inter-penetration of interest groups are needed to give the full picture. It is their absence which accounts for the negative form in which some of the following propositions are expressed.

— The existence of an accessible polity allows a wide range of educational demands to reach the central decision-making arena and many groups can work through the system of parliamentary coalitions in seeking to negotiate their demands.

— The extreme disunity of elite relations in the accessible polity prevents the consolidation of stable units for political manipulation (parties, alliances and coalitions) and leads to legislative immobilism. This, however, is as damaging to the interests of government as to those of opposition at any given time. It means that there is no steady downward flow of polity-directed changes in education: indeed non-decision-making is just as important as the legislation actually passed. Over time those policy changes which are introduced do not consistently and exclusively favour one section of the governing elites: instead the dominant policy tendency is 'centrism' and compromise. Unlike the impenetrable polity, Government and Opposition both share in the determination of policy at all times: it is rarely the sole perogative of the former.

— The combination of an accessible polity with heterogeneous governing elites encourages the mobilization of interest groups, but also places a premium on large, well-organized, national associations. However, when interest groups themselves are also divided and incapable of co-operation, this prevents the formation of stable associations with consistent political sponsorship. The disunity of governing elites and of educational interest groups together amplify the negative effects of one another.

- The profession enjoys a greater corporative role in the accessible polity, as far as the defense of its vested interests are concerned, and also a wider consultative role on educational matters in general. Nevertheless, it has to go outside the educational system in order to pursue educational change and has to overcome official resistance to its organizing with this in view. The contribution of the profession is not limited to negative obstructiveness: teachers and academics can initiate policy via extra-parliamentary associations although these still require political sponsorship to be effective.

- There is a premium on professional and external interest groups coalescing in organizations which operate as pressure groups in education. However, lack of superimposition of interests produces a fissiparousness in such associations, which is counter-productive since it precludes the prolonged unity of action which exerts continuous political pressures.

III. PATTERNS OF INTERACTION IN THE SEMI-PERMEABLE POLITY
FRANCE: The Fifth Republic from 1958-1975

The establishment and development of the Vth Republic represented a considerable reduction in political accessibility compared with the two previous regimes, without involving a departure from parliamentary government itself. It was a search for a constitutional remedy for political instability, as the constant overthrowal of governments in the past was attributed to the *régime d'assemblée* and not to the destructive behaviour of the political parties. To Michel Debré, who was instrumental in framing the new Constitution, it mirrored a 'strong preference for a *régime parlementaire* as a golden mean between the discredited *gouvernement d'assemblée* of the Third and Fourth Republics and the more thorough-going *régime présidentiel* of the United States'.[128] To De Gaulle, for whom it was designed and for whom it's acceptance was a vote of confidence in his leadership, it was equally important that 'our new democratic institutions should themselves compensate for the effects of our perpetually ebullient politics'.[129] Thus both endorsed a shift in the balance of power away from the Assembly and sought an antidote to past instability by conferring constitutional powers on President and Government which would preclude a powerful and unruly legislature. The regime has proved itself to be more than a vehicle for De Gaulle's charismatic leadership. Having now withstood two crises of Presidential succession, it has established its credentials as a formula for political stability. However, this section does focus on the Gaullist period and its continuation under Pompidou, rather than the last three years when the relationship between President, Party and Parliament changed in some important respects.

Limitations on Internal Initiation

The formal position of the profession did not alter with the advent of the Fifth Republic: professional rights to organization and to consultation remained intact, but the spirit in which these relations were conducted on the part of officialdom was one of frigid mistrust. Many teachers had publicly refused to support De Gaulle in the 1958 referendum, on good republican grounds of commitment to open government, distrust of right wing militarism, and total repugnance for Catholic conservatism. The old hussars of the Republic, and their colleagues at secondary and higher levels, suffered an unprecedented political alienation once the 'Republic of Professors' had ended for good. Paradoxically their formal powers now outstripped their informal influence over educational policy.

The new climate of relations between teachers and government was exemplified by the choice of the first Gaullist to hold the portfolio for education. Christian Fouchet, whose tenure of this office was the longest in French history, was no academic and his previous military and political record, including a stretch in Algeria, did little to endear him to the profession. It resulted in consistent rebuffs, such as failures to consult the appropriate commissions. Since the Fourth Republic had accentuated the advisory role of the profession and the consultative channels for the expression of expert opinion on educational matters, this new dismissive attitude rankled greatly, especially as the new government multiplied advisory organs in other areas.

However this was only one index of the new official approach whose general effect was to reduce both professional influence and the autonomy of teachers and academics. In particular the new ministerial style of direct control of instruction by very detailed decrees meant that the profession was subject to a great number of policy directives which it had neither helped to shape and which it was powerless to modify. The situation was exacerbated by the fact that this tougher official attitude towards the teachers was paralleled by a much softer line towards the Church in education: in other words, the laïcist profession witnessed its old enemies become favoured as the new educational allies of government.

In practical terms the profession's direct links with the central decision-making arena were reduced and its local and classroom activities became more circumscribed. Teachers and academics had little freedom to respond positively to external community demands or to the internal demands voiced by pupils disoriented, for example, by the almost annual changes in the Baccalauréat, or by students bewildered by the changing course requirements attending the ministerial programme of modernization. Wherever their sympathies lay, teachers could make few direct responses to such demands, nor could they act as effective sponsors, backing them higher up in the political decision-making process, and thus play an indirect role in initiating such changes.

It was this feeling of ministerial oppressiveness (shared with the pupils and students) and of professional powerlessness, which led many of those in secondary and especially higher education to support the May events and the principal educational demands advanced by the students. As in the impenetrable polity they had been forced to go outside education and educational channels to impress their views on policy, but in doing so they had the advantage of the professional unions and associations which had been organized and legitimated during the intervening period of republican government. It was significant that the concern of teachers and academics during the elaboration of reforms after the May events was first and foremost for autonomy: financial and administrative autonomy of the university, curricular autonomy for degrees and diplomas, and pedagogical autonomy to determine teaching methods and materials. Formally they succeeded, and autonomy in all the above senses was firmly inscribed as one of the three co-ordinates of the 1968 *Loi d'orientation de l'enseignement supérieur*. Informally, as we shall see, the political application of the law (aided it must be admitted by entrenched academic conservatism), operated to reduce professional enjoyment of its refound freedom.

Limitations on External Transactions

As far as the private sector was concerned, the policies of the Fifth Republic showed somewhat greater continuity with the Vichy government of Marshal Pétain than with the republican secularist tradition. On the other hand, in the grand post-revolutionary tradition (from which only the first decade of the Second Empire and the Vichy interregnum itself deviated), no educational concession to confessionalism was allowed to dilute the étatist control of instruction or the State definition of instruction.

The Vichy regime brought temporary financial relief with local and central payments to free schools, but their withdrawal in 1945 coupled with inflation involved closures and falling teacher salaries. Partisans of private education organized and the *Association de Parents d'élèves de l'enseignement Libre* put pressure on candidates at the 1951 elections to support unconditional aid to free schools in Parliament. Elected deputies kept their promise and against very considerable opposition introduced laws (1951) enabling private pupils to obtain grants and giving a per capita subvention to private education. The Vth Republic attempted to provide a stable solution to the situation by confirming aid (a substantial concession to Catholic pressures) but linking it to increased control (ultimately a greater bonus to their opponents than any perceived at the time). For the Loi Debré (1959), refusing to recognize an independent and monolithic private sector, offered separate contracts between the State and individual establishments. Such contracts of association provide for public instruction under central control within the private school, in return for the State undertaking all expenses. (A simpler contract involving lesser aid and lesser loss of autonomy was allowed for ten years and by 1967-68 over 80 percent of all types of private school were under contract). Although the law recognizes the 'special character' of the different schools involved, this is severely threatened by other clauses which insist that they should be open to all, and should respect freedom of conscience, quite apart from its undermining by the need to follow the rules and programmes of public education. Effectively the Loi Debré was a central charter for educational standardization for its result was to spread uniform bureaucratic practices to the last strongholds of diversity in instruction. The degree of pluralism introduced *into* the State system by the association of free schools appears small because of lack of internal autonomy, compared with the diversity lost *outside* it with the incorporation of the private sector. As Prost has argued 'Dans la réalité des faits, le pluralisme idéologique est incompatible avec les exigences du service public'.[130] Reversal of the integration process is extremely unlikely and 'en conséquence on peut penser que les futurs débats politiques porteront, non pas sur l'éventualité d'un retour en arrière, mais plutôt sur les modalités d'une intégration plus pousée à l'enseignement public'.[131] Because of this standardization the French system has deprived itself of an external shock absorber and source of independent innovation. In effect this lack of external diversity invites discontented groups to address themselves directly to the cause of their frustrations, the State educational system. And when coupled with the internal inflexibility of the centralized system it constrains them to do so in a particular way, through a process of political manipulation.

POLITICAL MANIPULATION IN A SEMI-PERMEABLE POLITY

A. The Framework of the State

A(i) The Accessibility of the Political Centre

The unusual combination of quasi-presidential and traditional parliamentary government,[132] which was intended to achieve political stability without sacrificing rule by consent, also involved a greater closure of the decision-making arena.

Presidential powers in both principle and practice have subtracted from those of Assembly and concentrated them away from Government and parliament alike. As such they are devices which can be used to override group demands and to resolve issues imperatively, since they carve out an independent area of decision-making. Certainly many of the powers accorded under the new Constitution existed in previous Republics, (Presidential choice of Prime Minister, appointment of Ministers, or the right to ask Parliament to reconsider legislation), but certain new ones clearly strengthened the hand of the executive against Parliament (in particular the right of dissolution, of assuming emergency powers, and of holding popular referenda). Further provisions gave the President more elbow room, and his right to appoint the Prime Minister without submitting his nomination to Assembly meant that the Constitution 'gave him ample leeway to become the effective head of government as well as head of state'.[133] Especially after 1962, when the President was elected on the basis of universal suffrage, he acquired a personal legitimacy greater than that of Premier and Government,[134] which augmented his direct control over policy.

In reality, however, the extent of Presidential powers derived more from Gaullist practice than from the Constitution itself, whose built-in checks he sometimes nullified. For example, two of the four referenda which were held as personal votes of confidence on policy issues were generally regarded as unconstitutional, in their by-passing of Parliament, as was the emergence of a presidential sector of decision-making.[135] Nevertheless, the position of the President ultimately rests on consent, and even if De Gaulle was often guilty of manipulating confidence, parliament and the electorate had frequent opportunities to withhold it — three general elections, three referenda and a presidential election, before his defeat in 1969. Furthermore the Constitution firmly establishes the Government as the executive and the powers of the President would be very much more restricted without the backing of the Chamber. 'This is in practice why De Gaulle had to make sure that the majority of the National Assembly was loyal to his policies and the development of the disciplined Gaullist party is thus a direct consequence of the existence of a parliamentary system'.[136]

Governmental powers, however, represent a further series of devices which insulate government itself from parliament, and which have reinforced Presidential powers in the context of durable Gaullist working majorities. In effect they provide for a manipulation of the decision-making arena to exclude certain issues and interests and to give preference to the expression and execution of policy demands made by government supporters. Once again their rationale is to limit the ability of Parliament to overthrow or obstruct government, in the interests of political stability. Firstly, the abolition of the *interpellation* procedure protected Ministers from being called to account for their policies, whilst the separation of functions (whereby Ministers automatically cease to be Deputies or Senators) cuts down on party pressures upon them and cuts off some of the upward flow of demands. Secondly the

Constitution circumscribes the area of legislative power which means, on the one hand, that Parliament's field of action is no longer for Parliament to determine, and on the other, that a sphere of executive perogative is created. Government can introduce measures by decree which previously had to be passed as laws, and thus implement policy without parliamentary scrutiny, modification or opposition. Finally, a provision by which the Government can make a Bill a matter of confidence on which it would resign if censured,[137] provides them with additional leverage on legislation, as the granting of official aid to Catholic schools shows. Whilst some of these devices exist in other European democracies, their cumulation makes them particularly stringent in France. Together they add up to a loss of control over rule-making by the Assembly to the Government, the latter being able to pursue its own programme whilst the former often cannot obtain consideration of alternative policies or raise certain problems. This is reflected by the great majority of Bills now being Government ones, whilst legislation which is not officially sponsored has only crept up to 10 percent of the whole, compared with 30 percent during the IVth Republic.[138] In sum the hold of Assembly Parties on Government has been loosened and political closure has increased.

Parliamentary powers nevertheless remain the bedrock of the Vth Republic, for Government could make the position of the President untenable, and in turn Parliament and the electorate can overthrow governments. On a day-to-day basis Government has to take heed of Assembly: to protect its majority it makes concessions to the local demands of its deputies, and to negotiate its policies it has to reduce tension by accepting oppositional amendments. Moreover a belligerent Assembly could extend its legislative influence in a parliament which is still not fully institutionalized and an opposition majority in the Chamber would undercut the Presidential aspect of the system. Both would require a strong party organization from the opposition, which in turn makes the nature of elite relations of supreme importance for the working of the Constitution. Since the Vth Republic rests essentially on consent it continues in the parliamentary if not the republican tradition,[139] but because of certain constitutional provisions and political practices it became significantly 'detached from the usual parliamentary and democratic instruments of the political parties, labour organizations, the press and public opinion'.[140] Thus it is classed as being a semi-penetrable polity.

A(ii) Elite Relations

The Constitutional bias favouring Government has been reinforced rather than undermined by the nature of elite relations under the Vth Republic. The political unity of Government groups, compared with the fragmentation of oppositional ones, has made the successful nego-tiation of policy the virtual preserve of Government and its supporters. In this context it is the degree of Party organization achieved by the various parliamentary groups which has been the decisive factor. *The general character of political parties* derives from the endurance of a 'sectional' social structure in France, with a strong geographical basis. The continued existence of a large propertied peasantry (the percentage engaged in the primary sector of the economy remained much higher than in other north western countries), and the predominance of villages over small towns had the overall effect of increasing the importance of constituency politics with its local leaders and interests at the expense of national political organization. Furthermore the enduring salience of the urban-rural cleavage in the post-war period has undercut any possibility of an alliance between peasants and workers and reduced the potential for political solidarity on the Left. In a country with relatively few large businesses, this has been paralleled on the right by antagonism of the small shopkeepers and artisans to big industry. In consequence parties are not clear class parties – the right includes the opponents of the technological revolution, peasant farmers, tradesmen, whitecollar workers and the left embraces not only middle class intellectuals but also what might be termed 'republican professionals'. Nor in important respects are they clear cut ideological parties, despite the endemic character of ideological debate. Certainly the clerical/anti-clerical divide continues to be important; for example, De Gaulle received four times the number of votes from practising Catholics in the 1965 presidential election than from those with no religious affiliation, whilst Mitterand gained nine times more votes from agnostics and atheists than from Catholics.[141] But the predominantly Catholic union (CFTC) and political party (MRP) has moved to the left and been accepted, albeit suspiciously, in various alliances. On the other hand foreign policy has found the Communists curiously closer to the Gaullists than to supporters of NATO or the EEC on the left.

Since cleavages cut across parties 'no French party is controlled by one social interest or depends on it for the bulk of its vote in elections; similarly no social interest is to be found wholly in the ranks of one party, and except for the industrial workers no important social interest is to be found mainly in the ranks of one party. Each party is a medley of social groups and is responsive to pressures of several kinds, even conflicting ones'.[142] This weakens all parties which must simultaneously organize and work at national level whilst blending and aggregating local and sectional interests. It contributes a vast potential for party splits and factionalism and a lasting barrier to durable alliances. Nevertheless the development of mass politics has taken a stride forward under the Vth Republic, but the most crucial aspect of elite relations is that this has not been a symmetrical process on the Right and the Left. 'It is the discipline of the Gaullist party, not the new Constitution, that has been responsible for transforming the first 12 years of the regime from one of stable oppositions and unstable Governments to one of stable Governments and unstable oppositions'.[143]

The Gaullist Political parties, the UNR and its successor the UDR, signal the growth of unity and organization among the elite in government. The heterogeneous Gaullist movement, cemented by personal loyalty rather than political programme, was slowly turned into an effective parliamentary machine which gave the General a firm hold over the decision-making arena. It was 'at first a ministerial team, then a Central Committee for the selection of candidates, then the largest group in Parliament, and – at last – a party'.[144] In 1958 the UNR had no clear policy, even on Algeria. It contested the election as an indeterminate centre party but 'its very equivocations served it; the traditional enemies, Socialist and Conservative, anti-clerical and ardent Catholic, often found it easier to vote for the UNR rather than for one another'.[145] The electoral system, designed by de Gaulle, produced 'one of the most disproportinately constituted assemblies in French history',[146] and gave the UNR a parliamentary hold, whilst the 1962 election gave France a majority party for the first time. But 'the new majority rested on no deep agreement of principle or policy. The basis for unity was personal and therefore transient. The UNR was still very far from being that *grand parti conservateur français* of which moderate right-wingers had often dreamed. It was a supporters' club, not a fully fledged political party'.[147] It had a weak structure, practically no popular membership and functioned mainly as a parliamentary group and electoral organization.

Between 1962-68 it elaborated its party platform, firstly stressing its commitment to *l'efficacité* (translated on the left as 'technocracy') and then in the Lille programme of 1967 extending this concept to include expansion, modernization, efficiency, administrative and regional reform, social democracy and national independence. From 1968 onwards efforts were made to create a strong organized party with improved contact between Government and Parliamentary group and between Parliament and the rank and file. This streamlined Party, renamed the UDR, was structurally sound enough to withstand the transition from De Gaulle to Pompidou and to maintain its political unity, despite the withdrawal of charisma and the coexistence of different ideological strands within its ranks. What is more, by the 1970s it had succeeded in gaining general acceptance for the Gaullist Constitution and legitimating its political institutions. In the four successive elections of 1962, 1967, 1968 and 1973 more than two fifths of the electorate cast their votes as a block for Gaullist candidates, the highest percentage for any one party, and enough to ensure the overwhelming predominance of the Gaullists in all government coalitions. Party organization thus gave De Gaulle 'the advantage, hitherto unique in Republican history, of having for ten years a continuous working, or near working, majority in the National Assembly'.[148]

The fragmented opposition parties were themselves the greatest force for Gaullist stability and predominance in policy matters. Whenever they failed to consolidate an effective opposition, both the Centre and the Left preferring fission to fusion, they gave an electoral, parliamentary and governmental bonus to the Gaullist Party. In this context political arithmetic made coalition imperative among the four major oppositional parties. The Socialists continued on a downhill path, polling only 15 percent of votes in 1958 (compared with 25 percent in 1936) whilst the Communists too reached their lowest electoral ebb, despite representing the only other organized party and gaining the next largest number of votes from 1958-68. For the Centre the recovery of conservative organization in the UNR precipitated an even speedier decline among the Catholic MRP and the Radical Parties. But if streamlining of the Right forced them to contemplate alliance it did not solve their coalitional dilemma. The Socialist party was pivotal in the consolidation of a broader opposition force and basically it could ally with both the Communists on its Left and the Centre Parties on its right.

The Socialist dilemma was two fold. First, neither of these alliances was likely to be stronger numerically than the Gaullist forces, yet a condition of each was the non-inclusion of one of the partners of the other. The Centre was uneasy at the prospect of an alliance including Communists, while an alliance between Socialist and Centre parties alienated both the Communist party and sections of the Socialist Party. Second, even if an electoral coalition stretching from Centre to Communists could have succeeded in winning an election, the victors would have found it impossible to agree on a Governmental pro- gramme.[149]

On the one hand a coalition of the Left has been consistently un- dermined by the possibility of a Centre coalition. The Radicals in particular have been continuously torn between federation with the Left and attempts to rejuvenate the Centre, especially as the UDR evolved into a more traditional conservative party. Although the Centre declined almost to political irrelevance between 1958-70, (the MRP ceasing to exist in 1967 and the whole centre only polling about 1/6th of the vote), it remained of destructive significance in relation to a consolidated opposition. In 1965 disagreements with the MRP (aid to Catholic schools being a major stumbling block) were largely responsible for the failure of a non-Communist Left coalition, the MRP opting out to try to develop a *Centre Démocrate*. Later attempts, spearheaded by the Radicals, to revive the Centre in a *Mouvement Reformateur* proved equally incohesive but had the same effect vis-à-vis the Left and in fact followed their desertion of the Socialist Federation in 1969. Essentially the activities of the Centre have hindered the polarization of opposition which is necessary to challenge the UDR.

On the other hand the major cause of weakness of the Left is the division between Communists and Socialists which seems to prevent a trend towards a two-party system. It was this antagonism which prompted the Socialists under Deferre to attempt a non-communist coalition in 1964, which was doomed not only because of dissension from the Centre but by the simple numerical need for Communist support. Following its breakdown the Socialist Party undertook to create a democratic federation uniting Radicals, Communists and smaller left-wing parties in 1966. In fact little more than an electoral alliance emerged, and although effective in cutting the Gaullist majority in 1967, the parties came no closer to a common programme, each contributor wanting unity on its own terms. The demoralization pro- duced by the Gaullist landslide victory after the May events provoked further dissension which was underlined by the failure to agree on a common left-wing presidential candidate in 1969. A new attempt was made by Mitterand to form a Union of the Left committed to gaining a 'socialist majority', but internal disputes focusing on the Communist issue meant that by 1972 'left-wing unity seemed more remote than at any time during the twelve years of the regime. The Gaullists were well aware, even if their opponents were not, that the divisions and un-certainties of the non-Communist opposition were among their own most powerful political assets'.[150]

The Communists, on the other hand, with a vote stabilizing at about 20 percent during the Vth Republic, recognized the strategic necessity of unity on the Left. They were prepared to make policy concessions to bring it about — an endorsement of the 'peaceful passage to Socialism' and a grudging recognition of the EEC — but these had the unintended consequence of undermining the Party's revolutionary appeal, especially given its conservative role in the May events. It had thus become less acceptable to its own supporters without becoming any more acceptable to the rest of the Left. The improved performance of the Left at the 1973 general election and the narrow defeat of Mit-terand in the 1974 Presidential election indicate some recovery but does not yet begin to point to the emergence of a credible alternative to government by the Right.

Thus the 'most important single political reality of the Fifth Republic is not the emergence of strong Governments, but the non-emergence of strong Oppositions able to prevent the majority from doing what any majority will do if it can . . . namely, to take advantage of their position'.[151] In other words, the nature of elite relations, with unity the preserve of Government whilst disarray characterized oppo-sition, intensified the constitutional and electoral biases towards majority domination in policy matters. The failure of the Left thus played a major role in increasing political closure towards a host of social demands. Because of it 'neither government nor Parliament provided that *circuit de confiance* between the State and public opinion which they were in theory supposed to provide'.[152]

A(iii) The Structure of Educational Interest Groups

Since the opposition parties were too disunited to effectively introduce educational demands into the decision-making arena, interest groups became the main channel for their expression. 'With the failure of the parties in the Assembly to regain their former position, the onus is firmly with the groups to secure an articulation and an aggregation of interests, but it is doubtful if they are fit to this task'.[153] For the sectional character of social structure which accounts for the overall weakness of party organization is similarly responsible for a lack of superimposition among interest groups.

Precisely the same cleavages are at work and affect the whole range of interest groups through which educational demands are expressed — professional associations, trade unions, employers' organizations, student groups and parental lobbies. France's occupation structure, distinctive among advanced industrial societies for the endurance of the urban and rural 'little man', has spawned a variety of action groups which have succeeded the outburst of Poujadism in the Fifties. As particularistic associations their main effect has been to weaken employers' organizations and unions alike — two of the main types of bodies whose national organization should otherwise favour political manipulation for educational change. The main industrial organization, the *Conseil National du Patronat Français* 'may not have acquired, even by the 1970s, genuine recognition from business as a whole. Despite its growth, it suffered from not being really representative of the small firms whose leaders, for reasons similar to those of many workers, preferred not to join any organization'.[154] Trade Unions do not organize more than a quarter of the active population, a fact partly due to the occupational structure, but for which their politicization is even more responsible. Although the salience of the religious divide between them has almost disappeared, with the secularization of the CFDT, traditional ideological cleavages continue among the four main unions and preclude rapprochement between them. This not only weakens their impact, in the absence of concerted action, but also cancels out the advantages of their rational and national structure. Furthermore these divisions prevent a direct link-up with professional associations of teachers, which, like under the IVth Republic, dare not put all their eggs in one basket. Finally religion has not ceased to be of importance — Meynaud mentions at least twenty interest groups of different kinds with distinctive religious orientations and these were always ready to mobilize to get State aid to Catholic schools onto the political agenda.

Given this endemic lack of superimposition the most that can occur are lightening opportunist alliances, which are essentially impermanent because they are linked to particular issues. In fact, as the 1968 events revealed, these may be concluded as much against other interest groups as for the cause itself, and joint participation does not lead to durable alliances or strengthened organization. Indeed organizational weakness is their second major characteristic. Blondel has maintained that the only really representative organizations, for a period in the fifties, were the middle class group of teachers and doctors and student unions.[155] The plethora of associational groups of all kinds which developed at the end of the decade (Meynaud lists over three hundred) contributed to particularism, factionalism and the narcissism of small differences. This was equally true of the extreme right wing groups springing into prominence with the Algerian problem and the left wing *groupuscules* flowering in the mid-sixties, both of which became involved in educational conflict. The small numbers belonging to each of these groups, the eternal preoccupation with inter-group squabbles and the tendency to split rather than coalesce, were forces for organizational diffusion rather than the consolidation of united national associations, necessary to confront the centralized State effectively.

As we have seen in the past, sectional interests on both the right and the left have sought the sponsorship of political parties whilst avoiding exclusive commitment to any particular one in a multi-party system. This pattern of action continued on the part of trade unions and teachers' associations, in the absence of a united Left, but it carried a new penalty in the face of a united Right. For the lasting divorce between these interest groups and opposition parties introduced an asymmetry of influence in which right wing pressure groups had the ear of government whilst their left-wing counterparts scarcely had a hearing in the National Assembly. This asymmetry was to prove particularly favourable to the Catholic schools lobby. In turn the failure of parliamentary manipulation by interest groups on the Left encouraged extra-parliamentary activities. Cut off from political influence or the prospect of it, which are powerful forces for group discipline and the aggregation of demands, the opposite occurred — the clubs and factions spawned and their internecine conflict intensified. A vicious circle developed — the powerlessness of opposition fostering the *groupuscules* and the conflict of the latter working against the unity of the Left.

In reality, the political Clubs of the 1960s (and presumably of the 1970s) do not represent 'new thinking' as they claim or hope to do. They constitute a very old approach to politics. They represent that combination of intellectualism, universalism and individualism that has characterized French reformist and revolutionary politics since the eighteenth century, and that, perhaps more than anything else, has helped to prevent the consolidation of stable and disciplined democratic parties.[156]

The demotion of Parliament and the emergence of strong Government under the Vth Republic has meant in general that direct pressure on Government is more likely to be effective than working through Deputies, once the parliamentary majority ceased to be precarious. Although a more covert process, there seems little doubt that it has selectively ignored demands from unions, students and teachers' associations and been more responsive to the claims of more conservative industrial and confessional interests. There is thus a marked asymmetry in the effectiveness of political manipulation which stems from the differential accessibility of government to different interest groups.

Government itself has encouraged the substitution of consultation for confrontation with the interest groups, as the existence of 500 Councils, 1,200 Committees and 3,000 Commissions at the national level indicates. But this

> proliferation of consultation does not at all mean that the interests hold sway: neither the government nor its bureaucracy is subject to an adverse vote, and given the fundamental disunity of the individual interests, it is not difficult to rule through division. Furthermore, the guiding principle of the Fifth Republic has all along been to tame the power of the political intermediaries – the interest groups as well as the parties.[157]

Where interests failed to get a response from Government, their reaction to rejection was identical – a resort to a direct action displayed first by the small agriculturalists, then by small shopkeepers, students, left wing factions, and teachers' associations and finally by trade unions.

B. Educational Interaction

During the Fifth Republic educational interaction followed precisely this pattern of a build-up of demands, the frustration and repudiation of educational interests, and their eventual explosion into direct action. The major trade unions, together with many teachers and academics, had voted against De Gaulle in the initial referendum to legitimate his assumption of authority and were to pay continuously for their opposition. Before 1968 the focal points of interaction marked a return to the earlier preoccupations with secularization, democratization and modernization. In each area changes were introduced and the processes involved had three things in common. Each measure reflected the use of government powers (not only their parliamentary majority but also decrees and motions of confidence). Each was passed in the face of substantial opposition from the teaching profession and external interest groups. Each in turn contributed to a growing reservoir of discontent, accumulating outside and inside the educational system.

Desecularization

The Loi Debré of 1959, giving aid to Catholic schools, was an immediate and blatant slap in the face for professional anti-clericalism and for Republican opinion in general. When the Barangé Law had permitted allocations towards teachers' salaries and buildings in the private sector in 1951, an MRP Deputy called this the 'breach through which the flood will pass'. Given the strength and vociferousness of its opponents this seemed remarkably unlikely. However in the first National Assembly to be returned in the Vth Republic, two-thirds of Deputies belonged to the Parliamentary Association for Free Schools, a Catholic intergroup in search of permanent State underwriting for its establishments. Immediately the Prime Minister established the Lapie Commission to examine the question and recommend legislation, and equally quickly the National Committee for Secular Action (CNAL) aggregated and articulated objections to subsidizing the confessional sector. Defense of laïcité was perhaps the one issue upon which the gamut of professional associations and the majority of trade unionists were deeply and fundamentally united. Nevertheless, their demands were overridden, the Government instead rewarded its Catholic supporters by embarking on a new policy of financial co-operation between public and private education.

The strength of opposition ruptured the Government's majority, led to the resignation of the (Socialist) Minister of Education (when additional amendments were introduced favouring the Church schools), and the resignation of half of the *Conseil Supérieur* on the grounds that it had not been consulted as was proper with major changes. Despite this De Gaulle made the bill a matter of confidence, and the threat of dissolving the National Assembly produced a vote of 427 for, 71 against and 18 abstentions — the new style of government had asserted itself in educational politics. A series of decrees and circulars issued in the next two years allowing chaplaincies to be attached to public schools on parental request[158] added insult to injury for any group standing to the left of the Radical Party. To them it threw in doubt the whole concept of a secular system and a neutral Université. Publication of the vastly increased sums flowing to the confessional schools under the Loi Debré added to their grievances. Already in 1967 the CNAL was preparing for massive demonstrations in favour of a single secular system incorporating all schools which had accepted public funds. Its target was the review of the Debré law, scheduled to begin in 1969, but meanwhile it represented a growing pool of dissatisfied people who recognized that these concessions to Catholic opinion hinged on the continuation of a Right-wing majority and Gaullist manipulation of constitutional and governmental powers in favour of their supporters.

Democratization

The Decrée Berthoin of 1959 put an end to the 'war of the projects' and was intended to defuse and diffuse the discontent which had built up following the repeated failures of the *école unique* movement. As such it was a compromise, intended to give a little to those who had wanted so much more democratization, yet to take away little from those who feared losing most of their vested interests in the educational status quo. 'La réforme de M. Berthoin . . . réalise en effet ce qui peut l'être des écoles moyennes, si l'on veut ménager les corporatismes rivaux'.[159] In creating a two-year observational cycle which took place in existing establishments the reform turned its back on structural change: it did not create a middle school in any real sense but contented itself with harmonizing programmes in primary and secondary schools for this two-year period. It was imposed imperatively by decree whilst De Gaulle still possessed the special powers granted to him before the new National Assembly had met. Thus it stemmed directly from the Presidency without there being any opportunity for Parliamentary intervention or modification.

As is typical of compromise measures it satisfied no-one. Its enactment had been opposed by the secondary teachers (SNES). The expansion of secondary education had already affected this part of the profession, worsening its working conditions, increasing its size, and lowering its academic qualifications. The reform could only hasten this degradation by providing a lower quality of pupil and delaying the start of the lycée curriculum proper. Thus to the SNES 'la démocratisation consiste à supprimer tous les obstacles à la sélection des meilleurs'.[160] The *Société des Agrégés* was even more categoric in its condemnation of any mixing of teachers, methods and subjects and was joined by *Franco-Ancienne* in its insistence that selection should be completed before the 6th class so that Latin could be started there, as was traditional in the lycée.

On the other hand, the instituteurs (SNI), technical teachers (SNET) and students (UNEF) condemned the reform as half-hearted because it had refused to create a fully autonomous middle school. Similarly the *Syndicat Général de l'Education Nationale* (affiliated with the CFDT) continued to advocate that such *écoles moyennes* 'ne sont pas une condition suffisante mais une condition absoluement nécessaire de la démocratisation'.[161] They condemned the endurance of preparatory classes to the lycées as a perpetuation of privilege and unmasked the class interest concealed in pleas for the early start for the secondary curriculum because it had to be absorbed slowly. 'Il y a quelque illogisme à éxiger une impregnation lente par une durée maximum des études tout en pretendant ne s'intéresser qu'aux petits génies qui saut une classe sur deux pour devenir bachelier complet à 15 ans'.[162]

This degree of dissatisfaction indicated that the 1959 compromise was not the final solution to grievances which had rankled for half a century. Continued pressure from the latter group produced some further concessions. Fouchet as Minister of Education conceded that the object of orientation was largely defeated by its occurring for some in primary schools and for others in collèges or lycées. He was responsible for creating *collèges d'enseignement secondaire* (CES), by decree in 1963, which combined part of the traditional primary syllabus and part of the curriculum which by tradition belonged to the secondary level. 'Surtout, la réforme vient trop tard. Réalisées à froid, en quelque sorte, par création d'établissements nouveaux — de type polyvalent — elle n'aurait menacé aucune situation acquise. Mais elle se fait à chaud, par transformation d'établissements déjà existants'.[163] By happenning at all they incurred the hostility of those defending the status quo, by taking place so slowly these transformations did little to satisfy democratic reformers. By 1968 there were only 1,500 CES, a third of children were still receiving terminal primary instruction and it would clearly be years before all lycées transformed their first cycle of studies into semi-autonomous middle schools. In sum the concessions made to modify the Berthoin solution, which had been imposed imperatively, drew off little of the discontent stimulated by undemocratic institutions and practices.

Modernization

Unlike the secularization issue which concerns all parts of the system equally, and the democratization question which focuses on points of pupil selection and transition from school to school, pressures for modernization are concentrated on the stages preceding entry to active life. The Fouchet reforms passed between 1963-66 and covering aspects of secondary, technical and university studies were all concerned with improving vocational preparation for the labour market. Although the Government was undoubtedly more in tune with this kind of demand, it is also the case that the changes introduced correspond more closely to its own national technocratic goals than to the specific requirements of given industries, professions or businesses in particular areas. This is clearly illustrated by the way education is incorporated in the National Plans. Educational levels are calibrated with occupational qualifications and the two are combined with indicative manpower planning. Traditionally, planning has been a bureaucratic rather than a democratic exercise which involved an official interpretation of group interests rather than groups negotiating their demands directly.

> The Plan is symptomatic of the downgrading of parliamentary institutions, alongside the shackles imposed by the constitution. To convert this to 'democratic planning' by allowing for a wide functional consultation stumbles on the power position of the higher bureaucracy; and the evocative term 'technocracy' endows the state-machine with a political purpose. As long as this retains its cohesion and is looked upon favourably by the government of the day, then the 'political' and the 'official' status of group interests are kept in a subordinate position.[164]

Nevertheless, since representatives of large scale economic interests generally figured among the government's supporters, if not its most enthusiastic ones, they did gain some satisfaction of their requirements from the Fouchet reforms.

> Les diverses mesures prises au cours des dernières années en vue de développer la formation professionnelle (réforme et développement de la scolarité aux niveaux des enseignements techniques du second cycle long et court, création des IUT, développement de la formation professionnelle post-scolaire dans le cadre de la loi du 3 décembre 1966) repondent dans une large mesure aux besoins exprimés par les porte-parole de l'économie.[165]

However, with the single exception mentioned above, these measures were passed by decree, thus overriding the opposition of other groups and illustrating the asymmetry of educational influence of different interests in politics.

In other words, one of the main consequences of the Fouchet reforms was to add to the growing pool of discontent on the Left. The Caen Colloqium of teachers held in 1967 and the Amiens Colloqium held a year later provided a running critical commentary on the reforms. The major student organizations condemned the internal chaos resulting from their application, and the Left generally viewed the introduction of 'short' courses at secondary and higher level as the creation of an inferior form of qualification which would perpetuate class differentials. Yet with typically military humour, M. Fouchet confided to a close friend in 1967 that 'in fact the University does not mind so much being raped'[166] – a year later she was certainly not lying back and enjoying it.

Thus the first decade of the Vth Republic had seen a gradual build-up of discontent outside the political arena. The antagonism which had existed between the profession and Gaullism in 1958 had never been overcome: there had been a persistent rejection of professional demands – in sum a complete failure of political manipulation on the part of the latter which finally led them to take extra-parliamentary action. 'Si, comme c'est le cas en France depuis 1958, l'orientation politique dominante du corps enseignant et celle de la majorité dont est issu le Gouvernement ne coincident pas, la méfiance du premier vis-à-vis des initiatives prises par le second est un facteur supplémentaire d'immobilisme. Dans une telle conjuncture il n'y a de déblocage possible que par la base'.[167] But the other groups who might join with them in concerted direct action, that is those on the Left and among the student body whose grievances ran equally deep, were still divided and sub-divided among themselves.

Although in 1967 the Communist Party published an issue of *L'Ecole et la Nation*, condemning Gaullist reforms as mere shunting operations, the instituteurs' SNI passed a motion at its September Congress condemning the government's economic, social and political policy, and in November students went on strike at Nanterre over the application of the Fouchet reforms, this signalled the general growth of frustration shared by parties, students and the profession rather than the emergence of real unity between them. Although teachers themselves had some unity within either the FEN or the SGEN, the latter was affiliated with the CFDT, whilst many members of the former belonged to the CGT, which were not themselves on good terms.

Furthermore, many university teachers (members of SNESup) and students looked to the parties (PSU) and factions of the extreme Left which were viewed with the utmost suspicion by the CGT and Communist Party which had experienced difficulties with its dissident youth section (UEC) since 1963.[168] The general innaccessibility of politics to left-wing educational interests led them to explode into direct-action, but their internal divisions prevented them from forming other than temporary alliances, cemented by the euphoria of revolt, and never holding together long enough to consolidate real educational gains.

THE MAY EVENTS

The events taking place between May and June 1968 are frequently subdivided into three phases; the period up to 14th May, generally termed the University phase, saw the development of the student movement from Nanterre to the Sorbonne and to other universities, culminating in large-scale fighting and the famous 'night of the barricades'; the period between the 15th and the 27th May, frequently called the economic phase, witnessed the outbreak of strikes among technical and professional employees as well as industrial workers, reaching the unprecedented total of eight million strikers, many of whom occupied their factories and work places; after this date followed the political phase of the crisis, in which the parties and unions struggled to regain control of the situation and the defence of the Vth Republic appeared less than certain. As I have given a detailed analysis of the events and their literature elsewhere,[169] only a brief examination of these phases and the links between them will be presented here. Implicit in it, however, is a rejection of the official chain-reaction account, endorsed by Government and Communist Party alike,[170] which interpreted the events as a fortuitous series of episodes, tenuously linked by accident and opportunism. Instead the perspective adopted is closer to that of Chombart de Lauwe,[171] who viewed the events as the explosion of grievances accumulated in the context of political inaccessibility and educational centralization.

The strike taking place in November 1967 at Nanterre, a new faculty of the University of Paris designed to decant the student overflow, concerned certain applications of the Fouchet reforms. The ministerial indifference with which it was met itself contributed to the politicization of the movement since it presented a handle to extreme left-wing groups stressing revolution rather than reform and whose activities had recently been heightened by the South-east Asian situation. The invasion of the administration building in protest over student arrests during a Vietnam demonstration led to the formation of the *22 mars* movement and the first closure of the faculty. After repeated protests in April, eight students were commanded to appear before the disciplinary council of the University of Paris. The way in which this Nanterre affair mushroomed to become a national concern owes much to the centralized structure in which it was embedded.

On the 3rd of May the crisis shifted to Paris. In the meeting summoned by minority left wing factions[172] to protest outside the Sorbonne about the disciplinary procedures, the ensuing battle with the police, and the closure of the Sorbonne itself, some see only the militant activities of the groupuscules. Without denying the importance of these groups for organization, mobilization and even militarization (some of their members had experience during the Algerian crisis), this conspiracy thesis simply cannot account for the numbers involved nor for the popular support given to the movement during the university stage (a public opinion poll on 8th May showed 80 percent of Parisians to be in sympathy with the students). More important appears to be the very centralization of the educational system itself, which traditionally had led to a parallel organization of student bodies at the national level. Whether one takes the subsidized national union of students (UNEF) or the student branches of political parties or factions, their national structure reflected the fact that collective bargaining must be central rather than local, and that by the very definition of the educational system, local affairs were national ones.

The attitudes of students participating during this phase were a complex mixture of political contestation and privileged idealism, of condemnation of technological production and fear of unemployment, of desires to turn the universities into red bases and of simply wanting a more rational relationship between university studies and future life. The typical product of this amalgam was a 'transgressive' association — the '22 Mars' movement — for whose members 'role images are either unavailable because of the uncertainty of the professional future or unacceptable because of their opposition to the traditional system of social roles'.[173] The university phase was fundamentally dualistic — it cannot be fully assimilated to a new form of class conflict in post-industrial society, as Touraine[174] suggests, for one strand was more preoccupied with existential demands, was more concerned with 'making art' than revolution and instituting the fête rather than the *base rouge* in the Sorbonne and Odéon. Nor, however, can the movement be seen as purely idealist in nature, for this has the obverse difficulty of neglecting the political engagement of many participants. Its dualism was its strength. The movement only acquired such magnitude because the anti-rationalism of students deprived of realistic academic goals fused with the political ideologies of students rejecting academic goals to produce, for a time, a common vocabulary and solidarity of action. But this dualism was its ultimate weakness because the moment of fusion passed precisely when political and educational concerns ceased to be complementary.

The economic phase which amplified the university outburst can only, with great difficulty, be seen as stage-managed by the student political factions, whose membership was numbered in dozens only two months earlier. Certainly contact had previously been established between students and young workers in particular areas. The two Trotskyite groups, JCR and CLER, as well as the pro-Chinese UJC (M-L), had published student-worker papers, been active in the apprentice centres, where the CGT was especially weak, and generally established channels of communication with industry, which would have facilitated the spread of student ideas. Vastly more important however was the willingness of the CFDT, the second largest trade union, to declare strikes, though it did so more in opposition to the CGT than in direct support of the students. 'It looked as if, with the cement of Catholicism gone, the CFDT was seeking to substitute a Socialist cement, which might perhaps help to explain its more sympathetic attitude to the 1968 revolutionary students and strikers'.[175] This degree of worker support was apparent rather than real — it reflected a bandwagon effect through which different elements profited from the occasion to seek different ends. 'Poussé par les éléments les plus jeunes, l'ensemble de la classe ouvrière a profité de cette occasion pour reprendre une conscience plus claire de ses revendications de base'.[176] Perhaps the participation of certain architects, doctors and barristers had more to do with the educational issues involved, but equally it may simply have reflected the chance to get something done, as, for example, the telecommunications strike sought to throw off the governmental hold over the media. Finally, the belated participation of the CGT (dragged in because a leader must follow his movement) completed the amplification of the strike to unprecedented proportions in France. Its entry was described by Séguy as a blow against those *provocateurs* who had sought to engage the working class in revolution and as a redirection of the conflict towards traditional union claims. This above all underlined the conflicting aims of the different elements active during May. 'The student revolt acted as a detonator for the strike of workers, but despite appearances the latter was the *inverse of the former*; while students sought to transcend the consumer society, the workers attempted to gain a greater share in it'.[177]

The political phase of the movement was not only a crisis for Government but for the official Left too, 'y compris Fédération de la Gauche et Parti Communiste, témoins muets, impuisants, ignorés par le torrent de mai qui se déchaînait en dehors d'eux et aussi contre eux'.[178] The leadership of the groupuscules, who increasingly channelled the movement without ever fully controlling it, never viewed victory as a replacement of De Gaulle by Mitterand, and least of all as the establishment of the first Communist government in Western Europe. But their increased influence was ultimately destructive for it sought to clarify the vague vocabulary of revolution which tenuously articulated the movement, to organize student-worker relations rather than letting them rest on the emotive isomorphism between occupation of university and of factory, and to treat educational questions not only as secondary but as a source of diversion. 'It is here that the rich and triumphant unity of the student commune began to crumble and the political commune to detach itself and sometimes to oppose itself to the university commune'.[179] The fissures reappeared, enabling De Gaulle to re-interpret the movement as the product of these provocateurs, to ban these extremist groups on declaring the June election, and to win a decisive vote in favour of the restoration of order. Division within the movement allowed the government to tackle it piecemeal, with punitive measures reserved for the groupuscules, financial concessions to the workers ('rien de ce point de vue n'est aussi révélateur que le décalage entre l'immensité de l'arrêt de travail et le minceur des revendications avancées par les directions syndicales'),[180] and university reform to remove the educational detonator.

The *Loi d'orientation de l'enseignement supérieur*, prepared by Edgar Faure, was a typical piece of panic legislation adopted in the National Assembly in October by 441 votes to 0, the Communists and 6 gaullists abstaining. The major political parties had restricted themselves to textual criticism and minor amendments, the whole tenor of debate being summed up by one Deputy who commended Faure's text for having the merit of existing.[181] The parties of the Left no less than those of the Right had an interest in defusing the educational problem. In the face of virtual parliamentary unanimity on the bill, the teachers' associations and student organizations were hopelessly divided — because the movement had never been fully politicized it had not been able to retreat, re-organize and reformulate its strategy after the electoral landslide. No concerted extra-parliamentary opposition impeded either the passing or the implementation of the act, and the events of 1968 were to prove too damaging to those who had taken part for this to have re-occurred by the mid-seventies.

The Events were disintegrative in two different respects. On the one hand, the failure to impose the changes sought caused the membership of many participant organizations to sink. 'What had happened was that students' and teachers' organizations — or at least the great majority — had ceased to be effective representatives of educational interests and had become purely political bodies'.[182] This was particularly true of the UNEF which collapsed into a number of factions, the largest being the communist dominated UNEF—Renouveau. In turn this meant that 'splits and almost complete disorganization put students, at the time of their increased legal influence in university administration, in a wholly ineffective position'.[183] On the other hand, the links which temporarily had been forged between different kinds of educational interest groups were broken and with them the opportunity for aggregating educational grievances was lost. The breach between the two main trade unions widened with the CGT reaffirming its interest in concrete wage demands and condemning the leftist trend in the CFDT as 'revolutionary infantilism'. Simultaneously, however, both closed trade union ranks, shrinking from the destructive influence of the PSU, and reaffirming their traditional independence from political parties. This attitude was also marked in the UNEF-Renouveau which restored primacy to educational issues. But this rejection was reciprocal, the official political parties being equally wary of student activism and the Communist party playing a moderating role in this respect.

The early seventies was thus a period of enduring grievances and continuing disunity. The 1968 law seeking to modernize the university provided little satisfaction for the student body. Their political factions, banned after the events, reformed themselves with increased optimism about a 'proletarian alliance' and an overt commitment to violent action. Yet this resurgence of faith in the revolutionary character of the working class has been accompanied by few signs of willingness on the part of the latter to provide a carrier organization, and not only because of stricter union surveillance. This has resulted in the common pattern of violence being turned inward against the university itself. The outbreaks taking place in 1970 showed very little attempt being made to find an educational pretext which justified political confrontation. Nevertheless, these are the groups, together with their symathisers among teachers, who may be expected to react violently against any further modernization whose effect is to harness higher education more closely to the mixed economy. On the other hand, the majority of students who, without enthusiasm, seemed prepared to wait and see the outcome of the reforms, retain realistic grievances about the divorce between university and active life. And it is not only the outcome of the modernization issue which has left behind seething discontent. An amendment to the Debré Law in 1970 brought the old anti-clerical pressures to the surface and indicated that official policy towards catholic schools rests on the continuation of the Right majority. Similarly, the virulence of debates about the teaching of Latin, a smokescreen behind which the battle for equality of opportunity is fought, shows the question of democratization to be unresolved. Given disunity among the discontented parties, their grievances are likely to grow for they will not be able to exert effective political pressure. The pattern of accumulation of dissatisfactions and their ultimate explosion seems likely to continue, but the next explosion is itself conditional on the disunity of opposition being surmounted.

GENERAL PROPOSITIONS

As an example of a semi-permeable polity the Vth Republic is a clear case of the powers of Assembly being weakened by Constitutional alterations. This coincided with a rather idiosyncratic set of elite relations which defy simple classification as either disunited or cohesive. During the period of the Vth Republic covered here there was substantially more cohesion amongst the ranks of Government than those of opposition parties. This in turn operated to intensify the constitutional provisions favouring President and Government at the expense of parliament. In other words, the predominantly Gaullist period which is dealt with here was distinctive in that the President's party consistently dominated the Assembly thus precluding a strong countervailing influence from parliament. Yet this is not a universal feature of the Vth Republic; it was a characteristic of Gaullism which has undergone considerable modification under the Presidency of Giscard d'Estaing. On the other hand, a lack of co-operation on the Left and an absence of superimposition of groups interested in educational change have all the appearance of durable features of French politics in the Twentieth century.

— The existence of a semi-permeable polity produces a distinct bias in the kinds of educational demands which can reach the central decision-making arena, as the manipulative action of government excludes certain issues and interests. This is exacerbated by a disunited opposition, but not caused by it for it derives directly from the loss of rule-making from Assembly to Government. Thus there is a built-in asymmetry of access to different interest groups which favours government supporters, giving preference to the expression of their demands.

— The semi-permeable polity in conjunction with a united government leads to the downward flow of policy-directives which (unlike the impenetrable polity) serve government supporters as well as the party in office itself. The role of the parliamentary opposition is much weaker here than in the accessible polity and it is not a continuous participant in the shaping of policy. Instead legislation is imperatively designed and systematically skewed towards serving official ends, whilst taking into account manifest and dangerous sources of discontent. Its provisions are compromises calculated to give away as little as possible to oppositional interests without stimulating increased hostility. Sometimes these calculations are wrong, changes being too slow, too minor, or too grudging to keep the lid on seething discontent and its outbreak necessitates a more generous compromise measure.

— In the semi-permeable polity there is again a strong premium on the combination and joint-action of professional and external interest groups of all kinds at the national level. However, the social heterogeneity of those who are dissatisfied with current education does not favour the emergence of a solidary organization exerting consistent political pressure. Although the government will seek to tame such groups, it does not (unlike the impermeable polity) fundamentally undermine the legitimacy of unions and associations or prevent their use of non-violent political action: in the semipermeable polity official constraint preventing educational organization is less important than the social composition of those seeking change, in reducing the effectiveness of educational conflict.

— The absence of a cohesive opposition movement intensifies the tendency for educational demands to be expressed through extra-parliamentary action, for the former leads to continuous failures in political manipulation above and beyond the legislative bias towards government interests. There is a pattern of the build-up of demands for change, political frustration, and explosion into direct action, the latter being the main source of policy concessions, which are gained via the panic legislation which ensues. Such alliances will be of temporary duration because of the fundamental lack of superimposition of the groups involved: in general there are many associational groups but few durable coalitions.

— The profession is in an intermediary position in relation to the other two kinds of polities. Its corporate and consultative role is smaller than in the open polity, whilst its degree of organization is greater than in the closed polity. It shares with the former the ability to organize and form alliances with parties, unions, and interest groups outside the educational field, and it shares with the latter the inability to play other than a negative role of obstructiveness within educational institutions. These two aspects are closely intertwined in the encouragement of revolt.

NOTES

1. A distinction drawn and maintained by Anthony Giddens, 'Elites', *New Society*, Vol. XXII, No. 528, 16 Nov. 1972, pp. 389-92.

2. In this debate evidence about the existence of semi-autonomous elites, of antagonism between elite groups, or cross-cutting membership (all of which refer to elite relations), has been systematically confused with governmental openness, diversity and decentralization (all of which pertain to the framework of the State). Not only did some cold warriors use evidence of disunity or distinctness among elites as an argument in favour of Western constitutional arrangements, but some of their opponents also thought they attacked this form of government by pointing to the solidarity and super-imposition of elites. This meant that much of the debate was conducted at cross-purposes.

3. John Rex, 'Capitalism, Elites and the Ruling Class', in P. Stanworth and A. Giddens (eds.), *Elites and Power in British Society*, London, 1974.

4. A. F. Bentley, *The Process of Government*, Cambridge, Mass., 1967, p. 257.

5. Steven Lukes, *Power: A Radical View*, London, 1974, pp. 21-22.

6. Reductionism does not *necessarily* follow from the failure to distinguish the form of government, (a), from relations among governing elites, (b), because statements about institutions (a), may be translated into statements about collectivities (b), both of course being group terms. Nevertheless, to conflate governmental structure (a) with elite organization (b) does appear to encourage individualism, and what is more important to discourage examination of 'systemic' or 'organizational' effects, where the mobilization of bias results from the form of organization.

7. E. E. Schattschneider, *The Semi-Sovereign People*, New York, 1960, p. 71.

8. David Nicholls, *Three Varieties of Pluralism*, London, 1974, p. 24.

9. Cf. Robert A. Dahl, *Who Governs? Democracy and Power in an American City*, New Haven, 1961, p. 93 f.

10. Cf. P. Bachrach and M. S. Baratz, *Power and Poverty. Theory & Practice*, New York, 1970, esp. pages 23-50.

11. Steven Lukes, *Power: A Radical View*, op. cit.

12. Robert A. Dahl, *Who Governs? Democracy and Power in an American City*, op. cit., p. 92.

13. Margaret Scotford Archer and Salvador Giner, 'Social Stratification in Europe', in Archer and Giner (eds.), *Contemporary Europe: Class, Status and Power*, London, 1971.

14. John Rex, 'Capitalism, Elites and the Ruling Class', in P. Stanworth and A. Giddens, (eds.), *Elites and Power in British Society*, op. cit., p. 213.

15. Gordon Smith, *Politics in Western Europe*, London, 1972, p. 37.

16. Patrick L. Alston, *Education and the State in Tsarist Russia*, Stanford, 1969, p. 150.

17. Ibid., p. 110.

18. Ibid, quoted from Tolstoy, p. 83.

19. Cf. Nicholas Hans, *The Russian Tradition in Education*, London, 1963, Ch. IV.

20. Patrick L. Alston, *Education and the State in Tsarist Russia*, op. cit., p. 89.

21. Ibid., p. 143.

22. Ibid., p. 156.

23. Cf. Jaan Pennar, Ivan I. Bakalo and G. Z. F. Bereday, *Modernization and Diversity in Soviet Education*, New York, 1971, pp. 141-145.

24. Control and content were clearly linked since 'any weakening of the maturity system would weaken the interlocking foundations of scholastic formalism – European academic standards, institutional bifurcation and State control'. Patrick L. Alston, *Education and the State in Tsarist Russia*, op. cit., p. 153.

25. Loc. cit.

26. J. Pennar, I. I. Bakalo and G. Z. F. Bereday, *Modernization and Diversity in Soviet Education*, op. cit. 'The teaching community was close to the people. The number of teachers had been increased by training peasant youth for teaching. Joining the ranks of the teachers, who were held in high esteem by the people, were also those intellectuals who dedicated themselves to serving the people. It is not surprising therefore that teachers who were in the armed forces joined the revolutionaries during the first days of the February revolution of 1917'. p. 145.

27. Loc. sit.

28. Cf. R. Karça, 'A General View of Soviet Education', and Jaan Pennar, 'Party Control over Soviet Schools', in G. Z. F. Bereday and J. Pennar, *The Politics of Soviet Education*, London, 1960.

29. Patrick L. Alston, *Education and the State in Tsarist Russia*, op. cit., p. 120 ff.

30. Ibid., p. 246.

31. J. Pennar, I. I. Bakalo and G. Z. F. Bereday, *Modernization and Diversity in Soviet Education*, op. cit., p. 260.

32. Ibid., p. 236-237. In discussing the Baltic region (Estonia, Livonia, Latvia and Lithuania) the authors point out that the number of private schools increased after 1905 when the Russian language policy was relaxed. For example, educational societies were maintaining 36 private schools in Estonia by 1910, but these were largely auxilliary to the general education system and could not issue valid diplomas. Upon annexation of the Baltic States by the Soviet Union, radical educational re-organization took place and all existing private schools were placed under the jurisdiction of the State.

33. Patrick L. Alston, *Education and the State in Tsarist Russia*, op. cit., p. 214.

34. E. H. Carr, *The Bolshevik Revolution 1917-23*, London, 1952, Vol. II, p. 273.

35. R. N. Carew Hunt, *The Theory and Practice of Communism*, London, 1963, p. 230.

36. Ibid., p. 231.

37. N. Hans, *The Russian Tradition in Education*, op. cit., p. 174 ff.

38. E. H. Carr, *The Bolshevik Revolution 1917-23*, op. cit., p. 270.

39. R. N. Carew Hunt, *The Theory and Practice of Communism*, op. cit., p. 226.

40. Cf. Paul Gregory, *Socialist and Non-socialist Industrialization Patterns*, New York, 1970.

41. R. N. Carew Hunt, *The Theory and Practice of Communism*, op. cit., p. 269.

42. Cf. Gerhard Simon, *Church, State and Opposition in the USSR*, London, 1973.

43. Samuel N. Harper, *Civic Training in Soviet Russia*, Chicago, 1929, p. 207.

44. V. I. Lenin, quoted in A. P. Pinkevitch, *The New Education in the Soviet Republic*, New York, 1929, p. 375.

45. Cf. V. I. Lenin, *The Impending Catastrophe and How to Combat It*, in his *Collected Works*, Vol. 25, London, 1960.

46. J. Pennar, I. I. Bakalo and G. Z. F. Bereday, *Modernization and Diversity in Soviet Education*, op. cit., p. 97.

47. G. Z. F. Bereday, W. W. Brickman and G. H. Read, *The Changing Soviet School*, Cambridge (Mass.), 1960, p. 87.

48. J. Pennar, I. I. Bakalo and G. Z. F. Bereday, *Modernization and Diversity in Soviet Education*, op. cit., p. 101.

49. Cf. M. N. Deineko, *Forty Years of Public Education in the U.S.S.R.*, Moscow, 1957, pp. 14-21.

50. Cf. Jaan Pennar, 'Party Control over Soviet Schools', in G. Z. F. Bereday, and J. Pennar, *The Politics of Soviet Education*, op. cit.

51. Nigel Grant, 'U.S.S.R.', in Margaret Scotford Archer (ed.), *Students, University and Society*, London, 1971, p. 85.

52. Nicholas De Witte, *Soviet Professional Manpower*, Washington, 1955, p. 23.

53. G. Z. F. Bereday, W. W. Brickman and G. H. Read, *The Changing Soviet School*, op. cit., p. 132.

54. Nigel Grant, 'U.S.S.R.', op. cit., p. 86.

55. Thomas Fitzsimmons (ed.), *RSFSR: Russian Soviet Federated Socialist Republic*, New Haven, Human Relations Area Files, 1957, Vol. II, p. 338.

56. Jaan Pennar, 'Party Control over Soviet Schools', op. cit., p. 47.

57. For historical changes in, and contemporary functions of this Council see, J. Minot, *L'Entreprise Education Nationale*, Paris, 1970.

58. Paul Gerbod, *La condition universitaire en France au XIXᵉ siècle*, Paris, 1965.

59. In 1821 the syllabus examined for the Baccalauréat was divided up into numbered questions and in 1840 the Ministry published a list of 500 questions which could appear as part of the examination. This exercised the most far reaching constraints on educational activities. Programmes developed which were based not on teaching or learning requirements but merely on the need to prepare for the examination. Between 1864-74 the Baccalauréat programme was limited to the last two years at secondary school, the list of questions was suppressed and the final examination divided into two parts. This lightened constraints but did not lift them. Cf. J-B. Piobetta, *Le Baccalauréat*, Paris, 1937.

60. R. D. Anderson, *Education in France 1848-1870*, Oxford, 1975.

61. Within two months of the passing of Loi Falloux, 800 instituteurs suspected of holding socialist opinions were dismissed from their posts, in the universities several chairs were suppressed and throughout programmes of study and examinations became limited in scope. Luc Decaunes and M. L. Cavalier, *Réformes et Projets de Réforme de l'enseignement français de la Révolution à nos jours (1789-1960)*, Paris, 1962, p. 33 ff.

62. Cf. Georges Duveau, *Les Instituteurs*, Paris, 1957. For the earlier period see, M. Gontard, *L'Enseignement primaire en France de la Révolution à la Loi Guizot, 1789-1833*, Lyons, 1959.

63. Antoine Prost, *L'Enseignement en France, 1800-1967*, Paris, 1968, p.73.

64. Between 1842-1877, 45 percent or more had social origins among the artisans, small farmers and shopkeepers. Op. cit., p. 76.

65. By 1877, 16 percent of secondary school teachers were sons of secondary teachers, 11.5 percent sons of instituteurs, a further 10 percent sons of other Civil Servants. Loc. cit.

66. P. Gerbod, *La condition universitaire en France au XIXe siècle*, op. cit., p. 642.

67. Cf. A. Delfau, *Napoléon 1er et l'instruction publique*, Paris, 1902.

68. Cf. A. Aulard, *Napoléon 1er et le monopole universitaire*, Paris, 1911.

69. Cf. Georges Weill, *Histoire du Catholicisme en France 1828-1908*, Paris, 1925.

70. Luc Decaunes and M. L. Cavalier, *Réformes et projets de réforme de l'enseignement français de la Révolution à nos jours (1789-1960)*, op. cit., p. 47.

71. Antoine Prost, *L'Enseignement en France*, op. cit., p. 158-9.

72. David Thomson, *Democracy in France since 1870*, London, 1964, p. 15.

73. Eric Cahm, 'Political Parties', in J. E. Flower, (ed.), *France Today*, London, 1973, p. 34.

74. David Thomson, *Democracy in France since 1870*, op. cit., p. 14.

75. D. W. Brogan, *The French Nation*, London, 1961, p. 129.

76. Antoine Prost, *L'Enseignement en France*, op. cit., p. 159.

77. Ibid., pp. 155-159.

78. Montalembert quoted ibid., p. 178.

79. Edgar Quinet, *L'Enseignement du peuple*, in *Oeuvres complètes*, Paris, Vol. XI, no date, p. 118.

80. Rouland (Minister in charge of education in 1856), quoted in J. Maurain, *La Politique ecclésiastique du Second Empire de 1852-1869*, Paris, 1930, p. 457.

81. R. D. Anderson, *Education in France 1848-70*, op. cit., p. 123.

82. Ibid., p. 67.

83. Ibid., pp. 136-137.

84. Ibid., p. 213.

85. Ibid., p. 245.

86. Ibid., p. 199.

87. 'L'enseignement primaire supérieur et l'enseignement professionnel c'étaient, il y a un demi siècle, deux idées nouvelles et distinctes, deux mots nouveaux qui ne semblaient pas synonymes. Et, en effet, ils ne le sont pas. Mais le cours des choses les a sensiblement rapprochés, ils convergent de plus en plus, et bien qu'ils ne se confondent pas, ils se touchent de près aujourd'hui'. F. Buisson, *L'enseignement primaire, supérieur et professionnel*, Paris, 1887, p. 4.

88. D. W. Brogan, *The French Nation*, op. cit., p. 131.

89. R. D. Anderson, *Education in France, 1848-1870*, op. cit., p. 144.

90. David Thomson, *Democracy in France*, op. cit., p. 112.

91. Cf. Jacques Fournier, *Politique de l'éducation*, Paris, 1971. In discussing teachers and their professional organizations he concludes that 'les clivages à l'intérieur du corps enseignant sont, en France, plus prononcés que dans beaucoup d'autres pays', p. 155.

92. Quoted in *Revue Internationale de l'Enseignement*, 1897, I, p. 293.

93. Antoine Prost, *L'Enseignement en France, 1800-1967*, op. cit., p. 387.

94. To Jules Ferry, if teachers were allowed to form 'cette coalition de fonctionnaires, outrage vivant aux lois de l'état, à l'autorité centrale, au pouvoir républicain, il n'y a plus de ministre de l'instruction publique, il n'y a plus d'inspecteurs, il n'y a plus de préfet'. Quoted in Louis Legrand, *L'influence du positivisme dans l'oeuvre scolaire de Jules Ferry*, Paris, 1961, p. 172.

95. Cf. Gérard Vincent, 'Les professeurs du second degré au début du XXe siècle, essai sur la mobilité sociale et la mobilité géographique', in *Revue d'histoire moderne et contemporaine*, Spring, 1966, pp. 49-86.

96. The numbers registered in private confessional schools fell between 1901-06 from 1,257,000 to 188,000 pupils. Ibid., p. 208.

97. Jacques Fournier, *Politique de l'éducation*, op. cit., p. 64.

98. John E. Talbott, *The Politics of Educational Reform in France, 1918-40*, Princeton, 1969, p. 54 ff.

99. David Thomson, *Democracy in France*, op. cit., p. 96.

100. Ibid., pp. 109-110.

101. Gordon Smith, *Politics in Western Europe*, op. cit., p. 205.

102. Cf. Maurice Duverger, 'The Eternal Morass: French Centrism', in M. Dogan and R. Rose, (eds.), *European Politics: A Reader*, London, 1971.

103. D. W. Brogan, *The French Nation*, op. cit., p. 170.

104. Maurice Duverger, 'The Eternal Morass: French Centrism', op. cit., p. 243-244.

105. S. M. Lipset, *The First New Nation*, London, 1964.

106. P. H. Williams and M. Harrison, *Politics and Society in De Gaulle's Republic*, London, 1971, p. 144.

107. Harry Eckstein, *Pressure Group Politics*, Stanford, 1960.

108. Luc Decaunes and M. L. Cavalier, *Réformes et projets de réforme de l'enseignement français de la Révolution à nos jours*, op. cit., p. 94.

109. Cf. E. Dolléans, *Histoire du Movement Ouvrier*, Vol. III, Paris, 1953, p. 147 ff.

110. Luc Decaunes and M. L. Cavalier *Réformes et Projets de Réforme*, op. cit., p. 103.

111. James M. Clark, *Teachers and Politics in France*, Syracuse N.Y., 1967, p. 102.

112. Roger Hagnauer, 'Dans l'enseignement: Bilan de six années d'autonomie', *Revue Prolétarienne*, December, 1953, p. 338.

113. Henry W. Ehrmann, 'French Bureaucracy and Organized Interests', *Administrative Science Quarterly*, Vol. V, 1961, p. 547.

114. Alfred Cobban, *A History of Modern France*, Vol. 3, op. cit., p. 24.

115. Cf. Louis Legrand, *L'influence du positivisme dans l'oeuvre scolaire de Jules Ferry*, op. cit.

116. Luc Decaunes and M. L. Cavalier, *Réformes et Projets de Réforme* op. cit., p. 71.

117. John E. Talbott, *The Politics of Educational Reform in France 1918-40*, op. cit., p. 65-66.

118. Ibid., p. 121.

119. Ibid., p. 132.

120. Ibid., p. 160.

121. Jacques Fournier, *Politique de l'éducation*, op. cit., p. 250.

122. John E. Talbott, *The Politics of Educational Reform in France 1918-40*, op. cit., p. 215.

123. D. R. Watson, 'Educational Reform in France, 1900-1940', *Past and Present*, Vol. 34, July 1966, p. 97.

124. Luc Decaunes and M. L. Cavalier, *Réformes et Projets de Réforme . . .* op. cit., p. 125.

125. Jacques Fournier, *Politique de l'éducation*, op. cit., p. 255.

126. Luc Decaunes and M. L. Cavalier, *Réformes et Projets de Réforme . . .* op. cit., 'Le conflit, on le voit, se situe autant sur le plan social que sur le plan scolaire, d'ailleurs inséperables l'un de l'autre. Il éclaire l'opposition traditionelle entre enseignement du premier degré et enseignement secondaire, les representants du premier préconisant une démocratisation de l'éducation par la fusion ou l'unification des enseignements (c'est le plan Langevin), les representants du second restant souvent, pour majorité, encore attachés à une notion hiérachique des études et souhaitant maintenir la prééminence de l'enseignement secondaire', p. 160.

127. Ibid., p. 162, note (1).

128. David Thomson, *Democracy in France since 1870*, op. cit., p. 263.

129. Quoted ibid., p. 261.

130. Antoine Prost, *L'Enseignement en France*, op. cit., p. 480.

131. Jacques Fournier, *Politique de l'éducation*, op. cit., p. 66.

132. Cf. Maurice Duverger, 'Les institutions après De Gaulle', *Le Monde*, 26 November, 1969.

133. Gordon Smith, *Politics in Western Europe*, op. cit., p. 140.

134. Cf. Maurice Duverger, *Institutions politiques et droit constitutionnel*, Paris, 1970, p. 735. See also his *La Ve République*, Paris, 1959.

135. For De Gaulle the Presidential sector comprised foreign affairs and defence, Algerian and Community Affairs, the 'open sector' being defined residually: in the former the President was initiator and executant, in the latter the Government.

136. Jean Blondel, *Contemporary France: Politics, Society and Institutions*, London, 1972, p. 51.

137. In fact the 1958 Constitution stacks the cards even more heavily in the Government's favour since only those endorsing censure register their vote while Government supporters abstain. It is a negative system of assessing support since all abstainers are counted as being on the side of Government. Cf. M. Prélot, *Pour Comprendre la nouvelle Constitution*, Paris, 1958.

138. Gordon Smith, *Politics in Western Europe*, op. cit., p. 205.

139. André Siegfried, *Le Figaro*, 30 July, 1958.

140. David Thomson, *Democracy in France since 1870*, op. cit., p. 292.

141. Pierre Avril, *Politics in France*, Harmondsworth, 1969, p. 261.

142. Peter Campbell, cited in Dorothy Pickles, *The Government and Politics of France*, Vol. I, London, 1972, p. 159.

143. Ibid., p. 154-155.

144. Jean Charlot, *L'UNR. Etude du pouvoir au sein d'un parti politique*, Paris, 1967, p. 23.

145. P. M. Williams and M. Harrison, *Elections Abroad*, London, 1959, p. 81.

146. The 200 deputies of the UNR were returned by 3½ million electors whilst the 50 socialist and communist deputies represented approximately 7 million voters. For a description of the electoral system see Peter Campbell, *French Electoral Systems and Elections Since 1789*, London, 1965.

147. David Thomson, *Democracy in France since 1870*, op. cit., p. 295.

148. Dorothy Pickles, *The Government and Politics of France*, op. cit., p. 145.

149. Ibid., p. 184.

150. Ibid., p. 204.

151. Ibid., p. 96.

152. David Thomson, *Democracy in France since 1870*, op. cit., p. 304.

153. Gordon Smith, *Politics in Western Europe*, op. cit., p. 71.

154. Jean Blondel, *Contemporary France*, op. cit., p. 19.

155. Ibid., p. 21. Cf. Jean Meynaud, *Les Groupes de pression en France*, Paris, 1957.

156. Dorothy Pickles, *The Government and Politics of France*, op. cit., p. 262.

157. Gordon Smith, *Politics in Western Europe*, op. cit., p. 71.

158. F. Ponteil, *Histoire de l'enseignement, 1789-1965*, Paris, 1966, p. 379-81.

159. Antoine Prost, *L'Enseignement en France*, op. cit., p. 422.

160. Luc Decaunes et M. L. Cavalier, *Réformes et projets de réforme . . .* op. cit., p. 224.

161. Syndicat Général de l'Education Nationale (SGEN), *Réforme de l'enseignement public*, Roneoed, Paris, March 1957, p. 14.

162. Ibid., p. 21.

163. Antoine Prost, *L'Enseignement en France*, op. cit., p. 424.

164. Gordon Smith, *Politics in Western Europe*, op. cit., p. 72.

165. Jacques Fournier, *Politique de l'éducation*, op. cit., p. 51.

166. *Le Monde*, 9-10 April 1967.

167. Jacques Fournier, *Politique de l'éducation*, op. cit., p. 61.

168. As early as 1963 the PCF was having difficulties with its dissident youth section and after this time the Party virtually lost control over its student group, the U.E.C., many of whose members left to join other factions. In this context Waldeck Rochet criticised those 'bourgeois ideologists who flatter youth so as to prevent them seeking what is really new. Towards this end they fabricate an artificial conflict between the generations'. Cf. his *La Place des étudiants dans la bataille pour le progrès, la paix, la liberté, le socialisme*, Paris, 1963, p. 11.

169. Margaret Scotford Archer 'France' in Archer (ed.), *Students, University and Society*, op. cit. The most complete descriptive account of the events is found in L. Rioux and R. Backmann, *L'Explosion de mai*, Paris, 1968.

170. The general chain-reaction account is presented in Jacques Perret, *Inquiète Sorbonne*, Paris, 1969, p. 16 f. Epistémon, *Les ideés qui ont ébranlé la France*, Paris, 1968, p. 21 f. Edgar Morin, et al., *Mai 1968: la Brèche*, Paris, 1968, p. 66 ff. A conspiracy version from the extreme right is provided by F. Duprat, *Les Journées of Mai '68*, Paris, 1968. For Communist versions which also include an element of conspiracy see: F. Fonvieille-Alquier, *Les Illusionnaires*, Paris,

1968; Georges Marchais, in *L'Humanité*, 3.5.68, L. Salini, *Mai des Prolétaires*, Paris, 1968.

171. P-H. Chombart de Lauwe, *Pour l'université*, Paris, 1968.

172. A list of these can be found in L. Rioux and R. Backmann, *L'Explosion de Mai*, op. cit., pp. 9-12, a summary of their development is given in P. Searle and M. McConville, *French Revolution 1968*, London, 1968. Those of major importance include the U.E.C. (Union des étudiants communistes), the official communist student group which gradually freed itself from Party control in the mid-sixties; U.J.C. (M-L) (Union des Jeunesses communistes (Marxistes-Leninistes)), and pro-chinese; J.C.R. (Jeunesse communiste-révolutionnaire), the Trotskyite youth group of the French Section of the 4th Internationale, F.E.R. (Féderation des étudiants révolutionnaires), a Trotskyite group of those breaking away from the 4th Internationale; J.A.C. (Jeunesse anarchiste communiste), anarchist youth group; I.S. (Internationale Situationniste).

173. F. A. Pinner, 'Tradition and Transgression: Western European students in the post war world', *Daedalus*, Winter, 1968, p. 144.

174. Alain Touraine, *Le Mouvement de Mai ou le Communisme Utopique*, Paris, 1968.

175. D. Pickles, *The Government and Politics of France*, op. cit., p. 274.

176. P. H. Chombart de Lauwe, *Pour l'université*, op. cit., p. 22.

177. André Philip, *Mai 1968 et la foi démocratique*, Paris, 1968, p. 15.

178. Edgar Morin, 'Une révolution sans visage', in Morin et al., *Mai 1968: la Brèche*, op. cit., p. 65.

179. Edgar Morin, 'La commune étudiante', ibid., p. 23.

180. Alain Griotteray, *Des barricades ou de réformes*, Paris, 1968, p. 27.

181. For the discussion of the law in the National Assembly see *Le Monde*, 5-12 October 1968, and for the text of the law 17-18 November 1968.

182. D. Pickles, *The Government and Politics of France*, op. cit., p. 288.

183. Jean Blondel, *Contemporary France*, op. cit., p. 22.

7 INTERACTION: In the Decentralized System

The greater complexity of interaction in the decentralized system has already been stressed. The reason for it is the equal importance of Internal Initiation, External Transactions and Political Manipulation as processes through which various groups and collectivities can bring about educational change. Furthermore, these different types of negotiation proceed simultaneously and have consequences which affect one another. This much was clear from the basic diagram presented at the end of Chapter 5. Instead of the simple convection current pattern of the centralized system (in which grievances were cumulated, passed upwards to the political centre, negotiated there through political interaction, before being transmitted downwards to educational institutions as polity-directed changes), a more complicated pattern of cross currents characterizes interaction and change in the decentralized system.

However, just as the basic diagram for centralized systems had to be expanded to give a less simplified picture of interaction, this is also true here and for exactly the same reasons. Again the three types of parties involved (political elites, external interest groups and professional educators), were represented as being undifferentiated and distinct, as if

393

there were no subdivisions within them or overlap between them. In turn, this resulted in a gross oversimplification of interaction itself, for it glossed over the complex transactions between sub-groups, parties and collectivities of which it is made up in reality. Thus a similar kind

FIGURE 6

Processes of Educational Change in Decentralized Systems

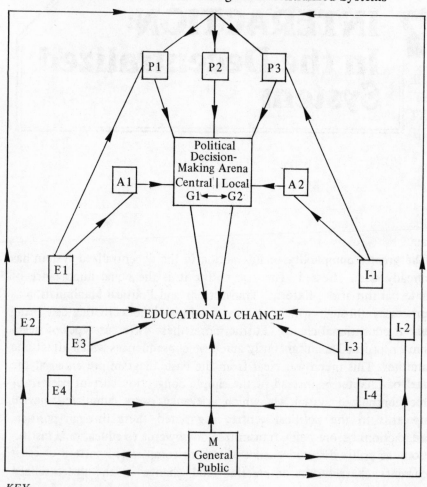

KEY
P = Political Party or faction
G = Government Body or Authority
I = External Interest Group
A = Advisory Council or Committee
E = Professional Educational Interest Group
M = General Public

of expanded diagram is needed for the decentralized system. Once again, although it comes closer to representing real patterns of interaction it still simplifies them in various ways — only one line, *illustrative* of each main interrelationship has been included in order to keep the diagram clear; overlapping membership between groups is not indicated; all interactions appear to be of equivalent importance and qualitative differences between them are of course omitted completely.

THE EQUAL IMPORTANCE OF
INTERNAL INITIATION,
EXTERNAL TRANSACTIONS
AND POLITICAL MANIPULATION

As was the case with centralized systems in the last chapter, the object of the subsequent discussion is to conceptualize and theorize about educational interaction in a way which will help to explain and understand the real events taking place in the decentralized systems of England and Denmark. However, the analysis which follows must be very different — hence the format of the present chapter — because of the greater complexity of the interaction processes involved. The supreme importance of political manipulation in the centralized system had two consequences for analysis. Firstly, it was possible to *describe* educational interaction as a political story, with characters, plot, and outcome, which could be told chapter by chapter and volume by volume for both France and Russia. Secondly, it was possible to *explain* educational interaction in terms of the changing interrelationships between the *political* structure and the structure of educational interest groups. When dealing with decentralized systems, the nature of both description and explanation differs considerably.

On the one hand interaction cannot be described as *a* story (political or otherwise), because three different kinds of negotiation are going on simultaneously and are taking place at three different levels (those of the school, community and nation), instead of being restricted to the last of these. There are only themes, not a continuous story. Furthermore the telling of each episode, e.g. 'going comprehensive', 'introducing child-centred learning' or 'founding new universities' is done in the knowledge that other episodes are taking place at the same time, which may be completely separate in terms of the issues, actors and levels involved. However, whilst they can be separate they are not usually independent of one another. The themes which dominate each kind of negotiation at any time are intertwined, and the outcome of one episode at one level affects the context in which other issues arise and are worked out at other levels or through another type of negotiation. Thus there is no historic saga, but only a vast collection of short stories, in which some of the same characters reappear and some of the same problems are tackled by different personae in different ways. Sometimes what happens in one story influences the outcome of the next, and always the tales vary in their scale and scope. This serves to indicate the problems of describing interaction in decentralized systems, but it also helps to define the problem to be tackled when attempting to explain such interaction.

Explanation involves making sense of this myriad of episodes. To theorize about interaction is to relate these episodic events to a set of more general relationships which underlie them and account for their patterning. However, in the decentralized system such relationships are not narrowly clustered around the intersection between education and the polity. Because the three forms of negotiation are of equal importance, then theories of educational interaction must also be broad enough to embrace those transactions conducted autonomously by the profession and those introduced directly by external interest groups, as well as those taking place in the political decision-making arena. Since each process of negotiation involves the exchange or use of resources, (including political power, but also liquid assets and expertise), it is argued that we should theorize in terms of the general relationships pertaining between resource holders in the decentralized system. In other words *educational interaction will be explained here by reference to the changing interrelationship between the structure of the resource distribution and the structure of educational interest groups.*

One of the principal tasks ahead concerns the conceptualization of these general relationships. The problem of conceptualizing the distribution of social resources in the decentralized system parallels that of delineating the distribution of political power in the centralized system, and it will be dealt with in a very similar way. However, before proceeding with this task, the manner in which the three processes of negotiation all involve the exchange and use of resources needs to be spelt out more explicitly in order to show why the analytical framework adopted is apposite. This approach is derived unslavishly from both exchange theory and *general* (i.e. non-organic) systems theory.

From the former is taken the basic notion that exchange transactions and power relations are inextricably linked with one another. They jointly account for the emergence of either reciprocity or control in the educational interaction between different groups: if a party is not sufficiently endowed with the appropriate resources to reciprocate for those it needs to receive from another, then the other can make such supplies dependent upon the compliance of the former in the educational issue which is at stake between them. Exchange theory assumes that the resources which are exchanged are varied (which is what distinguishes the decentralized from the centralized system), but not that these resources have an exact price in terms of a single medium of exchange. This is not a methodological problem, it is a matter which is unspecific to the actors involved.[1] They have no conversion table in front of them from which to read-off constant prices, for example, to be paid by industry for obtaining a particular form of technical training from public education. On the contrary, rates of exchange are socially determined and thus vary over time. Indeed one of our main descriptive tasks is to trace through these changes for the two systems examined here, and one of our principle theoretical problems is to account for the particular rates of exchange which are established upon the emergence of a decentralized educational system and their modification through subsequent interaction.

From general systems theory we take the notions that the overall distribution of resources provides the context within which all transactions occur and that negotiations completed in one quarter have repercussions in another. This is quite a different statement from the vague Parsonian assumption that every part of the social structure affects every other. Instead general systems theory is concerned with establishing the existence, the weight, and the precise effect of particular repercussions. Indeed the positive effects of feedback, as influences which amplify change within the system itself (morphogenesis or structural elaboration), are its problematic and what makes it of relevance here. Finally, unlike normative functionalism, this type of systems theory insists that exchange transactions and power relations must be examined in their own right, and not just via the norms restraining them and the values reinforcing them, if the dynamic aspect of the social structure is to be understood. This is an equally fundamental assumption as will be seen as we now turn to an initial examination of the various types of negotiation.

Internal Initiation

The principal resource commanded by the educational profession is its expertise. This includes the specialist knowledge possessed by teachers, their capacity to impart skills, and their techniques for inculcating values. Expertise therefore refers to their command of teaching material and teaching methods. Basically internal initiation involves the profession exchanging the expert services it can offer for other kinds of resources which it needs in order to achieve its own goals. These goals are various but their attainment always depends on the profession obtaining the financial means and legal rights to translate them into reality. To do this depends on getting a good rate of exchange for educational services against the financial resources supplied, in return, by external interest groups. But these transactions themselves may be subject to political veto so the profession also has to increase the value of its expertise to the political authorities in order to prevent their imposing such embargoes. The latter is merely one aspect of a broader negotiation with the polity in which expert services are exchanged against increments in autonomy (the legal rights to do x, y and z). Only if the profession succeeds in improving its wealth and autonomy in these ways will it be able to increase the amount of educational change produced by internal initiation and ensure that its direction coincides with professional interests. *Thus the main task, on whose accomplishment internal initiation depends, is the exchange of expertise for financial resources and legal rights on favourable terms.*

External Transaction

The principal resource commanded by external interest groups is their wealth, or more strictly their liquid assets, which can be devoted to the quest for educational services of various kinds. External transactions fundamentally consist in the exchange of financial resources for educational expertise — for example, a professional undertaking to receive certain pupils, provide a particular form of instruction, or produce a specific kind of output in terms of the knowledge, skills or values of those completing the course of study. The financial resources offered against expert services have to be sufficiently attractive to the profession to overcome their inertia (unwillingness to add new teaching burdens, devise new curricula or invent novel methods of assessment), and any repugnance or reluctance felt towards performing and providing the services required (if, for example, they involve a distraction from research, an extension of teaching hours, a collaboration with non-professionals, an alteration of teaching locale, a diminution of entry standards, or a limitation on the knowledge to be inculcated and assessed). Simultaneously the external interest group must be able to evade or overcome any political resistance to these transactions taking place; for only if it does both will it be able to instigate those educational changes needed to service its particular institutional operations. *Thus the main task, on whose completion external transactions rely, is the successful exchange of financial resources for expert services.*

Political Manipulation

The principal resource commanded by political authorities (both central and local) is their legal authority and capacity to impose negative sanctions. This includes their ability to pass laws and impose regulations, to withhold benefits and recognition, as well as to penalize irregular practices and offending parties. Political manipulation therefore consists in those groups who dominate the central or local decision-making arenas using their official powers to extract the educational services desired and to preclude undesirable outputs. At either level it involves the exchange of politico-educational privileges (ranging from salary increases to teachers, through the institutionalization of professional advice, to the recognition and regularization of internal initiatives) in return for increased educo-political services. Alternatively it can involve the application of political sanctions, in other words the withholding of certain rights or commodities in order to overcome professional resistance or to veto unwanted transactions. The services extracted or supressed in this way are used to keep educational activities in line with political requirements. *Thus the main task, on whose execution political manipulation rests, is the exchange of power resources for expert services.*

Obviously the designation of these 'main tasks' involves a considerable oversimplification, because in fact each of the groups concerned (be it professional, institutional or political) possesses more than one type of resource which comes into play in processes of negotiation. Professional groups not only command expertise but also enjoy certain powers (associated with the autonomy they retained upon the emergence of the decentralized system), and possess some financial resources of their own (which were preserved during incorporation or earned since then, through the use of this very autonomy to conduct direct transactions with the community). Similarly external interest groups not only have wealth, but also status (that is the capacity to confer reflected glory or disrepute on the profession with which it seeks to deal), and power (through the positions its members may occupy on central and local authorities, the coalitions they may form with political elites at various levels, and the sanctions they may be able to exercise on educational outputs, like refusal to employ certain kinds of school leavers to recognize certain qualifications). Even clearer or course is the ability of political authorities to manipulate wealth and status as aspects of power itself. Power partly consists in the capacity to withhold benefits, and two of the most important of these as far as education is concerned are the financial resources it receives from central and local government and the status conferred on its practitioners, processes and products through formal public approbation. The significance for interaction of each group possessing all three resources, to some degree, will be taken up a little later. The point of highlighting 'main tasks' above was to show that different *kinds* of resources are involved, in contrast to centralized systems, in the negotiations which produce educational change. Thus it follows that their *distribution* is of great importance in determining who can participate in the processes of change and how they can go about it. These qualifications were inserted here simply to stress that the distribution of all resources was not so uneven as to be a question of total monopoly or complete deprivation on the part of any of the three groups involved. Thus it follows that each type of negotiation is a complex multi-dimensional process, whatever its superficial appearance.

THE AVAILABILITY OF
RESOURCES IN SOCIETY

Access to resources affects which groups will be able to negotiate change in just the same way that the accessibility of the political centre influenced which parties could engage in political manipulation in centralized systems. Indeed the availability of resources can be conceptualized in much the same way as accessibility of the political centre, for the two have many characteristics in common. Both change over time, largely in response to non-educational factors, and thus while they are introduced here neither of them can be explained within the framework of the present analysis. As with political accessibility, all that can and will be done is to trace through changes in the availability of resources over time in conjunction with corresponding changes in educational interaction. Availability will be identified in exactly the same way as was used for political penetrability: resources are considered as inaccessible according to the degree to which socially significant parties do not possess them and cannot make use of them, and the extent to which other social groups can employ them to exclude these parties, their interests, and issues from processes of educational negotiation.

The *overall* availability of each resource (as opposed to its availability to any particular group) varies with the shape of its distribution i.e. distributions differ in terms of concentration from time to time and from place to place. As a general statement this appears to be uncontentious and it is endorsed by most sociological perspectives. For example, whilst Marxists stress the universality of a Ruling Class, commanding and cumulating scarce resources, they do not assume that its size is in constant proportion to the mass of the population (either within similar social formations or between different ones). Indeed the changing distribution of resources is vital to various aspects of the Marxist theory of change itself — the concepts of 'capital accumulation', 'increasing emiseration' and 'class polarization' are but a few instances of this. Equally, functionalist propositions about the way in which the resource distribution parallels the contributions made to social requirements, entail no assumptions about the extensiveness of the latter and hence the concentration of the former. Finally, elite theory in general, because it distinguishes different numbers and kinds of elites who enjoy different degrees and types of privileges in different epochs and areas, obviously incorporates the notion of variability in resource distributions.

The significance of this assumption here is that the greater the *concentration* of resources, the *fewer* the number of parties who will be able to negotiate educational change. Resource concentration in the decentralized system is thus the equivalent of political closure in the centralized system. In other words, the degree of concentration affects two basic aspects of educational interaction. Firstly, it influences the steepness of the gradient between elites and masses and hence their respective opportunities to participate effectively in processes of negotiation. Secondly, it follows that the degree of concentration also helps to determine the volume and kinds of educational demands which can be negotiated from different parts of society.

RELATIONS AMONG RESOURCE HOLDERS

Once again such relations cannot be conflated with nor derived from the fact of concentration alone, but they are of great importance for the nature of educational interaction and change. Resource holders may be superimposed, homogeneous and united, or they may be unlike one another, mutually antagonistic, and in pursuit of independent goals. The same was argued about political elites in the centralized system, but there the issue was simpler for we were only concerned with the relations found among one kind of resource holder, i.e. amongst the politically powerful. In the decentralized system the question is more complex for it involves discussion of the relations *between* different kinds of resource holders as well as *amongst* each of them. Obviously as far as the former is concerned, the extent to which the distributions of the different resources are superimposed is the crucial variable — for this determines whether one is referring to the same group of people or section of society when talking about those who command most financial resources or political power or expertise. Even if there is a high degree of superimposition, the second question remains — as it does in centralized systems — namely how far do elite members get on with one another and pull together to attain joint or mutually compatible goals.

Elsewhere[2] I have argued that there are no logical reasons for assuming that the class, status and power dimensions of social stratification are superimposed on top of one another, rather than significant discrepancies being found between the positions of given groups on the three hierarchies. Instead it is maintained that superimposition is a matter of contingency and degree, which have to be established in each particular case and place. The same approach characterizes the treatment of resource holders: they are neither presumed to be a single elite whose privileges extend over all that is scarce and socially valued, nor to consist of a plurality of elite groups which are distinct from one another in terms of the resources upon which their privileged positions are based. Thus the analytical framework employed here is not committed in advance to either a undimensional ruling class model or a pluralist picture of multiple elites. Again it is neutral in the sense that if one of these models holds universally, or works well for the two countries examined, this will show through the analysis presented. Thus the degree of superimposition amongst resource holders will be established empirically, and it is this which then determines how far educational interaction approximates to a uni- or multi-dimensional affair.

As in the centralized system the greater the superimposition and unity among the relevant elites, the more standardized are the educational changes introduced or the existing practices which are defended. However, there are some very important differences between the two kinds of system. Firstly, standardized action will be much less common here because those seeking change do not have to accommodate their goals with others, thus diluting their precise requirements in order to be able to exert greater political pressure. Because there are three different channels through which demands can be negotiated and satisfied, the structural conditions encouraging the cumulation of demands are greatly weakened. Secondly, this means that there is a lower premium on the unity of elites in the decentralized system, since different resource holders can obtain the educational services they want through independent transactions. Indeed united inaction (in repulsing the educational ambitions of the resourceless masses) is probably the most important form of concerted action, for where positive changes are sought, the sub-elites will tend to pursue their specific institutional requirements. Finally this does indeed imply that the less the unity among resource-holders, the greater the diversity of educational changes introduced. Unlike the centralized system where all protagonists cluster in and about the political arena, often blocking one another and producing overall immobilism, the existence of three processes for negotiating change reduces the extent to which groups cancel-out one another and contribute to stasis.

THE STRUCTURE OF
EDUCATIONAL INTEREST GROUPS

Clearly the social distribution of resources and the structure of educational interest groups can change independently of one another. However, our first concern is with the *original* institutionalized distributions of wealth, power, and expertise *at the time* when the new educational system emerged. For this implies important limitations on some of the basic aspects of negotiated exchanges.[3] In particular the contemporary distribution of resources restricted

(i)   the nature and number of people admitted to educational transactions.
(ii) their initial bargaining positions.
(iii) the volume and kinds of demands which could be negotiated at first.

The *original* distribution of resources does not exert such influences for all time, partly because interaction itself will bring certain interest groups into a better position vis-à-vis resources and partly because their distributions are constantly changing in response to various independent factors, thus increasing and decreasing the resources available to particular interest groups. Hence as far as the analysis of interaction is concerned, our task is to follow through the constraining influences exerted by the changing resource distributions on negotiations between educational interest groups. However, when we come to the study of educational change itself, we will see that the original distribution of resources facilitated a series of changes in the earliest days of the new system, which then constituted the context for further interaction and strings of subsequent changes. Later change may reverse earlier developments, but this does not mean that the former escapes from having been conditioned by the latter, and it does not remove the imprint of the original distribution of resources upon the development of the decentralized system.

At all times every educational interest group will have a place on the hierarchical distribution of each of the three resources considered. The general position of a group is made up of its placings on the hierarchies of wealth, power and expertise. Methodologically it is impossible, at least at the present time, to express these general positions in precise mathematical terms. I have discussed the reasons for this in more detail elsewhere,[4] but the basic obstacles consist in;

(a) doubts about the national character of any hierarchy which is highly dependent on the subjective attribution of prestige — here this is particularly relevant to 'expertise';

(b) difficulties in specifying and ranking all positions on a hierarchy — this is significant for the power dimension where it is desirable to include its more informal and intangible aspects (influential power) as well as official power positions;

(c) problems of commensurability between the three hierarchies, in the absence of a common denominator to which all resources can be reduced. In view of this we are forced to work in rather gross terms, merely designating groups as having high or low access to particular resources, and are constrained to avoid detailed comparative statements about the relative availability of different resources to given groups.

However, working within these limitations, it is possible to advance three propositions which link groups and resources to educational interaction:

1. groups with low access to all resources will be in the weakest negotiating position.
2. groups with differential access to the various resources will be in a stronger negotiating position.
3. groups with high access to all resources will be in the best negotiating position.

A fourth proposition concerning educational change follows from the above, namely that groups are likely to receive educational services in reverse order. Therefore it is groups in the latter position who will tend to be responsible for the majority of changes, whereas those in the first position will probably not be able to introduce significant educational modifications. It must be remembered, however, that the crucial overall relationship is between the position of the educational interest groups and the availability of the resources themselves. In other words, the less concentrated the distribution of resources, the fewer the number of parties who will find themselves in position (1), and the greater the proportion of groups who will be able to participate profitably in educational transactions. The opposite is equally true; a very high concentration of resources places a very restricted section of society in position (3). Along the same lines a differential concentration of the three resources maximizes the number of interest groups finding themselves in position (2).

However, these propositions deal only with one side of the equation, because when an interest group commands a resource(s) this represents a necessary, but not a sufficient, condition for successful negotiation (just as to have political access was a necessary but not a sufficient condition for producing change in the centralized system). The very meaning of the term 'negotiation' involves two parties, so it is inadequate to concentrate upon what one of them alone brings to the relationship. The propositions advanced above concern the relative *bargaining positions* of different interest groups, but this is a unilateral concept. For such a group to have real *negotiating strength* it must stand in a particular relationship to the other party involved. This concept is a bilateral or relational term, it is not a generalized capacity, possessed by some groups but not by others, but pertains to interaction itself. Negotiating strength arises in exchange situations, i.e. where group X commands resources which are highly valued but lacking (or lacking in sufficient quantities) by group Y, when Y in turn possesses resources of a different kind which are sought by X. It is a matter of degree, which ranges from the ability of X to make Y utterly dependent on the resources it supplies, through a balanced situation of reciprocal exchange between X and Y, to the opposite pole of imbalance, where X is totally dependent on the resources supplied by Y.

With this in mind we can now turn to the structure of educational interest groups, in relation to effective negotiation, and note a significant contrast with centralized systems. It has already been argued that the most crucial factor is the relationship between the social distribution of resources and the national distribution of those seeking educational change. Now we are concerned with relationships among the latter and whether any particular combinations or characteristics of interest groups improve their prospects of goal attainment. In the centralized system it was maintained that maximal effectiveness occurred when those experiencing educational grievances were superimposed and well organized, for this enabled the greatest leverage to be exerted on the political centre. However, in the decentralized system, where three processes of negotiation operate simultaneously, superimposition and organization are not necessary for effective transactions.

For example, a quiet informal transaction may be more productive than a publicly organized one which might alert hostile counter-pressures — a series of local firms working independently may be able to gain the services they seek from the colleges in their vicinity much more readily than if an industrial confederation sought the transformation of colleges of further education en bloc. It is also probable that the innovations introduced independently are much more satisfactory to their recipients, because of their specificity, precision and relevance, than the more general changes likely to stem from organized action. Furthermore the superimposition of grievances may do little to help their alleviation. For instance, the overlap between the Catholic population and certain working class and immigrant groups does not improve the position of Church schools, decrease class discrimination, or advance the educational rights of migrants. On the contrary, limited resources are spread too thinly in seeking to negotiate improvements on all these fronts, whereas one can speculate that if only the religious issue were at stake, confessional schools would be better defended.

These considerations lead to an important conclusion, namely that the superimposition and organization of interest groups are only advantageous in decentralized systems to the extent that they increase collective resources. The increase can be purely quantitative, such as rich groups getting together to found high quality private establishments, or it may involve spreading the type of resources available to the collectivity, as for instance when a prestige group adds respectability to the financial resources of another, and improves their joint negotiating strength. Unless this condition holds, collective action carries no automatic bonus in processes of negotiation. There is, however, one particular process − political manipulation − for which this condition nearly always does hold. The greater the intensity of organized pressure, whether at the level of voting in elections, shaping party policy, or influencing decision-making, the stronger the impact − because numbers, commitment and organization are the stuff from which power is made. And this of course is why superimposition and organization were always advantageous to interest groups in centralized systems, for to them political manipulation was the only process of negotiation available. Another way of looking at this is that the centralized system is a special case where collective action always increases resources. However it is only a particular case of a more general rule, whose full workings are only displayed in the decentralized system with its three processes of negotiation, namely that combination only promotes effective transactions when it enhances the bargaining position of educational interest groups.

PROCESSES OF INTERACTION IN THE DECENTRALIZED SYSTEM

Earlier we described the 'main tasks' involved in each of the three kinds of transactions which bring about educational change, but these were discussed in the abstract and were not related to real processes of social interaction. At a formal level it was seen that interaction consists in using resources to transact exchanges with others in order to attain goals, whose target may be either educational stasis or change. However, although the importance of the initial *bargaining positions* of groups was stressed (i.e. the amount of resources at their disposal), no indication was given of even the most general conditions under which negotiations were likely to be successful, or of the type of interaction which would be involved. These two questions will be the concern of the present section and they are inextricably linked to one another. To specify the conditions under which educational changes are transacted is to indicate what, in addition to their initial bargaining position, gives a group negotiating strength. Since negotiating strength is a relational term, this means that the answer is necessarily phrased in terms of the relationships between groups. Automatically this implies examining the interaction between educational interest groups.

Let us start this analysis by isolating three crucial elements of any given piece of educational interaction, namely

(i)   the participants, (at least) two educational interest groups, X and Y:

(ii) the resources they respectively command, X^{r1} and Y^{r2}, which constitute their bargaining positions:

(iii) the exchange (or non-exchange) of $r1$ and $r2$, which expresses the relative negotiating strengths of X and Y.

These elements determine the degree of change, if any, occurring in this particular case. They also decide who exercises educational control in this situation; it can be X, if Y finds $r1$ irresistible, or Y if X cannot do without $r2$, but control is not necessarily a zero-sum matter, for a reciprocal exchange of $r1$ and $r2$ gives X and Y shared control and joint responsibility for the changes introduced.

We can now begin to consider the nature of the relationship between these two groups and what will give one high negotiating strength vis-à-vis the other. It has been argued that an interest group has the best chance of concluding an educational transaction in its favour the more irresistible are the resources it supplies to the other party involved. In his discussion of exchange and power in social life Blau has provided[5] a useful classification of-the situations in which such irresistibility arises. X will have the highest degree of negotiating strength when it supplies resources to Y under four conditions. These are when Y cannot reciprocate, cannot get the needed resources from elsewhere, cannot coerce X to supply them, and cannot resign itself to doing without them. From these can be derived the strategies required to attain or sustain educational control on the part of X in relation to Y. X must try to establish rates of exchanges which are highly favourable to itself; bar Y's access to alternative sources of supply through monopolizing the resource or legally controlling the processes of exchange; discourage any attempt at coercion on Y's part; and prevent Y from being indifferent to the benefits it offers. Equally Y's defensive strategies, aimed at keeping up its own negotiating strength, can be deduced by corollary. It must do everything it can to avoid being reduced to complete dependence on X. This involves a constant effort to prevent the exchange rate from becoming too unfavourable, by increasing the desirability and exclusivity of its own resources or services to X. It must work at keeping alternative supply lines open and accumulating supplies, thus increasing independence from X; developing strong organizations to compel X to behave differently; and propagating counter-ideologies which undermine X's right to use resources in the way it does.

In combination these aggressive and defensive strategies which are deployed in negotiation draw attention to the four basic aspects of educational interaction:[6]

(a) the possibility of reciprocating benefits points to the importance of the initial resource distributions to subsequent exchange processes and to resulting changes in the resource distributions over time.

(b) the possibility of alternative suppliers of the same resource points to the importance of legal, normative and competitive features of the emerging exchange structure.

(c) the possibility of coercive power being used points to the significance of the general political power struggle, the formal organization of power positions and of opposition parties, coalitions and alliances, vis-à-vis education.

(d) the possibility of resignation to the loss of a resource points to the importance of educational values, the formation of new ideologies, and of conflicts between systems of ideas.

All of these will play their part in the multiplicity of transactions which we seek to describe and explain. However, their precise significance will become clearer if we now look at the three processes of negotiation in turn — political manipulation, external transactions and internal initiation — and at the particular groups involved and their 'main tasks'.

Political Manipulation

Obviously political manipulation in the decentralized system shares certain features with this phenomenon in centralized systems and indeed with political interaction in general. As far as pressures on the polity are concerned, these include the articulation, accumulation and organization of interests, and where political control is concerned, they involve the formation, implementation and regulation of policy. Beyond such universals, differences in institutional structure produce diverse patterns of interaction. The less unified nature of the decentralized system means that the very political decision-making arena, officially concerned with educational matters, is broader and embraces central government organs and local authority bodies. This is the first aspect of our earlier statement that the initial distribution of resources (here power) upon the emergence of the system, affects the extent and nature of persons admitted to transactions. In the decentralized system those in official political positions of educational control are a more extensive group, they are found locally as well as centrally, and are of a more varied character ranging, for example, from local Councillors to the Minister of Education. Relations between these levels of decision-making is a whole dimension of interaction which is lacking in centralized systems, but this will be examined later, for at the moment we are concerned with the general nature of political negotiation where decentralization prevails.

This involves giving more consideration to *how* those who have acquired official positions in the administrative framework (i.e. have accumulated power resources vis-à-vis education) go about influencing or impeding educational change. In the decentralized system, political acts of this kind are negotiated actions, and not merely in the universal sense in which every parliamentary or politburo policy is shaped by the manoeuvrings of those concerned. Here much broader sets of transactions are involved, beyond those directly responsible for the formal introduction of legislation or regulations. These include negotiation with professional interest groups to ensure the implementation of regulations, and with external interest groups to prevent the vitiation or evasion of legislation.

In centralized systems it was possible to concentrate almost exclusively on interaction which culminated in the passing of legislation, decrees, or instructions because their implementation was relatively unproblematic. Educational interest groups, both internal and external, had little alternative but to accept these measures since the polity was continuously in an unassailable position. In terms of our earlier notation, the polity X supplied resources to education under the four conditions which made the professional groups Y^1 completely dependent upon it, and unable to increase their autonomy through dealings with other interest groups Y^2. The rates of exchange between X and Y^1 consistently favoured the former, the profession having neither the finance nor the freedom to alter its services and thus manipulate a more reciprocal rate; X's political veto on direct transactions between Y^1 and Y^2 prevented resources from being acquired elsewhere; whilst neither Y^1 nor Y^2 could resign themselves to the situation. The profession, both as a body morally committed to providing educational services for the community and as individuals with vested interests in job security, could not dispense with centrally provided resources. Moreover, in the modern period, we have already seen that few external groups can remain indifferent to the receipt of educational services. The only weak point in the polity's control was its capacity to contain counter coercion on the part of Y^1 and Y^2, precisely because the negotiating strength of X itself generated so much discontent and opposition. Hence, of course, the pattern of intermittent explosions directed against X, which were traced through as a major source of change in centralized systems. In the emergent decentralized systems, however, the very different distribution of resources did not leave the polity in an unassailable position, and made its 'main task' of exchanging power resources for educational services considerably more complicated.

Here the original distribution of resources was much less favourable to the political centre. Other groups are also in strong bargaining positions and education is not exclusively dependent on resources supplied (or withheld) by the central political elite. We can look at professional and external interest groups together, because it is partly the relations between Y^1 and Y^2 which provide education with good defensive strategies against control by the central polity in decentralized systems.

(i) The profession starts from a better bargaining position. Some educational institutions possess financial resources of their own (buildings, endowments, scholarships, equipment etc.) which were retained during incorporation. Most establishments, to different degrees, have the capacity to earn more because of their relative institutional autonomy which was also protected as the system developed. This in turn allows the achievement or maintenance of high status, independent of its confirmation by the centre. These original resources are, of course, all mutually reinforcing — for example, high status enables a high price to be charged, these earnings increase autonomy, can improve the attractiveness of the services offered, and thus enhance the value of professional expertise. Their net effect is to enable the profession to establish and maintain a decent rate of exchange, for what it has to offer is not exclusively dependent upon what it has received from the State in the first place. Furthermore, the very fact that it transacts with both central and local authorities (which derives from the structure of the system itself) improves its negotiating strength vis-à-vis government, since it will be receiving resources directly from the opposition (where this controls local authorities) as well as from the governing elite. In turn these resources amplify the reinforcing cycle sketched above, thus further improving the professional bargaining position in relation to the political centre and protecting reciprocity in exchanges between the two.

(ii) The profession has alternative suppliers outside the political arena altogether and this renders it better able to resist the application of negative political sanctions and government threats of withholding supplies. Here the relationship between internal and external interest groups is mutually supportive, for both have interests in the maintenance of external transactions. The process of incorporation legitimated the historical practice of certain external groups supplying resources directly to education in exchange for particular services. Such rights were jealously guarded (by groups like the Churches in England and the Agricultural Co-operatives in Denmark), and acted as precedents for other parties seeking to instigate and institutionalize the same practices, at least in the private sector if not in public education.

(iii) Organizations formed to resist central encroachment on professional autonomy and on the acquired rights of external interest groups developed during the incorporation phase (the Headmasters' Conference is a good example of both), and strengthened and diversified after the emergence of the system. Here the defence by the local authorities of their own rights against the centre did as much to aid the interest groups as their own efforts. Given a decentralized structure, the aim of interest groups was to insert themselves at all levels of decision-making so as to cushion the impact of political directives on education. Examples of protective intermediary bodies involving professional groups include the University Grants Committee and the Consultative Committee. Insertion also occurs through the insistence on professional and interest group representation on the influential advisory committees to government, through coalitions on local educational committees, and through the collective bargaining of unions and associations. Surrounding this insertion into official positions and formal processes is of course a plethora of organized pressure groups working to repulse the coercive application of political power in the educational field.

(iv) Complementing such activities are a set of defensive ideologies which counter political intervention in general, or seek to protect particular practices, institutions, or acquired rights against central infringement. Prominent here are professional values stressing academic freedom and classroom autonomy, but equally important are those values propagated by interest groups whose common denominator is the maintenance of a free educational market — whether these are expressed in terms of parental choice, religious freedom, regional diversity, linguistic protection, ethnic rights or job relevance. Obviously many of these are contradictory in their aims and intentions, but by addressing different audiences in different areas they mobilize opposition to central vetoes on external transactions of vastly different kinds. Collectively the propagators of such values patrol the politico-educational boundaries, although individually they only police their own check-points. Here too, then, the internal and external interest groups reinforce one another in defence of their own vested interests.

In view of this the polity's 'main task' of translating power resources into expert services is made more difficult. Over time the central authority seeks to strengthen its educational control through educational interaction in order to be able to attain its own goals. It does so in the following four ways, all of which it should be noted are hedged by the initial and subsequent distribution of resources.

1. The first strategy is to try to reduce the capacity of education to reciprocate for the resources supplied to it by the State. The aim here is to attain the educational equivalent of the State's position in a command economy, where it controls the rate of exchange, prices, pro-

duction and distribution. Education would be unable to reciprocate because everything it had to offer would itself depend on public resources, as in extreme examples of centralization. Since the polity's main educational leverage consists in its ability to withhold benefits and impose penalties, the success of this strategy hinges on both being substantial. Hence the ever-readiness of the State to increase its invest-ment in education, even when it has become the majority supplier. Given a steady growth in the proportion of GNP commanded by governments, higher rates of absolute investment in education have been the rule, whilst economic recessions have not damaged the relative position of the State since they have had similar effects on other suppliers. As a strategy, however, this can prove double-edged, for to invest generously may be to allow the internal accumulation of surpluses with which the profession can pad itself against political prods whose thrust derives from the withholding of resources. The financing of English Universities would prove a fascinating study from this angle. However, if Tactic 2 is successful then dependence on State can be coupled with a low rate of exchange.

2. The effectiveness of the first strategy is also clearly dependent on the success of the second — barring access to alternative suppliers. We have seen that this cannot be achieved by monopolization of the resources used by education — the best the State can do is to become the majority supplier, for the initial resource distribution endows others with significant reserves. What it can do is to seek to limit the processes of exchange, via its control of legal machinery. Here it will refuse legal recognition to certain diplomas, establishments, personnel or courses, thus reducing the attractiveness of the services that the profession could offer to external groups. This discourages external transactions by damaging the professional bargaining position, but it is only one branch of a two-pronged attack. The other involves the imposition of legal vetoes and the refusal to authorize certain negotiations at all. The crucial element in this respect is the degree to which the external interest group is itself politically influential (and can deflect projected embargoes) or is capable of marshalling legal defence (to repulse or lift such vetoes). Ironically this means that the polity's strategy will be most effective against the weaker suppliers, who have least to offer the profession and have little power and status in addition to their financial resources, but who also present least threat to the educational ambitions of governing elites.

3. Political strategies for containing counter coercion all hinge on

blocking the access of educational interest groups to political power. Although in some respects the decentralized nature of the system is advantageous in this context (for example, student unrest remains localized and focused on the particular university authorities concerned and does not confront the polity directly), in other ways we have seen that it promotes the insertion of interest groups at the various levels of decision-making. Since the main problem for the governing elite is resistance to its policies, its strategies are concerned with undermining the autonomy which makes this possible. Thus legislation can reduce local and institutional autonomy, making the system more responsive to central directives, if the governing elite is strong enough to deploy the whole battery of central sanctions to this end. But two things may stand in its way: the political influence and positions already acquired by educational interests and the hostility of opposition parties (who may indeed accept State intervention in principle, but fear the consequences of placing this instrument in the hands of its opponents). This is a parallelogram of forces which results in few education Acts and few educational explosions.

4. Nevertheless, most political elites will promote ideologies favouring political intervention, often justified on totally different grounds but sharing the self-righteous assumption that it would be justly used in their hands alone. Thus the Left will stress the need for increased State control to ensure equal opportunity and the end of social discrimination in education, whilst the Right usually underlines that it is needed to guarantee efficiency, order and value for taxpayers' money. The former seeks to identify State intervention with avoiding unfairness and class perpetuation; the latter with abolishing wastage and anarchy. Both strands are met by opposing ideological cross-currents from amongst their own supporters, i.e. educational interest groups broadly aligned with left or right but supporting autonomy because it advances their aims, and this itself constitutes a powerful normative contribution to the maintenance of the status quo.

Thus in the decentralized system political manipulation involves a struggle, not only on the part of those wanting to influence governmental policy, but also in order to translate official policy into educational practice. Because of the initial distribution of resources, the polity is not in an unassailable bargaining position and since the enduring aim of interested parties is to defend if not to improve their own positions of influence, this tends to keep it that way. In this context, parts of the system continually escape political control and introduce changes independently, thus creating new problems for government: whilst with equal pertinacity the polity struggles to contain such developments and to keep education in line with governmental policy.

External Transactions

The 'main task' of translating financial resources into the expert services required involves direct negotiation with professional groups. The political aspects of such transactions have already been discussed in the previous section, so here we will concentrate on the factors determining the relative negotiating strengths of external and internal groups when they face one another in interaction. Obviously the bargaining positions of the various external interest groups differ according to the resources at their command, and this will be subject to change over time. Although wealth of resources is usually translated into a high level of negotiating strength, it will be extremely rare for any external interest group actually to reduce education, or a particular part of it, to a position of total dependence. Instead, when transactions occur they are more likely to be of a reciprocal nature because the profession is in a good strategic position to defend itself and to bid up the value of its expertise.

1. The fact that a professional group has been approached for services means that it has something of value to offer in the eyes of those making the advances. This it can play upon in negotiations – possibly by proferring a tailor-made package – and can thus make its contribution even more attractive to the purchaser who will improve on his original terms, thus inflating the value of expertise.

2. Any particular external interest group which approaches the profession in this way is one among several as far as the latter is concerned. Given that State funding provides for the majority of educational overheads, few professional groups are ever completely dependent on their outside earnings (except of course in the private sector). Thus, as they are not desperate, they can pick and choose among these alternative suppliers of resources, bidding up the rate between them and only settling on advantageous terms.

3. External interest groups cannot force the profession to supply services it does not want to provide (on normative grounds) or does not think are worth providing (at the price offered). On the contrary, the

onus is upon the external group to make its terms as attractive as possible to the educational institutions involved.

4. Finally as far as any particular transaction is concerned, the profession may resign itself on normative grounds, on calculative grounds (not putting-off a better supplier), or because it considers the additional effort unworthwhile, to rejecting this specific order.

Given this good defensive position on the part of the profession, what the external interest group must try to do is to ensure that a transaction takes place at a price *which is reasonable to it*. It will be most likely to succeed when four conditions hold: *Firstly*, when the external group has considerable resources at its disposal and thus can propose an exchange rate which is not considered cheesepairing by the profession (i.e. leaves the latter a substantial surplus over the actual cost of providing the services required): *Secondly*, when the offer it proposes compares favourably with those made by other interest groups. However, in relation to both of these points it must not be forgotten that such offers are not made exclusively in financial terms. If the profession believes that it gains reflected glory or promotes its own goals through association with a particular group, the cash element will play a smaller part in the transaction. On the other hand, if the profession feels it is degrading itself or jeopardizing its governmental supplies through sailing too close to political veto, the financial induce-ment will have to be considerably greater. Nevertheless the two above conditions hold good because wealth always enables an interest group to transact with the private sector, even if it makes no headway with public education: *Thirdly*, we have argued that it will rarely be possible to coerce educational services from an unwilling profession, but if a group can 'square' a deal in advance with the polity, through the political influence or favour that it enjoys, the educators are more likely to get down to the negotiating table for fear of future political reprisals. Additionally the more attractive the external group makes itself, through tactics like the recruitment of prestige figureheads, the greater its appeal: *Fourthly*, the more convinced a group is that it cannot dispense with educational services, the more likely it is to obtain them — partly because it will devote a greater proportion of its available resources to getting them, and partly because it will strive to meet the above conditions if it did not do so in the first place.

If the final condition holds, yet the group in question fails to bring about a direct transaction, it can still pursue its educational goals through political manipulation: indeed many groups will be engaging in both forms of negotiation simultaneously. However, it is important to note that repeated repulsion by the profession can lead some groups to resign themselves to doing without educational services altogether. These will be the poorer groups whose lack of resources had given them weak bargaining positions with the profession, and especially those whose political influence was equally low. For minority groups in particular, their failure in one kind of negotiation may produce general discouragement and mean that the profession has played a part in organizing certain issues and problems out of educational politics. This is unlikely to be the case for large lower class groups with strong collective organizations which will champion their cause politically, although certain enclaves within the working class may find themselves in this position, e.g. workers in declining areas, agricultural labourers, those with handicapped children etc. On the whole, however, the consequence of professional rejection will be greater among poor minority groups, such as immigrants, migrant workers, members of smaller religious sects, or ethnic groups, and those whose mother tongue is not an official language.

Internal Initiation

Here, where the main task is the translation of educational expertise into other kinds of resources (which increase autonomy and internal self-determination), different sections of the profession find themselves in different bargaining positions. The initial distribution of resources, vertically among the various educational levels and horizontally among different kinds of institutions, gave certain groups of teachers and academics better starting points in terms of wealth, prestige and autonomy. These were identified for England and Denmark at the end of Chapter 4, and they will be taken up again in the substantive discussion. However, this needs to be borne in mind when recalling the points made about professional negotiating strength in the discussion of the other two processes. Rather than repeating these again, we can extract from the earlier analysis the conditions under which the educators are most likely to succeed in transactions, and express these in such a way that they can refer to the profession as a whole or to particular parts of it.

From the foregoing discussion it appears that professional groups will do best in negotiation, and in turn be able to introduce more of the internal innovations they desire, when they can do the following:

1. Offer services which are attractive in terms of their inputs, processes and outputs. One of the most important aspects of this is professional upgrading through which a higher quality of service is made available. By raising expertise itself, a higher exchange rate can be asked, thus increasing the market value of professional skills. However, all this depends on teachers and academics possessing adequate financial surpluses and sufficient autonomy in the first place, i.e. upon the emergence of the system.

2. Control the certification of expertise, both in terms of the quantity and quality of those admitted to the profession, so as to create a *de facto* if not a *de jure* closed shop which bars alternative supplies of 'teachers' or 'lecturers', or so raises the prestige of the certificated professional that the latter are at best 'instructors' or 'trainers' and at worst 'crammers' or 'unqualified'.

3. Participate in official processes of educational control and administration in order that they themselves play a part in moulding official policy rather than being reduced to modifying, resisting or sabotaging it at the stage of implementation.

4. Reinforce and legitimate the above activities, as well as encouraging the need for expert services, through disseminating appropriate educational values. In this the profession alone can make *direct* use of the learning situation to spread its values, and also by its very nature it can make good use of public media.

This completes the analytical discussion of the three processes and the parties involved, except in one important respect. So far, in the interest of clarity, attention has been focused on each kind of negotiation in turn. The very fact that cross-references were continually made to other processes of interaction serves to indicate that only in the most artificial way can one forget the fact that all forms of negotiation proceed simultaneously and their consequences have implications for one another. Finally, then, these mutual influences must be examined, in their own right, by taking an overview of the interrelations between the three processes.

INTERACTION AND NEGOTIATIONS

There are two important respects in which the different types of negotiation are related to one another in terms of interaction; one direct and the other indirect. Firstly, it is indeed many of the *same people* who engage in the three kinds of transactions: some members of the population may only participate at the lowest level in one of them (e.g. by voting), a much smaller number will participate in all three (e.g. an active member of a political party, a Parent-Teacher Association, and a Chamber of Commerce), whilst between these extremes there are varying degrees of participation and of overlap between participants. It seems common-sense that experience gained in one context influences behaviour in another — indeed we have presented one example of how discouragement may become generalized, but it is equally important to allow for the reinforcing effects of experiences of successful negotiation. Above all the existence of overlap points to the actors' own knowledge of the fact that what happens via one process then has an influence on others, and that there is more than one way of getting what they want.

This is related to the second and indirect relationship, namely that the *consequences* of one kind of transaction influence subsequent interaction in the other kinds of negotiation. In other words each transaction brings about a shift in educational control and the definition of instruction which alters the context in which other transactions occur, and these effects may be cumulative. This can be pictured most graphically by presenting different hypothetical scenarios, in which one of the three processes of negotiation was consistently more effective than the other two over time.

(a) The greater the effectiveness of political manipulation, the more educational change is polity-directed and educational activities are politically controlled. Consequently, the lower will be the autonomy of the profession to introduce internal changes and the smaller the volume of external transactions which are allowed. Because of both, the financial resources earned by the profession will fall, thus lowering the attractiveness of the services which can be offered to external groups, above and beyond the political embargoes which might be placed on these anyway. As education becomes increasingly dependent on the polity for supplies, the rate of exchange falls and hence there is a decrease in surplus resources, as well as of professional freedom, which will reduce the amount of internal initiation possible. The end result in this scenario is one in which the relations between education and society become like those in the centralized system. This is because, as in those systems, educational control rests on political power, and negotiations are largely confined to that single medium of exchange. This has come about through a string of transactions, in which power resources have been progressively revalued (because the polity has pursued successful strategies in negotiation), whilst professional expertise and private finance have been correspondingly devalued (because their bearers have adopted less satisfactory tactics in negotiation).

(b) The greater the effectiveness of external transactions, the more educational operations are responsive to other social institutions and the control of change is in the hands of their elites. It follows that the polity has a declining ability to monitor or maintain a given definition of instruction. Instead, as external transactions proliferate, instruction becomes increasingly diversified and differentiated and moves outside the orbit of State control. (Hence this is the exact opposite of the case above, where education became progressively more standardized and unified). Simultaneously, however, as education becomes more dependent on external supplies, it may well be less possible to protect professional expertise or to defend academic values. True, the existence of a multiplicity of external suppliers would offer some protection, but in an increasingly open educational market it would be more difficult for educators to maintain the other three conditions which keep rates of exchange up – they would tend to loose control over the certification and training of teachers (for if the end-product of instruction is externally determined, so to some extent is the nature of its producers) – they would be less able to insert themselves into positions of educational control (which would now be situated in Company Boardrooms, Union Headquarters, Church Hierarchies, Commercial offices etc.) – and would have less capacity to propagate 'pure' academic values (since these would contradict many of their current activities and the piper has little love of that tune). As exchange rates fall, so too does the profession's capacity to introduce internal innovations, and it may finally come to regret the protection it derived from the political control of dealings with the community. These then are the consequences of transactions in which expertise and power are devalued in relation to wealth.

(c) The greater the effectiveness of internal initiation, the more the profession itself becomes master in its own house. Its progressive gains in autonomy free it from political tutelage and allow educational change to be introduced in accordance with professional values, whether this involves simple self-serving or response to (acceptable) external demands. Resources earned in this way not only strengthen teachers against threats of State re-intervention, but also underwrite various activities which increase their standing — for example, up-grading of professional skills, increasing academic specialization, improved facilities and conditions of work. This is part of a reinforcing cycle in which the refinement of expertise then increases professional prestige, which in turn raises the exchange rate for educational services supplied to external parties. As interest groups pay more, professional surpluses accumulate and are used for new forms of internal innovation. These increments in self-determination lead to a less unified educational system and a more specialized, but also a more academic, definition of instruction. This end-state will only occur if expert resources have been well defended and advantageously exchanged against political power and private wealth.

Each of these scenarios, crudely sketched in, is merely meant to bring home how the results of one kind of transaction alter the context in which other kinds subsequently take place. For it is rare to find cases where the effectiveness of one process has so consistently outweighed others that the final state of play approximates to one of these sketches. The reason for this is precisely because the three processes *do* go on simultaneously, and the continuation of each of them represents an important vested interest to particular social groups. This they will tend to defend, by bringing additional resources to bear, if the balance tips too far in favour of the other processes which give advantages to different groups and interests. This seems to be what Blau implies when he argues that 'the forces set in motion to restore equilibrium in one segment of the social structure, are typically disequilibrating forces in other respects, or in other segments. The success of some organized collectivities, which produces optimum conditions for meeting internal requirements, spells the failure of others, with consequent internal disruptions.'[7] However, there is nothing automatic about equilibration — this depends upon interaction, and thus upon how strongly the groups involved feel, how far they are prepared to extend themselves and how much of their resources they are willing to invest. Indeed at any one time the chances are that the balance does favour the greater effectiveness of one process of negotiation over the other two. Also over a period of time there is nothing *logically* which *precludes* this balance from shifting sequentially to render political manipulation, external transactions or internal initiation the most important process in determining educational control and the definition of instruction. All that is universally the case is that the three forms of negotiation always have consequences for one another, and that each of them shapes the action contexts in which the others take place.

DENMARK

The Distribution of Resources and Relations among Resource Holders

It was argued that the availability of resources affects which groups can participate in educational negotiation and that the more concentrated are these resources, the fewer the number of groups actively transacting changes in education. The power and wealth distributions are the most crucial for the population at large, for it is these resources that they will seek to exchange against educational services: the professional bearers of educational expertise will automatically be involved in negotiations, given their position in the new educational system. Basically in twentieth century Denmark the availability of both power and wealth has increased progressively to wider and wider sections of the population. This de-concentration of resources can be demonstrated by taking their initial distributions in 1902 as the base line and then showing how growing political accessibility and income equalization have resulted from the continuous redistribution of power and wealth.

The base line itself is extremely important for this original distribution affects the volume and kinds of demands which can be negotiated at the beginning of the system, which in turn of course influences subsequent educational interaction. In 1902 power remained highly concentrated in Denmark: the great liberal reform Party, Venstre, had come to office 30 years late by European standards,[8] the Upper House (*Landsting*) was still an enclave of the right and a barrier to democratic legislation, whilst the provisions of the 1866 Constitution involved gross inequalities of suffrage and of representation as well as the lack of Ministerial responsibility to Parliament. Although Venstre represented all farming interests in Parliament, those of the big land-owners were dominant. The Conservatives, forced into a secondary role after 1901, were a city party for the commercial and industrial middle classes.[9] The Social Democrats,[10] receiving growing support from Copenhagen and the ports, and with built-in union participation,[11] only enjoyed limited *Folketing* representation and remained committed to their 1876 programme for the redistribution of power and wealth.

The distribution of wealth itself was highly concentrated and heavily biased away from the urban and rural lower classes. Since agriculture remained of supreme importance (distinguishing Denmark from the usual pattern of industrialization, because its economic development was not closely correlated with urbanization),[12] land ownership was a crucial issue of enduring importance. Whilst Venstre was committed to independent land ownership as the basis of the social structure, the less affluent farmers and agricultural labourers were equally determined to see its extension through increasing the number of smallholdings, now viable because of the flourishing co-operative movement handling farm produce. Given the economic importance of agriculture, no political party could neglect it and the Social Democrats advocated redistribution through a voluntary transition to State land ownership.[13] The distribution of industrial wealth was equally uneven. Industry had grown slowly, mainly producing goods for the home market, but was unusually decentralized since many enterprises were linked to agriculture and fisheries (in the absence of great fuel, mineral or timber reserves), and thus it had not entailed any large-scale rural depopulation — all of which presented barriers to unionization.

In terms of relations amongst resource-holders, the turn of the century was marked by substantial differences of interests, but not ones which were strongly antagonistic, a fact helped by the remarkably homogeneous social structure,[14] lacking those kinds of cleavages which can threaten political stability.[15] The contrast between rural and urban interests was strong, but conflict between them was minimized because the export of foodstuffs meant that it was not the price that could be extracted from the urban domestic consumer which counted.[16] More important were the divisions between the two elites and *their* respective masses. Nevertheless differences of interest between large and small farmers were tempered by social mixing, the sons of both often working together as labourers when young before acquiring their own land,[17] and by the labourers' aspirations to become small-holders themselves. Similarly in industry, the potential for revolutionary conflict between workers and employers had already started to give way to rules of procedure — abolishing the wild-cat strike whilst confirming union rights to organize and negotiate.[18] Thus in 1902 the picture was one of non-antagonistic elites pursuing different interests in a political structure which they dominated, whilst the rural and urban masses sought the crystallization of a representative party structure and the redistribution of wealth through non-revolutionary means. At the beginning of the century we should therefore expect this concentration of resources to be mirrored in the domination of educational negotiations by elites, but with divergent elite interests producing diverse changes in education. Subsequent changes in the distribution of resources, which substantially transformed this initial picture, can be examined in five different phases.

The First Two Decades

The first twenty years was a period of a closed legislative elite and changes in its composition were channelled through the parliamentary parties. There were two main changes in the power distribution, the first consisting in the crystallization of a new Party structure, which allowed more interests to be directly and powerfully defended in Parliament, the second in constitutional changes which were possible because of this new balance of powers in the legislature.

Party re-formation was almost immediate. Venstre's first action on coming to power was to pass taxation reforms favouring the large farmers at the expense of the smallholders. This led to a schism, with the Radical Party splitting-off in 1905 to become a liberal party supporting the small farmer or 'little man', by advocating general social welfare measures. This was important in two senses. On the one hand it meant that the four main parties had taken shape in the first decade, along the two main lines of cleavage in Danish society – the primary versus the secondary sector of the economy, and workers versus employers. Thus the Conservatives were the party of employers and top civil servants, Venstre the agrarian liberal party, the Radicals had the support of small farmers and urban intellectuals, while the Social Democrats represented industrial workers. In other words, all the main sections of the social structure had party political representation and could seriously aspire to legislative influence. Furthermore as co-members of the governing elite, these four parties were to 'constitute a closed interaction and decision system, capable of resisting attempts at intrusion by new parties'[19] for several decades.

On the other hand, the crystallization of four major parties constituted a political predisposition towards coalition government. The formation of the Radical party provided a coalition partner, not only for Venstre, but more importantly for the Social Democrats, once their initial resistance to co-operation with the bourgeois Left was undermined.[20]

The reform of the Conservative Party, which became another middle class party, completed the spectrum of possible coalitions, by giving Venstre a potential ally on its Right. In general this meant that governmental influence did not depend upon an outright majority: in particular its main effect was to speed the Left into power. In 1913 the Radicals were in office supported by the Social Democrats, and a coalition of these two parties governed between 1918-20. Given the subsequent complexity of ministries a Table of winning coalitions is included for reference on the opposite page.

One of the immediate consequences of the new balance of parliamentary power was the passing of a new Constitution by the Radicals in 1915, which spelt a further and substantial dispersal of political power. In fact it did not meet with very strong opposition: to Venstre it was a return to the old Liberal Constitution, to the Conservatives its voting provisions benefitted a Party losing electoral support. However, the deconcentration of power implicit in universal suffrage, Cabinet responsibility, curtailing of the Upper House, proportional representation and a general referendum for any future constitutional change[21] was later to benefit the smaller parties and thus to increase political accessibility. In fact about 20 new parties have participated in *Folketing* elections since 1920, but this did not seriously affect the big four until after the second world war.

In terms of economic distribution, the first major change involved the spreading of land ownership and control, partly through Venstre governments increasing State loans to expand peasant ownership, and partly through the Radicals leasing out many smallholdings from old Church lands.[22] Although the question of ownership divided these two parties, their conflicting policies together halted the drift from the land, swelled the ranks of the rural middle classes considerably, and ensured the enduring political importance of agrarian propertied interests. The second consisted in the spreading of real income through improvements in workers' wages. Denmark's dependence on foreign trade created severe problems during the first world war and the consequent rise in food prices only benefitted profiteers and farmers whilst the 'gulasch age' lasted. The workers were hit hardest, with falling living standards and high unemployment, and responded with radicalized unions which put pressure on the Social Democratic Party. From this resulted the first governmental intervention for price and rent control which

TABLE 2

The Patterns of Coalition Formation: Winning Coalitions 1901-1975[1]

Period	Prime Minister	Maj. gov.	Min. gov. with supp.	Min. gov. without supp.	Parliamentary basis of gov. = winning coalition (Governing party without distinct support to form a majority)
1901-05	J. H. Deuntzer	x			*Reform-Liberals*
1905-06	J. C. Christensen	x			*Reform-Liberals*
1906-09	J. C. Christensen/ N. Neergaard	x[2]	x		*Reform-Liberals* + Moderate Lib.
1909	N. Neergaard			x	(Liberals)
1909	Holstein-Ledreborg			x	(Liberals)
1909-10	C. Th. Zahle			x	(Radicals)
1910-13	K. Bernsten			x	(Liberals)
1913-20	C. Th. Zahle	x[3]	x		*Radicals* + Social Democrats
1920-24	N. Neergaard		x		*Liberals* + Conservatives
1924-26	Th. Stauning		x		*Social Democrats* + Radicals
1926-29	Madsen-Mygdal		x		*Liberals* + Conservatives
1929-40	Th. Stauning	x			*Social Democrats* + Radicals
1940-43[4]	Th. Stauning/ V. Buhl/ E. Scavenius	x			all-party coalition
1945	V. Buhl	x			all-party coalition
1945-47	K. Kristensen		x		*Liberals* + Cons + Radicals
1947-50	H. Hedtoft			x	(Social Democrats)
1950-53	E. Eriksen			x	(Liberals + Conservatives)
1953-57	H. Hedtoft/ H. C. Hansen		x		*Social Democrats* + Radicals
1957-60	H. C. Hansen/ V. Kampmann	x			*Soc. Democr. + Rad. + Justice P.*
1960-64	V. Kampmann/ J. O. Krag	x			*Soc. Democrats + Radicals*[5]
1964-66	J. O. Krag			x	(Social Democrats)
1966-68	J. O. Krag		x		*Social Democr. + Socialists*
1968-71	H. Baunsgaard	x			*Radicals + Lib. + Conservatives*
1971-73	A. Jørgensen		x		*Soc. Dem. + Socialist Peoples Party*
1973-75	P. Hartling			x	(Liberals)
1975-	A. Jørgensen			x	(Social Democrats)

1 Italics denote governing parties. Two short-lived caretaker governments in 1920 are ignored, as well as the so-called ministers-of-control representing the opposition parties 1916-18.
2 Majority government 1908-09 through representation of former support party.
3 Majority government 1918-20 through representation of former support party.
4 Confronted with an ultimatum issued by the German occupiers the all-party coalition government resigned in 1943 but the resignation was not formally accepted by the King. In practice, Denmark was ruled by the leading civil servants 1943-45.
5 Winning coalition including one of the two, normally neutral, representatives of Greenland who became a minister.

Source: principally taken from Erik Damgaard, 'The Parliamentary Basis of Danish Governments: the Partners of Coalition Formation', *Scandinavian Political Studies*, Vol. 4 (1969), p. 33.

culminated in the construction of a cost of living index according to which wages and salaries have subsequently been regulated,[23] despite its inflationary tendencies.

1920 to the Second World War

'Thus, in 1920 the stage was set for a new era of parliamentary democracy in Denmark. At the September 1920 election to the Folketing the four old parties polled a total of 96.2 percent of the national vote'.[24] It was their period in two senses: in the virtual exclusion of other parties from politics and in the sequential assumption of all four to power – each party in fact enjoying a share of office twice. During this period the balance of power showed a distinct shift left-wards; the first Social Democratic government (with Radical support) took office between 1924-26, these two parties governed solidly as a coalition between 1929 and the outbreak of war, and the Radicals obtained a never surpassed 46 percent of the vote in 1935. Nevertheless, the Radical presence in coalitions moderated socialist policies and prevented the polarization of Danish politics, as did the concessions necessarily given to the other large parties. Three consequences for the distribution of power stemmed from this period of moderate government by the old four parties.

Firstly, the fact that the Social Democrats could gain a majority in the Upper House (1936) indicated that despite its undemocratic basis of representation, the Landsting was no longer a barrier to democratic legislation. This enclave of power which benefited the Right had been undermined, though its final abolition had to await the next period. Secondly, the extent of government powers increased dramatically as a result of an all-party agreement undertaken to solve the economic crisis of the 1930s. Although this gave something to each party it took a warrant from all of them for further State intervention. To Venstre this meant the abandonment of liberal free trade policy in return for devaluation and agricultural aid, to the Social Democrats it spelt State interference in collective bargaining in exchange for protection of workers' wages, to the Right it resulted in Exchange controls over production and foreign marketing which had to be set against cheaper money. Thirdly, this overall increase in government powers had repercussions on local government which was increasingly used as an instrument for the implementation of central policies. However, this development was only part of a two way process, for it was paralleled by the formation of national associations of town, district and county councils which in turn formed inter-municipal bodies to protect local influence, interests and autonomy.[25]

Small steps towards economic redistribution were taken before, during and after the depression, their precise nature reflecting the to and fro, the checks and balances of the four main parties. Thus the Venstre government (1920-24) passed further legislation extending State loans to buy smallholdings, whilst the first Social Democratic ministry countered with a major redistributive measure, a once and for all wealth tax on large estates, which it failed to carry because Radical support was withdrawn. It had also failed to pass its public works programme, intended to reduce unemployment, which was now running at over 20 percent, and the return of a Liberal Ministry with Conservative support (1926-29) represented the last serious attempt at a lassez-faire solution, with its concomitant concentration of resources — as manifest in the reduction of public expenditure through cuts in the social services and the deliberate weakening of the unions in order to bring about wage restraint.

A Social Democratic and Radical coalition returned to face the depression of the thirties with a common legislative programme geared to welfare redistribution rather than nationalization, and committed to action against unemployment, the expansion of smallholdings, the broadening of social legislation and an attack on monopolistic firms. After further Liberal losses in the 1933 elections (when unemployment reached an unprecedented 43 percent, agriculture was hard hit by the fall in international prices and British limitations on dairy imports, whilst employers were demanding a 20 percent decrease in wages), the government still needed support from the centre right in order to implement reforms since this continued to control the upper house. The party compromise, the Kanslergade agreement between Social Democrats, Radicals and Venstre, already mentioned, paved the way for further redistributive measures since it contained the promise of Liberal support for extensive social reforms, on which the Democrats had been working for ten years.

These proposals became law in 1933 and covered unemployment insurance, health, pensions and accident provisions, welfare services and public responsibility for providing adequate housing at reasonable prices. In conjunction with this, progressive taxation was used to begin equalizing financial resources, with direct and indirect taxes increasing to about 15 percent of earnings. Although this provoked an outcry in the agricultural community it did not prevent the government from being returned with a substantially increased vote. Nevertheless the Social Democrats continued to steer a course which avoided major political splits, concentrating on taxation and welfare not nationalization, involving the unions in compulsory arbitration and equating socialism with the provision of economic security through social legislation. Few had gained during the crisis,[26] but towards the end of the decade some moves had been made towards equalization and these were of additional significance in the Danish context, where industry was less monopolistic than in the rest of Europe and where the growth of rural proprietorship had increased the overall size of the middle classes, whilst preventing the influx of unskilled, and thus poorly paid, labour into the towns.

Until the outbreak of war the relationships amongst the political elites mirrored relations between institutional elites, given the closeness with which party structure was modelled on social structure. At this stage 'the four old parties had already attained stable relationships with the most important groups of voters, such as farmers, workers, and employers, thus virtually emptying the "support market" and leaving no major "openings" to new parties'.[27] This had two main consequences for relations amongst resource holders. On the one hand, it enforced constant compromise between the four major interest blocs because of the political balance between their parties. We have seen how the Social Democrats had to please the Radicals as well as themselves in 1924-26 and 1929-40 and that the Radicals would oppose them if necessary, bringing down the government in 1926 over the agricultural wealth tax. The Radical role enforced a rightist socialism, but in turn *this* new power combination forced the Liberals to consider and to accept Conservative support (1926-29). Simultaneously the Radicals, often holding the balance of government in their hands, not only moderated the Left but also opposed the Liberal/Conserative alliance as one which tended towards an undesirable polarization of politics.[28] In terms of political arithmetic this has meant that since the 1920s all governments have either been coalitions or minority ones — after 1939 even the Social Democrat Party had to resign forever its ambitions of gaining an absolute majority.[29] Coalitions have always been between partners adjacent to each other on the right-left continuum (or formed by two parties flanking a third in the sequence),[30] but partners or supporters have always diluted policy and functioned to keep the polity on a steady centrist course in which none of the elites could pursue their interests untrammelled by others.

On the other hand, this parallelogram of political forces did ensure the consistent political sponsorship of divergent social interests and meant that the different demands of resource holders had immediate political representation. Increasingly, however, such elites were brought further into government in their own right (rather than through their elected representatives), via advisory and regulatory agencies such as the Foreign Currency Council. 'Throughout the 1930s the Foreign Exchange Office exerted a decisive influence on Danish economic policy. It became necessary to have it under the control of a Foreign Currency Council, on which, practically speaking, all branches of Danish commerce and industry were represented . . . the need to have one's views represented encouraged the more efficient organization of industry into what amounted to pressure groups'.[31] Official incorporation was thus the other face of State intervention.

Second World War – 1960

In politics this was the last period of hegemony for the old four parties and one of the factors ending it was dissatisfaction with the very centrism it produced. The minority status of most governments promoted a pronounced consensus in the final legislative divisions in the Folketing. The first Liberal government (1945-47) and the first Democratic ministry (1947-50) both relied on Radical support which pulled them towards the centre: even the first 'bourgeois' government since the twenties (Venstre and the Conservatives 1950-53) had to appease the Radicals and make major concessions to the Left. The impossibility of majority government favoured legislative co-operation, rather than bringing the government down, and a distinct preference for non-controversial bills.[32] The 1957 elections finally indicated a fracturing of support for parties whose mutual counterbalancing prevented any of them from delivering the goods to the interests they represented. The results left the Radicals and Social Democrats with insufficient seats to form a government, and after negotiations they were joined by the Single Tax Party[33] to make up a coalition. Paradoxically this made the Triangle government the strongest for many years and one capable of carrying out social reforms, but in the longer run it was the first indication of political fragmentation.

The only major move towards the redistribution of power consisted in revisions of the Constitution, which came into force in 1953 after a referendum. These included abolition of the Upper House in favour of single chamber government, a lowering of the voting age to 23, a legislative referendum for the protection of minorities, the introduction of the Ombudsman and the use of proportional representation as the basis for membership of advisory committees and investigating commissions.[34] In the economic field the war had produced a general decline, with agriculture and industry being hit equally hard. Although no absolute improvement was registered until the end of the fifties, relative redistribution continued, without going very far during this period. An ironic effect of centrism was that the three main measures introduced were formally enacted from unexpected quarters: the Social Democratic government increased State land purchases in 1947 to provide further smallholdings (an example of how the Radicals claim to have tempered socialism), the Liberal-Conservative ministry stuck to the regulation of wages by the cost of living index (despite its inflationary tendencies and their deflationary preferences), and the Triangle government extended the agricultural support system since agricultural wages were rising slower than others (in an attempt to buy traditional liberal votes).

Despite certain shifts among the electorate, at the end of the fifties the old parties still got their votes from their old supporters, even if all now had to appeal to the 'new middle classes'.[35] And the backbone support groups still expected their parties to deliver very different goods reflecting their very different interests. On the other hand the parties themselves had gradually moved towards a general consensus — all supporting a society in which 'few have too much and fewer too little'. Disagreement was confined to specific aspects of policies such as rent control and the scope of public aid, but this was non-ideological for all accepted the existing framework of the welfare state and claimed some credit for it. The consensus and compromise encouraged by coalition did little to advance the special interests of institutional elites. One sign of dissatisfaction with immobilism was the intensified organization of interest groups. In 1957 the Committee for Businessmen's Politics was founded to get its members elected to the Folketing and was followed by similar associations for Merchants, Retailers, Civil Servants, Salaried Employees, Smallholders, and craftsmen, in addition to the well-established trade union and agricultural organizations.[36] All of these can be interpreted as the actions of a heterogeneous group of resource holders in pursuit of independent goals which were being ill-served by political immobilism. In many ways the very redistribution of resources, which had proceeded steadily throughout the twentieth century, had been responsible for this differentiation of so many heterogeneous special interests.

1960-1973

The 1960 election was a landmark since it ended the relatively closed legislative elite made up of the four old parties. The Socialist People's Party (led by the ex-communist leader) cleared the electoral threshold at the first attempt, thus transforming the possible combinations for coalition governments. The old Social Democratic policy of cutting itself off from those further on the Left (i.e. the Communists who had always been small and in decline after the war) could no longer work: the Radicals ceased to hold the balance (since they had lost out together with the Liberal and Single Tax Parties) and were no longer a necessary ingredient for Centre-Left government. In the 1966 elections, the improved position of the SPP eroded the resistance of the Social Democrats, for the possibility of a new left majority coalition now existed,[37] and the SPP moved into the supporting position previously held by the Radicals. This produced disunity within the SPP (and the schism of the Socialist Left): 'the left-wing members felt that the Socialist People's Party as a whole was in danger of becoming a mere appendix to the Social Democrats, in contra-distinction to many others outside the two parties who felt that the People's Socialists were in danger of becoming the tail that wagged the dog'.[38] Certainly government for the first time was subject to direct and intense influence from the extreme Left. Correspondingly the Radicals could no longer work in the left alliance, and when the 1968 elections looked like a round repudiation of socialist policies, they interpreted this as a mandate to move right[39] and join a three party coalition (Radical Liberal, Conservative). Together these obtained the largest majority enjoyed by any government since 1935 and they stayed in power until 1971. Then the new left coalition assumed office, a Social Democratic government with SPP support, and the four party system had finally factured towards the left and become a five party one.

This breakthrough of the socialist left is itself the most important aspect of power redistribution during the period. Nevertheless local government reforms, implemented by the Rightwing coalition between 1969-70, respresented an important dispersal of powers. It not only rationalized, by reducing the number of country municipalities, but also constituted a move towards decentralization and democratization. This to one observer was part of 'a growing tendency to shift the responsibility for more tasks over to the municipalities and to place a larger part of the economic burden on the local units. Since the local units have been simultaneously larger, one could say that the offices in local councils now carry more power and influence'.[40] The local councils had always been important as democratic agencies, since lists of candidates standing for community issues or interests could be nominated alongside party lists, and stood a good chance of gaining seats as proportional representation was also used at this level.[41] In addition, however, the reform introduced greater democratization of control since the new country councils were to elect their own chairman, instead of having a higher civil servant centrally appointed in this capacity.

The Social Democratic Government (1960-64) intensified State economic intervention, for purposes of redistribution, with an incomes policy linking wages, salaries and profits to a national economic plan. This was carried despite Liberal opposition, though the latter was probably responsible for agricultural prices being tied to the incomes policy and for an extensive programme of farm subsidies. It was also its actions which brought the government down over a land reform bill which would have given local authorities options on land purchase (to set up more smallholdings), but which involved too great an encroachment on individual rights for the Liberals. However with the move leftwards, pushed by SPP support, the Social Democrats introduced a redistributive fiscal reform in 1967, which ended preferential tax reductions, favouring the upper income brackets, and also succeeded in implementing a 'housing guarantee arrangement', giving all families an equitable relationship between rent and income.[42] The influence of the SPP undoubtedly speeded up the use of fiscal and financial measures for equalization. These operated in a direct fashion to equalize incomes between industries (improving the wages of small farmers and fishermen) and to maintain the cost of living indexing of wages and salaries (despite inflationary consequences). They also worked indirectly by increasing public revenue for collective welfare spending on items such as housing subsidies. The extent of these redistributive measures (e.g. the fact that the majority were losing about 50 percent of their income in taxation at the end of the period) led the principal opposition parties to condemn them as 'LO solutions' — that is policies dictated by the trade unions.

In terms of relations amongst resource holders, the period witnessed the crumbling of the legislative consensus underpinned by the parliamentary balance of the four old parties. This had been real enough in the early sixties when one study of 59 laws on welfare and housing, which were debated between 1964-69, found 46 having no votes cast against them at the final reading.[43] The different interests in society had persisted, but their relationship to party policy had been blurred by the all-party need to appeal to a broader electoral base. And despite their persistence the different dimensions of the social structure had altered in importance. The rural middle classes remained significant, after all about 30,000 *new* farms had been established with government aid in the twentieth century and decentralized enterprises had continued to make headway in the countryside; nevertheless there had been a continued reduction of the agricultural sector and an expansion of industry. To some extent this was mirrored in the voting figures,[44] with rural-urban differences showing some decline, the Conservatives improving relative to Liberals given the growth of white collar workers, and both the Social Democrats and SPP being able to recruit from urban areas without necessarily subtracting votes from one another.[45] But this had produced a fracture towards the left, rather than a steady shift leftwards within the existing party political structure. 'Summing up, we can say that on the basis of voting changes it is not possible to describe the Danish Party system as a undimensional system; however, the left-right dimension seems to be the most dominant'.[46] Equally significant was the fact that the great block interests of the institutional elites were getting little satisfaction from their parties, which only differed about the speed at which society should move towards social democracy.[47]

The 1973-75 Period

The 1973 elections brought both a rightwing backlash and further fragmentation as the extreme left and right mobilized. Given the nature of the electoral system, disenchantment with the efficacy of the old parties had immediate parliamentary consequences. As the proportion of the vote received by the old four slid from 90 percent to 60 percent of seats, ten parties took their place in the Folketing:[48] on the Right a new 'Progress Party' was launched which appealed to those tired of tax burdens and abuses of welfare provisions, in the middle the Center Democrats broke away from the now leftist Social Democrats over the issue of property taxes on home ownership, the two together gaining nearly a quarter of the vote and substantial representation. At the other extreme the Left Socialists separated from the Social Democrats, while the SPP and the Communist Party polled more votes. In addition, this election saw the rise of a Christian People's Party based on the moral condemnation of certain liberal and welfare matters, including abortion and pornography. The results of the 1975 elections showed that these new parties were not transient phenomena: all were again returned.[49] In both cases this fragmentation of the parties produced minority governments (Liberal in 1973, Social Democrat in 1975), which were so weak that they could only keep going on the basis of ad hoc coalitions for different bills.

In examining relations amongst resource holders throughout the twentieth century, the discussion of power redistribution has been closely integrated with an analysis of the development and change of political parties. This approach accords with Pedersen's view 'that the most significant changes in the social profile of the elites, i.e. the "transfer of power from old hands to new", were closely related to the major changes in the party system' and that the proper perspective from which to view elite transformation is 'as part of and a component in the general political development of Danish society'.[50] Progressively this had witnessed the incorporation of sections of the electorate which had previously been passive (when considered as large social blocs), until, in the most recent periods, many finer shades of opinion obtained access to the central decision-making arena.

Most recently more and more interest groups of different kinds have inserted themselves in Parliament: in 1976 out of 179 Folketing members, 61 were public or civil servants and a minimum of 17 were overt representatives of interest organizations.[51] The horse-trading which resulted produced shifting combinations on particular issues. It was particularly blatant in the seventies, but in fact this was only a special variant on a general theme which was rendered more obvious because most institutional elites now had direct access to parliamentary power. 'In the Danish political system no single socio-economic interest carried into the elites by a specific group of politicians has ever been allowed to materialize in authoritative political decisions . . . No single party has ever been free to carry through its intentions, but has always had either to abstain from legislative influence in the short run or to enter a compromise at one point or another in the decision-making process. The essential mechanism of decision-making in the Danish political system has always consisted in the formation by organized factions and parties of coalitions in the elites and between the elites. These coalitions have cross cut — and have had to cross cut — the various cleavages in the elites and in society, in particular the cleavages between upper and lower social strata, and between town and country-side'.[5 2]

At different times this resulted in give and take between the parties, consensus on the uncontroversial, or even a political immobilism somewhat reminiscent of Fourth Republic France. In the most recent periods, given the general tendency for minority governments anyway to have a lesser rate of legislative achievement, together with the new variety and range of competing cross-pressures, legislation is unlikely to be dramatic or contentious — despite the fact that growing State intervention has convinced interest groups that central political representation is vital to the advancement or defence of their causes, and that the electoral system has facilitated this. In other words the progressive redistribution of power has increasingly placed most important social groups and institutional elites in a position from which they can *engage* in political manipulation for educational change or defence of the educational status quo. But simultaneously it has produced a political situation in which none will be able to gain all that they want, in educational terms, because of the parliamentary balance of powers. From this we should expect to find intense politico-educational activities throughout the twentieth century, but also an equally intensive use of other processes for negotiating change in education, since political manipulation will leave a large proportion of special demands unsatisfied.

The significance of the parallel redistribution of economic resources during the twentieth century is found here, for it has meant that more and more groups progressively acquired the wealth needed to engage in external transactions to obtain the educational services they required. Various surveys have indicated the cumulative effects of increased national prosperity and the consistent application of welfare policies. In the most recent period an EEC report showed the Danes to be the most heavily taxed peoples in Europe, with half of the GNP being taken in taxes and a 60 percent tax rate being common amongst the middle class.[53] Concurrently the social security safety-net is placed high, allowing only a short fall, unemployment benefits, for example, providing a steady income of 90 percent of the normal wage. In other words, since the start of the century there has been a steady redistribution which has meant that fewer and fewer interest groups find themselves low on both economic and power resources. Where education is concerned, this should spell the active use of all three processes of negotiation and a diversity of educational changes matching the different interests of resource holders.

EXTERNAL TRANSACTIONS

Thinking purely in terms of Bargaining Power, and having seen that economic resources are highly concentrated at the start, it is to be expected that most of the early external transactions will be negotiated by the wealthier institutional elites. At the start of the system it is the agricultural interests of the large farmers which are likely to be most successful, given their wealth and the parliamentary dominance of their party, which was in a position to give political protection to their transactions. Commercial and industrial interests are next well placed, in view of their growing wealth throughout the twentieth century and their constant representation within the four big parties. The smallholders, unions and popular groups of all kinds are expected to have least impact through external transactions at the beginning of the period because of the concentration of wealth, but its progressive redistribution should lead them to make more use of this form of negotiation over time, especially since their political sponsorship occurs early and improves over the decades.

Thus, from inspection of the resource distributions alone, it appears that many groups were in good bargaining positions and that the potential existed for a growing richness of external transactions as the century progressed. This potential of course was increased by the prevalence of coalition government and party compromise, which in this context served to prevent strong powers of political veto from being used to outlaw external transactions. However, bargaining power is not automatically translated into Negotiating Strength — the latter involves standing in a particular relationship with another party. Hence in proceeding to analyze external transactions, the relations between the external interest groups and both the *polity* and the *profession* have to be examined in closer detail to discover whether they were such as to permit the translation of financial resources into the provision of educational services.

The Polity and External Interest Groups

Earlier it was argued that to attain its own goals and to prevent education from escaping government control and creating problems for official educational policy, the Parties would constantly monitor external transactions, not repressing all, but rather concentrating their powers of veto on developments incompatible with their own educational aims. When such developments occur it was suggested that the governing party would use four tactics in its overall strategy for strengthening political control over education:

1. monopolizing supplies to education;
2. barring alternative suppliers through the use of legal embargoes;
3. undermining local and institutional autonomy of educational establishments;
4. propagating values justifying State intervention.

At one time or another during the twentieth century all of these tactics were deployed against the activities of different external interest groups, and often several of them were used in combination. At times the enterprises founded by various external interest groups were suppressed, marginalized or rechannelled, but overall this did not prevent external transactions from being a consistently important source of educational change.

From the start of the system there was a built-in principle that the State was not the only supplier of educational resources. Private schools, freeschools, technical schools and Folk High Schools were incorporated in the loose organic connection established under Venstre's auspices, and this did not involve dispossession of property or loss of control. Thus the emergent educational system was such that certain external interest groups had a financial and a legal foothold in it, which constituted a vested interest for them to maintain and a precedent which others later tried to emulate through further external transactions.

The first two decades were broadly a period during which the groups most active in external transactions were from the centre right (the affluent farmers) who increasingly came up against the power of political veto from the left, which had been speeded into power. In crude terms the Social Democrats used their power resources to try to prevent a socially privileged group from deriving additional educational advantages from their economic resources. The main tactic that the left employed in seeking to enforce their embargo was (2), the barring of alternative suppliers to education. However, we have argued that the application of such vetoes is maximally effective when those they are used against are politically uninfluential, and when other parties do not oppose their implementation. We have also seen that this was the time at which the four main parties crystallized, reflecting the major cleavages in society, and balanced one another in the central decision-making arena. In fact, the relative political balance between Venstre and the Social Democrats (who alternated in office between 1910-30), coupled with the fact that many of the external transactions taking place were in the Grundtvigian tradition (practical forms of agricultural instruction), meant that they were approved by Venstre and defended by its members in the Folketing. Thus the first decades of the twentieth century can be seen as a time of struggle between Venstre and the Social Democrats over the degree to which the State should control processes of exchange in education.

The opposition of the Social Democrat Party to private, and private but subsidized, education (i.e. the main types of external transaction legally recognized and incorporated into the new system) was apparent the moment it became a significant political force either locally or centrally. When it first gained a majority on the Copenhagen town Council in 1917 the Social Democrat party announced that the subsidy to private secondary schools could not continue indefinitely. By 1918 the Radical government, pressed by its Social Democrat supporters, had prepared a law providing for the State to take over those private schools that were agreeable, and only to continue State aid to others where 'their instruction and whole organization are in pattern with the public school, accept pedagogical supervision and economic control by the State, and do not in the entrance examinations – beyond the test of ability – have the stamp of being reserved for a special social class'.[54] This also of course implied the use of tactic (3), undermining institutional autonomy, by the most tried and tested method – the minimization of differences between public and private instruction. Thus State

control was clearly viewed as a concomitant of educational democratization, and the transfer of primary and secondary schools from private
to public auspices was pursued vigorously during the first Social
Democratic ministry (1924-26). In 1910, at the secondary level, of 45
schools, 25 were private, 13 State and 6 communal. By 1925, thirty-
three belonged to the State, thirteen were communal and private
schools had fallen to ten in number. By the same date nine tenths of
primary school pupils were attending public schools.

One of the last acts of the Radical-Social Democrat government,
before falling in 1920, was to establish a Great Commission to examine
education in general, under the Chairmanship of Klausen, a leading
Social Democrat, and with representatives from other parties and the
teaching profession. It reported in 1923 and this document indicated
the wide divide separating the Liberals and the Social Democrats on the
questions of educational centralization and the degree of State control
which was desirable over private schools. The Left, including the NUT,
were opposed, on democratic grounds, to any firm financial committment to private education and saw State control as the price for
receiving any aid at all. They proposed that public Directors should
supervise Folk School, Gymnasia, Real and Youth Schools alike. The
latter two were mainly private networks which had been developed
through external transactions: the one met parental and employer
demands for an extended practical instruction at the end of the folkschool, the other comprised rural and urban schools working in the
Grundtvigian tradition. Both had the support of Venstre: the Youth
Schools had always been particularly close to the heart of its agricultural supporters, and its defence of the Real schools perhaps became
warmer as the Liberals began to need Conservative support to hold
office (1920-24 and 1926-29).

Venstre consistently defended subsidies to private education without rigid State control, thus protecting its autonomy and repudiating
tactic (3), 'so that there is an opportunity for men and women with
special pedagogical gifts to set up schools representing their ideas and
outlook in a way different from that possible in the circumstances of
the public school'.[55] The Liberals obviously feared placing too strong
an instrument of educational control in the hands of the growing Social
Democratic party. During the first two decades Venstre was successful
in protecting the networks of those external interest groups which it
favoured (the Real schools, the Folk High Schools and the Youth
Schools), thus preserving the official legitimacy of external trans-

actions, which other interest groups then sought to use themselves. Very importantly, in 1921, the Liberals gave State aid to private training colleges, which outnumbered public ones by 12 to 7. They defended these largely because they were of Grundtvigian or Home Mission origin,[56] but by corollary they prevented teachers in general from becoming agents formed and trained by the State. All this had been possible because of the equal political strengths of the two parties in Parliament. Nevertheless, the growing power of the left had succeeded in imposing more stringent controls on mainstream primary and secondary education and was beginning to marginalize external transactions, confining them to private, terminal or adult education.

The thirties, with a strong Left majority in power throughout, witnessed the third tactic coming into play, namely that of undermining the local and institutional autonomy of public education in order to increase its responsiveness to the central polity, thus diminishing its ability to deal directly with external interest groups. Essentially the governing coalition was an alliance, in educational terms, of left-wing populism on the part of the Social Democrats and Grundtvigian populism on the part of the Radicals. Both wanted the *people* to participate at grass-roots level in the schools, but neither were willing to give organized interests the freedom to operate in education, unlike the Liberals. Hence the dual intention of the Minister of Education was 'to give parents a strong concern and pedagogical influence with the school where their children attend, and to introduce an academic supervision in place of the Church supervision'.[57] The local participation of parents and the central intervention of State were equally legitimate, the involvement of organized interests, community associations, and institutional elites were not. Thus the 1933 Education Act made provision for Parents' Boards at individual schools,[58] but otherwise placed public and private, evening and youth schools under similar and intensified supervision. Secondly, rules were established for giving State aid to private schools, which involved the inspection of these institutions by a Ministry approved 'supervisor', upon whose adverse report the subsidy could be withdrawn. Finally, the publication (by Ordinance) of the timetable for the Gymnasia in 1935, to cover State, communal and private schools alike, had the double effect of preventing the gymnasium from responding to outside demands because its activities were prescribed in such detail and decreasing the attractiveness of private educational enterprise by restraining its diversity.

The thirties thus represented the lowest ebb for external transactions, with strong State curricular control debarring them in the public sector, and supervisory controls limiting them in private or proprietory schools. The external interest groups were forced not merely into the private sector but were also restricted to transacting courses which led to no public examination. This of course was the period of Left majority Government, with the Social Democrats obtaining the largest poll ever in 1935, thus giving it the political power to exercise educational vetoes. It was also the era of the depression, of falling workers' wages, which temporarily cancelled out the significance of economic redistribution for external transactions. It meant that the poorer social groups were unable to engage seriously in this process of negotiating educational change, and that therefore its savage political curtailment only damaged the opponents of the governing party — those industrial and commercial elites who still had the wealth to continue founding technical, clerical and mercantile courses and establishments at all levels.

After the war, in the forties, fifties and early sixties, both of these factors became inoperative. Politically there was a return to minority government — concession, consensus and centrism — whose dual effect was to lift official embargoes on external transactions whilst increasing the activities of external interest groups because of the educational immobilism of government. Economically the slow return to prosperity, coupled with growing equalization, created more interest groups with more resources who were now in a bargaining position to make use of this method for negotiating the educational services they required.

The National government of the postwar recovery period brought some immediate relief, with a law in 1942 recognizing the Junior Folk High School, for those under 18, as similar to the Folk High School, with respect to subsidies and minimal supervision.[59] More important was an amendment to the 1933 Act, which was introduced by the Liberal government with Radical and Conservative support, giving *Fri* schools the right to choose their own supervisory authority and thus enabling diverse provisions to be introduced at elementary level via external transactions. 'Their position is very free, they are as a rule not supervised by the local authorities, but can choose their own inspector, who, moreover only has to see that the standard of instruction in Danish, written and oral, writing and arithmetic is satisfactory.'[60] By 1948 there were 228 schools of this kind with over 10,000 pupils and the Ministry expected their enrollments to rise with a recent increase in government grants. Still, however, State controls of a curricular and supervisory nature effectively precluded direct transactions with *public* instruction at primary and secondary levels, and thus forced different external interest groups to make a variety of private provisions. Unintentionally this contributed to the proliferation of independent specialized institutions completely outside the aegis of the Ministry of Education. In particular networks of agricultural, technical and commercial schools were gradually being established, ranging from the lowest apprenticeship course to the highest level.

In the late forties and fifties, the long period of minority governments and of give and take in policy, compromise dominated in the educational field as in others. The Left still wanted to extend State control in the interests of democracy: the Liberals still wanted to protect educational free trade and to defend the acquired rights of congenial interest groups. The compromise formula, accepted because no party could get its own way politically, was very like that which had given rise to the system itself — a further phase of incorporation, which gave legal recognition to existing transactions and sought to bring the public and private sectors into a new 'organic connection'. The Left hoped to use this compromise as tactic (1), the pouring in of State resources to all kinds of instruction, in the belief that financial dependence would spell State control: the Liberals were ready to employ it in order to give legal recognition to the established networks, knowing that they themselves were in a position to ensure that incorporation did not cost too much in terms of autonomy. In part too the compromise was genuine, for on the one hand Liberal opinion was now less hostile to welfare provisions, and on the other the Social Democrats were aware that the Unions, Craft Guilds, Townsmen's Associations and Co-operatives were beginning to be seriously involved in external transactions.

The legislation passed bore the marks of these differing party motives but, as in 1902, neither dispossession of property nor managerial subordination were involved. The first regulation of 1950 embraced the complex network of commercial schools, which remained in the hands of the Business Associations which had founded them, but accepted inspection by the Ministry of Trade in return for a 40 percent State contribution towards expenses. More importantly still, the acquired rights of the commercial elites were translated into formal positions of control, in what now became official and compulsory training for business apprentices, thus inserting these external interest groups into the administrative structure in such a way that they could defend themselves in the future. Specifically a Commercial School Board, with membership drawn jointly from the Ministry of Trade and the Business Organizations, was formed to operate in a consultative capacity to the Inspectorate and an Examination Commission, which in turn were composed of businessmen and teachers, who jointly set the papers and conducted assessment.[61] In other words, the long arm of central curricular control did not reach down to regulate the definition of instruction here. These details have been given because this was the pattern which, with minor variations, was extended to the private networks of technical, trade and agricultural institutions of education between 1954-60. A proper examination of their component courses and establishments will be delayed until the next chapter.

A general law on further education, covering Youth Schools, Junior Folk High Schools, Evening Schools, Agricultural courses, Folk High Schools and Continuation classes was passed in 1954 and endorsed their decentralized administration.[62] It did not undermine the links between the teaching given and the practical work for which it was designed, it did not prevent the receipt of financial resources from the institutional elites or the local authorities, and it did not go beyond the appointment of a State Consultant for Further Education, whose supervision was exercised in conjunction with inspectors appointed by the founding associations.

Taken together these provisions meant that during the fifties the external interest groups had gained both legal recognition and public aid for the external transactions they had previously concluded in the private sector. Given that much of this legislation specified compulsory attendance for various categories of school leavers, young workers and apprentices, it meant that the external interest groups were the acknowledged masters in pre-vocational and vocational instruction, and that external transaction was the recognized process governing changes in practical training. However, mainstream education (the folkschool and the gymnasium) remained inaccessible for the external interest groups, because of the enduring stringency of State control exercised via the centralized management of knowledge. Only with the concerted action of the teachers was this somewhat relaxed in 1970 and will thus be dealt with in the next section. The final political point to note, however, is that this change was accomplished under the last majority government to date, the Radical-Liberal-Conservative coalition of 1968-71. The centre-right had thus been consistent throughout the

century in its willingness to lift political embargoes on external transactions. Doubtless its critics from the left would argue that this was
because its supporters consistently benefited from such a process —
which is true, except that by the seventies the range of external interest
gorups making use of this form of negotiation certainly could not be
characterized as exclusively 'bourgeois'.

The Teaching Profession and External Interest Groups

At *primary level* we have seen that external transactions were confined
to the establishment of private schools, largely on the public pattern,
until the mid-century. Then the legal right was gained to instruct pupils
throughout the period of compulsory education in private, but State
aided, *friskole*. Certainly these provisions introduced diversity at this
level, for it now included 'schools which follow a different course from
the publically run schools, on religious, or pedagogical grounds, or on
grounds of national-linguistic difference, such as schools for the
German minority',[63] but the embargo on transactions with *public*
elementary schools remained because of their controlled curricula.
Nevertheless this fund of experimentation in the private sector may
have contributed to professional restlessness during the fifties and 'the
repeated request that local authorities should seek the permission from
the Minister to introduce experiments in developing the schools of an
area, which implements the growing desire in Denmark for more local
initiative'.[64] By 1966 the Danish Union of Teachers were showing
public dissatisfaction with this 'initiative by license', and advanced their
own programme for primary school development. This included more
flexible syllabuses facilitating co-operation with parental demands,
employers' requirements and the new forms of further education now
available. It was indicative of professional willingness to engage in
external transactions at this level, and to lift the political vetoes
preventing them. It was also symptomatic of a desire to link up public
primary schooling with those forms of further education which had
been independently founded and were now publically recognized.

Much of the 1966 teachers' programme was embodied in the 1970
Education Act, passed by the majority government of the Right.
However, since the primary teachers had been consistent protagonists
of equality of educational opportunity this could not be interpreted as

a purely rightwing move, which perhaps facilitated its passage. The main provision concerned pupils who were not proceeding with academic instruction (entering secondary education proper), nor leaving (to attend one of the independent vocational schools already discussed), but continuing in an 8th, 9th or 10th class of post-compulsory schooling. This last option was now intended to be related to practical life and 'the Ministry only put forward a number of rulings on matters of principle concerning this teaching and attached a series of suggestions worked out on a broad and general basis, but has otherwise left it to the Local Authorities to establish their 8th to 10th classes on the basis of local conditions'.[65] Furthermore these classes can be 'divided into streams, adapted to the pupils' future activities in different branches of commerce or industry, without, however, actual vocational training being given'.[66] Since this specialization can begin in the 7th year, with pupils taking specialist options (such as agriculture, languages, practical workshop and domestic science) alongside general subjects, the way was finally open for external transactions to penetrate *public* primary instruction. That this is restricted to the later forms is probably little loss to the external interest groups, most of whose specialist requirements are concentrated on the terminal classes since they rely on the prior acquisition of basic literacy and numeracy. The combination of a willing profession, interest groups ready to invest heavily, and a majority government sympathetic to the enterprises in question, had been necessary to bring this about.

At *secondary level*, however, the Ministry of Education retained its grip on non-specialized schooling throughout the period and the Gymnasium remained barricaded against outside initiative behind its tightly prescribed curriculum. Private Gymnasia continued (there were 14 out of the total 97 in 1970)[67] but were straight-jacketed into the same regimen as part of the leftwing policy for undermining social privilege. Thus external transactions were mainly concerned with the establishment of post-compulsory courses and institutions. The enormous success in developing this kind of instruction, in effectively providing several alternative kinds of secondary education (which will be discussed in the following chapter), must partly be attributed to the willingness of the teaching profession to provide the necessary expertise. This willingness derived from two factors, one normative the other calculative. Firstly, the fact that the majority of teacher training remained in private hands throughout the century meant that there was nothing unorthodox in trainees being appointed to private schools once qualified. Indeed, in the case of the Colleges of Grundtvigian origin and those established in the fifties to meet local needs, training was oriented in this direction. Secondly, the private sector represented a way for non-graduate teachers to enter the secondary field, which had attractions for those unqualified to teach in the Gymnasia and had the additional advantage of carrying a lower workload than was general in the communal schools.[68] Thus various external interest groups made offers which were attractive in terms of career prospects and working conditions, and which did not involve any violation of professional values. In this way the Agricultural Associations, Agricultural Cooperatives, Danish Federation of Industries, Craft Guilds, Townsmens' Associations, Businessmens' Organizations and Trade Unions elaborated three main alternatives to academic secondary instruction and each contained a range of practical, branching options.

In *higher education* the failure of the external interest groups to enter into negotiations with the universities of Copenhagen and Aarhus cannot be attributed to political veto or any strategy on the part of central government, for both institutions enjoyed a very high degree of autonomy from the start. They possessed property of their own, were partially self-supporting, and had largely independent governing bodies (for example, at Aarhus the Board of Governors was made up of three members elected by the Friends of the University, three by the city Council, the Rector of the University and one State representative).[69] In turn this implies considerable professional freedom to maintain or modify the prevailing definition of higher learning. But the academics themselves have consistently endorsed maintenance rather than change, repulsing the overtures of the external interest groups on normative grounds — their freedom, status and wealth enabling them to do so with impunity. Hence the faculty rejected pragmatic external requirements, thus forcing the interest groups to establish networks of independent, unaffiliated Colleges and High Schools, since they remained convinced about the indispensibility of specialized training to them. Thus the 'comparatively large number of institutions of higher education in Denmark may be explained by the fact that the two universities have limited their activities to the disciplines coming within the faculties dating back to the Middle Ages'.[70]

Hence each of the independent networks of agricultural, technical and commercial training developed an apex within tertiary education giving instruction at graduate and post-graduate levels, but outside the universities. None attracted political censure, for to Venstre, and all parties on its left, the Universities were bastions of traditional high culture which they had consistently condemned because it underpinned social privilege. In modern times the parties themselves found the universities obstructive in terms of their anachronistic outputs. Thus each independent establishment has attracted official aid and legal recognition as being of university status, largely because various Departments of State were themselves wanting to recruit types of graduates which the old universities steadfastly refused to train. It is significant in this connection that these moves were not engineered by the Ministry of Education in an attempt to integrate higher education, but instead were transacted on an ad hoc basis by the Ministries of Agriculture, Commerce, Industry and Shipping. Yet subsidy and supervision have done little to undermine the rights of the external interest groups in relation to these institutions: on the contrary they have been legally underwritten. Their position as suppliers of resources to higher education is recognized and all continue to receive research and training services in return for financial contributions.

INTERNAL INITIATION

At the start of the system the profession as a whole possessed expertise, alternative suppliers of resources, and some degree of insertion into positions of educational administration. However, the profession was not a whole: the 'organic connection' which had created the system had done so by incorporating two different cultures, two types of school, and with it, two types of teachers. The graduates, with their long training and commitment to high culture, who staffed the Gymnasia and University had little in common with the 'men from the plough' recruited by the Teacher Training Colleges to later stock the Folkschool and Middle School. These two parts of the profession differed not only in background and cultivation, but also in their Bargaining Positions at the beginning of the system.

Initially then, teachers in the Folk and Middle Schools had relatively low expertise, as judged objectively by the short duration of their training, or subjectively by its grounding in popular culture. Any resources at their command or disposal were only found in the private sector, although the independent status of the Training Colleges themselves gave a significant amount of financial freedom at the apex of the non-graduate profession. In public elementary education their autonomy was severely limited, for although all permanent teachers formed a consultative Council in each school, its powers were restricted to matters concerning instruction in that establishment alone. Furthermore, the economic powers of the local Communal Council and curricular control by central government (the timetable for the Folkschool was published in 1900 and for the Middle School in 1904) were strong constraints on professional initiative at this level. Gymnasia teachers shared the same low autonomy, since stringent curricular controls had been imposed as part of Venstre's attack on classical learned culture, and the same shortage of disposable financial assets, with the exception of the private schools which were nevertheless subject to the above controls and thus able to make little use of their capital to support innovation (the timetable for the Gymnasium was published in 1906). They differed, however, in being the bearers of considerable expertise since all of them were graduates. Only in higher education did the staff of the Royal University of Copenhagen enjoy high expertise, control considerable resources accumulated from past endowments, and experience substantial professional autonomy. These differences in the initial bargaining positions of teachers at the three levels are summarized in the following table:

	Non-Graduate Teachers	Graduate Teachers	
	Folk and Middle School	Gymnasia	University
Expertise	Low	High	High
Wealth	Low	Low	High
Autonomy	Low	Low	High

However, it is relationships with other groups that determine how far bargaining power can be translated into negotiating strength, thus enabling the profession to engage in a significant amount of internal initiation. From the initial bargaining positions it appears that only the faculty of the University of Copenhagen was well placed for this: all other parts of the profession suffered from deficiencies in expertise, freedom or finance. In reality the negotiating strengths to emerge from interaction bore little resemblance to the expectations engendered by the initial resource distribution. This was because the strategies pursued by different sections of the profession, with more or less success, brought about a gradual redistribution of resources, thus altering their bargaining positions in relation to one another. As a whole we will see that the profession managed to slough off financial poverty and political constraint, and, via a series of transactions, established a more reciprocal exchange relationship. This in turn permitted more internal initiation to take place, thus allowing the profession to make an increasing contribution to educational change. It is these transactions which must now be analyzed.

The Polity and the Profession

Earlier, when examining external transactions, we saw how the polity eventually failed to block alternative or additional suppliers of wealth to education at all levels. This obviously increased the resources available to the profession, but would have been of little use for internal initiation unless enough autonomy was gained to enable this wealth to be devoted to teachers' goals and values. In order to increase their autonomy vis-à-vis the polity, which was very low except in the Royal University, the primary and secondary teachers had to make use of the following tactics:

1. to increase the value of their expertise by raising and upgrading it;
2. to monopolize and monitor expertise by controlling certification and training;
3. to participate in educational administration in order to cushion the impact of the polity upon them and to mould policy rather than passively to receive it;
4. to legitimate such professional activities.

As a broad generalization, the primary teachers were fully successful in their use of all four tactics to increase their autonomy, whilst the Gymnasia teachers failed to make significant headway, despite their initial advantage of possessing a much higher level of expertise. The crucial factor distinguishing between them was the nature of their relationships with the polity, which allowed the non-graduate teachers an incomparably greater negotiating strength. The fact that historically Venstre had backed the Grundtvigian 'school of life' against the learned 'school of death' left a permanent mark on the system, because parties from the Liberals leftwards never ceased to view the elitist graduate teacher with suspicion, whereas 'the man from the plough' ranked among their supporters and was an important symbol in egalitarian imagery.

The Non-graduate Teachers

In the twentieth century this part of the profession was strikingly successful in all four respects, and these reinforced one another over time. From the beginning they benefited from the Liberal concern to advance this group of teachers at the expense of others, higher in the system. Although the Social Democrat party did not have the same organic and historical connection with this group, and often found its own desire for political control over education at war with their advancement, its attitude was not hostile. Partly this was because Folk and Middle School teachers never functioned as a bourgeois group in politics or society, and partly it must be attributed to the influence of its main coalition partner, the Radicals, who shared the same Grundt-vigian links with teachers as did Venstre.

In the first two decades professional autonomy was immediately at issue. Already by 1907 the NUT was showing organized resentment about the supervisory arrangements imposed at the beginning of the system and counter-proposed that they should become their own 'advisors' (i.e. self-inspecting) and be inserted on local authority bodies. This was accepted by a government Committee, reporting in 1911, which also took issue with teachers being wholly paid by the State since 'they will feel themselves to be State officials and not bound in the same degree to the locality in which they work'.[71] This was part of a more general Liberal recognition that the 'State's influence on the schools' direction and its control over the school and its life and work will necessarily be increased when the State's subsidy to the school expenditure rises'.[72] This shows Venstre to be aware of the appropriate political counter-tactic (an influx of public resources to produce financial dependence) but to be unwilling to use it, partly so as to avoid placing central control within grasp of the Social Democrats. Although the Liberals failed to pass a bill incorporating changes in supervision they did prevent the Social Democratic government (1924-26) from instituting 12 Advisors (who would have been non-professional inspectors), and from passing a bill centralizing control over teacher training, on the grounds that it should not be a State monopoly.[73] Given policy conflict between the two parties, the profession benefitted during this period of political balance which precluded determined central constraints, to make small but significant advances on a number of fronts before 1930.

Firstly, the NUT took a step towards insertion in 1919 by gaining recognition and consultative status in salary negotiations with the Ministry. Secondly, the official acceptance of private Teacher Training Colleges as having the same status as State ones (and therefore to be subsidized for 2/3rds of their costs) served to protect the basis for subsequent increments in professional independence — it later allowed a wedge to be driven between expertise and officialdom. Finally the very absence of legislation (due to deadlock between governments and oppositions) enabled the traditional Folkschool teacher silently to upgrade himself by moving into the communal Middle School and establishing his right to teach the 'secondary' age group, which was eventually extended to 17. However, despite the Klausen Committee's flowery commendation of 'the rich fruits which the encouragement of the child's self-activity in school work can bring', central syllabus control continued to circumscribe class room activities and the Social Democrats remained adamant about the impossibility of curricular freedom, since 'it is too costly to experiment with the whole country's school system'.[74]

In the period of government by the Social Democrat-Radical alliance between 1929-40, further moves towards professional independence, insertion, and the definition of instruction were achieved. The Radical influence was probably important in modifying the Democrats' attitudes to this part of the profession, but equally significant was the fact that the NUT members of the Klausen Committee had supported the Social Democrats in their condemnation of private schools and had thus won their egalitarian spurs. Continued Venstre defence still played a role, given a moderate government heedful of opposition, as the first step forward illustrates. In 1930 the Teacher Training Colleges increased their self-management when college lecturers gained charge of entry examinations. This turned out to be an important control over recruitment. It prevented a closed circuit of academic reproduction in which only those with State certificates (i.e. gained through having followed a centrally determined programme) could enter. Most immediately this was due to Venstre defending the historic rights of the 'man from the plough', but its unintended consequence was to leave the profession free to determine its own entrance criteria. Additionally the Certification examination was administered by College lecturers with Censors appointed by the Ministry. Independence had increased but it had not gone far: college syllabuses were still given in detail for private and State establishments alike, and the State Advisor for the Folkschool supervised the colleges and chaired the Certificate examination.

The 1933 Act on educational administration, although based on the Klausen Report, included a number of concessions to NUT opinion, many of which increased professional insertion. These have to be seen against the background of the multi-party Kanslergade agreement and the general policy of bringing elites into government. In particular, the old advisor-inspector problem received a compromise solution, whereby experienced teachers themselves became the new County School Advisors — the Directorate's pedagogical advice-givers. Teacher representatives took part in the Parents' Boards which could now be established at each school, thus allaying apprehension that popular participation would introduce parental power over the profession. More important still was the provision that all teachers within a town or commune would form a Joint Teachers' Council, which carried their consultative rights beyond the confines of the single school.

Finally in the same year, the NUT, backing experiments conducted with the terminal classes in Copenhagen (possible, because of the greater autonomy of the Capital), advocated an integrated method of teaching in the Folkschool for which curricular freedom and flexibility were pre-conditions. For the first time, the 1937 Primary School Act made concessions in this direction since it was 'a framework within which Local Authorities are required to set up an educational system based on certain principles which to some extent enable Local Educational Authorities to adapt the system as they think fit'.[75] Two of its most important provisions specified that the last Middle School classes should concentrate on subjects (undefined in law) which had 'regard to the children's future activities in practical life',[76] and that there was no legal obligation to keep subject areas discrete when teaching them. This breach in curricular rigidity was confirmed in 1941, when the 1900 Circular, giving detailed instructions on all Folkschool work, was recalled and no new Circular issued, since it would be 'unnecessary and unfortunate, when there ought not to be any plan to lead instruction on predetermined tracks'.[77] Instead of ordinances and regulations[78] there were merely 'Suggestions', which themselves endorsed the notion that 'each teacher must seek the way of working which stems from his nature and with which he believes he can best adapt his instruction'.[79]

Thus the central management of knowledge was abandoned at this level and teachers became free to respond to the community, to experiment, and to borrow from private practice — but only where the primary and non-examination Middle School were concerned.

In the immediate postwar period attempts were made to extend this freedom into the examined sector. After the Occupation, a delegation from teachers' organizations went to the Ministry to request that experimental activity be recognized and supported within the existing administrative framework. An Act of 1948 gave permission to experiment with instruction and examination in the Training Colleges, in the primary and Middle Schools (1950) and in the Gymnasia (1952), provided these departures did not adversely affect the tasks allotted to the type of school concerned. Basically what this sanctioned was the addition of subjects over and above the legal requirements. In the same vein the 1945 Act abandoned the attempt to prescribe curricular for the Youth Schools, merely enjoining that a third of the timetable was to be devoted to subjects connected with working life and community affairs.

The 1958 Law passed by the Triangle government, establishing the undivided school and introducing a leaving certificate at 14, effectively gave legal recognition to further curricular freedom, for not only did schooling up to this age already include optional subjects geared to pupils' future occupations, but also this was recorded on the final Certificate. Furthermore the Real examination, now the earliest in Danish Schools, provided for options and additions to the curriculum, given Ministerial approval, and again noted each subject studied on the Certificate. All of this indicated a lifting of political control over what was taught and a complementary freedom for the profession to manage knowledge at these levels. Nevertheless this remained a limited freedom, pertaining only to the lower forms of examined, but nonetheless terminal instruction. Those pupils wishing to proceed to the Real course or the Gymnasium found their preparatory subjects curtailed, and, in the case of the latter, that the curriculum remained as centrally directed as ever. In this respect the 1970 Act reinforced rather than transformed the situation: it left the Local Authorities free to organize their 8th-10th classes in relation to local conditions, but the Ministry still lays down syllabus and examination requirements for each subject in the Gymnasium, thus restricting professional innovation.

After the war considerable progress was also made towards professional control of certification. Increasingly the assessments of

College lecturers were substituted for formal examinations and the 1954 Law embodied this principle for many subjects, including teaching practice. Only the final examination in a reduced number of papers was conducted by the College in conjunction with a moderator appointed by the Ministry. This legislation also officially recognized the de facto upgrading, which had been taking place over half a century, with College trainees staffing the Middle Schools: for the Colleges' task now formally included training to teach in the whole school (i.e. 1-10th grade and 1st-3rd Real classes).[80]

A further move to improve the quality of expertise was mooted by the Teacher Training Committee in the mid-sixties, its aim being to raise the quality of entrants without restricting the social basis of recruitment to the Colleges, or bowing to the Gymnasia definition of instruction by insisting that all applicants possessed the *Studenter* certificate. The profession was successful in persuading the Ministry to develop a new qualification, the Higher Leaving Examination (1965), which would provide preparatory teacher training (as well as an introduction to other careers), but which itself had no formal entry requirements thus making it 'open downwards as well as upwards'.[81] This had the dual function of preserving traditional access to the Colleges for the 'man from the plough', whilst not dragging teacher training down to the level of his acquirements. This two-year preparatory course, held initially in the Colleges themselves and later in the Gymnasia, brought about a substantial upgrading. Forty of these courses had been established by 1970 and it has been estimated that only half of the 1966 College entrants would have qualified for enrollment under the new law.[82] In turn this enabled College standards to rise, and the level of expertise attained in specialist subjects is now accepted to be the rough equivalent of Part I in university examinations.[83]

Finally, the recognition of the Danish Higher College of Education (founded 1856) as an institution of Higher education, able to award Candidate, Licenciate, and Doctoral degrees[84] capped the upgrading process by eliminating the *necessary* non-graduate status of the Folk-school teacher. The full significance of this increase in expertise can only be appreciated when taken in conjunction with the simultaneous growth of control by the Colleges over their own activities and programmes, which itself derived from the progressive insertion of teachers into the formal structure of educational administration.

The 1948 Law on the local direction and supervision of the system had accorded Teachers' organizations a more prominent position, emphasis being laid on consulting the Joint Teachers' Council on matters of professional concern. More importantly, the Chairman of the area Joint Council gained a place on the local School Commission alongside the School Director and Inspector. In the fifties the practice of serving teachers acting as examiners, moderators and inspectors for other schools was extended, thus increasing academic autonomy since the teacher was less at the mercy of pressures from all quarters.[85] The legal right given to the Joint Councils to express their views on all school developments and instruction plans,[86] was paralleled at College level in 1954 by the establishment of an Advisory Committee to the Ministry, to be consulted on general questions of training and the appointment of examiners. Its composition reflected acquired rights (the fact that 19 out of 29 Colleges were still private) and organized interests, by including private and public Principals, together with representatives of the NUT and the National Council of Student Teachers.[87] Its existence fostered considerable freedom and flexibility within the Colleges, including staff-student negotiation of the plans used for teaching each special subject and the introduction of free courses of study which can be proposed by the Students' Council.[88] The most significant outward indicator of this new internal autonomy is the fact that the Colleges now differ significantly from one another.

Throughout the twentieth century the non-graduate teachers had succeeded in raising the value of their expertise through up-grading, in gaining greater autonomy by lifting political controls on teacher training and curricular development, inserting themselves into positions from which they helped to mould policy, and legitimating these advances through the work of their professional associations. In these ways they acquired the freedom for internal initiation, either in response to community requirements or in pursuit of their own goals. This will be discussed in a moment, but first we must examine the lesser success of graduate teachers in extending their capacity to introduce change in the more 'academic' parts of the educational system.

Graduate Teachers

From the start of the system it was the Gymnasium which Venstre attacked and sought to control as the bastion of traditional culture: the accession to power of parties much further to the left did nothing to persuade governing elites to relax their grasp on this level. Thus the crucial factor differentiating between the graduate teacher and his non-graduate counterpart was that the latter enjoyed political confidence and sponsorship whereas the former encountered hostility from all but the Conservative party. Obviously the attitudes of governing elites determine the force with which they employ the four political counter-strategies to contain aspirations towards professional autonomy. Moreover they will be more successful strategically the less they are divided, for this deprives the profession of parliamentary protection. The progressively weakening role of the Conservative Party, and its self-defensive insistence that it too was a party of the Centre, was detrimental to the Gymnasia teachers in this connection. It meant that successive governments never relaxed the political vetoes barring alternative suppliers at this level, thus keeping the Gymnasia in a state of financial dependence which precluded serious bids for increased autonomy, especially given that professional insertion in educational administration was not allowed to advance far.

Thus, although the level of expertise possessed by the Gymnasia teachers remained very high, the majority having followed university courses of at least five years duration, their autonomy never rose to a commensurate level. The increments they did gain were a pale reflection of those attained by non-graduate teachers — the right to experiment under Ministerial licence in 1952, to form a Teachers' Council in each school with the right to be heard on certain matters, and, in 1970 to have internal assessments count towards and appear on the *Studenter* certificate. All of this left curricular control in Ministerial hands (syllabus and examination requirements being specified in detail for each subject) which clamped down on innovatory methods. Since the same regulations were enforced in private schools, this part of the profession was given no freedom to make use of its capital resources for initiating change. In both sectors, staff lacked the autonomy to respond to parental or pupil demands, even if their values had predisposed them to do so. Finally the main professional association also appears to have been less than successful in inserting itself in administrative positions so as to cushion the direct impact of political controls — the Gymnasia Teachers Union only gained official recognition as the formal agency for negotiating pay and conditions of work with the Ministry.

In terms of the four professional tactics the graduate teachers only made headway with the first — the revaluation of expertise and the improvement of the exchange rate. Although successive governments had consistently employed the counter-tactic of pouring in enough resources to produce dependency, and thus give the polity control of the exchange rate, and despite the fact that the increased expertise of the Folkschool teachers might have threatened and devalued that of the graduate – several related factors militated against this outcome. Firstly, the Gymnasia teachers were products of the universities which were themselves autonomous institutions, largely independent of political control. Additionally, as we shall see, they had used their autonomy in the service of academic values, and its result was a small, elitarian output who had undergone lengthy courses of the highest standing. Consequently the expertise of the graduate teacher was not challenged by improvements lower down in the profession, and, as a scarce commodity, he was in increasing demand by various alternative employers. The most serious achievement of the GTU occurred in 1960, when it capitalized on the shortage of experts and negotiated a new 'contract' appointment, enabling teachers to opt for non-civil servant status. The main attraction of this option, taken up by just under half in 1967, was higher pay.[89] It represented an improvement in the exchange rate for expertise, but no further increment in professional autonomy. Though contract appointments carried with them the right to strike, whilst remaining a government employee, the potential of this as a tool with which to influence educational change was largely nullified by the greater insecurity of these untenured appointments.

The contrast with university teachers could not be more striking, given that these stood and stand no higher in the general political regard. This difference is due to the high initial position of the university sector on all three dimensions, and the fact that these are mutually reinforcing over time. The traditional autonomy enjoyed by the University of Copenhagen has been retained and indeed shared by the University of Aarhus (founded privately but officially recognized in 1931),[90] and to some extent by other institutions of higher education. Curricular control is minimal, 'the governing bodies of the universities themselves decide on the subject-matter to be taught within the various fields of study, the educational methods to be employed, the books to be used, and the general course of study, right up to the prescribed university examinations'.[91] Insertion on the other hand is maximal, for 'the universities exert a very strong influence on the drafting of the general rules governing examination systems and the organization of the university, items which still legally come within the jurisdiction of government, and which consequently are provided for by Royal Decree or Ordinance. Also the initiative for making amendments to the existing decrees and ordinances is in most cases taken by the governing bodies of the universities themselves'.[92] This in turn has prevented the financial indebtedness of these institutions to the State from being translated into academic dependence on government. Moreover the property they possess and their capacity to earn further resources (unlike the Gymnasia) protect them from any such threat materializing. Indeed, given increasing social demand and restricted outputs of graduates the negotiating strength of the universities appears to have widened rather than narrowed the scope of academic freedom. Recent discussions of this relationship with government — all of which were premised on political dissatisfaction with university performance — neverthelesss accepted 'the assumption that the autonomy granted to the universities and other institutions of higher education in academic affairs will be unchanged'.[93] As at the debut of the new educational system, its apex remains the part which is most free to engage in internal initiation.

The Community and the Profession

Again it is necessary to distinguish between the non-graduate and graduate teachers because they differed not only in terms of their relative autonomy, but also in the nature of their organization, values and relationship to the community. Before the First World War, teachers in the public Folk and Middle Schools lacked the freedom to mediate community demands: they were busy consolidating the tactics which would enable them to do so. The democratic character of their recruitment meant that the primary teachers came from the people and the Grundtvigian inspiration of their training ensured that they remained close to them. This identification with popular values was witnessed by the profession's willingness to staff the independent Youth, Evening and Folk High Schools, for pay could not have been the inducement. Yet this natural and spontaneous affinity with the people had nothing in common with political populism. Ironically the Social Democrat policy of imposing parental participation in education met with suspicion and hostility, for the profession correctly diagnosed the socio-political model on which it was based and rejected it. The Social Democrat ideal of a government which responded directly to the masses, without the intervention of organized secondary groups in pursuit of sectional interests, may have been conceived with bourgeois pressure groups in mind, but to the teachers it cut both ways and appeared equally antagonistic to their own professional organizations and interests.

Thus primary teachers resisted the notion of Parents' Boards, which the 1933 Law specified should be formed in each school, for this could give parents more influence than they themselves possessed and would constitute an additional source of control over them. The teachers were willing to respond voluntarily to the community, but not to have it imposed as the local watchdog. Thus the NUT advanced a counter proposal — that parental voices should be heard by giving them half the seats on the School Commission — a neat 'solution' which would simultaneously have diminished the number of 'political' members on local authorities. In effect the NUT was telling the Social Democrats that real populism involved sharing political power with the masses, not using the people to reduce the authority of the teacher. Neither plan became common practice: the NUT proposal was brushed aside for the Social Democrats were not contemplating devolution of control, but their own ideological conception of the Parents' Boards was not effective given the teachers' resistance and their own unwillingness to endow them with real powers. Thus 'the parents were apt to find themselves between upper and lower grindstones, the communal authority reluctant to devolve responsibility and the teachers objecting to more and more supervision'.[94]

Thus in the pre-war period community demands could rarely be met in the *public* primary schools, either through the official channel of the Parents' Boards or through unofficial professional initiative, and they were thrown back on external transactions with the private sector as has been seen. However, as sufficient autonomy was gradually acquired in the postwar years, this part of the profession was willing to put much of their new freedom at the service of the community. The fact that they retained their identification with the people, despite their own collective upgrading, prevented them from pursuing autonomous academic values at variance with local culture. This responsiveness became clear in four different types of activity.

Firstly, the Youth Schools and Folk High Schools continued to make vocational provisions in the light of local occupational outlets, thus providing practical further and adult education which did not ape 'academic' general instruction. Secondly, before the inception of the undivided school in 1958, the Middle School and Real classes continuously added subjects beyond the legal requirements, including topics of obvious utility like bookkeeping, typewriting and needlework as well as song, drawing, additional languages and latin. The latter category may appear more indicative of professional values than community demand, but these subjects should be seen from the Grundtvigian perspective of education for personal awakening, which was firmly rooted in the countryside. Thirdly, teachers of the terminal forms in the Folkschool reacted immediately to the curricular freedom granted them in 1958. 'To make the upper grades attractive to pupils, the school authorities have obtained the co-operation of trade and industry. This has resulted in an increase in the number of students who stay beyond the school leaving age, since they receive the type of training which makes them acceptable to employers in the office and in the factory'.[95] Finally, the simultaneous incorporation of the highly differentiated types of private, secondary and vocational training, largely staffed by non-graduate teachers, bore witness to their flexibility in meeting the complexity of community demands, although in this case it was reinforced by the concomitant upgrading of those involved. In general then this level of instruction was responding actively to its environment in the postwar period. Certainly there was some bias towards meeting employers' requirements, with expertise being exchanged with those who could offer the best rates, but some of the new found professional autonomy was also devoted to meeting non-vocational demands and to serving the community in institutions like the Folk High School and its Junior counterpart.

In complete contrast, graduate teachers used what freedom they had, (small in the case of the Gymnasia, extensive in the universities) to further professional goals. These jointly reflected their social background, intellectual training, and vested interests in maintaining academic standards after their own long apprenticeships. We have already seen that as the teacher shortage persisted and was aggravated in the postwar period, 'the strong bargaining position of the academic unions'[96] was used to improve their work, status and financial positions. They capitalized on the shortage to negotiate overtime work at high rates of pay, unlike other civil servants, which had the dual function of increasing remuneration whilst keeping out less qualified teachers. Their negotiating strength allowed them to maintain favourable differentials with the Folkschool teacher, to arrange lower workloads, better staff-pupil ratios, extra allowances for those committing themselves to five hours overtime per week,[97] and the new 'contract' appointment already discussed. Thus 'though all teachers have been able to improve their standard of living along with the entire working community, the special conditions surrounding shortages of university graduates in general, and gymnasia teachers in particular, have led to a wide range of attractive incentives to graduates to enter gymnasia teaching'.[98] Certainly collective bargaining represented their major professional advance, but it is doubtful if greater freedom would have been harnessed to any purpose other than the defence of traditional academic standards. The similarity of their values with those of the university teachers was blatant in their joint opposition to the 1958 Act, establishing the undivided school, a stance which was endorsed by the Conservative Party alone. Additionally there is circumstantial evidence from the way in which the university faculty behaved, given the greatest autonomy in the system.

Consistently the universities have used this to pursue professional goals, reinforcing an academic, isolationist and conservative policy, often at variance with community and government alike.

> The government recognizes that the universities direct their activities with a view to achieving certain goals of their own, such as research for the sake of research, and instruction aimed at a liberal education or the development of innate capacities; but at the same time it expects the universities, along with the state railways, the hospitals, post offices, and so on, to contribute towards the implementation of the goals it has set for the benefit of the community and its growth. The professors, however, are responsible for their special subjects, the cultural heritage; they are prepared to fight for this and give it preference over other considerations brought up by the government.

As far as graduate teachers in both Gymnasia and the universities were concerned, their actions (and most especially their inaction in any cause other than their own interests) were a great spur to external transactions with private education. It is unsurprising that these flourished at secondary and higher levels and that successive governments took a positive view towards such private initiative, leaving the traditional institutions to their own devices. Yet external transactions are particularly expensive at these levels and thus tend to be restricted to the richest groups in society. In other words there was a considerable residue of discontent, satisfied neither by internal initiation nor external transactions. This was greater amongst the mass of parents, concerned about their children's overall educational experience and opportunity, than among the institutional elites whose specialist demands had largely been met through external transactions.

POLITICAL MANIPULATION

Some aspects of political relationships with education have already been examined in previous sections: this is the main difficulty of treating the three processes of negotiation as analytically separate, when in fact they are co-terminus. Thus the section on internal initiation separated out the relationships between the polity and the profession during the twentieth century, and charted a general trend towards greater reciprocity between them. More specifically different levels of instruction moved into different types of relationships with the polity, as the outcome of their interaction over time – the Primary school one of reciprocity, the Gymnasium one of dependence and the universities one of independence. This implies that during the twentieth century the profession has become a more important force in educational change, not only through internal initiation, but also (because of their insertion and autonomy) in processes of political manipulation.

Similarly, the section on external transactions isolated the relationship between the polity and outside interest groups and traced how political embargoes were progressively lifted, thus expanding the possibilities for direct negotiation. This implies that over time the external interest groups have also become more important sources of educational change, with the wealthier ones gaining substantial satisfaction from external transactions, whilst only the poorer ones remained exclusively dependent on political manipulation. The first section examined changes in the distribution of power in Danish society and showed a shift over the last seventy years towards economic redistribution and parliamentary government from the left. This implies that the political structure becomes increasingly accessible and that leftwing forces gradually become more important than rightwing ones in political manipulation. It remains to put these various elements together in order to elucidate the *processes* of political manipulation taking place.

The task then is to *capture the processes* of political manipulation over time, without too much repetition but also without ex post facto elisions. The method used will be to concentrate on the major Education Acts (1937, 1958, and 1970), treating these as sequential snapshots. For each Act the two sides of the equation will be analyzed: on the one hand, which groups were trying to influence government action for educational ends; on the other hand, the degree of political negotiating strength in relation to education. In dealing primarily with the Acts, which by definition represent successful pieces of governmental intervention, however little they might satisfy those attempting to use political manipulation, the significance of political *in*action must not be neglected, whether due to party deadlock or lack of government negotiating strength.

The new 1902 structure was immediately questioned, and this signalled a long debate about the articulation of the component parts of the educational system. The Liberal Committee of 1909 and the Klausen Commission reporting in 1923 revealed neither political nor educational consensus about its restructuration. While the university authorities and the Conservatives condemned the Middle School and wanted to return to the previous situation where the Higher schools could start early with their lengthy academic drill, the non-graduate teachers and Radical opinion sought to bolster the role, activities, and age group covered by the Folkschool. Three things became clear in the debate which followed. Firstly, it showed that it was the Middle School which was the battlefield for opposing opinions, an early indication that political manipulation was to concentrate on the equality of opportunity issue. Secondly, it demonstrated that the most powerful section of the profession at that time, the university staff, were hostile to the Middle School, whereas the less influential NUT supported it, thus underlining the future unlikelihood of united professional action on this issue. Thirdly, it revealed that dissension amongst the political elites was equally profound — disagreements on every issue reflected the representative composition of the Klausen Commission and were a foretaste of the disunity which was to characterize the political side of the equation for several decades.

Given the minority status of all governments between 1909-29 and the corresponding balance of parliamentary powers, there was no possibility of introducing legislation to bring about major changes in the structural co-ordination of education, in the absence of consensus between the parties. Inaction protected the status quo of 1902, but with it went the various forms of dissatisfaction with the existence and role of the Middle School. 'There was little contention about the nature of elementary schooling, now that it was universal and conferred no social and economic privilege, compared with the main argument which centered on the purpose and programme of secondary education'.[100] Only after the Social Democrats gained the largest poll ever in 1935, and formed a strengthened majority government with the Radicals, could a bill be formulated with serious hopes for its passage.

Even so the 1937 Act, creating the non-examination Middle School, was a product of low political negotiating strength. This was partly due to the opposition of influential groups in parliament which blunted any clear cut political thrust and prevented government from using many of the sanctions potentially at its disposal. Stauning's ministry still depended on coalition with the Radicals and the Act showed the same moderation as the rest of its social legislation — the result of lengthy political compromise and educational consultation. Negotiating strength was further reduced because on the other side of the equation official policy incurred the hostility of the most autonomous and influential parts of the profession, the universities, which moreover enjoyed the political protection of the Conservative Party. In this context the government realistically talked about educational improvements, not reform.

What was at stake was still the Middle School and the question of its function, given the manifest wastefulness of the numbers starting but not finishing the course. Broadly, to the Secondary and Higher teachers and much of Conservative and Liberal opinion its function was to prepare for further education, and it was not doing this to an adequate standard because of the weight of numbers and the quality of pupils. The NUT and most Grundtvigian opinion took the opposite view; its function should be practical and it failed through being too academic and irrelevant to those wanting more than Folkschool instruction, but not proceeding to higher education. Various solutions were advanced by political and professional groups, producing different patterns of support and opposition from the late 1920s onwards, but none elicited any degree of consensus.

A Liberal-Conservative Commission (1928), under the Chairmanship of the Inspector of Gymnasia, had wanted primary schooling to end without an examination and a system of Preparatory Schools then to prepare for entrance to the Gymnasium. However, they had coupled this with a branching Gymnasium course, with a two year Real option, and thus incurred the wrath of both graduate and Real teachers. The National Union of Gymnasia Teachers prompted a second investigation (1933), under Social Democratic auspices, and it managed to get the final report to endorse the broad, traditional, academic curriculum. The National Union of Real Teachers opposed the delaying of their course until 14 and resisted any assimilation to the Gymnasia or its curricula. The NUT was in full agreement with the latter sentiment, but it counter-proposed a longer (than 14) and more practical Folkschool.

The eventual compromise formula was suggested by teachers from the Copenhagen schools who had taken advantage of their greater autonomy to experiment with the later classes of the Folkschools. Copenhagen, it should be remembered, had been the Social Democrats stronghold in local and general elections. The government invited them to put forward a plan (1932) and a Committee established under Kaalund-Jørgensen produced a report entitled 'the Practical Middle School' in 1935. This advocated two Middle Schools running in parallel, the one to be an examination school preparing for further education, the other would be more practical in orientation, more flexible in teaching methods and more elastic in its programmes, and would not lead to an examination. The NUT immediately backed the new approach to curriculum and teaching methods proposed by the Report: the government endorsed it since the formula appeared to be a democratic response to manifest social demand. In 1935 the Minister of Education Jørgen Jørgensen, A Grundtvigian Radical, introduced a Bill modelled on the earlier report and providing, side by side with the 4 year examination Middle School, a non-examination Middle School 'in connection with the Folkschool and taking as its aim life's work for those not "bookishly endowed" '.[101]

When the Bill came to the vote in 1937, other parties only introduced minor amendments. It was a true compromise measure which gave something to most people and took little away from anyone. Since the traditional examination schools were left untouched, and now gained a more selective entry, there was no reason for opposition from Gymnasia or University — their main points had been conceded. Since the examination Middle School could have an extension into Real classes, this removed the fear of diminished autonomy through assimilation to the Gymnasium. Since the Folkschool was given increased scope and an extended range of subjects, the NUT was satisfied with the greater classroom freedom and teaching autonomy it gained. Although there was some Conservative opposition, most Liberals welcomed the greater practical orientation — especially as it was couched in Grundtvigian vocabulary. As far as the Social Democrats were concerned they genuinely appear to have believed that given the same staff teaching in both, then 'the non-examination Middle School will immediately be placed on a par with the examination Middle School in people's estimation'.[102] At all events, had the government contemplated a more radical (and less Radical) formula, they would not have had the negotiating strength to enact or implement it. The 1937 Law lasted as the major legal instrument co-ordinating the principal parts of the system until the Act of 1958.

The most significant difference between the two Acts was the degree of political unity which prefaced them. Professional divisions were similar, though more intense over the latter Bill, but the negotiating strength of government was greatly enhanced when a completely divided profession now faced a polity concerted on educational policy. Not only did this deprive professional opposition of effective political protection, it also strengthened the government's hand in terms of the sanctions it could deploy against groups of recalcitrant teachers.

Postwar reactions to the non-examination Middle School showed something of the same consensus as that which then characterized parliament, with its succession of minority coalition governments promoting centrism. There was fairly unanimous agreement that the new Middle School had failed. The Minister for Education in the Liberal-Conservative ministry pointed out, in 1951, that not only was it unattractive to employers, who still looked for an examination certificate, but also that it lacked the saving grace of being more democratic, for 'practically speaking, only the least gifted pupils from poorer homes remain'.[103] This was echoed a year later in a report issued by the organizations of teachers involved at this level. It stressed that these courses were simply second best rather than being a more practical alternative, whose vocational relevance ought anyway to be marked by the awarding of appropriate certificates. The failure to run the two Middle Schools in double harness was because their main distinguishing feature was superiority and inferiority. On this most were agreed, but two opposite conclusions could be drawn from it: either that their differentiation should be accentuated to make them real alternatives, or that they should be collapsed back into single school which would avoid social discrimination whilst offering no less in terms of academic specialization.

Different groups did draw different conclusions, but the political majority was to favour the latter. This time the winning formula was produced by members assembled from the Grundtvigian 'Home and School Society', chaired by Jørgen Jørgensen. Generally known as the Askov Committee, its report recommended that schools should be undivided and exam-free until 14. Following this there should be a voluntary 8th class, practical in orientation, a three year continuation school, divided into branches and including the Real course, or a five-year Gymnasium with various specialist streams. Whilst this commanded Social Democratic and Radical support, it also aroused intense opposition from Gymnasia and Real school teachers on familiar grounds — the former afraid of falling standards, the latter fearing the loss of autonomy. In this they were joined by the Conservative Party: 'the historian might note with irony that the Conservatives were now supporting the law of 1937 (which they had voted against) and were discovering too late that a virile and successful alternative to the examination Middle School was essential if that school was to be preserved'.[104]

The government reaction was typically centrist when faced with opposition from one of the old four parties: it compromised and tried to concede something to everyone. The Bill the Social Democrats introduced in 1955 was for a school divided horizontally rather than vertically. A five-year Groundschool would be followed by a three-year Headschool for all, but the latter would be sub-divided into a bookish side and a practical side. Both would carry certificates but only the bookish stream would lead on to a two-year course for the Real exam or a four-year Gymnasium course. Each provision seemed carefully calculated to undermine a particular pocket of resistance, but eighteen months of protracted negotiations followed, during which different sections of the political elite and teaching profession struggled to enlarge the concessions made to them.

Technically the stumbling block had been Venstre's unwillingness to endorse raising the school leaving age to 15, as specified in the original bill — something the liberals had traditionally opposed in the interest of farming families. Negotiations revealed, however, that a majority could be recruited for the more radical Askov proposals, if the notion of necessarily propitiating every major party were abandoned, i.e. if it were advanced in the face of Conservative opposition. Support had been progressively mobilized by two successive Ministers of Education, Julius Bomholt and Jørgen Jørgensen: 'The former who for some years had been the cultural leader of labour, secured the support of his party: the latter who is the chairman . . . of the Radicals (the left wing of the Liberals) and at the same time generally accepted as the most prominent political spokesman of Grundtvigian and Folk High School aspects, obtained support from practically all liberal members and from the greatest professional association, the National Union of Teachers, in all elementary and post-primary schools. With this background new legislation could be issued'.[105] The new bill was an amalgam of the Askov proposals and Venstre's reservations about them: the raising of the school leaving age was abandoned, but the undivided school from 7-14 now became government policy.

The hostility of secondary and university teachers was immediately vocalized. After the age of 14, the bill specified a two year Real course, followed by either a final Real class (16-17) or a three year Gymnasium course. To the higher levels of the profession this broken-up pattern could only mean a devaluation of the whole of secondary education. It was seen as a threat to standards in those schools which had tradition-ally prepared pupils for higher education, and in turn for university standards themselves. 'None of them participated in the compromise that ended the discussion; nor did they hesitate to draw political and public attention to the fact that the prospective laws were defective on the point in question. But their arguments and eventually their protests were neglected. So, perhaps for the first time in Danish educational history, a reorganization of the higher school was carried through, not only without co-operative support from the institutions of higher learning but directly against their will, and against the demand of practically the whole academic world. In Parliament the Conservatives shared in the criticism and voted against the reform. In fact the episode was another phase in the continuing battle about the school, and confronted by the working and farming classes, under purposeful leaders, the champions of academic and social conservatism were the losers'.[106]

It is doubtful that they would have been such heavy losers if the last stages of these negotiations had not coincided with the beginning of party fragmentation and rejection of centre immobilism. The 1957 elections which resulted in the Triangle Government of Social Demo-crats, Radicals and the Justice Party ironically produced the strongest ministry for many years – in fact the first majority government since the all-party wartime coalitions. Given that Venstre already supported the Bill, this only left the Conservatives, with their seats now reduced (to 30 out of the total 175) ready to vote against it. This situation represented a considerable increase in governmental negotiating strength compared with 1937, for the massive Parliamentary majority in favour of the bill allowed sanctions to be employed which were unavailable twenty years earlier, when strong opposition had precluded their use. Indeed the Conservatives were to complain that the Govern-ment abused its political strength to impose its 'camouflaged compre-hensive school'.[107]

In one sense the governing elite could argue that this was untrue, after all, it had the support of the majority of teachers, the large NUT. In another sense the criticism was apt, for political determination was matched on the other side of the equation by professional division, and to pass the Bill was to override the secondary and university teachers coercively. The negotiating strength of the Gymnasia teachers was weak to non-existent; their financial dependence and lack of autonomy meant that they could only make ideological appeals to the country at large about the fall of national standards. For them, as for the university teachers, the reverse face of political consensus was the loss of parliamentary protection. The university teachers, with their greater autonomy and independence could resist more strongly, and intervened during the second reading of the bill to threaten that holders of the School Certificate would no longer automatically be considered as qualified for higher education, and that it might be inevitable for the university to institute supplementary courses and selective tests.[108] The spokesman for the Committee in charge of the bill refused to yield to this threat in the belief that the universities could be brought to heel when their anxieties were proved groundless. He practically told them to mind their own business and in parliamentary terms there was nothing else they could do: the bill passed, unamended, by 110 votes to 31.

It was a victory for political manipulation from the left: a major indicator of the way in which the redistribution of power in society gave new classes the means of initiating educational change despite traditional and professional opposition. It was equally significant that political manipulation had been used for educational democratization, for meeting the demands of those who could not negotiate changes through other channels. The new shift to the left in Danish politics had finally attained the target set by the old left in the 1860s, that 'fundamental education up to 14 should be acknowledged as the common basis of *all* higher education'.[109]

Subsequent changes did not alter this principle or the new structuration of the system which embodied it. They were mainly initiated by professional organizations, especially those of the non-graduate teachers, taking advantage of their new negotiating strength to transact a number of modifications that were not very politically contentious. The development of the Higher Leaving Examination at the instigation of the Teacher Training Colleges has already been mentioned. This was welcomed in the Gymnasium for specialization had as its corollary selectivity – and this became the main method of defending standards in secondary schools whilst formally accommodating themselves to the 1958 legislation. It was paralleled at primary level by a programme, initially produced by the NUT in 1966, for abolishing streaming and then dividing teaching into two levels, with pupils choosing between them and the different examinations for which they prepared. Neither proposal aroused political hostility or dissension: the Social Democrats acceded to the former in 1966, the Radical-Liberal-Conservative alliance to the latter in 1970, as part of a general reform of local government. However, the changes embodied in the laws and decrees of the late sixties and early seventies are more properly viewed as out-comes of internal initiation or external transactions, which were suc-cessful in obtaining official endorsement, than as cases of political manipulation. They were not innovations promoted by the polity in the interest of a mass constituency, like the 1937 and 1958 Acts, but rather changes that successive governments sanctioned in the belief that they did not contradict the interests of their supporters.

In general, the first half of the seventies was not an active period of political manipulation. There appears to be independent evidence to support the view that this was due to lack of pervasive discontent rather than to difficulties of gaining parliamentary action in the context of increasing party fragmentation. One survey indicates that, between 1971 and 1975, education was perceived as the least important social problem on a list including Economic conditions, Wages and Public Spending, Housing, Social Problems, the Environment, Traffic etc.[110] Thus the lull in political manipulation can perhaps be attributed to a temporary lack of widespread educational grievances, given that internal initiation and external transactions allowed many sectional interests to negotiate the educational changes they sought.

ENGLAND

The Distribution of Resources and Relations among Resource Holders

As in Denmark the distribution of power and wealth remained highly concentrated in England at the beginning of the twentieth century, thus severely limiting those who could participate in any type of educational negotiation. However, the English case displayed a much greater superimposition of the two dimensions at the turn of the century which meant that there were very few groups indeed with differential access to power and wealth, and thus in an intermediary bargaining position. Instead different sections of society either had high access to both, or little access to either — the overall concentration of resources placing the vast majority of the population in the latter category. Again, like Denmark, the twentieth century witnessed a progressive, though not steady, redistribution of resources which increased the number and diversified the nature of those participating in processes of educational change compared with the baseline of 1902.

Indicators of the concentration of power in 1902 include the absence of universal (male) franchise, the want of a political party primarily representing the masses in Parliament, and the lack of legislative supremacy for the representative body, the House of Commons. Despite the enlargement of the electorate, after the 1884 reform bill,[111] politics remained dominated by the traditional Liberal and Tory parties who monopolized the parliamentary arena. Only in socio-economic terms, however, did these represent a homogeneous elite, for relations within and between them had been characterized by disunity and antagonism in the immediate past. The Liberal party in particular had been torn over home rule for Ireland, one consequence of which was the defection of both Whigs and Radicals to the Tories. This lucky break for the Tory Party, and the realignment of parties on the issue of the Union with Ireland, had brought with it a dilution of the conservative nature of Conservative philosophy and policy. Most importantly it injected a powerful new dose of economic protectionism which struggled hard, in the pre-war years, against the endemic commitment to free trade. In addition to internal party divisions, the disputes over the 1902 Education Act had reanimated antagonism between the two parties of privilege.

This concentration of power was matched by a similar distribution of wealth. Real wages had been stationary from 1896-1902, and though higher incomes fared no better than lower ones, this left a great divide between them,[112] whilst the bulk of capital remained in the hands of the top few percent. It was this very superimposition of wealth and power which caused the masses to seek simultaneous improvement on both dimensions, through the joint processes of Trade Unionism and Party organization. Both were fostered by recent socio-economic changes which had increased the homogeneity of manual workers and in turn encouraged solidarity. On the one hand, although manual wages as a whole had not improved relative to those of higher occupational groups, intra-class differentials had shrunk, with the rise in wage levels of unskilled workers. On the other hand, the weakening of local, regional and religious cleavages decreased those forms of differentiation which had made it common to refer to the 'labouring classes' in the plural, rather than to a solidary working class, in the nineteenth century.

Trade Unionism had increased and included about 12 percent of potential members in 1900: its recent growth embraced more of the unskilled workforce whose new wage gains could be abruptly eliminated, given a slump in trade. In general the Unions were threatened by legislature and judiciary alike. Firstly, the Employers' Parliamentary Council was seeking official protection for entre-preneurial interests, in addition to their lock-out strategies. Secondly, the House of Lords, in its judicial capacity, had financially undermined the Unions by holding their funds liable for the tortious acts of officials and had threatened their effectiveness by limiting the right to picket.[113] Against this background, the quest for direct labour repre-sentation in parliament emerged and developed. That this should be independent representation was due at least as much to Liberal rebuffs as to political philosophy. The Liberal Party refused to act as a carrier organization partly because of the priority it gave to the interests of business, the professions, and non-conformism, and partly because local associations would not adopt working men as candidates and shoulder their election expenses and upkeep.

The Labour Representation Committee was founded in 1900, but from the start it was not a united body. Union support was variable, although accounting for 2/3rds of the membership in the first year. It was greatest among the new unskilled unions and those most disrupted by recent technical changes (printers, boot and shoe operatives, Rail-way Servants), and least among long-standing groups like the miners who already had electoral arrangements (for Lib/Lab candidates), thanks to their geographical concentration. In addition there were various associations, the Independent Labour Party founded in 1893, the marxist Socialist Democratic Federation, and the Fabians, all of whom gained a disproportionate number of offices. Almost im-mediately schismatic tendencies manifested themselves, with the SDF dissociating itself two years later when unable to secure endorsement of its class warfare approach. This was counter-balanced by greater Union participation[114] following the Taff Vale judgment of the Lords. LRC membership doubled between 1901-03, and of the large Unions, only the miners remained unaffiliated. It was precisely what its title indicated, a labour organization rather than a Socialist Party; it was based on no coherent political philosophy, but placed an umbrella over the various strands of radical thinking endorsed by component elements — marxism, parliamentary socialism, guild socialism, Fabian gradualism etc.

Thus in terms of the distribution of resources, the picture at the beginning of the century was similar to the Danish one. Their concentration led to the same situation where very few groups were in a strong bargaining position for negotiating educational changes, and a similar expectation that these socio-economic elites alone would have their educational demands met. However, although elite domination of the earliest negotiations was expected in England as in Denmark, the greater antagonism prevailing between different sections of the elite, and particularly between the two parties of privilege, intensified the hostility of negotiations in English education. Subsequent changes in the distribution of power, which later transformed this picture, also represent differences between the two countries. Most importantly, perhaps, it was the Liberal party which lost out in England (largely for internal reasons) and lost heavily, whilst in Denmark it was the Conservatives who declined (mainly because of social factors), though their fall was cushioned by the multi-party system favouring coalition government. Differences between the two countries in their electoral and political systems also account for variations in factors like the speed of the left to power, the constitution of governing elites, and the degree of policy dilution enforced by political arithmetic, all of which have an immediate bearing on the three processes of educational negotiation.

1902-1918

This period witnessed a certain redistribution of political power which was without counterpart in the economic domain. Primarily it consisted in the Labour Party moving from the status of a pressure group to become a parliamentary party at the end of the war. This involved a deconcentration of power by giving a new section of society political representation, and thus allowing the majority of the population to think in terms of influencing legislation for the first time. Meanwhile, collaboration with the Liberals produced reforms of a limited redistributive tendency, but the whole period was more of a prelude to full parliamentary democracy than the phase in which it was accomplished. After all, by the end of the war, the registered electorate was still only about 60 percent of the total male population,[115] the 63 seats won by Labour were less than those held by Sinn Fein, and its prospects of attaining and alternating in office were remote. Moreover the state of the parties in 1918 allowed no projections and fostered no certainties about the future character of Government and Opposition: indeed abandonment of a two party system seemed more likely than its intensification. In other words, the rise of the Labour party, and its ultimate attainment of office in the next period, cannot be attributed to some inexorable upsurge in popular mobilization but to the machinations of party politics.

The election of 1906 gave the Liberal party its one resounding victory after the split in 1886. That it was also a success for Labour is only true in a much more restricted sense: it had crossed the electoral threshold with its gain of 29 seats, and had returned a new kind of candidate with a Trade Union background and working class origins. But this too was dependent on an electoral pact, only 3 Labour men were returned against Liberal opposition. The Liberal Party received 50 percent of the total vote and, with a majority of 84 seats over all other parties, was not reliant on support from Labour members in parliament. Labour had floated in on the Liberal tide and until the war it functioned as a pressure group in much the same way as landlords, lawyers, brewers, financiers and miners had done for the last two decades.[116] As such it was neither united nor secure. Internally the Labour movement was torn by socialist dissension (the marxist SDF splitting off for three years between 1911-14 in an attempt to found a British Socialist Party), and by syndicalist factions which sought to substitute industrial action for parliamentary politics. Financially it was crippled by the Osborne judgment, upheld by the Lords, which made illegal any compulsory levy on Trade Union members for political purposes. Parliamentary representation was a tenuous bridgehead which gained no reinforcement before the war. Labour's electoral support shrank in the 1910 elections, by 1914 it had only 38 MPs, and the loss of by-elections from 1911 to 1914 indicated some further decline.

In turn these factors meant that the Labour party had to work to keep the Liberals in office after 1910, and to act as clients in obtaining concessions from them. 'The necessity of supporting the Liberal government during the difficult years when the Osborne judgment was in operation completed the subordination of the Parliamentary Labour Party to the position of "handmaiden of liberalism" ".[117] Only in so far as the specific interests of the Unions were concerned did it make an independent stand, and then because of the vigorous extra-parliamentary pressure exerted by different Trade organizations, making use of their new political instrument. Beyond this the Party would frame no programme and make no undertaking to challenge capitalism: neither practically nor ideologically did it distinguish itself from liberal radicalism.

Nor could Labour take much credit for Liberal reformism, which was only attributable to Labour pressures as far as the legality of the Trade Unions was concerned (reversal of the Taff Vale decision by the Trades Disputes Act, 1906) and their right to make a political levy (reversal of the Osborne judgment by the Trade Union Act, 1913). Nevertheless their alliance produced some reforms of limited redistributive significance before the First World War. These included provision of school meals, old age pensions, limitation of mining hours, starting graduated income tax and the levying of super-tax for the first time. In general these were more indicative of changes in principle about government intervention, to counter-balance the severities of market economy, than as practical steps towards redistribution. More important here was the negotiation of payment for MPs, which was gained in return for Labour support of the 1911 National Insurance Bill (a contributory scheme which fell far short of the Health Service advocated by the Fabians), and the reduction of the powers of the House of Lords by the Parliament Act of the same year.

When the Labour Party was invited to join the first wartime coalition government in 1915, this was not due to its strength in the House but because of the size of the Trade Union movement affiliated with it[118] and the need for industrial co-operation in the war effort. It was the split in the Liberal leadership, starting in 1916 and leaving Lloyd George beholden to conservative support, which created the real breach in prevailing party alignment. The 1918 election results indicated that Labour was there to stay — the acceleration of Union membership during the war[119] assured it, given TUC commitment to Parliamentary representation (45 percent of Union members being affiliated to the Party). But it did not represent a new or conclusive shift in the balance of political power. The door had been pushed open to give access to wider interests, but it was by no means clear that class would constitute the new axis of party politics or that the door might not swing to with a Liberal recovery or a Labour breakdown, through torments over the Russian Revolution.

The factor which ensured that the Labour presence in parliament would be heavily manipulated for the political negotiation of educational change by the working class was the unchanging nature of the national distribution of wealth. For political advance, however limited, had for the first time placed this group in a *differential* position vis-à-vis the two resources. There had been no significant improvement in real wages during the 15 to 20 years preceeding the war[120] and no tendency for the lower paid classes to do better than the higher ones, the mean deviation for male employment categories standing at 67 percent for 1913-14.[121] Given that the average wage of moderately skilled manual workers left, on the most generous calculations, the margin of a few shillings a week after deduction of necessary expenses,[122] together with the relatively high rates of pre-war unemployment,[123] it cannot be expected that the mass of people played much part in the external transaction of educational change. This process, especially in its usual capital intensive form, is still expected to have remained the preserve of the richer classes. Anything that the working class attempted before the war was likely to have been dogged with financial difficulties. The only economic trend which gave any hope of reducing this traditional disparity was the growth of Trade Union funds, which might forseeably free the transactions of this class from dependence on individual contributions. Nevertheless immediately after 1918, despite a slight rise in real wages, political manipulation must have held out much greater promise as a strategy. Indeed the four point policy statement, adopted by Labour in 1918, included a heading on 'the surplus for the common good' — which pledged the party to devote the balance of the nation's wealth to expanding educational opportunities.[124] However, given the parliamentary representation of all classes in addition to religious interests, the political negotiation of educational reform was bound to be a hard fought and multi-dimensional process.

The Interwar Years

The economic situation between the wars was not of a kind to extend the range of those able to satisfy their educational demands through external transactions: on the contrary the protracted crisis was accompanied by widening income differentials, thus reducing the absolute and relative earnings of the working class for most of the period. In 1920 wage rates and manual earnings plummeted down in the wake of unprecedented unemployment and drastic falls in prices. This downward drift of money earnings, more accentuated among manual than non-manual workers and more pronounced among the unskilled than the skilled, continued until 1934 when the fall in wage rates was finally reversed.[125] Crisis and depression had hit the lowest earners hardest as indicated by the increased size of the mean deviation for male occupations, which rose from the 67 percent of 1913-14 to 73 percent by 1922-24, and still stood at 70 percent in 1935-36.[126] Although manual earnings registered an absolute increase after that date, showing a maximum growth rate of about 30 percent between 1938-40, this did not represent a consistent improvement relative to other occupational categories.[127] Furthermore, the percentage of those unemployed, which was disproportionately concentrated in this class, remained in double figures throughout the period, peaking at over 20 percent in 1931-32.[128] Not only did it remain high until the end of the war, but its effects were exacerbated by a substantial rise in prices after 1935. Certainly the picture is somewhat lightened if allowance is made for the simultaneous improvement in welfare provisions, particularly pensions and insurance,[129] and for the smaller size of families which reduced stringency in most sections of society.[130] Nevertheless, the margin of disposable income for the average worker was not the kind of surplus which could sustain external transactions, even in the unlikely event that education was given priority over a slightly improved diet.[131] In general the effects of the depression are likely to have reduced the overall importance of this process of educational change throughout the period, confining its availability even more narrowly to those sections of society on which they impinged least.

In this context it is significant to note that teachers fared *relatively* well, compared with the working class and also with certain other professional groups. The pay of certificated teachers rose two and a half times between 1914 and 1924[132] and did not fall as far, proportionately, as did manual earnings. In addition, although unemployment was lower than average among professionals and clerks in the thirties, in teaching it was almost non-existent at its peak in 1931. As we shall see this involved a struggle, and in subjective terms it must have seemed a losing battle, but the fact remains that the profession did succeed in protecting the value of its expertise under the worst economic conditions, and this may give some indication that it was also in a position to keep the process of internal initiation going.

Turning from the distribution of individual wages and earnings to the question of collective and corporate wealth, we find a parallel decline in the assets of working class organizations. Few educational transactions could be expected of the Unions during this period, since the effect of the General Strike and depression led membership and income to come tumbling down from the mid-twenties to the middle thirties. By 1944 the density of Union membership had only just recovered to surpass the level attained in 1918. On the other hand, inter-industrial organization showed a rapid rate of growth: the FBI, founded in the First World War, registered a six-fold increase in affiliated firms by 1925.[133] Moreover it expanded among the bigger businesses thus mirroring the strong trend towards economic 'rationalization', or rather cartelization, in the twenties which was inhibited by no anti-trust legislation as in the USA. Quite the contrary, the attempts of firms to free themselves from the vicissitudes of market competition, as the depression deepened, found the Conservative party bowing to the pressures of the FBI, city banks, and the Associated Chambers of Commerce, in 1931, to endorse a new protective policy. This was only part of a closer harmony between the main holders of power and wealth during the period, which was all the more significant because it coincided with the most acrimonious relations amongst their counterparts — the Labour party and the Unions. In turn, as we shall see, this effectively nullified the considerable redistribution of power which took place between the wars.

Signposts to these changes included the extension of the electorate from 10 million in 1918 to 22 million in 1929, the arrival of the Labour Party in office, the decline of the Liberals and the concomitant realignment of politics on the basis of class. From the end of the war Labour had been playing for ascendancy in the intervening by-elections, and it consolidated its position as the major opposition party after the general election of 1922. In the process it endorsed the rhetoric of socialism and nationalization — a consequence as much as a cause of the break with the Liberals, but one which was encouraged by the enlarged TUC. However, it was the split and downfall of the Liberal Party, whose complexities cannot be reduced to a simple and ineluctable rise of Labour,[134] which transformed party alignments and the basis of national politics. In the early twenties the Liberal party was still gaining 30 percent of the vote whilst tearing itself apart, by 1929 they polled

23 percent in their last serious contest, after which they never gained more than 12 percent of votes until 1974. The source of transformation was not a direct switching of support from Liberal to Labour, in fact the Conservatives gained more from this, as Labour's growth was achieved through the mobilization of workers with non-political backgrounds.[135] Much more important was the fact that 'the displacement of the Liberals as the Conservatives' main opponent is one of the keys to the displacement of religion by class as the main grounds of party support'.[136] But the début of class politics also saw a rather different Labour and Conservative Party at either end of the new political axis, in the absence of a strong Liberal intermediary. In other words the parties which now shared government and opposition between them did not remain unchanged — a fact which became clear when Labour entered office for the first times in 1924 and 1929 and when the Conservatives again assumed power after the landslide election of 1931.

Taking office as a minority government the Labour Party had to choose between bold socialist measures, symbolic actions which would fail but would establish intent, or a policy of moderation which would certify their fitness to govern. In opting for the latter, and only taking measures for which there was Liberal support, this ministry which lasted only a few months induced a fissure in the Labour movement. The ILP wanted a direct attack on unemployment, later embodied in its policy for a 'living wage': many of the Unions wanted direct action and had bruited about a general strike since 1921. When the Strike came and collapsed within days in 1926, the failure of militancy merely confirmed the political leaders' view that Parliament was the appointed path to salvation, but it substantially weakened their support base.

The manner of the General Strike's collapse is immensely important in the history of the Labour movement. The miners' plight, the worsened circumstances of other wage earners, the vindictive Trade Dispute Act of 1927, the loss of members and of financial resources which the Act entailed for the Labour Party and the trade unions — these were some of the consequences of what happened in May 1926. But as important is the fact that the surrender immeasurably advanced the transformation of the workers' movement into a tame, disciplined trade union and electoral interest.[137]

There is truth in this, but the tameness and accommodation of the TUC did not go so far as to subordinate it to an even more accommodating parliamentary leadership.

After another brief ministry of prudence, Macdonald sought to lead Labour into a National Government in 1931, after failing to gain

Cabinet endorsement of a 10 percent cut in employment benefits. Both the NEC and TUC, who were now ready to collaborate in a parliamentary democracy which promoted efficient capitalism, balked at this direct attack on the 'interests of labour'. This repudiation of its leader was something from which the Party did not recover until 1945.[138] With Labour weakened in Parliament and the Unions enfeebled in the country, both the result of the same internal division, the 'interests of labour' were left to the mercy of Conservative government and economic depression. Union decline meant that the 'Government was able to ignore their direct representations and they had no alternative to using the Parliamentary Labour Party as a means of contact with the Government'.[139] In this consisted the need to repair relations between Party and Unions, and it was largely accomplished by Bevin and Citrine, who steered the TUC on a middle course between militant anti-capitalism and the extortion of piecemeal reforms, whilst exercising 'indirect rule' over the parliamentary party for a few years.[140] Under Atlee's leadership the TUC acquired its desired role as a partner in the making of socio-economic policy: the next step, which the war accelerated, was the continuation of this role which ever party was in office.

Meanwhile, however, the immediate beneficiary of disunity in the Labour movement was Baldwin's immensely strong Conservative government of 1931. But it was soon clear that this was a new kind of Conservatism which was willing to break with free trade, to move towards the managed economy and to take on board the policy of providing a 'decent minimum' standard of living for all – changes which were held necessary if the party of the smaller class was to be returned by the nation. Protectionism, initiated under the Import Duties Act of 1932, gave the polity a lever on industrial development. 'Making protection work meant using the State to force industrial concentration or co-ordination. State grants and the conditional offer of tariffs were used to try to "reorganize" home industry'.[141] This was only the preface to a number of Keynesian methods of economic intervention which the National Government began to use during the war in co-operation with industry.

> Group consultation had been on the rise for many years. But it is not too much to say that the scale and nature of state intervention under the National Government founded a system of quasi-corporatism in which industry and government were brought into regular and continuous contact. Labour at the time had not yet achieved such governmental 'recognition'.[142]

Thus the industrial and Conservative elites were drawing closer together in the thirties, at precisely the time when relations within the Labour movement were at their worst. Given the economic context, it is clear that the lower classes could only look to political manipulation for the satisfaction of their educational demands. Given this relationship amongst resource holders, it is equally clear that what they could get would be on Conservative terms. Before the end of the war the National Government acknowledged that a lot was expected of politics in the educational field, and it included reform in its plans for postwar reconstruction. The new deal, to save Churchill in peacetime, expressed the new collectivism – the social face of economic corporatism – but one whose features resembled the 'decent minimum' more closely than any more egalitarian parentage.

1944-64

If the previous period was one of new party alignments, of dramatic rises and falls in party fortunes, and of class polarization in politics, the postwar era was the exact reverse. With the exception of 1945 when the Labour Party swept to power, the balance between the parties was remarkably stable in the next twenty years, with electoral support for Labour levelling off after several decades of growth. Although the Conservatives enjoyed considerably more time in office, they did not hold it on terms which allowed them to ignore Opposition inside or outside Parliament. This political balance influenced elite relations and prompted a substantial convergence between programmes, as both parties were constrained to appeal to a broader section of the electorate than their 'own' class alone. On the one hand this spelt a further deconcentration of power, since the two parties increasingly made bids for support amongst the interest groups, whose influence on policy grew accordingly. On the other hand consensus politics in a two-party system carries with it the same danger of political immobilism as does centralism in the multi-party system.

Intimations of convergence in socio-economic policy were contained in Churchill's Four Year Plan for reconstruction, which entailed a 'great mass of social legislation', endorsed, in his view, by 'the leading men in both the principle parties'.[143] Though it is probable that they would have proceeded more slowly and on a more limited scale, judging by the lukewarm reactions of most Conservatives to the Beveridge report

(1943), electoral defeat in 1945 precipitated a new conservatism, which spelt a more generous undertaking in social policy than the 'decent minimum'. It was this that allowed Eden to assert that only differences of 'degree' and not of 'principle' now separated the parties – a statement confirmed by the publication of the Conservative Industrial Charter in 1947, accepting both the managed economy and Welfare State.

With its first parliamentary majority and a five year lease on office, the Labour government moved fast to implement its manifesto for social reconstruction, passing acts covering National Insurance, Assistance, the Health Service, Rent Control, Housing, and a more progressive taxation system. On the other hand, whilst it also carried out important measures for nationalizing the Bank of England, fuel, power, and transportation (as well as taking a step towards controlling restrictive practices), Labour's economic policy showed a progressive disenchantment with direct control of the economy by public administration. Instead of nationalization and manpower planning, it was increasingly attracted towards indirect controls, using Keynesian methods of market manipulation. In the last years of Atlee's ministry a wages policy took the place of manpower directives, the unions became closely involved with negotiating the terms of wage restraint and extracted their quid pro quo in the form of profit reductions. Thus Labour's acceptance of economic management necessitated union involvement in the control of the mixed economy, and this established a new balance of power in economic planning between Government, Labour and Capital. In the broadest terms the Labour Party's economic policy had shifted appreciably closer to the Conservative pattern, whilst in social policy the move had been the opposite direction.

Such convergence was encouraged by the narrow electoral margin which meant that the two parties were never more than a few percent apart in the next five elections of this period. For the first time Labour's support declined in 1950, 1951, 1955, and 1959. Partly, at least, this was due to the long term fall in the proportion of the active population engaged in manual work, which was more accentuated after the war[144] when the upwardly mobile tended to affiliate with the party of their new class. Since collective mobility was not symetrical,[145] this loss was not compensated by Labour gains from among the downwardly mobile. Partly too, the flattening out of support was the result of past conversion rates between the parties, which now produced roughly equal numerical flows, away from, and towards Labour.[146] Be this as it may, the Party itself blamed this situation on its working class image and the unpopularity of national-ization. It sought a remedy in extending its appeal beyond the manual workers, and thus toned down the rhetoric of class conflict, smoothing away ideological antagonism. Although Conservative support increased in the same four elections, the Party was well aware of the constant need to make a national appeal in a country where both objectively and subjectively about 70 percent of the population belonged to the working class, especially as the Tory manual vote came mainly from the oldest cohorts in the electorate.[147] Thus both parties intensified their efforts to maximize cross-class voting, yet their overall balance meant that in each election campaign they were both reduced to the wooing of amenable interest groups. 'Correspondingly, general elections con-sisted less of pitched battles between opposing social philosophies than of small raids on interest groups. As class and ideological contours faded, groups appeared as more prominent features of the political scene'.[148]

This was the background against which a new harmony in elite relations developed in the fifties. On the Labour side it resulted from a victory for revisionism, consummated in the election of Gaitskell as Leader in 1955, which not only accepted the mixed economy but also considered that the elimination of inequality should be confined to provisions which were consonant with maintaining financial incentives and stimulating competition. On the opposite side, Conservatism 'imperceptibly smudged into corporatism, and in particular, pluralist corporatism'[149] through which the unions were brought into 'partner-ship'. The maintenance of the same priorities as Labour in the field of social policy and a similar pattern of public spending on social services were indicative of the collectivism associated with economic corpora-tism. Hence the monumental continuity of 'Butskellism', with its bi-partite endorsement of the managed economy, the welfare state, and political pluralism. This was also a formula for social and economic intervention in which government was 'predicated on the assumption that it will be advised, helped and criticised by the specialised know-ledge of interested parties'.[150] Particularly for the large and well organized interest groups like the FBI (which now included 6/7ths of industrial concerns), the TUC, and the professions, this was a formula which gave them an influence on policy, independent of their parlia-mentary representation. In educational terms it widened the channels of political manipulation beyond those of Westminster and Whitehall.

However, neither harmony between leaders nor policy consensus should be confused with unanimity within or between parties. Although no union left the Labour party over the issue of revisionism (indeed the proportion of union members affiliated to the party increased to 54 percent by 1964), this departure from socialist economics was an anathema to some, as was the discarding of socialist fundamentalism to certain groups in the NEC. Both dissent and discontent were present, even if muted by unpopular Tory moves like the 1961 pay pause, which was especially resented by teachers. At the same time the Conservative party was undergoing a kind of lower middle class revolt from those who felt that the burden of public expenditure and taxation fell disproportionately on them − class interests still rankled under the veneer of official unanimity. In other words, there were important social groups − part of organized labour, sections of the middle class, some of the professionals like teachers − who were not getting what they wanted out of consensus politics, despite their greater involvement in government. For the first time in the century, the change in economic circumstances placed a large number of such groups in a position where they could take independent action to satisfy, or at least assuage, their grievances in particular areas like education.

One of the most striking features of this postwar period was the extremely low level of unemployment, compared with the end of the Great War. With it went an upward movement of money earnings which represented a steady increase in real incomes above pre-war levels, despite inflation. Until 1950 these improvements took place within an unchanged pay structure; they represented absolute gains in disposable income, despite the fact that the relative differences between occupational categories remained unaltered. Whether the subsequent period of affluence resulted in a deconcentration of economic resources, through a reduction of wage differentials, has been the subject of intense debate.

On the one hand some economists, noteably Lydall and Paish,[151] maintain that the expansionist economy in the fifties produced a bias towards a greater equality of incomes and that an increasing share of income then came from wages rather than rent, interest or dividends. Simultaneously they accept that capital remained concentrated, and had only been spread within the top 20 percent of the population.[152] This view is supported by others like Routh, whose mean deviations for male occupational groups have been cited throughout, and which registered a drop from 70 percent in 1935-36 to 48 percent in

1955-56.[153] On the other hand, Titmuss in particular has questioned these calculations, which are based on treating income and wealth as separate entities. To him this fails to make any allowance for the ways in which income and wealth could be converted into one another, especially when this proved advantageous to the richer groups.[154] This is not a debate which can be entered here, except to note certain points of agreement which have important implications for educational change. First and foremost, the absolute improvement in real incomes is not contested and, as Bottomore suggests, it is 'plausible to argue that a few years of economic growth at post-war rates makes a greater difference to working class levels of living than any redistribution of wealth and income could achieve'.[155] Secondly, the bulk of wage earners were now above the poverty standard of the thirties: poverty still existed among the old, the immigrants, the declining areas, but it was no longer a phenomenon coterminus with social class. Thirdly, steady welfare expenditure coupled with high employment virtually eliminated one of the most severe pre-war differentials between classes. In other words what is being stressed here, because it seems most important in relation to the external transaction of educational change, is that the increase in disposable income throughout society brought this process within the reach of a much greater section of the population, despite the fact that the very wealthy remained specially privileged in this respect too. Furthermore it appears correct to place the emphasis here, when seeking to characterize the period as a whole, since there is also some measure of agreement that in the early sixties income differentials once more began to widen.[156]

1964-75

The actions of the Labour government from the mid-sixties onwards effectively ended the Social Democratic phase and with it the co-operative relations between the three elements of the new oligarchy: the State, Capital and Labour. Yet these actions themselves were partly the political repercussions of further industrial concentration: a development that successive governments had encouraged but which now threatened to escape their control. Both parties had contributed not only to 'taming the traditional violence of markets'[157] but also to the reversal of the classic relationship between market dictates and industrial production, which Galbraith characterizes as the 'revised sequence', i.e. the inversion of classical economics.[158] Growth of corporate planning, industrial rationalization, and institutional investment (with the pension funds playing their part) had fostered the giant concerns whose internationalism progressively freed them from control by national governments. Correspondingly the task of economic management became increasingly transnational, operating through agencies like the EEC and IMF. In other words, as the markets and interests of the multinationals widened, they dissociated themselves from their host countries, and became iess responsive to the national polity: those in office had to work *within* an economic context moulded by such companies, and not one which the State could manipulate with ease. Obviously this was not a sudden development of the mid-sixties, indeed Britain's postwar expansion had been part of a world boom, which it had not created, but from which it benefitted. What was unpleasantly novel about the sixties was that the British position in the international economic system was deteriorating, and this represented a new backcloth to party politics against which the previous harmony between State, Capital and Labour dissolved. Given that the middle element of the three was now less amenable to control, it was the struggle between the former and the latter which occupied this period, as the State sought to alter the Labour side of the equation in order, literally, to balance the books.

x   We have already discussed how the Conservative party had played its part in the consensus politics of the fifties. Throughout the boom it had not inhibited the spread of affluence: 'Wage claims, wage rates, and wage earnings rose buoyantly during the early fifites. And while from time to time the Government asked in vain for restraint, not only did it not interfere with this upward movement on the wages front, but on critical occasions it took action to help the workers win their demands'.[159] Thus it contributed to maintaining the Social Democratic society. 'The alliance between State and Unions remained the linchpin of the status quo, and it was the central guiding need to sustain that alliance which determined how far the Conservative Government made changes in all fields of union powers, on wage settlements, on the Welfare State, or on the public sector, despite constant pressure and criticism from the neo-Liberals.[160] It was the Labour party which ruptured this alliance and terminated the Social Democracy phase.

Labour returned to office in 1964 with a small majority which precluded the fulfillment of its election pledges, except for introducing Capital Gains Tax and Corporation Tax. Gaining a substantial majority

in 1966, its main strategies for tackling the economic situation showed
that it held itself aloof from the Union movement and was not about to
act as its party in office.

> The Labour Government tried to carry to its logical extreme the alliance
> between the State and the Unions, but using the unions to control labour on
> behalf of the Government. Of course elements of this had always been a vital
> part of Social Democracy, but the unions had made a bargain: in return for
> their loyalty, there were specific benefits for their members. Reformism
> worked within certain limits. But now the unions were expected to sacrifice
> more than before with little or nothing in return: a wages freeze, an incomes
> policy, and finally, proposals for a labour law which would permanently
> inhibit organized labour's power to challenge the Government. Labour
> demanded all this and more, without any quid pro quo. There was no
> bargain.[161]

The Industrial Relations Bill intended to prevent unofficial stoppages,
was only withdrawn after bitter union attacks on its penal sanction
clauses.

> Under Labour, the alliance between State and unions snapped. And by that
> rupture, the long thraldom of Conservatives to Social Democracy was ended.
> If the TUC was powerless, there was no longer any point in Conservative
> self-restraint. If the unions could not deliver worker loyalty, they were no
> longer worth cultivating, soothing, bribing. A whole strategy for conserving
> the status quo was no longer valid. If *The Industrial Charter* heralded the
> Conservative acceptance of Social Democracy, the Industrial Relations Act of
> 1971 proclaimed its rejection of it.[162]

Many have seen the recrudescence of class conflict in the actions taken
by both political parties to contain and control the unions, be it in the
direct interest of business or because of a more indirect concern for
economic growth. But there is one element of the current conflict that
this interpretation plays down, namely the extent to which it is a
struggle between the organized Leviathans, whether parties or unions,
from which the majority of both classes are, and feel, excluded.[163] To
a significant degree, power has been displaced from party politics onto
the organized corporations, the conflict between political parties now
being no more important than that between the government and the
unions, which takes place outside the parliamentary arena as much as
inside it. In a way this displacement parallels the tendency in the
economic realm for the State to be superceded by multinational
companies whose investment income outstrips the national budget,
only there it is financial resources which are being concentrated away

from the State. In other words, where wealth and power are concerned this is a period of their relocation rather than their redistribution.

Furthermore, the class character of party alignment has declined considerably during this period. Contributory causes include the fact that both Labour and the Conservatives presented less of a class stimulus, in terms of leadership and policy. Indeed the postwar cohorts of voters had grown up with 'Butskellism', in which similar problems were given similar solutions whichever party was in office.[164] The parties themselves contributed to it, for whilst both sloughed off consensus, neither formulated a coherent philosophy but preferred to make sectional appeals to interest groups in the hope of building support by accretion. This was particularly true of the Opposition:

> In Conservatism today, the shadowy fragments of a commitment to free competition co-exist with continuing attempts to regulate and damp down competition; the defence of free enterprise co-exists with the acceptance and even the desire to extend State ownership; of self-help with public welfare provisions; of imperialism with decolonization; of individualism with collectivism. Each fragment represents a different element in the party's history and a different segment of support.[165]

Labour, in office, displayed no greater coherence of policy but nursed different categories in turn — with food subsidies, first child allowances, tax relief for the lower middle classes, encouragement to first home buyers — giving with one hand whilst axing public spending with the other. The result has been a volatility of Party support, unknown in the fifties, a fall in voting turn-out at general elections, and the progress first of Liberalism and then of Nationalism.[166]

In summing up the significance of the relocation of resources for the negotiation of educational change during this period, it seems likely that the process of political manipulation will be disproportionately influenced by organized extra-parliamentary interest groups, particularly the unions given Labour's considerably longer term in office. Equally a substantial amount of party antagonism can be anticipated in view of the salience of education for numerous support groups. The alienation or disillusionment of certain sections of the electorate, especially among the middle class (the self-employed, the rate-payers, the shopkeepers, the 'semi-professionals' and quasi-intellectuals), will produce one source of external transactions, despite the fact that their major grievance is progressive impoverishment. Nevertheless, this is expected to tail off towards the end of the period as inflation bit further into disposable income. Another source however, which will not show the same sensitivity to national economic fluctuations as personal income, is large-scale industry, whose concentration of wealth on a multinational basis should have allowed them to continue with equally large-scale transactions to gain the training or research desired, at least until the world recession deepened in the seventies.

EXTERNAL TRANSACTIONS

The settlement of 1902, and the negotiations leading up to it, recognized a number of groups as suppliers of educational resources: the various religious denominations whose voluntary schools were incorporated but not nationalized, the entrepreneurs whose technical schools and colleges gained recognition and financial support, the upper middle classes whose independent network constituted the prestige private sector. Only working class definitions of instruction were excluded because this movement had concentrated its resources on the Board Schools which the Act deliberately eliminated, leaving a small toehold in university extension work as its sole purchase on the new educational system. Since the terms of this settlement had been drawn up by the Conservative Party, it remains to be seen how far political realignment and a substantial redistribution of power affected them in the next 75 years. Equally the terms bore a close if imperfect relationship to the concentration of wealth at the end of the nineteenth century, and it is anticipated that the redistribution of income and relocation of wealth should have brought about a series of external transactions which modified the original settlement over time.

To the End of the First World War

Until the end of the First World War, the concentration and superimposition of power and wealth placed only a small number of groups in a strong bargaining position, gave very few groups differential access to one over the other, and left most people deprived of both resources. In turn this meant that the economic elites alone were likely to satisfy their educational demands through external transactions, if they could translate their financial resources into educational services. Success of course depended on negotiating strength not bargaining power, on the external interest group standing in a particular relationship to the profession (such that the teachers are willing to negotiate), and the polity (such that it does not veto or hinder negotiations). In relation to the latter, disunity among the political elites, especially the antagonism between the two parties, was likely to have coloured and complicated educational negotiations. In general it appears that the distribution of resources at the time when the new system emerged did exert a strong influence on the volume and type of demands which could be negotiated at first.

Four different kinds of groups were active in the defence or advancement of external transactions before the end of the war, and their respective relations with both polity and profession must be examined to discover whether these permitted them to convert financial resources into educational services. Firstly, two religious interest groups, the Anglican and Catholic Churches, fought to protect their recognized rights as suppliers of denominational instruction. With the Liberal electoral victory in 1906, freechurchmen looked to the government for changes in legislation which would reduce the favourable position accorded to voluntary schools in 1902. The educational secularism of the nascent Labour Party seemed propitious in this respect, although it appeared to favour the more extreme measure of imposing a political veto on denominational schooling (Tactic 2) altogether.

Aware of the financial strain that Anglican schools placed on the resources of the Established Church, the Liberal government sought a formula for the transference of voluntary institutions to public control. Three different Bills, framed between 1906-08, represented political attempts to reduce the autonomy of denominational schools, by making them more financially dependent on public spending (Tactic 1): they presented a choice between handing over the voluntary schools to the LEAs in return for being allowed to give a limited amount of denominational instruction in *council* schools,[167] or contracting out of the public system altogether and thus foregoing rate-aid. Many Anglicans were tempted by this formula — the right to proselytize without the need to pay[168] — but the Catholics who were still expanding their schools while the Anglican network was in decline, dreaded the loss of rate-aid if forced to contract out. The primary teachers too were hostile, partly because they feared having to give denominational instruction in the public sector, and partly because conditions were sure to deteriorate in schools which contracted into the private sector.[169] Labour fervour for secularism cooled markedly as Catholic outrage threatened to split the working class movement.[170] Conservatives, particularly in the House of Lords, were strong in support of the Established Church and quick to protect it from dispossession or coercion by blocking government bills. The 'Liberals had to recognize that even a large majority in the Commons could not ensure victory in this difficult and dangerous field'.[171] Antagonism between political elites (coupled with opposition from the profession) had served to protect external transactions between institutionalized religion and public education in their 1902 form – perhaps a mixed blessing for the Anglicans, but an undoubted benefit to the Roman Catholics. All that the Liberals had been able to do for their nonconformist clients was to initiate a fairly long-term assault on the denominational character of teacher training; firstly by establishing more Local Authority Colleges (i.e. Tactic 1, the pouring in of resources), and secondly by insisting that denominational colleges must not reject candidates on religious grounds for half of their available places (i.e. Tactic 3, the undermining of institutional autonomy).

No other case (with the exception of industrialists and the universities) was concerned with the *defence* of external transactions, but rather with the right of other social groups to develop this process of educational change. Furthermore, apart from the denominational issue, disunity among resource holders was not a powerful factor in determining the outcome. The rise of the 'New Education' movement was the simplest of these cases, since it confined itself to the private sector throughout its genesis. The 'progressives' were a loose association of prominent and often wealthy individuals who endorsed new methods of teaching and learning, accentuating 'freedom' and 'individualism' along the same broad lines as Montessori. They became a more organized interest group after the Conference on New Ideals in Education in 1915. The movement gained early encouragement from the profession when Edward Holmes, the ex-Chief Inspector of the Board of Education, published his attack on the conventional school, *What is and What Might Be*. 'Reformers who had been on the defensive gained unexpected support and defenders of the status quo were shaken when so eminent an educationalist joined the ranks of their attackers'.[172] This was augmented by other books, like Caldwell Cook's *The Play Way* written from the Perse School in Cambridge, and by a large number of teachers who voluntarily enrolled on progressive courses. Nor was official sympathy lacking, especially as the movement took advantage of anti-German sentiments when castigating formal methods as 'prussianization': H. A. L. Fisher as President of the Board took the Chair at an official reception for Maria Montessori. But at this time the progressive movement sought little from either polity or profession except their interest: they were prepared to maintain and staff new schools on an experimental basis, they constituted no threat and made no demands, but were merely an extension of the existing independent network.

The final cases are especially instructive because two groups, one from the most affluent section of the population, the other from the least wealthy, both tried to negotiate directly with the same educational institutions — the universities. The support of business had been a precondition for the establishment of the civic universities from 1850 onwards, whether this had taken the form of sponsorship by local industry (e.g. Sheffield, Birmingham and Manchester), funding by a particular firm (e.g. Bristol and Wills tobacco, Reading and Palmer's biscuits), or industrial support by a national concern (e.g. Newcastle and Mining). This drawing together of industries and the universities was greatly extended before the First World War and came to include Oxbridge as well as the civic institutions. Why then this relatively new industrial demand for educational services, and why too the collaboration of the profession and the compliance of the polity which enabled it to be realized and to be met more and more fully?

The formation of the very large firm following a burst of amalgamations, especially in textiles, brewing, iron and steel, underpinned the growing demand for graduate trainees, post-experience courses, and above all scientific research. In granting Charters to the civic colleges, the Conservative Party recognized and legitimated the external transactions with industry upon which their existence depended: 'It was evident that without massive support from industry no university movement stood much chance of successful development'.[173] Equally Haldane was clear that a major function of these institutions was 'to be able to minister to the wants of the manufacturers'.[174] On the whole, however, this general political permissiveness stemmed from a low official estimate of the value of academic expertise. This rendered both Parties indifferent to activities which were irrelevant to government policy, but were strongly endorsed by some politicians like Joseph Chamberlain. The scientific contribution of the universities to the war

effort transformed government opinion about their peripheric importance. It led directly to the foundation of the DSIR, in 1916, to act as a
broker between manufacturers with problems and the universities with
expertise. Henceforth transactions between industry and university
enjoyed all-Party support, now that the centrality of expertise to
economic life and national defence had been acknowledged.

What then of the negotiating strengths of these two institutions, left
with an official blessing to come to terms with one another? As an
external interest group, industry was in an exceedingly strong position.
It had considerable resources at its disposal and could pay lavishly, by
university standards, for the outputs it required. Moreover, the offers it
made could not be bettered by any other social group. Finally, under
the stress of foreign competition, the largest firms were convinced that
their viability depended on acquiring research and development
services, as well as what would now be termed further education, and
that only the universities could supply these.

In comparison, the negotiating strength of the university profession
was distinctly weaker. Certainly they had been approached, and in
some cases 'implored' by industries which recognized the value of their
scientific expertise and its scarcity. 'The importance of this is further
enhanced when it is appreciated that there are no state centres for
industrial research, save possibly the NPL, no research associations, and
that research within the firm was in its infancy in the 1890s and 1900s.
The civic universities were thus proportionately more important in this
regard than possibly ever again'.[175] Nevertheless the universities had no
other supplier on this scale (unsurprising since the entrepreneurial elite
was the wealthiest in society), and, as State grants did not begin to
cover overheads, they were in no position to pick and choose among
offers from rival interest groups. Even Cambridge, rich in endowments,
was under-going financial hardship and resolved to tap the benefits of
links with industry. On the other hand, the struggles experienced by
Colleges which had sought to develop on the basis of professional or
civic support, such as Leicester and Southampton, or which did not
receive the backing of big business (Nottingham and Exeter), provided
salutory lessons on the indispensability of the hundreds of thousands
that companies alone were willing and able to supply. True the profession could not be coerced, but the terms offered were generous. The
acquisition of new laboratories, equipment and libraries had academic
attractions which counterbalanced any repugnance felt towards
investigating the bio-chemistry of cheese-ripening, the composition of

detergents, or the commercial environment of the jewellery trade, not that most projects were so banal. All the same it was industry which paid the piper and the academics who had to play the tune. Sometimes this involved personal constraints (like the Sheffield Professor who could not publish his results, thus revealing trade secrets) and sometimes it spelt serious reductions in curricular autonomy. However, the civic universities as a whole made it clear that one of their main purposes was research and training for industry, thus indicating that a considerable section of the profession gave normative assent to such transactions.

In other words industry was the stronger element and its negotiations with the profession represented an imbalanced exchange between the two. In the initial scramble for Charters and the subsequent competition for students, the universities laid themselves out to woo industrial support and this necessarily gave the latter a substantial element of control — at Bristol firms becoming annual subscribers could virtually buy their way onto the governing body.[176] It meant that research programmes were often determined outside the universities and that taught courses, especially in the new faculties of Commerce, were tailor-made to business specifications — for Alfred Marshall, planning the economics syllabus at Cambridge, it became a question of how far he was 'really willing to go to help the businessmen and still remain academically respectable'.[177]

This responsiveness to industry and deference to its demands contrasted strikingly with university reactions to the working-class movement for Adult Education. The unfavourable nature of the 1902 settlement meant that no instruction was left under working-class control, while the unequal distribution of resources confined organized labour to *cheap* and peripheric educational activities — Socialist Sunday Schools, Co-operative Classes and Clarion Clubs. Within the Labour movement the component factions agreed on the necessity of education for the Member of Parliament and Trade Union Leader, but diverged significantly over the form it should take — the SLP seeking independent marxist courses for political self-education, the TUC preferring access to the universities rather than a substitute for it. The Association to Promote the Higher Education of Working Men, formed by Labour supporters and TUC representatives in 1903, tried 'to construct a working alliance between university extension and the working class movement' which would widen the only form of external transaction left to them. Initial approaches to Oxford were well received by liberal academics who saw themselves as cementing new relationships between the social classes. At the annual conference four years later, Morant was present and promised the support of the Board of Education in bringing the universities into closer contact with the working classes. 'With the approval and support of Church and State, of Oxford dons and leaders of the Labour movement, the WEA was well and truly launched'.[178]

Although enjoying a euphoric début, adult education was in constant need of funds and the resource distribution placed its organisers at the mercy of philanthropy, the profession, and the polity. As an external interest group it proffered the begging bowl not the wallet, its negotiating strength was practically non-existent and, as in all transactions between unequals, the stronger party dictated the terms. The imbalance in this exchange favoured the universities. It was skewed in the opposite direction from that characterizing university relations with industry. The significance of this imbalance became clear when developments in adult education affronted the dons and threatened to confront the government.

Originally the Oxford Colleges had been approached for financial aid with which to start WEA Tutorial Classes. Eight had begun work and 'the "impartial" study of historical and economic questions so fostered was something very different from the Marxist studies promoted by socialist groups which had inherited the earlier Socialist League slogan: educate-agitate-organise'.[179] The 'impartial' approach was not merely what the profession offered, it was the only type of instruction they thought *ought* to be available. Thus the foundation of Ruskin College as an independent institution, by American philanthropy, was a thorn in the side of the university and it pricked harder when its SDF Principal encouraged a definite socialist bias. Those dons who were on its staff and governing body believed that its approach should be 'non-partisan', the Vice Chancellor Lord Curzon concurred. Negotiations followed in which the university tried to subsume Ruskin, as a kind of preparatory college, rather than leaving it as a self-standing Labour College. In return for sacrificing its independence, especially in defining the content of instruction, Oxford offered financial assistance and some university places for its students. The Ruskin Principal and the student body opposed integration, first by strike action and then by forming the Plebs League 'to bring about a more satisfactory connection of Ruskin College with the Labour movement'.[180] The strike could inflict no damage on Oxford itself; it only illustrated the fact that external interest groups cannot coerce the profession. Instead the onus is on the former to make the terms attractive to the latter — all the more so when the imbalance of exchange means that the weaker party must submit to the stronger if transactions are to continue. Submission took place, the Principal was removed, and all hopes of winning Oxford for the service of Labour had to be abandoned.

If this attempt at independence had been restrained by the profession, the genuine Labour Colleges which the Plebs League tried to found, as a provincial system of adult education for the working class, met with resistance from the polity. The College, its district and divisional classes had a hard struggle for financial survival, depending on contributions from the militant unions and often from rank and file support over the heads of their union leaders. Its stated objectives cut it off from paternalistic donors. Unrest in the Welsh mines was partly attributed to CLC activities in the coalfields, where forty classes had been established. Significantly the Commission of Enquiry into Industrial Unrest (1917) contrasted the propagandist instruction of the CLC most unfavourably with the WEA spirit of knowledge for its own sake. The political lesson was pointed, 'non-partisan' activities would have the blessing of the Board, the committed approach would incur negative sanctions.

Both polity and profession hustled the adult education movement along WEA lines, by giving tutorial classes legal recognition and financial support provided they worked to a university syllabus under academic surveillance. By undermining institutional autonomy (Tactic 3), the Board had ensured that adult education was harmless to government and had also backed up the dons in their defence of the traditional definition of instruction. Weakness in the negotiating strength of the working class meant that they were not able to introduce a different form of education through external transactions, and one which was specifically fitted to class requirements. The contrast with the tailor-made courses offered to industrialists could not be greater, and is a direct reflection of the respective bargaining positions of these two external interest groups.

The Interwar Years

In the interwar years we have suggested that economic crisis, high unemployment, and growing income differentials would contract the range of groups able to engage in external transactions. In other words, this period is not likely to be of the richest in educational changes introduced through this process. No new external interest groups are expected to start direct negotiations, and those whose financial bargaining position was weak before the war will generally be in worse circumstances now — the various churches, the adult education movement and also the 'progressives'. Political redistribution in favour of the Left is expected to have been neutralized by the damage inflicted on the unions by the General Strike and on the Party by the repudiation of its leader. On the other hand, the quasi-corporatism developing between Conservatism and industry in the thirties appears to have augmented the bargaining position of business groups — the only ones to have bettered their position during this period. It now remains to examine how far these factors were influential and to what extent their impact was modified by the relative negotiating strengths of the parties involved.

The postwar period found the voluntary schools in straightened circumstances. Building costs had risen whilst subscriptions fell away, partly because of the trade depression and unemployment, and partly due to falling religious affiliation. Their comparative position worsened as the Fisher Act improved standards and expanded provision in public education. References in the Spens report to parity of amenities between all types of school, and in the Hadow report to reorganization involving vast amounts of new accommodation, were challenges to which denominationalism was unequal. Since the Churches could not afford to provide the new establishments, children would automatically proceed from the voluntary primary school to the council secondary school, unless foregoing further education.

> Moreover it was not now a question of some dramatic and forcible seizure which might be denounced and resisted as intolerable persecution; the new schools could be provided 'to fill up the gaps' as the board schools had been, and the parents left to decide whether they wished to take advantage of the new facilities or to continue to send their children to the existing inferior 'all-age' voluntary schools.[181]

In this context the Anglicans were divided between those willing to transfer their schools to the State in exchange for the right to give religious instruction in council schools (which the NUT opposed), others favouring the concentration of their resources on Training Colleges, and some wanting to join the Catholics in pressing the State to build denominational secondary schools. The balance between the three political parties in the late twenties meant that each scrambled for new votes and could not afford to alienate old supporters. The Conservatives were uncomfortably aware that a policy of naked denominationalism would now be of more benefit to the Catholics than to their Anglican supporters. At the same time Labour's hands were tied by an internal struggle between secularists, nonconformists and Catholics. The latter were particularly militant within the Labour Party because they had lost parliamentary sponsorship by the Irish MPs, following the creation of the Free State in 1921. Labour saw the red light after the Catholics actually fielded independent candidates in local elections, because of the schools issue. It did nothing when in office from 1929-31: to have acted for or against the voluntary schools would have split the Party. The decline of the Liberal Party was the real salvation of denominationalism, for with it freechurchmen lost any hope of killing the dual system. If this had not been possible when their party was at the height of its powers, it stood no chance whatsoever afterwards. Behind it was left a Conservative Party which wanted to protect Anglican interests and a Labour Party with a lot to gain from Catholic demands being satisfied, especially if it was not the agent manifestly ministering to them.

The strong National Government of 1936 initiated a compromise solution whereby for three years (a limited period at NUT insistence) the LEAs would make 50-75 percent grants towards building voluntary secondary schools necessitated by the raising of the school-leaving age and reorganization of provisions. In other words, the dual system was to continue and to be projected onto the secondary level, largely at public expense! This paradox is resolved when it is recognized that the Churches now occupied a differential bargaining position, enjoying a political influence disproportionate to their resources, whilst gaining an artificial increment in negotiating strength because neither Party could allow the other to protect one denomination alone. In terms of political tactics, the two parties could not countenance legal vetoes against voluntary schools (Tactic 2); their respective defence of different denominations limited the sanctions which could be used to undermine institutional autonomy (Tactic 3); whilst the savage cuts in public expenditure during these years[182] discouraged use of the least contentious strategy, namely pouring in funds to increase dependence on the State (Tactic 1). The temporary formula was in fact a limited version of Tactic 1, and it was clearly the most politically attractive solution for it assuaged nonconformist and secular opinion whilst not involving confrontation with the Churches.

Towards the end of the war the government recognized that the contribution of the voluntary schools would be necessary in the plans for educational reorganization, although the denominations would require assistance to bring their networks up to standard. The fomula employed was a neat version of Tactic 1, which had the political beauty of making closer integration with the State a voluntary matter determined only by the denominations' financial self-sufficiency. The Churches could opt for complete public support, involving almost complete public control and limited facilities for denominational instruction, or limited support and control but unrestricted facilities for denominational instruction. For those who disliked the one, Butler could point to the other, and what was also important, the profession was not opposed to this settlement which spelt an overall reduction in the number of teachers appointed on religious grounds. 'In effect a Conservative minister had once again intervened to ensure the continuance of the dual system'.[183]

The activities and enthusiasm of the progressive movement continued immediately after the war, with a spate of new independent schools being founded upon experimental lines – a boarding school for working class children (the Caldecott Community), another for war orphans (Tiptree Hall), the Forest School, a piece of rural romanticism, Summerhill, the best known 'demonstration' school, Beacon Hill run by the Russells, the Malting House School, which Susan Isaccs used to study child development, and many others including those experimenting with the Dalton Plan. But most of them experienced perpetual financial difficulties, some schools were of short duration, and the situation worsened with the downturn in the economy. 'The new schools founded after 1926 were not necessarily of less interest or importance than those which had been founded before, but they were fewer and the atmosphere generally was less hopeful'.[184] The schools stood as concrete demonstrations of progressive ideas in action, but with the onset of financial austerity they were in danger of becoming isolated showpieces or follies depending on one's point of view. Whilst the established Public Schools were able to survive the economic crisis by drawing on their endowments to keep fees below costs,[185] the new independents had no such resources upon which to fall back.

With the Depression their example might have lead nowhere, were it not for the headway that the movement continued to make in winning over the profession. Hence the future success of the movement did not depend on the fluctuation of resources, which facilitated or retarded expansion in the private sector. Although this kind of external transaction has continued up to today, and has continuously provided demonstration models of new methods at primary and secondary levels,[186] the rest of the progressive victory was accomplished through internal initiation. The seeding of the profession in this period produced its harvest during the sixties, after the elimination of selective secondary education and its downward constraint on the primary curriculum. This theme will be taken up again when examining negotiations between teachers and the polity.

Even more susceptible to hard times was the movement for adult education. However, this suffered as much from the internal divisions and the resulting weakness of the Union movement and the Labour Party alike, as from financial starvation. Unlike the Churches, rescued by their political allies, and the progressive movement, kept in protective custody by the profession, independent adult education went to the wall, for there was nothing in the negotiating strength of the working class to offset the deterioration in its bargaining position. In the early twenties the two strands — the WEA and Central Labour College — had struggled to advance towards national status. At this time the General Council of the TUC had failed to co-ordinate them under its own control, thus engendering a larger, more comprehensive network. The General Strike was the final deathblow for the radical socialist tendancy: many members of the Plebs League went over to the Communist Party while others abandoned their marxist convictions and worked on a reduced scale to promote education for particular Unions. Alongside this, the Clarion movement and Labour Churches were also in decline. Thus only the WEA approach continued to develop, and this in the 'non-partisan' form which had been shaped by political and professional pressures in the preceding period. Precisely because it was a transaction which did *not* provide services *specific* to the working class,

> it would seem reasonable enough that a major part in promoting adult education should be taken over by the educational system, if still in cooperation with outside organizations. Although the trade union and cooperative movement continued to promote educational activities on the part of their members, the labour movement as a whole now made no further move towards founding institutions designed to teach from a specifically Labour standpoint.[187]

After this severe check, and following the Party's achievement of its

first parliamentary majority in 1945, the energies of the Labour movement were henceforth withdrawn from external transactions and redirected towards political manipulation.

Exactly the opposite was the case with industry. As it moved into
closer contact with government, industrialists received strong official
encouragement to extend external transactions with higher education,
in order to surmount the economic crisis and re-establish their position
in international competition. This political go-ahead preceded the emergence of quasi-corporatism in the thirties. It was the heritage of the First
World War and the cult of science which led government to increase its
own spending at this level throughout the inter-war years (whilst
cutting back at others), and to look favourably on industry and commerce doing likewise. In this period when organized research became
one of the leading sources of invention and the amalgamation of
companies accelerated greatly, the demand for graduate labour in
scientific departments and managerial positions developed accordingly.
'Industry moved towards the universities and the universities were more
than willing to meet it half way'.[188]

However, changes in the negotiating strength of the profession
vis-à-vis these industrial interest groups led to greater reciprocity in
transactions between the two: imbalance of exchange was certainly not
eliminated, but the universities lost their supine dependency. Firstly,
aware of the wartime revaluation of their expertise and the swelling
demand for their services (graduate employment weathered the Depression well), academics began to bid up the exchange rate amongst firms
and generated a surplus which could be used for their own ends. Thus,
for example, while Manchester directly serviced Metro-Vickers, the
Chloride Electrical Storage Company, the British Dyestuffs Corporation
(later ICI) etc., it was also able to develop pure science, unrelated to
local industrial interests, under Rutherford, Bohr, Lawrence Bragg and
others.[189] The general development of the PhD rather than the MA
course is part of the same picture.

Secondly, the increased contribution of the State to the Universities
(grants from government were less than one quarter of university
income in 1920 but rose to one third ten years later) provided a steady
income for covering a portion of overhead costs which allowed the
colleges to be more selective about their clients. There is some indication that both faculty and graduates were more prepared to meet the
demands of 'new' science-based industries than those with less allure –
broadcasting, films, aircraft, and aeronautical engineering were well

serviced. Furthermore, the formation of the bipartite UGC, to administer government grants, represented a buffer which sheltered academics from the cruder demands of companies: it looked with suspicion on University Colleges which behaved like local technical schools.

Thirdly, the onus was beginning to be on industry, though not yet on commerce, to make its offers attractive, not merely in financial terms (the laboratories, donations, and Chairs) although these remained tremendously important, but also in the form of interesting research problems, graduate training schemes, and the abandonment of the traditional premium apprenticeship system for new recruits. None of this suggests a major change in the industry/university relationship, only a shift in degree towards greater reciprocity. The imbalance remained, as is witnessed by Bristol's overtures to local industries to induce them to fund research fellowships: 'Thus you might select some subject of research connected with the problems of your own business. You would have full access to the research and prior knowledge of the results obtained'.[190] But on the whole it was rare to find Colleges now laying themselves out in this way, though commerce departments were still having to do so.

It is in this context of improved negotiating strength that an academic sub-group became vocal in its normative rejection of the linkage with industry. Flexner and Laski claimed that the external financing of research was moulding university development without regard to academic considerations, whilst Bernal and Huxley concentrated more on the misdirection of scientific development which this engendered. Those hostile to industrial involvement came from various disciplines; it was not a simple cleavage between Arts and Sciences. On the other hand, this outlook was counterbalanced by many who legitimated the linkage, and some, like the Vice Chancellor of Birmingham, who wanted to make links between industry and the universities even closer, 'not by waiting for Business to come to them, but for them to go out and capture Business'.[191] It was the latter view which prevailed, partly because the academic opponents of industry tended to be the political opponents of the Conservative government but more importantly because their objections were drowned by the Second World War in which the universities were deeply involved from the start. And this meant close co-operation between university scientists and firms, particularly GEC, BTH, EMI, ICI and Metro-Vickers.[192] If it was any consolation to its opponents — and it was a great source of satisfaction to its advocates — the proliferation of external transactions with industry had ensured that 'in contrast to almost every other form of educational activity not even the most severe years of depression marked a declining rate of growth'[193] for the universities.

The Post-War Period

The post-war period of economic recovery and political consensus was expected to be very rich in external transactions. This was indeed the case and the changes that can be attributed to this process show that its intensified usage was due both to private affluence (personal investment) and corporate growth (collective investment). The former is what is novel to this period, at least on the scale at which it took place, the latter represents a continuation of institutional exchanges from the previous period, but at a greatly increased rate.

In teasing out the educational developments introduced via external transactions, it is important to be aware of their masking by other factors. The unprecedented increase in public educational expenditure (itself the result of political manipulation), at a rate which exceeded the growth of national income after 1945,[194] often conceals or obscures the degree to which other resource holders were translating their wealth into educational services, especially when figures are presented in relative rather than absolute terms. This is particularly significant because it was those areas of increased public spending (secondary, further, and higher education) which were also the main loci of external transactions. There are obvious exceptions, where direct exchange was used to fill lacunae in State provisions (such as nursery schooling), but, in general, this process too begins to desert the primary level which had been the predominant concern of the nineteenth century networks. This tendency, and it is no more than that, is due to the *general* rise in expertise, transmitted through instruction, which makes all forms of primary education essentially 'preparatory', whereas external transactions always show clustering around terminal points, and thus tend to concentrate on progressively later age groups as school leaving is delayed.

This is not merely a tendency produced by collective patterns of investment (e.g. firms interested in immediate pre-entry training) but is also the product of personal investment, although this trend does not

exhaust the forms taken by the latter. Expenditure on private education rose steadily to reach an estimated 30 million in the fifties.
Spending on private schooling increased sharply with children's age: as
a proportion of the school population those in private establishments
jumped from 7 percent at 11, to 11 percent at 14, 33 percent at 15 and
50 percent at 16.[195] Parental investment was clearly being made at the
points where it yielded highest returns. This remarkable development of
the private sector was clearly related to growing affluence:

> the class from which the existing independent school population springs has
> shown every sign of increasing since 1944 and the expected annual rise in the
> national income will make expenditure on education a less onerous burden on
> individual families. The higher income groups are almost unanimous in their
> support of the private sector. Although 65% of those earning £1,000 or over in
> 1954 had been educated privately 95% of their children were attending private
> schools.[196]

The range of schools which were developed or expanded in this context
represented the usual contribution of external transactions to the
diversification of provisions. Certainly much of this parental investment
was directed towards the traditional public schools, whose fees combined with their endowments meant that their facilities became more
lavish. In turn it was increasingly difficult to bring even the grammar
schools up to the standards of the best of private education. If the
competitiveness of the public schools was protected in this way, other
components of the private sector also benefited, especially the experimental progressive schools which perhaps gained most support from
professional parents without a family tradition of public school attendance. However, it was not affluence alone which prompted these
developments, although it was a necessary condition for them: equally
important were the unintended consequences of the official policy of
selection. As far as the grammar schools were concerned it 'is likely that
the substitution of children of higher ability displaced children whose
parents could afford to pay fees at a higher scale than those charged
(with subsidy) by the pre-1944 secondary schools. The rising incomes
of this class of parent, followed by an increase in the number of their
children above the age of eight, has created a demand for additional
places in independent schools'.[197]

Furthermore, selective secondary education also had the effect of
stimulating new private efforts at primary level. For the lower middle
class family, which could not contemplate meeting public school fees,

the selective grammar school was an ideal institution, provided of course that their children could gain admission. For all that has been written about the positive discrimination of 11+ intelligence tests in favour of this class, parents at the time worried about their children getting through, especially if they appeared to be of average or lower ability. As the cautious class, the heirs of the white-collar clerks obsessed with 'security', the struggling home owners impressed by the safety of bricks and mortar, the willing clients of the man from the Prudential, their collective reaction was to take out educational insurance in the form of the private crammer. These schools, for which no statistical data are available, represented a limited investment (often pupils only attended for the crucial two years from nine to eleven), on reasonable terms,[198] which paid good dividends in high pass rates, whatever their educational shortcomings. Many of the crammers were blatantly entrepreneurial and often relied on semi-qualified staff, but their expansion only drew together a set of diffuse and undocumented external transactions which the middle and lower middle class had already developed as their incomes allowed – the elocution teacher, the dancing class instructor, the piano mistress, the maths coach and other 'front-room' tutors. In this way the lower middle class, the group who thought the Conservative Party was not doing enough for them, exchanged their resources with the private sector at primary level in order to ensure access to the best of State instruction at the secondary stage.

A final area in which private provision expanded during these years was nursery schooling, to be followed later by the burgeoning play group movement, and pushed even further back by more informal mother and toddler groups. Partly this was a response to an obvious deficiency, due to repeated delays in opening public nurseries, partly it reflected a rise in women's wages which made it worthwhile to continue working. As with the crammers, many of these arrangements for child-minding were far from satisfactory. As has been stressed before, the process of external transaction in no way protects against the development of the inferior or the second-rate. In England during this period personal investment produced some of the very best and very worst of educational practices.

Turning to institutional transactions, both industry and commerce displayed an unprecedented rate of activity which was unhindered by the polity: consensus politics meant that both parties fostered the linkage between industry and the universities because of its contribution to the managed economy. However, to a greater extent than before, these exchanges were with further education as well as higher education. This additional emphasis must be attributed to a number of factors which operated in conjunction — changes in the occupational structure increasing the number of positions requiring technical skills, severe competition for graduate output (which itself forced industry to reach further back and to sponsor schoolboys through university in order to secure them upon graduation), greater industrial representation on consultative committees where they could make their demands known, and, finally, the existence of colleges whose constitutions were vague enough and whose inclinations were strong enough for firms to be able to negotiate services to meet their local requirements. Under the provisions of the 1944 Act 'the attitude towards the functions of further education could not have been more permissive whether with regard to the public it was to serve or the nature of the service that this public was to be provided with'.[199] Industry and commerce were ready and able to pay for the privilege of supplying the definitions.

The polity registered no objections: on the contrary it was willing to encourage these developments both directly and indirectly. When constituting the Percy Committee on higher technological education it included an unprecedented number of industrialists, even in a period when advisory committees to government were becoming increasingly representative.[200] Consequently the report published in 1945 'was the work of technologists and technical HMIs who were all committed to the advancement of technology in its educational and professional contexts'.[201] The recommendations, dealing both with content and control, were formulae favourable to industry which also commanded official support. Basically they sought to bridge the gap between the universities, turning out research scientists, and the Technical Colleges, producing technicians and laboratory assistants. A number of Colleges of Technology should be developed from amongst the latter which would provide sandwich courses, post-graduate and refresher courses, without being hampered by university formalities. Regional Advisory Councils would consult local industrial requirements and co-ordinate technological instruction nationally, whilst the representation of industrialists on the governing bodies would ensure responsiveness to changing local demands. The Labour government reacted enthusiastically, viewing these proposals as an aid to reconstruction, and implemented most of the recommendations immediately. The relevant Circular of 4.46 was concerned with 'the freedom of action (within financial limits) to be enjoyed by such bodies; with ensuring that colleges met regional and national needs; and with developing national schools as separate entities, to be supported by industry and financed by direct government grant'.[202] At this level the industrial employer became the recognized expert on further educational development, whilst his role as supplier of resources gained full legal recognition.

The prevailing political consensus is important here, for the Conservative government simply continued where Labour left off. It finished implementing the Percy recommendations (giving 24 colleges the special grant for advanced technological studies) and proceeded to new changes in the same vein. In 1956 the creation of Colleges of Advanced Technology was announced (9 in number), together with Regional Colleges, and an award entitled the Diploma in Technology. If one adds to this the establishment of Industrial Training Boards for each sector of the economy (1963) which imposed levies (refunding them to firms making adequate provisions, and otherwise passing them on to support further education), we have the educational counterpart of Conservative corporatism. Here the partnership of State and industry involved the legal legitimation of external transactions and the official acceptance of a flexible framework for further education through which industrialists could negotiate their subsequent or supplementary requirements.

As far as the universities were concerned, this period witnessed a complete shift from a buyers' to a sellers' market. This reversal destroyed the imbalanced nature of exchange between the two institutions, which until now had been biased in favour of industry. Indeed, perhaps for the only period to date, the exchange rate was to the advantage of the universities since a market existed for practically anything they chose to produce at that time. Advisory reports, appearing immediately after the war, like Percy (1945) or the Barlow Committee on Scientific Manpower (also 1945) signalled shortages in university output and endorsed considerable expansion. As at the lower levels of technical training, so here political consensus espoused the industrial cause. Full university status was conferred on a number of colleges which had developed through past external transactions — Nottingham (1948), Southampton (1952), Hull (1954), Exeter (1955), Leicester (1957), and in a rather different category, Keele (1962). This expansion, unparalleled since the 1900s, together with increased public spending on higher education, constituted the official policy of providing a suitable environment in which industrial demands could be met. Neither political Party tried to coerce the universities into making

expansion synonymous with an increased number of science and technology graduates, perhaps because this seemed unnecessary. After all, in
the past the universities had been only too willing to respond to
industrial overtures.

However, the negotiating strengths of the two sides were now
reversed and this altered what could be transacted. As an external
interest group industrialists were fully convinced of their need for
research and manpower services from the university. In these years
industry for the first time became the single largest employer of
graduates.[203] Companies like ICI, which had absorbed 30 graduates per
1000 employees in 1932 were taking 70 by the mid-sixties. A decline in
manual and semi-skilled occupations was registered in the 1950s
whereas scientific, professional, and higher technical posts which required degrees rose by 72 percent.[204] In this context the FBI and
Confederation of Management Associations were clamouring for larger
outputs and had 'squared' this with the polity. Industry was now
booming, it had still bigger resources at its disposal, and, apart from the
State, could offer terms with which no other interest group could
compete. Its bargaining position was better than ever before, but
negotiating strength is a relational concept and it was precisely the
relationship between buyer and seller which had changed.

For the first time the academic profession had an expertise which
was considered almost invaluable and for whose services they could
charge higher and higher prices. 'Apart from their greedy absorption of
graduates which reached new peaks, industry also in the mid-fifties very
greatly increased its private finance of universities and even more
strikingly its finance of research'.[205] Secondly, as firms vied with one
another for their services, the universities could pick and choose
amongst them, deciding not only which they would supply but also
how far they would go to meet specific requirements. Indeed, an
unintended consequence of increased State funding, via the UGC, was
to reinforce this very independence vis-à-vis industrial demands,
whereas the political motive·had been the exact opposite — public
resources were intended to enable higher education to respond more
fully. Thus science degrees as a whole did not account for the majority
of new places, whilst degrees which were specifically technological only
represented a third of those in science. Again the PhD was developed
rather than the MSc. The universities did not lay themselves out as
before, they often put academic concerns first in their development
decisions, and used their surplus to develop arts, humanities, and social

science rather than degrees in pure and applied science. They got away with it because when industrialists could not get the science recruit that they sought, they tended to take the Arts graduate instead[206] and convinced themselves, or allowed themselves to be convinced, that they were acquiring valuable 'personal qualities' in the process. Thirdly, since academia was less open to coercion than ever before, the universities firmly placed the onus on the Companies to make their terms attractive. They did so where research projects were concerned and also in the field of graduate recruitment. Firms competed with one another to provide seductive forms of graduate training – in the mid-fifties 300 companies were arranging vacation courses for over 2,000 students.[207] The universities were not uncooperative, they created new Appointments Boards and the AUT also ran various conferences in conjunction with the FBI. They still wanted to negotiate, but on better terms, and these were now normative as well as financial. Finally, the universities could afford the luxury of a conscience: they could resign themselves on normative grounds to foregoing particular transactions without this threatening their survival. They could defend standards, integrity and expertise by declining offers, and do so all the more easily since the technical college network was ready and glad to enter such negotiations in their stead.

This displacement of transactions onto non-university institutions had another interesting twist which takes us full circle back to the discussion of private education and its enhanced importance during this period. In the attempt to increase the throughput of those enrolling for science degrees, the Industrial Fund for the Advancement of Scientific Education was formed to provide grants for science buildings in independent and direct grant schools.[208] About £3 million were presented, in 1955, to improve and expand science accommodation. It is impossible to calculate what harvest industry reaped from this long-term investment, but there is no doubt that it improved the facilities of the public schools in one of the areas in which they were relatively weak.

Of all the groups to engage in external transactions during this period, only the Churches had to be content with holding their own rather than making progress. Their falling membership and reduced resources made it increasingly difficult for them to maintain a large network of schools. On the other hand, their very decline in society also meant that the polity had less to gain, in terms of political support, by appeasing them. Government policy was mainly concerned with striking a balance between the competing claims of Anglicans and Catholics. The latter were still in a position to contemplate running new secondary schools and thus approached the State for 75 percent grants for building voluntary establishments. The Anglicans, who had accepted 'controlled' status to a much greater extent, only sought improved maintenance grants since building-aid would benefit Catholics more than the Established Church. The 1959 Act was a compromise between the two since it conceded grants for new schools but restricted these to the provision of 'secondary moderns'. However, this legislation involved more than just striking a balance between competing claims, it also firmly delineated two types of secondary institution (the Grammar and Technical Schools) where the State would give no encouragement to the Churches. This effectively confined religious transactions to the inferior part of secondary education, given the declining resources of these interest groups.

At the primary level too there was no question of advance by the Churches, but merely of stabilization. Here two factors interacted to protect denominational schooling. On the one hand, the teaching profession gradually withdrew its objections to the State assisting voluntary schools, for this brought working conditions up to public standards, and teachers also felt that the legal safeguards against religious Tests now gave them adequate protection. On the other hand, the growth of ecumenicalism took the heat out of the internicine debate, and led the freechurchmen finally to withdraw their political opposition to denominationalism in education. The last obstacle, the nonconformists' objection to the endurance of single school areas, held in Anglican fief, disappeared as the Established Church and Free Church Federal Council co-operated to give the latter representation on the Management Boards in such areas. In 1961 the Free Churches at last admitted that voluntary denominational schools were an integral part of the educational system.[209] This rapprochement *amongst* religious interest groups was vital to the continuation of their external transactions in a period when neither polity nor profession would have gone very far out of their way to defend this traditional process.

1964-75

The last period, 1964-75, does not mark a radical change as far as external transactions are concerned: there are continuities both in the patterns of personal investment and of collective transactions. Since this was a time of relocation rather than redistribution of resources, it is unsurprising to find that negotiations with the private sector remained the preserve of middle class groups, for nothing had changed to bring them within reach of working class parents. Expenditure on private education grew to around £60 million, which in real terms represented a slight increase over the previous period, and rising personal incomes continued to make this form of instruction possible for more families, even though they still tended to be drawn from the same class. A substantial part of this investment went to the old public schools, whose annual fees passed the £1,500 mark, but the progressive and experimental schools continued to benefit, as did the politer versions of the earlier crammers. Unfortunately no exact data are available on the schools of 'the new suberbia or, possibly, to put the point another way, the elements of respectability that refused to be satisfied with an elementary school but could not afford a Headmasters' Conference or a Preparatory School'.[210]

An interesting sub-development along the same lines was a tendency for parents to make use of 'voluntary aided', and especially Catholic schools, as preferable to the local primary or comprehensive school. This feeling that 'the Convent' provided a better standard of instruction and discipline (especially for girls) appears to have manifested itself regardless of religious affiliation and may yet become a significant factor in perpetuating the voluntary schools. Given that all Parties agreed that Church schools should not suffer from comprehensive reorganization and should receive 80 percent building and maintenance grants for any type of school,[211] the existence of a ready clientele should preserve the remains of the dual system.

Developments in technical and higher education in relation to collective investment were rather more complicated. To begin with political attitudes retreated from the simplistic view that industry and the universities should merely be encouraged to get together. The polity, and particularly Labour which was in office for most of this period, definitely fostered educational services to industry, but it also sought to monitor this process more closely. 'Labour and noteably Mr Wilson recognized the intrinsic importance of science and technology and also saw it as an issue with which to refashion a classless "technocratic" image for the party. Most importantly, in contrast to the Conservatives, their emphasis was on science for industry rather than on prestige "big science" for atomic energy that had marked the achieve-

ments of the fifties.'[212] In this connection official policy rapidly
passed from an optimistic phase, a continuation of Conservative attitudes from the previous period, to a more pessimistic view of the
controls needed to place higher education at the service of industry.

In accepting the Robbins Committee's proposals on university expansion, the Government clearly anticipated that a doubling of student
numbers in the sixties would produce a swing towards applied science
and this was just as important a motive as educational egalitarianism.
To this end the eight English CATs were brought under the UGC in
1965 to constitute Technological Universities alongside the new plateglass universities. These ex-Colleges of Advanced Technology brought
with them an unapologetic closeness to industry and its requirements,
while some of the new universities, especially Essex, Lancaster and
Warwick, rapidly engaged in transactions with industrialists. On the
other hand Sussex, East Anglia, York and Kent remained almost
completely disengaged from industry. Furthermore, all the new
universities promptly developed the social sciences whilst the politicians
were still talking about the growth of applied technology. Socialization
of students was on academic lines: 'the ethos transmitted by the staff
to their students that research itself was the goal and that production,
being regarded as of less intrinsic interest, could be left to others,'[213]
was officially regretted. All this was evidence of university autonomy,
of the reciprocity of exchanges between industry and academia which
had been established in the previous period, yet from which the new
universities benefited as they were endowed from the start with the
freedom to design their own courses. What the polity appears to have
bemoaned is that it accorded the new universities an autonomy which
they turned more to their own account than to that of the national
economy. If this is the case then it had largely itself to blame, for it was
the fact that central government provided three quarters of university
expenditure by 1965 which blunted responsiveness to external overtures. The lesson learned by the polity was not this one: instead what it
determined to do was to see that this freedom went no further than the
existing universities.

In 1965 the government called a halt to the establishment of further
universities for the next ten years. A year later it announced its 'binary
policy' which replaced the previous programme of incorporating the
whole of higher education into the universities. Significantly the binary
policy was introduced without the usual lengthy consultative process in
which the profession played an increasingly important role. The desig-

nation of twenty-seven Regional Colleges as Polytechnics, concentrating on advanced work and preparing for degrees, yet under LEA control, was an official attempt to alter the professional side of the equation. The balance of exchange between industry and the universities had swung too far in favour of the latter: in the other part of the binary system the profession would neither be allowed to develop such negotiating strength nor possess the freedom to pursue self-determined goals with surplus resources. At least this seems to have been the idea in theory. In practice the workings of Local, Area, and Regional Colleges and the Polytechnics have given little indication that the LEA can deliver a greater fidelity to government policy than the UGC had succeeded in doing. The reason is the same in both parts of the system — the growth of professional autonomy in the wake of its re-valued expertise.

After 1966 the government gave concrete encouragement to strengthening links with industry by means of special awards for students entering companies on graduation, co-operative awards for those working on joint industry-university research projects, and six university based industrial units supported by the Ministry of Technology, to take on research contracts for local firms. Similarly the UGC gave 'pump-priming' assistance to specific university schemes promoting closer ties with industry, and industrial liaison posts were financed in a number of universities to make contact with industrialists and discover how the university could help them. At the same time the CBI and Committee of Vice-Chancellors created a Joint Committee on the Relations of Industry and the universities. None of this indicates that the universities held back from industrial involvement, they did not — they transacted as readily as ever, only rather more selectively and on better terms which allowed them simultaneously to pursue their self-defined goals. Furthermore the 1,500 unfilled university places in science and engineering at the end of the sixties[214] supported the academic view that this should not be their exclusive role. Yet despite autonomous action within higher education, 'the sixties also saw a remarkable and unprecedented creation of administrative arrangements as linking mechanisms binding the universities and industry more formally and closely together than ever before'.[215]

There is nothing mutually exclusive, outside Labour thinking, about internal initiation and external transactions: on the contrary they are logically linked in a number of ways. What often lay behind public controversy and criticism was not so much the universities taking undue advantage of their enhanced negotiating strength, as a good deal of industrial uncertainty about the services it should transact – whether it wanted general science teaching for future adaptability or specialized training for current job requirements – or sometimes one and sometimes the other. However with the serious downturn of the economy in the seventies industrial transactions were cut-back hard, reducing the resource flow to the universities and increasing their dependence on the State. Then the connection between the two processes became abundantly clear, for as external transactions dwindled so did the internal initiation which had fostered the development of new departments, subjects and specialisms in the sixties. The withdrawal or serious reduction of financial supplies from industry placed the universities in an entirely unprecedented position of vulnerability towards the State – never before had they confronted it without the protection afforded by a committed alternative supplier.

INTERNAL INITIATION

The initial Bargaining Positions characterizing different sections of the teaching body immediately after the introduction of the 1902 Act were stronger than those of their counterparts in the new centralized systems. However, the differences between the academics at one extreme and the elementary school teachers at the other were so great that their attempts to translate their bargaining positions into negotiating strength have to be treated separately. Although all parts of the profession were successful in producing a greater reciprocity in their exchanges over time, their starting points were so dissimilar that the respective action sequences proceeded on qualitatively different planes. Nor, as will become clear, are we dealing with a simple linear progression in which the conditions favouring internal initiation steadily improved over time, so that one part of the profession consistently lags behind the vanguard, but covers the same ground at a slower pace. Nevertheless, because the various kinds of teachers all did make headway, at one time or another, with their main task of exchanging professional expertise against financial resources and legal rights, one of the most important consequences was the development of internal innovations *between* different parts and levels of the system, which altered the nature of systematization from the inside by changing the inputs, processes and outputs at one particular level in relation to others.

Expertise

The initial distribution of resources was least favourable to the most numerous section of the profession – the elementary school teachers. Their expertise, gained through the Pupil Teachers Centres and Training Colleges was not in itself particularly high, a result as they were well aware, of being trained to execute the Revised Code – a process of being crammed in order to cram, reminiscent of earlier monitorial practices. In turn this low level of training was further diluted by a number of side entrances to the classroom which shepherded in two groups without either academic or professional pedigree – the uncertificated and the untrained. The joint responsibility for this lay with the two main suppliers of resources to the elementary level, the Board of Education and the religious denominations: the former continued to hold an 'Acting Teachers' examination allowing those who passed it to teach, although they had undergone no systematic academic preparation or vocational training, whilst the voluntary schools depended heavily on cheap, unqualified teachers. At the turn of the century the situation was deteriorating rather than improving in these two respects.

> The impression that emerges of the teaching staff is of a small band of trained certificated teachers immersed in a growing flood of untrained certificated teachers, assistant teachers, additional women teachers, pupil-teachers and probationers. This flood of cheap, untrained labour was mainly female. The teachers were beginning to see that an expansion of the training college system was necessary to reduce the 'army of unqualified practitioners.[216]

In other words they were very conscious that they must increase their overall expertise in order to upgrade the whole profession before they could hope for a better exchange rate.

Wealth

Although the school teachers had two suppliers of resources, the serious impoverishment of the one, the voluntary schools, prevented them from being played off against one another to improve either pay or facilities. On the contrary, the rock bottom remuneration, poor conditions and reliance on the unqualified in the voluntary schools, which remained uncompetitive despite rate-aid, exerted a downward pull on council schools, which did not have to pay much in order to pay better. Furthermore, wealth and expertise had been deliberately manoeuvered into a negatively reinforcing relationship by the polity. The sudden demand for teachers following the extension of elementary schooling in 1870 had been met by an imperative lowering of the standard of the certificate, in order to secure staffing, rather than improving pay to attract more recruits.[217] The after-effects of the revised code were not limited to the artificial 'pegging down' of salaries (which this distorted version of laissez-faire concealed)[218] but also involved a loss of status and of independence in the classroom.

Autonomy

The low autonomy explicit in teaching under the code had carried over into the general conditions of employment of teachers. A number of extraneous duties (playing the organ, parish work) were imposed as terms of employment, especially in voluntary schools, whilst 'obnoxious interference' and excessive regulation by local employers imposed humiliating limitations on teaching and discipline. Coupled with this, teachers had little security, were subject to capricious dismissal, had no access to the Inspectorate or right of appeal against individual decisions or against 'black-listing' by the Department. In some ways, the 1902 Act intensified low autonomy, for in killing the School Boards it abolished the one agency through which the teachers had acquired some influence which could be used for professional self-protection.[219] With their demise the school teachers were convinced of the need for insertion at both the parliamentary and local authority level in order to protect and advance professional freedom. Since 1885 they had tried to safeguard their interests by successfully sponsoring parliamentary candidates. Now they were convinced that a strong national organization was more than ever essential to exert pressure on policy formation at both levels, for they had little confidence in Morant's statement that their 'interests' should be 'represented' on the new Education Committees.[220] For a substantial improvement in negotiating strength, such representation had to be direct and organized — so far the NUT had been preoccupied with building up its membership and developing negotiating techniques, next it had to accomplish insertion. To teachers at the turn of the century their union was the key element in achieving their trio of aims, improved expertise, remuneration and autonomy — in other words the pre-conditions for internal initiation. In the following sections we will see that the NUT steadily increased the negotiating strength of the school teachers up to the Second World War, placing them in a position to engage in a considerable number of far reaching innovations and giving them an agency through which to play an important role in political manipulation.

Expertise

At the other end of the profession was the tiny group of academics, numbering under 2,000 in total, and divided approximately equally between Oxbridge Dons and Civic University teachers, although of course a large proportion of the latter were Oxbridge graduates. Consequently their expertise was high at the start and was to get higher, broader and deeper as the scope of academic knowledge itself became wider and more specialized. However, uses to which this expertise should be put was a matter which divided the profession on historical lines. On the one hand, there was the 'professorial' orientation, best exemplified in the University of London tradition, which stressed the lecturing and research role of academics accentuating their expert knowledge and its contribution, in the broadest terms, to society. On the other, was the 'collegiate' orientation, best illustrated in the colleges revitalized by the Oxford movement, which emphasized the ideal of service and pastoral care by the personal tutor. The two traditions were not incompatible with professionalism but they centered on different aspects of it − technical expertise and service to clients[221] − which meant that university teachers did not start with a common definition of the role which they should collectively strive to win for the university in society. What most could agree on from the start, however, was that their financial resources and legal rights should be brought up to the same high level as their expertise.

Wealth

The universities themselves, with the partial exception of Oxford, were poor, but their staff, and especially the growing ranks of untenured assistants, were disproportionately worse off. The newly chartered civic universities were virtually dependent on industrial financing: colleges like Leicester which had tried to develop on the basis of local and professional contributions failed to make headway as did others which were too reliant on a single founding benefactor, like Sheffield in the early days of Mappin.[222] Whilst the capital value of buildings and equipment was high, most of the new universities, like the voluntary schools before them, met with less generosity over maintenance costs. It was good personal publicity or company advertising to name a library or a laboratory, but with the exception of endowing chairs, it was less rewarding to underwrite mundane running costs or the salary bill. Although they varied widely in their annual endowment income (from £23,000 at Manchester to £400 at Nottingham) the mode was around £6,000[223] and meant that their plea that they could not pay their staff more was genuine enough. Oxford and Cambridge, on the other hand, were property holding corporations, although at the turn of the century Cambridge was in great financial difficulties. Furthermore, much of the Oxbridge wealth pertained directly to the colleges and could not be redeployed for university developments. Thus, despite their plurality of suppliers and diverse sources of income, the universities as a whole were far from being an affluent body. It is in this context that the 'growth of Government finance, although potentially a threat to university autonomy, was the assistant staff's best hope of ameliorating their condition'.[224] Much of the action initiated later by their organization, the AUT, was aimed at obtaining State support without allowing this threat to materialize. And until the most recent period they were remarkably successful in doing so — in bidding up the rate of exchange for expertise against wealth with successive governments, whilst maintaining the same relationship with the State as with their other suppliers.

Autonomy
Though the polity did not infringe university autonomy, this did not mean that academic staff constituted a self-governing community. Academic authority over the most academic of concerns, curriculum and examinations, was technically the preserve of the lay governors, in a tradition stemming from the University of London. 'By the end of the century, as a result, English university education outside Oxford and Cambridge was in effect organized on a university college system in which teaching was divorced from academic control. In short, scholars were deprived of almost all discretion in the management of their affairs'.[225] Certainly these bodies exerted most of their powers in the field of financial expenditure rather than staff supervision, and admittedly too the new Charters specified teacher representation on the Councils, but the balance had still not tipped away from lay government and towards the academic Senates at the start of the century. In these struggles with local trustees to establish the basic elements of academic freedom, the Oxbridge background of many civic university

teachers was important in enabling them to counterpose the model of the traditional academic guilds.[226] But a new phenomenon, the rapid rise of non-professional staff who now just outnumbered the professors, and were both the products and victims of institutional poverty, was to be more actively responsible for increasing self-government. This enlarged category of young assistants could no longer expect automatic promotion to the professoriate in the fullness of time – they were too numerous. Neither therefore could they confidently await representation on the governing bodies of their institutions which went with a chair, and this left them in no position to influence their pay, conditions of work or intellectual environment. This groundswell appears to have been crucial in pressing Senates to become more egalitarian and to assume broader academic powers, and in pushing professional representation further upwards to give it a stronger voice in Council decision-making. Thus the attempt to increase professional autonomy was spearheaded by one and the same group active in improving the financial situation of the academics – the assistant teachers – which is unsurprising since this subgroup exemplified the massive disjuncture between high expertise on the one hand and relatively little wealth or autonomy on the other, in its most extreme form. Interaction throughout the rest of the century can be read as a sustained attempt to close these gaps by raising the latter to the level of the former, thus eradicating the inconsistencies in initial bargaining position.

As with the elementary school teachers and the secondary teachers, situated in an intermediary position, the academics appear to have made consistent progress in acquiring the conditions for substantial internal initiation, up to and following the Second World War. However there was no inevitability about this: it depended upon negotiating strength which is a relational term. The most recent period clearly underlines the fact that interaction can produce reverses over time, narrowing professional powers to direct educational development, as well as advances which widen their influence over the definition of instruction.

The School Teachers, 1902-1908

To increase negotiating strength in relation to both central and local authorities (for the latter was never merely the agent of the former), involved co-ordinated professional action. From 1870 onwards this advancement was seen to hinge on an organizational unity which was inconceivable until then since the voluntary system had split the teachers into different camps, sectionalizing their interests and undermining any common cause by a divisive religious partizanship. The foundation of the National Union of Elementary Teachers in that year was the first move towards professional association and this was taken a stage further in 1889 when the word 'Elementary' was dropped. 'From its inception, its prime object was nothing less than the creation of a teaching profession, by uniting teachers of all types in a single combination'.[227]

However, organizational unity was a far-off goal given a number of structured cleavages within the teaching body — voluntary and council teachers; headmasters and class teachers; graduates and non-graduates; collegiate trained and untrained; men and women; certificated and uncertificated. These vested interests encouraged separate associations at different levels (the 'Joint-Four' — secondary organizations of Headmistresses, Assistant Mistresses, Headmasters and Assistant Masters which were quite unrelated to the NUT), and at the same levels (the National Federation of Class Teachers, of Women Teachers, the National Association of Head Teachers, of Non-Collegiate Certificated Teachers and the National Union of Women Teachers which had independent status and variable relations with the NUT).[228] Beatrice Webb commented of these sectional organizations that 'in so far as they correspond with a genuine differentiation among the membership (they) may have been necessary, if the union was to continue all embracing. But such internal sectional developments have certain harmful results. They distract the energy, which might otherwise have been given to the advancement of the interests of the NUT or of the profession as a whole to internal intrigue'.[229] The NUT was well aware of this and its ultimate aim was for a united profession in a unified educational system, the two being seen as closely related to one another and involving a transformation of both central and local authorities for education.

The ten point declaration of the NUT's objectives in 1870 also reveals the methods by which it thought to attain them. In fact the ten points coincide closely with the four conditions under which the profession can increase its negotiating strength, and they have been grouped accordingly.

Upgrading   — More stringent requirements for entry into the teaching profession.

	– Adequate Salaries.
	– Security of tenure and a standard contract of service.
	– Restoration of an adequate pension plan.
Self-Regulation	– Control of entrance to the profession and teachers' registration.
	– Freedom from 'obnoxious interference' in internal school affairs.
	– Freedom from compulsory extraneous duties.
Insertion	– The right of promotion for teachers to the Inspectorate.
	– The right of appeal against an Inspector's recommendation to cancel a teacher's certificate.
Normative Influence	– The revision of the educational code.

Upgrading

An improvement in their collective expertise was seen by the NUT as the key to full professional status. As their President stressed in 1901, 'the organized thousands of the National Union of Teachers have aspirations toward that high intellectual plane which has come to be embodied in one word – "culture" '.[230] To this end large and increasing numbers of teachers had tried to upgrade themselves independently by taking external degrees which was possible from the Training Colleges attached to universities. This practice was deliberately discouraged by the Board of Education as part of the general policy of keeping ex-elementary teachers out of secondary schools, because they were officially viewed as 'uncultured and imperfectly educated . . . creatures of tradition and routine'.[231] The Board thus exhibited a 'caste' attitude which rebuffed the upward aspirations of elementary teachers by imposing a firm dividing line between elementary and secondary studies and enforcing its own concept of elitist secondary instruction.

The nature of teacher training was obviously crucial to the increase of expertise. Thus the teachers initially welcomed the idea of amalgamating the Pupil Teacher Centres with secondary schooling and the Training Colleges with the universities, which would then prepare both elementary and secondary teachers. However, this hope of acquiring culture backfired, for the replacement of the PTCs by bursarships to secondary schools proved a route which was too long and expensive for the traditional hardcore of working class recruits. Falling recruitment in turn made it impossible to drive out the hoard of 'supplementary' teachers: in response to LEA pressures the Board conceded their right to remain during this period, and by legalizing this practice the State was manipulating the legal machinery against professional upgrading in a clear use of Tactic 2. This of course was diametrically opposed to the NUT aim of weeding out the untrained and partly qualified as well as terminating the Board's Acting Teachers Examination.[232] Furthermore, the amalgamation of the Training Colleges and Universities did not take place, and the stereotype of the LEA municipal day-training college for the elementary teacher and university for the secondary teacher still held good. The latter never contemplated teaching at elementary level until driven to it by unemployment in the 1940s.

The NUT was equally aware that attempts at upgrading were foundering upon low pay and low status, the latter the fault of the Board, the former of the LEAs, which failed to attract a high calibre of entrants. There were many struggles with separate LEAs, often involving strike action, militant tactics and mass resignations, but it was obvious to the Union that ultimately only a national salary scale, underwritten by the State, would solve the problem. Militancy proved influential for the Board required professional co-operation to implement the Fisher Act of 1918, and was alarmed at the degree of professional alienation. Nevertheless, although the introduction of the Burnham Committee and its minimum pay scales represented a gain in procedural terms, the actual cash settlement left the teachers marginally worse off in real terms than before the war. In other words upgrading, either of the level of expertise or its rate of exchange as measured by remuneration, had not got very far during this period.

Self-Regulation

Just as upgrading was seen as the key to professional status, independence was perceived as fundamental to professional influence:

> The average teacher looked upon the average doctor or lawyer with envy, not because of their superior emoluments but because of their superior independence. The teaching profession was crushed beneath the downward thrust of external authority. They suffered from a multitude of masters — the Board of Education, the local authority, the general public.[233]

Against this background W. W. Hill put a resolution to the NUT for 'professional self-government and full partnership in administration'[234] and this ambition was the main reason why school teachers turned their backs on the TUC. As an interim step the first priority was to put certification into the hands of an independent representative body to protect the value of their diplomas from government tampering and to drive the unqualified out of the profession.

These aims were also in the interests of secondary teachers but in addition the latter sought to distinguish themselves from the elementary category. Consequently they pursued the notion of a Teachers' Registration Council as the mechanism through which a self-governing profession could be constituted and protected against the incursion of the unqualified. The NUT was in full agreement but was forced to oppose the College of Preceptors which had sponsored a Bill for the registration of secondary teachers alone, since this would constitute a new legal barrier denying its members entry to secondary posts. As the only body which had been trained to teach and as one which considered that many of its current tasks fell within the secondary field, the NUT was bound to resist any attempt to impose a precise definition of elementary schooling or restrict the title of 'professional' to those holding posts in grammar schools. But the polity intervened to support the interests of the secondary teachers, using its legal powers to issue the 'caste' register of 1902 which prescribed a double column entry listing separately those qualified to teach in elementary and in secondary schools. This use of Tactic 2 (legal intervention) to revise the single alphabetical list which Parliament had sanctioned in 1899 and for which the NUT had campaigned, infuriated the elementary organization. In the uproar that followed (the register was never actually printed) the Board would have been delighted to drop the Council altogether and revert to the traditional procedure by which it itself determined the 'recognition' of secondary schools. However, confronted with the choice between no professional council at all or compromise with the elementary teachers, a rapprochement took place between the secondary associations and the NUT and they jointly endorsed the single column Register. Although Morant dragged his feet, fearing the influence elementary teachers would exert on it, the Teachers Registration Council was finally established in 1912. In principle the profession had achieved a major step towards self-regulation: in practice the Board refused to cede any legal powers to the new Council. The TRC made the distinction between the qualified and the unqualified but had no sanctions to compel registration or penalize those who remained unregistered or unsuitable for registration. As a move towards self-government the Council had been wrecked by a professional disunity on which the polity had capitalized to enfeeble its powers.[235]

This division between elementary and secondary teachers was also mirrored in their differential progress towards the autonomous control of classroom activities in the two types of schools. On the one hand the secondary teachers achieved a considerable extension of professional powers over examinations which also involved public recognition of their expertise. The Secondary Schools Examination Council (1917), founded to co-ordinate the various university bodies conducting secondary examinations and to produce broadly comparable School Certificates, was more than an advisory committee to government. Its composition included teachers representatives, it carried out administrative functions on behalf of the Board, and it only referred back in controversial cases.[236] This was extremely important as it gave the secondary teachers substantial formal control over curricula and examinations since, together with university representatives, academic members outweighed educational administrators. This new foothold was to be extremely important – it gave the classroom back to the teacher, it meant that the downward influence always exerted by examinations was now engineered by academic colleagues rather than imposed by officialdom, and it provided a recognized platform from which the profession could influence further policy.

As far as the elementary teachers were concerned this particular battle over the management of knowledge had already been waged and won in the 1890s, with the abandoning of the Revised Code. Their victory was clearly inscribed in the government *Handbook of Suggestions for the Consideration of Teachers* (1918 edition);

> the only uniformative practice that the Board of Education desire to see in the teaching of the public elementary schools is that each teacher shall think for himself and work out by himself such methods of teaching as may use his power to the best advantage and best suited to the particular needs and conditions of the school.[237]

Thus their problem was not about the definition of instruction but about the supervision of teaching. At the local level a significant degree of self-regulation had been achieved by the appointment of ex-teachers to the LEA inspectorate, in contrast to the HMIs who were usually public school men from Whitehall. The leakage to the press of the

'Holmes-Morant' circular, in which the local inspectors were berated as 'uncultured' and 'routine', revealed the Board's attitude to the elementary teacher. It also explained the real reason why official policy prevented this category of teacher from aspiring to the central Inspectorate but instead placed those whose background included no experience of state-aided schools in a supervisory capacity over them. If, on the one hand, this revealed how far the elementary teachers still had to go towards self-governing status, the ensuing fracas indicated that the NUT had made some headway in political insertion and influence.

Insertion

At the local level, the constitution of the new LEAs made some insertion possible as teachers were eligible to serve on a council outside the area in which they were employed. The NUT ensured that full advantage was taken of this provision and by 1904 nearly 600 teachers were already members of Education Committees or advisory bodies. Nevertheless, this was inadequate to modify local policy, particularly where money was at stake, and the whole period witnessed a protracted struggle between teachers and the LEAs over the related questions of pay and unqualified staff. So acrimonious were these relations that H. A. L. Fisher briefly toyed with the unprecedented (and unliberal) idea of making teachers civil servants.[238] Meanwhile the profession was slowly managing to insert itself at the level of the central administration. The 1902 Act had provided for a Consultative Committee to advise on matters submitted to it by the Board. Although the latter made sure that it did not participate in administration and steered clear of contemporary policies, it established a valuable precedent which was commended by the 1918 Committee on the Machinery of Government. It was the first of many advisory committees on education which were to come, and although all remained strictly consultative they did represent public channels for the national diffusion of professional values and policies. Furthermore the aftermath of the Holmes-Morant affair, in which the NUT 'humbled the government' by forcing Morant's resignation (largely because the Conservatives used this stick to beat the Liberals), also issued in a more conciliatory attitude on the part of the Board. Basically however the profession was not yet sufficiently inserted to have much positive influence on policy or to provide a protective cushioning for its members against the impact of central and local policies upon them.

Professional Values

Neither the professional associations nor unions had elaborated a coherent set of values which commanded general consensus. Perhaps the strongest common denominator at this time was the general endorsement of professionalism in education, not merely as a polite name for a closed shop, but as a normative conviction that what was good for the teacher was also good for education and vice versa. The school teachers also gave their championship to expansionism, especially in secondary and technical education. Beyond these two dominant themes, professional values trailed off into a diffuse sponsorship of various humanistic courses — the half-timer, the undernourished, the unhealthy and the feeble minded. Neither part of the profession had as yet been seriously influenced by the progressive movement which was to provide it with a well-delineated value system, the new orthodoxy of the next period. Until the end of the war the profession had no collective conspectus on educational development, it was too preoccupied with the perennial concerns of trade unionism, and its negotiating strength was too weak to act as a spur to the elaboration of detailed blueprints which were condemned to remain as academic exercises at this time.

The Academics, 1902-18

Unlike the school teachers this was not yet to be a period of collective action on the part of the academics or the university institutions: but then again, unlike the school teachers, it was not an era in which academia was subject to strong political control. Instead it was a time during which all the various universities were making their separate bids for financial survival and what could literally be called the primitive accumulation of capital. These actions were only to have a cumulative effect for higher education because by and large all university institutions, confronted with the same problems of poverty and the same array of potential suppliers, responded in broadly similar ways. They sought to increase their earnings by offering services to a wide range of social groups, but to do so in such a way as not to infringe their fragile autonomy; for not only was the development of self-government a prime goal in its own right, but a certain degree of academic freedom was also a pre-condition of being able to earn resources. Without sufficient freedom to devise the training and research programmes which would attract capital and produce a surplus to be devoted to internally defined goals (which in turn reinforced their autonomy), the academics would remain trapped in their initial bargaining position. Instead they attempted to break out by deploying their limited freedom of action to offer rather more attractive services and to steadily amplify the scope of both, until they had brought about the positive feedback loop just outlined — which leads to morphogenesis rather than morphostasis. This strategy was underway before the First World War but it did not achieve the conditions necessary for substantial internal initiation until later on. That it actually got off the ground was because the polity took a permissive attitude towards links with industry as was seen in the discussion of external transactions. Even when the polity had itself become a significant supplier, it did not attempt to use financial dependence or any other tactic to strengthen its own control over the universities. Fundamentally this seems to be because the political requirements which crystallized during the war were well serviced by the universities (as part of their own strategy of course) and there was no obvious sense in which government would get a better deal through increased control. At all events this permissiveness played a vital part in letting the university teachers start off on the long road to improving their negotiating strength in the four relevant respects.

Attractive Services

For the universities there was no question of upgrading, their expertise was already very high and growing yearly, so the main concern was to improve the exchange rate which it commanded. The basic tactic was very straightforward, and consisted in offering attractive services in terms of research and training to those who would pay for them, industry being the most obvious target. What we examined under external transactions was the university *response to explicit industrial demands*, but 'in so far as industry valued the universities before the First World War, it was chiefly for their science and technology'.[239] Yet some academics were convinced that a broader range of disciplines could contribute to industry and commerce and set about *creating industrial demand* for new kinds of university services. Often, like the attempt to harness economics to commercial education, the initiative was taken by particular individuals from within their own institution in the face of disapproval from colleagues and indifference from the market. Since it was very much a buyers' market, the onus was on the universities in question to promote their services through agencies like their own Appointments Boards, but once a new offering was taken up other universities were quick to imitate and make the service generally available. The earnings gained in this fashion were received in two ways, which corresponded roughly but imperfectly to their research and training services: the first was through donations, subscriptions and endowments, the second through student fees, which often represented the single most important source of university income before the war, and averaged out at about 30 percent of their total revenue.[240] Obviously the two sources of earnings were reinforcing — the better the reputation of a given centre for a special line of applied research, the more students would apply (or be encouraged to apply by firms and technical schools) for courses in that subject. In turn graduates, entering industry in growing numbers, took with them a knowledge of the research facilities available at their *alma mater*.

Over a decade later the universities gained a relatively new customer with considerable purchasing power. At the beginning of the war, as H. A. L. Fisher noted, 'there was a most inadequate apprehension of the results which might be derived from the laboratories and brains of the universities'.[241] Official recognition of their research contribution and effective industrial training techniques (for munitions workers, mechanics, engineers and aeronautical instructors)[242] led to a 'cult of technology' and a new official demand for what the universities had to offer. Official demand was backed-up with official funds. Government grants had been paid since the 'whisky money' of 1889 but they had remained relatively small and a substantial proportion was to cover the costs of teacher training.

The war marked both a quantitative and a qualitative development of government investment in higher education. Prodded by resolutions from professors and deputations from the Royal Society as well as their own immediate experiences, the Government undertook much more responsibility towards science and its practical applications. The foundation and funding of the Department of Scientific and Industrial Research to encourage 'research of special timeliness and promise'[243] did two important things: it represented a new buyer, for it gave direct financial assistance to research projects in different university departments, and it actually encouraged industry, the academics' main alternative supplier, to make more intensive use of their professional expertise.[244] This felicitous influence, which owed everything to the successful wartime co-operation of firms, scientists and officials, had far reaching consequences for the strategy of academics. It allowed them, and even encouraged them, to approach the two richest institutions in society — industry and the State — to offer what they would in exchange for what they could get. In obtaining two wealthy suppliers the academics had achieved the main condition for improving the rate of exchange and accumulating a surplus to devote to its own ends. Before they could do the latter, however, the profession had to strengthen its autonomy (self-determination) and influence (insertion) to prevent the use of its new resources from being pre-empted by others and it also had to consolidate a collective value-system, specifying the goals the university teachers sought to achieve.

Self-Regulation

Industry and the State, the universities' dual suppliers, both represented a threat to professional self-government. The close involvement with industry did lead to some fears of encroachment, which dated back to the foundation of the civic universities and was the price paid for the generous injection of capital which had enabled them to be launched. In this period the acquisition of a second major supplier in the State, although involving a threat of government intervention, was wholly beneficial in its proximate consequences. It enabled the universities to play-off its two suppliers against one another to their own advantage. In discussing this point Sanderson argues that industrial encroachment 'was nothing like so serious as the danger that would have arisen from the withdrawal of business interest and support. More important in our view was the way in which many of these institutions which might have remained merely technical colleges were moulded to become genuine multi-disciplinary universities by the pressures of Victoria, the London external degree and the government grant'.[245] The latter, administered by an Advisory Committee on University Grants provided a body behind which the universities could shelter, protesting that they would prejudice their position if they concentrated on banal research projects or schemes of vocational training. It was mainly a device for politely declining unwanted external transactions, but it also provided the funds and the encouragement for broader academic developments, with few official strings attached, as did the DSIR. The reasons for this situation rather than the materialization of government intervention, are properly part of the insertion theme.

Insertion

The early history of what was to become the University Grants Committee is instructive in this respect. Grant income was originally distributed by an ad hoc Committee on Grants to University Colleges until 1904. Then, as the grant increased, this task passed to a more prestigious but *still ad hoc* University Colleges Committee under R. B. Haldane, one of the few politicians to forsee the wartime contribution of university science and to try to make 'an English Charlottenburg' out of Imperial College and other Charlottenburgs out of the regional universities.[246] This in turn recommended the formation of a permanant advisory body to disburse exchequer grants, as part of a general attempt to stabilize the tenuous position of the civic universities. Significantly, the first chairman was a Professor (later Sir William McCormick), who went on to become the first chairman of the Advisory Council to the DSIR and of the UGC itself until 1930. By 1911 the Advisory Committee on University Grants was composed *entirely of academics* and it was under the influence of such a body, directly responsible to the President of the Board of Education (H. A. L. Fisher, himself an ex-academic historian), that the grants 'were paid over without earmarking to the universities' general income to be expended at their discretion'.[247] The threat of State 'dirigism' which had formed some part of Haldane's approach[248] in 1905 had been averted. The cushioning effect of this insertion on the UGC was vital in insulating the universities from direct political control, but it was the effect of insertion by influential individual academics or their close collaborators, not of collective professional or institutional associations.

Only towards the very end of the war was there any realization of the advantages to be derived from professional organization either in pay negotiations or in policy formation. In the early years of the century

> the very real autonomy of the universities and colleges led to a great variety of pay and conditions and ... the absence of a national paymaster, made it pointless to organize nationally ... Yet these same reasons also made it inevitable that the pressure for national organization, when it finally came, should come from the non-professorial staff of the civic universities and university colleges.[249]

With the growth of government financing they saw for the first time the possibility of deflecting some of these monies towards better pay and conditions. This was worth organizing for, and the junior teachers were not deterred by abstract fears about a loss of institutional autonomy from which they had never themselves benefited. Ironically it was precisely this anxiety that *any* inter-university organization might *itself* infringe institutional independence which had caused the universities to hang back from any type of co-operation. 'Another effect of the growth of government aid, of ultimate advantage to the unification of the academic profession, was the dim yet growing realization on the part of university chief administrators that unity had advantages when facing a common paymaster'.[250] These two movements, the one towards professional organization, which was later to crystallize into the AUT, and the other towards institutional organization, which was to develop into the Committee of Vice-Chancellors, finally took root at the end of this period. They were to transform insertion from a personal phenomenon dependent on the reputation and contacts of individual academics into a professional, organized and representative phenomenon in the interwar years.

Professional Value System
Equally the emergence of any collective opinion about the place of the universities in society had to await full professionalization. Disparate normative perspectives emanated from various institutions, but although statements of intent, proclamations of ultimate goals, and exhortations to normative change abounded, it was never very clear whom these views represented or whether they were at all representative. Only organizations, speaking on behalf of a wide and well defined constituency, could answer these questions with conviction and make claim to a public hearing and an influence on policy, after, that is, they had aggregated and articulated the diffuse and diverse values propagated in academic circles before the war.

The School Teachers, 1918-44

The interwar years saw the profession making progress towards all the four conditions which improve negotiating strength vis-à-vis the polity and this leads to the expectation of a significant amount of internal initiation for the first time. Improvement on at least three of these conditions is attributable to the activities of professional organizations, especially those of the NUT. By 1918 its membership was 100,000 and rising: it had embraced the uncertificated teachers and was reaching out in the hope of forming a single professional union with the secondary associations — the Joint Four, the ATCDE (which indicates that the college teachers were seen as an integral part of the teaching body), as well as with separate elementary unions, the NAS and NAHT. The formula for federation was as weak as it was uncontentious; the 'profession would thus show a united front on matters on which all associations were agreed, but each union was free to act in opposition. In practice, federation on these terms offered teachers nothing which they did not already possess; it did not require a formal constitution to permit unions to co-operate among themselves in areas of common agreement, and the proposed structure did little to bring unions together on issues which divided them'.[251] The problem was that objective differences in the vested interests of various parts of the profession had not been tackled, and the disunity which continued to emanate from them was a reason (or an excuse) for denying a greater degree of self-government.

Upgrading

Although the proportion of uncertificated staff was now falling, there was fear of postwar dilution by the untrained given that the profession had not gained control over entry. This threat did not turn out to be severe and by the nineteen-thirties an increase of graduates among elementary personnel and of trained teachers amongst secondary staff was pronounced. In 1921 only 1.3 percent of elementary teachers had graduated, by 1938 this had risen to 7.3 percent, whilst by the same date a clear majority of secondary teachers had received training on top of their degrees.[252] Nevertheless, these improvements in qualifications still had a long way to go and, as the product of individual self-help, they were undoubtedly repressed by the socio-political context in which they took place, since it afforded little incentive for making the personal sacrifices on whose accumulation this collective upgrading then depended.

The level of teachers' remuneration reflected the low esteem in which their expertise was held by central and local government. Partly this was due to the general economic crisis, but even here the low status of the teachers made them vulnerable to more savage cut-backs than those experienced by their university colleagues. The Committee on National Expenditure (Geddes) had imposed a 5 percent reduction of salaries and transferred superannuation to a contributory scheme, a regressive move of rather dubious legality. Although the Burnham Committee protected salaries from another 15 percent cut which the LEAs sought in 1924, and to some extent stabilized wages, the Committee on National Expenditure (May) tried to dock a further 20 percent in 1931, while the strongest protest only commuted this to 10 percent. At last in the 1930s freedom from unemployment and falling prices appeared to be associated with a rise in professional status in society. The NUT was quick to digest this lesson and from the 1930s onwards increased expertise, professional upgrading, and high secure remuneration were seen as inextricably linked.

This was clear in the NUT Report (1939) on 'The Training of Teachers and Grants to Intending Teachers'. Its first and most important recommendation was that 'in the interests of a unified educational system and a united profession, it is essential that every teacher should be of graduate status and trained'.[253] In other words the union had determined that their members must acquire the only qualification which the authorities respected, the university degree, if they were to obtain a decent rate of exchange from them. The NUT report was submitted to the Government Committee (McNair) set up to investigate the recruitment and training of teachers in 1942. The McNair recommendations concluded that in future only qualified teachers should be recognized – but went no further towards the NUT ideal of a unified graduate profession. The latter welcomed it, nevertheless, because it laid much stress on improving salaries, and immediate past experience had convinced the NUT of the ineluctable connection between status and remuneration. For exactly the same reason it greeted the 1944 Act enthusiastically; it seemed to raise the barrier holding back the upgrading of elementary teachers and to allow the school teachers to break out of the vicious circle of low pay – low status – low expertise. Thus to its Secretary the 'most magnificent thing in this Bill is that it removes the word "Elementary" from the nomenclature of British Education. And with that goes the badge of inferiority that has so long clung to the elementary schools. Implied in that one clause is the unification and consolidation of the teaching profession'.[254] This speech was made to the Campaign for Educational Advance, formed to press for the introduction of the 1944 Bill, and it seems clear that one of the main reasons why teachers championed it was great professional expectations about what it would do for their own upgrading.

Self-Regulation

At the local level the period witnessed a growing partnership between the NUT and the Association of Education Committees. Better relations led to specific improvements for the profession – the end of 'obnoxious interference' or 'extraneous duties' and the establishment of joint machinery to avoid cases of capricious dismissal. In general the LEAs began to involve the NUT in any school reorganization which affected teachers and to acknowledge professional rights to consultation, participation and autonomy. This was reinforced by the entry of elementary teachers to the Inspectorate which liberated them from the classroom criticism and censure of those not conversant with the practical problems they confronted. This new harmony with the HMIs was to be of considerable importance in encouraging innovations in teaching and learning as the two came to share a common set of pedagogical values in this period. At central level, however, the most important advance came when the Board terminated the Acting Teachers examination and relinquished the responsibility of examining for certification. Henceforth the Board's certificate would endorse the award made by the academic authority in question. Thus, after 84 years, certification had passed out of direct government control. By 1930, eleven groups of Training Colleges had been formed around the universities and two NUT representatives had been invited to sit on the National Committee for the Certification of Teachers, which surveyed the work of these regional bodies. The new examining arrangements of 1930 had not introduced any constitutional linkage between colleges and universities or any formal integration of their activities: but the NUT was now stating that it wanted both as a way of acquiring greater freedom and intellectual upgrading at one and the same time. Its (1939) report on teacher training insisted that 'every training college should become an integral part of a university and should provide an alternative but equivalent form of training to that followed by the student working for a degree'.[255]

The reaction of the McNair Committee (1942) was sympathetic; it opposed centralization in teacher training, it envisaged closer administrative links between the colleges and the universities (via Institutes of Education), and it advocated financing the colleges through a block grant to the universities which would greatly have increased their financial autonomy. The kernel of this Report was rejected as the LEAs insisted on keeping administration and finance in their own hands. Thus 'the close co-operation and pooling of resources which McNair saw as essential to the success of the School of Education idea in no sense became general in the twenty years after 1944'.[256] The LEAs rejected direct financing as they were to do again after the Robbins report, for their ensuing autonomy would have decreased college responsiveness to political control (Tactic 3). This audacious attempt to shift the balance of power towards self-government had failed in its structural aspects, although not in its cultural ones, as intellectual tutelage had now passed to the academics.

Insertion

Considerable progress was made in inserting the profession at both central and local levels in administrative, political and consultative positions, enabling the profession to influence both the formation and application of policy — giving professional proposals a serious hearing during decision-making and allowing it to cushion and modify political directives before these reached the schoolroom. Their advisory influence was extended because of the sheer quality and the public importance attached to the seven Reports (including the Hadow ones) produced by the Consultative Committees between the wars. They were infused with professional values and the attention they progressively commanded amongst educated opinion ensured the national diffusion of the new pedagogy. The Consultative Committee to Government was to be of lasting significance in relation to educational policy and the zone of influence it had won for itself was recognized in the 1944 Act where it was replaced by a similar body — the Central Advisory Council for England. This had a wider brief — to advise the Minister on 'such matters connected with educational theory and practice as they think fit, and upon any questions referred to them by him'[257] and, for the first time, the legal right to initiate its own investigations on topics of its choice. Furthermore the purely consultative influence of such organs had begun to be amplified by an overlap between their membership and that of parliamentary pressure groups. R. H. Tawney, for example, was an active member of the Hadow Committee and also dominated the Council for Educational Advance pressing for the introduction of the 1944 Bill. The overlapping of personnel between political agencies and advisory organisms spelt further integration between the shaping of opinion and the introduction of policy — a link between educational ideas and political action.

At the local level relations between the NUT and the LEAs improved considerably, partly again because of a growing overlap between the two categories, many Directors of Education and LEA Inspectors being ex-elementary school teachers and NUT Members, and partly through working together on the difficult salary negotiations of the period. Relationships with the Board got off to a good start after the profession had supported Fisher's Act of 1918 and remained cordial under his successor. It became common to refer to a 'friendly and conspiratorial triumvirate' made up of three long serving officers: Sir Frederick Mander (Secretary of the NUT 1931-47), Sir Maurice Holmes (Permanent Secretary of the Board of Education 1936-45) and Sir Percival Sharp (Secretary of the Association of Education Committees 1925-45). The progressive insertion of the teaching profession and of its main organization, the NUT, especially in the late thirties and early forties, probably made the school teachers one of the earliest beneficiaries of the new conservative corporatism which continued to develop after the war.

Professional Value System

Besides the continuing endorsement of professionalism, expansionism and egalitarianism, these general themes were also integrated into a highly articulate pedagogical system during this period. Increasingly the progressive philosophy which had been hammered out in experimental schools in the private sector now spread to the profession in general. The process involved was not one of vague cultural diffusion, instead the path taken by influential educators can be logged fairly precisely and it is important to note that the positions and platforms from which they disseminated their views would not have been available, but for the progress that teachers in the public sector had made towards academic self-government.

The progressives had always set themselves up as opinion leaders and increasingly they inserted themselves in influential positions for moulding professional attitudes. Percy Nunn as Professor of Education at London University had provided the progressives with a text book, *Education: Its Data and First Principles*, which affected the outlook and practice of a generation of trainee teachers.[258] Increasingly the colleges and university departments provided a haven for those seeking to spread progressive ideas and methods, like Susan Isaacs who became Head of the new Department of Child Development at the London Institute of Education, and provided a platform from which they could evangelize. By the mid-thirties they had succeeded in consolidating a new educational orthodoxy which was spilling over beyond the profession itself. Thus progressive ideas became the established educational theory. By 1939 a substantial majority of opinion leaders worked within the progressives' intellectual orbit. Most of those who wrote books on education, spoke at Conferences, produced official reports or sat on important committees, trained teachers, or contributed to the educational journals came to accept progressive views as a basis for their own thinking.[259]

The Academics, 1918-44

In terms of professional organization the academics lagged behind the school teachers: they were not yet a united body though they were preoccupied with becoming one in this period. Consequently in their interactions with different social groups, university teachers were not steering towards a collectively defined goal. Again then, the improved negotiating strength of the academics between the wars must be attributed to the cumulative influence of active individuals, departments and institutions as much as to the nascent AUT. Equally important, especially whilst the professional association was being rapidly and belatedly consolidated, was the absence of political constraint — of any of the four tactics resisting the search for resources and the quest for autonomy, which are the pre-conditions of internal innovation. Given this political permissiveness, internal initiation would have been much richer had it not been for the prolonged economic crisis which hit the universities' two major suppliers equally hard. In this gloomy context the range of innovations taking place is surprising and gives some indication of the directions internal initiation would take and the ends it would serve when released from financial stringency in the next period.

Attractive Services
In this economic situation new suppliers and sources of income were obviously not forthcoming and the task of the academics was to maintain the flow of resources from its two main clients, industry and government, despite the financial difficulties of both institutions. It was not an encouraging background against which to hope for an improvement in the exchange rate, but on the other hand the demands for their services increased substantially in the aftermath of war. More of the (demobilized) students were oriented towards careers in science and technology; factory production had received the usual wartime spur to the development of new techniques and industry was thus offering

contracts and consultancies to academics; and various Government agencies besides the UGC and DSIR looked to the universities to conduct research projects in areas like medicine, agriculture and fishery. 'Not that these multiple demands on their services were unwelcome to the universities and their staffs. Far from it: they were only too glad to extend their activities in any interesting and intellectually profitable direction, provided only that the money was available to support them'.[260]

This was the basic problem. Although industry was prepared to pay quite well, especially in the fields which had developed during the first world war, a war of chemistry, thus helping to establish a more reciprocal exchange rate between them, their demands were limited to a fairly restricted circle of disciplines. Government demands, however, which were spread more widely, were also coupled with a really firm determination to keep the exchange rate down.

> There, however, was the rub. For the government and the public which demanded so much and increasingly more from the universities was less than willing to pay adequately for it. On the other side from the constant public pressure for expansion there was, paradoxically, an equally constant public pressure for retrenchment. Whatever the universities did by way of development and service was too little, whatever they asked for by way of financial support was too much.[261]

This was the consistent reaction of the polity throughout the period. The Geddes axe (chopping 20 percent off the recurrent grant) and the further cut in the great slump of 1932 only intensified the underlying attitude, given the dramatic worsening of economic conditions. There is no doubt that successive governments were well aware what they were about, that to keep the exchange rate down was to inhibit internal academic developments and that protest could be silenced by threats to university autonomy, the essential pre-condition for attracting more resources. Thus a deputation of university representatives to the Chancellor of the Exchequer, over pay and superannuation in 1920, provoked this revealing reply from Austin Chamberlain:

> The universities have extended beyond their means. They have been more anxious to extend than to pay their existing staffs properly; and accordingly, the salaries are much too low. My opinion is, you ought not to extend into new fields until you have been able to pay decently, I do not say extravagantly or richly, because I think it will never be a well paid profession.[262]

He proceeded to remind them that the government grant had recently topped the £1 million mark, warning that any further dependence on State aid might entail a loss of university autonomy, and suggesting that they earned more resources themselves by putting up student fees.[263]

Thus the overall effect of relations with the polity was to keep the exchange rate down and thus to reduce the surplus resources which could be devoted to internally defined ends. Nevertheless, the universities were not in a position of financial dependence, the State still only contributed about 30 percent of their income despite absolute increases. Nor, as Chamberlain's attitude shows, did government seek to bar alternative (industrial) suppliers, or actually reduce the academic autonomy essential to higher earnings, despite its threats to this effect. The universities continued to transact with industry, to the limits of the latter's ability, and to accumulate what they could; but the combined effect of political retrenchment and industrial crisis prevented the exchange rate from tilting towards them. Consequently, although university teachers wished to develop a wider range of services to other social groups and to undertake new intellectual developments, these innovations were limited though not eliminated by the shortage of funds.

Self-Regulation

The universities became much more solidary bodies in the interwar years and this was to lead to a grand conception of an integrated self-governing profession of *all* teachers, with the universities at its apex. The non-professional staff gradually won security of tenure and representation in university government before the war, as part of a secular and liberal trend away from the traditions imposed by the founders of the civic universities. It was accompanied by a shift towards a more academic form of internal government which integrated the NPS during the general retreat from lay control.[264] But academic self-government was not just a defensive concept: with the growth of internal unity and disappearance of old divides, it became increasingly expansionist. With the appearance of the McNair report on teacher training during the Second World War the universities sought to snatch the initiative and to transform their traditional role in teacher training into cultural hegemony and financial control over the whole profession. In asserting their claim to supreme authority over teacher training in general they were obviously seeking to unify the profession and turn it into a self-regulating body immune from State interference. Thus the AUT argued 'that as the highest stage in the hierarchy of educational institutions, they ought to do what they could to strengthen the whole system; that they had the prestige and ability to establish and maintain academic standards without the rigidity and uniformity of a centralized body, and that they alone were in a position to unify the training of the whole profession, graduate and non-graduate'.[265] Although only academic authority but not financial control was ceded to the universities, this was a step towards professional unity which allowed the academics to reach down and influence school policy, thus helping to shape their own external environment, and permitted the two groups of staff to work together, moulding school and university relations in ways independent of central or local administration.

Insertion

The reasons which had delayed the emergence of a professional organization were also to keep it relatively weak and uninfluential in the two decades following the formation of the AUT in 1919. It was consistently small, there were only 2,277 full time teachers outside Oxbridge at its inception and less than 4,000 in 1939, so that at its best it represented under 2,000 teachers in the 1930s. It had a minute income, a highly amateurish organization and had only just established itself in Oxford and Cambridge before the outbreak of war. The AUT was obviously dependent on joint membership with other professional associations and abandoned the aim of sponsoring its own parliamentary candidates after one attempt in 1922. Above and beyond these considerations was the AUT's own decision to give first priority to improving pay and conditions, rather than to influencing educational policy. Thus its Chairman 'pointed out that the idea which had brought the Association into being was of a trade union character, but he expressed the hope that, when material conditions had been satisfactorily improved, educational matters generally would form the essential points on which discussion would take place'.[266] This early unionist stance and its preoccupation with tenure, status, grading, salaries and superannuation was obviously inimical to insertion in agencies with a wider concern for educational policy.

In the same year, 1919, two other bodies emerged in their final shape, the UGC and the Committee of Vice-Chancellors, completing a triangle of parties whose interaction was powerfully to influence university development and to protect it from undue external or official interference.

The coincidence has an explanation, however; it grew out of the post-war difficulties of the universities, the demand for a much-expanded government grant, and the consequent need for a body to advise the Treasury (rather than the Board of Education) on the size of the grant and control its disbursement, and for two other bodies to watch the interests respectively of the universities as institutions and of their academic staffs as employees and professional men.[267]

In this period a 'watchdog' role is the most that can be assigned to the AUT until the last years of the war, when the pay scales fell from its eyes and it first began to hammer out a comprehensive policy of its own for university development on the basis of an articulated set of professional values.

Professional Values

After the first world war university teachers were divided amongst themselves over the contradictory demands for expansion or retrenchment, technology or culture, utility or elitism. Although it cannot simply be assigned to one side or the other, the AUT was firmly rooted in the unendowed civic universities which depended on recruiting financial support and could not afford to turn their backs on expansion, technology or utility. Given this context the AUT was not won over by the ideological opposition to industrial involvement which was held by some in the thirties to involve serious capitalist interference (Flexner and Laski), neglect of the human sciences (Huxley), or to imply secrecy and censorship (Bernal). Yet if it steered clear of this basically left-wing critique, it heartily endorsed the social democratic position, taking part in the Council for Educational Advance and elaborating its own liberal approach in a sub-committee set up in 1942 to examine Postwar University Development. This advocated both expansionism and egalitarianism, opening the universities 'to all who can profit thereby' (backed up by generous maintenance grants). It indicated a very clear willingness to serve a great diversity of groups and especially the immediate community and region, proposing Extra-Mural departments, People's Colleges and Folk High Schools. This was indicative of a professional value system which now exceeded the pursuit of vested professional interests — pay, sabbatical leave, research time and facilities — which had preoccupied the AUT in its first two decades. However, the pursuit of such values was expensive, and the report acknowlegded the universities' need to earn the necessary resources by continuing to meet demands for practical training and research. Thus point four stressed that the 'universities are part of society both morally and intellectually, and bear a direct responsibility to it. They must therefore study the application of organized knowledge to practical problems, and train men and women for particular tasks.'[268] Nevertheless this was clearly subordinate to point one, which simply stated that 'an essential function of the universities is the pursuit of knowledge not controlled or guided by any private or corporate interest'. In elaborating their collective values the profession was fully conscious of the indispensibility of both academic autonomy and financial resources to the achievement of their internally defined goals for university development.

The School Teachers, 1945-65

With the Act of 1944, the goal of a united profession seemed in sight, but these gains still had to be translated into improved negotiating strength. Once again internal professional disunity reduced organizational effectiveness. Although many of the sectional subgroups (class teachers, heads, Labour, Conservative and Communist teachers; all-age, primary, technical, modern and grammar school teachers) had now been incorporated within the NUT, it still proved impossible to bring about federation with the various unions outside it (the Joint-Four, the secessionist NAS, the National Union of Women Teachers and the new Graduate Teachers Association). New attempts at confederation (1946-51) failed to bring them all into a common Institute of Education, largely because their separate vested interests endured, providing lasting reasons for independence. Nevertheless the NUT was becoming more representative of the whole profession. Its grammar school membership more than tripled between 1938-54, and since two-fifths of graduate teachers now worked *outside* these schools, the NUT was no longer the union of the non-graduates. Both its strength and its weakness were to be crucial in this period of political consensus.

Upgrading

This is the area in which teachers did least well in the post-war period. Obtaining a good salary was seen by the profession as the key to upgrading — and it was in political hands: the polity determined the rate of exchange and kept it low throughout these years, despite militant action on the part of the teachers.[269] Collectively the NUT failed to capitalize on the teacher shortage, critical because of 'the bulge', and this was met by an Emergency Training Scheme which brought 35,000 new teachers into the profession, without Union opposition. Many inside the NUT argued that this shortage could have been used to bring about a general salary rise. However, the quid pro quo for accepting it was a plan to do away completely with the unqualified. Retrospectively it seems that these opponents were right: there is not a trade-off between upgrading and pay. Instead the two are positively correlated, and furthermore any recruitment outside normal channels was regressive in terms of the ideal of a graduate profession.

The salary question was linked to upgrading in another way. When the separate primary and secondary Burnham Committees were collapsed into one, after much controversy it was decided to pay an increased 'graduate allowance'. In one way, this provided a financial incentive for higher qualifications, in another it was a procedural precedent for improving the exchange rate selectively, rather than improving the base rate for the profession as a whole. With the shortage of maths and science teachers in the fifties, when the bulge arrived in the secondary schools, the government recognized that the exchange rate had to rise in order to compete with industry, but it sought to allow this only where it valued professional expertise, by a system of special allowances for those subject specialists. These were introduced by Burnham, and the most the NUT could gain in terms of concessions was an elaborate scheme of special allowances, starting in 1955, for those teaching above 'O' level, which were not confined either to grammar schools or science subjects. The NUT agreed reluctantly, but it did so at a price — namely acceptance of the State's valuation of different phases of a child's education and the subsequent encouragement of the best qualified teachers to concentrate on the older age groups. This also served to undermine the growing professional unity, reflected in a new 'traffic of teachers between schools catering for different age ranges'.[270] Instead it acted to reinforce the old primary/secondary divisions by 'directing' the graduate teacher to the upper forms of the examination school. In addition, anything which reduced unity had further consequences for the other three conditions of internal initiation.

Self-Regulation

The persistent demand for self-regulation continued. The ill-fated Teachers Registration Council was finally snuffed out in 1949, to be followed by NUT pressures for a National Teachers' Institute to control recruitment and dismissal. Disagreement over its form within the profession was the cause or excuse for it making no headway at first.[271] However, a fully representative working party of the NUT, Joint-Four, NAS, NAHT and the ATCDE, with observers from AUT and Headmasters' Conference, was established in 1960 and agreed on seeking a Teachers' General Council, on the same lines as the GMC, to determine entrance qualifications and professional standards. It would be an independent statutory body, with which the unions could negotiate, elected by teachers (unlike the old Registration Council) and free from government control.

Yet having achieved organizational unity — the previous or supposed stumbling block — the Unions received a clear cut answer from the Minister turning down these proposals in 1964. The reasons were principled: it was argued that in a democracy it is the State's duty to control the number, training and qualifications of the teachers in the public interest and a dereliction of those duties to hand them over to a closed self-governing profession. Although redolent of the new political collectivism, and the rhetoric legitimating intervention, this governmental response could be justified legally by reference to the 1944 Act. The Explanatory Memorandum (1943) had stressed that the Bill itself involved 'a recognition of the principle that the public system of education, though administered locally, is the nation's concern'.[272] In other words, a political veto was imposed on a self regulation which would have enhanced resistance to central or local directives.

To some this was a fitting verdict on the status aspirations of a group which had turned its back on the organized working class movement: their aim of joining the traditional professions of the upper middle class had been fundamentally misconceived. No doubt that towards the end of this period many teachers began to see things this way, and no doubt too that as power began to be relocated amongst the organizational Leviathans, in the mid-sixties, it was better to join one of them than to remain in the limbo of semi-professionalism. Nevertheless, whilst Butskellism and the stable balance between the parties lasted, this was the era of the interest groups and in an attempt to woo them, many aspects of self-government were granted separately, even if in toto they fell short of the concerted ideal of the Unions.

The government, as has been seen, had divested itself of examining powers for the certification of teachers, it had created the Central Advisory Council from which professional opinion exerted a powerful influence, and had allowed the Inspectorate to assume the role of senior colleagues not government agents. Most importantly of all, neither the central nor the local authorities provided more than rough guides to school activities and this provided considerable operational autonomy, especially in the non-examination schools.[273] Teaching methods and curriculum were the preserve of the individual schools: technically the only subject prescribed in the 1944 Act was religious education. 'The statutory limitations on what can be done in a school are very few indeed'.[274] Enough security, self-control and autonomy had been gained to allow positive innovations to be undertaken at the level of the schools, and, as we shall see next, enough insertion had taken place to enable the instigation of policy reform at the national level. Although the polity had refused self-governance 'there has been a strong tendency through most of the present century to leave more and more of the question concerning the content of education to local authorities, schools, training colleges, area training organizations and the like. The amount of devolution of authority from the centre that has taken place here is not fully recognized'.[275] In this period it became increasingly visible.

Insertion

During this period when organized interest groups exerted a disproportionate influence, the profession inserted itself like a series of wedges at all levels of decision-making. Writing in 1957, Tropp argued that 'the last few years have in no way lessened the external influence of the NUT. There is a group of twenty-three NUT members in the House of Commons (twenty-one Labour and two Conservative) and teachers and ex-teachers are prominent in local government and all aspects of local, social, political and cultural life. Through its representatives on local educational authorities, area training organizations, universities and education bodies of all kinds, the union's influence is widely spread'.[276] Indeed throughout this period of consensus politics, the NUT developed its informal contacts with the DES, and with officials of the local authority associations. What is crucial here is that in 'many matters the local authorities share the view of the NUT rather than the DES. They do not appear to the NUT to be simply another local dimension of government'.[277]

It is significant of the importance attached to professional influence at the local level that the teachers' unions have consistently opposed subsequent plans for administrative reorganization which would have reduced local control and have augmented that of the centre — such as the Maud report on local government and the Bains report which threatened to erode the powers of the education committees. It is equally important that the AEC, the only local government service with its own national association and representative rights, defended itself with the aid of the teachers against frequent claims that there was no good reason why one part of the service should be so strongly and separately organized. In other words, the NUT and AEC played a mutually supportive role in protecting their extensive autonomous powers of decision-making.

Thus, as Coates[278] has documented, the tradition of close knit relations which emerged in the preceding period was strengthened in the postwar political context. It is this which led Manzer to regard the profession as part of a cordial consensual network underpinning a triumvirate of DES, LEA and the profession.[279] This was not new but it seems clear that the contemporary state of English politics accorded it considerable prominence and ensured that as far as internal initiation was concerned it would not be hampered by continuous political vetoes.

Professional Values

The progressive value system, diffuse and varied as it was, now became the new orthodoxy, not just of the profession itself but of educated and official opinion as well. The professional associations were

> a strong force in creating opinion about the style, organization and content of education. By their membership of successive committees and commissions, on all of which they have had some members even when, as with the CAC appointments, these were 'personal', they were part of the progressive, liberal and child-centered movement which has predominated in British education and which has affected official policies on school examinations, as with the Secondary Schools Examination Council reports from Norwood onwards which regarded examinations as at best a necessary evil, and as in the 'new orthodoxy' which assumes that open schooling in the primary school is best.[280]

Simultaneously, the Inspectorate, now less than ever the right hand men of the Ministry, were also won over and threw their expert weight behind the new approach: 'In the past, HMI's might have been a force for uniformity. They are now a force in favour of school freedom, progressive methods in the primary schools and the right of teachers to develop creatively their own ways of securing progress'.[281]

However, whilst the profession as a whole was fully committed to this parcel of cultural changes (and the classroom practices that accompanied them) it was much less decisive and determined where structural reforms were concerned (and about the political pressures needed to accomplish them). It favoured a general expansionism, a variety and an experimentation in the organization of secondary schooling, and it echoed the call for equality of opportunity. What it did not do was to swing behind a policy for comprehensive reorganization during the whole of this period. Partly this was because of the enduring strength of the Grammar School teachers in the NUT, partly because there seems to have been a lasting fear, from the Spens report onwards, that a single type of secondary school would spell standardization. Also the profession appears to have had more confidence in measures which its members could introduce 'on the ground', in the interests of children, than in legislative reforms dealing with the broader interests of social classes.[282]

The Academics, 1944-64

The university teachers emerged from the war with a greatly enhanced reputation and a much clearer idea of where they were going. This time they had been involved in war activities from the start and their contribution to the development of radar and atomic energy was the supreme vindication of the disengaged research projects which had been autonomously undertaken in physics departments earlier on.[283] A closer co-operation between industry, university and government had come into being, anticipating the managed economy, the consensus politics and technocratic orientation which were the major characteristics of the postwar political scene. This time the AUT was ready with its wholesale review of higher education, published between 1944-45 as a Report on University Development, thus anticipating the disproportionate influence that expert interest groups were to play given a stable balance between the parties and the social democratic consensus.

Attractive Services

The war had convinced society that what the universities had to offer was worth having and its end marked a dramatic shift to a sellers' market. Student numbers rose and kept on rising, the courses which had been treated with indifference by employers ten years earlier (economics and commerce) were suddenly in vogue, and even the arts graduate (not just the language specialists) were readily absorbed by industry. For the first time the university teachers confronted a sellers' market and taking stock of this situation they began to exercise their new powers of discretion as to what should be made available.

Firstly, they reviewed their relationship with industry and put this on a more considered footing, giving due weight to its ethical aspects and insisting that transactions only be concluded at the highest intellectual level – two refinements the profession had not previously been in a position to afford. The profession now tended to advise their industrial clients about their needs, rather than university teachers providing services in direct response to industrial demands. With this went a growing university disinclination to accept subsidized ad hoc research in universities, unless it presented intellectual stimulation, as this might lead to an alien commercial domination over scientific development. Similarly they toughly resisted some of the more anti-intellectual demands emanating from the FBI in the fifties – as epitomized in the retort that we 'cannot put on courses on running the rugger club'.[284]

However, within the parameters of academic excellence the university teachers were more than willing to continue to service industrial management and science: they were simply much more selective and expensive. In the fifties industry was equally willing to pay the price. There was an extraordinary doubling of its benefactions to the universities (from £12 million in 1952-57 to £24 million in 1957-63) and an even more remarkable rise in what these outside bodies were prepared to pay for research (which rose from 6.5 percent of university finance in 1956-57 to 11.1 percent only four years later), representing the largest rise in any source of university income.[285] What is particularly significant about these figures is that they demonstrate how the exchange rate had tilted to favour the universities. By the mid-fifties the AUT established that about 20 percent of the resources of scientific and technological departments, or approximately 5 percent of the total finance of universities, was being devoted to industrial research. In other words, if this 5 percent is compared with the 11 percent above it provides some indication of the positive resource balance now produced for the universities by the higher exchange rate. This surplus was devoted to internal developments, to the forms of diversification and specialization of knowledge sought by academics themselves. Partly this meant an intensification of the 'pure' rather than the 'applied', but partly too it enabled the universities to respond to causes like adult education, which could not pay their way yet were approved by the professional value system, and to service the demands of other professions by taking over the training of their recruits. The financial scope for internal initiation had never been wider, and for the time being their autonomy matched it.

Self-Regulation

Following the unprecedented postwar expansion of student numbers, the universities were receiving an equally unprecedented amount of financial support from the State. The governmental contribution doubled from the end of the last period (34 percent of university income in 1938-39) to the middle of this one (66.5 percent of university income in 1951-52).[286] As long as industry was pouring in money equally enthusiastically, i.e. throughout this period, the question of financial dependence on State did not present itself. Perhaps it is truer to say that whilst the universities were revelling in their new found wealth and public esteem they did not heed the danger signals, which retrospectively seem to have been clear enough. Already in 1946 the formal terms of reference of the UGC had been extended and now included a new task ... 'to assist, in consultation with the universities and other bodies concerned, the preparation and execution of such plans for the development of the universities as may from time to time be required in order to ensure that they are fully adequate to national needs'.[287] Soon the UGC was introducing earmarked grants, supplementing the recurrent grant, to encourage vocational study and research in officially approved areas (e.g. medicine, agriculture, dentistry and youth leadership). The universities protested at this interference with their autonomy and the channelling of their efforts into politically defined areas, but were rebuffed with the argument that none needed to accept this additional revenue which did not affect their block grants. Grants earmarked for such purposes continued to rise from £8.9 million in 1947-48 to £16.6 million in 1951-52 and came to represent 30 percent of the total recurrent grant.[288] Moreover, such 'dependence on public finance on an unprecedented scale was accompanied by a new pattern of relations between the Government and the universities. The machinery remained ostensibly the same, but the University Grants Committee acquired a more initiating and executive role'.[289]

Tactic one, the manipulation of financial dependence on the part of the polity, had shown the first signs of coming into play; all that restrained it and prevented it from being linked with Tactic 3, under-mining institutional autonomy, was the existence of enthusiastic alter-native suppliers. In retrospect, the university teachers proved poor strategists, they seem to have got off on the wrong foot from the start of the period. Their 1944-45 Report, criticizing the consequences of ad hoc industrial research, proposed rationalization by establishing a separate Research Council for each industry under the general direction of a Government body which would funnel State and industrial funds to the appropriate universities and institutes. This academic attitude demonstrated no awareness that their best protection against State intervention lay in the maintenance of the strongest and most proxi-mate links with its non-government suppliers, so as to ensure that the State could not reduce the universities to financial dependency. Although none of these dangers to autonomy materialized whilst the recovery and postwar economic boom continued (on the contrary it was the richest period yet for internal initiation), the profession was now in a strategically vulnerable position. Any collapse of industrial support (i.e. the natural equivalent of Tactic 2, the barring of alter-native suppliers) would immediately leave the profession at the financial mercy of government (Tactic 1) and would open the door to forces ready to undermine autonomy (Tactic 3).

Insertion

The history of postwar insertion on the part of the universities is a mixture of the successful exploits of a pressure group and the successive failures of a would-be corporation. On the one hand the AUT made great efforts to ensure the political circulation of its postwar report and held a meeting with MPs in 1944 after which it issued the 'Memo-randum on University Needs'. That so many of its proposals were achieved is indicative of its influence and adoption in political circles. Similarly it was wholly successful in condemning a project which the Labour Government appeared to favour, between 1949-51, for tech-nological institutes outside the universities. The AUT view was that such developments should be secured by university expansion and that no branch of technology should be excluded from university depart-ments. Again an all-Party Meeting with MPs was followed immediately by a White Paper recommending a Technological University, and, with the return of the Conservatives, by a new policy expanding Imperial College. The examples could be multiplied, and would include successful expansionist pressures pre-dating Robbins, and all point to a condition of considerable political influence during this period of consensus government favouring pressure groups.

However, the opposite appears to have been the case whenever the profession and the universities attempted to acquire a more corporate role in policy formation. The only end product of the campaign for an Academic Council for the co-ordination and planning of university development was the Home Universities Conference, a pale reflection of the original concept since it merely involved an annual meeting of Vice-Chancellors, academics, lay governors, AUT and UGC representatives, which aired views but passed no resolutions and could take no action. New attempts were made to generate a more permanant and effective co-ordinating body and the AUT weighed the notion of a British Council of Universities only to discard it as too unwieldy in size. Subsequently there was some attempt to revivify the HUC and increase external contracts by subordinating it to a joint conference with industrialists, but this also failed to prove an effective formula.

Failure at corporate insertion was closely paralleled by a similar fate for professional organization. The establishment of uniform salary scales for university teachers was a symptom of UGC encroachment. 'This was an objective for which the AUT had striven from its earliest years, but the manner of its achievement underlined the weakness of the Association and indeed of the universities in face of the growing domination of the State'.[290] The professional association was accorded no official negotiating role with regard to salaries: the UGC was not even compelled to give it a hearing. Although the AUT shed its traditionally amateur organization and attempted to become as professional as those with whom it had to deal, it neither succeeded in inserting itself in the governing elite nor in equalling the countervailing powers of the trade unions. Certainly in the fifties it finally saw the establishment of a formal salary negotiating machinery made up of the Vice-Chancellors, the UGC and AUT but in a sense this came too late, slippage had already occurred in academic relativities with other professions, as the National Incomes Commission concluded in 1964.[291] At the same time the NIC rejected the notion of an independent review body which Robbins had proposed and the AUT had welcomed. Instead, the monitoring of university salaries was passed to the Prices and Incomes Board which turned the AUT's demands down flatly, in a way few employers could have done, on the pretext of breaking the inflationary chain of wage settlements. As a trade union the AUT had made a poor showing which, as an inherently small association, was presumably what encouraged it to take part in the foundation of a Confederation of Professional and Public Service Organizations in 1962. However the diversity of professional interests deprived this body of the socio-economic solidarity of the TUC: the Confederation made little headway, failed to win representation on the National Economic Development Council, and the AUT withdrew in 1964. Thus by the end of this period the AUT had failed to make the transition from interest group politics, which had served it well so far, to the new large-scale corporatism with which it had to contend from the mid-sixties onwards.

Professional Value Systems

Expansionism and egalitarianism were the dominant normative themes of the AUT 1944-45 Report on university development, and commitment to both strengthened throughout the period. On the one hand expansionism was reinforced as a diversity of bodies steadily clamoured for the same thing — the Percy Committee (1945), the Barlow Committee (1945-6), the NUT, the FBI, the Confederation of Management Associations. On the other hand, the advocacy of egalitarianism was probably strengthened by the growing proportion of non-professorial staff in the AUT (86 percent in 1953-54) and in the universities themselves.[292] The two themes were inextricably linked in professional thinking — at least all could agree that 'more would be fairer', if nothing else. The consensus among university teachers on these two points was such that they made a quick transition from normative exhortation to policy drafting. In 1957 a Report on a Policy for University Expansion was published with AUT approval stressing the need for at least five new universities, to be established as new autonomous institutions with full degree-giving powers. From policy formation they moved to practical planning when the Chancellor of the Exchequer approved expansion *without* endorsing new institutions for the purpose. The AUT established a Committee on New University Institutions which merged with its Committee on University Expansion and began to hold discussions with various LEAs interested in opening a university in their towns. How far such AUT pressures were responsible for swinging UGC opinion behind the idea of expansion through new institutions is impossible to determine, for it was only one of a number of groups seeking to press forward in this direction *before* the Robbins Committee reported. One thing, however, is quite clear — when the

Robbins Committee produced its final report, it reflected the values of the university teachers, it did not create them.

The School Teachers, 1964-75

The comprehensive reorganization of secondary schools undercut the vested interests of the grammar school teachers and largely removed the reason for independent organizations at the secondary level. The separate unions did not disappear, the Joint-Four continued in federation, the NAS remained, but was now committed to maintaining academic standards rather than defending the male teacher, whilst the Head Teachers NAHT and college teachers ATTI and ATCDE worked in closer partnership with the NUT. The latter was undoubtedly strengthened in terms of numbers and representativeness of the whole profession. In 1965 its members included 70 percent of all primary and secondary staff, which, allowing for those belonging to no union, meant that the vast majority of organized teachers fell within its purview.

However, despite growing professional unity and the increasing capacity of a single body to speak for the profession as a whole, the polity appears to have said 'so far but no further' at this time. The profession kept what it had already gained and was able to add to this, but all four political tactics — financial dependency, legal control, undermining autonomy and the propagation of etatist values — were brought into play to try to prevent it from acquiring an even better position from which to extend independent innovations, thus guiding educational development from inside. Given this political outlook, in conjunction with the relocation of power amongst the largest corporate interests, the profession reassessed its situation. With the breakdown of consensus politics it could not expect to command the same continuous attention as an interest group; with the onset of governmental resistance, if not hostility, its prospects of acquiring professional self-governance were gloomy; with the counter-development of corporatism amongst the trade unions, it was obvious that it had the support of neither of the 'great powers'. Eventually the profession threw in its lot with organized labour, for if one Leviathan was trying to restrain it, the other might provide the only means of advancing it. Nevertheless, despite this increased militancy much of the influence exerted by the teachers in this period was due to the semi-professional status acquired over the preceding decades.

Upgrading

Although there was only one representative of teacher education appointed to the Robbins Committee, to the dismay of the Association of College Lecturers (ATCDE), the final Report 'placed teacher education firmly within the orbit of higher education, and made a series of recommendations regarding the future of the colleges that were closely related to the wishes of the bodies directly concerned. The most important of these from the point of view of many of those engaged in training teachers related to the creation of a new degree, the Bachelor of Education'.[293] It appeared to consumate the ideal of an all-graduate profession and had the added merit of recognizing expertise in teaching as well as academic competance in some particular field of learning. Certainly the Robbins Report had carefully specified that the BEd course would be for those college students capable of working at degree level, but in practice it did not begin to take over in a wholesale fashion to produce the dramatic upgrading which its enthusiastic reception by the colleges and universities alike would have seemed to imply. In the sixties only about 10 percent of students continued on the four year course leading to the degree and thus remained overshadowed by the much bigger traditional group. The reason for this was the failure to establish the closer administrative and financial links between colleges and universities, which Robbins had advocated, rather than the inability of college students to take honours degrees. This failure, which will be discussed below, prevented the integration of teaching and learning between the two kinds of institutions, and linked them only by the formal bonds of 'validation' and 'moderation'.

Even less progress was registered towards salaries which would enable teachers to sustain a professional life-style. Here the polity was clearly trying to maintain financial dependency and keep the exchange rate down. Pay negotiations[294] assumed the character of confrontations and at the end of the sixties the teachers were engaging in increasingly militant action in support of their claims. This was intensified by growing national economic austerity which was to culminate in education cuts of various kinds and in Government pay and price policies in the seventies. The reciprocal 'attempts to form alliances outside education which cluminated in the NAS, ATTI and NUT becoming members of the TUC by 1971, and the formation of the Rank and File in the NUT, were all movements outside the old framework of consensus. By joining the TUC the associations looked outside the educational system towards general incomes policy'.[295]

Thus in the contemporary period the profession succeeded neither in improving the financial exchange rate for its expertise nor in substantially improving the collective level of expertise so as to justify a more generous recompense.

Self-Regulation

The Robbins Report had recommended the integration of Colleges, Departments and Institutes of Education into university Schools of Education, with administration and finance being transferred from the local authorities to the universities themselves. This proposal to bring the colleges wholly within the university framework was met with 'general rejoicing' by the teacher trainers (ATCDE) as a measure which would enable them to share the autonomy traditional to university institutions. The Conservative Party immediately dissented from the proposal, but it was the new Labour Secretary of State who finally vetoed it in 1965. His reasons for this had already been outlined in his speech earlier the same year, issuing in the Binary policy. In it he made a clear distinction between the 'autonomous sector' in higher education (the universities) and the 'public sector' (including the colleges), arguing that 'a substantial part of the higher educational system should be under social control, directly responsible to social needs'.[296] A firm break was thus placed on institutions upgrading themselves through higher academic standards until they attained the independence of the universities, as the final recognition of their intellectual worth. In other words, this was a clear combination of political tactics (2) and (3) – the refusal of legal recognition and the denial of institutional autonomy, both of which were legitimated (Tactic 4) by the now familiar etatist doctrine of public responsibility for the educational policy of the nation. Yet there is also no doubt that a good deal of party political purpose was concealed by this rhetoric of government responsibility – 'to a government concerned with using the educational system as an instrument of social policy, and desirous of adopting a substantial volume of centralized educational planning, the extension of such freedoms to a wider area of post-school education can only serve to diminish the effectiveness with which such goals can be pursued'.[297]

Thus collegiate autonomy was rejected by the polity – the most that was conceded after the Weaver Report[298] was a liberalization of college governance, i.e. the establishment of governing bodies which were no longer sub-committees of the Local Authority but included university and teacher representatives. This did represent a softening if not a change in LEA attitudes, and the ATCDE accepted the recommendations as 'the best compromise solution in the present situation'.[299] It became law in 1967 and whilst by no means conferring self-government on the colleges it did mark a shift towards academic control and some increase in the powers of self determination which could be devoted to the pursuit of the pedagogical values endorsed by the profession.

On the other hand, at the level of the schools the scope for autonomous action on the part of the teachers was widening both quantitatively and qualitatively. At the beginning of the period Government had 'little, if any, direct hold over the patterns of curriculum and methods. The only way in which the centre has its say, and not the last say at that, is through the inspectorate and through its membership of the Schools Council for Curriculum and Examinations'.[300] Both of these were at least as responsive to the profession as to the polity, thanks to the insertion of teachers into each of them. Certainly the schools were still subject to local authority control, but many LEA's were now making use of their own discretionary powers to engage in forms of reorganization and experimentation in which teachers were their close accomplices – comprehensive plans, community colleges, etc. Most important of all, the abandonment of objective selection tests increased the power of the teachers' subjective assessments: simultaneously the profession gained more control over the day to day definition of instruction and more power over its pupils accomplishments and destinies.

> Until recently, the individual teacher's decision making has played a relatively minor part in the processes by means of which the educational system exercises its selective and differentiating functions. These have been carried on by the system rather than by the individual teacher, structurally rather than personally . . . with the abolition of the eleven plus and the coming of comprehensive schools, the selective and differentiating functions move from the system to inside the school, and impose new demands on the teacher.[301]

The profession has thus acquired new powers over the management of knowledge and new choices about socio-educational reproduction: with it they also have to assume a new responsibility for the educational services given to the community. This new professional freedom in primary and much of secondary schooling raises the question of the relationship between the pedagogic value system and the needs of different parts of society in its most crucial form to date in English education.

Insertion

In general, the profession has continued to be successful in inserting itself on various decision-making agencies by virtue of its recognized expertise and, via both formal and informal channels, it has a growing influence over policy formation and ability to cushion its implementation. The NUT is represented on 125 official educational bodies and advisory committees set up by government departments and public corporations, and other unions hold seats on various similar agencies.[302]

In 1964 the NUT had thirty-seven MPs in the House of Commons.[303] It gives evidence to royal commissions and the Ministry usually seeks its views on preparatory drafts of policy statements. The centre is not legally obliged to obtain the advice of teachers and this regular practice involves a constant recognition of professional expertise. At the local level teachers can be co-opted onto the Education Committees where they sit as full members and most LEAs now have at least one such representative. The fact that teachers gave their support to local rather than central control of employment was demonstrated in the various controversies over local government reorganization. The way in which the professional unions successfully worked with the AEC and Society of Education Officers to retain an Education Committee as a statutory requirement in the new larger local authorities (established in 1974), can be seen as the teachers defending administrative agencies which were favourable to them.

However, the main advancement in insertion came with the setting up of the Schools Council for Curriculum and Examinations (1965), 'to assist the Secretary of State to carry out his responsibility for the direction of policy and the general arrangements for secondary school examinations and to discharge on his behalf the functions of a central, co-ordinating authority'.[304] In 1964 when the Minister (David Eccles) attempted to found a Curriculum Study Group, infelicitously mentioned as a 'commando-like unit', fears were immediately aroused about a resumption of State intereference after three-quarters of a century of 'hands off'. The teachers' unions together with local authority associations successfully killed this project and convinced the Ministry that the only workable entity would be an autonomous body outside the Department.[305] The unions rightly take credit for insisting that the majority control of the new Schools Council should rest with teachers and not with Ministry officials. In other words the chief central agency concerned with examination development and curriculum content — two major aspects of the definition of instruction — officially reversed the respective roles of profession and polity as inherited from the nineteenth century.

Nevertheless the purview of the Schools Council did not exhaust all aspects of the definition of instruction: it has a strong influence upon what kinds of education are available, but little say on *who* gets them. Significantly this was one of the areas in which an exceptionally important change of policy and principle was introduced from the centre without prior consultation with the profession, namely the issuing of Circular 10/65. Here a firm distinction was drawn between the principle of ending selection, seen as a social question which the Ministry must resolve on behalf of the community, and the practical reorganization of schools involved in its implementation about which the profession should be closely consulted. In other words, there is a general political philosophy about a reserved sector of decisions taken by government in the public interest — of which Circular 10/65 and the Binary Policy, are clear examples. In sum, the profession is sufficiently well inserted to cushion itself against the rigid imposition of central policy (as was the case with both of these examples), but is not invariably in a position to mould and monitor all policies which are centrally instigated.

Ideology

The contemporary period probably witnessed the high water mark of professional normative consensus with the publication of the Plowden Report in 1965, the culmination of half a century of progressive pedagogy and humanitarian concern for the disadvantaged. In many ways it was also the pinnacle of the liberal NUT influence over professional values — values which had consistently protested 'the need for informality in schools, for curriculum related to children's interests, for the emancipation of schools from the artificial pressures imposed by external examinations or the demands of employers'.[306] The cracks began to appear soon afterwards: they were both organizational and ideological and their destructive dialectic was to dissolve professional consensus by the 1970s. The contributory causes were varied: partly there was the material failure of the unions to deliver satisfactory pay settlements which led to strike action and a more militant pose and vocabulary: partly there was the withdrawal of Circular 10/65 by the Conservatives which to some demonstrated the impossibility of making educational advance according to the traditional rules of the political game: partly too the failure of the Educational Priority Areas, the climateric of compensatory policy, caused some to decide that it was the other side of the equation which needed changing – not the children but 'bourgeois' definitions of school achievement. Added to this were two equally important factors. On the one hand there was the mobilization of parents in organizations like CASE and their demands for participation, which both echoed and amplified the Plowden view of parents as a 'fourth party' in education. This encouraged a radical commutarian concept of the school which seemed to blend together the traditional idea of working class community and the current idealization of the commune in student culture. On the other hand educational journalism expanded enormously,[307] thriving on the trendiest experiments and ensuring the international diffusion of the most arresting views (such as deschooling – free schooling had always been good copy), with scant attention to their socio-cultural contexts or proven efficacy.

After the mid-sixties internal criticism mounted of the way in which union executives 'have maintained their respectability in order to maintain their educational influence and agreed only reluctantly to more militant action. Younger teachers and, in the NUT, the Rank and File, have argued that militant action was not only necessary on pay but that strong union action was required on other topics in order not so much to come to an agreement with central government and local authorities as to force their hand'.[308] Formed in 1968 the Rank and File has been more influential than numerous, but its magazine has become a vehicle for the radical leftists, the International Socialists and the diffuse anti-authoritarianism of student politics. This new radicalism produced its own critics both within the profession (the Black Papers) and from society (the Campaign for the Defence of Academic Standards).

The Academics, 1964-75

The Robbins Report, welcomed enthusiastically by the academics, recommended an integrated system of higher education which was legally vetoed by the polity (Tactic 2). Moreover, university autonomy to develop along self-determined lines was also to be curtailed (Tactic 3) through the growing 'dirigisme' of the UGC. That those tactics were now brought into play by the polity partly reflected the end of the social democratic phase in politics and the emergence of a more aggressively interventionist State, unrestrained by the need to sustain parliamentary consensus. Equally, however, they resulted from the development of financial dependence of the university on government funding. In the last period this was seen to be growing, but not yet to have had deleterious consequences for the universities because of the equally ready supply of industrial resources. Given the general world recession and the particularly high rate of English inflation, in the late sixties and seventies, the universities' alternative suppliers began gradually to dry up. The withdrawal of their financial support as the economic crisis worsened left the universities alone for the first time with the State, not just as their major supplier, but as the sole agency on which they depended for operating and development funds. The political strategy of pouring in more and more funds until all the universities had to offer was itself reliant on government resources (Tactic 1), had paid off with the emergence of financial dependence: and this in turn allowed Tactic 2 to be activated, the use of political veto, which is always more effective in the absence of alternative suppliers. Once financial dependency was established, the exchange rate could be lowered, thus reducing the surplus available for internal initiation, and the way was also opened (in the absence of protection by alternative suppliers) for more direct state intervention — Tactic 3 — lowering institutional autonomy. All these consequences did not take place immediately: there were two or three years during which the Robbins proposals took on flesh and revealed their final form, in which the last vestiges of the social democratic phase of politics were dispersed, and in which the economic downturn established itself as here to stay. Thereafter the negotiating strength of the universities vis-à-vis the polity declined from year to year. By 1966 they had won everything they were going to achieve for a long time: the rest of the period concerned their defensive action to protect what they could of the conditions favouring internal initiation.

Services

The Robbins Report was accepted in principle by both Labour and Conservative parties in one of the last acts of consensus government and as the climacteric of university influence. The new universities were created with the power to grant their own degrees from the start, including the upgraded CATs. Given such freedom it was unsurprising that the new institutions developed along different lines providing a diversity of services. Certainly there was a swing towards applied science, due largely to the new technological universities which continued their servicing of local industry, but the overall proportion of non-science places remained as large as before the war at 43 percent.[309] In spite of the official stress on scientific education the main growth point in the new universities was social studies, which left the relative position of the Arts as a whole, undiminished. In using their resources and autonomy for a massive development in social studies, the universities behaved as if they still confronted a sellers' market. Their approach was a direct continuation of attitudes fostered in the previous period when the demand for their output was such that academics could define what they were willing to sell rather than being instructed on what they should produce: they stepped up the output of social scientists and expected industry, commerce and bureaucracy to absorb them in the same way they had accepted the arts graduate a decade earlier. In fact this proved a mismatch, partly because industry had somewhat clarified its views and increasingly favoured a *broad* scientific background and partly too because of the anti-industrial orientation of many young social scientists who thus brought neither the right skills nor the right values into management.

The universities' defence consisted in pointing out that they were serving public demand, or more precisely student demand, since the Dainton enquiry[310] had confirmed that the proportion of 'A' levels gained in science and mathematics had declined after 1960, and anyway that the *available* places for degrees in science and technology were not being filled in the mid-sixties. Thus by the end of the decade there was 'a clash here between higher education for technology and industry and expansion as an act of social justice in which the latter predominated',[311] as one would expect from the more radical nature of the professional value system. Yet expansion in the face of dawning economic recession 'has almost completely eroded the financial basis of autonomy, converting the universities to this extent into state dependencies and thus placing the burden of maintaining academic freedom on the beliefs and sentiments of those who wield power in the modern system of government and of administration'.[312] But the polity with its new weapon of financial dependency decided to drop some of the burden immediately by taking greater powers of intervention upon itself, and to prevent it growing in weight at future times by calling a halt to the emergence of universities.

Self-Determination

The AUT submission to the Robbins Committee had concluded that 'we fully accept the need for a greater degree of co-ordination of the various forms of higher education. Such co-ordination should, however, stop short of state control and direction'.[313] The academics had long wanted to integrate the Colleges of Education and it was their policy to take an overall responsibility for scientific education. In this context Robbins also judged that the UGC mechanism linking universities and government was the best compromise between the universities' legitimate demands for autonomy and the State's equally legitimate demand for the right to supervise the spending of public funds. But the UGC did not remain what it had been, it 'became imperceptibly the agent of the DES rather than the neutral mediator between the universities and the government'.[314] It closely scrutinized new developments, proposed the winding up of a department for the first time, and instigated its letters of 'guidance' starting with the 1967-72 quinquennium. For the first time too the universities became directly financially accountable to Parliament and, in event of complaint, to the DES. This 'transfer of responsibility from the Treasury to the DES is an assertion of the existence of education as a system of related parts which requires central planning and decision-making. The UGC, in this sense, accepts a "socialist" rather than a "liberal" role'.[315]

The Robbins Report had wanted to keep the door to university status open and proposed a dramatic innovation whereby all Colleges of Further Education should be eligible to apply to grant degrees for special subjects under a new Council for National Academic Awards, which was intended as a half-way house to university status. The AUT had its reservations about this scheduling of centres of excellence, preferring the traditional process of competition, but its real concerns were, firstly, that the academic currency of the degree should not be debased, and secondly, that this half-way house should not be used as an *alternative* to the attainment of full university status. They succeeded in the former, largely through their own determination to make the CNAA work as a highly respectable and discriminating body, but failed utterly with the latter when the Binary policy got underway in the mid-sixties. Its introduction revealed the polity using all four tactics to prevent other parts of higher education from going the same way as the universities — it was a political condemnation of the purposes to which academics had devoted their powers of internal initiation and a determination that the Colleges should never acquire the preconditions for doing likewise. Firstly there was the obvious manipulation of financial dependence (Tactic 1) to keep College staff separate and more controlled than university teachers — 'separate but equal development has come to mean an unequal policy of on the one hand deliberately raising the starting salaries in the state colleges above those of university teachers . . . and on the other making the college lecturers pay for their initial financial advantage in heavier teaching loads, less time for research, and much less say in the government of their institutions'.[316] Secondly, legal constraint and lowered institutional autonomy (Tactics 2 and 3) were used in conjunction to reduce resistance to central directives on the part of the thirty colleges which were scheduled as Polytechnics. These were to concentrate on degree level work, but to be firmly denied the right to aspire to university status or to the academic freedoms customary to degree-giving bodies.

Undoubtedly these developments represented a decline in the negotiating strength of the academics but they did not signal the withdrawal of all the achievements of the previous sixty years. It was more a case of 'so far but no further' — the new universities had taken off and the others continued to enjoy a considerable degree of self-determination despite financial dependence. Their accumulated expertise attracted too much public recognition for the exchange rate to do more than tilt back against the universities: it has done so more and more with public spending cuts in the seventies, but it still represents a basic reciprocity unknown before the last war. The binary policy is of course a breach in this, since it in fact establishes two different exchange rates for a single commodity, and it is equally important as a kind of 'cordon sanitaire', thrown round the universities to prevent their freedoms from becoming contagious. Nevertheless, however 'powerful external pressures on universities may be, they remain for the most part pressures rather than directions. The universities are still today required to make up their own minds, individually, on a great range of their activities; even where the choice may be strictly limited, it still has to be made. . . It is part of the conventional wisdom to believe that he who pays the piper calls the tune. But there are limitations. To start with, it is no use calling outside the piper's repertoire, and there are things some pipers will not play. But in any event the universities are not only pipers: they are also composers'.[317]

Insertion

In view of the special and delicate nature of interaction between government and the universities, the Robbins Report had recommended a special Ministry dealing with the universities and research. As it was, all education was brought under the DES and this signalled a halt to any advance in professional insertion. It was paralleled by a similar rejection of the proposed independent salary review body for university teachers. The latter were clearly not going to be assigned a specially influential place in the new unificatory framework of educational administration. Linked with this of course was the 'loss' of the UGC as a genuine intermediary body, cushioning the profession against central policy directives. In the general social relocation of power taking place, the universities were unwillingly being assimilated to the State.

In this context the profession made further attempts to consolidate some kind of Academic Council to co-ordinate action and defend self-government. The next version to replace the old Home Universities Council was a small Joint Consultative Committee (1967) comprising representatives of the AUT and Vice-Chancellors – its very composition denying the distinction between freedom of the academic and loss of autonomy for the university. One of its first discussions centred on the UGC letter of guidance for the 1967-72 quinquennium. Since then it has represented 'one more step in the direction of the integration of the academic profession for the purposes of self-knowledge, self-expression, self-criticism and, regrettably perhaps in what often seems an increasingly hostile environment, self-defence'.[318] However, to the profession as a whole these attempts to generate an effective Academic Council, which had not succeeded in times of warmer government relations, were less likely to make headway now, and the profession itself was changing. Expansion had increased its size and modified its composition, bringing in a mass of new young lecturers, more attuned to the style of student politics of the sixties than to the long drawn out and usually inconclusive negotiations habitual in the AUT. Its consequence was to radicalize the AUT and above all to convince the more active university teachers that their collective organization could not remain in the limbo of professionalism where the two corporate Leviathans, the State and Labour, would grind it between them. Since the relocation of power had taken place, the fate of a small profession could not be defended independently and it was increasingly clear to the more politicized lecturers that their own organization had to join with one side or the other and profit from their greater strength. That the profession threw in its lot with labour, and steered the AUT into the TUC, can only be explained by fundamental changes in the professional value system which owed much to the new influx of post-Robbins lecturers.

Professional Value System

Given that a considerable expansion had taken place, academic circles necessarily debated the ends towards which this should be devoted. Within them a growing anti-industrial tendency crystallized, whose common denominator was a commitment to university disengagement. At one extreme this manifested itself as a simple disinterest, amongst scientists, about the industrial applications of their discoveries:[319] at the other, as an almost rabid rejection of a role in the reproduction of the forces of capitalist production. The disengaged stance incorporated a number of different and often mutually contradictory positions — academic self-absorption in the intellectual enterprise — mental adventurism, closely allied to the progressive philosophy of the school teachers, stressing the same themes of spontaneity, participation and relativism — and a radical political stance which saw disengagement as a temporary preliminary to re-engagement for revolutionary ideological ends. There seems little doubt but that the various troubles of the late sixties accelerated a shift from self-absorption to radical commitment, as well as enlarging this latter perspective. It no longer held that the university should simply disengage from industry but also sought a general withdrawal from maintaining the social structure as such. The integration of the profession, in which the NPS had obtained considerable influence prior to the troubles, prevented a total split between academic conservatives and student supporters, as in many European countries. It also meant, however, that the radicals and the radicalized continued to work from within to dominate the formal channels for the expression of academic values. Some polarization of course took place. At one extreme the Council for Academic Freedom and Democracy was formed to resist a situation in which academics 'cannot prevent their work being dictated by the needs of government, industry or commerce',[320] and at the opposite extreme an Independent University was founded which was free *to* respond to industrial demands. In general, however, radicalization did not spell fragmentation, the struggle remained within the profession and principally within its traditional organization the AUT (although some academics joined more politicized unions). The radical elements sought to win, drag or drive its members, often kicking and screaming, towards a new orthodoxy of values in which the university was to contest rather than to serve society.

POLITICAL MANIPULATION

The Education Act of 1918

The Education Act of 1918 was the last great piece of Liberal legislation in the educational field, and although it was quintessentially liberal in character, it was the product of hard fought political negotiation, not the inexorable result of twentieth century liberal thought. Nothing had been clearer after the Party's landslide electoral victory in 1906 than that the principal educational commitment of the Liberals was to undoing the damage inflicted on nonconformists by the Tory settlement of 1902. The Bill they immediately introduced to this effect (and which was blocked in the Lords) contained no reference to secondary education, and in fact their first action in this area was to raise secondary school fees. The continuity with Tory policies greatly outweighed any affinities with the approach of the Labour movement towards educational democratization, which it was having to advocate through political manipulation *faute de mieux*. Despite party political antagonisms the old governing elites were still in accord about areas of political inaction.

The Labour movement as a whole had declared its opposition to the developing scholarship system (with the exception of the Fabians, who had promoted this 'capacity catching'), and were in no doubt that the part of the 1902 Settlement which *they* sought to overthrow was the killing of the School Boards and the implicit closure of post-elementary instruction to the working class. In 1906 the TUC came out categorically in favour of secondary education for all, free and in reach of every child through comprehensive bursaries, and on a full-time basis until the age of 16. That it refused to endorse Parliamentary candidates who would not subscribe to this policy is both an indication of the importance attached to the issue and a recognition that this goal could only be achieved through political manipulation. Although Labour had crossed the electoral threshold in 1906, the Liberal Government was not dependent on their support and there 'was little the Labour movement could do on a national level during these years other than to reiterate their standpoint, to clarify their· policy, and to win support for its implementation'.[321] Except that is for one important thing – it turned the question of secondary education, and of access to it, into a political issue, which the other parties would have preferred not to debate but to determine by administrative fiat and strategic inaction.

The 1906 Report on Higher Elementary Schools by the Consultative Committee (not yet an organ of the teaching profession) revealed the totally different conception of secondary education which had guided official policy since 1900, and continued to do so despite the change of Government. It was a concept involving the negative principle of hierarchical organization: whereas the higher elementary school was 'end-on' to and 'continuous' with the elementary school, so that the two 'form a series', the secondary school was 'not continuous in the same way' and was unintegrated with the ordinary elementary school, having its own primary departments. This kind of systematization reflected and reproduced class relationships: 'the two types of school prepare for different walks of life – the one for the lower ranks of industry and commerce, the other for the higher ranks and for the liberal professions'.[322] The NUT immediately launched a crusade against this official policy of class prejudice, and the elementary teachers showed the greatest readiness to reinforce TUC protests against the fee increase which would slam the secondary school door shut on the working class, forcing them into the cul-de-sac of the Higher Elementary School.

It was only *after* this furore that the Liberal Government made the concession of an increased grant to those secondary schools willing to offer 25 percent of their places as free places for pupils from elementary schools. To observers like Tawney it served to demonstrate the yawning divide between the Labour movement's view of secondary education as a right and the Liberals conception of it 'as an exceptional privilege to be strained through a sieve, and reserved, so far as the mass of the people were concerned, for children of exceptional capacity'.[323] The divide widened as the TUC and Labour Party extended their attack to embrace the misuse of endowments, intended for the people, by the Public Schools and universities, but as it did so it underlined the powerlessness of the Labour Movement and the unimportance attached to it by a self-sufficient Liberal government – Asquith as Prime Minister simply refused to see a deputation on this matter in 1913.

Certainly prewar industrial unrest encouraged some Liberal unbending but only within the parameters of its bifurcated policy. The abortive 1911 Bill, abandoned for lack of time, contained the concessions it was willing to make within the framework of these principles, and is important since the 1918 Act was to widen the concessions without altering the principles on which they were based. Essentially it was willing to abolish the half-time system by raising the leaving age for full-time education to 13 but saw the subsequent instruction of the majority as taking place in part-time continuation classes, quite separate from the secondary schools.

If this had taken place in a period of declining Labour votes when the left had to work to keep the Liberals in office (1910-14), the inclusion of Labour in the War government of 1915 and the brief appointment of Arthur Henderson as President of the Board of Education seemed slightly more propitious, despite the fact that Henderson's post was simply a seat from which to conduct industrial relations and that it was only the strength of labour organization in the TUC which had prompted this inclusion of the Party. More important, however, was the general commitment of the national government to postwar reconstruction, in which education figured largely. Equally significant was the appointment of H. A. L. Fisher, as the first academic President of the Board, by Lloyd George on the grounds that educational reform would be more acceptable from an educationalist than a politician[324] — the political hostility and alienation of the teaching profession was both noted and feared. With the Prime Minister's undertaking that money would be found for ambitious educational measures the polity was clearly geared up for educational reform in order to appease the joint public and professional demand.

In 1916 then, the parties and pressure groups began to line up, to articulate policies, to ally with and dissociate themselves from others, and generally to intensify political manipulation now that legislative change was in view. The most radical stance was initiated by the Bradford Trades Council, which was quickly endorsed by thirty others, and then adopted by both the ILP and Labour Party at their annual conferences in 1917. Thus the official Labour programme was for universal, free, compulsory education until the age of 16 in a common secondary school. All other groups stopped short at secondary education for all, including the WEA and NUT who supported considerable expansion but on a selective basis. An Educational Reform Council formed in the same year articulated the views of liberal educationalists like Fisher himself and detailed the model which was to dominate policy in the 20s and 30s. In it elementary schools were to be divided into Junior forms (5-11) and Senior forms (11-14); at 11 some would be transferred by scholarships and free places to *both* grammar schools *and* higher elementary schools; the notion that elementary and secondary instruction were of different kinds and were non-continuous thus remained intact. Again the majority of schemes recommended part-time continuation education until 16 or 18 and only the Bradford Charter, aware that it could be substituted for raising the school leaving age, pressed for full-time education until 16.

The Labour movement remained in the weakest parliamentary position from which to advance such a policy and its chances of persuading the Liberal Party to take its view were small indeed, given Lloyd George's dependence on conservative support after 1916. The Labour Party's only successful piece of manipulation consisted in the Report of an inquiry which Henderson had instigated whilst at the Board of Education. The Lewis Report on Juvenile Employment made a timely appearance in 1917 and revealed that the use of exemption clauses had been employed by local authorities, in response to manufacturing interests, to swell the category of part-timers and make nonsense of educational extension. It therefore recommended full-time instruction until 14, without exception, and part-time education until 18. To the TUC this was a necessary but derisory minimum, which involved side-stepping the basic issue of the class nature of the educational structure, but Fisher took it over in detail when drafting his first version of the Bill in 1917, supplementing it with some of the proposals originated by the Educational Reform Council.

The Bill was an amalgam: it took its two most basic provisions — full-time education until 14 with no exemptions, thus ending the half-time system, and part-time continuation education until 18, for those who were not receiving full-time instruction until 16 — jointly from the Liberal Bill of 1911 and the Lewis Report, borrowing from the latter the exact details of the continuation scheme. It threw a concession to the WEA and NUT expansionists by way of an enabling clause lifting the 2d limit on rates raised for non-elementary instruction; it doffed its cap to the Reform Council by proposing to develop the Higher Elementary School; and it sought to avoid the wrath of the Churches by including not one reference to religion. As an amalgam it bid for a safe passage and it already had the backing of the full range of Professional Associations.[325]

The Bill failed to make parliamentary progress because of two main sources of opposition. On the one hand, northern manufacturers saw the end of the half-time system as resulting in major industrial dislocation; the Lancaster cotton producers claimed, for example, that it spelt an 8 percent reduction of the labour force in the textile industry. On the other hand, whilst they carefully endorsed its educational provisions, the 'most powerful opposition to the 1917 Education Bill came from the local education authorities who ... felt that under certain of the administrative clauses, such as the procedure for submitting schemes to the Board for the reorganization of education in an area, the powers of the Board (the central authority) would be enlarged at the expense of those of the local education authorities'.[326] This they pressed on the Government through the AEC, the County Councils Association and other organizations[327] as part of their deep antagonism towards centralization, with the aim of having the clauses altered or removed. Given this opposition, Fisher expressed disappointment at the lack of assistance he received in the House from Labour MPs. Coolness was the keynote of reactions in the Labour movement: to the TUC it was an inadequate settlement in relation to their requirements, to the WEA it was only a measure abolishing the half-timers, to the Party it failed to deal with the main problem — the class nature of education — or to tackle it by structural reorganization. They were cool not because they disapproved of the Bill's provisions but because of the massive act of non-decision-making which it concealed, namely the determination not to change the basic structure of the educational system.

The 1917 Bill was withdrawn for subsequent reintroduction. The Labour Party urged amendment of the text to make it 'a complete charter of National Education from the Primary School to the University',[328] which was less a call for amendment than for the replacement of the Bill by the Bradford Charter. More powerful was the intervention of the FBI, reporting on the unfavourable reaction of 2,000 firms it had surveyed to the creation of continuation schools, and its determination to eliminate this proposal, or cut it to the bone, during the committee stage of the Bill. The revised text ignored both, and its provisions remained unchanged except for modification of the administrative clauses. Although these retained the kernel notion about the submission of reorganization schemes, the initiative for educational development was placed firmly with the local authorities in a partnership with the centre, in which the latter would act more as an advisory body.[329] These alterations were acceptable, they banished the spectre of stronger unification.[330]

In the House, industrial interests, spearheaded by the Lancashire group of MPs, fought for amendments on the lines advocated by the FBI. Although refusing these, Fisher made an unexpected concession at committee stage by postponing the introduction of the continuation schools for seven years, a concession without which he believed the Bill would have failed to reach the statute book.[331] To Fisher the continuation school had been the most important part of his Bill and he believed that he had at least secured them in principle; the alternative judgment was that the Act had done nothing more than abolish the half-time system. Retrospectively its main importance is undoubtedly as a piece of non-decision-making, for the 1918 Education Act 'was governed by the principle that as much development in education as possible would be brought about through the existing structure of education'.[332] At the time, the Liberals did not know that their failure was as great as it was and that economic depression would prevent the principle of the continuation school from becoming established practice: nor could the FBI know, the the same reason, that its victory was nearly complete and that its policy of full-time secondary education for the selected few[333] had actually passed by default.

The 1944 Education Act

In the interwar period of economic depression and realignment of the political parties the distribution of resources had two consistent implications for this process of change. On the one hand, the economic situation made the majority of the population exclusively dependent on political manipulation for expressing their educational demands. On the other hand, the political situation meant that the Labour Party was never in a position to manipulate political power so as to satisfy these demands. This strand was woven through the protracted interaction which led up to the 1944 Act, but the pattern itself was more complex and involved constant interplay between the four agencies officially concerned with educational decision-making – the political parties – the advisory committees to government – the Board of Education – and the Local Authorities. Their involvement made for a more intricate form of political interaction than in the centralized system, which lacks the central/local dimension to both conflict and change. By pursuing its own goals, each of the four agencies altered the context in which the others had to negotiate, lending to a continuous process of mutual constraint, reaction and modification, taking place at the ideological as well as the organizational level. The major struggle dominating political manipulation during these two decades was over the nature of system- atization (the positive or negative principle of hierarchical integration) and the degree of differentiation which should accompany it.

The 'coupon' election of 1918, returning a coalition government under Lloyd George, dominated by 'hard faced' conservative industrialists[334] but with Fisher still at the Board, issued in a period of parliamentary tension between Liberals and Conservatives in educa- tional matters. This was soon to be passed on to relations between Labour and the Conservatives and these became much more stressful when politics were realigned on the basis of class after the Liberal decline. Thus 1920 witnessed the contradiction between Liberal ex- pansionism, when the Hilton Young report, prompted by Fisher, advocated increasing free places in secondary schools from 25 percent to 40 percent, while conservative retrenchment in fact brought the implementation of the 1918 Act to a complete halt. The weakness of Liberal counter pressures, even though reinforced by the small parlia- mentary Labour party and the local authorities (AEC), tilted the balance of power firmly towards the Conservatives and made this halt a prelude to full retreat when the Geddes axe fell in 1922. Cuts in public spending, as the answer to economic depression, meant an assault on free secondary places, teachers salaries, and the minimum 50 percent grant payable by the Exchequer to match local authority spending, under the 1918 Act. Fisher stayed on at the Board to try to deflect economies in education, but although he rescued the percentage grant and took the edge off other proposals, he collected flack from both the TUC and the FBI for the middle course he had steered – a foretaste of the polarization which was soon to dominate national politics.

The terms of the forthcoming debate were set during the two short ministries which followed, each lasting only a year – the Conservatives (back in 1922 with a clear majority for the first time since 1900) and the Labour Party (forming its first government in 1924 with Liberal support). Baldwin, replacing Bonar Law as Prime Minister, steered firmly down the retrenchment path, allowing no relaxation of the Geddes cuts and arguing against the expansion of secondary schooling which would only lower its standards, especially if it became available to all. Tawney, publishing *Secondary Education for All* as a Labour

Party document provided an answer to conservative philosophy which used the need to defend standards in secondary education as an argument against a strong ladder between elementary and secondary levels. In the interest of equality the levels should be 'two stages in a single course', but *differentiation* should characterize the definition of post elementary instruction, thus avoiding the levelling down effect of uniformity. This important departure from the Bradford Charter became official party policy — 'equality of educational provision is not identity of education provision, and it is important that there should be the greatest diversity of type among secondary schools'.[335] But when in office Labour was is no position to introduce any charter, its hands were tied by its Liberal supporters. Even more importantly, it was constrained by the situation inherited from its predecessor, by the need to devote itself chiefly to negative tasks — to undoing Geddes and reversing the engines. In positive terms it could not push ahead with 'secondary education for all'. It had to content itself with extending secondary places, free places, and maintenance grants, ameliorating provisions but not transforming the existing structure.

The return of the Conservatives in 1924, with an overall majority guaranteeing a five year term of office, marked a new round of educational economy at precisely the time when the Labour movement was least able to prevent it, for the acrimony between the TUC and the Party over the general strike neutralized the new redistribution of political power. Conservative cuts, which again attempted to remove the percentage grant, despite the virulent protest of the AEC and County Council Associations, were restrained not by the Opposition but by their own fears of what they now saw as a revolutionary situation, following the collapse of the General Strike. It was in this context that the Consultative Committee, under the chairmanship of Hadow, produced its report on 'The Education of the Adolescent' in 1926. The Hadow Report was not a Labour initiative, it was the product of a political struggle between the Consultative Committee, now the main official outlet for expert educational opinion, which wanted to investigate the curriculum between the ages of 11-16, and the Board which had limited its terms of reference to courses in schools other than secondary ones, up to the age of 15.[336]

With an academic membership of the Committee which included Hadow (Vice Chancellor of Sheffield), Tawney and Mansbridge (representing adult education),[337] this first report reconceptualized systematization according to the positive principle, whereby education was seen as a continuous process of progressive stages. The term 'elementary' was replaced by 'primary' to denote the Junior stage until 11, and the concept of 'secondary' was detached from a single type of school and re-applied to all forms of post-elementary instruction.[338] The new Secondary education should last until 15 (involving raising the school leaving age) so as to give all at least a four-year course after the primary school. It urged that this increase in equality should not involve a growth of uniformity: pupils should go forward on different paths to a range of schools suited to 'varying interests and cultivative powers' so that 'selection by differentiation takes the place of selection by elimination'.[339] The report acknowledged the logicality of placing all post-elementary instruction under a single set of regulations but also accepted that it was not empowered to make recommendations involving the traditional secondary school and thus had 'to build with materials inherited from the past on pain of not building at all'.[340] In practice, this meant endorsing and fostering the post-elementary outgrowths, the Central schools, Junior Technical schools and higher tops which had been developed locally by a process analogous to the emergence of the Higher Grade schools in the nineteenth century.

The Report was well received by all, but largely because they stressed different parts of it. Nevertheless since all focused on the same document, their reactions represented a clarification of educational goals in relation to one another and against a fixed reference point. In particular the responses of the Conservative Party and the Board were clearly distinguished from the interpretations advanced by Labour, the NUT and the local authorities. The reformulation of Conservative educational philosophy was triggered off by an AEC deputation urging the implementation of Hadow. This was informed that the Government agreed on all essentials, except raising the school leaving age, and in the last three years had itself been working towards the ideal of universal post-elementary education of different kinds.[341] Eighteen months later the Board issued *The New Prospect in Education*, purporting to inform local authorities on how to undertake 'Hadow reorganization' but in fact presenting a substantial reinterpretation of Hadow. Reorganization itself was referred to as 'a readjustment of the existing elementary system', the right of those over 11 was to 'intermediate education' (a term alien to Hadow) in schools set apart for this, whilst secondary schools for pupils over 16 must remain unaltered and take in fewer numbers,[342] whereas Hadow had wanted 'many more'. Class politics were starting to bite, but it would be a misrepresentation to reduce the emerging Conservative philosophy to a *simple* bipartite policy, bending the Hadow recommendations to reinforce and reproduce class stratification. It was concerned with the latter of course, but it was also beginning to conceptualize secondary education in a way very different from Morant's single academic school and a way, which, if it had been followed up, would have incorporated the *Real* definition of instruction which has never developed forcefully in England. In *The New Prospect*, the Central Schools were the prototypes of a practically oriented education which the Board envisaged as reaching upwards to matriculation and leading onwards to the Technical Colleges. This too would be selective and would thus leave the majority of pupils in new senior 'non-examination' schools, to borrow Danish terminology. To this extent it retained negative systematization, but it advocated a differentiation which was foreign to bipartitism and showed that the Conservatives too had been converted to the need for variety. Thus Baldwin's 1929 election promises included higher education for all *and* a link between schools and 'the great technical colleges'[343] *as well as* the universities.

If the Conservative ideal was one of selection and differentiation, the Labour reaction to Hadow was the endorsement of differentiation without selection, in other words a preference for diversity of provisions in conjunction with the positive principle of hierarchical integration. Undoubtedly Labour put the raising of the school leaving age at the top of its list of 'Hadow' priorities, as a precondition for *any* serious post-elementary course, but the annual conference of 1927 also moved towards the ideal of a single multilateral school.[344] This was advocated with greater precision by the teachers' unions, and at least one of the secondary associations. The NUT argued that a single school to which all transferred would create equality of opportunity, whilst its courses and departments of different types would avoid uniformity or the emergence of the status differentials encouraged by differentiated institutions. The gradual endorsement of the multi-bias school represented a formulation distinct from the Bradford Charter (which discountenanced differentiation) and from Tawney's 'Secondary Education for all' (which would have had to countenance some form of selection).

In fact, however, in the late 20s and 30s neither ideal was translated into the practical policy of either political party, for both were the victims of circumstances, including those circumstances they created for one another. Labour's second ministry began in 1929, already entangled in 'the toils of a conservative predisposition',[345] namely the mobilization of the Churches to resist any Hadow reorganization until their own place in the new secondary scheme was guaranteed. It ended in economic crisis two years later, having failed to raise the school leaving age, alter the existing structure, or do anything more than encourage the active LEAs to reorganize through offering building grants and add a further 10 percent of free places in the secondary schools. The 1931 election, returning a national government under Macdonald, was what the 'coupon' election had been to the Liberals in 1918: it was a split from which Labour did not recover until the war and a political breach through which the Conservatives could drive the most stringent economy measures yet — the May recommendations which claimed back the 50 percent exchequer contribution which had encouraged progressive authorities, stopped Hadow reorganization in mid-stream, and abolished free places in secondary schools, substituting remission of fees for the very lowest income levels. The significance of government control being synonymous with financial control had never had greater implications than in this period — 'with the Labour movement weakened, neither the teachers nor local authorities could deflect a policy of freezing expenditure right across the board'.[346] When economic recovery began in the mid-thirties neither party thought in grandiose terms of structural transformation, and both reduced their sights even lower than Hadow reorganization. Labour no longer waged a generous campaign for secondary education for all, the effect of fifteen years of spending cuts had limited its horizons to the raising of the school leaving age, for which numerous groups were now pressing in the School Age Council. What followed were the sordid wranglings over the Conservative Act of 1936, raising the leaving age to 15, with exemptions for 14 year olds in 'beneficial employment'. It was met with general contempt; the AEC called it a travesty of a reform, but the whole episode represented as much of a retreat from the Conservative vision of Hadow as from the Labour interpretation of the Report.

Both parties had merely tinkered with the existing structure rather than implementing their different readings of Hadow. Labour had encouraged reorganization into junior and senior schools and had increased the numbers of free secondary places, but it had not made any advance towards establishing multilateral schools. The Conservatives had played the percentage game, with secondary places and local grants, in the opposite direction and instead of consolidating Real education linked to the Technical colleges, it had lapsed into bipartism by allowing the elementary system to reconstitute itself afresh. Again it was the Consultative Committee which jerked political attention away from the grubbier class wranglings of party politics over a maintenance grant here and an exemption clause there, and, with the worst economic restraints removed, forced them to re-address macroscopic questions of structural reorganization and philosophical problems about the social functions of education.

In 1934 the Consultative Committee had a new remit to consider secondary education, including 'the organization and interaction' of schools other than elementary, with special reference 'to the framework and content of education of pupils who do not remain at school beyond the age of about 16'. In themselves these terms of reference indicated the Board's animosity towards the Hadow principle of secondary education as an organic whole. 'It is not difficult to see how this fitted in with the Board's line of policy. If it could be shown that pupils leaving at 16 needed a different kind of curriculum, then, taking account of the intention to maintain existing secondary schools unchanged with a higher leaving age, the only conclusion could be that another type of school to accommodate such pupils would be necessary'.[347] On the other hand, the profession, the local authorities and the Labour movement were quick to submit their recommendations to the Committee, and at the top of their list of priorities was a single code of regulations for all post-elementary schools and an equality for the Senior schools which would enable them to dispense a secondary education with the same facilities and staffing as was traditional in the secondary schools. Collectively this group (the NUT, AEC, CCA, TUC, L.P.) sought to avoid two hermetically sealed compartments at secondary level. They were committed to the positive principle of systematization, whose logical implication was a single school, in the view of the Labour Teachers, or at least a common curriculum until 14, in the opinion of the NUT. The concept of the multilateral school had been reanimated.

When the Committee reported four years later its recommendations represented a blending of the two perspectives which had emerged on the Left and Right following Hadow, stressing their common denominator, i.e., agreement on the need for differentiation, and seeking a compromise on what divided them, namely the positive or negative principle of systematization. The title of the final report was significant of this attempt to blend a new consensus: *Secondary Education with special reference to Grammar Schools and Technical High Schools.* It criticized the academicism of Morant's secondary school and took up the earlier Conservative idea of remedying this neglect of science and technology by building up a new form of technical secondary school. Similarly it was in the Tory vein that differentiation should take place in different types of schools (grammar, technical and secondary modern), but beyond this the recommendations for common regulations, social availability and for a shared curriculum were in the Labour tradition. There should be a common code making all post-elementary education secondary in character and encouraging parity of staffing and facilities, together with the complete abolition of fees. Although the Spens Report stopped short of adopting the multilateral school, except experimentally in sparsely populated areas and on new housing estates, it argued nonetheless that 'the multilateral idea, though it may not be expressed by means of the multilateral school, should permeate the system of secondary education as we conceive it'.[348] This, in conjunction with insistence on equivalent status and conditions for the three schools and ease of transfer between them, were the ways in which Spens tried to avoid the undesirable consequences which could stem from a form of hierarchical organization whose only positive aspect was still to be the selective ladder.

Like the Hadow Report, Spens could be read in different ways by accentuating different sections, and this was immediately apparent in the reactions of the two parties who subjected it to their differing class biases. Thus the Labour movement considered that it leaned too far to the right, the TUC, in particular, stressing that the separation of the three types of schools could only reinforce social stratification and that as long as selection remained 'it is in practice useless to talk of parity in education or equality of opportunity in after life'.[349] Similarly the NUT condemned the restriction of grammar school places to 15 percent of that age group, which involved a retreat in many areas. These aspects which were criticized on the left were perfectly acceptable to the Conservatives, whose own reservations related to the administrative provisions (welcomed on the left) — the single code of regulations, essential to Spens if parity were to have a chance, and the financial increases concomitant on giving all schools the same amenities. Both of the latter the Conservative Party turned down flatly. The Board's enthusiasm was restricted to welcoming the new type of technical school. The Consultative Committee's proclivity to address structural and administrative problems attracted its opprobrium and it would have liked to have suppressed it or at least to deprive it of the independent status of an advisory committee, since it refused to confine itself to what the Board recognized as its only area of expertise, curricular development. Consequently the related question of secondary school examinations was referred to the narrower Secondary Schools Examinations Council which, in presenting the Norwood Report, went 'beyond its brief to produce a veritable ideology of "tripartitism" to fit a projected organization of secondary education which could effectively maintain the old hierarchical pattern'.[350]

The wartime National government played a significant role in this context for it meant that demands frustrated over the failure to raise the school leaving age and the shelving of the Spens Report were continually expressed within the governing elite, and that the Labour Party could sustain and transmit the external pressures for large scale reform and 'no tinkering' to the political centre.[351] R. A. Butler, as President of the Board, formally initiated the run-up to a major piece of legislation when he circulated the green book on 'Education after the War' in 1941. This itself advocated secondary education for all on a tripartite basis, but with Labour ministers in the government the alternative case gained a public hearing. 'In the course of these exchanges the multilateral school was more widely discussed than ever before'.[352] The annual conference of the Labour Party in 1942 resolved in favour 'of a new type of multilateral school which could provide a variety of courses suited to children of all normal types': the TUC, slightly more cautiously, called for 'really substantial experiments in the way of multilateral schools'.[353] These specific pressures advocating a particular form of structural reorganization overlapped with more general demands for reform. In November 1942 the TUC, NUT, WEA, and Co-Operative Union together formed the Council for Educational Advance to obtain 'immediate legislation to provide equality of educational opportunity for all children',[354] without explicitly predicating this on a single common secondary school. This position was also adopted by the AEC and the CCA. The impetus was there for a Bill but there was no political, administrative or educational consensus on the provisions it should introduce.

In July 1943 the Board issued a white paper on 'Educational Reconstruction' which reiterated the tripartite recommendations of the green book but stressed flexible transfer between the schools, which in some circumstances could be combined on a single site or in a single building. The protagonists of multilateralism, who were even more vocal in the Parliamentary debate, were making headway and Butler was clearly wavering, though in vague enough terms, when he told the Commons that 'I would say to those idealists who want to see more than one form of secondary education in the same school – sometimes called multilateral schools – that I hope that more than one type of secondary education may from time to time be amalgamated under one roof'.[355] Almost immediately counter-balast was provided by the publication of the Norwood Report (*Curriculum and Examinations in Secondary Schools*). With its pseudo-psychological justification of three kinds of schools for three kinds of minds this new report perverted the Spens notion of parity of status between secondary schools by ranking the three types hierarchically, with the Morant grammar school unchallenged and unmodified at the top. It was a neat inversion, wholly congenial to Board policy, but it was not, popular belief to the contrary, directly translated into the Education Bill.

As drafted and as passed the Bill was a cautious document, exceedingly careful to exploit any element of consensus and to alienate no large body of opinion fundamentally – in short it was a grand piece of political manipulation. Butler recognized that there was a significant difference between the positions taken by the Campaign for Educational Advance, desperate for a Bill raising the leaving age, abolishing fees, providing uniform amenities, the same pupil-teacher ratio and per capita spending throughout secondary education, and by the protagonists of *a particular form of organization*, the multilateral school, in which these broader aims would be accomplished. Accordingly the Bill gave secondary education for all: it made no mention of types of secondary school beyond stressing variety, and was mute on the subject of curriculum at either primary or secondary level. The key phrase making it the duty of local authorities to offer 'such variety of instruction and training as may be desirable in view of their different ages, abilities and aptitudes, and of the different periods for which they may be expected to remain at school',[356] could, and to Butler did suggest tripartite reorganization, but it *in no way legally prescribed it* and was thus no barrier against supporting the Bill. Moreover, what Butler had also made clear *was the legality* of the multilateral school, on the same terms that the Spens Report had proposed. The Labour Parliamentary Secretary to the Board, James Chuter Ede wrote in *The Times* after the final Bill had been introduced in the House of Commons, 'I do not know where people get the idea about three types of school, because I have gone through the Bill with a fine toothcomb and I can find only one school for senior pupils and that is a secondary school. What you like to make of it will depend on the way you serve the precise needs of the individual area in the country'.[357] The beginning is disingenuous, comically so from one attached to the Board, but the conclusion is valid enough; it was not the 1944 Act which shackled secondary education to tripartitism.

What the 1944 Act did do was to create the necessary but not the sufficient conditions for imposing a tripartite, *or any other* organizational scheme on the system, to a much greater degree than had ever been the case in this decentralized structure. The Act strengthened unification, it created a Minister to 'control and direct' a 'national policy',[358] with more effective initiative and sanctions than the Board had ever possessed. The Explanatory Memorandum of 1943 justified the increased powers accorded to the centre in terms of 'a recognition of the principle that the public system of education, though administered locally is the nation's concern, the full benefits of which should be equally available to all alike, wherever their homes may be'.[359] This increase in unification meant a complementary contraction of local decision-making powers and a reduced capacity on the part of the local authorities to 'make what they liked' of parliamentary legislation when now constrained and monitored by a more powerful central administration. It is thus in its overt administrative reforms, and not its covert psychological assumptions, that the 1944 Act contributed to subsequent organizational standardization, to a degree unprecedented in England. Nevertheless, increased unification is *only* a necessary condition for this outcome, the sufficient conditions require in addition that the governing elite pursues a policy of organizational uniformity. The sufficient conditions were never lacking, and the history of political manipulation in the three following decades is largely the story of how the Conservative and Labour Parties in turn used the new central powers to direct organizational change along two different lines – tripartitism followed by comprehensive reorganization. Since, even in its strengthened form, unification in England remained much weaker than in centralized systems, the next thirty years were also the history of other groups fighting back to repel organizational uniformity.

Comprehensive Reorganization

The question of how to organize secondary education dominated political manipulation for the three decades following the 1944 Act.

The attention of the lower classes remained rivetted on political negotiation when other social groups turned to make use of external
transactions or internal initiation, since both processes widened out
after the war. Given a parliamentary context in which they could
command continuous political attention, the non-privileged used
political manipulation to press for increased educational opportunity,
and then for equality of educational opportunity. It is no exaggeration
to say that the working class dictated the topic of political debate, if
not its terms or conclusions. Essentially the debate was about equality
in education: technically it was about systematization, about how the
different parts of secondary schooling were linked to one another and
with the primary schools: specifically it was about whether the positive
or the negative principle of hierarchical organization should prevail.

The 1944 Act left these questions to be determined between the
local authorities, who would submit development plans, and the
Ministry which would consider them for approval. The 1944 Education
Act increased the unification of the system and the new powers
attaching to the administrative centre appeared to threaten the traditional initiative of the local authorities, which had rested on their
long-standing autonomy. The first clause of the Act stressing that
educational development was to take place under Ministerial 'control
and direction' might seem to indicate a highly centralized system with
education typically responsive to the central polity.[360] Yet the Act
had not redistributed powers so fundamentally as to destroy the basic
decentralized structure: the Minister does not have complete executive
responsibility, his powers are limited and specific whilst other powers
and duties are assigned directly to the LEAs, and the latter are not
central agents, in some matters they require ministerial approval but
they have considerable scope for initiative and discretion especially as
their authority stems from Parliament and it not delegated to them by
the Minister. Moreover to 'describe central controls is, however, to
paint a very incomplete picture of central-local relations in the educational service: first because much of what flows from the centre is not a
control or directive, and secondly because there is a considerable flow
in the reverse direction'.[361] It is into these two flows that most of the
postwar struggles over the reorganization of secondary education were
canalized. Under the Act the central-local partnership remained,
although the partners were less equal than before. More Ministerial
control could be expected, and it was not lacking from either the
Labour or the Tory governments in the first decade. In the mid-fifties,

however, the reverse flow became more important, and the running was made by the Local Authorities, who took it over from government and ministry in a manner inconceivable in the centralized system.

The provisions of the new Act, designed by Conservatives within the National Government, were first tried out by the Labour Party which took office immediately after the war. Although Labour came to power with a mandate for comprehensive reorganization, the annual conference of 1942 having pledged support for the multilateral school, when it left office in 1951 there were only twelve such schools in being. Instead it was the policy of the Ministry, the Norwood philosophy of the old Board, which survived the change of political administration. A month before Ellen Wilkinson took up the education portfolio, the Ministry had issued *The Nation's Schools* specifying the direction of postwar development on Norwood lines, with no effort to conceal the social discrimination concomitant with tripartism: the modern schools, it stated, are for those children 'whose future employment will not demand any measure of technical skill or knowledge'.[362] Nevertheless, she defended it before a hostile Party conference in 1946 and although the pamphlet was not reprinted, its successor *The New Secondary Education* (1947) embodied the same determination to impose tripartitism and was not withdrawn until 1958, a good index of the continuity of Ministry policy.

Why then did the two Labour Ministers of Education (George Tomlinson followed Ellen Wilkinson in this office) accept and implement the Norwood philosophy despite internal party opposition? Their reasoning is significant, and not to be dismissed as rationalization, for there was nothing to prevent either from taking a tougher line with their civil servants. Wilkinson's justification rested on the need for differentiation and appealed to an impeccable if naive socialist view of the division of Labour and a rejection of the Morant definition of secondary instruction. 'Not everyone wants an academic education. After all, coal has to be mined and fields ploughed, and it is a fantastic idea that we have allowed, so to speak to be cemented into our body politic, that you are in a higher social class if you add up figures in a book than if you plough the fields and scatter the good seed on the land'.[363] For those who could then believe in parity of occupational esteem it was no more ingenuous to envisage parity of status between different types of schools. Tomlinson, on the other hand, reflected a respect for the Grammar Schools common among many Labour politicians who had made their own way up this ladder: to them the abolition of fees meant that only merit would determine which children climbed it in future.

Furthermore, the tripartite philosophy was widely endorsed by expert opinion, especially by psychometricians, and at the same time opposition to the multilateral alternative had also hardened amongst educationalists like Eric James, Kandel and Dent, and most importantly among administrators like W. P. Alexander, the long serving Secretary of the AEC. In the same vein, a resolution condemning tripartism was heavily lost at the NUT conference of 1948. Against this background of pressures the Labour Party as a whole appears to have remained suspicious but irresolute. The Labour Party Conference of 1947 deprecated the current policy but merely urged the Minister 'to take great care that he does not perpetuate under the new Education Act the undemocratic tradition of English Secondary Education'.[364]

Thus tripartite reorganization got underway, with the Government backing the Ministry, which in turn advised Local Authorities to think in terms of three kinds of schools when drawing up their development plans. 'Judicious experiments' with multilateral or bilateral schools were to be sanctioned, according to *The Nation's Schools*, where LEAs were adamant to try them, especially in 'sparsely populated areas'. Nevertheless, this was the smallest trickle and Tomlinson had no compunction at turning down the Middlesex Plan for a fully comprehensive system, as advocated by its Labour controlled council, a decision he justified on the grounds that 'comprehensive schools are still (the) subject of violent controversy in educational circles (and) would alienate a large vocal and influential section of opinion'.[365] Only in the last two years of the Attlee government did the National Executive firmly condemn the tripartite system and counter-propose wholesale comprehensive reorganization in *A Policy for Secondary Education*. 'Thus in 1951 as the Labour Party relinquished office it became for the first time fully and publically committed to comprehensive reorganization of secondary education'.[366]

The return of the Tories ensured the continuity of policy — 'A Conservative administration applied in an open and single minded fashion the policy which Tomlinson had pursued with a measure of confusion'.[367] The nature of secondary reorganization had not figured largely in the election manifestoes, it had been a minor issue in the 1952 election, and was to remain restricted to squabbles with a limited number of local authorities for another four years. In other words, the policy for secondary education mirrored the general political consensus dominating this period. The balance between the parties meant that both feared the alienation of support (and thus did nothing dramatic) and both consistently wooed the interest groups (and therefore made concessions to determined elements).

Thus the new government pressed on with tripartism and those LEAs seeking comprehensive reorganization had to fight hard for ministerial permission. Florence Horsburgh, the first Conservative Minister, continued to allow 'limited experiments' provided comprehensive schools were not the only form of secondary education available in a local authority area. In accepting the Coventry Plan it was stressed that this was strictly experimental and that the schools should be built in such a way that they could later be split up if this proved desirable. The LCC and other areas which were now establishing comprehensive schools received no official encouragement; on the contrary permission was restricted to regions with limited populations and those, like Coventry and London, which had to engage in postwar rebuilding anyway. Moreover, those which were allowed had to be big schools, with over 2,000 pupils, so that they could provide the three types of education under one roof, a proviso which in fact extended the tripartite definition of instruction to them and imposed it on them.

In other words, the similarity of approach to secondary reorganization by the two Parties could not have been closer. Together both the Labour and Conservative governments had supported Department policy and used the new central powers to introduce tripartite organization, despite the reservations and opposition of a number of local authorities. In the first decade after the 1944 Act they had jointly brought about a higher degree of systematization than had ever before characterized the English educational system. Administratively it was neat and tidy, all children entered one of these types of school by selection at the end of the primary stage; only two of those led on to higher education; and any further experimentation had been quantitatively limited and had been rendered qualitatively compatible with the prevailing definition of instruction. The principle of hierarchical organization was predominantly negative since 75-80 percent of children entered the terminal secondary modern schools, the ladder only being extended to the minority selected for the Grammar and Technical schools. Yet from the mid-fifties onwards, this centrally guided push towards systematization, and the negative principle on which it was based, was increasingly resisted and disrupted if not reversed by opposition from local authorities.

By 1953 the LCC plans were well underway and Kidbrooke school was due to open as the first purpose-built comprehensive the following year. A row blew up, as Horsburgh refused to allow it to incorporate a local girls' grammar school, which had far reaching reverberations, starting with the AEC protesting to the Commons about this infringement of local autonomy in education. It was both the beginning of the Conservative earnest to save the grammar schools and of local determination to reassert the role of the LEA in policy formation. Thus David Eccles, who succeeded as Minister in 1954, asserted that no comprehensive school should be allowed to compete with any existing school — 'one must choose between justice and equality, for it is impossible to apply both principles at once. Those who support the comprehensive schools prefer equality. Her Majesty's present government prefer justice. My colleagues and I will never agree to the assassination of the grammar schools'.[368] Immediately he followed this up by rejecting proposals from Manchester and Swansea for multilateral schools on the above grounds. Effectively this meant that only on new housing estates could such schools be opened in urban areas — thus frustrating the postwar plans of various LEAs and freezing the existing state of play. Hence 'the mid-1950's were marked by a series of conflicts between local authorities wishing to establish comprehensive schools, and the Ministry, wishing to prevent this development except on its own terms'.[369]

The cause of the progressive LEAs was being strengthened by a change in expert opinion which to date had been the main prop of tripartism. The British Psychological Association produced *Secondary School Selection* in 1957, criticizing the use of intelligence tests for this purpose. Even more importantly the accumulation of sociological evidence drew attention to the systematic social bias of tests which reflected environmental influences as much as hereditary endowments. Increasingly the sociologists replaced the psychologists as sources of expert opinion and their views were received by and transmitted through the Central Advisory Committee in the Crowther Report (1959). Concurrently over fifty comprehensive schools were now functioning, were attracting considerable attention in the press, and making their own pragmatic contribution to the debate about educational opportunity.[370]

Nevertheless, when the Conservative Government published its White Paper on *Secondary Education for All, a New Drive* it gave priority to the development of advanced courses in secondary moderns, reiterated its defence of the grammar school, and reasserted the purely experimental nature of comprehensive schools. It too could command expert approval, particularly among educationalists like Eric James, Harry Rée and G. H. Bantock, though collectively it was becoming clear that its main support was from the Grammar School Teachers, the White Paper receiving its warmest welcome from the Joint-Four. Yet this paper was itself a concession to discontent with the secondary modern school in many areas. However, whilst the central response was to shore it up by allowing it to provide advanced courses instead of functioning as an educational cul-de-sac, the reaction of many local areas was to dispose of it altogether, jettisoning selection procedures at the same time. Although plans for comprehensive reorganization continued to be rejected (Newport and Darlington in 1959), the Leicestershire experiment crept in under the net by using existing buildings and stimulated more counties to plan a similar transition — including Derbyshire, Devon, Cornwall, Gloucestershire, Lancashire and Staffordshire. The Crowther Report appearing in 1959 and underlining the need for a more flexible structure of secondary schooling preceded a new wave of plans from the north of England which was moving determinedly towards general comprehensive organization. Significantly Edward Boyle sanctioned Bradford's two-tier system in 1964, making it the first city fully to abolish the 11+, a sign not so much of Conservative conversion to comprehensive schemes, as of snowballing antitripartism amongst local authorities.

> In the early 1960s there was apparent the beginnings of a movement to do away with the selective system at the secondary stage, one which represented a reversal of the position established in the late 1940s when the central authority had firmly contained development on these lines. Now it was the central authority that retreated before local authorities, though still uttering some final vetoes as it went.[371]

The end of the social democratic consensus in the mid-sixties issued in a more hostile period of party politics which was fully reflected in the field of educational policy, given the salience of this issue amongst the electorate. The next pair of governments (Labour 1964-70, Conservative 1970-74) displayed a hardening of antithetic policies towards secondary organization, only modified in *both* cases by the resistance of different sets of local authorites. In a period of growing corporatism, in which power was increasingly displaced onto the most strongly organized collectivities, it is not surprising that the local authorities proved very influential – they were always there to press their various cases, which ever party was in power, and with the growing volatility of electoral support, they were obvious candidates for the strategy adopted by both parties of appeasing sectional interests. Hence followed a decade in which the Labour ministry sponsored the more 'progressive' authorities and the Conservative government replied, not simply by an equivalent sponsorship of the more 'traditional' areas, but also by restoring to the LEAs as a whole much of their freedom for self-determination which had been lost under the 1944 Act. Thus thirty years later, by 1974, the respective positions of the central and local partners had again been reversed, with the Authorities becoming more influential than the Ministry as a consequence of political interaction in the last ten years.

When the Labour Party returned to power in 1964 it was, once again, already committed to the establishment of the comprehensive school and the abolition of the 11+. In deploring the selective tripartite system, the new Secretary of State, Michael Stewart, immediately drew attention to the successful comprehensive experiments operating in many areas and determined to make this national policy. 'Thereafter the former position, whereby local authorities desiring comprehensive reorganization had been impeded from above, was reversed. It was now the Ministry which, exercising its powers of control and direction in pursuance of a comprehensive policy, took the lead in promoting change and criticized or rejected the plans of local authorities which still wished to retain selection in open or concealed form'.[372] But if it was convinced of the rightness, importance and immediacy of this policy why did the Government follow the path of persuasion rather than legislation?

The main reason, of course, was their tiny majority in the House of Commons, until re-elected in 1966, added to which the DES set its face against legislation in the hope of avoiding controversy. As in 1945 the Ministry and the Party leadership were in agreement, for the controversy feared by the DES was precisely what the Government feared would lead any such Bill to fail. Consequently it decided to proceed by departmental circular rather than parliamentary reform, a method whose most important implication was 'its inbuilt shedding of responsibility for initiating reorganization by the central department'.[373] Circular 10/65 which requested all LEAs to submit proposals for the reorganization of secondary education on comprehensive lines thus gave specific priority to local initiative and policy. Moreover it was to progressive local practice that the government had turned when drawing up the circular with its six recommended models for reorganization. 'All six of the schemes suggested were either in operation or proposed through local authority initiatives. The "central guidance" that 10/65 claimed to give in effect amounted to passing around to all authorities what the DES had found in its suggestion box in 1965'.[374] Beyond this the Government merely stated its preference for the all-through 11-18 model, the simplest of the plans, the closest to the party's historic ideal of a common secondary school, and the most obvious embodiment of the positive principle of hierarchical integration. The sixth form college scheme or the middle school formula were considered too daring to recommend, except in limited numbers, but this central advice was quickly swept away, given the absence of sanctions to impose it.

This indeed was the fundamental difficulty of reform by persuasion: reorganization could neither be compelled or unified. Circular 10/66 was intended to provide some back-up since it refused to permit any school building that was not designed to fit in with reorganization. Since the government were not making any new funds available *for* comprehensive reform, building grants could not be manipulated to encourage amenable authorities and penalize recalcitrant ones. At most Circular 10/66 constituted a partial negative sanction, for some authorities did not need new schools and many did not need new grammar schools which were the only buildings discountenanced by the circular. Yet between them these two circulars were the only governmental instruments of reform and they could deal with neither of the main stumbling blocks to reorganization. On the one hand, there was local resistance and although the DES played it down, it was known that 50 percent of Authorities had no plans which could meet the 1966 deadline for submission.[375] Moreover, the swing towards the Conservatives in the municipal elections of 1967-68 encouraged many authorities to stall and retreat from reorganization. Finally, the ultimate irony was that if development plans were rejected, then the Authority simply returned to its old selective status quo. 'Although 10/65 claimed to be laying down national policy and giving central guidance, the failure to write the comprehensive principle into the law and to co-ordinate it carefully from the centre meant inevitably that the centre remained without real responsibility for pursuing reorganization and in an exposed position vis-à-vis those areas where local impetus was lacking'.[376] Simultaneously others could exploit this exposed position, and 'save our schools' committees sprang to the defence of local grammar schools whilst the National Educational Association grew out of a successful parental action in the Courts against the introduction of comprehensive schools in Enfield.[377] On the other hand the redevelopments which were taking place meant that the term 'comprehensive' was simply a label covering the greatest diversity of organizational arrangements and internal practices. 'A national reorganization policy that in effect amounted to permission for local authorities to go their own way could not genuinely be a national policy and it naturally resulted in a piecemeal state of affairs'.[378]

Eventually the Government was convinced of the need to increase unification if it was to make any more headway with reform and decided to introduce a Bill in 1970 to exert leverage on intransigent LEAs. Its terms were exceptionally mild, another indicator of central government stepping lightly where local autonomy was concerned, and in fact did not require anybody to do anything. The LEAs were to have 'regard for the need' to abolish selective secondary schooling: the Secretary of State could require the submission of development plans, but not their implementation. It would not have subtracted greatly from local initiative, but in any case the general election intervened in June before it had reached the statute book. The Labour government had failed to bring about comprehensive reform — the overall 'effect of the introduction of the circular was to accelerate rather than to begin — or to complete — a process',[379] and one which was anyway essentially local in character. It remained so under the Conservatives, for the weak unification which had prevented the execution of comprehensive reform and which Labour had belatedly sought to rectify, was weakened still further by the new government which stood to gain educationally from local intransigence and politically from defending local rights.

The new Party hostility was clearly apparent as the incoming government immediately withdrew the two Labour circulars, replacing them with circular 10/70 which stated that secondary policy was now to be guided by 'educational considerations in general, local needs and wishes in particular, and wise use of resources'. In other words the central polity, in direct deference to the 1944 Act, was *not* going to impose a particular form of secondary organization but to permit local variations, which might mean going comprehensive, staying selective or a mixture of both. The new circular 'also said no existing pattern of schools would be broken up it seemed to be working well, for it was good schools Conservatives wanted, not schools conforming to any one monolithic pattern. Under 10/65, even though meaningless legally, Conservatives felt authorities had been under a compulsion to organize in one way. Under 10/70 they were free to organize as they wished'.[380]

In practice this issued in a policy of co-existence — at the national level between different areas which organized secondary education in different ways, and at the local level between different kinds of schools which would thus offer parental choice. The latter was often the product of the Ministry accepting a comprehensive plan for a town or area, providing that it did not incorporate the grammar school(s). Thus the Conservative government decelerated and diluted comprehensive organization rather than stopping it (in fact Margaret Thatcher, as the new Secretary of State, accepted many more comprehensive schools than she rejected), such was the distribution of local preferences. Nevertheless the official switching of priorities and resources to the replacement of buildings at the primary level acted as a further brake on secondary redevelopment and this waning impetus served to activate the pro-comprehensive lobby as never before. It was the Conservatives' turn to be told that there is no such thing as a non-controversial educational policy, even (or especially) a laissez-faire one. Thus the TUC, NUT, NAHT, The Association for the Advancement of State Education and Stop the 11+ groups mobilized nationally and locally, while diversity continued to be the keynote of central provisions.

It is perhaps worth quoting Benn and Simon's conclusions at length about the decade following the first circular (throughout which the Secretary of State had no powers to compel LEAs to introduce comprehensive schools) because the links that they make between the analysis of change, egalitarian educational values and future political strategy are those towards which the Labour Government stumbled after 1974.

> The net effect of both the Labour Government's circular 10/65 and the Conservative's 10/70 has been to force the demand for comprehensives, and the campaigning, down to the local level. The local community is the essential building block of the educational system, where participation in education is most possible for ordinary citizens. But there is a limit to what the local authorities or the local pressure groups can do alone. The time is long overdue when central government aid, central government co-ordination and directives, central government advice, central government legislation, and central government long-term planning — with fair criteria and coherent standards laid down for comprehensive schools of all kinds, together with the extension of these criteria to all secondary schools — must be made. It is a comprehensive system

which is required, not merely a few more comprehensive schools; and only a national decision will make this possible. Without this necessary national action, the reform will always remain half way there.[381]

This is a call, frankly based on commitment to egalitarian values, for greater unification in order to enforce the positive principle of hierarchical organization, and one which also accepts and welcomes the increased standardization which would accompany higher systematization.

The Labour Government of 1974 entered office with its values clearly established but less than sure about how to attain them. The new Secretary of State, Reg Prentice, continued the battle of circulars, issuing 4/74 as a sterner version of 10/65, which required LEAs to submit plans for full comprehensive reorganization by the end of 1974, if they had not already done so. From the start, however, he showed a readiness to back this up with greater sanctions — the manipulation of building programmes to ensure LEA co-operation, the threat of withdrawing financial support from the voluntary aided schools if they resisted, and abolition of direct grant status to enforce the co-ordination of these schools. Nevertheless, though persuasion was now brutal it still stopped short at compulsion, and left seven Local Authorities in open defiance of the Department as well as a number of others who were stalling or producing unacceptable schemes. This time the Government was quicker to conclude that it would have to obtain new powers through legislation if it were to impose its will — a new Bill was promised in the Queen's Speech of November 1975.

Yet for all that it seems unlikely that events will follow the scenario sketched by Benn and Simon for going 'all the way there'. Certainly the issue of educational equality is a government priority — it has dominated political manipulation since the war, given the growing corporate power of the unions and the predominance of Labour Governments. Clearly too the present government has accepted the indispensibility of more unification to the universalization of comprehensive policy. However, it seems likely that it will stop there, with the formal introduction of the positive principle of hierarchical organization, rather than proceeding to impose Benn and Simon's 'fair criteria and coherent standards' for establishments bearing the name of comprehensive, an ideal redolent of the common school enshrined in the Bradford Charter. To begin with, the government has already manifested some reluctance towards legislation; it could have come to office with a Bill already prepared and dispensed with another round of circulars. Yet, understandably, both parties hold off from legislative encroachments on local autonomy, not only because of their certain unpopularity, but also, given a fairly regular alternation of governments, because to give oneself the advantages of a more centralized apparatus more responsive to the polity today is to hand it to the other party tomorrow. Thus the mildness of the 1970 Bill, scarcely augmenting unification to a point sufficient for the basic task, is a more realistic prototype to envisage than one which greatly increases systematization. Secondly, the comprehensive movement has gained the support it enjoys, precisely because it has *not* spelt standardization but has allowed teachers, administrators and communities to experiment with different forms of organization and curriculum. Consequently their attachment is more to this new freedom to *make* their own comprehensive schools than to some doctrinaire characterization of 'the' comprehensive school. Finally the sequence of political interaction, encouraged by both political parties as they gave local initiative its head, has now structured a series of vested interests in contemporary patterns of secondary organization (in Sixth form Colleges, Middle Schools, Upper Schools etc). These in themselves will condition a resistance to standardization which will continue to limit the degree of systematization which can be achieved — and there are many on both the left and the right who will not deplore the continuation of this tradition of weak systematization in English education.

NOTES

1. P. M. Blau, *Exchange and Power in Social Life*, New York, 1964. See Chapter 4, 'Social Exchange'.

2. Margaret Scotford Archer and Salvador Giner (eds.), *Contemporary Europe: Class, Status and Power*, London, 1971, pp. 1-28.

3. As Eisenstadt argues 'the institutionalization of exchange . . . sets normative and organizational limits to some of its basic properties and elements, such as the rates of exchange, the initial bargain positions, and the extent of persons admitted into the exchange'. S. N. Eisenstadt, *Review* of P. M. Blau's *Exchange and Power in Social Life, American Journal of Sociology*, Vol. LXXI, No. 3, 1965, p. 334.

4. Margaret Scotford Archer and Salvador Giner (eds.), *Contemporary Europe: Class Status and Power*, op. cit., pp. 14-19.

5. P. M. Blau, *Exchange and Power in Social Life*, op. cit., Chapter 5, 'Differentiation of Power'.

6. Cf. Walter Buckley, *Sociology and Modern Systems Theory*, New Jersey, 1967, p. 202.

7. P. M. Blau, *Exchange and Power in Social Life*, op. cit., p. 337.

8. Cf. J. Bukdahl et. al. (eds.), *Scandinavia Past and Present*, Copenhagen, no date, p. 831-35.

9. The Conservative People's Party (Det Konservative folkeparti) was formed on the foundations of the old Conservative party in 1916, as an organizational response to the Liberal victory in 1901. See Nils Andrén, *Government and Politics in the Nordic Counties*, Stockholm, 1964, ch. 3.

10. For a brief discussion of the Party's nineteenth century origins, see J. Bukdahl et. al. (eds.), *Scandinavia Past and Present*, op. cit., pp. 853-63.

11. The Executive Committee included Union representatives and one from the co-operative associations. The higher party organs thus included a large number of non-elected members from such organizations. However, the Party's Folketing group does not have an autonomous position like the British Labour Party. Cf. Kenneth E. Miller, *Government and Politics in Denmark*, Boston, 1968, pp. 60-69.

12. Unlike Britain the chief industrial units, other than in Copenhagen 'are closely bound to the agriculture both in the site of the factory units and in the supply of raw materials'. A. C. O'Dell, *The Scandinavian World*, London, 1957, p. 197.

13. At the party congress of 1880 the Social Democrats had adopted a resolution stating that gradually the State should become the principal landowner, but rejecting the obligatory introduction of collective forms of agriculture.

14. Jan Stehouwer, 'Long term Ecological Analysis of Electoral Statistics in Denmark', *Scandinavian Political Studies*, Vol. 2, 1967, p. 111.

15. 'Denmark is a country totally lacking those cleavages which elsewhere produce bitter conflict among the citizens and among parties in the legislature. No minority problems exist, such as religious, ethnic, regional or other types of subcultures, within the territorial borders. In the post-war period no party – not even the communists – has stated as its goal an alteration of the structure of the political system; there has been no "opposition of principle".' Morgens N. Pedersen, 'Consensus and Conflict in the Danish Folketing 1945-65', *Scandinavian Political Studies*, Vol. 2, 1967, p. 160.

16. S. S. Nilson, 'Political Parties', in J. A. Lauwerys (ed.), *Scandinavian Democracy*, Copenhagen, 1958, pp. 107-126.

17. A. C. O'Dell, *The Scandinavian World*, op. cit., p. 193-94.

18. National Trade Unions formed the Federation of Trade Unions in 1898 and the Employers' organization developed almost simultaneously. Serious conflict between them produced the lockout of 1899, involving an unprecedented 30,000 men. The 'September Settlement' which resulted involved recognition of the unions, and their official rights to negotiate, whilst establishing rules of procedure for the declaration of strikes which ruled out the wild-cat strike, common since the 1870s. Cf. J. Bukdahl et. al. *Scandinavia Past and Present*, op. cit., p. 858 ff.

19. Erik Damgaard, 'Stability and Change in the Danish Party System over Half a Century', *Scandinavian Political Studies*, Vol. 9, 1974, p. 108.

20. Kenneth E. Miller, *Government and Politics in Denmark*, Boston, 1968, p. 60 ff.

21. Details of the 1915 Constitution and the modified system of proportional representation by district are given in J. Andenaes, 'The Development of Political Democracy in Scandinavia', in J. A. Lauwerys (ed.), *Scandinavian Democracy*, op. cit., pp. 93-107.

22. Cf. W. Glyn Jones, *Denmark*, London, 1970, pp. 134-35.

23. Ibid., pp. 116-19.

24. Erik Damgaard, 'Stability and Change in the Danish Party System over Half a Century', op. cit., p. 104.

25. 'On the one hand the organizations take the initiative in approaching the central administration with problems which the municipalities consider important, on the other, the ministries rarely make decisions of far reaching consequence without first ascertaining municipal opinion through written or oral inquiries to the organizations. In addition to all this there is the work of the numerous committees and commissions appointed by the government to investigate questions of municipal importance – The municipal organisations are nearly always represented in these and as a consequence frequently exert a determining influence on their reports – an influence which is developed in legislation by numerous municipal leaders who sit in Parliament'. Bertel Dahlgaard, 'Local Government', in J. A. Lauwerys (ed.), *Scandinavian Democracy*, op. cit., p. 181.

26. For a time workers suffered about a 7 percent drop in living standards, by withholding wage claims, as prices began to rise, in order to limit unemployment. Wages only began to rise again at the end of the decade. W. Glyn Jones, *Denmark*, op. cit., p. 161 ff.

27. Erik Damgaard, 'Stability and Change in the Danish Party System over Half a Century', op. cit., p. 116.

28. 'Party leaders have claimed that Radical participation in coalitions with the Social Democrats has restrained the socialist tendencies of the larger party and helped to prevent the emergence of "two bloc" politics in Denmark, with a socialist and an anti-socialist group belligerently confronting each other. The Radicals have occasionally supported or offered to support Liberal Minority Governments but have drawn the line at formal collaboration with the Conservatives, for whom they have seen no place in any liberal-minded reform movement. They have thus opposed the Liberal-Conservative alliance as tending toward an undesirable polarization of political blocs and have tried to separate the Liberals from it'. Kenneth E. Miller, *Government and Politics in Denmark*, op. cit., p. 83-84.

29. 'That year (1939) the decline at the election to the Folketing and the defeat at the referendum for a new Constitution signaled the beginning of a new period in which the Social Democrats had to share the same conditions as the other parties, with shifting ups and downs at the elections to the Folketing. The time of triumphal progress had ceased'. Palle Svenssen, 'Support for the Danish Social Democratic Party 1924-1939 – Growth and Response', *Scandinavian Political Studies*, Vol. 9, 1974, pp. 127-46.

30. Erik Damgaard, 'The Parliamentary Basis of Danish Governments. The Patterns of Coalition Formation', *Scandinavian Political Studies*, Vol. 4, 1969, p. 43.

31. W. Glyn Jones, *Denmark* op. cit., p. 156.

32. Morgens N. Pedersen, 'Consensus and Conflict in the Danish Folketing, 1945-65', op. cit., p. 160-61.

33. Based on the single tax theory of Henry George and known as Rets-forbundet. It returned members to the Rigsdag and Folketing from 1926. In 1957 it helped form the Triangle government, but was wiped out from the Folketing in the 1960 election.

34. Nils Andrén, *Government and Politics in the Nordic Countries*, op. cit., p. 43.

35. For details of changes see Jan Stehouwer, 'Long Term Ecological Analysis of Electoral Statistics in Denmark', op. cit., pp. 104-15.

36. Kenneth E. Miller, *Government and Politics in Denmark*, op. cit., pp. 116-23.

37. Erik Damgaard, 'The Parliamentary Basis of Danish Governments: The Patterns of Coalition Formation', op. cit., p. 52.

38. W. Glyn Jones, *Denmark*, op. cit., p. 208.

39. Morgens N. Pedersen et al., 'Party Distances in the Danish Folketing 1945-68', *Scandinavian Political Studies*, Vol. 6, 1971, p. 101.

40. Ole Riis, 'The Local Council Elections in Denmark 1970', *Scandinavian Political Studies*, Vol. 6, 1971, p. 217.

41. However, proportional representation at both levels of government also means that, unlike Britain, party strengths in local elections are not strikingly different in various parts of the Country from Folketing ones. This presumably means that overall the two will show less policy variation from one another than can be the case in Britain. Cf. Kenneth E. Miller, *Government and Politics in Denmark*, op. cit., p. 197.

42. Curt Sørensen, 'Denmark: Politics since 1964 and the Parliamentary Election of 1966', *Scandinavian Political Studies*, Vol. 2, 1967, pp. 263-65.

43. Kenneth E. Miller, *Government & Politics in Denmark*, op. cit., p. 221.

44. Cf. Ingemar Glans, 'Denmark: the 1964 Folketing Election', *Scandinavian Political Studies*, Vol. 1, 1966, pp. 231-36, and 'The Danish Parliamentary Election of 1966', *Scandinavian Political Studies*, Vol. 2, 1967, pp. 266-72.

45. Cf. Jan Stehouwer and Ole Borre, 'Four General Elections in Denmark, 1960-68', *Scandinavian Political Studies*, Vol. 4, 1969, pp. 133-48; Morgens N Pedersen, 'Preferential Voting in Denmark: The Voters' Influence on the Election of Folketing Candidates', *Scandinavian Political Studies*, Vol. 1, 1966, pp. 167-87; Raimo Väyrynen, 'Analysis of Party Systems by Concentration, Fractionalization, and Entropy Measures', *Scandinavian Political Studies*, Vol. 7, 1972, pp. 137-55.

46. Jørgen Elklit, Ole Riis and Ole Tonsgaard, 'Local Voting Studies of Total Electorates: The Danish General Election of 1971', *Scandinavian Political Studies*, Vol. 7, 1972, p. 211.

47. Cf. Ole Borre and Daniel Katz, 'Party Identification and its Motivational Base in a Multiparty System: A study of the Danish General Election of 1971', *Scandinavian Political Studies*, Vol. 8, 1973, pp. 69-111.

48. Ole Borre, 'Denmark's Protest Election of December 1973', *Scandinavian Political Studies*, Vol. 9, 1974, pp. 197-203.

49. Ole Borre, 'The General Election in Denmark, January 1975: Toward a New Structure of the Party System?', *Scandinavian Political Studies*, Vol. 10, 1975. See Table II, p. 213.

50. Morgens N. Pedersen, *Political Development and Elite Transformation in Denmark*, London, 1976, p. 55.

51. *The Times*, 29 April, 1976.

52. Morgens N. Pedersen, *Political Development and Elite Transformation in Denmark*, op. cit., pp. 56-57.

53. *The Times*, 29 April, 1976.

54. Law of 20 March 1918, quoted in Willis Dixon, *Education in Denmark*, Copenhagen, 1958, p. 119.

55. Cited by Willis Dixon, ibid., p. 130.

56. Tage Kampmann, 'Primary School Teachers', in Danske Selskab, *Schools and Education in Denmark*, Copenhagen, 1972, p. 131 ff.

57. F. J. Borgbjerg, Social Democrat Minister of Education, cited in Willis Dixon, *Education in Denmark*, op. cit., p. 136.

58. There was even an attempt to prevent organized interests working through the Parents Boards. 'When at least a third of the parents and guardians (if the school roll were not over 100, at least one-half; if the school roll were over 400, at least a sixth) made a petition to the Communal Council, a Parents Board of three members must be elected for the single school. The voters would be parents and guardians with children at the school and the right to elect the Board lapsed if less than the proportion of voters representing the petitioner minimum stated above took part in the election – an interesting provision this, to prevent the arising of cliques and try to guarantee a sustained interest in the business'. Ibid., pp. 137-38.

59. Eigil Thrane, *Education and Culture in Denmark: A survey of the Educational Scientific and Cultural Conditions*, Copenhagen, 1958, p. 24 ff.

60. Ministry of Education, *Survey of Danish Elementary, Secondary and Further (non-vocational) Education*, Copenhagen, 1951, p. 18.

61. Cf. Eigil Thrane, *Education and Culture in Denmark*, op. cit.

62. Ibid., p. 21.

63. Herman Ruge, *Educational Systems in Scandinavia*, Oslo, 1962, p. 23.

64. Willis Dixon, op. cit., p. 225.

65. Hjalmar Thomsen, 'The Primary School in Denmark', in Danske Selskab, *Schools and Education in Denmark*, op. cit., p. 55.

66. Loc. cit.

67. Aksel Nelleman, 'The Gymnasium School in Denmark', in Danske Selskab, *Schools and Education in Denmark*, op. cit., pp. 76-104.

68. OECD, *Study on Teachers: Denmark, Italy, Luxembourg: Training, Recruitment and Utilization of Teachers*, Country Case Studies, Primary and Secondary Education, Paris, 1968, p. 89.

69. Danish Ministry of Education, *Higher Education in Denmark*, Copenhagen, 1954, p. 8.

70. Ole B. Thomsen, 'Governments and Universities: A Danish View', in D. F. Dadson (ed.), *On Higher Education*, Toronto, 1966, p. 94.

71. The 1911 Committee Report cited by Willis Dixon, *Education in Denmark*, op. cit., p. 129.

72. Loc. cit.

73. Ibid., p. 134.

74. Both cited ibid., p. 126.

75. Hjalmar Thomsen, 'The Primary School in Denmark', op. cit., p. 11.

76. Cited by Willis Dixon, *Education in Denmark,* op. cit., p. 157.

77. Official announcement cited ibid., p. 163.

78. 'The Primary School law is to a large extent merely a framework. This is particularly true of the method of teaching . . . Nor are there any ordinances or Ministerial regulations directing how the objects of the primary schools are to be attained. All there is, is a circular of 24th May 1941 giving very briefly what should normally be attained in the seven years of compulsory education', Eigil Thrane, *Education and Culture in Denmark*, op. cit., p. 17.

79. From 'Suggestions for Instruction in the Non-examination Folkschool' (1942), cited by Willis Dixon, *Education in Denmark*, op. cit., p. 163.

80. OECD, *Study on Teachers*, op. cit., p. 123 and 126.

81. Tage Kampmann, 'Primary School Teachers', op. cit., p. 133 ff.

82. OECD, *Study on Teachers*, op. cit., p. 151.

83. Those university students with the Part I examination can transfer to the Teacher Training College and have it counted as their specialist subject. However no equivalence has been established in the opposite direction, enabling transfer *to* the universities. See Tage Kampmann, 'Primary School Teachers', op. cit., p. 141 ff.

84. OECD, *Study on Teachers*, op. cit., pp. 191-93.

85. Cf. Willis Dixon, *Education in Denmark*, op. cit., p. 207-08.

86. William W. Brickman, *Denmark's Educational System and Problems*, Washington, 1967, pp. 5-10.

87. The Teacher Training College Council has 16 members, 3 appointed by the Principals of the State Colleges, 3 by Principals of Private Colleges, 1 by the Teachers' Council of the Royal Danish School of Educational Studies, 1 by the Danish NUT, 2 by the National Council of Student Teachers, 3 by teachers of the State Colleges and 3 by their private counterparts. See Tage Kampmann, 'Primary School Teachers', op. cit.

88. Cf. ibid.

89. OECD, *Study on Teachers*, op. cit., pp. 70-74.

90. Danish Ministry of Education, *Higher Education in Denmark*, op. cit. 'The University of Aarhus has property of its own and is a self-supporting institution; its constitution and regulations, however, must be approved by the Minister of Education. Its administration is in the hands of a Board of Governors, at present consisting of 8 members, viz 3 elected by the Society formed by friends of the university, 3 elected by Aarhus City Council, the Rektor of the University, and a representative of the State', p. 8.

91. Ole B. Thomsen, 'Governments and Universities: A Danish View', op. cit., p. 101.

92. Loc. cit.

93. Ibid., p. 104.

94. Willis Dixon, *Education in Denmark,* op. cit., p. 170.

95. William W. Brickman, *Denmark's Educational System and Problems*, op. cit., p. 34.

96. OECD, *Study on Teachers*, op. cit., p. 45.

97. Ibid. The standard weekly load of Folkschool Teachers was 32 lessons, compared with 24 for Gymnasium teachers.

98. Ibid., p. 53.

99. Ole B. Thomsen, 'Governments and Universities: A Danish View', op. cit., p. 118.

100. Willis Dixon, *Education in Denmark*, op. cit., p. 142.

101. Ibid., p. 153.

102. T. Hauberg, a Social Democrat and a Head Teacher defending the Bill, cited ibid., p. 154.

103. Cited from *Paedagogisk – Psykologisk Tidsskrift*, ibid., p. 200.

104. Ibid., p. 225.

105. F. C. Kålund-Jørgensen, 'The Relation between Secondary Schools and Universities – Denmark', in G. Z. F. Bereday and J. A. Lauwerys (eds.), *The Yearbook of Education* London, 1959, p. 457.

106. Ibid., p. 458.

107. Cited by Willis Dixon, *Education in Denmark*, op. cit., p. 230.

108. Cf. F. C. Kålund-Jørgensen, 'The Relation Between Secondary Schools and Universities – Denmark', op. cit., p. 472 ff. During the second reading of the Bill the Faculties of Philosophy and Arts submitted a memorandum in which they maintained that the altered pattern would devalue pre-university education to such a degree that it would have to be considered whether the holders of the higher school certificate should be accepted in future. The governing body (Konsortium) of Copenhagen University put forward a memorandum on the same lines stressing that professional requirements were increasing just when it was proposed to dilute secondary education. Aarhus supported Copenhagen in this.

109. Ibid., p. 472.

110. Ole Borre, 'The General Election in Denmark, January 1975: Toward a New Structure of the Party System', op. cit., p. 212.

111. Cf. Andrew Jones, *The Politics of Reform, 1884*, Cambridge, 1972..

112. Guy Routh, *Occupation and Pay in Great Britain 1906-60*, Cambridge, 1965, p. 32.

113. Henry Pelling, *A Short History of the Labour Party*, London, 1968, p. 11 ff.

114. Idem. Membership of the Labour Representation Committee rose from 376,000 in 1901 to 861,000 in 1903.

115. David Butler and Donald Stokes, *Political Change in Britain: the Evolution of Electoral Choice*, London, 1974, p. 179.

116. Samuel H. Beer, *Modern British Politics: A Study of Parties and Pressure Groups*, London, 1965, p. 113.

117. Henry Pelling, *A Short History of the Labour Party*, op. cit., p. 30.

118. George Sayer Bain, Robert Bacon and John Pimlott, 'The Labour Force' in A. H. Halsey, *Trends in British Society since 1900*, London, 1972. In 1915, 2,054,000 union members were affiliated to the Labour Party, representing 47.1% of the total union membership. p. 125.

119. Idem. Union membership reached a peak in 1920 of 4,318,000 members which was not surpassed until after the second world war.

120. A. L. Bowley, *Wages and Income in the United Kingdom since 1860*, Cambridge, 1937, p. xviii.

121. Guy Routh, *Occupation and Pay in Great Britain 1906-60*, op. cit., p. 106.

122. A. L. Bowley, *Wages and Income in the United Kingdom since 1860*, op. cit., p. 39. See also Ch. IV, 'Earnings and Needs'.

123. George Sayer Bain, Robert Bacon and John Pimlott, 'The Labour Force', op. cit. The peak rate of unemployment between 1902 and 1914 was 7.8% in 1908, the average for these years being 4.3%, p. 119.

124. Cf. Sidney Webb, 'Labour and the New Social Order', a policy statement adopted by the Party conference in 1918 and which constituted its basic platform until 1950.

125. Guy Routh, *Occupation and Pay in Great Britain 1906-60*, op. cit., p. 123.

126. Ibid., p. 106.

127. Ibid., p. 125-32.

128. George Sayer Bain, Robert Bacon and John Pimlott, 'The Labour Force', op. cit., p. 119.

129. See Bentley B. Gilbert, *British Social Policy 1914-1939*, London, 1970, especially chapters 3, 5 and 6.

130. A. L. Bowley, *Wages and Income in the United Kingdom since 1860*, op. cit., pp. xviii-xix.

131. On the calculation that the free margin for the average worker in employment had risen to £1, Bowley comments that 'No doubt the allocation of this margin varies greatly from family to family. In some cases they will have moved to new houses at higher rents. Very likely more fuel and light are used, and more variety of clothes are bought. The rest may be saved, used as a reserve for unemployment, or for re-establishing the budget after resuming work, spent on travel, tobacco, cinemas or in any other way'. Ibid., p. 39.

132. Guy Routh, *Occupation and Pay in Great Britain, 1906-60*, op. cit., p. 116.

133. Samuel H. Beer, *Modern British Politics*, op. cit. With a tendency to represent the larger firms the FBI, at the end of its first year, included 62 trade associations and 350 individual firms. By 1925 these had risen to 195 associations and 2,100 firms. p. 333.

134. Maurice Cowling, *The Impact of Labour 1920-1924*, Cambridge, 1971. 'If, however, there had been no division at the top there is no reason to suppose that the trimming leadership given by Asquith or Lloyd George could not have continued indefinitely. There would have been serious conflict. The atmosphere would have changed. There would have been leftward shifts. Some Liberals would have left when they occurred. But what destroyed the Liberal Party was not the inevitability of the Labour predominance in an enlarged electorate but a combination of the loss of Ireland in 1918, the timing of general elections, splits among the leaders, depression in the Liberal Party at large, and the will of the Conservative Party and the energy, ruthlessness and intelligence of Labour propaganda'. pp. 420-21.

135. David Butler and Donald Stokes, *Political Change in Britain*, op. cit., pp. 168-77.

136. Ibid., pp. 165-66.

137. Ralph Miliband, *Parliamentary Socialism*, London, 1961, p. 148.

138. Robert McKenzie and Allan Silver, *Angels in Marble*, London, 1968, p. 13.

139. V. L. Allen, *Trade Unions and the Government*, London, 1960, pp. 29-30.

140. Henry Pelling, *A Short History of the Labour Party*, op. cit., p. 140.

141. Nigel Harris, *Competition and the Corporate Society: British Conservatives the State and Industry 1945-1964*, London, 1972, p. 43.

142. Samuel H. Beer, *Modern British Politics*, op. cit., p. 298.

143. Churchill quoted ibid., p. 305.

144. G. S. Bain, *The Growth of White Collar Unionism*, Oxford, 1970. He estimates that between 1950 and 1965 the proportion of the active population engaged in manual occupations fell by 5%.

145. Cf. S. H. Miller, 'Comparative Social Mobility' in C. S. Heller (ed.), *Structured Social Inequality*, New York, 1969, pp. 325-40.

146. David Butler and Donald Stokes, *Political Change in Britain*, op. cit., pp. 177-78.

147. Ibid., p. 182.

148. Samuel H. Beer, *Modern British Politics*, op. cit., p. 242.

149. Nigel Harris, *Competition and the Corporate Society*, op. cit., p. 261.

150. S. E. Finer, 'The Political Power of Private Capital', Part 2, *Sociological Review*, No. 1, Vol. IV, 1956, p. 14.

151. Cf. H. F. Lydall, *British Incomes and Savings*, Oxford, 1955 and his 'The Long Term Trend in the Size of Distribution of Income', *Journal of the Royal Statistical Society*, Series A. Vol. 122, Pt. 1, 1959 pp. 1-46; F. W. Paish, 'The Real Incidence of Personal Taxation', *Lloyds Bank Review*, New series No. 43, Jan. 1957, p. 1-16.

152. H. F. Lydall and D. G. Tipping, 'The Distribution of Personal Wealth in Britain', *Bulletin of Oxford University Institute of Economics and Statistics*, Vol. 23, 1961, p. 83-104.

153. Guy Routh, *Occupation and Pay in Great Britain, 1906-60*, op. cit., p. 106.

154. Richard M. Titmuss, *Income Distribution and Social Change*, London, 1963.

155. T. B. Bottomore, 'Class Structure in Western Europe', in Margaret Scotford Archer and Salvador Giner (eds.), *Contemporary Europe; Class, Status and Power*, London, 1971, p. 392.

156. Cf. S. Pollard and D. W. Crossley, *The Wealth of Britain*, London, 1968, Chapter 9. Guy Routh, *Occupation and Pay in Great Britain, 1906-60*, op. cit., p. 133.

157. Andrew Shonfield, *Modern Capitalism*, Oxford, 1965, p. 368.

158. J. K. Galbraith, *The New Industrial State*, Harmondsworth, 1969. The unidirectional flow of instructions from consumer, to market, to producer, is characterized as the 'accepted sequence' of classical economics. This is no longer held to correspond to reality. Instead the firm reaches forward to control its markets and or beyond that to manage market behaviour by shaping the attitudes of those it ostensibly serves. This is termed the 'revised sequence' which dominates among the larger firms of the technostructure whilst the 'accepted sequence' still operates in the smaller entrepreneurial firms.

159. Samuel H. Beer, *Modern British Politics*, op. cit., p. 360.

160. Nigel Harris, *Competition and the Corporate Society*, op. cit., p. 270.

161. Ibid., p. 271.

162. Ibid., p. 272.

163. David Butler and Donald Stokes, *Political Change in Britain* op. cit. 'By the end of the decade the fraction of the electorate which felt that trade unions had too much power had grown from one-half to two-thirds. In contrast, the period from 1963-1970 saw a drop in the percentage of respondents thinking that big business had too much power', p. 198.

164. Ibid., pp. 193-97 and 203-04.

165. Nigel Harris, *Competition and the Corporate Society*, op. cit., p. 255.

166. David Butler and Donald Stokes, *Political Change in Britain*, op. cit., p. 207.

167. 1906 Birrell's Bill; 1908 McKenna's Bill; 1908 Runciman's Bill; See James Murphy, *Church, State and Schools in Britain, 1800-1970*, London, 1971, pp. 96-100.

168. Ibid., p. 98.

169. Ibid., p. 99.

170. Ibid., p. 100.

171. Ibid., p. 99.

172. R. J. W. Selleck, *English Primary Education and the Progressives, 1914-1939*, London, 1972, p. 26.

173. Michael Sanderson, *The Universities and British Industry, 1850-1970*, London, 1972, p. 78.

174. Cited ibid., p. 82.

175. Ibid., pp. 93-94.

176. Ibid., p. 103.

177. Ibid., p. 202.

178. Brian Simon, *Education and the Labour Movement, 1870-1920*, London, 1965, p. 309.

179. Ibid., p. 311.

180. Cf. W. W. Craik, *The Central Labour College*, London, 1964.

181. James Murphy, *Church, State and Schools in Britain, 1800-1970*, op. cit., p. 106.

182. John Vaizey and John Sheehan, *Resources for Education*, London, 1968, pp. 36-40.

183. James Murphy, *Church, State and Schools in Britain, 1800-1970*, op. cit., p. 114.

184. R. J. W. Selleck, *English Primary Education and the Progressives, 1914-1939*, op. cit., p. 32.

185. John Vaizey and John Sheehan, *Resources for Education*, op. cit., p. 28.

186. Cf. W. A. C. Stewart, *The Educational Innovators*, London, 1968, Vol. 2.

187. Brian Simon, *Education and the Labour Movement, 1870-1920*, op. cit., p. 141-42.

188. Michael Sanderson, *The Universities and British Industry, 1850-1970*, op. cit., p. 250.

189. Ibid., pp. 252-53.

190. Cited ibid., p. 307.

191. Cited ibid., p. 310.

192. Ibid., pp. 346-48.

193. John Vaizey and John Sheehan, *Resources for Education*, op. cit., p. 122.

194. 'We may note a rise in real outlays from £128.1 m. in 1921 to £152.9 m. in 1930. This expansion of about one sixth was a substantial one during a period marked by depression. It was maintained at a slower rate to 1938, when expenditure was £165.0 m. Thereafter there was a fall, during the war years to £139.3 m. in 1944, but the post-war period soon made up for this. By 1948 expenditure had reached £215.3 m., two thirds more than in 1938. By 1953 the total was £287.3 m., three quarters more than in 1948, and by 1955 the total was probably £300.0 m. or nearly double the 1938 figure. Between 1955 and 1965, the total rose to £451.4m. that is to over twice the 1948 figure. Thus, we see, there was a notable expansion in the total amount of expenditure in real terms during the forty years we have studied, and that the major part of this expansion has taken place since 1955', ibid., pp. 131-32.

195. Ibid., p. 107.

196. Ibid., p. 116.

197. Ibid., p. 120.

198. Two schools of this kind, known to the author, were charging £17 per term in the mid-fifties in the North of England.

199. B. Tipton, *Conflict and Change in a Technical College*, London, 1973, p. 19.

200. See M. S. Archer, 'Grande-Bretagne', in Georges Langrod (ed.), *La consultation dans l'administration contemporaine*, Paris, 1972, pp. 754-83.

201. Maurice Kogan and Tim Packwood, *Advisory Councils and Committees in Education*, London, 1974, p. 60.

202. Ibid., p. 59.

203. P. E. P., *Graduates in Industry*, London, 1957, p. 43.

204. Michael Sanderson, *The Universities and British Industry 1850-1970*, op. cit., p. 364.

205. Ibid., p. 359.

206. See Audrey Collin, Anthony M. Rees, and John Utting, *The Arts Graduate in Industry* (Acton Society Trust), London, 1962.

207. Michael Sanderson, *The Universities and British Industry, 1850-1970*, op. cit., p. 353.

208. Ibid., p. 352.

209. James Murphy, *Church, State and Schools in Britain, 1800-1970*, op. cit., p. 122.

210. John Vaizey and John Sheehan, *Resources for Education*, op. cit., p. 107.

211. James Murphy, *Church, State and Schools in Britain, 1800-1970*, op. cit., p. 124.

212. Michael Sanderson, *The Universities and British Industry, 1850-1970*, op. cit., p. 364.

213. Ibid., p. 386.

214. Ibid., p. 375.

215. Ibid., p. 378.

216. Asher Tropp, *The School Teachers*, London, 1957, pp. 117-18.

217. Ibid., p. 114 note.

218. The Revised Code made it difficult to substantiate salary claims, since it allowed the Authorities to retort that teachers' pay would rise if their pupils were more successful, since grant income for salaries depended on the number of examination passes. It was an instrument for dissimulation, since it appeared to make remuneration dependent only on personal expertise.

219. The School Boards had given teachers the chance of executive action, for although they could not hold positions on the Boards under which they served, they could be elected in other areas, and private teachers, ex-teachers and union officials were able to hold seats. Given the cumulative voting system used, school teachers often ended with considerable influence on the Boards, which helped to release them collectively from the mercy of their employers.

220. See P. H. J. H. Gosden, *The Development of Educational Administration in England and Wales*, Oxford, 1966, p. 181 ff. In a Memorandum of 1903 Morant specified five interests which should always be represented: University education, Secondary education, Technical, Commercial and Industrial education, Teacher Training and Elementary education in Council and Voluntary Schools.

221. Harold Perkin, *Key Profession: The History of the Association of University Teachers*, London, 1969, p. 15.

222. Michael Sanderson, *The Universities and British Industry, 1850-1970*, op. cit. 'The most successful movements were those where support was excited in a wide range of firms and industries, as in Manchester, Birmingham, and Liverpool, with no obvious single supporter. If the civic movement were merely channelled into the routine forms of local government then this was little better than a kiss of death as the anaemic early history of Nottingham, Southampton and Exeter indicated', p. 80.

223. Ibid., Table 6, page 78.

224. Harold Perkin, *Key Profession*, op. cit., p. 33.

225. Graeme C. Moodie and Rowland Eustace, *Power and Authority in British Universities*, London, 1974, p. 28.

226. A. H. Halsey and M. A. Trow, *The British Academics*, London, 1971. 'They often had to engage in struggles with local trustees to establish the elements of academic freedom and self-government which they held to be appropriate to their professional status and which many of them had brought to their new universities from the traditional academic guilds of Oxford and Cambridge. They quickly won academic freedom in practice, if not in formal constitutions', p. 149 note.

227. Norman Morris, 'England', pp. 44-82, in Albert A. Blum (ed.), *Teacher Unions and Associations, a Comparative Study*, Illinois, 1969, p. 47.

228. See Asher Tropp, *The School Teachers*, op. cit., pp. 154-59.

229. Cited ibid., p. 159. See also p. 174.

230. Cited ibid., p. 171.

231. Phrases contained in the 'Holmes-Morant' Circular of 6 January, 1910. Reprinted ibid., pp. 271-72.

232. Although in 1911 the Board did recognize a four-year course given in 'training departments attached to university institutions', after considerable NUT and collegiate pressure, this did not overcome the fundamental bifurcation between the formation of elementary and secondary teachers.

233. *The Schoolmaster*, 26 April 1919.

234. See Asher Tropp, *The School Teachers*, op. cit., p. 268.

235. Henceforth, 'if self-government were to be anything more than a dream, the unions would first have to come to terms with themselves. A profession which was divided by conflicting interests and aspirations was not likely to be entrusted with the right to administer its own affairs ... Further progress seemed to depend, therefore, on the construction of some overall organizational framework', Norman Morris, 'England', op. cit., p. 74.

236. P. H. J. H. Gosden, *The Development of Educational Administration in England and Wales*, op. cit., p. 120 ff.

237. Cf. Maurice Kogan, *The Government of Education*, London, 1971, p. 14.

238. This 'policy disclosed such a prospect of danger to educational freedom and to a wholesome variety of experimentation, such a menace to local responsibility and so formidable to accretion of work and power to the Board at Whitehall that I dismissed it from my mind'. H. A. L. Fisher, *An Unfinished Autobiography*, London, 1940, p. 97.

239. Michael Sanderson, *The Universities and British Industry, 1850-1970*, op. cit., p. 184.

240. Ibid., p. 116.

241. H. A. L. Fisher, *The Place of the University in National Life*, Oxford, 1919, p. 6.

242. See Michael Sanderson, *The Universities and British Industry, 1850-1970*, op. cit., pp. 231-32.

243. Ibid., p. 234.

244. This had never been antithetic to government thinking. Haldane as the disciple of Green and Adam Smith did not wish for financial dependence on the state, but rather endorsed the principle that government grants should be paid in proportion to the Colleges' income from other sources, and obviously these would be mainly industrial. This principle guided the various committees successively disbursing the grants before the development of the UGC. In Liberal thinking in particular, this encouraged university initiative without fostering parasitism on the State. Cf. Eric Ashby and Mary Anderson, *Portrait of Haldane at Work on Education*, London, 1974, p. 74 f.

245. Michael Sanderson, *The Universities and British Industry, 1850-1970*, op. cit., p. 119.

246. To Haldane 'what would appeal most really to the public would be the proposition to add to the local Universities thoroughly equipped organizations for the development of the application of science to commerce and especially industry. This we might put forward as an entire policy ... of course a thoroughly practical plan would have to be elaborated, with the special character of Midland industries in view. The Birmingham Charlottenburg should have its own special characteristics', cited in Eric Ashby and Mary Anderson, *Portrait of Haldane at work on Education*, op. cit., p. 72.

247. Harold Perkin, *Key Profession*, op. cit., p. 33.

248. See Eric Ashby and Mary Anderson, *Portrait of Haldane at work on Education*, op. cit., p. 78 and p. 100.

249. Harold Perkin, *Key Profession*, op. cit., p. 26.

250. Ibid., p. 34.

251. Norman Morris, 'England', op. cit., p. 75.

252. Asher Tropp, *The School Teachers,* op. cit., p. 246 note.

253. Cited ibid., p. 246.

254. Cited ibid., p. 243.

255. Cited ibid., p. 246.

256. William Taylor, *Society and the Education of Teachers*, London, 1969, p. 68.

257. Cf. P. H. J. H. Gosden, *The Development of Educational Administration in England and Wales*, op. cit., p. 117.

258. R. J. W. Selleck, *English Primary Education and the Progressives, 1914-1939*, op. cit., pp. 46-47.

259. Ibid., p. 120.

260. Harold Perkin, *Key Profession*, op. cit., p. 59.

261. Loc. cit.

262. Cited ibid., p. 60.

263. Ibid., p. 69.

264. Graeme C. Moodie and Rowland Eustace, *Power and Authority in British Universities*, op. cit. 'In the nineteenth century the internal powers of court and council were virtually unqualified. In this century, however, council's powers have been steadily reduced by insistance upon the need to consult senate and by the grant of specific powers to the latter including, in particular, the vesting in senate of the initiative in important areas', p. 34.

265. Cf. Harold Perkin, *Key Profession*, op. cit., p. 127-28.

266. Cited ibid., p. 46.

267. Ibid., p. 35.

268. C.f. Ibid., p. 115.

269. Given the low basic pay scales a campaign started in 1954 to raise them. This showed a clear connection between good pay and upgrading. The campaign was aimed at 'building up public appreciation of the value of education and the worth of the teacher' – an attempt to get the public to value them more than the State did. This did not make any significant gains despite actions like refusing to collect school savings and 'dinner-money'. Cf. Asher Tropp, *The School Teachers*, op. cit., p. 252-53.

270. William Taylor, *Society and the Education of Teachers*, op. cit., p. 72.

271. 'One of the reasons for the NUT's failure was lack of positive support from other unions. Self-government, on the basis of one man one vote, implied government by teachers in elementary schools. The secondary school unions could not accept this, nor could the British Government, whose members were drawn from the same social and educational class as secondary school teachers . . . Even if a central council for the profession were to be established, it could only govern for as long as its members pulled in the same direction. Further progress seemed to depend, therefore, on the construction of some overall organizational framework within which teachers could pursue matters of general concern in concert, without placing their particular sectional interests at risk'. Norman Morris, 'England', op. cit., p. 74.

272. Cf. P. H. J. H. Gosden, *The Development of Educational Administration in England and Wales*, op. cit., p. 115.

273. Even there the very nature of examinations did not escape strong professional influence, secondary teachers and academics having the majority of members on the reconstituted Secondary Schools Examination Committee of 1946 — which was the forerunner of the Schools Council. Ibid., pp. 120-21.

274. Maurice Kogan, *The Government of Education*, op. cit., p. 31.

275. P. H. J. H. Gosden, *The Development of Educational Administration in England and Wales*, op. cit., p. 220.

276. Asher Tropp, *The School Teachers*, op. cit., p. 261.

277. Maurice Kogan, *Educational Policy Making: A Study of Interest Groups and Parliament*, London, 1975, p. 111.

278. Cf. R. D. Coates, *Teachers' Unions and Interest Group Politics*, Cambridge, 1972.

279. Cf. R. A. Manzer, *Teachers and Politics: The Role of the National Union of Teachers in the making of National Educational Policy in England and Wales since 1944*, Manchester, 1970.

280. Maurice Kogan, *Educational Policy Making*, op. cit., p. 10.

281. Maurice Kogan, *The Government of Education*, op. cit., p. 22.

282. In the words of the General Secretary of the NUT, Sir Ronald Gould, 'I have heard it said that the existence in this country of 146 strong, vigorous LEAs safeguards democracy and lessens the risks of dictatorship. No doubt this is true but an even greater safeguard is the existence of a quarter of a million teachers who are free to decide what should be taught and how it should be taught'. *The Schoolmaster*, 10 September 1954.

283. This fusion between abstract theory and military applications 'allayed some suspicions that Cavendish physics was having a baleful effect on British University physics in the interwar years by turning it away from practical industrial technology'. Michael Sanderson, *The Universities and British Industry, 1850-1970*, op. cit., p. 347.

284. Cf. ibid., p. 356.

285. Ibid., p. 358.

286. Harold Perkin, *Key Profession*, op. cit., p. 132.

287. Cf. ibid., p. 133.

288. Loc. cit.

289. Ibid., p. 132.

290. Ibid., p. 134.

291. Ibid., p. 181.

292. Ibid., p. 142.

293. William Taylor, *Society and the Education of Teachers*, op. cit., p. 74.

294. Under the 1965 Remuneration of Teachers Act, the Teacher panel of the Burnham Committee (as opposed to its counterpart, the Management Panel) is appointed by the Minister from the various teachers unions. He can thus manipulate with whom he negotiates by raising or lowering their number of seats and justifies this key role by reference to the Ministry's democratic accountability for the amount spent on pay and its distribution.

295. Maurice Kogan, *Educational Policy Making*, op. cit., p. 124.

296. Cf. William Taylor, *Society and the Education of Teachers*, op. cit., p. 90.

297. Ibid., p. 92.

298. A study group, established by the Secretary of State and including Local Authorities, the ATCDE, the voluntary providing bodies (a quarter of Colleges were still denominational), and, after a struggle, some university representatives, had been at work and produced its report in 1966, which became known as the Weaver Report. See *Report of the Study Group on the Government of Colleges of Education*, London, 1966.

299. William Taylor, *Society and the Education of Teachers*, op. cit., p. 83.

300. Maurice Kogan, *The Government of Education*, op. cit., p. 20.

301. William Taylor, *Society and the Education of Teachers*, op. cit., p. 50.

302. See Norman Morris, 'England', op. cit., p. 70, Table 3, 'Sample List of Committees or Organizations on which Unions are Represented and the Number of Seats held by each Union'.

303. Maurice Kogan, *Educational Policy-Making*, op. cit., p. 112.

304. P. H. J. H. Gosden, *The Development of Educational Administration in England and Wales*, op. cit., p. 121.

305. Cf. R. A. Manzer, *Teachers and Politics*, op. cit.

306. Maurice Kogan, *Educational Policy Making*, op. cit., p. 109.

307. Ibid., p. 134 f.

308. Michael Locke, *Power and Politics in the School System*, London, 1974, p. 35.

309. Michael Sanderson, *The Universities and British Industry 1850-1970*, op. cit., p. 365.

310. *Enquiry into the Flow of Candidates in Science and Technology into Higher Education* (Dainton Report), London, 1968.

311. Michael Sanderson, *The Universities and British Industry 1850-1970*, op. cit., p. 376.

312. A. H. Halsey and M. A. Trow, *The British Academics*, op. cit., p. 64.

313. Cf. Harold Perkin, *Key Profession*, op. cit., p. 218.

314. Ibid., p. 223.

315. A. H. Halsey and M. A. Trow, *The British Academics*, op. cit., p. 87.

316. Harold Perkin, *Key Profession*, op. cit., p. 222.

317. Graeme C. Moodie and Rowland Eustace, *Power and Authority in British Universities*, op. cit., p. 47.

318. Harold Perkin, *Key Profession*, op. cit., p. 201.

319. See Michael Sanderson, *The Universities and British Industry, 1850-1970*, op. cit., p. 387.

320. Ibid., p. 381-82.

321. Brian Simon, *Education and the Labour Movement 1870-1920*, op. cit., p. 256.

322. *Report of the Consultative Committee on Higher Elementary Schools*, 1906, p. 22.

323. R. H. Tawney, *Secondary Education for All*, London, 1922, pp. 83-84.

324. Lawrence Andrews, *The Education Act, 1918*, London, 1976, p. 17.

325. The National Union of Teachers, The Incorporated Association of Headmasters, the Headmistresses' Association, the Association of Assistant Mistresses, the Incorporated Association of Assistant Masters, The Association of Technical Institutions and the Association of Teachers in Technical Institutions, as well as the Education Policy Committee of the Headmasters' Association and the Headmasters' Conference, were content with the Bill. Ibid., p. 25.

326. Ibid., p. 27.

327. Ibid., p. 28.

328. Cited by Brian Simon, *Education and the Labour Movement 1870-1920*, op. cit., p. 356.

329. Lawrence Andrews, *The Education Act, 1918*, op. cit., p. 78.

330. H. A. L. Fisher's own reaction was that 'It is always dangerous to interfere with vested interests. I bowed to the storm. The measure was carefully stripped of every feature which might make it obnoxious to the public bodies (i.e. the local authorities) who would be required to work it'. Cited by H. C. Dent, *1870-1970: Century of Growth in English Education*, London, 1970, p. 85.

331. Lawrence Andrews, *The Education Act, 1918*, op. cit., p. 53.

332. Ibid., p. 35.

333. Ibid., pp. 49-50.

334. Of the 484 members returned on Lloyd George's coalition coupon, these were predominantly conservatives and included 179 company directors and a further 86 with commercial or financial interests.

335. Cited by Brian Simon, *The Politics of Educational Reform*, London, 1974, p. 63.

336. Ibid., pp. 116-18 and 126.

337. From a total membership of twenty, for whom incomplete records survive, more than half are known to have been teachers, academics, or educational administrators and the committee probably only failed to be the microcosm of the educational service which its secretary intended, by its bias towards grammar and public schools and the universities. See Maurice Kogan and Tim Packwood, *Advisory Committees in Education*, op. cit., pp. 90-91.

338. *The Education of the Adolescent*, (the Hadow Report), 1926, p. xxi.

339. Ibid., pp. 78-79.

340. Ibid., p. 77.

341. In the words of the Parliamentary Secretary when questioned in the Commons: 'The Report will be of the utmost assistance to authorities in enabling them to define and regulate their policy, but for the most part it appears to call for continuity of administrative action by the Board rather than for any new departure at this stage', *Hansard*, 14 February 1927.

342. See Brian Simon, *The Politics of Educational Reform, 1920-1940*, op. cit., pp. 137-38.

343. Cited ibid., p. 153.

344. The Conference endorsed a memorandum which defined the aim as being to 'develop a new type of secondary school which offers a variety of courses suitable to children of different aptitudes and capacities, but is otherwise on a level with the present day Secondary School'. Cited ibid., p. 136.

345. Ibid., p. 151.

346. Ibid., p. 307.

347. Ibid., p. 257.

348. *Secondary Education with Special reference to Grammar Schools and Technical High Schools*, (The Spens Report), 1938, p. 202.

349. Cited by Brian Simon, *The Politics of Educational Reform, 1920-1940*, op. cit., p. 266.

350. Ibid., p. 269.

351. H. C. Dent, *1870-1970, Century of Growth in English Education*, op. cit., p. 115.

352. David Rubinstein and Brian Simon, *The Evolution of the Comprehensive School 1926-1966*, London, 1969, pp. 23-24.

353. Cited ibid., p. 24.

354. See Asher Tropp, *The School Teachers*, op. cit., p. 240.

355. *Hansard*, 29 July 1943.

356. Cf. H. C. Dent, *The Education Act, 1944*, London, 1969, p. 13.

357. *The Times*, 14 April 1944.

358. See H. C. Dent, *The Education Act, 1944*, op. cit., p. 47.

359. C.f. P. H. J. H. Gosden, *The Development of Educational Administration in England and Wales*, op. cit., p. 115.

360. J. A. G. Griffith, *Central Departments and Local Authorities*, London, 1966, p. 98.

361. D. E. Regan, *Local Government and Education*, London, 1977, p. 33.

362. See Brian Simon, *The Politics of Educational Reform, 1920-1940*, op. cit., p. 329.

363. Cited in David Rubinstein and Brian Simon, *The Evolution of the Comprehensive School, 1926-1966*, op. cit., p. 38.

364. Ibid., p. 39.

365. C.f. Michael Locke, *Power and Politics in the School System*, op. cit., p. 86.

366. D. E. Regan, *Local Government and Education*, op. cit., p. 49.

367. Rodney Barker, *Education and Politics 1900-1951: A Study of the Labour Party*, London, 1972.

368. *The Schoolmaster*, 7 January 1955.

369. David Rubinstein and Brian Simon, *The Evolution of the Comprehensive School 1926-1966*, op. cit., p. 73.

370. The following publications contributed to the debate in the mid-fifties: M. Cole, *What is a Comprehensive School?*, London, 1953; R. Pedley et. al., *Comprehensive Schools Today*, London, 1954; R. Pedley, *Comprehensive Education, A. New Approach*, London, 1956; B. Simon (ed.), *New Trends in English Education*, London, 1957; S. C. Mason, *The Leicester Experiment*, London, 1957; N.U.T., *Inside the Comprehensive School*, London, 1958.

371. Caroline Benn and Brian Simon, *Half Way There*, Harmondsworth, 1972, p. 53.

372. David Rubinstein and Brian Simon, *The Evolution of the Comprehensive School, 1926-1966*, op. cit., p. 89.

373. Caroline Benn and Brian Simon, *Half Way There*, op. cit., p. 70.

374. Ibid., p. 56.

375. Ibid., p. 65.

376. Ibid., p. 69.

377. See R. Buxton, 'Comprehensive Education: Central Government, Local Authorities and the Law', pp. 99-120 in Gerald Fowler, Vera Morris and Jennifer Ozga, *Decision Making in British Education*, London, 1973.

378. Caroline Benn and Brian Simon, *Half Way There*, op. cit., p. 69.

379. Ibid., p. 56.

380. Ibid., p. 89.

381. Ibid., p. 97.

8 STRUCTURAL ELABORATION: Two Patterns of Educational Change

The examination of patterns of change brings the analysis up to the present time. It involves a discussion of current educational practices and problems, but it consistently links these back to prior processes of interaction and to even earlier processes of structural conditioning. In other words, the contemporary characteristics of educational systems and the activities that take place within them are grounded in history and cannot be explained without reference to their genesis and subsequent development. The task of this Chapter is not to describe these historical changes or to assess the performance of modern educational systems — these are the preserves of the educational historian and the comparative educationalist. The sociological contribution consists in providing a theoretical account of macroscopic patterns of change in terms of the structural and cultural factors which produce and sustain them.

So far it has been argued that educational systems with Restrictive or Substitutive origins emerged with different internal structures and different external relations to society. These were characterized as

Centralized and Decentralized systems respectively. In Chapter 5 the ways in which these two kinds of system conditioned subsequent processes of educational interaction were outlined in detail – stressing both the universal influences of State systems of education (of which the most important was the transition from competitive conflict to negotiated exchange as the principal form of interaction) and the different influences exerted by the two types of system. Chapter 6 then concentrated on the Centralized system and examined how interaction was constrained to focus on one particular process of negotiation, political manipulation. In contrast, Chapter 7 sought to demonstrate that the decentralized system encouraged the use of three different processes of negotiation, each of which was of equivalent importance – external transactions, internal initiation and political manipulation. *Thus the final stage has now been reached, where it remains to link processes of interaction to patterns of change.*

This will represent the last phase of the modern cycle of Structural Conditioning, Social Interaction and Structural Elaboration. Again it involves forging theoretical links between the three phases, rather than simply describing the third as the outcome of the preceding ones. As such it implies that further sociological propositions will have to be advanced about the relationship between the interaction which has already been examined, for the two kinds of system, and the large-scale changes which have taken place since their emergence. Once this has been accomplished it completes the discussion of the modern cycle and constitutes the end of the present study; but in reality, of course, it only signals the debut of further changes and of an indefinite number of succeeding cycles. For the patterns of change that will be discussed now are no more the fixed and permanent features of educational systems than were their immediate, or more distant predecessors, which gave way to the current characteristics and were also partly responsible for shaping them. In the ceaseless process of social intereaction and structural change, the elaborated characteristics which we are about to transfix analytically are already conditioning new forms of interaction and thus planting the seeds of their own transformation.

However, the prime concern here will be the *patterns* of change taking place, rather than the specific and necessarily transitory changes themselves. Here the first problem is to link these back to the processes of interaction producing them, and this will occupy the bulk of the analysis. But the last problem is to ask whether the *accumulation* of these changes is such as to alter the patterns of change to be expected in the immediate future. In other words, have these changes added up to *enough* of a change in educational systems to destroy the structural features which condition this *patterning* of change? Specifically this question asks whether the changes which have occurred in centralized and decentralized systems since their inception have so transformed these systems that they will no longer continue to generate different patterns of change. After all, conditional influences are not determinants and it is quite possible, both logically and empirically, that subsequent interaction has produced modifications leading to systemic convergence. In this case the old centralized and decentralized systems would no longer engender two distinctive patterns of change, because the structural differences generating them would have been removed.

More generally this question asks whether the last cycle has finished, or is finishing, in 1975, where this study ends. As has been underlined throughout, the delineation of cycles is a matter of analytical convenience, determined only by the nature of the problem in hand. Nevertheless it is an important question to pose and it is quite valid to ask and to answer it *within* the frame of reference *used here* for the identification of *these* cycles. The reply is identical to the one given above — this cycle can only be said to have finished and a new one started if the elaborated characteristics have so transformed the systems that they no longer exert the same kinds of conditional influences. Practically this means that the cycle ends when it is no longer possible to characterize public education in terms of *State systems*, which are *multiply integrated* with different parts of society, and whose organizational structures can be classified as either *centralized* or *decentralized*. (It should be clearly understood however that these parameters can remain constant whilst all sorts of other changes take place, particularly those at a less macroscopic level, which is why researchers with other kinds of problematics will delineate different analytical cycles). I will try to answer this question at the end of the chapter, but will postpone it until the comparative data have been reviewed for the four countries because the terms used above (like centralization and decentralization) do not just carry the vague connotations of ordinary language usage (which make questions about continuation or termination a matter of dispute over meanings), but have specific organizational referents (like unification and systematization or differentiation and specialization). It is therefore necessary to examine the empirical changes which have taken place in these referents before arriving at conclusions about the fate of the broader characteristics which these denote.

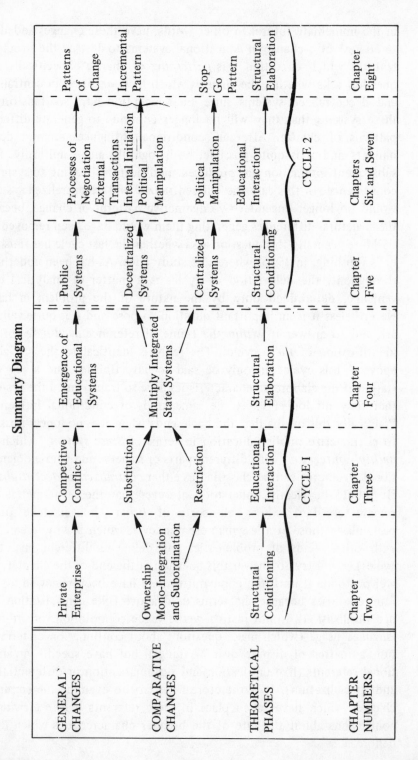

Figure 7

Summary Diagram

GENERAL CHANGES	Private Enterprise	Competitive Conflict	Emergence of Educational Systems	Public Systems	Processes of Negotiation	Patterns of Change
COMPARATIVE CHANGES	Ownership Mono-Integration and Subordination	Substitution	Multiply Integrated State Systems	Decentralized Systems	External Transactions Internal Initiation Political Manipulation	Incremental Pattern
		Restriction		Centralized Systems	Political Manipulation	Stop-Go Pattern
THEORETICAL PHASES	Structural Conditioning	Educational Interaction	Structural Elaboration	Structural Conditioning	Educational Interaction	Structural Elaboration
		CYCLE I			CYCLE 2	
CHAPTER NUMBERS	Chapter Two	Chapter Three	Chapter Four	Chapter Five	Chapters Six and Seven	Chapter Eight

Figure 7 provides a *Summary Diagram* of the theoretical and comparative field covered throughout this study and the last column is the subject of the present chapter.

Turning now to patterns of change themselves, the main argument concerns their linkage with the processes of interaction which have already been examined. Here it appears that different patterns of change are found in the centralized and the decentralized system. In the centralized system, political manipulation, the process of interaction which accounts for the bulk of macroscopic changes, is also responsible for patterning them in a distinctive way. As we have seen, demands for change have to be accumulated, aggregated and articulated at the political centre, they have to be negotiated in the central political arena, and, if they are successful, they are then transmitted downwards to educational institutions as polity-directed changes. Changes are evidenced and documented at the centre by laws, decrees and regulations – they are not always dramatic but they are normally quite definite. A number of features are associated with this political negotiation of educational change – polity-directed changes are usually slow and cumbersome to bring about, they involve concession, dilution and compromise, they are general and national in application rather than specific and local. The significance of all of these aspects will be examined a little later, for the moment the crucial point is that they represent a punctuation of educational stasis, for education can change very little in the centralized system between such bouts of legislative intervention. Patterns of change therefore follow a jerky sequence in which long periods of stability (i.e. changelessness) are intermittently interrupted by polity-directed measures. This has been termed the '*Stop-Go pattern*', and its precise derivation from educational interaction in the centralized system will occupy the next sub-section.

It is contrasted with the pattern of change common to decentralized systems. In the latter we have seen that three processes of negotiation are of roughly equal importance for introducing educational change and that the three types of transactions proceed simultaneously. In other words, all demands do not have to be passed upwards to the political centre; some can be negotiated autonomously within educational institutions, others can be transacted independently by external interest groups. Consequently change is never-ending, it is constantly being initiated, imitated, modified, reversed and counteracted at the level of the school, the community and the nation. Equally, however, it is usually undramatic, frequently indefinite, and commonly specific and local in application. The three processes taking place together at the three levels, intertwine and influence one another, sometimes positively, sometimes negatively, to produce a seamless web of changes. This has been termed the *'Incremental pattern'*, signifying that macroscopic change is made up of small increments, of minor modifications introduced from different sources, whose sole significance may lie in their accretion. Once again a separate sub-section will be devoted to the ways in which this pattern derives from interaction in the decentralized system.

In proceeding to make this connection between processes of interaction and patterns of change, it should perhaps be stressed for the last time that what is presented does not constitute a complete theory of educational change. What are being traced through are the effects of structural conditioning on *how* social groups bring about educational changes and the imprint of this on the resulting patterns of change. Such a theory cannot itself explain the composition and characteristics of social groups at any time, or their norms and values, for these require general theories about social structures and cultural systems.

THE CENTRALIZED EDUCATIONAL SYSTEM AND THE STOP-GO PATTERN OF CHANGE

As has already been seen, the centralized system, in which unification and systematization are the predominant characteristics, encourages the build-up of frustrated demands outside education and in the wider society. This is because professional educators lack the autonomy to initiate change internally in schools and colleges, thus satisfying some of their own goals, responding directly to student and pupil demands, and meeting those external requirements which are acceptable to them. Instead of these demands being propitiated by direct negotiation at the local or institutional level, thus drawing off discontent on a day-to-day basis, dissatisfaction accumulates. To effect educational change *all groups* must move outside the educational field to engage in political interaction at the national level. Political manipulation involves the cumulation, expression and negotiation of educational demands through the 'normal political channels', whatever these may be in society at that time. In Chapter 6 the conditions under which this enterprise was likely to be successful were considered in relation to the accessibility of the political centre, the nature of governing elites and the positions of those voicing educational demands in the socio-political structure. A number of generalizations about these relationships were advanced, specifying the conditions under which a particular volume and type of demand could be transacted. These will not be recapitulated here, for it is the consequences of success or failure in bringing about legislative change which are of interest now, not their causes. The following discussion will follow through the respective consequences of success and failure in order to pinpoint their contribution to the overall pattern of educational change in the centralized system.

As far as the successful negotiation of demands is concerned, the nature of the political structure and of elite relations influence *whose* requirements are met (and in what qualitative or quantitative terms) but have much less effect on the *form of change* which is introduced. Polity-directed changes are very alike in form, or at least their similarities outweigh their differences, despite considerable variation in the political contexts in which they occur. *Thus changes which are routinely negotiated through political manipulation are like in kind and it is this similarity between the products of successful transactions which partly accounts for a common pattern of change in centralized systems.* (The contribution of unsuccessful groups working via irregular forms of political interaction – which completes the pattern – will be discussed later on). When it is argued that the form of change is very alike, this is with reference to three distinct aspects – the initiation, the legislation and the execution of change(s). By examining these in turn, and discussing the mechanics involved in each of them, we can jointly describe how it is and explain why it is that centralized systems generate the same kind of pattern.

(a) The Initiation of Change

Basically changes are slow and cumbersome to bring about in the centralized system: and this is the case regardless of the type of political structure or elite relations which prevail. On the one hand, they are slow in the *accessible polity* because of the time it takes between the first articulation of a demand by a social group and its final translation into legislation (which will be used as a portmanteau term to include decrees, ministerial instructions and regulations). In between lie lengthy processes of aggregating demands, gaining political sponsorship, winning space on (party) political programmes, achieving power, obtaining legislative priority, overcoming oppositional challenge or amendment, before finally entering the statute books. At each of these stages a particular policy demand can suffer repeated reversals, and the history of the French *école unique* movement provided an exceptionally clear example of how protracted all this can be. Of course the use of devices like ministerial instructions can and do shorten the process by skipping some of these stages, but in an accessible polity these will quickly be challenged and made a parliamentary matter, thus introducing at least half of the above problems. The opposition will always keep a sharp eye open for any ministerial attempt to introduce a substantial change of policy through the accumulation of seemingly innocuous regulations. It might be interjected at this point that the same is true of decentralized systems (with accessible polities), and this is indeed the case — but since political manipulation is not the only means of producing change there, it is much less crucial for the patterning of it. (Incidentally, decentralized systems are certainly not notable for the frequency of major legislative changes in education).

On the other hand, change is also slow and cumbersome in the *impenetrable polity*, for reasons quite other than the need to marshall consensus. Here the governing elite monitors educational development in relation to its own goals and to changing circumstances. It hesitates to introduce a major change until there is pressing evidence that current policies are not working or are not appropriate, and it does so for several reasons. Firstly, since the change will be national, it necessitates a considerable amount of detailed planning — involving factors like teacher retraining, manpower forecasting, building schedules, design and production of equipment and texts, reviewing local or regional problems — even if these tasks are not thought of in terms of their contemporary complexity. Secondly, it is obvious that all of these elements are extremely expensive and will not be embarked upon lightly, given the inevitable competition of other priorities for public spending. Finally the elite will hold back as long as possible because what is involved is a jump in the dark.

This restraining force is in fact shared by governing elites of all kinds — it is generic to the centralized system. For these systems do not contain within themselves any fund of experimentation, they lack the local, private or autonomous institutions which provide concrete models of new ideas in action and thus furnish a practical basis for argument and a firm precedent for action. Instead new policies must be discussed in the abstract, their pros and cons debated in academic terms with reference, at best, to foreign practices taking place in quite different social contexts. Certainly there appears to be a growing tendency for governing elites themselves to initiate experiments (in a restricted area, a particular type or level of school, and for a limited duration) and we find examples of this in modern France and Russia. Nevertheless State experimentation, whilst providing concrete data, carries with it many of the disadvantages common to legislation itself. After all, the decision to undertake an experiment is a political decision: and by and large this means that it will have to be promising, acceptable, responsible, justifiable and any number of other things which will distinguish it from the fund of spontaneous experiments in decentralized systems, which are both more *diverse* and more *radical*. State experimentation functions in many ways as a negative feedback loop, which minimizes gross deviations from the status quo, by exercising a preliminary exclusion of radical, but possibly workable alternatives. Thus leaps in the dark are resisted, until pushed by political supporters or force of circumstances, and when they are taken they will be unadventurous, unless produced by a new group assuming power.

Because the political centre thinks long and hard before it legislates and because the intervening changes brought about through other processes are minimal in comparison, then long periods of relative educational stasis are typical in the centralized system. During these, grievances of course accumulate, and are normally exacerbated by the very limited degree of internal initiation which does take place between legislative changes. Constrained as the profession is, its main contribution, as we have seen, is restricted to obstructing the application of central directives — to playing a negative, and usually conservative role. Beyond this it can only operate as a vested interest group, advancing those academic concerns which are perceived as irrelevant to the polity and therefore do not attract its sanctions. Generally these spell an academic inwardness, which at one extreme involves a mechanical routinization of intellectual tasks and a calculative pursuit of material rewards, and, at the other, an academicism which dissociates the teaching and learning process from any end but itself. Both involve displacement of the goals which have been politically defined for education. The former replaces them with the officially approved procedures and methods, which are adhered to ritualistically. The latter substitutes an abstract intellectualism, intensifying commitment to pure knowledge rather than practical skills, and frequently fostering a high status culture which both stratifies the various courses taught and encourages all of them to emulate the prestige elements (classicism, *culture générale*, literary culture, etc.). The overall effect of both routinization and academicism is to increase the slippage of educational practices in relation to political goals, but to do so in a way which does not enhance educational services to dissatisfied groups in society.

The periods of stasis are not necessarily very long (i.e. a matter of decades), but an interval of relatively high educational stability always intervenes between successive pieces of legislation. Bearing in mind the universal deterents to speedy political redirection of educational development, which have just been discussed, the circumstances leading to *protracted* stasis can be specified more closely. Given an accessible polity, the quicker the *alternation* of *majority* governments the shorter the period between polity-directed educational changes. Conversely, if the same governing elite remains in office, if parliamentary parties lock in immobilism, or produce weak centrist coalitions, stasis will be prolonged. Given an inaccessible polity the quicker the *succession* of elite factions *dominating* decision-making or the more dramatic the changes in domestic or foreign circumstances, the faster polity-directed changes will succeed one another in education. Conversely a durable elite and a stable political environment will foster educational continuity.

(b) The Legislation of Change

Legislation in the centralized system always involves concession, compromise and dilution of the goals pursued by those who help to pass it. This is most obvious, because witnessed at its most extreme, in the accessible polity with a weak government. For if it succeeds in legislating at all, it produces the most innocuous compromise measures and the greatest discrepancies between the change introduced and the goals of *any* of the groups which participated. The introduction of experimental *classes nouvelles* instead of the universal *école unique* illustrates the compromise enforced between the primary teachers and the Left on the one hand, and professional and political conservatism on the other, in the last decades of the Third Republic. However, the same is also the case in the semi-penetrable polity, in which concessions have to be made to government supporters (like the Loi Debré rewarding Gaullist catholics despite the hostility evoked in most other quarters) and compromises with dangerous opponents (like the decré Berthoin, intended to pacify the leftwing proponents of educational democratization without alienating the right-wing defenders of educational elitism). Equally, the closed polity, with strong elite disunity, publicly betrays the same tendencies — the attempt to find formulae which give something to everybody who counts and take away as little as possible from any of them. The wranglings over modern, technical and professional instruction during the Second Empire revealed the design of two compromise policies (of bifurcation and then of special education), calculated to mobilize adequate support — in fact the second was an admission that the first had failed and represented a re-run at the same problem, which elite pressures would not allow to be buried.

Nevertheless these tendencies also characterize the closed polity with highly superimposed and integrated elites, though they may not be worked out in public to the same extent. The reason is simply that, however harmonious their relations, different sub-sections of the governing elite want different services from education, and if none wish to reduce educational responsiveness to the polity by relaxing unification then all have to work doubly hard to dovetail their requirements with one another so that the resulting form of systematization avoids clashes between them. Obviously this involves a series of compromises on matters like the contents of foundation schooling, the ages at which specialization can begin in one direction without prejudice to others, the routes and qualifications giving entry to higher levels and so forth. However, these are not simply operational problems to which some objective and optimal solution can be applied, they are political and ideological problems and both power and values will determine *how* they are solved at any time — these will dictate the nature of the compromise. Thus throughout Soviet educational history, for example, there has been a continuous tension between the use of education to produce socialist society and to service the planned economy. In the post-revolutionary period the utilitarian functions of education were subordinated to the egalitarian ones: the Stalinist period reversed these priorities. These two extremes of course mirrored the political supremacy of different sub-groups, but subsequently Soviet leadership appears to have hunted for a compromise formula which would enable the two functions to be performed simultaneously. Sometimes its composition has meant that it leaned more towards the one than the other, and the oscillation of compromise is perhaps the dominant theme of the later decades.

In other words, concession and compromise are general characteristics of legislative change in the centralized system, whatever the
political structure or elite relations which go with it. Above all this
means that no polity directed change is ever *precisely* what anyone
wanted. Even if a group successfully pilots its demands through into
legislation, this will not give it exactly what it sought, for the change
introduced will be tempered by the requirements of powerful others.
Sometimes the compromise will be so gross that it represents something
that nobody really wants. In brief, legislative change often fails to
satisfy and never satisfies fully in the centralized system. The most
successful use of political manipulation still means that demands are
met without precision, and this lack of precision is fundamental to
legislation which is national in scope and at best meets the highest
common denominator of those educational interests enjoying political
expression. Because of this each polity-directed change does not
significantly reduce the pool of discontent. Even among those to whom
it gives something, it also falls short: they continue to exact more or
better and remain ready to extract it if political circumstances permit.
Thus they stay armed for further political manipulation and give the
educational system no respite from the pressure of their demands.
Typically, legislation has tepid supporters and brutally hostile critics in
the centralized system.

(c) The Execution of Change

Educational legislation is national and uniform both in conception and
application in the centralized system. The commitment to maintaining
strong central control, in the interests of educational responsiveness to
the polity, and a high level of co-ordination, to avoid conflict between
the different services education is to provide, have a number of consequences for patterns of change. First and foremost this means that
change will be confined to measures which do not challenge unification
and which dovetail with the current form of systematization.

On the one hand, this means that the logic of central control
perpetuates the illogic of educational uniformity. Instead of allowing
for variations to meet local conditions or for adaptation in response to
changing circumstances, each legislative change imposes a standardized
formula on the relevant part of the educational system. Usually this
involves too gross a response to the variety of initial social conditions,

and further tensions are generated given the inflexibility of such measures in the face of social change. The obvious corrective which consists in allowing sufficient local and institutional autonomy for self-regulation is precluded by the fear of its abuse, i.e. fear that the parts will escape central control, pursue their own ends or prove more responsive to groups other than the polity. Often this straightforward dread of losing control is not confessed but is concealed behind an etatist ideology which stresses the positive connections been uniformity and social justice, standardization and national integration, or identity of provisions and geographical mobility.

On the other hand, the logic of strong systematization produces absurdities whenever the polity attempts to extract specialist services from education. We have already seen that one solution to this, namely permitting strongly differentiated units to develop a range of specialist outputs, is ruled out by the retention of unification. The alternative is polity-directed specialization, and this is what takes place, orchestrated from the centre and organized so as to fit in with other centrally approved goals for education. This entails a high degree of educational planning with branching specialisms and co-ordinated linkages with higher levels. Once again this means that a number of demands will be rebuffed because they do not easily fit in. Furthermore, it implies that the rationality of centrally planned specialization can be nullified by social action and social change. Thus, for example, student failure rates or the decisions of pupils not to pursue their specialisms can wildly distort numerical targets, just as social, economic or technological changes can render them obsolete. These consequences are just as pronounced in imperative Soviet planning as in the indicative French plans, for they are not problems whose solution depends on the availability of sanctions.

In other words, the uniformity with which change is applied and the tight co-ordination of specialist developments mean that changes both fail to satisfy and frequently fail to work. Once again they leave behind them a pool of discontent whose proportions increase as the dysfunctional consequences of change amplify over time. This trend will continue whilst-ever the polity refuses to cede some degree of unification and systematization, for the attempt to introduce more differentiation and specialization without weakening the predominance of the first pair of characteristics can only lead to further absurdities, maladaptions and undesired consequences. These educational systems are the sites of a fundamental contradiction between attempts to increase diversification without extending decentralization. However, the problems this produces and the discontent which it stimulates receive a very different solution, given commitment to the centralized structure. Instead of a move towards decentralization, they prompt the movement from one national and uniform plan to another – legislative inadequacy is met by more legislation in these 'over-controlled' systems. In this lies another part of the mechanism which produces the 'stop-go' pattern of change, and one which operates in all types of political structures.

So far attention has been directed towards successful political manipulation and its consequences in terms of the changes introduced and the attitudes of the groups who helped to shape them. It now remains to examine what happens if and when the political negotiation of educational demands proves impossible – either for one particular group or for a number of groups. When discussing interaction in Chapter 6 considerable variation was noted in whose demands could be transacted in different kinds of political structures, but it was also seen that each type of structure was capable of frustrating a substantial volume of demands. In general then, if demands are consistently refused, the strains which produce them continue and grievances grow and accumulate. However they do so outside the 'normal' political channels, whatever these may be, for the legitimate procedures have already failed them repeatedly. Thus demands continue to build up in society, and whether this reservoir of discontent bursts depends partly on the political action taken and partly on the social constitution of the frustrated groups and the type of contestation in which they are willing to engage.

That centralized systems can 'tolerate' considerable discontent there is no doubt, for they do so all the time, but the political centre can react in different ways if it reaches alarming proportions. Direct repression is most common in the closed polity. Here a battery of threats, sanctions and punitive examples are used. The educational status quo is also buttressed by other social institutions (whether these be the churches, youth organizations or the security forces) and widespread ideological indoctrination is disseminated through the media and education itself – all these serve to keep the lid on. They do so by subtracting from the potential participants in disorderly outbursts and thus rob these of a mass character if intimidation and dissimulation are successfully applied. Indeed, when repression is supremely successful the collective character of discontent disappears, to be replaced (seemingly) by individual manifestations of 'dissidence' which can be dealt with on a personal basis. If these techniques work, widespread discontent is contained and the educational status quo remains undisturbed from below. In other words change or stasis continue to be determined by the political elite and to follow the 'stop-go' pattern for polity-directed changes already discussed. However, this policy of continuous surveillance is expensive and time-consuming to maintain — it has to be very efficient to be really effective — and since it contains the problem rather than resolving it, educational grievances can break out at the first hint of political instability.

Alternatively, and this is more typical of semi-penetrable and open polities, though it is not exclusive to them, concessions can be made when dissatisfaction appears to reach a dangerous level, the aim being to keep it within 'manageable' proportions. Thus some changes will be conceded, both to reduce the overall amount of discontent and also if possible to break up any solidary groupings of dissatisfied parties. Again these will follow the 'stop-go' pattern of polity-directed change. However, the assessment of danger levels and the estimation of the size of concession needed are both delicate matters of political judgement and they can be wildly wrong. Whether the polity is made to pay for such errors depends upon the extent to which the disgruntled groups can work together and recruit support from other parts of society for extra-parliamentary action. The result is an explosion, like the May events in France in 1968, which is bigger if educational grievances are augmented by others, as they were then. If dramatic, their participants may even envisage toppling the polity itself (the Fifth Republic looked very insecure for a month). Were this to succeed then political change would precede educational reform, and the *result* would be very similar to cases where grievances break out in inaccessible polities which reveal instability, as during the Russian Revolution. The action sequences would differ: in the former educational discontent would be the detonator and other factors would amplify the explosion; in the latter educational discontent would capitalize on political disintegration rather than causing it. In both, however, political change would signal a new 'go' phase of educational reform.

The explosion of educational grievances may not reach this point, and obviously the governing elite will seek to put out the fire and to stop it from spreading. In this context panic legislation takes place to defuse the situation and restore order. Promises of unheard of concessions are made, unprecedented shifts of principle take place, entrenched positions are yielded and a major reform is hurried onto the statute books. If and when the furore dies down, and the government again feels secure, it may well try to back out of its more radical undertakings and the disillusionment this causes leads to the re-accumulation of discontent. Whether a new explosion takes place depends on the degree of unity retained (or forged anew) among the proponents of educational change, the sensitivity of government to signs of unrest, and its flexibility in propitiating them before flashpoint is reached.

Thus whether educational changes are polity-directed though peaceful political manipulation or are the products of explosion followed by panic legislation, they constitute a distinctive 'stop-go' pattern. Periods of stasis are punctuated by legislative reforms and change advances by jerks rather than the slow accretion of modifications. The pattern remains the same whether it is produced through the legitimate political channels or not. In all cases universal reforms fail to satisfy; they are followed by a period in which grievances build up and finally result in another universal reform, the cycle repeating itself indefinitely. Thus after each reform, new strains are generated and whether these are (temporarily) resolved by negotiation or lead to a new explosion depends upon their political reception.

PATTERNS OF EDUCATIONAL CHANGE
IN THE USSR

Given the impenetrable nature of the polity the vast majority of educational changes were directed from the political centre: processes other than political manipulation and groups other than political elites were relatively insignificant, as during the Second Empire in France, our other example of an impenetrable polity. However, the fact that relations between Soviet elites were very close throughout the post-revolutionary period leads to quantitative and qualitative differences in the patterns of change observed in Russia compared with Imperial France. There has been more change in the Soviet Union because the different sub-elites have not acted in a mutually obstructive fashion, to impede legislation: instead this has taken place in accordance with changing educational priorities or circumstances. Secondly, when reforms were introduced they were imposed in a standardized manner and did not provide for much differentiation since little attempt was made to serve a large range of diverse interests simultaneously.

Change was therefore initiated by central legislation and imposed throughout the country, for the 'steel girding of the Soviet school is only superficially concealed by the outward decentralization . . . The various arrangements by which the fifteen republics and the union government parcel out the responsibility do nothing to conceal the unity of organization which has hitherto been the main source of support, financial and administrative, of the Soviet school system.[1] However, education consistently tended to be too responsive to the polity — it was over-controlled in Etzioni's terms,[2] and often what started out as a purposeful plan ended up being implemented mechanically by those called upon to administer it. Indeed the very inflexibility of the predetermined programme produced frictions and difficulties which were met by further legislation rather than by any slackening of the tight unification and systematization which had produced them. This hunt for an optimal legislative formula has been continuous, producing the stop-go pattern of change characteristic of all centralized systems. 'Attempts to legislate educational change result in no more than a series of schemes, each rapidly succeeding the other, each equally limited in its application. The course of pre-revolutionary as well as Soviet educational history was weakened precisely by such spasmodic legislation'.[3] The pattern remains unaltered from Tsarist times because the structural features producing it are also unchanged; unified control of instruction being equally prized by the two regimes.

> Although the Soviet educational system follows the course set for it by the revolution, its administration and style have been pre-revolutionary in character. The course of action set in 1917 has been pursued without much thought to the changes that might be required of it in the future. When difficulties occur and the system threatens to explode, an emergency occurs, and everyone dashes forward with remedies to douse the fire. When this is overcome and when things are all right again, not much thought is given to new creative revolutionary policies.[4]

The changes introduced in the immediate post-revolutionary period firmly subordinated educational standards to the needs of socialist reconstruction and political reintegration. Instruction was a precondition of the working class becoming the ruling class in the fullest sense, for to Lenin 'an illiterate person stands outside; he must first be taught the ABC. Without this, there can be no politics; without this there are only rumours, gossip, tales, prejudices, but no politics'.[5] But if education were to be universal and if higher education were to be egalitarian, then the old admissions' requirements, examination certificates and academic curricula had to go: with a mass intake they were as unattainable in practice as they were undesirable in principle because of their divisive nature.

Hence the introduction of the Unified Labour School, where subject centered teaching was down-graded in favour of a progressive curriculum whose child-centredness made it accessible to all, and of the workers' faculties which prepared, rather than qualified, peasants and proletarians for university entrance. In itself the Unified Labour School represented the maintenance of a high degree of systematization for it was a *single* institution, covering *all* grades, and implied no real break between 'primary' and 'secondary' levels. The negative Tsarist principle of hierarchical organization had been exchanged for an extremely positive one, which encouraged the masses to move freely up the entire system. Simultaneously it represented no diminution in unification. Its universality was necessary to prevent bourgeois resurgence via special institutions and its uniformity was a prerequisite of egalitarianism — both of these justified the retention of a strong administrative framework. Unification was therefore extensive, aiming at a state monopoly, and intense, that is closely monitored to prevent deviation or regression.

Since the Unified Labour School was an undifferentiated institution and since standards fell throughout education, the supply of certain technical skills dried up altogether and the level of professional and scientific training dropped accordingly. At first this appeared as a temporary sacrifice, necessary for transition to the new society, but which would not be too costly to the regime in the short-run. This reflected Lenin's initial belief that the administration of the State would be reduced to 'accounting and control' which could be 'performed by every literate person' for 'workmens' wages'.[6] Already by 1920 this was seen to be unrealistic. The development of socialism required experts and specialists yet these were mainly members of the bourgeoisie, who still demanded high salaries and forced the regime 'to administer with the help of people belonging to the class we have overthrown'.[7] Yet this was only part of the cost involved, for when Lenin recanted it was in relation to the lack of administrative training alone, and it was not until the 'new economic policy' ended that the lack of technical training finally registered as the largest debit in the educational accounts.

The revolt against the polytechnic principle at the end of the twenties was prompted by two related factors; firstly a considerable change in the concept of State educational interests following the commitment to economic planning by the new elite leadership, and secondly, on the eve of the first 5 year plan, Sturmilin's demonstration of a close connection between instruction and labour productivity.[8] Despite the opposition of many teachers, of those communists who clung to ideological egalitarianism, and of the 'pedologists',[9] the political reaction was to impose a legislative package containing a new utilitarian definition of instruction. Between 1932-36, in the midst of the treason trials and party purges, the Central Committee resolved that schools must prepare students more satisfactorily for the technikums and higher education (1931), it decreed a revision of all courses of study, a reintroduction of discipline, and a restoration of the teacher as leader (1932), it demanded 'real textbooks' which imparted systematic knowledge (1933), it restored grading in schools (1935), and it condemned pedology as an anti-Marxist perversion (1936). The main contours of the reformed system were actually layed down in Article 121 of the new constitution, which states that the citizens' right to instruction 'is ensured by universal and compulsory education; by free education up to and including the seventh grade; by a system of state stipends for students of higher educational establishments who excel in their studies; by instruction in schools being conducted in the native language, and by the organization in the factories, state farms, machine and tractor stations, and collective farms of free vocational, technical and agronomic training for the working people'.[10] Thus selectivity, specialization and vocationalism were to be the guiding principles of an education at the service of economic development.

However, Stalin's reforms meant no reduction in unification or systematization; they merely introduced that degree of specialization and differentiation which was compatible with them and necessary for meeting the new economic goals. Indeed in many ways the predominance of the first pair of characteristics was intensified with the introduction of the new general secondary school, and the return to academic formalism. 'With the reorganization of the system went reorganization of the curriculum. A rigid, centrally determined curriculum was established for the whole Soviet Union and "stabilized" textbooks were introduced'.[11] The reinstatement of the Maturity examination in 1944 was a further index of the growth in standardization, for through it the State could define and manage educational knowledge as well as testing and rewarding its acquisition in all parts of the Union. Centralization thus increased and 'the principle of independence of each nationality was curtailed in order to achieve overall economic co-ordination and better training of technicians. The attitude of the ruling Communists to the principles of *narodnost* depended on the circumstances'.[12] With the defection of the Ukraine and other non-Russian areas to Germany during the war, 'circumstances' were held to warrant the sovietization of the national republics. In education the slogan 'national in form, socialist in content' spelt a decrease in diversity and a growth of unification whose only educational justification was, significantly enough, in terms of increased systematization — namely that it gave students everywhere the freedom to apply to any higher institution in the country. More convincing reasons are the facts that national languages and culture were barriers to federal communications, the development of federal industry, and the unity of the Red Army.

Specialization of a different kind was necessary, however, to provide the range of technical and scientific skills called for in economic planning. Lower technical training of skilled workers covered over 500 occupational specialisms and was placed under the general control of the federal Ministry of Labour Reserves in 1940. Intermediate training of a technical and semi-professional nature was provided in Technikums, Teacher Training Institutes and Correspondence Schools. It was under the jurisdiction of the appropriate ministry but also under the general direction of the Ministry of Higher Education, as far as curriculum and programmes were concerned. Advanced training was the perogative of the multi-faculty Universities and Institutes. These arrangements were intended to provide the bulk of school leavers with useful qualifications whilst ensuring that the highest level of technical expertise would also be developed. The specialized nature of lower level training presented no problems for higher education; the latter recruited the majority of its students from those who remained for an extra three years in the general secondary schools, and not from working youth.

The differentiation of other types of school only occurred when it corresponded with some pressing need of State, and then under close supervision. Special boarding schools for the Army and Air-force (Suvorov schools) and Navy (Nakhimov schools) were opened in 1943. A year later a decree of the Central Committee established a two year Party school, which prepared for lower party and governmental positions, a Higher Party School, and the Academy of Social Sciences which trained instructors in these sensitive subjects. Even here the same general curriculum was followed and because of the screening of instructors and students alike there was little threat to central control. On the contrary, since these establishments recruited for high positions in the State apparatus, positive inducements as well as negative constraints prevented any abuse of their differentiated status.

However, the inflexibility of this system in relation to burgeoning numerical demands for more instruction and in the face of changing economic circumstances, produced two unintended consequences. Moreover, the fact that the system remained virtually unchanged until after Stalin's death in 1953 greatly intensified the unacceptability of both of them. It had been a rigidly planned system, but also a mass system. 'The essence of a plan is that it attempts to plot the course of progress. The essence of mass pressure is that it defies such restriction . . . These two characteristics are plainly incompatible. It was virtually certain that an exclusive concentration on academic study would throw out of balance an orderly supply of highly trained manual workers',[13] just as it was certain that stringent selectivity would halt the development towards an egalitarian society. Opposition built up as these consequences were perceived as dysfunctional to the social and economic goals of the political elite itself.

On the one hand from 1940, if not earlier, the system had encouraged the formation of a new Soviet elite along intellectual, technical and professional lines. As other avenues of mobility closed and 'all really powerful occupations (were) now accessible only through formalized educational training',[14] this technocratic elite threatened to become a 'new class'. The refusal to expand university places beyond the quotas provided for by the economic plans, whilst the secondary schools produced more and more qualified aspirants, increased the friction between the now-established intelligentsia and the masses. Vigorous selectivity had severely limited equality of opportunity and the hardening of new lines of stratification was a threat to political stability. During the Stalinist period this was contained exclusively by repression since concession to mass demands was held to imply serious disadvantages for economic policy.

On the other hand retention of the system was not simply a matter of choosing to meet economic goals at the expense of social ones, for the two were intimately related. As more pupils stayed on at the ten year school because of the privileges to which it led, and yet only about

20 percent actually proceeded to higher institutions, a dangerous and expensive form of wastage increased. 'The kind of instruction given to these students in the senior school encouraged them to think of themselves as destined for "white collar" jobs rather than for assembly lines and collective farms',[15] although this was the destination of growing numbers of them. They were untrained for it, they were 'ignorant of production' since their schooling had been 'divorced from life' and had merely instilled a 'contempt for physical labour',[16] to use Khruschev's words of condemnation. What is more they were withdrawn from productive work at precisely the time when the labour force had reached a particularly low point (because of the falling birth-rate during the war years) whilst the new seven year economic plan represented the most ambitious attempt yet to overtake the western world. Lastly the rapid rate of economic development was producing corresponding shifts in job specifications and frequent labour dislocations which the rigidity of educational programmes only exacerbated.

Strong dissatisfaction was finally expressed along these lines at the 19th and 20th Party Congresses and resolution of the leadership issue, three years after Stalin's death, allowed Khruschev, as Party Secretary, to tackle its source. The means used was an archetypical piece of 'total' legislation — the 'stop' phase was over and education was forced to 'go' in a new and centrally determined direction. But equally typically, what was promulgated was panic legislation, introduced after a brief period of partial experimentation under State auspices. It was of course imposed uniformly on the whole country and the judgement pronounced on it by a team of contemporary foreign observers appears to have been substantially correct . . . 'the reform enacted in December 1958 can be considered a poorly thought out, ad hoc piece of legislation that is going to disappoint everyone concerned. It will neither bring about a greater dedication to manual labour nor prevent the deterioration of preparation for university training'.[17]

The essence of the reform was a transition to an eight year compulsory school which would give general polytechnic instruction, later to be combined with socially useful work. This school which finished at 15 was considered as an incomplete 'Labour Polytechnic School'. Secondary education was completed by following one of three types of instruction, each involving labour, for which eligibility was determined by examination at the end of the eight year school. Since productive work was also inserted between secondary and higher instruction, elitarian attitudes and inequalities of opportunity were expected to diminish simultaneously. Alongside this, the economy was supposed to benefit from the fullest use of manpower: in the short run from an injection of labour[18] and in the longer term from all acquiring a skill.

The reform did involve some diversification of provisions, for a multiple track system stood end on to the eight year school. Pupils could attend vocational schools for young workers or farmers on a shift system (whilst in full employment), or a general polytechnic school, attached to a plant or a collective farm, with its own workshops (often on a part-time basis), or finally a technikum, a specialized school where general education was completed and a medium level specialist qualification acquired. Thus although the eight year school retained a standardized curriculum, which even the special purpose schools (retained from the Stalinist era) taught in full besides their specialism, the polytechnic stage which followed was more closely geared to the needs of local industries. This did not, however, represent a significant move towards decentralization, for the concession of greater local control over lower levels of training was more than cancelled out by increased central control of higher levels. On the one hand the regional economic councils, established in 1957, were given some powers to regulate elementary vocational instruction in their areas, whilst on the other, the technikums, whose curricula had been regulated by the appropriate ministries, were now placed in the hands of the Ministry of Higher and Secondary Specialized Education. Other administrative adjustments at the Republic and local government level meant 'the bulk of financing, the curriculum, personnel, management and inspection – the four cornerstones of control – are completely in the hands of governmental hierarchy'.[19] Thus limited diversification had no weakening effect on unification and had less influence on the prevailing form of systematization than might have been expected. The reason for this was that the alternative shift schools for working and rural youth, which enrolled almost three-quarters of the age group, functioned as educational dead-ends. Thus the most diversified part of education which might have dovetailed with difficulty, simply did not link-up with higher levels of instruction.

Dissatisfaction arose immediately the reform went into full operation, and much of it centered on the absurdities produced by diversification without decentralization. In other words, the system again generated tensions because of its inflexibility. Deficiencies in central manpower planning were already apparent by 1960, and surveys revealed that only 1/4 of those with production training were employed in the type of occupation for which they had been trained at school. Two-thirds of those enrolling for higher education entered courses of study different from the specialism they had followed at school.[20] Thus quite apart from sheer inaccuracy and miscalculation[21] in man-power *forecasting*, the economy was not receiving the benefits intended. Even the short-term release of labour was a mixed blessing, for it was often too short to usefully assimilate the student into production and was resented in factories where management and employees shared bonuses for exceeding production quotas.

As an egalitarian policy the reform produced different kinds of dissatisfactions, all of which, however, related to the fall in educational standards consequent upon the insertion of practical work. At one extreme, the intended beneficiaries saw no dramatic improvement in their opportunities for the majority of 15-18 year olds (attending schools for working youth) were deprived of any reasonable chance of a non-vocational education. Furthermore since this type of training was limited by the kinds of factories and farms present in the community, it also narrowed their occupational choices and prospects. If training at higher levels was too formal, that at lower levels was too primitive, for it did not confer 'a wide spectrum of skills and give pupils a basic knowledge of production necessary for working in enterprises in a variety of branches of the economy, as well as in enterprises in the particular town or *raion* (district)'.[22] At the other extreme the 'new class' objected to practical work training, which they hoped their children would never use, for interfering with their studies and delaying their university entrance. To many others it seemed that the reform, which was expensive to operate, levelled down in terms of instruction without levelling out in terms of stratification: the technocratic State had less skills at its disposal, but socialist society was no closer.

'The crowning point for the reaction against mass reforms was reached in 1964, when the entire substance of the reform was abandoned',[23] and the familiar process of legislative change again took place. The 1966 resolution of the Central Committee and Council of Ministers, 'On measures to improve the training of specialists and perfect the guidance of higher and specialized education in the country', represented a swing back to the principle of high standard, selective, specialist instruction. In principle the resolution appeared to accept that more flexibility was required, that curricular standardization should be diluted, and that increased institutional independence was a concomitant of efficient specialized training. In practice, however, the State seemed unable to bring itself to weaken unification and allow the devolution of authority necessary for such specialization. Instead it made a provision for the Ministry to assume direct control over a number of higher educational institutions, and there to develop teaching materials, compile textbooks, and train instructors. Clearly 'exhortation and example was not enough; control was felt to be necessary ... hence, presumably the direct take-over of the intended model-institutions; hence, too, the mounting of a full-scale governmental inspection of *all* higher institutions in the country "with a view to strengthening control over the quality of the training given to specialists" '.[24] At secondary level the fact that numbers would grow, without a proportionate increase in those proceeding to the tertiary sector, encouraged 'a search for a diversification of training to meet different purposes and aptitudes. This search is a sharp departure from the established Soviet principles of a common one-block education for all children'.[25] However, the actual moves taken in this direction have been rather tentative — the development of maths and science schools for the specially gifted and the introduction of some elective subjects. For the search has gone on in the context of further unification, following the creation of a single Ministry of Education for the USSR in 1966. As with higher education the aim has been to increase differentiation and specialization without conceding substantial devolution of authority or a significant reduction in systematization.

Comments

Throughout the post-revolutionary period educational change has been polity-directed by an elite which has remained closely knit despite personal changes in leadership. It might be thought that such political continuity is conducive to educational stability, and this is true in two senses. Firstly, the major structural characteristics of the system have remained unchanged, because they have consistently been seen as advantageous to the Party. Despite changes in leadership all have wanted to retain the responsiveness of education to political control which a centralized structure provides. Secondly, continuities in elite goals and priorities have been reflected as stable elements in the educational field. Perhaps the most important example of these is the strong scientific-utilitarian bias which has been maintained in the curriculum through all the changes in school policy. The following Table

illustrates this by comparing the syllabus of Tolstoy's Tsarist gymnasium, with the opposition's blueprint on the eve of the Revolution,
and Khruschev's polytechnic reform of 1958.[26]

TABLE 3

Hours per week throughout 8 years

	1871	1915	1959
Humanities	154	80	87
Maths and Science	47	73	84
Physical Culture, Practical Work & Arts	–	34	93

Source: N. Hans, *The Russian Tradition in Education*, London, 1963, p. 157.

However, it is clearly not the case that formal continuities in educational control lead to a lack of change and an ultra-stable system. For
on the other hand, changes in leadership and changes in circumstances,
failure to make optimal decisions and practical obstacles to effective
planning — these factors in conjunction account for the substantial
volume of change observed — but for all that the demands negotiated
were exclusively elite ones. Popular demands had only the most indirect
form of expression, as dumb numerical pressures within the system.
Patterns of school leaving, of application to one type of institution and
neglect of another represented the aggregate results of popular preference, but as such they were dealt with imperatively (for example by
manipulating incentives to make unpopular establishments more
attractive), rather than being matters of negotiation. However 'the
biggest problem, perhaps, is not so much what is happening inside the
institutions as the pressures building up outside'.[27] This is common in
all centralized systems, but what is distinctive about the USSR is the
success with which the political elite has prevented this from gaining
organized expression at any time. The armory of repressive controls and
the network of manipulative devices which enmeshed the population
have insulated educational policy from external discontent. Only in so
far as the latter was perceived as a potential threat by the political elite
did it enter into their educational calculations. Thus the different
phases of the 'stop-go' sequence were not prompted by dramatic public
outbursts but rather by the slow dawning awareness on the part of the
elite that the system once more required major adjustment, if, among
other things, such outbursts were to be avoided.

PATTERNS OF EDUCATIONAL CHANGE IN FRANCE: THE SECOND EMPIRE

Given an impenetrable political structure the crucial point is not merely that educational change is polity directed — for this is true of political manipulation in all centralized systems — but that it remains the perogative of a tight circle of people (whose interests are equally circumscribed) whilst other demands are systematically repulsed. Had Napoleon III possessed a clearer idea of his optimal definition of instruction and assigned education a more prominent role in the imperial design, there is no doubt that he could have left a more significant mark on the system. As it was the changes taking place were those for which his three Ministers of Education could recruit parliamentary support. Legislation was based on neither external nor internal demands, for community requirements remained as unheeded as professional opinion: it was initiated *at* the political centre and its fate was determined there. Frequently political deadlock disposed of ministerial proposals, and Duruy, in particular, was quite open about his willingness to permutate three different projects, involving compulsory, free, and special education, to arrive at a combination which would command a majority. Given a divided elite, the proposals that passed were the weakest form of compromise legislation: modern studies gained a firmer foothold, but not real parity in secondary education; primary schooling tended to become cheaper, but not free; and professional instruction was watered down into special education, but not comprehensive training at all levels.

These measures were unsatisfactory because this lowest common denominator of political agreement was imposed uniformly on the whole educational system. Thus neither of the two most ambitious reforms of the Second Empire (for a full secondary education based on modern subjects in the 1850s, and for a shorter practical form of secondary instruction in the 1860s), was received with any enthusiasm by those expected to provide it, the local authorities; to present it, the teachers; or to profit from it, the parents and pupils. Insistance on uniformity was the root of dissatisfaction. Already we have seen how the teaching body rejected the earlier bifurcation policy and obstructed its implementation throughout the national network of *lycées*. The experimental Technical schools introduced by Foutoul, at the same time, had a disasterously identical syllabus, regardless of region. The government was not willing to allow the flexibility of programmes and the scope for local initiative that was essential for their acceptance, and municipal councils withdrew their subsidies accordingly. The State's 'educational ideal could not easily be reconciled with the kind of vocational specialization which *enseignement professionnel* seemed to demand. The university was a national body which believed in imposing uniform programmes, while the success of enseignement professionnel depended on variation to fit local needs'.[28] The Special Education of the 1860s met with the same reaction for again it lacked local relevance. To the merchants, landowners and industrialists who dominated the municipal councils it was not specialized enough, for in rural areas they wanted training in agriculture and viticulture, in Grasse, the chemistry of perfume making, in Aubusson, carpet design and so forth. To the majority of parents too, 'elle écartait ... l'élément véritablement professionnel, en d'autres termes la préparation à un métier, l'apprentissage d'un état agricole, industriel et commercial'.[29]

Thus the polity-directed changes steadily repulsed any increase in the *specialization* or *differentiation* of the educational system for fear of the corresponding autonomy this would give to the community and the profession. They reinforced *unification* and the standardization which accompanies it and retained the existing form of *systematization* virtually unchanged. 'The logic of the French educational system seemed to have no room for an education which was secondary in spirit but too short and practical to fit into the traditional secondary pattern'.[30] In this context the contributions of other groups to educational change were largely negative: instead of being able to initiate changes internally the profession could only block central directives by withholding academic approval, and instead of being able to transact new provisions the community could only obstruct governmental plans by withholding financial support. The reforms that the polity did introduce left the majority of specific demands unsatisifed, and created by their uniform application more dissatisfaction than they removed.

During the Second Empire education was characterized by rigidity and stasis, but because political action had the effect of strengthening unification and systematization it also had the unintended consequence of damming-up resistance inside the system and creating a reservoir of discontent outside it. Only changes in the political structure itself could release this flood, and, as we have seen, the educationally dissatisfied groups were getting themselves organized to profit from governmental instability and were ready to contribute towards it by 1870. This stasis, apart from polity-directed changes, accompanied by the accumulation of educational discontent, is typical of the impenetrable political structure. It is a distinctive part of the 'stop-go' pattern of educational change common to centralized systems. The Second Empire represented the 'stop' phase, and only with the advent of the Third Republic in 1870 did change begin to 'go' again, as organized educational opposition took advantage of political transformation and the increased accessibility of government organs. In effect this was merely one cycle of the secular French pattern, for 'political and legislative changes in nineteenth century France tended to come about through the alternate application of rival programmes, rather than through the gradual evolution of consensus'.[31]

PATTERNS OF EDUCATIONAL CHANGE IN FRANCE: THE THIRD AND FOURTH REPUBLICS

Although educational change was polity-directed, being imposed nationally through central legislation, it was the product of hard and often unproductive negotiation in which extra-parliamentary groups and opposition parties were often as important as government, rather than a semi-private process in which a unified elite hunted for an optimal formula, as in the Soviet Union, or a disunited one slogged it out in a closed political arena, as in the Second Empire. Nevertheless despite great differences in political structure and elite relations, the same 'stop-go' pattern of change was just as marked in IIIrd and IVth Republic France. The same structural cause was at the root of it — the predominance of unification and systematization — and the same political motive perpetuated it — the unwillingness of any groups when in power to throw away the seemingly self-evident advantages of central educational control.

The spate of Republican legislation in the eighties, covering all types and levels of instruction, represented the 'go' phase. It occurred as soon as the Republic had been secured and was a great undamming of frustrated demands which had built up outside the system during the Second Empire. Above all it gave legislative expression to anti-clericalism, but along with this it sought to satisfy demands for educational modernization in an increasingly industrial society. Through this war with the Church, the *formal* structure of education was confirmed rather than changed. The aim was to buttress the Republic and prevent political integration from being undermined by incompatible modes of religious socialization; instead it would be reinforced by the influence of public education. Thus to Ferry, 'quand nous parlons d'une action de l'Etat dans l'éducation, tendant à maintenir l'unité, nous attribuons à l'Etat le seul rôle qu'il puisse avoir en matière d'enseignement et d'éducation. Il s'en occupe pour maintenir une certaine morale d'Etat, certaines doctrines d'Etat qui importent à sa conservation.'[32] The introduction of free, compulsory and secular public schooling, which was to consolidate republican society, in fact increased the unification and systematization which already marked French education.

On the one hand the extensiveness of unification increased. For the provision of *secular State schooling* could not by itself produce the national unity required. Firstly, the expense would still leave the masses outside the educational pale and, secondly, there was the danger of the bourgeoisie making private arrangements or patronising the confessional schools. Thus 'gratuity' and 'obligation' were added to 'secularism' in order to undermine religious competition to public instruction and the class threat to national solidarity. 'L'unité d'éducation est essentielle-ment conçue comme un instrument de fusion morale et affective et comme le moyen de vulgariser l'idéal republicain. La généralisation de l'instruction est d'autre part, liée au fonctionnement du système parle-mentaire et du suffrage universel'.[33] Because of compulsory attendance and gratuity the scope of primary schooling under State control in-creased considerably: because of the political role instruction was to play, there was no diminution in the intensity of unification. Indeed like every political elite which inherits a highly unified, and thus politically responsive, educational system the 'Republicans found the hierarchical lines of authority running from Paris to the provinces quite satisfactory; they saw little reason to change them'.[34]

On the other hand, a high degree of systematization was also retained and the negative principle of hierarchical organization re-mained unaltered. The Act of 1886 was the charter for primary instruc-tion, which effectively established its structure and defined its pro-grammes for eighty years. At the primary level three integrated stages succeeded one another — the *écoles maternelles* and infant classes, the *écoles primaires élementaires*, and the *écoles primaires supérieures* and classes of this type attached to ordinary primary schools under the

name of *'cours complémentaires'.* Programmes were standardized, dovetailed with one another, and protected from local or temporal deviations. This degree of systematization was partly due to the strength of
unification, the two characteristics being mutually reinforcing, for 'sans
une forte structure administrative son unité aurait peut-être été
menacée; mais l'organisation était si cohérente que les écoles primaires
ne forment toujours qu'une seule institution'.[35] At the secondary level
consistent and successful attempts were made to improve the integration between the *lycées* and *collèges* and the different forms of higher
education in university faculties and *grandes écoles.* But no attempt
whatsoever was made to link primary and secondary levels.

The political ideology was republican not egalitarian, it sought to
eliminate class conflict rather than to provide equality of opportunity.[36] Thus, although to Ferry it was impossible to produce 'cette
confraternité d'idées qui font la force des vraies démocraties si, entre
ces deux classes, il n'y a pas eu le premier rapprochement, le première
fusion qui résulte du mélange des riches et des pauvres sur les bancs de
quelque école',[37] the organic society did not require this mixing to
extend beyond the basic primary level. Between the two levels the
negative principle prevailed – secondary education proper was reserved
to the bourgeoisie and *primaire supérieur* instruction or the professional
schools were for the people – there was no need to dovetail their
programmes, for transfer between them was not to take place. Nothing
indicates this principle more clearly than the fact that pupils entered
the first class of secondary studies at the age of 10 plus, whereas the
certificat d'études primaires was taken at the age of twelve. Thus
parents had to opt early for the *second degré*, and their only option was
a seven year long, fee paying course. Many of the bourgeoisie of course
opted earlier still, sending their children to the fee paying preparatory
classes of the lycée: a practice not at all discouraged by republican
government which sanctioned it by a special certificate for its teachers
in 1881. Thus as secondary education grew downwards (the preparatory classes received 16,000 in 1881, 31,000 in 1913 and 55,000 before
the Second World War), the primary level sprouted its own secondary
tops. The two sub-systems continued to develop in parallel, each of
them highly systematized in itself, but not positively linked to the
other.

However, the retention of strong unification and systematization
during the 'go' phase of the eighties also perpetuated the traditional
rigidity of the system. In the decades preceding the Great War the

maintenance of these characteristics militated against the achievement of the Republicans' own goal of educational modernization. The failure of three different attempts to link education more closely to contemporary life — (a) to develop modern technical training, (b) to diversify and update secondary studies, and (c) to found real university centres of teaching and research — all pointed to the same lesson. It is impossible to increase specialization and differentiation (necessary for all three projects) without accepting some weakening of unification and systematization.

(a) From its inception the French educational system had serviced administrative requirements and neglected economic ones: 'Former le producteur, l'enseignement français y repugne. Son rationalisme tourne à l'intellectualisme'.[38] Thus at the beginning of the IIIrd Republic five out of six started work without any vocational training, a fact deplored by syndicates, industry and the Ministry of Commerce alike. The initial attempt to found apprenticeship schools in 1880 foundered because of disputes about curriculum and funding between the Ministries of Public Instruction and Commerce under whose joint control they were officially placed. Essentially the former refused to finance a training of the practicality demanded by the latter. Twelve years later a much more modest project, converting the most vocational *écoles primaires supérieures* (EPS) into *écoles practiques du commerce et de l'industrie* (EPCI) was successful. It allowed the development of specialized courses linked to practical work.

This was possible because unification was suspended as far as they were concerned, since these schools passed into the hands of the Ministry of Commerce and were no longer subject to administrative standardization or the need to dovetail with other parts of the educational system. However, their contribution to the creation of a skilled workforce was a drop in the ocean (in 1914 the 69 EPCI enrolled under 14,000 students) they formed a small skilled elite but did nothing for the mass of workers: 'en fait, il faudra attendre les années 1950 pour que les pouvoirs publiques prennent vraiment conscience du rôle capital de l'enseignement technique de la vie de la nation'.[39]

The government was prepared to go no further in weakening unification to solve this problem. Ferry was resolutely hostile to any abandoning of authority to industry, or to any adaptation of the definition of instruction to its specialized interests . . . 'Dans une société démocratique surtout, il est de la plus haute importance de ne pas livrer les études aux entreprises de l'industrialisme, aux caprices des intérêts à courte vue, aux courants impétueux et contradictoires du monde affairé positif, tout aux soucis de l'heure présente'.[40] Apart then from several model *écoles nationales professionnelles,* which operated at a level even higher than the EPCI, this left the professional sections of the EPC as the only other major source of vocational preparation. Yet although their recruitment increased considerably (and attracted the old clientele of Special education, once this became part of the *Baccalauréat*), a decreasing proportion registered in the professional sections, this falling to 13 percent in 1908. The EPS were thus providing a short general education rather than a preparation for active life: they were guiding their best pupils upwards to the *écoles normales* rather than outwards to industry and commerce. 'Ce glissement insensible est en fait une mutation: l'enseignement primaire supérieur conduit plus souvent à d'autres études. Bientôt, comme tout enseignement qui ne prépare pas ses élèves directement à la vie, il se veut 'culturel' ... Le système éducatif français s'avère ainsi incapable de prendre en charge la formation des producteurs'.[41]

(b) Exactly the same systemic rigidity repulsed attempts to diversify secondary studies, giving them a more modern content and greater practical utility. In establishing the shorter course of 'special education' at the end of the Second Empire, Duruy had acknowledged the inappropriateness of the classical humanities for those entering agriculture, industry or commerce. These 'special' courses had fulfilled the original intentions insofar as the vast majority of their intake returned to practical life rather than pursuing further education. However, they were now used as a vehicle for modernizing the secondary level *as a whole* — for injecting science into the curriculum and diversifying the classical definition of instruction. From 1881 the Republicans made the special education course more sequential, increased its length, and then enobled it with the creation of a *baccalauréat (spécial)* which gave entry to the faculties of science and medicine. These developments were not opposed by the defenders of the traditional humanities: a separate modern section was the best defence against *overall* modernization and hence the undiluted classical culture could continue to be addressed to the intellectual and social elite. It was, for its prestige was unassailable, but with undesirable consequences for modernization.

Once 'special' education was sanctioned by a Baccalauréat, it dropped practical exercises in favour of academic study; in becoming purely intellectual it increasingly imitated the method of classical instruction (with *dissertations, explications de textes, versions* etc.) both because of its prestige and the standardizing influence of Baccalauréat procedures; in becoming imitative it lost its distinctiveness, and its practicality. Special education gave way to a classical instruction without latin, and as such never attained the status of the traditional humanities. Any chance of modern studies being established as different but equal was lost; they became the same but inferior.

The integration of modern studies was completed in 1902, when 'special' education disappeared altogether, to be replaced by sections without latin in a single secondary education, permeated by *culture générale* but branching into four different Baccalauréat options – A. *Latin-grec*, B. *Latin-langues vivantes*, C. *Latin-sciences*, D. *Sciences-langues vivantes*. The aim of this reform was the 'réalisation de l'unité de l'enseignement, tout en introduisant dans cet enseignement plus de variété.[42] In fact unity prevailed over diversity, for section D remained inferior, the best pupils being directed away from it, whilst it became less different for the curriculum of the first four years was shared with other sections. If modern education could have taken place in separate establishments, on the lines of German *realschulen*, it might have won its own prestige and retained a distinct character. Such institutional differentiation was never even contemplated by government, but without it diversification of educational functions could not go very far, given the entrenchment of classicism.

Paradoxically, although the aim had been diversification, the effect was to destroy the distinctiveness of 'special' education, and with it, the possibility of a radical modernization of secondary studies. This failure can be attributed to the strength and standardizing influence of systematization and unification. Whilever the official Baccalauréat dominated secondary education (and remained an essential element of State control) it placed a straight-jacket on curricular development: whilever its possession conferred a legal right to higher education, its syllabuses prepared for further study rather than active life. In other words, they were defined by the need to co-ordinate with the faculties and grandes écoles within the system and not by the need to provide services required by different parts of society outside the educational system.

(c) Finally, the Republicans addressed themselves to the modernization of higher education, to the development of scientific studies and the creation of centres of research. 'Or, en France, même l'enseignement supérieur est uniforme: d'une université à l'autre, on retrouve les mêmes matières, enseignées dans le même esprit, pour préparer aux mêmes grades. Le mouvement universitaire des années 1880, décentrali-sateur et inspiré par l'example allemand, échoua à briser ce carcan'.[43] Partly the aim was to envigorate the State institutions so as to protect them from competition from private Catholic establishments, and to this extent it was successful. A building programme, including the construction of the Sorbonne, extended State provisions: the creation of grants and teaching positions gave birth to the first generation of students in science and letters faculties. But the reformers recognized that an efficient higher education had to be specialized (concerned with deepening competence in a particular area), had to take place in large centres (to accommodate minority disciplines), and had to be differ-entiated (to allow the free development of scientific activity). In other words, they for once accepted the necessity of a concomitant decentral-ization. This was not to involve a profound weakening of unification. The head of the new universities was still to be the Recteur, as a representative of the central administration rather than autonomous, self governing institutions being created. But the new university coun-cils and assemblies would have greater powers over personnel, pro-grammes and development.

However, the reformers were constrained to work with what existed, the isolated groups of traditional faculties, and to proceed cautiously so as to avoid the political charge of abandoning State control over an integral part of public education. It was fear of such parliamentary condemnation which led the Republican leadership to do what it could by decree, rather than exposing the projected reform to the vote. Essentially this meant that they tried to structure new universities by co-ordinating the old faculties, creating councils and assemblies and decreeing a budget to the component faculties in 1890. But here opposition from the Senate weighed in favour of the status quo — 'par souci d'égalité, par sens administratif de l'uniformité des institutions, le Sénat veut transformer en université tout groupe de facultés, même limité à deux . . . C'est la caricature de l'idée universi-taire, mais les intérêts locaux sont puissants au Sénat, et les centres lésés par la réforme auraient été beaucoup plus nombreux que ceux qu'elle aurait promus à la dignité d'université'.[44] Thus appeal was made to the old argument that standardization meant fairness to all parts of the nation. It was one the reformers found hard to resist since their own strategy had strengthened the faculties and dealt in terms of regrouping them. But the idea of a few grand centres capable of specialist teaching and interdisciplinary research was forfeited if any couple of faculties were deemed to constitute a university.

The differentiation of universities required a profound restructuration, it could not be accomplished additively by collecting together the few faculties in a particular town, or nominally by a change in appellation. Yet this is all that was accomplished by the law of 1896. This act.

> 'généralement saluée comme l'acte de naissance des universités, est donc au contraire leur acte de décès. Elle ne crée rien de neuf: elle change seulement une étiquette. Les corps de facultés s'appellent désormais universités. Ce sont donc quinze universités, une par académie, le triomphe du principe posé par le Premier Empire et confirmé par le Second en 1854! ... Le poids des structures heritées de l'université impériale – les facultés – et qu'ils avaient imprudemment renforcées pour parer au plus pressé, avait finalement raison de leurs théories réformistes'.[45]

Fundamentally all three attempts at modernization were failures because government was unwilling to transform the major structural characteristics of the system. *Thus during the 'go' phase the Republicans were successful in secularizing public instruction for this was perfectly compatible with the maintenance of strong unification and systematization, but failed with modernization because they were politically unwilling to relinquish any element of central control or any degree of central co-ordination of the system.* In other words, they tried to accomplish modernization without any diminution in centralization, by inserting reforms within an unchanged structure. But the effect of the system was to repulse them ... 'les réformes imposées au système d'enseignement sont souvent diluées, digerées, dénaturées, réinterprétées dans le sens de finalités qui ne sont pas les leurs ... En d'autres termes, des mesures isolées, fragmentaires, risquent fort d'échouer car elles ne remettent pas en cause l'équilibre général du système et laissent intacts les méchanismes grâce auxquels il peut les absorber'.[46]

Thus the educational system which entered the twentieth century frustrated two major demands in society. It left unsatisfied the demand for modern professional training, especially for the lower levels of production, agriculture and commerce, and it had not begun to meet the demand for democratization. It served the haute bourgeoisie, guaranteeing class reproduction and the cultural confirmation of status, but it did not service the economy, except at the highest levels, by producing the skills required. On the other hand, the bifurcated system denied the masses the chance of educational mobility, whilst the shortage of technical training reduced their opportunities for occupational mobility. The two demands were related, as the *Compagnons* were quick to see, and they shared something else in common – both represented onslaughts on the prevailing degree of unification and type of systematization and both basically failed to gain satisfaction during the 'stop' phase which lasted until the fall of the IVth Republic.

The *école unique* movement has already been examined in terms of interaction, but it was clear that it registered little success in overcoming the bifurcation between primary and secondary instruction and establishing the positive principle of hierarchical integration. Practical achievements were minimal and can be summed up as the introduction of free secondary studies, the inception of *classes nouvelles*, and a bridging move between the two levels in terms of teaching training. Gratuity only made a small contribution to democratization, for the length of the baccalauréat course still made it an expensive and hazardous investment for the masses. The classes nouvelles, started in 1937 and extended throughout the first cycle of the second degré in 1945, remained experimental. In 1950 only 750 such classes were being operated in 200 establishments of different kinds, and although three years later they were extended to cover the full range of secondary instruction (under the name of *'classes pilotes'*), they were still only available to about 7,000 pupils. Although this scale of official experimentation was novel and provided concrete information on the practicability of orientation and of diversified courses, its contribution was to the political debate rather than to solving the educational problem. Finally, the abolition of the *brevet supérieur*, and its replacement by the baccalauréat, in the écoles normales after the Second World War, went some way towards reducing the caste division between *instituteurs* and *professeurs* which had paralleled and reinforced the divide between primary and secondary levels. With the baccalauréat, instituteurs now had the possibility of acquiring the *licence, diplome d'études supérieures* and *l'agrégation*, and thus the right to teach in lycées. Correspondingly, places were opened in écoles normales for ordinary bacheliers to gain professional training, and pedagogical certificates were now required of professeurs. But 'pour utiles qu'elles soient, ces mesures restent fragmentaires et ne modifient pas la physionomie générale de l'enseignement public. Aucune d'entre elles n'annonce la refonte d'ensemble que les circonstances et l'évolution technique et sociale réclament impérieusement depuis des années'.[47]

Although modernization fared rather better, technical instruction suffered from the irrisistible tug of unification and the fact that progressive differentiation and systematization were forced to go hand in hand. The Astier law of 1919 tackled the problem of producing a skilled work force by founding part-time schools and making it obligatory for municipalities to run them, for employers to release their apprentices and for school leavers under the age of 18 to attend them. Its provisions implied decentralization, for such schools were to be controlled by the Ministry of Commerce, organized by local commissions (which included delegates from Chambers of Commerce etc.) 'en fonction des besoins de la localité',[48] and financed by a tax on employers. 'Certes, le technique conserve une autonomie réelle, mais elle recule peu à peu'.[49] By 1920 it had been reintegrated with the Ministry of National Education, by 1930 it had ceased to be voted a separate budget, and its successive directors were busy increasing its general educational content at the expense of vocational specialization. As irrelevance increased so did evasion by apprentices and employers, thus by the outbreak of war apprenticeship training was still grossly deficient in quantitative and qualitative terms. Wartime unemployment prompted the formation of *centres de formation professionnelle* (renamed apprenticeship centres in 1949), and shortage of job opportunities accounted for their greater success. Although the use of instructors from industry offered some protection against displacement towards general education, it was the constant threat to their relative autonomy which led many of those involved to advocate the attachment of these schools to the Youth Secretariat rather than the Education Ministry.

Indeed the higher the form of technical instruction, the more acute was this threat. At the very bottom, the part-time apprenticeship courses training artisans were still organized by local *Chambres de métiers*, because as terminal forms of instruction their autonomous activities had no effect on the rest of the educational system. Above that level the creation of a series of national technical qualifications, each conferring rights to further education, resulted predictably in uniformity. In particular, the establishment of a Baccalauréat technique in 1946 exerted a powerful downwards influence, standardizing curricula in *cours complémentaires*, the appropriate sections of secondary schools, and the *écoles nationales professionnelles*. In one way this recognition signalled the success of modernization (the existence of a complete hierarchy of technical studies), but in another it caught technical education up in the system — and loss of specialization, differentiation, and direct practical relevance were the prices paid.

Because of two world wars (which gave the usual impetus to scientific education) the period did not represent a complete 'stop' phase in the development of technical instruction, but the academic hierarchy to emerge was not what had been sought by either employers' or workers' organizations.

Thus the structure of the educational system whose major characteristics successive governments were so loath to modify, left the demand for democratization completely unsatisfied and that for modernization still largely frustrated at the end of the Fourth Republic. 'La centralisation, en effet, rend difficle les réformes: il manque cette diversité qui donnerait l'idée d'innovations souhaitables et permettrait d'éprouver les réformes qu'on projette. Il faut donc courir le risque d'une réforme générale, venue d'en haut, qui constitue un véritable saut dans l'inconnu, ou bien se resigner à supporter encore des maux tolérables, puisque connus. La centralisation est ainsi un obstacle au progrès, qu'elle n'autorise que par le détour de crises.'[50] The final question remaining, then, is why this immobility on the part of the system during the Third and Fourth Republics did not give rise to crisis? Why in other words did the discontent which continuously built up outside the system not burst out in some form of collective action which could not be ignored? The answer I believe lies quite simply in the accessibility of politics during the entire period. Demands could always find political expression, pressure groups could find political sponsors, and interests could find political coalitions. The decision-making arena was perpetually open and in continuous use: it must have seemed to many groups, but particularly to those on the left, that they constantly hovered on the point of breakthrough. Another election, a further coalition, a new Bill, and reform would be within their grasp – next time. And they would not have been deluding themselves if they could have held together: meanwhile their great political expectations defused the explosive potential of discontent.

PATTERNS OF EDUCATIONAL CHANGE IN FRANCE: THE FIFTH REPUBLIC

Whilst-ever powers of educational control are concentrated at the centre, this remains the source of change – whether it is introduced by political negotiation or induced by political disruption. Both processes were important under the Vth Republic and their causes and consequences are closely intertwined. The first major reforms dealing with the issues of desecularization, democratization and modernization were polity-directed in a spirit of educational pragmatism. 'La démarche de la Ve Republique est en effet empirique. Elle n'applique pas un plan cohérent, qui se devoilerait à travers des mesures successives dont il assure la continuité; elle obéit aux situations'.[51] The situations it faced were inherited from the immobilism of the IVth Republic and the dissatisfactions which had accumulated around these three issues. The Debré, Berthoin and Fouchet measures can all be viewed in the same light, as piecemeal changes and pragmatic concessions intended to take the edge off discontent – giving away a little in order to conserve a great deal. As such these reforms tinkered 'à la marge' rather than indicating a willingness to engage in large scale structural change or devolution of educational control.

Precisely because these polity-directed changes protected unification and preserved systematization (in the interests of educational responsiveness to Government and its requirements) they did not increase the flexibility of the system by introducing the differentiation and specialization needed to satisfy a plurality of demands. The logic of centralized control thus perpetuated the illogic of educational uniformity. Public education remained, in the words of Christian Fouchet, 'the biggest enterprise in the world apart from the Red Army' and was not much more sensitive to the expression of sectional interests and local demands. This in turn was to engender the outbursts, which have already been discussed, and to be the key factor perpetuating the 'stop-go' pattern of change in France.

The Debré law of 1959, giving State aid to private and mainly confessional schools, was justified by specific reference to the 'indispensable unité'[52] of national education. This concession to Catholic supporters offered private schools one of four solutions to their financial difficulties – total integration with public education – a contract of association – a simpler contract – or the maintenance of the status quo. The first and last formulae were only used in a minority of cases; thus by 1967-68, of private primary establishments, secondary schools of 'CEG type', and 'Lycée type', respectively 92 percent, 87 percent and 81 percent were under one kind of contractual arrangement or the other. Both formulae mean that the State aids such schools and pays teachers providing that, whilst conserving their 'own character', each school teaches 'with complete respect for liberty of conscience' and conforms to certain requirements about number of pupils, qualifications of teachers and standards of physical environment. With the full contract, all expenses are undertaken by the State at the cost of a greater loss of autonomy, for the school also becomes subject to the rules and programmes governing public education. The simple contract, which provides for less aid but less State control, is however only a temporary formula.

Integration, loss of autonomy and standardization are all implicit in the Loi Debré, and its implementation leads one to wonder whether national education has not lost one of its few sources of diversity and the public system one of its few shock absorbers. 'Toute la question sera alors de savoir dans quelle mesure les établissements seront admis à conserver ce que la loi Debré appelle leur "caractère propre". La réponse à cette question serait évidemment facilité si – nous rejoignons ici le problème de la décentralisation – une plus grande autonomie des établissements était admise à l'intérieur de l'enseignement public lui-même'.[53] Since this was clearly not the trend of the following years, the reform which had raised so much anti-clerical hostility, also had the effect of subjecting public education to the closest Catholic scrutiny, since their own confessional schools ceased to constitute a real private sector.

The Berthoin reform of 1959 came as an anti-climax after forty years of struggle to establish an école unique, embodying the positive principle of hierarchical integration. A cycle of observation starting at the age of eleven and lasting for two years was was introduced for all pupils. At the end of their elementary studies pupils could continue at primary school, attend a *Collège d'Enseignement Général* (the old *cours complémentaires*), or enter a Lycée. Officially this 'placement' (effected either by teachers' recommendations, parental preference, or simply by pupils staying where they were) was not viewed as decisive, for after two years of observation pupils would be orientated to the appropriate secondary course. In other words, the observation cycle took place in different kinds of establishments, much to the satisfaction of the professeurs who had always opposed the idea of autonomous middle schools for all. Moreover the content of this cycle was not the same for all, for it was made up of the normal programmes followed in the 6th and the 5th classes in these different kinds of institutions. The notion of a lengthy 'tronc commun', followed by all pupils and used to establish the patterns of individual ability was reduced to a single term during which curricula were 'harmonized' in different kinds of schools. Yet even this half measure was a compromise 'entre les partisans de l'ordre ancien, qui voudraient voir reconstituer un véritable enseignement secondaire, et les partisans d'un ordre nouveau qui voudraient un enseignement commun d'orientation prolongé sur deux ou quatre ans. Le trimestre commun paraît *inutile* aux uns, parce-que, pour eux, l'orientation droit se faire d'abord par la sélection. Il paraît *insuffisant* aux autres, parce-que, pour eux, l'orientation droit se faire d'abord par l'observation'.[54]

At the end of the observation cycle, the *Conseil d'Orientation* in each school advised parents of appropriate further studies. *Classes passerelles* situated in the 4th class provided conversion courses for those who had somehow taken the wrong turning during the orientation phase. However, since assessments were made in establishments varying from the lycée to the primary school, and moreover were made on the basis of their respective curricula, it is not surprising that this should have resulted in very little individual mobility – only 1 percent of pupils transferring from the latter to the former. Because of the vested interests of different groups of teachers, the compromise reform had left existing structures intact, but in doing so it had merely perpetuated these interests and the activities associated with their defence. Devices like the harmonization of curricula and the classes passerelles had increased overall systematization, by linking different parts of the system, without providing the vast majority of pupils with more diverse educational opportunities, available on a democratic basis.

This tendency of the system to repel fragmentary reforms also vitiated attempts to correct the deficiencies of the Berthoin measures, by establishing a fully differentiated middle school – the *Collège d'Enseignement Secondaire* (CES). Theoretically these were to cater for the whole age group from 11-14, thus functioning as common or comprehensive schools. Some pupils would proceed from the CES to secondary establishments, others to full-time vocational training, and yet others to apprenticeship schemes. But the CES was to be formed by converting the first cycle of lycée studies into independent units and by transforming the existing CEGs into CESs – it was opposed by professeurs and municipalities alike. Had the reform engaged in audacious structural change and created new polyvalent institutions of a self-standing type, it would have overriden vested interests: as it was it placed itself at their mercy. On the one hand they resisted and delayed its implementation (there were only 220 schools of this type in 1964, and 1,500 in 1968, with many still refusing to transform themselves in the seventies). On the other hand they prevented it from operating as an integrated and purposeful institution. The CES was made up of a classical and a modern section from the secondary curriculum, a *'moderne court'* section from the CET, and the old *'classe de fin d'études'* from the primary school, but professional resistance has prevented them from melding with one another. 'The hope was, and still is, that fusion will take place and that flexibility will replace separateness, to the benefit of all pupils. This is not yet discernible outside a few pilot schools that have overridden the hourly divisions of the timetable, have built workrooms, classrooms, project rooms, reading rooms and common rooms of different sizes and for both heterogeneous and homogeneous groups. Juxtaposition by itself does not bring down institutional partitions'.[55] Thus even where structural differentiation took place, functional differentiation lagged far behind. It is this which leads Prost to conclude that 's'il semble bien qu'avec les CES l'école unique ait trouvé sa structure définitive, il s'en faut cependant qu'ils répondent à ses exigences pédagogiques'.[56]

The Fouchet reforms at secondary and higher level were a package of changes whose contents were intended to alleviate some very different kinds of discontent — that of students with the 50 percent failure rate at the end of the first year (likened by a subsequent Minister of Education to organizing a ship-wreck to find out who could swim), of large employers finding the encyclopaedic culture of graduates irrelevant to occupational needs, of staff at both levels facing rising numbers and falling standards, and of the Left in general, concerned about marked social discrimination. The same mechanism was adopted at secondary and higher levels and involved the differentiation of cycles of studies within them, giving a greater opportunity for vocational specialization. Simultaneously this was intended to satisfy students (by giving greater choice, better orientation and thus a lower failure rate), to produce school leavers and graduates better suited to occupational outlets, and to have a democratic appeal because it established shorter courses for those whose cultural or financial background had previously excluded them altogether.

Both at secondary and higher levels, the Fouchet reforms aimed at increasing the relevance of qualifications to future careers and jobs. They sought to diversify outlets for pupils of varying aptitudes and attainments by offering alternative short courses, parallel to the traditional 'long' academic secondary stream leading up to university. This challenged the dualism between the lycée and the post-primary forms of instruction, located in other establishments and staffed by a separate corps of non-graduate teachers. While the most able pupils were still to be channelled into the 'long' stream, they would cease to be segregated and training facilities would be provided in the other streams. The long-term aim was to break down the monopoly of the baccalauréat as a passport to all desirable employment — though it was impossible on political grounds to prevent it from remaining a permit for university entry. At least attempts were made to 'demystify' the baccalauréat by turning the terminal forms into specialized sections with different final examinations, relevant to future academic studies (instead of the former subdivision into two examinations separated by a one year course and emphasizing general literature, abstract reasoning and linguistic prowess).

At university level the complementary reforms introduced between 1963 and 1966 were mainly intended to obviate the disadvantages inherent in the lack of pre-entry selection. Faculties of letters and sciences were reorganized by creating three cycles, the first one to provide the basic knowledge required to bring entrants up to university standard. In this cycle, science students could choose between four sections (maths and physics, physics and chemistry, chemistry and biology, biology and geology), and letters students between nine sections (classics, modern literature, modern languages, history, geography, psychology, sociology, ancient history and archaeology). Two years of study in one of these sections led up to the DUES or DUEL diploma which gave the right to register for the second cycle where specialization began. Again there was a long or a short alternative towards which students could be channelled depending on their performance at DUES/DUEL level. One year in the second cycle (i.e. three years of undergraduate study in all) led up to the *licence*, whereas two years (four in all) led to the master degree. The third cycle consisted of research with a minimum period of two years for the preparation of a thesis.

In accordance with the philosophy of 'short' alternatives, the creation of *Instituts Universitaires de Technologie* (IUTs) alongside the university faculties constituted an added outlet for secondary leavers by offering two year courses for the training of cadres (at supervisory and lower managerial level). The overwhelming majority of entrants were *bacheliers* (up to 90 percent), though entry by examination was possible. The teaching staff were to be recruited partly from among university teachers and partly from among established specialists working either in nationalized enterprises or in the private sector. The subjects taught were to be selected for their vocational value, assessed in the light of economic needs, and the methods of tuition were to be more modern than in the faculties, with an emphasis on group work and practical projects in fields such as civil engineering, electronics, documentation and statistics.

In many ways, however, the maintenance of unified controls weakened the government's own desire for more differentiation and specialization at these levels. As usual the reforms were applied identically in all institutions, including the new universities created to cope with overcrowding. The reform was 'dans la forme comme au fond, d'essence technocratique: dans la forme car il s'agit d'imposer plus que d'inciter, et la centralisation demeure la règle; au fond car si un souffle extérieur s'introduit dans la définition de la politique d'éducation, il émane des managers de la société plus que de l'ensemble des forces vives de la nation'.[57] Even in technocratic terms the reforms were less than successful, to judge by the divergence between the proportions intended to follow science and technology courses under the National Plan and the much lower percentage of students enrolling in them. Not only did this spell manpower deficiencies vis-à-vis the economy, but also the continued growth of a body of pupils and students without clear vocational expectations or opportunities. In addition the chaotic application of the law (more than 2000 decrees and circulars were involved), placed many students in an anomalous position because of the constant changes taking place in their courses, and heightened the awareness of many staff to the continuous nature of ministerial interference. Finally the Left as we have seen was not impressed by the democratic intentions of a reform which created an inferior opportunity structure for the non-privileged.

Clearly many of the demands which the reforms sought to assuage were mutually contradictory, but it is precisely because of this that any attempt to impose a uniform solution, common to all schools and universities, was bound to satisfy no-one. Only a strategy willing to sacrifice some control and allow some institutional autonomy, so that truely differentiated establishments could provide specialist services, could hope to satisfy these conflicting demands simultaneously. The tenacity with which the government clung to central educational control again precluded this: 'if the Ministry were less concerned with control, administration and unification . . . then the Ministry could be an instrument of reform rather than an overworked, ponderous machine'.[58]

Of this groups inside and outside the system were fully aware. The Caen Colloquium of university teachers, meeting in 1966, rejected the napoleonic concept of a single national structure with identical regional establishments as more suitable for the post office or police than for education. Instead they sought the creation of diversified universities, autonomous in policy and administration, and for which the Ministry would merely ensure adequate financing, equipment and staffing. Such universities would develop their own courses, curriculum and examinations. The same demand for decentralization and the same condemnation of standardization was voiced in connection with secondary education at the Amiens Colloquium, only two months before the May events. But confronted with the highly unified system there was little that could be done by means of internal initiation or external transactions to mitigate its effects.

Cut off from the possibility of responding directly to the community or playing a constructive role in educational administration, much of the profession turned in upon itself, pursuing an academic conservatism vis-à-vis the definition of instruction which was not politically contentious. The changes introduced in this way reflected the vested interests of the profession at work, but they were important for their cumulative effect was to increase the disjunction between education and active life. Pierre Bourdieu's brilliant analysis of the professor confirming and securing his own status by reproducing himself in his students, highlights the irrationality resulting from treating all 'as apprentice professors and not as professional apprentices'.[59] A variety of professional practices all worked in the direction of reinforcing the *disciplinary* organization of knowledge, of creating subject-based 'baronries' which placed teaching assistants in a vassalage which was intellectual as well as personal, and of reducing academic influence to a process of 'co-optation controlée'.[60] For pupils and students the effect was to separate their present studies from any future relevance and to condemn them either to academic ritualism or intellectual adventurism. For employers in all sectors of society the consequence was similar, namely to deprive them of school leavers or graduates whose knowledge was organized on a *professional* basis. Certainly the professional training scheme of 1966 allowed for some external transactions in this area (it was partly financed by employers and supplemented by the State), but since these remained outside the educational system proper they could have no effect on its principle outputs or the definition of instruction which was reproduced.

Because the regime had been so unwilling to concede central control, it had virtually eliminated the other two processes through which change could have been introduced and grievances diminished. Instead it had imposed reforms uniformly and satisfied no-one by these compromise measures. The pool of discontent had grown and since power was concentrated at the centre this is where it was directed. To the participants in the May events, 'the political interpretation of reform — changes not too surely introduced (and not too clearly related to any coherent timetable or plan) as pressures become irrisistible at successive levels — had in their view proved inadequate or irrelevant. It had not yet translated 'democratization' (the politicians' own aim) into institutional terms. It had not dynamically swept away obstacles. It had not provided new channels for new forces which were bursting with grievance or idealism while politicians were trying to cope with problems set by a previous decade or century'.[61] Hence the outburst of May which heralded in a new 'go' phase of legislative change. As an educational revolt it represented a massive condemnation of the 'mania for centralization'[62] and a movement for educational autonomy and regional diversity contrary to the revolutionary, monarchical and republican traditions alike. It now remains to be seen how far the panic legislation introduced in 1968 showed a willingness to reduce unification and loosen systematization to solve the crisis.

The *Loi d'orientation de l'enseignement supérieur* adopted by Parliament in November 1968 broke away from the Napoleonic Université in each of the three main principles it endorsed — multi-disciplinarity, participation and autonomy. The speed of the operation was a condition of its success for these principles would never have received the almost unanimous support of Parliament had the scare been less recent. Indeed the grounds on which it was accepted or supported were very different — for some it was the fulfilment of long deferred hopes, for others it was an unavoidable concession intended to restore order. The law was construed by the Minister himself and by those who supported it on the left as widening educational opportunities and increasing the share of students in decision-making processes. However, the support of administrators and some of the right was due largely to a desire for more vocationalism and their alliance with Faure proved temporary. Similarly, the attacks made on the law before its enactment and continued during its implementation sprang from a strange coalition

between the conservative right, the gauchist 'desperadoes' and tradi-
tionalist academics. This complex political background was important
in shaping the interpretations given to the law in practice, especially as
these often contravened both its spirit and letter. The vagueness of
some provisions — due either to haste in drafting or the need for
compromise — facilitated re-entrenchment.

The new law was clearly intended to embody the concession of
greater differentiation and specialization. The basic unit on which the
whole system of higher education was to be founded was the university
not the *Université*. Each university was to become an autonomous
establishment from the financial point of view and free to draw up its
own statute — officially a complete departure from the previous
centralized pattern, but like most of the provisions, one which was not
to prove so radical in practice. Its size must be limited to avoid the huge
conglomorations which had grown under the IVth Republic, for the
argument that large universities could offer a wider range of courses was
considered less important than the advantage of adaptation in accordance with regional circumstances.

Of the three characteristics with which the loi d'orientation
endowed the new universities — multi-disciplinarity, participation and
autonomy — the first attracted most attention and stimulated the
keenest controversies among staff; the second pre-occupied the students
virtually to the exclusion of all other issues; yet it was autonomy which
underpinned them both and involved the greatest departure from previous precedents. As principles, participation and autonomy spelt a
weakening of unification, whilst multi-disciplinarity a reduction of
internal systematization in favour of linking higher education to future
careers. However, as Maurice Duverger commented at the time[63] the
future of the universities was more dependent on the application of the
law than its passing, and it is this which must now be examined.

Multidisciplinarity

Limited in size 'à l'échelle humaine', the new universities are qualitatively defined as 'multidisciplinary'. Article 6 of the law refers to the
desirability of an interpenetration between arts/letters and
science/technology within them, whilst recognizing the possibility of
'universities with a dominant vocation', i.e. grouping related
specialisms. This was already tantamount to admitting that pluri-

disciplinarity was a utopian ideal in the context of academic entrenchment in traditionally defined subject areas. The abolition of faculties – to which no mention was made in the first draft of the law, in order 'to kill them by omission'[64] and to which only one article of the final text alluded – was intended to eradicate administrative and pedagogic barriers between disciplines. The universities were to be 'organic groupings' of teaching and research units (UERs) which could transcend such divisions. However, the way in which these units could be devised and the difference between their coverage and that of the faculties were not made clear. Assemblies of staff – with or without the participation of students, depending on local conditions – were convened to decide on the reshaping of the former faculties and were free to do so without legal constraint. The only limitation on their planning was the maximum intake of 2,500 students per unit specified in the law (the minimum being 800). Thus a number of faculties survived under a new guise by constituting themselves into UERs. This was the case at Amiens, Besançon, Limoges, Nice, Orléans, Pau, Reims, Rouen, St. Etienne and Tours. In larger towns, the pressure of student numbers forced a split into several UERs per faculty, but few original regroupings of subject matters within each unit were actually adopted. Almost everywhere, after less conventional proposals were put forward and then rejected by a majority, it was the solution most akin to traditional habits which was adopted, the subdivision by subjects.[65] Thus faculties of science turned themselves into units of physics, chemistry, maths and natural science (as at Lyons and Toulouse) – in other words, a division along the lines of the major courses taught in the past prevailed. Faculties of letters displayed an even greater attachment to mono-disciplinarity – as at Bordeaux where philosophy became the basis of one unit or at Aix en Provence where three units (Letters, Literature and Language) were set up to coincide with the three existing chairs.

As an alternative to this approach, conducive to the creation of one unit per discipline, or major course, or group of related disciplines was a breakdown based on the cycle or level of study. Thus the faculties of science at Grenoble and Montpellier divided themselves into one 1st cycle unit for the basic training and orientation of university entrants, three 2nd cycle units for the scientific formation of teachers, researchers and technicians respectively, and then various research units. However, this type of division remained the exception, for a variety of reasons. On the one hand, the unit centred on one discipline was a group in which relations between a professor and his disciples had often remained unperturbed by the May events or in which a fruitful dialogue had been initiated in May. In neither case were outsiders invited. Whether the purpose was to keep revolutionaries or reactionaries away, political considerations came into play. In addition, the creation of units corresponding to cycles was feared as a threat to research. As the Centre National de la Recherche Scientifique (CNRS) and all its laboratories were excluded from the scope of *loi d'orientation*, some academics expected the government to cut research grants for universities and to turn them gradually into teaching institutions only. In order to protect their members against such a policy — which would run counter to the aspirations of academics — many faculties included research in each unit which they formed. Another fear experienced in connection with this type of subdivision was of an evolution towards American type 'junior colleges'. Neither teachers nor students (when they were consulted) favoured such a trend — the former wished to avoid any lowering of their own status, or worsening of their working conditions. The latter feared that 'horizontal' units would involve tougher selection procedures at the end of the 1st cycle. Hence the grounds on which decisions about future units were made could be related to considerations of self-interest or self-defence.

Participation

By September 1969 some 630 UERs had been set up to replace the former faculties (approximately 100) and endowed with statutes by delegates of their staff and students. According to the loi d'orientation a complex procedure of elections was organized separately for each category of teachers, students, administrative and technical staff. If they failed to agree on the statutes by March 1969, these could be introduced by governmental decree. The complex conditions with which the law surrounded representation of each category were intended to protect the interests of the professoriate, without depriving other members of staff, and to grant an opportunity for participation to the students. The established university teachers were granted 60 percent of staff representation although they were only about a third of the teaching personnel. The parity between staff and students promised in the aftermath of the May events was in fact reduced to a maximum of one third for students because of the differentiation between categories of university teachers. Staff representatives must be at least as many as student delegates and can be more numerous. In addition, the number of student representatives is limited by complicated provisions based on the ratio of voters to registered members of each student constituency. Furthermore, the limits imposed on participation are broad and exclude such areas as the drawing up of teaching programmes, the allocation of credits, the testing of aptitude and knowledge, the recruitment and promotion of staff, and all matters of selection. In sum this legal hedging contrasted sharply with the initial statements about equal shares in university management.[66]

Unwilling to share in the reorganization of bourgeois universities, the 'groupuscules' and the UNEF itself pronounced against the participation of their members in the first university elections. In an article entitled 'We shall not vote' a junior teacher at Vincennes University [67] summed up the main arguments for abstaining. After listing the advantages granted to the professoriate and the restrictions on student representation, he singled out the inclusion of local personalities in the councils (between 1/6 and 1/3 of their membership) as a symptom of 'the greater subordination of the University to the interests of large firms' under cover of participation. In fact, this attitude may have been widespread as only one student in four on average votes in university elections. However, whether as a result of political involvement or apathy, student representation turned out to be insufficiently representative, often improvised on the spur of the moment and generally inadequate in between elections.

The first responsibility of the council elected within each UER was to meet with the councils of other units with which the creation of a university was contemplated. This cumbersome process was suggested by Minister Faure as embodying the spirit which had prevailed in May — the return to grass roots, the initiation of reforms from the basic cells, in contrast to the centralized tradition of deciding at the top and then passing the decision 'downwards'. Attacks on the loi d'orientation have often singled out its lack of explicitness on the controversial issue of relationships between UERs and universities. While powers were granted to the new universities to undertake all the activities formerly incumbent upon the faculties, article 3 provided for the administrative autonomy of the units without specifying its limits in relation to the prerogatives of the universities. Hence the risk of future internal clashes and the temptation to 'play safe' by avoiding any co-operation with unfamiliar or politically uncongenial units. Whereas the initial stage involved problems about how to approach multidisciplinarity, it was quickly followed up by a withdrawal from 'compromising' entanglements and a return to safer forms of integration. Most pure scientists found the social scientists too politicized for comfort, as did lawyers, and the former juxtaposition of arts and social sciences within the *Facultés de Lettres* tended to endure in the new universities. The faculties of science and medicine, well endowed with research laboratories and staff, did not like to merge with poorer specialisms for fear of losing facilities. The Ministry opposed attempts to set up purely medical (or legal, or technical) universities in order to uphold the principle of multi-disciplinarity. As a result partnerships were often based on shared political attitudes rather than intellectual complementarity, 'a marriage of reason' between law and medicine representing a common pattern.

Autonomy

Prior to 1968, there was practically no pedagogical autonomy, since the faculties were neither free to select their students at entry (as the baccalauréat gave the right to register), nor to recruit their own staff (who were centrally appointed under the civil service statutes), nor to devise their own curricula (which were drawn up by the Ministry). Although pre-entry selection had been widely advocated in the sixties as a remedy to overcrowding and the lowering of standards, it was politically unacceptable after May.[68] Demographic and political pressures made any restrictions on registration appear retrograde, yet the right for autonomous universities to protect themselves against congestion was upheld by several speakers during the debate. Ultimately article 21 created a species of internal selection by empowering the university to set up post-entry probation periods (*stages d'orientation*) for newly registered students.[69] Autonomy with regard to staff selection was extended by article 31, whereby no limit is placed on the ratio of temporary contracts to formal appointments, though these are still chosen from a centrally drawn-up list of those eligible, thus ending the exclusion of foreigners and the traditional supremacy of full professors.

However, the major limitation on academic autonomy derives from the existence of national degrees and diplomas which imply that the corresponding courses will be based on ministerial regulations. The universities are of course now free to issue their own certificates, but even the most extreme opponents of centralization are unwilling to relinquish the State guaranteed qualifications to which future employers are accustomed. The scope for experimenting with curricula and even teaching methods is restricted since all UERs and universities are constrained to recognize each others' programmes. To these pressures in favour of homogeneity is added the right of students to be offered a similar bill of fare since they are not free to choose their cafeteria – the university in which they register must be nearest to their domicile. This limitation – intended chiefly to prevent the exodus of provincials to Paris – makes it impossible, at least in the first cycle, to select from among various curricula or approaches. Hence the alternative is either the arbitrariness of geographical accident or uniformity between universities at the level of the first cycle. Historical precedents have influenced academics in the latter direction, and experiments with new specialisms or approaches have largely been limited to the second and third cycles.

In terms of financial autonomy the only major reform brought about by the law is the allocation of funds and of posts to specialisms by reference to student numbers, without earmarking the exact purpose of each credit.[70] Because of it, academics are discovering the burdens of financial responsibility as much as profiting from new freedoms. Not only do universities own and maintain their own buildings and grounds since 1972, but the funds granted to cover the cost of the dismantling of the faculties have not always proved sufficient. In addition the UERs tend to hang onto the buildings, resources and money (as well as staff) of the faculties from which they emerge. The fight over shares in the budget tends to be particularly acrimonious wherever multi-disciplinarity has prevailed, as at Aix Marseilles II (law-medicine), Strasbourg I or Lille I (economics and science). Moreover, the approval of university budgets by their councils is always made difficult by the tendency of UERs to seek an increase in their own credits as against university expenditure which corresponds to the general services necessary to the operations of all units.

Lastly, *political* autonomy is implicit in the traditional definition of academic freedom. The loi d'orientation reasserts as basic principles the toleration of all opinions and the necessity of objectivity in the imparting of knowledge. It grants to students a freedom of information on political, economic and social problems, which constitutes a new right. Its implementation must not, however, interfere with either teaching or research, result in a monopoly or propaganda, or lead to a breach of the peace. Whenever possible, special premises are to be put at the students' disposal for this purpose in order to avoid political discussions in lecture theatres. This distinction seems difficult to maintain in practice. In fact the whole of article 36 raises delicate problems of interpretation about how propaganda is to be distinguished from information. The attempt to satisfy the gauchists by recognizing political rights on the campus and the moderates by circumscribing them seems to have rendered this part of the law virtually inapplicable.

Thus in the years immediately following the 1968 reform the energies of the universities were devoted to thrashing out the details of its practical application. This self-absorption and the parochial scandals and battles which the press recorded served to distract attention from a monumental act of non-decision-making also contained in the loi d'orientation. This was, its full title notwithstanding, an Act concerning the universities alone. It did not tackle the other part 'de l'enseigne-ment supérieur' — the grandes écoles, or for that matter the important CNRS, in whose agencies research is institutionalized. Typically govern-ment had been most willing to make concessions in those educational institutions which served its own requirements least proximately — the ordinary open-door universities, not the elitarian grandes écoles supply-ing ministerial technocrats. This 'alternative university' continues to co-exist with the reorganized universities. Many, though not all of them, are subordinated to technical ministeries for which they train specialists, not to the Ministry of Education. Ten different ministries supervise these various Schools whose common characteristics are selec-tion by competitive examination for entry, higher costs of tuition per student than in other educational establishments, and a monopoly — either legal or factual — of recruitment to certain careers. This privi-leged sector has remained outside the orbit of loi d'orientation, these Schools have retained the highest status and have preserved their distinctive elitarian features. Their insulation from the full impact of the Faure reform has been due partly to the efforts of powerful associations grouping their former pupils, and allegedly to the fact that President Pompidou went through Ecole Normale himself, which affected official attitudes to grandes écoles in general. Hence they continue to provide the precise degree of functional specialization which public administration (and to some extent private enterprise) require at the highest level, and for which the governing elite accords them the necessary autonomy — in fact the highest degree of differ-entiation in the whole educational system — safe in the knowledge that murderous competition for entry and appointment to elite positions on graduation, provide adequate protection against abusive tendencies i.e. escaping State control and pursuing autonomous goals. For example those gaining access to the *Ecole Nationale d'Administration* become Civil Servants *on entry* and have a choice of official posts which they can select, three years later, in the rank order in which they graduate. The selective, meritocratic, and technocratic elements are mutually reinforcing, and have been neatly captured in the term 'Enarchie'.[71] Thus in many ways there are two universities in France,[72] the one devoting itself to the settlement of its own political dilemmas, the other retaining the pattern of selectiveness and vocationalism inherent in the Napoleonic tradition.

Considered as a whole the loi d'orientation did not bring about a radical structural transformation. The new organizational differentiation that it promised succumbed substantially to traditional academic practices and vested interests, which reasserted themselves in the two or three years following the Act. The new rational specialization that it eulogized, with courses linked to career outlets, was mangled between the entrenchment of intellectual traditionalism on the part of staff and the repudiation of industrial vocationalism on the part of students. Thus although the Law did involve some diminution in unification and systematization, despite the fact that central powers were clawed back to a significant degree during its implementation, the subordinate characteristics have not grown well on the old tree — and partly at least because the old inducements to uniformity have not been completely withdrawn. The combined forces of administrative 'dirigism' and academic conservatism solidly outweighed the tentative and panic commitment of the polity to decentralization. Hence it is with somewhat more reason than elsewhere that the student movement in the early seventies turned in on the universities themselves and also attacked the State through the universities.

Comments

Change during this period of semi-penetrable government occurred in two different stages. The first, falling between 1958 and 1967, represented a polity-directed 'go' phase, in which the new Republic sought to propitiate the educational grievances which had accumulated over the preceding decades. But the principle governing reform was expediency, not a coherent educational philosophy, and in this it was typical of Gaullism, with its lack of any comprehensive socio-political ideology. The reform undertaken 'was in keeping with de Gaulle's distrust of theoreticians, an attitude reminiscent of Napoleon's contempt for "ideologues". Indeed, it might be argued that his distrust extended from intellectuals to general ideas, dismissed as superstructural and ephemeral, by contrast with interests which, being derived from geographical and historical factors, were both real and lasting'.[73] Thus two of the legislative changes (the Berthoin and Fouchet reforms) were pragmatic attempts to buy off two seething and vocal sources of discontent, whilst the Debré Law rewarded catholic interests for their political support.

These concessions gave very little satisfaction in educational terms, unsurprisingly since they did not attempt to tackle the two main educational problems (of democratization and of modernization) at their root, but only sought to eliminate the *political* discontent to which they gave rise. Indeed these measures were most important for what they did not do, namely alter the structure of the system by significantly reducing the stifling unification or removing the undemocratic principle on which systematization was based. As changes they were polity-directed from the top rather than being the products of public negotiation or parliamentary transaction. Their contents reflected De Gaulle's own conviction that 'Public opinion exists, but it doesn't count'.[74] As such they obviously did not 'go' far enough, and public opinion did count when the issue of democratization concerned the bulk of the population and the question of modernization involved the economic elites. The attempt to protect political unity by engaging in educational expediency involved a serious under-estimate of educational discontent which was nearly fatal for the regime. The paliative measures enacted up to the mid-sixties were the clearest indication that the 'wages of pragmatism were insignificance'.[75]

The May events signalled a moral radical 'go' phase, as the panic reaction to this politico-educational outburst. The legislation, passed in a hurry to avert the crisis, contained an overt commitment to reducing the degree of unification and systematization. It revealed an unprecedented acceptance of educational decentralization as the price to be paid for political restabilization. But as we have seen this concession was limited in scope, even within higher education itself, and became more limited in substance once the immediate crisis had been surmounted. The polity had been forced into declaring a policy of decentralization. This is a very important reversal of the administrative policy that has prevailed in France . . . and is not likely to be implemented as easily as the word is uttered by Ministers. The system is under pressure but the politicians cannot start from zero. It is the present system that they have to alter . . . The experience of a decade indicates that while the system is not immobile, the rate of adaptation to new pressures and new demands is so unsatisfactory that periodical recourse must be had to measures which are outside the administrative and the normal parliamentary procedure. Crisis occurs and during the upheaval some groups win what they can by way of monetary reward or institutional recognition. Power is redistributed and the machinery is restarted. Conservative forces reassert themselves, professional groups assert their rights and defend themselves against new pressures. But the machinery needs overhaul and modernization at so many points that partial breakdown must recur frequently until the system acquires a new flexibility'.[76]

In other words, the legislation of the Fifth Republic, including its panic concessions, has not assuaged frustrated demands, particularly those for increased democratization (which require a transformation of systematization) and for increased modernization (which necessitate a suspension of unification). Old demands remain outstanding and new grievances are added to them, the reservoir of discontent continues to fill and the measures taken do not tap-off enough to prevent the level from continuing to rise.

THE DECENTRALIZED EDUCATIONAL SYSTEM AND THE INCREMENTAL PATTERN OF CHANGE

As was seen in Chapter 7, the predominance of differentiation and specialization in the decentralized system means that although the educational status quo will give rise to a variety of unsatisfied demands at any given time, more of these can be fulfilled by direct negotiation because more change can be implemented internally or independently. In other words, the very structure of these systems encourages educational interaction to remain a matter of peaceful negotiation rather than of disruptive outburst. The availability of the three processes of change results in discontent being both less intense and less extensive at any time. In the decentralized system there is more satisfaction to be had, because demands are met by services of a greater specificity and relevance, thus reducing the intensity of grievances. There are also more ways of obtaining satisfaction and because the three processes continuously subtract from the pool of discontent, there is thus less superimposition of grievances.

In the decentralized system demands are not necessarily cumulated, expressed and negotiated at national level: they can be transacted locally or institutionally as well as at the political centre. This in turn leads to a much more complex pattern of change. On the one hand there are the sectional negotiations conducted between particular vested interest groups. These may take place endogenously, initiated by the profession in the relevant educational institutions, or exogenously, instigated by external interest groups in collaboration with the appropriate educational establishments. Both types of sectional demands are cumulated on a specific basis and it is their success in producing the educational changes sought which prevents the polarization of conflict: there is less build up of discontent among a series of groups who have all experienced a common unresponsiveness of the system to their requirements. On the other hand, political manipulation provides a channel for those groups who cannot get their demands satisfied in any other way, and it tends to work rather more effectively because it is not constantly encumbered by every kind of demand. Although all groups will keep a watchful eye on polity-directed changes, these are not the same zero-sum issues as in the centralized system. The lesser degree of unification and systematization means that such changes will not be imposed in uniform fashion and may have no effect on the level or type of institutions which are the site of particular sectional transactions. In other words, political manipulation is not the sole focal point of educational interaction and every interest group does not line-up over each piece of legislation to fight its clauses tooth and nail because they are bound to affect it. Instead political interaction is the main resort of lower class and underprivileged groups whose organizations engage in continuous political manipulation since they cannot gain much from internal initiation or external transactions.

As all three processes of negotiation operate simultaneously and successfully, educational change is ceaseless. There is no period of stasis between educational Acts and no sense in which these represent the largest or most important changes, except that they are the most public – they are the most audible if not the most visible. (This of course is why some are tempted to assign a class character to educational interaction as a whole: political manipulation is class based and it does command more attention by definition because of the public character of parliamentary proceedings.) Nevertheless the changes introduced by sectional transactions can be just as far reaching. What is really crucial in the decentralized system is that these different forms of interaction produce changes which have consequences for one another. Each one moulds the educational context in which the others take place; every change is intertwined with others and may reinforce or dilute the overall effect. In sum, there is a constant stream of modifications rather than a stop-go pattern of change.

In the decentralized system change is a combination of small localized shifts, possibly concentrated on one level or one establishment in a given area, whose effect is cumulative, and polity directed changes, which are intended to be larger in scope. However, for reasons which will be examined in a moment, even the legislative changes which occur here do not dramatically transform the system. These are modified, in their very conception, by the other on-going changes and are mediated, in their implementation, by local and institutional forces. They too bring about further increments of change rather than root and branch reforms. It is by following through the way in which the small localized shifts can accumulate to produce a significant scale of change as well as the way in which central policy directives are systematically reduced in scope that the overall pattern of incremental change is understood. The 'incremental pattern' is the result of both action sequences, in conjunction with one another.

The Accumulation of Small Localized Changes

Here we are concerned with the results of *external transactions* and *internal initiation*, that is with the contribution which these two processes of negotiation make to the overall pattern of change. Both show a strong tendency to introduce unit changes which fall far short of the macroscopic. Thus external transactions usually involve localized changes between interest groups and educational institutions. These may be, and may remain, extremely small in scale (like one firm negotiating a research contract with its local university) and thus depend upon replication and aggregation if they are to influence educational development. Alternatively an institutional interest group can engineer a series of transactions, in different localities, which produce a network of changes by accretion (like the Danish network of agricultural schools and colleges built up in this way). Similarly the innovations introduced by internal initiation normally involve small changes in teaching material and methods which take place in particular schools and classrooms. Again only by their repetition in a large number of establishments, whether by spontaneous imitation or orchestrated by a professional organization, can these add up to large scale educational developments. The rest of the argument is thus taken up with demonstrating two propositions: firstly that the accumulation of large scale change from both processes is a frequent and important occurrence, and secondly that the kinds of change introduced in these ways have distinctive characteristics which in turn affect the central governance of education.

Quintessentially external transactions provide services (to the interest groups involved) which are marked by their *specificity*. For negotiations are only successful when the buyer gets what he wants from a seller who is willing to supply him – dissatisfaction on the part of the former or reluctance on the part of the latter mean a break-down in negotiations. Obviously, as in any sort of dealing, there is some room for manoeuvre – for vendors to oversell their products and to try to tell the buyer what he wants, and for purchasers to be blinded by status considerations rather than being guided exclusively by their practical requirements. By and large, however, external transactions give interest groups the type of service they seek, or cease to take place. If this service is not forthcoming from public education then it can always be obtained from the private sector, provided the resources are there to pay for it. Clearly, the better the negotiating strength of an external interest group, the more these services will be tailor-made to its requirements.

In turn this specificity means that the new services which have been transacted represent a diversification of current educational practices. Incidentally this also works in reverse, when a particular kind of external transaction stops, either through lack of money or political embargo, the system loses one source of diversity. Thus, for example, the worsening finances of the established Church and most other denominations has meant the virtual withdrawal of a religious definition of instruction in England, with the exception of Catholic schools. However, this diversification often cannot be accommodated within the existing institutional, disciplinary and curricular frameworks, and involves changes in all three. Consequently external transactions foster the progressive segmentation of institutions, differentiation of courses, and specialization of knowledge, whether for teaching or research.

Both England and Denmark provide ample evidence of the way in which the accumulation of such transactions can alter the composition of the educational system. In Denmark, the growth by accretion of three differentiated networks devoted to agricultural, industrial and commercial instruction provides a very clear example of the importance of cumulative change, for this vocational instruction both paralleled and challenged public secondary education as well as linking upwards to its own tertiary institutions. In England too a whole range of educational institutions and activities would not have come into being were it not for external transactions. Of these the civic universities are perhaps the most important example and their development represented the aggregate effect of hundreds, if not thousands, of independent transactions on the part of industry. Each of these companies reacted to its own market situation in a similar kind of way, but their individual quests for scientific training and research produced this major change in university education and pumped successive waves of differentiation throughout the tertiary level.

Certainly many external transactions remain localized and without sequel, and do so necessarily if they involve unique requirements or special circumstances: indeed one of the main functions of such transactions is to bring educational services into line with regional problems and particularistic situations. Equally, however, some transactions which bid fair to introduce macroscopic change leave no lasting impression on educational development. Thus, for example, there has been a repeated failure in England to introduce a form of post-elementary *real* instruction despite at least two promising beginnings. However, the point here is not that all external transactions necessarily accumulate until they represent large scale changes, only that they *can produce macroscopic changes incrementally*. Which ones will do so is determined in the course of interaction and in relation to the other two processes of change.

Thus the cumulative effect of external transactions is to increase the overall differentiation and specialization of the system. Exactly the same is true of the products of internal initiation. Although this too is a logical connection, it is not quite so direct or obvious as with external transactions. The teaching profession seeks self-determination, which means that it tries to lift every barrier which prevents teachers from controlling the uses made of their expertise. In particular they attempt to remove central curricular controls, both because the curriculum represents the very heart of their expertise, and its control by others is a negation of professionalism, but also because it is the strongest barrier to self-determination. (The truth of this is clearly demonstrated in centralized systems where the restrictions imposed through political control of curricula and examinations limit teachers to the pursuit of their material interests and encourage an arid, socially disengaged academicism.) If they succeed in this, then teachers will pursue diverse values and interests as they take advantage of their autonomy in different ways. Here diversification will be the keynote because teachers in the decentralized system are never a unitary body. The profession, like the system itself, is incorporated from the independent networks and initially this involves teachers from different social backgrounds, with different forms of training, different interests, different values and often different pedagogical convictions. Indeed, as was seen in the last chapter, one of the most difficult tasks of professionalization is to weld these disparate groups into a single self-conscious organization. In neither country was this completely successful, for divergent interests were not fully eradicated and the divisive organizations defending them were correspondingly difficult to integrate. Historically teachers had never been a single *corps enseignant* sharing a common status as civil servants: in the modern period they remained divided. Consequently as their autonomy increased it was devoted to different ends and this signalled a diversification in definitions of instruction once the management of knowledge passed into professional hands with the lifting of curricular controls. Some of these ends were progressive, others conservative; some innovations were consonant with official policy, others contradicted it; some were inward-looking and academic, others were outward-looking and responsive to community demands.

Changes introduced through internal initiation often involve nothing more than personal experiments on the part of individual teachers in the seclusion of their own classrooms — indeed this is the basic unit of internal initiation. However, these *can* accumulate in a number of ways and result in macroscopic changes. Firstly and very importantly, concerted action orchestrated by a professional organization in pursuit of collectively defined goals can co-ordinate changes which become national in scope. The transformation of English primary education along progressive lines was accomplished without legislative intervention and was solely due to an exceptionally high degree of pedagogical consensus amongst teachers at this level, encouraged and spread by the NUT. Secondly, there are various mechanisms of mutual influence within the profession. Often innovations are generalized through imitation – e.g. the copying of early prototypes of comprehensive school by other LEAs. Similarly the growing demand for a particular innovation can lead to the rapid diffusion of this service through internal initiation – like the spread of business education in English universities once this had attracted the market. Related to this is the creation of positive feedback loops which amplify demand for an innovation, thus encouraging the extension of this service – a mechanism which was extremely important in the elaboration of research and development services to industry from tertiary institutions in both countries. Equally the proven workability and desirability of certain changes can result in their acceptance by institutions which would almost certainly have resisted a full-frontal attack or a straight proposal to diversify their activities – like the highly traditionalistic Gymnasia in Denmark which accepted and assimilated the Higher Leaving Certificate. Thirdly, a change which has prevailed at one level can acquire wider diffusion via the downward influence exerted by higher levels on lower ones, particularly through the agency of examinations – in this way the 11+ examination made all English primary schooling preparatory to secondary instruction; the traditional Danish Universities fostered academicism in the Gymnasia through the Studenter examination; and the English universities reached down to shape teacher training via the Certificate and BEd examinations.

Thus the constant stream of small modifications introduced by both external transactions and internal initiation can add up to bigger changes over time. The innovations which stem from these two pro-cesses affect one another, for each shapes the action context in which the other takes place. These reciprocal influences can be reinforcing (in which case they amplify morphogenesis) or contradictory (in which case they can neutralize one another, encouraging morphostasis, or counteract one another, leading to further structural elaboration). A striking example of mutual reinforcement is provided by the experi-mental progressive schools, founded in England through external trans-actions, and the progressive practices introduced in primary schools through internal initiation by teachers won over by this pedagogy. An illustration of counteraction is found in the Danish universities where professional freedom was used to buttress traditional academic values; so resistant were these institutions to social demands that alternative forms of higher education were developed through external trans-actions. Even if the two processes operate at different levels (and we have already seen that external transactions tend to cluster around terminal points which means that they have progressively concentrated on older age groups), their mutual effects will be experienced *between* levels and again can reinforce or contradict. In other words, not only do both processes lead incrementally to changes of larger magnitude, but the conjunction between the two will amplify *some* of these changes still further until they reach macroscopic proportions.

The full range of changes which are brought about through internal initiation and external transactions, including those which remain small and localized, are characterized by their untidiness. In institutional terms they are tacked on as unplanned extensions, they sprout out of the top of existing institutions, shoot up like a scaffolding against the mainstream schools, or sprawl out as new edifices built in their grounds. In terms of the definition of knowledge the changes are analogous; new disciplines are delineated, old ones are subdivided, existing distinctions are blurred, prevailing categories are recombined, the boundaries of educational knowledge are redrawn and status is redistributed. Thus because both external transactions and internal initiation intensify systemic differentiation and specialization, they threaten overall systematization. In other words, the changes they introduce jointly and separately result in anarchic structural elaboration.

The Modification of Polity-Directed Changes

The process of political manipulation produces compromise legislation (a term again used in the broadest sense) in much the same way as in centralized systems with accessible polities, but here the resemblance ends. In *content* polity-directed changes in the decentralized system are more exclusively concerned with the educational demands of the less privileged, as other groups have alternative outlets. This was intensified in both England and Denmark as both polities underwent a marked shift leftward during this century. Consequently the major Education Acts in the two countries were concerned *with the issue of democratization*, even if each legislative intervention did not increase equality of educational opportunity. In *form* polity-directed changes are more exclusively preoccupied with *systematization*, and not simply because the erection of an educational ladder (the positive principle of hierarchical organization) is a necessary concomitant of democratization. The political centre consistently seeks to increase systematization in order to prevent independent sources of differentiation and specialization from threatening the overall integration of the system and the achievement of politically defined goals. Its concern is to hold back these anarchic developments and to introduce order amongst them; the polity itself does not have to generate planned diversification in order to meet a plurality of goals, as in centralized systems, but to prune and train the independent developments into the required shape. It is in *scope*, however, that polity-directed changes in the decentralized system are most sharply distinguished from those taking place in centralized systems.

Here there are no grand reforms which radically transform national education and whose passage marks a complete change of direction or a large stride forward or backwards. Both the conception and application of polity-directed measures are modified by local and institutional forces whose general effect is to prevent legislation from introducing changes which are either uniform or universal. Instead such modifications mean that *each polity-directed change is itself incremental in its effects*. Its scope is reduced by resistance and its standardized provisions are distorted, redefined and adapted at ground level. Rather than ushering in dramatic policy changes from the top down, the effect of political manipulation is reduced to fostering and chivvying, to shooing development in roughly the right direction by the incremental influence of its sticks and carrots. In other words, it has been argued that there is no 'stop' phase in the decentralized system because internal initiation and external transactions maintain a ceaseless flow of small localized changes. Now it is being maintained that there is no distinctive 'go' phase, heralded by central legislation, because interaction at lower levels robs it of much of its impact. It is by examining these mechanisms that we complete our specification of the factors producing the 'incremental pattern' of change in decentralized educational systems.

(a) Polity-directed Changes are Affected by Existing Developments

Any projected legislation must necessarily take into account what is there – a truism whatever the structure of the educational system. However, at any given time the practices and provisions current in the decentralized system reflect the consequences of decentralization in the past. Their diversity and malintegration shape a practical context of considerable complexity which political intervention has *always* to confront. In other words, the decentralized structure constantly produces and reproduces an untidy patchwork of educational activities which condition what legislation can do with or to them. Thus any government proposing to introduce a change from the centre is faced not only by a much greater variety of practices and provisions but also by a much broader series of vested interests in their maintenance, compared with the centralized system. Vested interests in independence, in autonomy, in acquired rights, in continued services, in established privileges and, most basically, in having a say, all constitute constraints on political intervention and fundamentally limit its scale. Thus, for example, the first two Labour Governments were limited to extending free places in the grammar schools, to a slight democratization of what was there and was well defended, rather than being able to replace it by something altogether more egalitarian. In the same vein R. A. Butler reflected that his 1944 Education Act had merely succeeded in 'recasting' the system, not transforming it. These constraints (represented by vested interests) both stem from and duplicate the historical struggles over incorporation of the independent networks, in which each sought to retain its distinctiveness, thus lowering the integration of the whole.

Equally, the ongoing practices and provisions have as much effect on the conception and conduct of polity-directed change as does legislative intervention on current educational activities. Such changes follow just as much as they lead in the decentralized system. On the one hand, legislation is often *modelled* on experiments which have been conducted autonomously and have given concrete evidence of their effectiveness or at least provided a persuasive precedent. In many ways the fund of experimentation, made up from private, local and professional innovations, constitutes the Research and Development agency of the education industry. Thus, for example, the greater freedom of the Copenhagen schools, which had been conserved historically, allowed them to pioneer the Practical Middle School (subsequently adopted by the 1937 Act, which enjoined the general development of non-examination middle schools) and the flexible, applied curriculum at the end of the Folkschool (later incorporated into the 1970 Act, giving curricular freedom to local authorities for the last years before school-leaving). It is of course the most autonomous parts of the system which play the most influential exemplary role, which is one reason why their strong private sectors are so important in decentralized systems.

On the other hand, the *impetus* for central legislation itself often comes from below: for what takes place in different localities and institutions are not just isolated experiments but are in fact new developments. Because of their relative autonomy, the local authorities, the schools, colleges and universities can spearhead educational changes. These new developments take shape from below by a roll-on effect — from experimentation via imitation and accumulation to substantial innovation. Often the centre has to run to keep up, its legislative acts merely recognizing, legitimating and extending what has already taken place. The recognition and incorporation in 1954, of the three independent networks giving agricultural, industrial and commercial schooling in Denmark, are a good illustration; so too are the English moves to found new universities which were well underway before the Robbins Committee reported and the government accepted its recommendations. Slightly less overtly it was the LEAs which made the running with 'intermediate' instruction between the wars, who began to drop 11+ selection, and to pioneer comprehensive re-organization. When polity-direction finally came, it no longer had a clean page on which to draw a fresh design, but a set of burgeoning initiatives already in operation — a new set of existing practices to take into account and a new series of vested interests protecting them. Consequently political action bent with the tide: it gave recognition and it gave legitimation and what it sought to achieve in addition was universalization. Here both the Hadow proposals, as accepted by government, and Circular 10/65 are very revealing, for both based their six recommended schemes on ones which were *already in being*. What was to be universalized was not a centrally determined plan but progressive local practice. And since local practices varied, what in fact was generalized was their diversity. Thus both Hadow reorganization and Comprehensive reorganization never conceived or imposed a specific kind of change establishing a particular type of school: they merely pointed to bundles of acceptable practices which were nothing more than the prior initiatives taken by local authorities.

(b) Polity-directed Changes are
Mediated Locally and Institutionally

This dimension of interaction is almost entirely lacking in the central-ized system. Here local and institutional autonomy enables action to be taken at various levels which results in the modification of central directives. Because legislation is mediated by such forces it does not have a uniform effect wherever it is applied, and consequently it does not give rise to standardized changes in the institutions or processes involved. Autonomy can be used to modify polity-directed changes in two main directions; both can and do come into play simultaneously at the prompting of different groups who employ the same freedom in different ways.

Firstly then, the area or institutional authorities can be laggardly in their implementation of legislation or their response to central directives. Without downright defiance they can be slow, thus reducing the tempo of educational change, pleading local difficulties, special problems, the need for more information or any other delaying tactic. More importantly still they can make a minimalistic response, a symbolic gesture towards implementation, a ritualistic obeisance to the letter of the law whilst traducing its spirit, all of which will affect the texture of educational change. History shows that local authorities have often been laggardly with impunity: Hadow reorganization was barely half-finished by the outbreak of war; many areas never developed the Technical Schools which were an intrinsic element of the tripartite policy; schemes for comprehensive reorganization were not forth-coming from 50 percent of authorities when they fell due in 1966. It also demonstrates the ever present possibility of both ungenerous and ingenious interpretations of any legislation or regulation considered.

Secondly, mediation also operates in the other direction, pushing and stretching legal provisions as far as they will go, and often much further than was ever intended. Again this involves reinterpretation, the maximum usage of enabling clauses, the exploitation of precedents and the pleading of 'special cases'; ducking restrictions, circumventing regu-lations and capitalizing on any ambiguity or vagueness in the central directive. Thus between the wars a number of LEAs fostered a new outgrowth of post-elementary instruction, again blurring the official distinction between elementary and secondary schooling, in an action-replay of the Higher Grade School contest. Similarly after 1944 certain areas pleaded their population dispersal or their need to repair bomb damage in order to establish multilateral schools, which were not illegal under the terms of the Act but were being firmly resisted by administrative action. Most recently the sheer pressure of local authority opinion, as embodied in the schemes they submitted, led the Labour Government to withdraw its resistance to the 'middle school' formula for comprehensive reorganization and to accept it on the same footing as other legitimate models.

In this discussion of mediation the illustrations have been taken from the local authorities and the ways in which they use their autonomy, but exactly the same points hold at the institutional level. The crucial fact to underline is that the two types of modifications — the positive and the negative, the amplifying and the minimizing, those pushing forward and those holding back — affect each polity-directed change *simultaneously*, for local and institutional autonomy will be put to both ends by different groups in different places. Thus mediation means that a single central directive leads to a plurality of practices, according to the interpretations placed on it; practices which may be so disparate that their common denominator is hard to detect. Furthermore the balance of such modifications may represent a substantial shift away from central policy — like the predominantly bipartite organization of secondary schooling in a supposedly tripartite system. *In sum, mediation prevents central policy directives from introducing clear and uniform changes in national education.*

(c) Polity-directed Changes are Rejected by Parts of the System

Any given polity-directed change can be resisted or rejected by different parts of the educational system, but mainly those which are most independent or those which determine to push their relative autonomy to its very limits. The circumstances under which this will take place depend jointly on the nature of the projected change, its implications for component institutions and the goals and values of those associated with them. The consequence of these rejections is again to reduce the scope of legislative intervention. In other words, *not only do central policy directives fail to produce uniform changes in education, they also fail to introduce universal changes.*

In many ways resistance is an extreme form of the negative or minimalistic modification of legislation, just discussed. However, mediation does involve acceptance of laws and regulations, reluctant as this may be, and entails an attempt to modify their provisions which stops short of outright rejection. We are concerned now not with reluctance but with repudiation — a principled refusal to comply which often involves a public stand and precipitates a public debate. By contrast, reluctant compliance shuns publicity, it does not want to attract attention to its modificatory manouevres which might galvanize the central authorities into corrective action. Examples of the rejection of central policy directives include the recalcitrance of certain English LEAs vis-à-vis comprehensive reorganization and the refusal of the majority of Direct Grant Schools to associate themselves with it. In Denmark too the Gymnasia and university teachers went out on a limb in 1958 with their resistance to the extended Folkschool, dubbed a camoflaged comprehensive policy.

Certainly the use of political sanctions can sometimes overcome resistance, by undermining the autonomy of the recalcitrant part. This has been threatened in the case of the English LEAs and has already been used against the direct grant schools; in Denmark Gymnasia teachers were forced to comply and State intervention in university governance was threatened. However, the central polity is frequently impotent in relation to the fully independent sector of education, which is strong in decentralized systems. Often it cannot prevent private education from continuing its resistance and damaging the very conception of polity-directed change; for its actions not only limit the scope of central policy but also vitiate its workings. Thus the activities of the English public schools undermined the whole notion of meritocratic selection on which tripartism was based: the direct grant schools which have now joined their ranks are performing the same role in relation to the policy for comprehensivization.

Logically, of course, further political sanctions could eliminate these sources of resistance and disruption. After all there is nothing inconceivable or unprecedented about the abolition of private schooling. In practice, however, we now come full circle back to the beginning of our discussion — to the ineluctable fact that polity-directed change in the decentralized system is limited by what is there. Historically strong private sectors emerged, vested interests were associated with their maintenance, and these continue to condition their own defence. In short they represent extreme cases which serve to highlight a much more general phenomenon. They epitomize the fact that no polity in a decentralized system ever has, or ever can create, a *tabula rasa* on which it can freely design change. To a greater or lesser extent the polity has always to work within the constraints of what is there, and ultimately it has to resign itself to proceeding incrementally rather than radically towards the changes that it would like to introduce immediately and universally. Hence the results of political manipulation also contribute to the 'incremental pattern' of change, thus reinforcing the effects of internal initiation and external transactions.

Turning now to the patterns of change in Denmark and England, the contribution of each process of negotiation will be examined sequentially. Once their empirical contributions have been teased out it will be possible to assess their relative significance over time and to determine whether they have retained their rough initial parity of importance. This will also enable us to move on from this discussion of *patterns of change* to a consideration of the *products of change* in these two countries compared with our two case studies of centralized systems. From there we arrive at the final task of all – the assessment of whether a structural convergence has taken place, such that future developments will no longer bear the marks of educational centralization or decentralization.

PATTERNS OF EDUCATIONAL CHANGE IN TWENTIETH CENTURY DENMARK

External Transactions have been a potent force for educational diversification since the beginning of the century. The activities of external interest groups have been responsible for the elaboration of three differentiated networks giving agricultural, technical and commercial training, all more specialized and practical than the corresponding levels of public schooling. Each network comprises all stages from pre-apprenticeship training to an institute(s) of higher education preparing for the Doctorate. They thus represent three distinct alternatives which parallel post-compulsory instruction in the public sector. At times these products of external transactions have achieved an independence which threatens State control and the overall integration of the system since they have constituted a source of differentiation and specialization which has been consistently in advance of public provisions. However, the negotiating strength of their protagonists has been sufficient to repulse any hint of political repression and to ensure that incorporation and accommodation with the State system have not involved a loss of managerial control or a diminution in the specialist services provided to different parts of society.

Unsurprisingly the earliest successful ventures were undertaken from the dominant institutional sphere at the start of the century — agriculture. In the nineteenth century we have seen that the outstanding characteristic of agricultural education was its practical rather than elitarian nature: this continued to be the case as this specialized network was developed. At the bottom were certain Youth and Evening Schools in rural areas which gave a preliminary introduction to farm work alongside general civic and economic instruction. Then followed the agricultural courses proper, distinctive in that they were 'initiated by the agricultural associations, and by the close connection between the teaching given and the practical work with which the pupils are daily occupied'.[77] After that came the Junior Folk High School, and the Agricultural School (recognized as similar to the Folk High School and enrolling the 18 plus age group).

The latter were non-examination schools, which could be almost as specialized as the former, but not necessarily geared to work in the primary sector. Since 1844 over 177 Folk High Schools have been erected. They attained their maximum number of pupils in 1919-20, were at their lowest ebb during the depression, and returned to their high tide mark after the Second World War. Since then their annual number of pupils had been about 6,000, and Special High Schools have been differentiated off to emphasize particular subjects, such as artisam training, fishery or nursing. Today these Schools express various viewpoints ranging 'from the Grundtvigian and the Home Mission, to the social views of the Workers' High School, and in aims, from the gymnastic and sports High Schools to the work for international understanding of the International High School at Elsinore.[78] They can thus be seen as providing a range of religious, political, leisure, cultural and vocational services beyond those directly connected with agriculture.

At the apex are the Agricultural Colleges, part of higher education, which prepare for the *License* examination, give post-graduate courses and, after 1935, obtained the right to present Doctorates. The relationship between these levels is of peculiar importance for the recruitment of pupils, the relevance of outputs, and the reproduction of expertise —

the diffusion of scientific agricultural knowledge in Denmark is probably without parallel in any other country. The reason for this is the fruitful interchange between the Agricultural College and the characteristically Danish

Agricultural School, of which there are about 30, with some 3,000 students in all. They are non-examination, State-aided residential schools. The College receives a yearly quota from these schools, and the majority of the graduates return to country districts as teachers and agricultural advisory officers. Thus the link between the Agricultural College and the farming population is preserved and strengthened.[79]

Technical education was slower to develop due to the enduring conviction that prosperity lay in agriculture, but from 1912 onwards the Danish Federation of Industries played an important part in its establishment. As in agriculture, the relatively wide distribution of economic resources prevented these from becoming elitist establishments either in terms of their intake or their control. The Craft Guilds and Townsmen's Association were equally important in the foundation of these Trade and Technical Schools, and increasingly the Unions have come to share the control of apprenticeship training with employers' organizations. A similar, though perhaps more internally specialized, network of courses, schools and colleges to those in agriculture were developed, and again it is possible to move from the earliest type of apprenticeship training to attendance at the Technological University.

The Youth Schools provide for those between 14-18 who are not apprenticed but are destined for manual work and these have largely taken over from the Work Technical Schools which initiated industrial preparation for unskilled workers in 1940, but only received about 1 percent of the relevant work force. Currently the pattern is for short courses, organized trade by trade, proceeding from the elementary to the more advanced, which workers can follow sequentially as their skills increase. As with agricultural training, the gradual incorporation of this instruction under official auspices has not severed the direct connection with the interest groups which initiated it. Indeed in some ways the 1960 Act on Occupational Training for Non-Skilled Workers has both accepted and extended it. 'In order to ensure that the training offered by these courses corresponds to the work which those attending them will later have to perform, the co-operation of the organization of the trades concerned has been enlisted and they have been made *directly responsible* for the content of the courses. A trade which wants to initiate training under the Act can set up a Trade Committee comprising an equal number of representatives of worker and employer organizations. The main task of such a Committee is to plan courses on the required scale and to ensure that they are adequately carried out.'[80] Control is thus shared by the two sides of industry, both of which had helped to initiate it, with each contributing to operating costs, and jointly determining the degreee of future specialization and its contents.

At a somewhat higher level is vocational training at the Technical School, which is often combined with apprenticeship and learning on the job. In 1955 there were 350 such courses with approximately 48,000 in attendance. In addition Technical Schools provide one year courses for skilled industrial workers and for those straight from school, whilst some are devoted to a particular vocation like the Builders' Schools. Above this the Technical Colleges give students who have finished their apprenticeships, passed the Trade examination or acquired the *Real* certificate a more theoretical training for future posts as technicians, managers or contractors in independent enterprises. These generally have five specialist departments — electro-technics, mechanical engineering, shipbuilding, building and construction and house building, but offer various additional courses for hospital and laboratory technicians, boilermen, electricians, navigators, etc. Finally the Danish Institute of Technology gives the highest level of theoretical training to those who have matriculated in Maths and Science or passed the special entrance examination. It has four Departments of Chemical, Mechanical, Civil and Electrical engineering in which students can gain qualifications ranging from the Doctorate down to that of 'Academy Engineer', which is slightly lower than first degree level. The whole range of technical courses have been well subscribed and ironically this sector has experienced increasing difficulties with staffing because the demand for technicians has outstripped the supply. The schools and colleges have had to compete with richer recipients of their services when trying to recruit teachers from their own outputs.

The position of external interest groups as suppliers of higher educational resources is recognized, and all continue to make payments in return for research and training services. Thus, for example, the State provides funds for the Technical University in Copenhagen but 'certain large foundations such as Carlsberg, the Otto Mønsted, the Laurits Andersen, the H.C. Ørsted, the Tuborg, the Thomas B. Thrige, and several others, grant very considerable sums to the research work done in the Technical University laboratories'.[81] Moreover, entry requirements have protected the direct link between practical life, lower independent establishments, and admission to this part of higher education, although those with conventional Secondary qualifications can also enter. Hence direct links with industry are protected, since both inputs and outputs of specialist technical education remain geared to the demands of the relevant external interest groups.

Commercial education came comparatively late compared with the other two networks, and all such schools are private, owned and run by the local Businessmen's Associations or other organizations formed especially for this purpose. Again this complex of highly specialized courses constitutes a hierarchy, running from the day release commercial schools attended by about 46,000 trainees (approximately the same number as their counterparts on technical courses), to the 22 Business Colleges and 14 Advanced Colleges, before linking up with the two Higher Commercial Colleges which are part of tertiary education. Each level carries a certificate which enables its holders to proceed to the next, thus facilitating career mobility. These have been calibrated with primary, *real* and secondary qualifications in the public sector so that pupils can transfer to commercial training at any stage.

Again courses are highly specialized. The Commercial Schools for apprentices provide three basic alternative strands (without foreign languages, with modern languages, and clerical training). All lead to the preliminary examination in commerce which itself has several special branches, e.g. for book-selling, shipping, insurance and banking, as well as to more orthodox State examinations in shorthand, book-keeping, languages, etc. There are also special Schools for Clerks and Shop-Assistants whose curriculum is made up of languages, Danish, arithmetic, book-keeping, commercial studies, geography, economics, civics and typewriting. The Colleges give a more theoretical training in general business management and the Copenhagen School of Economics and Business Administration represents the highest stage of commercial education. This can award a degree in Commercial Science, for those taking up senior executive posts, or in languages, where the content is slanted towards interpreting and translating for import-export firms.

Most schools, whether owned by associations of businessmen or standing as independent foundations in receipt of local subsidies, can receive State aid which covers about 40 percent of overheads. Some, however, are run on a completely private basis by commercial, industrial and shipping firms, but receive State recognition. Thus it is still the case that all these schools

are owned and run by the commercial organization,. . . employer associations and trade unions are represented in a consultative body, the Commercial School Council. All examination papers are checked and controlled by private businessmen appointed by the commercial organization, and the bulk of the completed papers are examined by both educational and commercial examiners. The contact between teacher and businessman with regard to commercial training could not be closer.[82]

The development of these three different networks of schools and colleges automatically increased the diversity and complexity of Danish education. In other words, there is no doubt that external transactions represented a powerful but undramatic source of differentiation and specialization. Quietly, course by course, and school by school, different sections and regions of society could negotiate the changes that they sought; cumulatively these produced national educational changes and concomitantly they involved a recognition of the educational rights of the external interest groups. There is, however, another side to this picture of anarchic elaboration, namely the integrative force of the polity seeking to contain differentiation and specialization within an overall framework of unification and systematization. Since, as we have seen, the polity either did not want or did not have the strength to constrain direct negotiations, its twentieth century role consisted in integrating private initiative with public polity. *Thus external transactions continuously farthered progressive segmentation whilst governmental intervention consistently fostered progressive systematization, the two characteristics developing side by side with neither dominating the other in the pattern of educational change.*

Although isolated, sporadic pieces of legislation and decrees did indicate this tendency in the first half of the century, it became more pronounced after 1950. The formula of the 1954 Law, which unified and simplified the relations between the State and diverse forms of post-compulsory training was typical. Through it the State achieved rationalization, co-ordination and supervision, but on the other hand, the transacted networks obtained legal recognition, official status and public aid. Ownership remained in private hands, alternative suppliers of resources were acknowledged, and managerial autonomy was not substantially infringed by the State Consultant for Further Education. At its simplest, the external interest groups had defended the specificity of the educational services they sought, whilst the State had co-ordinated these diverse provisions with the mainstream of public education.

The 1956 law making Apprenticeship training compulsory also utilized the above formula, as did the 1960 Act on the Training of Non-Skilled Workers. In making both obligatory, the polity was in fact making attendance at independent institutions compulsory — perhaps the supreme form of legal recognition. Certainly it was only doing so because of the recalcitrance of secondary teachers about providing applied instruction, but the effect was to unify the networks by elevating them to play a national role. The advantages to the latter were clear — official endorsement and public aid without a corresponding loss of differentiation and specialization — those accruing to the State were equally obvious as far as unification and systematization were concerned. Thus the Ministry of Foreign Affairs writes about the provisions for non-skilled workers; 'As the training is developed it is the intention to co-ordinate it to the maximum possible extent with the education given in Youth Schools and the top years of the primary schools. It is also aimed to maintain close co-operation with the defense services and with other schools and institutions where non-skilled workers are trained, in order, among other things, to facilitate a smooth transition from the schemes for the non-skilled to further technical training'.[83] Less self-evident is the crucial fact that by accepting the results of external transactions graciously rather than grudgingly (for they could not be prevented), successive governments were thus deflecting educational grievances which would otherwise have been addressed to the central polity itself.

Internal Initiation took different forms, served different interests and had very different consequences at each of the three main levels. As far as the non-graduate teachers were concerned, their contributions to educational innovation were twofold. On the one hand, they willingly negotiated with external interest groups and staffed the wide range of institutions established for futher and vocational instruction by external transactions. On the other hand, their Grundtvigian values and popular social origins also prompted them to use their growing autonomy and administrative insertion to meet local community demands. Until the Second World War the stringency of the central management of knowledge prevented them from engaging in serious internal initiation within public education, largely confining their experiments with teaching methods and curricula to the private sector. Afterwards much of their improved negotiating strength was devoted to lifting those curricular controls which restricted internal initiation.

Already in the late twenties and thirties the NUT signalled its commitment to a Folkschool which met the practical demands of urban and rural communities, and the Union of Real School Teachers indicated their total unwillingness to be assimilated to the academic definition of instruction — 'The Gymnasium and Real courses were to be different, it was pointed out, or why have both'[84] Any element of autonomy which they gained was used to these ends, and we have already seen how the experiments undertaken in the freer Copenhagen Folkschools represented the groundwork for the 1937 Law. Its provisions were not only a significant step forward for internal initiation as a process modifying public education at the national level, they were also typical of the way in which this was to be used in the future. The Law did not define activities in the terminal classes of the non-examination Middle School and thus left the profession free to innovate at this level. That they did not succeed in developing an alternative definition of popular instruction there was due to a number of factors beyond professional control — the creaming off of the best pupils to the examination school, the traditional insistance by employers on an Examination Certificate, political refusal to raise the school leaving age to 15 and the hegemony of academic culture which was structurally supported by the selectivity of primary instruction. If the non-graduate teachers are to be criticized in relation to this Act, it is not for their unwillingness to respond experimentally to community demands, but rather for their desire to service immediate popular requirements by getting practical instruction underway on any terms, instead of considering the longer term issue of class advancement.

After the war this section of the profession pressed for greater freedom to innovate in the examination schools and gained Ministerial license to experiment in the Training Colleges and the main types of Schools between 1948-50. It was a limited freedom which allowed departures from the various centrally established curricula in so far as these did not adversely affect the tasks allocated to each type of school. In fact it mainly consisted in adding subjects to these courses in the light of public demand. This may not seem a major form of internal initiation but it had important ramifications. As teachers progressively inserted themselves in local administration and played a stronger role in the drawing up of the local Teaching Plan they could call upon their experimental experiences to recommend the inclusion of new subjects and as evidence of the practicality of broader syllabuses. Moreover they could influence political decision-making in the same way by flourishing concrete evidence rather than vague ideals. Their influence was very clear on the *standard* curriculum, adopted after the 1958 Law, for the first seven grades. This comprised seven years of Danish language, handwriting, arithmetic, religious knowledge, music and art; six years of physical education and handiwork; five years of history, geography and science; three years of woodwork for boys and two years of domestic science for girls; and finally two years of natural sciences and a foreign language.[85] As a basic curriculum it bears the clear impress of Grundtvigian values.

However, the 1958 Act also sanctioned the addition of a large number of extra and optional subjects in the Folkschool and the Real Course. These were related to active life and recorded on the school leaving certificate. Thus subjects in local demand like typing, book-keeping, languages, applied sciences, practical workshop and, for the first time in Danish Public Schools, agricultural subjects, became officially sanctioned and publically recognized.[86] Certainly these options were restricted to the terminal forms of Folkschool and Real instruction but this was a less important constraint given that the standard curriculum was now broad enough to constitute a basis and a preparation for them. Moreover, the more explicit community demands themselves focused on the preparaiton of school leavers rather than on the whole range of primary instruction.

The next major achievement on the part of non-graduate teachers carried their internal initiation into secondary education proper. The new Higher Leaving Examination was a two-year course instigated by the Training Colleges and accepted by the Social Democrat Government in 1966. Initially it was designed to raise the quality of professional training without restricting the social basis of recruitment. It gave a broad theoretical and applied instruction which became accepted for a large number of semi-professional careers and gave its holders access to further training in teaching, social work, physiotherapy, business economics, dentistry, hospital work, agricultural, vetinary and dairying courses, depending on the specialist subjects taken. Originally it was held in the Teacher Training Colleges themselves, but the forty or so courses established gradually took their place in the Gymnasium, as the Real courses moved downwards into the Folkschools. As a method of introducing change into the most traditionalistic of academic enclaves, this innovation had been infinitely more effective than any of the full-frontal attacks made upon Gymnasia curriculum. In this way a major form of differentiation was introduced into secondary studies, and was perhaps acceptable to its teachers precisely because it represented an addition to rather than an alteration of their principal activities. Indeed one of its side effects was to increase the prestige of the *Studenter* examination, since the Higher Leaving Examination was acknowledged to be of a lower level, yet also gave access to professional careers.

Simultaneously the NUT maintained its pressures for a more practically relevant primary school. From the mid-sixties onwards it supported changes proposed by the Danish Institute of Education and
initiated experimentally in Copenhagen schools. These added up to a
further plea for more flexibility in the curriculum and the addition of
new subjects which had already been taught successfully, such as road
safety, librarianship, hygiene, family and sex instruction. The autonomy they had previously gained had been used for initiating certain
changes in the Folkschool, whose success was now used as an argument
for a further extension of classroom freedom. The 1970 Act made
several important concessions to these forces for differentiation and
specialization at this level. It left the new Local Authorities to organize
the contents of their 8th-10th classes independently – a Liberal ack-
nowledgment of their ability to serve the manifest demands of the
community. Teachers were also given more influence in the drawing up
of Teaching Plans and were allowed to integrate primary and Real
instruction at their discretion.

The gradual post-war improvement in the negotiating strength of the
primary school teacher had been used to diversify compulsory schooling for all, and the opportunities available to those who stayed on
beyond the school leaving age. At secondary level we have already seen
how the suspicion with which Gymnasia teachers were viewed by the
public authorities was the complete antithesis of the confidence enjoyed by their counterparts at primary level. This contrast is equally
glaring if one now considers the relative contributions of the two parts
of the profession to the initiation of educational change. Because of
normative conflict between graduate teachers and the polity which was
exacerbated as governments shifted leftwards over time, the Gymnasia
remained closely controlled, and the 1970 Act still insisted on a tightly
prescribed curriculum. Given this lack of autonomy the graduate
teachers behaved in a way very similar to their counterparts in centralized educational systems. Since their action context was heavily constrained, their internal initiation was restricted to the pursuit of vested
interests – to the progressive improvement of their professional work,
status and financial conditions. None of these actions, excepting their
acceptance of the Higher Leaving Examination, made any significant
difference to structural characteristics of secondary education.

Only in higher education did the combination of expertise *and*
autonomy place this part of the profession in a position to engage in a
form of internal initiation which was in accordance with their own

values but normatively opposed to official policy. As we have seen this involved the pursuit of pure academic values, unrelated to socio-economic requirements, the prolongation of degree courses, indifferent to manpower demands, and the proliferation of abstract research, unconcerned with practical applications. In turn these autonomous developments threatened the overall co-ordination of higher education whilst depriving various institutional elites, including the polity, of the services they sought at this level. They were pursued despite public dissatisfaction: 'the idea of co-ordination does not appeal immediately to individual institutions of higher education, since to each it implies that it might see its wishes unfulfilled or only partly fulfilled for the sake of another institution'.[87]

In 1962 a University Administration Committee was established, including government representatives and presidents of institutions of higher education, in order to achieve greater systematization between its parts and responsiveness to external requirements. Given the un-assailable autonomy of the universities this task cannot be predicated on unification, it has to be engineered on a basis of voluntary co-operation. Thus the offical members of the Committee had to abandon hopes of establishing an intermediate agency for the administration of higher education since the universities flatly rejected this threat to their autonomy (one which had been realized in Sweden with the appoint-ment of a Chancellor for Universities). Instead the most to emerge from these deliberations was a number of co-ordination committees, created across faculty and institutional lines, whose opinions were to be con-sulted when individual institutions engaged in decision-making. It was written in 'that there would be no direct communication between any of the agencies and the Ministry; nor would the agencies be vested with any authority that might in any way disturb the picture of the institu-tion as an independent unit'.[88] Rather than unification these proposals aimed more modestly at voluntary systematization, since the higher educational institutions 'themselves would be vested with part of the responsibility for the interests of the overall system'.[89]

This formula was strengthened in 1965 with the establishment of the University Planning Committee, a consultative body charged with elaborating long and short-term development plans bringing together the presidents, faculty, students, governmental members and repre-sentatives from trade, industry and other interests. A National Research Council of similar composition was formed in parallel as an advisory body to government on research policy and funding. Both reforms aim to reduce the disruptive influence and unresponsive nature of the autonomous universities and

> will serve as a real touchstone to determine whether the universities are able to meet the test of practical application of the principle of self-government, i.e. whether they are able to control their own affairs in such a manner that will be satisfactory to the community as a whole. If they fail in this test – if the system is threatened by dissolution from within through internal disagreement – the idea of an intermediate agency between the government and the universities or some other type of increased government interference in the management of the universities will probably crop up again.[90]

There is, of course, an alternative to the coercive imposition of unification if the internal initiation of the universities continues to be unacceptable, and a more likely one, given that their autonomy is grounded in a fair degree of financial independence. This would consist in government leaving the universities to plough their own furrow, accepting their malintegration, but compensating for this by sponsoring and advancing other sections of higher education. Indeed

> history shows that if in such a situation the universities employ their power to defend and preserve an isolationist and conservative policy, their social importance will decline, and the government will gradually leave them to their own devices and resort to the establishment of entirely new institutions with a view to implementing its own objectives ... in Denmark the establishment of special colleges and high schools for the education of engineers, agronomists, vetinarians, indeed even surgeons, provides more recent examples of such a reaction on the part of the government.[91]

In other words the unintended consequence of politically unacceptable forms of internal initiation may be legal recognition and State support for aceptable changes introduced through external transactions. Higher education thus provides a very clear example of the way in which changes negotiated by one process of interaction alter the context in which other types of educational transaction take place.

Overall the process of internal initiation can be seen to have increased the diversity of Danish education, especially at primary and tertiary levels. The changes introduced are usually undramatic in themselves but cumulative in their effects, which may be progressive or conservative depending on the professional values involved. In general they function to weaken unification and to create problems for systematization. This is interpreted as threatening, rather than merely problematic, only when normative conflict with official policy or officially sanctioned demands occur.

Political Manipulation, as we have seen, remained pre-occupied with problems of educational democratization throughout most of the century. This was largely because of the growing importance of the Social Democrats and Parties further to the left, and the lesser ability of their supporters to influence change through the other two processes. Democratization had two specific aspects in this connection: on the one hand, it represented an assault on the prevailing form of systematization and an attempt to reorganize the relationship between parts and levels in closer conformity with the positve principle of hierarchical organization. As in the nineteenth century, this still involved efforts to advance the popular Folkschool at the expense of the elitarian Gymnasium. On the other hand, it constituted a challenge to the existing *type* of unification and the desire to increase popular participation at the expense of control by social elites. Neither of these aims should be interpreted as a desire for less unification or systematization, but rather for a change in their form and the interests they served. Questions about differentiation and specialization were closely intertwined with the above, partly because of parental pressures for a more relevant instruction, and partly because the struggle between the two halves of the profession was about precisely this issue.

Dissatisfaction with the role of the Middle School centered on the issue of hierarchical organization from the start. The Klausen Committee's members divided between those advocating progress towards the positive principle (through advancing the Folkschool), and those wanting a return to bifurcation between the elementary and Learned schools. Discontent with the traditional social basis of educational administration (the absence of direct voting to the School Commission and the birthright seat of the Parson) also surfaced during the same Committee's deliberations. The two laws introduced during the 1930s were direct responses to these demands, which took place as soon as the Social Democrat Party was in a parliamentary position to do so.

The intention behind the 1933 Law on the direction of the School system 'was to give parents a strong concern and pedagogical influence with the school where their children attend, and to introduce an academic supervision in place of the Church supervision'.[92] The Local Communal Council became the most important local authority and it nominated a School Commission (whose members need not belong to the Communal Council). Between them the two prepared the School Plan and Instruction plan for the area, consulted the Teachers' Councils and the Parents' Boards whose establishment was the main concession to direct parental participation. At County level supervision was exercised by the School Directorate which has a pedagogical advisor, who was an experienced teacher, nominated the Directorate and confirmed by the Ministry. Each County also had a School Council with representatives from component County and Town Councils in proportion to their populations. It was an attempt to get the balance between parliamentary, professional and parental powers right. As a device for democratizing control it was less than successful for the Parents' Boards failed to harness parental interest, given their limited consultative powers. Over the next decade their numbers declined, until only 10 percent of schools were operating them in 1944.

Equally unsuccessful from the democratic point of view was the 1937 Act on the primary school. The NUT and most leftwing opinion had sought positive hierarchical integration (a long Folkschool for all leading to a shorter branching secondary education) *together* with more differentiation in order to increase the relevance of instruction: 'the Folkschools practical department must have a significantly more practical form than it now has'.[93] The Liberals, Conservatives and Gymnasia teachers endorsed the negative principle of hierarchical organization since they wished the Primary School to end without examination, the Middle School to be abolished, and entry to the Higher Schools to be governed by a selective test which went beyond what was taught in the Folkschool. They also, and the graduate teachers, in particular, supported a relatively undifferentiated and unspecialized instruction. The compromise that was politically negotiated favoured the latter rather than the former, for it retreated from the notion of an educational ladder for all, spanning primary and secondary levels, and held out false hopes for differentiation which were soon dashed.

When the Union of Gymnasia Teachers, in co-operation with the Instruction Inspectorate, came out against secondary specialization and optional subjects and instead reasserted the value of the traditional broad curriculum, they won a major victory. For when the Social Democrat Government accepted this in the 1935 Ordinance on Gymnasia timetables, it re-established prestige secondary instruction on traditional academic lines and simultaneously delayed the start of the Real course until the end of the Middle School. In turn this created a problem for those pupils who wanted more education than the Folkschool, but for whom the Middle School was not relevant because it prepared for further academic instruction rather than active life. The proposed solution, to create a differentiated Middle School, a practical one running alongside the examination one, appealed to teachers and to popular opinion alike because of the opportunity it seemed to hold out for more specialized, relevant and applied instruction in this non-examination school. The report on the 'Practical Middle School', prepared by Copenhagen Folkschool teachers, stressed the importance of this and the NUT was attracted by the new approach to curriculum and methods it proposed in which freedom and elasticity were to predominate.

To the Social Democrats its implications were democratic as well as practical. 'The two schools will be equal in status, and, it is hoped, in common estimation, and will also be set equally so that the children who now weigh heavily on so many places in the Middle School will of their own inclination seek the non-examination Middle School and acquit themselves well there'.[94] The Ministry did not insist on closely controlling the activities of the new school. It was willing to give more freedom to the local authorities and to teachers. That both flexibility and specialization were acceptable to the polity was indicated in the Minister's statement that 'it is not clear whether elementary agricultural subjects, typewriting, shorthand, and so on, take their place as such in a school for children: how far in this respect one can go, experience will tell'.[95]

Yet as soon as the 1937 Act was implemented it became clear that the non-examination Middle School was neither democratic nor differentiated. Its failure in these two different respects was related, for together they constituted a vicious circle. To ensure egalitarianism the same teachers taught in both types of Middle School, but because of this they tended to use the same curriculum and methods. This was reinforced by the pressures exerted by academic secondary education to cream off the most able pupils: 'the examination urge from above – from the Higher School (Gymnasium) – renders any real pedagogical reorientation impossible, and in the non-examination Middle School, practically speaking, only the least gifted pupils from poorer homes remain'.[96] Thus most parents tried to get their children into examination schools, and they were encouraged in this by employers' preferences for certificated school-leavers. As the Conservatives and Liberals were quick to point out: 'The non-examination school, with the content it was possible to give it, had been expected to attract pupils and be appreciated by employers who, it was imagined, would be as ready to apprentice pupils from the non-examination school as holders of the Middle – or Real – examination certificates. This, however, has not been the case'.[97] What critics on the right failed to underline was that much of the reason for this lay in lack of differentiation, in the fact that the 'non-examination Middle School is firmly set on a curriculum similar to — although more restricted than — that of the examination school'.[98]

The 1937 compromise had brought about the worst of both worlds: it had achieved neither parity of prestige between the schools nor difference of function. Ironically it had only produced further unification. It had originated, as will be recalled, from experiments that teachers had been conducting in the more autonomous Copenhagen Folkschools and had been welcomed by non-graduate teachers precisely because it echoed their own tentative initiatives with new methods and subjects. By introducing the non-examination Middle School the Law had effectively imposed a legal framework on experiments then being conducted with the last classes of the Folkschool. Yet the new Middle School was not structured in such a way as to foster these practical innovations or to furnish the calibre of pupil who could make them a success.

Whilst the deficiencies of the Primary School reform were becoming gradually apparent, a small move was made towards democratizing local educational control. The Bill passed in 1949 was sufficiently broad to win parliamentary support, which had to be recruited given the minority status of the Social Democrat Ministry which ruled without a coalitional partner. The new regulations were an attempt to secure greater local representation. One of their most important provisions was to replace the more stringent local franchise by the parliamentary franchise for election to the School Commission. This body was charged with the local direction of schools, and parental participation was now engineered through a School Board if parents wanted one. If not it was guaranteed by their nominating representatives to the School Commission, on which teachers also had non-voting members. Parents as such still found themselves caught between the communal authority, which was unwilling to devolve much authority to them, and the profession, who remained hostile to their supervision, but members of the community gained a greater say and were now recruited on a wider social basis to the School Commission.

The first organized reaction of non-graduate teachers to post-war developments in primary education was a Report (1952) which contended that if the new Middle School were to be maintained it must be 'imbued with interest through a strong extension of the practical subjects with an eye to working life, short of the school itself giving vocational training'.[99] In other words, it must be more clearly differentiated from the generalist examination Middle School. The Report proposed that the curriculum should develop progressively towards four specialisms at the end of the course — technical, handicraft, commercial and housecraft — for which certificates should be awarded to give their holders a standing on the occupational market. The Askov Committee, meeting under Grundtvigian auspices, were of the view that yet more radical changes were needed: that given the vicious circle, differentiation could not succeed without democratization. Instead they advanced the notion of the undivided school until 14, thus reverting to the conviction that without positive hierarchical organization educational practices were bound to be socially discriminatory. This proved politically influential.

The Bill that was finally passed with the support of all parties, except the Conservatives, introduced positive systematization, since the last two years of primary education became both the end of elementary instruction and the beginning of secondary: this common elementary education now became the sole basis for all subsequent schooling — the policy which the Radicals had always sought to impose and the Gymnasia teachers to repulse. Whilst the Folkschool teachers welcomed this warmly on democratic grounds, they wanted the new school to be undivided socially rather than undifferentiated educationally in terms of curriculum. It is generally the case that these two aims co-exist with difficulty, for what are intended as branching horizontal alternatives quickly tend to become ordered hierarchically in terms of prestige. Since political commitment was to democratization, the Bill minimized internal specialization and talked at most of a 'mild diversion', giving the Conservatives some grounds for calling it a camoflaged comprehensive policy. Any kind of differentiated coursework had to be delayed until the sixth (penultimate) class, with pupils then being streamed by 'attainment, ability and interests' according to teachers' guidance, parental preference and pupil performance on tests in Danish and arithmetic. Even here the Minister indicated his willingness to sanction unstreamed 6th and 7th classes at the request of the school authorities and where a majority of parents of children in the 5th class requested it. In these ways the polity registered the higher priority it assigned to achieving positive hierarchical organization than to encouraging educational diversification at primary level. A strongly unified curriculum was seen as a safeguard of egalitarism. No bias in it should interfere with the one continuous and unbroken course of instruction which protected the right of all to transfer from one course to another and prevented the crystallization of elite routes.

The Folkschool now consisted of a seven year compulsory course up to the age of 14, after which pupils could stay on for a voluntary 8th or 9th classs or transfer to the three year Real course which could be followed there, in the Gymnasia, or in the private Real schools which continued to operate. In practice the amount of differentiation to develop (within the statutory limits) was determined by parents and teachers. Their democratic preferences were allowed some free play since the State could preclude abuses for undemocratic purposes because of substantial unification. Thus in the 7th, 8th and 9th years specialization related to active life could take place, provided it stopped short of vocational training. Similarly the leaving certificate recorded the subjects studied from the 5th year onwards and the marks gained in special subject examinations after the 7th class. Two factors encouraged specialization at the Folkschool to a degree which probably exceeded legislative intentions. Firstly, the Gymnasium increasingly declined to sustain Real courses, in line with its teachers' preference for 'pure' academic work, and this task developed on the Folkschools, thus improving their staffing and encouraging pupils to think of this course as readily available. Secondly, the possibility of one or two years additional schooling proved popular and there was an increasing tendency for pupils to stay on voluntarily, particularly when occupationally biased courses which awarded an examination certificate were available. The teachers as we have noted were keen to experiment with this kind of work and parental enthusiasm encouraged them to use their freedom for internal initiation to serve the community in this way.

Nevertheless, this type of initiative was limited, and in fact restricted to the terminal classes of elementary education. For those wanting to proceed to secondary education proper, the Ministry held written examinations (both for transfer from the second to third Real class and from the second Real class to the first Gymnasium class) and this obviously involved standardization of the preparatory curriculum: a fact which was reinforced by the Gymnasia teachers' commitment to maintaining standards and the traditional academic definition of instruction.

However, the Gymnasium was facing a major problem after 1958. Its teachers had strongly opposed the reform (in defending negative systematization) and gone out on a limb with the university faculty in declaring that their shorter broken-up course could not equip pupils for higher education. Yet paragraph 8 of the Law insisted that those with the Higher School Certificate had the right to matriculate at university and other institutes of higher education. As Kalund-Jørgensen commented at the time, their likelihood of getting the law amended was nil;

> It would be too hard a blow to the majority of the House if it had to admit its own mistake. Apparently there is only one way out of the dilemma. It is implicit in paragraph 2, where it is said that instruction in the Gymnasium shall be given partly on specialist lines. There are no limits set to this specialization. In that respect the new law is different from the former where only three kinds of specialization were legal. Now the studies and training at the learned institutes today are highly differentiated. It seems incredible that one single general education could be arranged so as to cover all the variety of branches.[100]

It was: the Gymnasium was trapped between the unification which had been imposed politically on primary instruction and the differentiation which had been introduced by external transactions in tertiary education. In this context the defense of standards could only be accomplished at the price of departing from the old broad curriculum.

Increased specialization was the result and it was encouraged officially by the Ministerial Curricula Committee's 1960 Report on the 'New Gymnasium'.[101] In this the Social Democrats were being fully consistent with their historical attack on the privileged classical culture of the Learned Schools: here, paradoxically, democratization was furthered by diversification. After this time teaching became 'even more differentiated than it was in the Gymnasium of 1903-65. On entering the Gymnasium pupils must decide between two streams, the language stream and the mathematics stream. Before leaving the first Gymnasium class each pupil has to choose between various sub-streams. The second and third Gymnasium classes in the language stream offer a choice of four sub-streams: modern languages, music and language, social science, and classical language sub-streams, while the second and third Gymnasium classes in the maths stream offer a choice of three streams: maths-physics, social science, and maths and science sub-streams'.[102] Although there is certainly no supremacy still attaching to classics (in fact only 17 out of 90 Gymnasia provided this sub-section in 1964),[103] nevertheless the total number of common lessons still outweigh the time devoted to specialist ones. To this extent traditional practices have endured, but another boost was given to differentiation with the introduction of the two year Higher Leaving Examination in 1966.

Initiated by the Teacher Training Colleges it was promulgated by the Social Democrats on egalitarian grounds;

> behind these recommendations for the establishment of essentially preparatory training prior to the teacher training course lay a desire to give those who had gone through the normal primary school, and then worked for a period in trade or industry, the opportunity of satisfying a subsequently developed urge for further education. Simultaneously there was a wish to create a course of education which would provide several alternatives and not require a final choice of career to be made right at the start of the course.[104]

Such courses gradually found their home in the Gymnasium where they have taken over from the Real activities which are more and more part of the Folkschool. They have been accepted because they represent an overall upgrading of secondary instruction and allow the Gymnasia increased scope for selectivity. This newly differentiated course provides a second chance for many who have missed the ordinary route into secondary education. It thus strengthens the positive principle of hierarchical organization and encourages social mobility since it prepares for many of the semi-professions.[105]

Ironically, given the preferences of their respective teachers, the sixties had seen the Gymnasium develop in terms of differentiation and specialization, whilst the primary school remained restricted by unifying legislation. The programme produced by the NUT in 1966 showed that primary teachers stood by their old principles, for they advocated 10 years of compulsory schooling with a flexible structure and many more options to facilitate co-operation with home, employers and further education. It was taken up by the Radical-Liberal-Conservative Government since the Right had consistently protested that the 1958 Act sacrificed practical requirements to egalitarian values. The note they circulated before tabling legislation was clear in advocating more differentiation. It proposed that subject teaching should be divided into two levels, with pupils choosing the level appropriate to the examination at which they aimed. There were to be two — a major leaving examination equivalent to the Real certificate and a minor leaving examination taken at the end of the ninth year.

These principles were embodied in the Act of 1970 which simultaneously devolved more authority for education on to the Local Councils. The conjunction between the two policies was important for the Local Authorities were left free to establish the 8th-10th classes in relation to community requirements. On this point the law only specifies that these classes can be divided into streams and adapted to future activities in industry and commerce. This specialization can begin in the 7th year with pupils taking practical options (e.g. practical workshop, woodwork, domestic science, typing or agricultural subjects) alongside their general course. Furthermore teaching in these classes was to be integrated with the Real course in an attempt to improve standards and increase the options which could be made available. Leaving examinations were held in the 9th and 10th classes for those who wanted them so that each additional year's schooling was publically marked and could earn commensurate rewards on the occupational market. A special combination of subjects, whose main emphasis was on physics, chemistry and maths could lead to the preliminary technical examination in the 9th class or the extended diploma of the same name in the 10th class. Thus at the end of compulsory schooling pupils could leave (and enter one of the Youth or Apprentice schemes of tuition), stay on for a practically oriented 8th, 9th or 10th class, or be promoted directly to the Real course.

With this Act Denmark elaborated a public educational system in which differentiation and specialization were pronounced at each of its three levels. Simultaneously more than half a century of democratic political pressure had ensured that the positive principle of hierarchical integration reigned throughout. All three characteristics are even more pronounced if activities and institutions in the private sector are taken into account. In relation to them unification is weak. Systematization had been achieved largely at its expense, for the gradual incorporation of external transactions at further, secondary, and higher levels, in order to integrate the whole in a co-ordinated fashion, has extended the partners admitted to educational control alongside the State. Furthermore, concession to local and parental demands for more democratic participation has also weakened unification from the centre. The polity's administrative and legal control remained strong enough to co-ordinate the diverse internal and external developments but not to eliminate these activities themselves.

PATTERNS OF EDUCATIONAL CHANGE IN
TWENTIETH CENTURY ENGLAND

External Transactions

External transactions, whether conducted via personal or institutional
investment, have been a force for educational diversification which has
been important at all levels, from nursery schooling through to Business
Schools for post-graduate training. Changes negotiated through this
process have increased the overall specialization of education activities
and differentiation of institutional arrangements. Frequently, however,
these threatened the integration of the system because of the problems
and exigencies they created for public control and government educational policy. Sometimes, when the external interest group had low
negotiating strength, such disruptive tendencies were contained by
reinforcing unification and systematization. At other times, stronger
external interest groups, particularly ones which enjoyed professional
support, escaped administrative controls and developed on autonomous
lines which disturbed the systematization of public education in proportion to their divergence from official policy. Here, of course, the
immediate reaction of the authorities was very negative, but in broader
systemic terms it is important to recognize that such developments
took the heat off public education by removing a demand which it had
failed to satisfy.

Primary and Secondary Education

In the last Chapter reference was made to a general tendency for
external transactions to move upwards through the three main educational levels over time. Exceptions like nursery schooling were noted
but there are also two partial exceptions, that is interest groups which,
by their very nature, do not desert primary education even though they
confirm the trend by taking a growing interest in the secondary level as
the century proceeded. These are the Churches, whose goal of religious
socialization, being universalistic, must necessarily transact at those
levels where the majority of pupils are found — and not until mid-
century did this include secondary instruction. Also in this same
category are the parental interest groups whose investment patterns
follow the points at which educational opportunities are determined

and at which socio-economic life chances are distributed. Again this means that personal investors cannot afford to skirt the primary level completely, although as a group they concentrate their efforts on the final years of schooling. Whilst the transactions of both religious and parental interest groups have added to educational diversity, they present an interesting contrast because the activities of the former have been sufficiently contained to prevent them from disrupting public education in the twentieth century, whilst those of the latter have done so seriously and continuously.

The main achievement of the Churches has been to remain in education despite their worsening bargaining position, following the secular decline in religious affiliation and hence subscriptions. Despite the favourable nature of the 1902 settlement towards denominational instruction, Morant himself clearly thought of this in the light of a reprieve. Writing to Balfour he commented: 'I agree with you that voluntary managers will find it a much more expensive business than they at present realize to bring and keep their buildings up the increasingly heightened standards of the local authority. And possibly there will be some twenty years hence another "intolerable strain" in that respect'.[106] Yet survive they did, though in decreasing proportion as the following table indicates, and with differing degrees of success, the Catholics still making headway as the Anglicans fell further and further and further behind.

TABLE 4

**Enrollment in all Schools, excluding Independent,
Direct Grant, Nursery and Special Schools**

Type of School	1900	1938	1962	1967
Council	47.0	69.6	77.6	76.9
Church of England	40.2	22.1	11.9	11.8
Roman Catholic	5.4	7.4	8.4	9.3
Other	7.4	0.9	2.1	2.0

Source: James Murphy, *Church, State and Schools in Britain, 1800-1970*, p. 125

Similarly they hung on in teacher training[107] and also gained public assistance in 1936 for building senior schools in order that their position should not be prejudiced by developments in secondary education. There is no doubt that the Churches were increasingly left behind in this respect: in 1939 while 62 percent of those in State schools were in senior schools, this was only the case for 16 percent of pupils in voluntary establishments.[108] It became even clearer when, under the 1944 Act, the denominations had to opt for either 'voluntary aided' status (where their schools remained fully denominational and they retained the right to give religious instruction, to appoint teachers and to nominate two-thirds of the managers), or 'controlled' status (where the school would be financed, maintained and governed like a Council school, except for religious instruction being given on two occasions a week if parents so desired by a 'reserved' teacher, specially appointed to give it). The Roman Catholics held out against 'controlled' status but the Anglicans largely gave in to it. Although the Catholic spearhead succeeded in embedding itself in secondary instruction and in obtaining 75 percent building grants in 1959, this was on terms which specifically excluded the foundation of Grammar and Technical Schools: in other words, the Churches were being confined to the inferior part of secondary instruction in so far as they were reliant on public funds. They profited, however, from comprehensive reorganization which, in doing away with these distinctions between schools, was consistent in assisting the Churches to build the new type of establishments, but generous in extending this aid to the building of primary, secondary or technical schools at the same 80 percent rate.

The Churches, as external interest groups, continued their trans-actions at the primary and then the secondary level, contributing something to educational diversity, but to a lesser degree than before because of their greater dependence on the State, induced by their dwindling resources. The activities of denominational schools became progressively easier to contain as they passed under the unified admin-istrative framework, and in the case of the 'controlled' schools became virtually indistinguishable from council schools. With increased unifica-tion went a simultaneous growth in systematization, for the schools of 'controlled' status had no chance of maintaining a distinct identity, atmosphere, and least of all a different definition of knowledge from State schools. For Anglicans in particular, even their greatest achieve-ment in political terms, the introducing of the compulsory Act of Worship in all schools under the 1944 Act, was perversely counter-productive. If all schools worshipped daily, then the two additional weekly sessions of religious instruction were hardly likely to give a distinctive character to Anglican schools, whose secular subjects were the preserve of State inspection anyway. Thus Anglican instruction became decreasingly different, less able to create exigencies for the public system of which it was now a part, but by the same token it experienced increased difficulties in recruiting support ,since it no longer offered an alternative educational service. Since the established Church had become a junior partner in the State enterprise it was largely left to the Catholics to give a distinctive religious stamp to their voluntary aided schools. The steady development of the Catholic network over three-quarters of a century indicates their success in this, although it may ironically be the case that some of their present clientele are more attracted by the general ethos and educational approach of Catholic schools than by their religious orientation. Considering denominational instruction as a whole, it seems clear that the Churches' loss of managerial control over time also led to a diminution in the specialist services provided by them. Their contribution to educational diversity has become literally ghostly.

Much more significant in this respect were the various institutions founded or kept in being by parental transactions – the Preparatory Schools, Public Schools, Experimental Schools, the Progressives, the 'Crammers' and the Tutorial Agencies. These added considerably to diversification – in teaching and learning methods, in the definitions of educational knowledge, in school administration and organization, and in the characteristics possessed by their leavers. Whether quiet or flamboyant, these schools taken together represented a fund of experimentation, took on the role of guinea-pigs, and worked out the practical implications of educational theories in ways from which the rest of the system was not immune. Although the vast majority of these transactions were confined to the private sector, and were possible because of this, they impinged in two ways on public education – by example and by interference. In the broadest possible terms the experimental movement exerted the strongest exemplary influence in the twentieth century, whilst the endurance of the traditional private schools constituted more of a hindrance to public policy.

The 'progressives were a small and loosely knit group of outsiders, sometimes ignored by the authorities, sometimes obstructed and occasionally helped, but never part of the public system. They were independent of the Board and the local authorities and frequently opposed to their policies, they did not follow a lead given by the authorities, but themselves had the initiative, they did not work from within the system for reform but stood outside and went their own way'[109] Some of their demonstration schools like Summerhill and Dartington Hall must be amongst the most visited in the country: others which succumbed to financial hazards, like the Malting House School, at least produced a literature. Since they remained strictly private, they avoided and evaded unification: since they attached little importance to public examinations or rejected conventional means of preparing for them, they remained unmoved by one of the main tugs towards systematization. Although they stood apart in structural terms, they had the largest cultural impact on professionals and educationalists. By the outbreak of the war 'the progressives had made great gains. They had established a firm foothold in the training institutions, especially the colleges; most of the educational theorists and textbook writers espoused their cause; opinion among influential but non-professional educationists, such as Hadow and Tawney, was swinging their way; the official documents reflected their view. They were making the running'[110] Nevertheless, while-ever the tripartite selective policy lasted, the progressive movement was confined to the private sector and limited to the transaction of exemplary institutions, a process which flourished after the war with the great improvement in economic climate.

However, with the gradual abandoning of the 11+, the development of comprehensive schools in which many pupils were not preparing for the GCE, and the raising of the school leaving age, the progressive approach breached public education at primary and secondary levels. The profession, which had been substantially converted to these views, introduced them (often blended with a politically inspired stress on community rather than individualism) in primary instruction and in secondary where possible. Details of the strains this created for systematization, of the growing outcry about falling standards, illiteracy and indiscipline in primary schools, which made the academic tasks of secondary instruction increasingly difficult and passed these problems on to vocational training, properly belong to the discussion of internal initiation. Nevertheless, these processes are only separated for analytical convenience, in reality they are contemporaneous, and it is important to recognize that the changes teachers introduced in public education were continuously sustained by ongoing experimentation in the private sector. The secular evangelism of the progressives, led by A.S. Neill, always had concrete points of reference in schools like Summerhill, Bedales, Monkton Wyld and Dartington Hall which demonstrated the ideals in practice. Twentieth century education 'has been a rich time for these pioneers. It has not sought them but neither has it turned them away. It is they who have provided the Research and Development of the industry'.[111] The influence of the progressives on public education has been a mixed blessing from the official point of view, but because it has taken place at the ideational level, whilst the experimental schools themselves remained independent and outside the grasp of unification, the State has been unable to contain them or their disruptive consequences for public education.

The more traditional forms of private education and the newer opportunist variants had an equal effect on the public sector through their interference with the type of systematization which constituted offical policy. When the latter consisted in meritocratic selection, with a ladder to be climbed only by those with the requisite ability, private practice introduced two kinds of distortions. On the one hand, the crammers shepherded a crowd of middle class borderlines, or worse, up the first extension of the ladder. Insofar as the self-fulfilling prophecy failed to work once these pupils were safely into the Grammar Schools, another range of crammers, more politely known as Tutorial Agencies, saw them up the second extension, into the universities. The Public Schools of course afforded even greater protection to the educational opportunities and occupational life chances of children from yet more privileged backgrounds. Together the two distorted the meritocratic principle and added substantially to the social discrimination already built into the tests used for selection. Their activities in this context served to fuel the political opposition mustered against this type of systematization.

However, when the selective system was replaced by comprehensive reorganization, in the name of equality of educational opportunity, the private sector hindered its achievement in a very serious way. The public schools, with their superior facilities and elite connotations, mocked the notion of a common school for all, whilst the direct grant schools continued to cream-off the best pupils in their area leaving the comprehensives with smaller sixth forms and lower records of achievement. Circular 10/65, which carried no statutory powers, had asked the direct grant schools to 'associate' themselves with Local Authority plans for comprehensive reorganization, a move which has been likened to asking the Atheneum to consider the ways in which it could become a Youth Centre.[112] By 1972 only two such schools out of a total of 172 had gone comprehensive[113] the remainder continuing to play their traditional selective role. But here the partially unified nature of these schools was a lever used to contain their disruptive influence at local and central level. Many LEAs gave notice that they would cease to take up places in direct grant schools once their reorganization was complete[114] whilst the official view condemned the continuation of selection as incompatible with comprehensive reorganization and argued that a definite choice must be made between them. The central polity was unwilling to wait for death by slow local attrition as the patient continued in excellent health.

It attempted to rid itself of the lesser hindrance, the direct grant schools, because it had a weapon it could wield against them which it did not command in relation to the public schools — namely financial dependence. The aim was to bring them to heel by forcing them to choose between complete unification (assimilation into the re-organized system like any grammar school) or total independence. In fact it appears that government underestimated the financial viability of these institutions, for even the relatively poorly endowed like the Girls' Public Day School Trust network felt that the market was strong enough to enable them to go independent. By and large political intervention had only succeeded in reducing interference with its policy from within the system at the expense of increasing it from without. Since independent schools are self-supporting and outside the State system, they remain non-unified, retain managerial control, and continue to supply the specialist services their clients seek. In this case their provision of a better education for the few than the State can give to all meant that private elitism was an ever present thorn in the flesh of public egalitarianism.

Adult Education, Further Education and Higher Education

It is these very different kinds of terminal instruction which progressively attracted most attention from the external interest groups. Largely this reflects an updating in the practice of employers: when elementary schooling was all there was for the vast majority, the nineteenth century entrepreneur was concerned about its content, when it bacame a preliminary grounding for futher education, then employers began to neglect the preparatory stage and to concentrate on the final years of formation. Also of importance was the growing industrial reliance on scientific research, which threw a new light on transactions with the universities and with the tertiary level in general. These were particularly significant given the offical protection of the academic grammar schools which rendered them unattractive and unamenable to external trasactions. Similarly, the increasingly 'progressive' conviction of the teaching profession made them unresponsive to the the nut and bolt requirements of interest groups in schools like the secondary moderns where negotiations could have taken place. The changes introduced into these forms of terminal instruction have all increased the specialization of studies and have furthered organizational differentiation, be it of universities, colleges, departments or courses. They have usually been transacted by groups with high negotiating strength and have often been incorporated into the system retrospectively without loss of distinctiveness. Only in the case of a particularly weak interest group whose activities were deemed specially disruptive did administrative control and organizational reintegration succeed in killing this transaction as a source of educational diversification.

The Adult Education Movement attempted in part to introduce a new definition of instruction – the committed Marxist approach as taught first at Ruskin and subsequently by the Central Labour College and classes. Simultaneously it sought the services of the universities for the working class, a service to which they felt they had a right in view of the misappropriation of endowments originally intended for the poor. This they wished to negotiate directly rather than awaiting the slow reform of secondary education as a means of gaining university entry. We have already seen how this movement was channelled along WEA lines, by a pincer movement of the profession and the polity. The Dons would only countenance the 'non-partisan' curriculum, which to the Plebs League was 'simply an inculcation of governing-class ideas';[115] the Ministry would not recognize the dissemination of ideas which were not only educationally but also politically disruptive. Together they did not preclude external transactions by the working class at this level, but defined the form they should take and monitored it closely. The WEA Tutorial Classes received an official subvention and were inspected by the Board whose regulations defined them as a three year course of study to a syllabus approved by the university and convened by a tutor which it appointed.

Thus adult education became unified under the Board and systematized in its relations with the university. Between them, official control and curricular integration strangled the WEA as a contributor to educational diversity – what it offered was the traditional liberal definition of instruction: only whom it was offered to had changed. And even here the promised quid pro quo for integration – entry to the universities rather than a poor substitute for it — did not materialize. WEA 'classes were successfully established which aimed to provide a higher education leading on to university work, but this aim was not achieved; the universities remained as exclusive as ever and it was only when scholarship holders from the secondary schools began to find their way up in the 1920s and 1930s that working class children at last began to have access to university education on a small scale'.[116] A still more far reaching consequence of the failure to introduce a radical form of adult education was that it destroyed the motivation of the working class movement to continue with external transactions, since the leadership was convinced of its inability to negotiate an independent education serving class needs.

The contrast with the influence exerted by industrial interest groups has already been reviewed. External transactions on the part of industry were responsible both for the modernization of traditional higher education and for the very emergence of the civic universities. This type of negotiation 'is one of quite recent origin in the long span of history of British universities, covering scarcely the last hundred years. Throughout this relatively short time, industry has become highly dependent on the activities of the universities, just as universities have had to take account of the needs of industry in ways which would have seemed inconceivable in the mid-nineteenth century'.[117] Cambridge's re-orientation to industry was precipitated by financial difficulties: it knew that it had to respond or to go under, and that response meant adaptation. Meetings were held with industrial and commercial leaders to consider the suitability of graduates for particular courses in banking, metallurgy, industrial chemistry, etc. Industrial advisors were quickly recruited to the new Appointments Board and included the Managing Director of John Brown's, a Director of the Asiatic Petroleum Company (later part of Shell), Sir William Mather for Engineering and Nathaniel Cohen for the City. Whilst these negotiations were largely concerned with the development of existing degrees, commercial interests were encouraging the establishment of an honours examination in economics with business management in view, and as an education particularly useful to businessmens' sons. Supportive statements were submitted to Senate by leaders in shipping, iron, paper, gas and electricity.

The civic universities, themselves of course a form of institutional differentiation for which industry was responsible, also present the clearest evidence of the scientific and educational specialization inextricably related to these external transactions. Leeds, which had received a total of £160,000 from the Clothworkers' Company by 1912 but was not otherwise well endowed, thus specialized rather narrowly on textile and leather technology. Birmingham, on the other hand, displayed a diversity of specialisms following the various types of Midlands industry which supported it — the Birmingham and Midlands Counties Wholesale Brewers' Association gave £28,000 for the School of Brewing, Sir James Chance of the glass firm donated £50,000 for engineering, John Feeney £20,000 for metallurgy as well as contributions from Cadbury's, Dunlop, GEC and various light engineering and chemical firms. Sheffield, developing along the lines set by its early benefactor, Mark Firth the steelmaster, became the premier School of Metallurgy and made enormous research contributions to the surrounding iron and steel industries.[118] Shipbuilding and naval architecture, as specialized forms of engineering, developed at Newcastle in conjunction with Swann Hunter and Wigham Richardson and also at Liverpool, aided by the Harrison Hughes laboratories which were used for work on marine propulsion engines. Examples could be multiplied. In the first years of the century the civic universities provided the teaching services required in their regions and these were as likely to be specialized courses for further education taken in the evenings by laboratory assistants as work of degree level. Research also became more specialized in those fields which were of concern to local firms.

> The contributions of the civic universities to industry, even in their early days, were thus remarkable and of considerable importance. They were now becoming a leading source of innovation for industry as Oxford and Cambridge never hitherto had been. The thrust bearing lubrication, colliery pumps, vanadium steels, chrome, leather, gas fires, sparking plugs and radio tuning, all owed much to the work of these professors while products like cheese, soap, beer and the quadruple expansion engine were all considerably improved by their work. Even more important than the spectacular innovation was the more routine but vital improvement of the practice of firms.[119]

Such transactions met with official approval, which deepened over the following decades as the State became more closely involved with industrial efficiency and economic development. In consequence the civic universities became incorporated into the system, they received legal recognition (in the form of Charters) and financial support from central grants; but they suffered no loss of diversity or distinctiveness in the process. The status of university was conferred on the most prominent differentiated units to have emerged through external transactions: the receipt of public support was not conditional on dropping any of the specialized services which had developed. The form of unification which took place was weak, for its main agency, the University Grants Committee, was of bipartite (official and academic) composition which in itself prevented direct ministerial control over the distribution of finance or decision-making.

In the interwar years a supportive triangular relationship thus emerged between government, industry and the universities, in which the latter not only serviced manifest demands but also played a part in industrial reconstruction — the rise of 'new' industries such as aviation, petroleum and electrical engineering and food processing. Correspondingly the involvement of university teachers in the practical problems for which research contracts had been negotiated, generated further academic and scientific specialization in its turn: 'the requirements of industry have opened up a whole range of new subjects and cross connections which would not necessarily have come about without these demands — the chemistry of glass, the mathematics of flight, the biology of the food fishes'.[120] The same could be said of a number of the taught courses to develop during this period: like business administration at LSE and Manchester, industrial psychology at Cambridge and statistics at Oxford. This pattern continues through the fifties, when in a second spate of incorporation full university status was conferred on the remaining civic institutions, which had developed more slowly precisely because they originally lacked an industrial hinterland from which firms clamoured for their services. Again this involved weak unification, the new universities enjoying the same autonomy as the old.

However, after the Second World War official attention was increasingly drawn to the need for greater systematization in technological education, especially by the influential Percy Committee of 1945. This pin-pointed two problems: firstly, the need to co-ordinate the work of the technical colleges and the universities in order to avoid wastage, overlap and duplication of functions at both regional and national levels; secondly, the need to upgrade college work in order to match a volume of industrial demand which the universities could not satisfy. To meet both of these needs simultaneously implied a much higher level of systematization, in which the functions of different institutions would be clearly defined and dovetailed with one another.

As far as the Colleges were concerned the 1944 Act

made local authorities responsible for securing the provision of education and cultural training and recreation for those over the compulsory school age. But whether this education should be general or vocational and what kinds of cultural and recreational activities it was proper for public money to be spent upon were questions that the Act did not pursue. Subsequently more detailed recommendations came down to authorities and colleges in circulars and administrative memoranda, but these merely exhorted them to carry out a miscellany of activities and were of little help with the problem of making choices and defining tasks'.[121]

In the decade after the war the colleges developed freely, progressively defining their form and functions via external transactions in exactly the same way that the universities had done half a century earlier. The White Paper and explanatory circular issued in 1956 represented the 'first major official comment after the Act on the emerging technical college structure . . . The circular implies that having let colleges develop freely so far, it was time that the Ministry exercised some kind of control over their development'.[122]

The aim was clearly systematization: for the first time these documents made reference to local, area, and regional colleges, implying a hierarchy of institutions engaged in distinct but complementary activities. Yet it seems clear from supplementary circulars that the Ministry was torn between wanting to take a firm hold, introducing order into further education, and its recognition that ultimately the utility of the colleges depended upon their responsiveness to local demands and circumstances. It compromised by designating certain regional colleges as places where advanced work would be concentrated (CATs), but did not regard this list as definitive, produced no firm guidelines differentiating between the other levels, and allowed that upgrading was a legitimate aim for the various colleges to entertain. The task of deciding which activities to pursue still rested then on the colleges themselves and the Local Education Committee.

This cycle was repeated with the 1966 White Paper, recommending that a limited number of polytechnics be designated in which both full-time technical instruction and sandwich-type higher education were to be concentrated, although these would still need to be supplemented by the work of other colleges, particularly in specialized fields. This series of changes indicates the way in which official policy tried to use upgrading to introduce systematization: each time the hope was that by clarifying the aims of the most advanced colleges and giving them legal and financial backing as well as status incentives, that the lower levels of colleges would be defined residually. That this never happened, and that instead an overlap of activities and a wastage of resources (through running too many courses in too many places for too few students) continued to be the case, serves to illustrate the impossibility of bringing about a high degree of systematization without a corresponding increase in unification. Yet a combination of external demands, the autonomy of the local authorities and professional vested interests worked together to repulse unification by modifying official directives, reinterpreting ministerial goals, exploiting loopholes in departmental circulars and creating precedents, exceptions and special cases.

Precisely the same problem was encountered with the universities in the sixties, when the Government sought a further systematization of advanced technological instruction, but had to do so in the context of weak unification (i.e. the traditional autonomy enjoyed and defended by these institutions). The strategy until the mid-sixties was to incorporate all higher technological education into the universities (by upgrading the CATs), with the dual aim of eliminating wasteful overlap and increasing the number of science graduates. Official dissatisfaction with this solution stemmed directly from the uses (or abuses) to which the post-Robbins institutions put their autonomy, which had been granted on the same basis as enjoyed by their predecessors. This enabled each university to respond as it chose to transactions proferred by industry. Kent, East Anglia and above all Sussex remained disengaged from industry, slightly more involved with agriculture, fisheries and food research but above all were concerned to meet student demand and to experiment with 'new maps of learning'. Surrey, on the other hand, deliberately put on courses relating to catering, hotel management and tourism with the support of appropriate firms, whilst Essex went out of its way to provide 'a firm basis for the student of electronics and other branches of engineering which are the leading industries of Essex'.[123] Warwick presents the clearest case of industrial involvement in the foundation, operation and government of the university with the traditional externally financed Chairs in Business Studies, Industrial Relations and Management Information Systems. If Warwick responded to the demands of the Midlands conurbation in which it was situated, Lancaster 'transcended its environment to establish all manner of enterprising links with industry that were not self-evidently dictated by the industrial conditions of its immediate region'.[124] It was not then that the universities were unresponsive to industry *in general* but rather that the negotiations which took place and the forms of specialized teaching or research which resulted were in no way co-ordinated with one another – they did not add up to a coherent national policy. Yet this is what a government more and more embroiled in making the mixed economy work is what it felt it needed.

Moreover, with their enhanced negotiating strength the universities were using their surplus resources to pursue some of their own academic goals, introducing new forms of specialization in pure and social science, which official opinion clearly felt that it did not want and which it believed industry did not require. As far as industrialists themselves were concerned they were not transmitting clear messages about their requirements to the universities. A confused debate went on amongst them over the merits of generalism, for future adaptability, versus the advantages of intense specialization for current job requirements. It was not until the mid-sixties that experience reinforced a clearer preference for science-based managers, so it is not surprising that the new universities, in planning their first courses, should have believed that there was an on-going demand for the non-technical graduate. It was certainly a 'fallacy of the time to suppose that as industry wanted a broader science education it also desired a broader arts and social studies programme, mixing economics with sociology, literature, history and so forth, as was to become common especially in the new universities'.[125] But it was a fallacy which industry had partly encouraged by its ready acceptance of the Arts graduate in the fifties, and its rationalization of this, to itself and others, in terms of his broad mental conspectus, managerial qualities and transfer abilities.

Post-graduate study was also a controversial aspect of university work in the late sixties and early seventies, with the Swann Report (The Flow into Employment of Scientists, Engineers and Technologists – 1968) and the Bosworth Report (Graduate Training in Manufacturing Technology) criticizing PhD training as too abstract, whilst the Eaborn Report (Relationships between University Courses in Chemistry and the Needs of Industry – 1970) and the Docksey Report (Industry, Science and the Universities) expressed satisfaction about the relationship of PhD research to industrial problems.[126] Certainly the development of the PhD rather than shorter graduate courses did reflect academic concern for the advancement of knowledge, and it is doubtless true that many of the rarefied topics undertaken had little relevance for industrialists. On the other hand, when business was decisive about its post-graduate requirements and put up the money in the usual way, the universities were immediately responsive. When the British

Institute of Management called for two Business Schools to provide post-experience courses and graduate training, the UGC in conjunction with the Foundation for Management Education (formed under Keith Joseph), quickly raised the requisite funds from industry and established two national business schools in London and Manchester, with the co-operation of their respective universities.

Whether official opinion was right or wrong in its desire for a more systematized process of scientific training and research, it recognized that it could not bring this about, given the autonomy of the universities. In other words, weak unification at this level meant that the forms of differentiation and specialization to develop would depend jointly on professional values and direct negotiations. If it was unable to contain and canalise specialization when unification was weak, then Government appears to have thought that it could achieve its aims by reversing this formula. Hence one of the reasons for the introduction of the binary policy, in which the less autonomous polytechnics were to become the new agents of a systematic technological education. However, the main lesson which seems to emerge from the mismatch in the mid-sixties and the debate on post-graduate training in the early seventies is that various industries have different requirements which cannot be met by a single blanket formula. The variety, changeability and incommensurateness of industrial and commercial demands are such that only a kaleidoscopic process of external transactions can meet them and keep meeting them. In this way new forms of specialization in both teaching and research are introduced, formulated, reformulated, abandoned and replaced with changing demand — changes whose flexibility is fundamentally incompatible with strong unification and systematization.

Internal Initiation

The School Teachers, 1902-18

Given the extent of professional disunity and the weak negotiating strength of school teachers vis à vis the polity after the 1902 Act, a significant degree of internal initiation could not be expected before the end of the First World War. Unlike the academics they started from a position of financial and administrative dependence on State and lacked the autonomy to break out of this by accumulating additional resources and pushing up the exchange rate. Moreover, the school teachers themselves lacked anything approaching the expertise possessed by their university counterparts and it is inconceivable that they could have commanded the same kind of market. Instead the teachers had to work the other way round, acquiring influence and increased autonomy through organization and insertion. Thus whilst the academics advanced their cause by first exchanging expertise against resources on the open market, the school teachers proceeded by upgrading their expertise and extending the legal recognition received from the political centre. In terms of legal rights the main gain in self-determination registered during the period concerned control of examinations, curricula and the management of knowledge in general. Consequently, the only significant acts of internal initiation possible to the school teachers were those which could be introduced within the confines of their classrooms. These tended to assume two important forms: on the one hand, elementary teachers appear to have struggled to give their working class pupils as broad a general education as possible thus keeping alive the spirit of the higher grade schools: on the other, inspection of school log books indicates a willingness to experiment with new subjects and to respond to the nature of the community in which they were located. Nevertheless, there is no doubt that the most dramatic and influential experiments with curricula and teaching methods were taking place outside the confines of State education, in the private progressive schools whose staff evaded all political constraints since they had chosen to work through external transactions rather than internal initiation. It is only when the public teachers and the private experimentalists came together in the next period, when the school teachers had improved their negotiating strength, that internal initiation began to exert a major influence on the development of State education. The same is not true of higher education, largely because it started from a better bargaining position in terms of its high expertise, but again the influence of internal initiation was also less important than processes of political manipulation and external transactions during this period.

The Academics, 1902-18

Academic innovation had to work within severe constraints: the universities were still cap in hand to industry, and did not acquire the State as a serious alternative supplier for more than another decade. Services were undertaken in return for resources at a low exchange rate which provided little surplus for the universities. Given that the majority of these services were to industry, internal initiation tended to be confined to the interstices between the training and research activities sponsored by different companies and parts of the field of production. The section on external transactions has already detailed the types of technical and scientific education which were developed in direct response to external demands of this kind. Here, however, it is important to accentuate the ways in which the profession manipulated their side of those transactions to produce outputs which embodied more than the blunt dictates of industry.

In terms of research this involved extracting every drop of scientific interest from the practical problems which constitued their brief. Research and development services were raised to a higher level through this application of expertise, but the interplay between practical demand and academic response also generated a new range of scientific specialisms which came into their own during the war — aeronautics, electrical engineering, chemical engineering, artificial fibres and wireless communications. In terms of teaching, the profession succeeded in initiating and sustaining degrees which were more broadly based than was stricly indicated by the requirements of industrial training. Most of the external transactions took place between companies and the Civic University Colleges which awarded University of London Degrees, and the latter insisted that students took certain literary subjects even if they were following a science course. This then was internally imposed by a senior academic institution on its junior affiliates and it meant that the 'colleges had to teach them, if not out of any conviction of their value then at least for the science students' degree work'.[127]

This internal insistence on an element of liberal education in conjuction with the high level to which academics had independently raised scientific research was to pay dividends when the universities confronted two alternative suppliers, industry and the State, by the middle of the war. The two could be played off against one another, not just financially but also in terms of the definition of instruction, to the advantage of the academics. Thus industry could be induced to accept the more broadly based degree which the universities could rightly plead was a condition of receiving the government grant, whilst the State was manoeuvred into endorsing technological specialisms as part of *university* education, without whose earnings the colleges could not have made their valuable contribution to the war effort. The most important consequence then of internal initiation was that

England was saved from the dual form of higher education such as existed in Germany and which many politicians of science wished Britain to emulate. It thus preserved the mutually beneficial linkages of science and technologies in the same institution, prevented the creation on non-technological universities which would rapidly have become chiefly narrow arts teacher training colleges, and so avoided a situation whereby a 'second rate' stigma would have attached to centres dealing purely with the technologies.[128]

Simultaneously, in an attempt to increase resources, various universities tried to discover latent demands and to transform them into manifest requirements, especially in academic fields that were not paying their way. The expansion of world markets, the development of London as a financial and banking capital, increasing bureaucratization, rationalization of companies and worsening industrial relations, all indicated to certain academics that a demand could be created for business and commercial training. Hence the initiative was taken internally to adapt economics teaching to those ends, in order to tap industrial pockets in a new way. This type of innovation was entirely unco-ordinated between universities — it resulted from the personal initiative of particular academic economists who read the market in rather similar ways, and the pioneering courses they established bore the marks of their different personalities and institutional affiliations.

Thus the BSc (Econ.) degree, established at the London School of Economics in 1901, demonstrated the basic pattern of building a business education on foundation courses in economics and statistics by adding options in railway economics, commercial law, immigration, banking, rates, the English Constitution, the structure of modern business, and later on, factory welfare and social administration. A similar development under Ashley at Birmingham met the businessman more than half way by accepting accountancy and commercial correspondence (in foreign languages) as university subjects. Again, under the broad umbrella of 'economics', a whole range of related sub-disciplines were brought into being or developed within the university framework — public finance, industrial relations, transport economics and so forth. At Cambridge Alfred Marshall had a rather different task of converting traditional economics teaching, which had never included the actual workings of companies or led to an examination, into a separate Economics Tripos which would be welcomed by businessmen wanting to send their sons to a traditional university. Although Marshall himself would not go so far as to incorporate accountancy (book-keeping in his view), the pre-war curriculum was of considerable practical utility (under the influence of Pigou) and included some original courses — the

localization of industry, joint-stock companies, trusts and cartels, fluc-
tuating demand, wages and conditions of labour, trade unions and
employers' associations, industrial insurance and government interference.

This major act of internal initiation received a cool and even hostile
reception from industry and academic colleagues alike. For three
decades most of the graduates from these commerce courses went into
teaching or research posts, and as the Goodenough Committee concluded in 1931 'Commercial faculties have not so far received any great
encouragement from employers'.[129] But at least this initiative had
succeeded in introducing and sustaining a new range of disciplines in
the universities. This diversification of courses, under the general aegis
of economics, constituted an important extension of the definition of
instruction and must be compared with the stagnation or inertia of the
other social sciences – sociology, psychology, anthropology and
politics, which remained both under-represented and under-financed.

Finally, and as a general comment on the role which internal
initiation plays in the social management of knowledge, it is worth
stressing that when demand was eventually forthcoming, commercial
education was quickly made readily available. The three concrete prototypes provided working models for imitation or adaptation, and the
other universities possessed enough autonomy for diffusion then to
take place exclusively via internal initiation.

> Under the influence of common long-term pressures and specifically stimu-
> lated by the example of the three main schools, other universities rapidly
> reformed their thinking of economics, expanding departments, creating dis-
> tinct examinations, and changing and widening the content of the courses.
> Most importantly, following Birmingham, some centres made the transition
> from economics courses pure and simple to commerce courses, fitting econo-
> mics into a context of languages, law, and other subjects.[130]

The university teachers had fostered a cumulative process in which
the meeting of external demands in turn stimulated further demands
which added new resources and broadened the scope for more
adventurous types of internal initiation. Thus for example 'by their
willingness to undertake testing for firms and by allowing firms to use
university equipment, they introduced and raised scientific standards
within the firm that often in turn induced them to begin their own
testing and research departments using the graduates they had now
grown to trust'.[131] In other words the academics had manoeuvred the
universities into a positive feedback loop in which their present activi-

ties were also creating their own future market, and with it they had improved their prospects of acquiring a positive resource balance to devote to their own internally determined ends.

The School Teachers, 1918-44

The gradual but consistent improvement in professional negotiating strength vis à vis the polity leads to an expectation of considerable internal initiation, especially towards the end of the period. However, two factors came into play sequentially, and both had the effect of restraining the teachers' internal contribution to educational development. Firstly, the economic depression and crisis of the twenties cut school budgets to the bone, leaving no surplus for experimentation or the pursuit of of internally defined goals, thus intensifying the consequences of a low rate of exchange. Secondly, just when economic recovery was in view, one of the major changes introduced through political manipulation began to exert its influence on primary and secondary schools alike – the development of the selective principle.

Thus the conquest of professional values by the progressive movement did not have an immediate impact on public instruction. During this period various devotees had tried to implement their views despite difficulties with the local authorities. There were isolated instances, like Prestolee in Lancashire of 'that rare phenomenon, a public elementary school which was unmistakenly progressive'[132] and of variations on the Dalton Plan which were used in secondary schools.[133] In general, however, a deep penetration of the public sector was prevented. On the one hand, constant stringency in school budgets and cutbacks in school building were practical barriers against the new methods which required space, adaptation of premises, and special materials. On the other, all primary schools were being turned into 'preparatory' schools in the face of selection at eleven. Curricular change was repulsed by this most conservative of educational influences, the examination. Thus the emergence of selective secondary instruction had the consequence of making public elementary education less accessible to progressive reformers, through its lack of curricular autonomy. The most important and ultimately the most influential expressions of the new values still took place in the private sector through the external transaction of experimental schools. It was not until the next period that progressive values could be implemented through internal initiation.

Nevertheless, although pedagogical innovation and policy influence were not yet great, it is still in order to ask in whose interests the teachers' improved negotiating strength was deployed. Here the facile equation of what was good for the teacher being good for education is less easy to maintain. There had been earlier problems about this: the growth of breakfast clubs, clothes clubs, boot clubs and dinner clubs had set up a tension between educational and humanitarian values on the one hand, and the fear of mortgaging professional interests by accepting new 'extraneous duties', on the other. This became more serious with the 1944 Bill, for which the school teachers pressed so hard. On one interpretation it could be argued fairly convincingly that they gained something important from the first flush of conservative collectivism – an Act which contained the hope of both a unified profession and education system. In other words, the two sides of the equation still complemented one another. Another interpretation, however, at lease raises a doubt as to whether this was not the point at which professional and educational interests begain to diverge. It queries whether the prospects of professional unity and freedom of movement between primary and secondary schools, so long the ambitions of the NUT, did not make the school teachers overwilling to accept secondary education for all on conservative terms.

Earlier they had welcomed the Hadow report because it recommended the universalization of secondary schooling, but they had been equally quick to stress that this should be within the context of multilateral institutions. Thus in 1928 the NUT had proposed that 'local authorities should be permitted to establish post-primary schools of multiple-bias type taking all children from the age of seven onwards and supplying some of them with an academic course leading to the university'.[134] Equally the NUT regretted that the Spens Report had approved the tripartite system and viewed the multilateral formula with disapproval. Nevertheless, whether willingly or unwillingly, in lending their support to the Bill the profession had helped to erect a structural obstacle to the accomplishment of their new pedagogic aims which it would take more than two decades to demolish.

The Academics, 1918-44

In the last Chapter it was argued that the low exchange rate for expertise, due to the financial difficulties of the two major suppliers –

industry and the State, did not provide the kind of surplus which would allow expensive forms of innovation. Consequently, we find that although the university teachers articulated various kinds of structural and institutional changes which they would have liked to see (e.g. Continuation Schools, People's Colleges and Folk High Schools), the main impact of internal initiation was in the less expensive areas of intellectual specialization, curriculum development, and changing methods of examination. In brief, professional innovations were largely confined to the management of knowledge.

At the disciplinary level some subjects continued to develop despite their lack of engagement with current industrial demands, and to do so in the intellectual directions defined by their practitioners. Thus, for example, chemistry was the predominant industrial science rather than physics after the First World War, when the former had shown what it could do in areas like explosives. Mainstream physics, which continued to be funded in well established departments, made use of its disengagement to undergo an important phase of theoretical development. 'The predominance of Cambridge theoretical physics, and its migration to most of the chairs in the country, swung the subject, notably at Bristol, Manchester and Liverpool, away from a concern with matters of immediate potential relevance for engineering'.[135] The same theoretical concentration was also evident in those disciplines which had courted industrial demand but failed, temporarily, to find a market. Thus the practitioners of the economic and commercial disciplines, which had been autonomously introduced in the hope of increasing resources, used the quiet period of rejection in the twenties and thirties to build up the intellectual level of these subjects. Internal support for the continuing development of such disciplines can be seen as long term academic investments, of a kind universities must constantly make, which eventually brought in good returns.

> In both cases the intellectual developments of the subject by a few people were of vastly greater significance than any short-term immediate services to industry. As their developments came to be appreciated, thus enormously raising the prestige of the subjects, so accordingly there followed at a gap of a generation or so the expansion of the routine output of students to industry — the nuclear physicists of the 1950s and the economists of the 1960s, both of which would have been impossible without the scholarly developments of the 1930s.[136]

Thus despite their limited means the universities did not submit all their developments to the direct requirements of industry. They supported their own research interests, not just in isolated theoretically oriented departments like physics, but more generally as witnessed by the introduction of the doctoral thesis (PhD), specifically awarded for original contributions to knowledge. Equally, whilst the universities were very willing to engage in any mutually advantageous transaction with industry, they fought shy of starting expensive developments which were unlikely to attract many students, and left those demands unsatisfied. Hence some things were not taught which industry wanted (metallurgy, oil and chemical engineering) whilst other things were taught in which industry was uninterested (physics, economics and commerce). Still further subjects were differentiated and developed from a combination of intellectual interest and practical demand, like languages, industrial psychology and statistics. These types of internal innovation and modification accounted for an increased specialization in certain directions and concentration on particular areas, over and above those directly attributable to external transactions.

To an even greater extent the universities were concerned with the internal regulation of examinations at degree, matriculation and school leaving levels. As concerns the first degree, university teachers were very ready to raise its academic level the moment an improved standard of entrants appeared to warrant abandoning the pass degree. There were obvious advantages, of course, in upgrading the expertise of their end products, as well as the attractions of teaching at a higher level. In the process the AUT strove to maintain diversity by developing broad general Honours degrees alongside more specialized ones, as real alternatives with a genuine parity of status. It was this model which developed strongly at Birmingham and Leeds. The same joint concern for raising intellectual standards whilst maintaining academic diversity characterized AUT discussions with the Secondary Schools Association over a common co-ordinated entrance policy. This was intended to overcome the confusion and duplication of syllabuses which the schools experienced because of the various University Examining Boards at work. Not only did the liaison sub-committee come to an extremely important agreement which represented a rejection of greater unification, but it also heralded an intimate and exclusive relationship between the universities and academic secondary schools. Firstly, in terms of entrance qualifications 'it called for a common policy, but resisted a single national examination as too unwieldy and stereotyped, preferring instead the existing system of separate Examining Boards, but with more co-ordination'.[137] Secondly, the university pressure for a higher standard of entrance exam was already present and signified a general pull from higher education which encouraged secondary schooling to become more academic. Thirdly, it was a small step from the discussion of entrance requirements to the comprehensive review of all secondary school examinations, as subsequent AUT Reports showed.[138] The universities were starting to reach down and influence school curricula and examinations quite independently of government.

The early trade union stance of the AUT explains the use of internal initiation to advance vested professional interests throughout the period. Hence the development of better facilities (the instigation of the inter-Library Loan system), of sabbatical leave, of research amenities and international linkages. But these characterize any national association of academics in any type of system. What was much more significant, with the emergence of a distinctive professional value system, was the extent to which the English university teachers looked forward to being able to satisfy a range of community demands which would never pay their own way. In other words, because of their normative convictions, they were willing to put some of their freedom of action, personnel and resources at the service of the community or region. The AUT Report on postwar educational reconstruction (1944-45) advocated extral-mural departments, to give refresher courses and generally to equip citizens for life in a democratic state; People's Colleges in every large centre of population, co-ordinating the cultural activities of the area, and Folk High Schools on the Danish model. It involved a very big concept of adult education, a generous definition of those whom it would serve, and considerable openness about the agencies with whom university staff would work in those institutions.[139] If the wider aspirations, involving structural changes and institutional developments, were ruled out by lack of resources, internal initiation brought about 'a revolution in the role and status of Extra-Mural Departments and the involvement of the universities in the adult education in their regions'.[140]

The School Teachers, 1944-65

The negotiating strength of the profession in relation to the polity was greatly reinforced during this period: it was well inserted, had won autonomy in the classroom and had a serious collective commitment to the progressive pedagogical value system. On the political side of the equation it benefitted from consensus government since neither party alienated this important interest group by use of repressive tactics: successive governments limited themselves to the strategy of keeping the exchange rate down, but even here the political need for and recognition of expertise produced movements towards greater reciprocity. This improvement, which slowly released the Unions from the thraldom of salary negotiations, was part of the general economic recovery which allowed the financing of educational reconstruction. The profession was ready. In the thirties, when its desire for change had been paralized by economic austerity and national enthusiasm for the selective principle, it had concentrated on teacher training – the one area in which it could freely manoeuvre (thanks to the academic connection with the universities, won in the last period) and had socialized successive waves of recruits. Thus 'the progressives had, by 1939, produced a reasonably uniform set of ideas and procedures (which owed a great deal to the naturalism made popular by the New Education). By that time a person who was being initiated into the educational culture of the English primary school, who read his textbooks and journals, took part in discussions or listened to the lectures at his teachers' college – such a person found that he was being constantly confronted with the ideas and practices which have been called "progressive" '.[141] This then was a context which seemed likely to produce a rich harvest of internal initiation, and this time other factors did not intervene to reduce it.

Internal initiation was responsible for the complete transformation of the primary schools in the postwar years – changes which owed nothing to Parliamentary legislation, government regulations or ministerial instructions, and everything to the independent actions of teachers in thousands of separate classrooms, directed by a common pedagogical value system. The co-existence of two other factors served to amplify this process of change, just as the prewar social context had effectually dampened it. The first was the gradual shifting of institutional concern towards secondary and terminal instruction, a product of the gradual rise of expertise which was noted in the earlier discussion of external transactions. In other words, primary schooling, the main focus of socio-educational conflict in the nineteenth century, was gradually abandoned by the external interest groups, whose demands were now addressed to later age groups. So long as the primary school *did nothing which inhibited* future learning and motivation (i.e. so long as it taught the basic skills and values on which secondary and vocational education depended), then whatever else it chose to do was of little interest in the other major institutional spheres. This desertion of the primary level left the teachers to follow their own internally defined goals, free from social as well as political intervention. Secondly, the move away from the selective principle and the 11 plus examination, which gathered speed throughout the period (and to which teachers themselves contributed through political manipulation), slowly freed the primary school from its enforced 'preparatory' status and gave it a new capacity for self-determination: 'For, however widespread progressive thought became in the colleges, however popular it was in the official reports or among writers on education, it could not easily be put into practice while primary schooling ended in an examination which enshrined many of the values the progressives opposed'.[142]

Thus, internal initiation became the most important of the three processes of change as far as the primary level was concerned. Obviously not every school was affected, for by its very nature this process depended on individual teachers using their freedoms in a particular way, but the progressive influence was marked by a general relaxation of discipline, dissolution of the formal curriculum, reduction of competition and the increased importance attached to art, drama, movement, music and self-expression — all of which put the child at the centre of the educational process and organized the school around his development needs. Grasping it gingerly at first, school teachers found that their freedom was genuine and extensive. They were the true managers of knowledge and they exploited the latitude of their new powers with increasing confidence, elaborating novel methods for stimulating creativity and breaking down old disciplinary barriers to the integrated curriculum. Yet it is still vital to try to get underneath the tremendous euphoria of the period and to ask whose interests these changes served. The euphoric answer was 'the child', but this child was an abstract concept of the developmental phychologist, he belonged to no social class or ethnic group, he brought no culturally induced values or skills to the drama of the learning situation. In short this answer ducked the issue of *social* responsibility, which was the inescapable counterpart of the teachers' new powers, as did the progressive philosophy itself. Taylor has argued pursuasively that the romanticism, the rhetoric, the structural vacuity and social dissociation of this ideology were endemic: it involved 'a suspicion of the intellect and the intellectual; a lack of interest in political and structual change; a stress upon the intuitive and the intangible, upon spontaneity and creativity; an attempt to find personal autonomy through the arts; a hunger for the satisfactions of inter-personal life within the community and small group, and a flight from rationality'.[143]

The community which the teachers served was not the immediate neighbourhood community of their catchment areas, any more than their service was a response to the actual demands of real working class or middle class communities. Instead 'community' like 'the child' was an abstraction — a legendary *gemeinschaft* of warmth and vitality, supposedly surviving in the interstices of advanced industrial societies and the hearts of all pre-school children. The profession did not filter community demands, it pursued its own goals in the interests of the community. It is significant in this context that the end of the period saw the mobilization of the parent movement, the last interest group with a stake in the primary schools, signalling their unwillingness to leave teachers with a free hand.[144] Initially it was very diffuse, a mixture of concern and consumerism, which did not represent parents but rather, as the Confederation for the Advancement of State Education (CASE) was to put it, the movement represented the rights of parents to be represented.[145] The crystallization of various parental groups pursuing particular demands did not properly confront the profession until the next period.

If internal initiation had transformed the primary school along progressive lines, its use at the secondary level was less purposeful because the profession had less concerted views about development. Thus whilst many teachers were actively supporting LEA moves towards comprehensive reorganization, throwing their autonomous influence behind this, others were encouraging their secondary modern schools to push themselves upwards to GCE standard, and the Grammar School teachers were by and large putting their weight behind the protection of their tradition of excellence. It is only at the level of higher education that the degree of concerted professional action matched that of the primary teachers, and led to the same magnitude of change. In the primary schools this autonomy and self-management had repulsed unification and many were coming to believe that it threatened systematization by failing to teach the skills and values required at later stages. Thus 'the freedom of the individual school makes it difficult for a national policy of education to be formulated and carried through, and difficult as well for the less able headteacher to be subjected to criticism and complaints from the authority and from parents'.[146] The universities won themselves the same freedom in this period, and they too were later to attract the same hostile judgements: but until the mid-sixties they could also enjoy the euphoria of unimpeded internal initiation.

The Academics, 1944-65

The growing number of student places in science and technology is the most obvious index of the intensive exchanges between industry and the universities during this period, and has already been discussed under external transactions. However, these figures repay scrutiny for they reveal some telling developments once the rate of exchange favoured the university. Of all first degrees in science and technology, degrees in technology represented a much smaller percentage of the whole than in other advanced industrial countries (36 percent compared with Canada 65 percent: France, 48 percent: Germany, 68 percent: USA, 49 percent).[147] In other words, it is argued that in the new sellers' markets, the academics used internal initiation to develop 'pure' science, with more reference to its intellectual interest than to its practical utility. This is not to say that university teachers in general or university scientists in particular disdained applied technology. Indeed, on the contrary, whenever they were *collectively* confronted with the question of where technological instruction should be conducted, their unanimous reply was 'in the universities'. What seems to have happened then is that whilst they *collectively* approved it, *individually* few of them undertook it, preferring to devote themselves and their students to more abstract theoretical problems. *Culmulatively* this represented a shift towards pure science in this time of ready resources.

This resource surplus for the first time enabled the universities to choose which social demands they would serve, without first ascertaining whether the client could pay or asking him to meet the bill in full. Naturally enough the academic profession was highly responsive to the demands of other professions. 'Indeed, much of the expansion of higher education is due less to the general demand for university places than to the particular demands of individual professions for the university to take over the training of their recruits'.[148] Examples from the years immediately after the war include accountancy, vetinary medicine, estate management, youth leadership and journalism. On the other hand, academia was deliberately seeking to serve the community by developing the extra mural departments, putting adult education on a sound footing and trying to gain adequate recognition for it from university government. Nor, given the range of local bodies and activities with which they started to work, can this be dismissed as cultural paternalism, much less as intellectual authoritarianism which had vitiated the old university extension work.

The keynote underlying these main changes — the curricula and research developments fostering intellectual interests and favouring the deepest vested interest of academics, the response to industrial and professional demands, and the new attempt at serving the community — was diversity. To service this range of requirements simultaneously involved the further differentiation of courses and increased disciplinary specialization. As a whole the profession possessed sufficient autonomy to devise and offer the kinds of degrees, diplomas and certificates required, and the absence of strong unification and systematization meant that each separate university could develop along different lines.

> Some idea of the expanding provision for specialized training can be gained from the proliferation of subjects on which advanced students were engaged, which rose from 123 in 1928-29 to 448 in 1964-65, including an increase from seven to twenty-six kinds of engineering and from one to five branches of economics. Even the trade unions and the police, the professions with the smallest proportions of graduates, are offered courses in industrial relations and criminology. Thus there is no major profession for which the universities do not provide specialized training, and none which does not seek to recruit from amongst university graduates.[149]

The co-existence of numerous external demands, the substantial improvements in real incomes, and the autonomy of the universities to determine their own development, represented an unbeatable recipe for diversification, especially in the management of knowledge. As Ben-David has argued, 'to recognize and develop innovation into new disciplines depended on the existence of a decentralized competitive market for academic achievements'.[150] Given postwar affluence and consensus government, which imposed no vetoes for fear of alienating a significant interest group, such a market had never been bettered.

Indeed it is possible that diversification and specialization could have gone even further in this period, had relations between university teachers not acted as a self-imposed brake upon internal initiation. In other words, what often held back new developments were not external constraints (political embargoes or shortages of funding), but a species of professional in-fighting between 'empire builders' and 'secessionists'. For instance

> one result of departmental organization is that teachers of a 'new' branch of a subject frequently find it difficult to expand and develop unless they are permitted to set up a new and independent department. But, precisely because recognition as an independent department makes it easier for a subject to develop, the demand for that recognition will encounter opposition at the faculty level from the existing departments most likely to suffer from its competition. Thus, it can be argued, the structure is an inherently conservative force.[151]

Finally it is important to stress that the central pressures towards unification and systematization were not simply weakened as a result of increased differentiation and specialization, although this was undoubtedly the case. They were also reduced by a direct assault on them during this period, an attack which focussed on the control of technological instruction. After the war the universities charged themselves with responsibility for the whole of scientific education at the tertiary level. Thus, for example, the AUT postwar report saw one of the tasks of the Extra-Mural Departments as providing regular courses for scientists in industry. Similarly in its concern to improve the quality and supply of laboratory assistants and technicians, it joined with the Association of Scientific Workers and the British Association of Chemists to work out a detailed scheme of certificates and diplomas with their respective syllabuses. This was then handed over to the City and Guilds of London Institute and implemented in various Technical Colleges during the 1950s. It was not that the university teachers necessarily wanted to provide these services themselves; indeed we have seen that their own orientation was towards 'pure' science, but collectively they wanted to monitor them, and in so far as they took place in other institutions, this should be under university sponsorship.

Hence their concern about the Colleges of Advanced Technology, founded in 1956 out of the larger technical colleges, to increase the numbers enrolled for degree standard work but awarding the Diploma in Technology, and their determination to bring them into the university framework.

> 'In retrospect this can now be seen as one more attempt in the long standing campaign by the Ministry of Education (now the Department of Education and Science) and the Local Education Authorities to break the universities' monopoly of granting degrees which culminated in the present 'binary system' and the degrees of the Council for National Academic Awards. If so, it

misfired, as the logic of the situation was that the CATs should seek to complete their upgrading by seeking recognition as universities'.[152]

The universities themselves encouraged this — it was the path their own development had followed and it accorded with their commitment to expansionism. Furthermore, it was necessary in order to guarantee the self-regulation of an integrated profession that they should share the autonomy which the universities had won for themselves. Consequently the AUT admitted CAT staff to membership in 1961, thus raising their prestige, and the Robbins report confirmed this upgrading by recommending that the CATs be given full university status. Thus the university profession out-manoeuvred the polity in this period — repulsing the attempt to bring part of higher education under stronger unification, which would have made it more responsive to central directives, and to introduce a form of systematization which would have divided tertiary science in two, making one part a poor relation, compelled to dovetail with other provisions of the local authorities, whilst destroying the integration between the staff, students and activities in the two parts. As a pressure group operating in a socio-economic context highly favourable to university expansion, the AUT was able to withstand and even defeat this attempt at State intervention: it was to be much less successful with the breakdown of consensus politics in the next period, because it stood apart from the two corporate Leviathans amongst whom power was progressively relocated.

The School Teachers, 1964-75

This was the time at which the polity, emerging from the permissiveness of consensus government, told the profession as a whole 'so far but no further'. But this did not take away most of the rights which the teachers had won historically, and as far as the management of knowledge was concerned, government was trying to shut the stable door after the horse had gone. Indeed when the profession succeeded in wresting control of the new Schools Council out of political hands, killing the notion of it as an elite commando unit, the school teachers successfully maintained the primacy of internal initiation as the process responsible for curricular development.

The Schools Council is undoubtedly a triumph of the established teachers' associations. The Schools Council claims that it does not prescribe developments or their take-up in the schools. Nonetheless the Council is one of the largest forces with resources for development work and the associations have a strong voice in determining what it does. In so doing, however, it perpetuates assumptions about institutional autonomy'.[153]

It does and it has to do so, for this autonomy is the very bedrock of internal initiation, without which no amount of professional consensus could be translated directly into change as it is here.

The examinations which had once restrained curricular freedom at all levels and placed an external brake on experimentation had one by one succumbed to professional control: the BEd and the university validated certificate now stood where official certification once held sway; the Certificate of Secondary Education could now dispense with the external authority of academic colleagues, a procedure which in its own day had replaced the Education Department's 'Standards'; the 11+ and the earlier scholarship examinations had given way to teachers' assessments and subjective recommendations. With the erosion of formal public examinations, the barriers between levels were broken down and progressive methods could have free play throughout the schools, rather than being confined to the primary level. The NUT threw its organizational strength behind these changes, partly because this integration between stages was favourable to the assimilation of primary and secondary teachers (and their salary scales) and partly because it had itself become a lumbering engine for progressive change.

'The Union has advanced views well in line with the progressive consensus. . . In its evidence to every consultative committee and central council it has protested the need for informality in schools, for curriculum related to children's interests, for the emancipation of schools from the artificial pressures imposed by external examinations or the demands of employers; and was thus party to the flexible arrangements for the Certificate of Secondary Education. It has therefore found common cause with the teacher training system, H.M. Inspectors of Schools and the doctrines enunciated by successive committees and Central Advisory Councils'.[154]

This common cause reached its climateric with the Plowden Committee Report, after which the progressive consensus was strained to breaking point by an internal radicalization which produced its own opponents through a polarization of values. The debate between them must be assessed in terms of the relationship between pedagogic values and the requirements of different parts of society, since the profession now had the power to meet or deny them. The new radicalism which permeated the universities and colleges influencing younger practising teachers and educational journalists, shades off into left wing political extremism, underground culture, encounter groups and the various liberation movements. Its common denominators are a repudiation of professionalism, an image of teachers as sources of information rather than expertise, an inversion of the teacher-pupil relationship where the latter becomes the guide, a rejection of positions of authority, privilege and control, a desire to see secondary schools as voluntary participatory communities, a diffuse wish to stop education maintaining the social structure and a disregard for educational standards as traditionally defined.

This new radicalism stimulated its own critics: first from the NAS, which found academic excellence a better cause than male chauvinism, from the Campaign for the Defence of Academic Standards, from the Black Paper group and from Dr Rhodes Boyson in Parliament. The media were as ready to document indiscipline, illiteracy and exercises of anti-authoritarianism as they had been to publicize trendy methods. This movement is equally eclectic, embracing many who simply think things have 'gone too far' and want to get the grammar books and maths tables out of the cupboard, the disciplinarians who also want the desks and cane brought back in, academics who have found that 'more meant a lot worse', and a variety of employers wanting greater application and a better attitude towards work. These various grievances have crystallized around reading ability for, as Robert Lowe explained a century earlier, this is the most measurable aspect of attainment at school. It was such pressures which culminated in the Bullock Committee on Reading Standards in the School. In many ways the great debate on literacy epitomizes professional divisions about how they should exercise their new responsibilities to the community in general.

The radicals refuse to devote their powers over the management of knowledge to the purpose of socio-economic reproduction. On the contrary, knowledge must be employed to transform the system of social stratification and this means withdrawing the traditional high status attached to 'bourgeois' knowledge and reattaching it to popular speech and culture. It is from this perspective that working class expression is held to have a vitality and virility unknown to formal language codes, a flexibility linked to creativity which is only stunted by grammatical rectitude, and above all a contemporary relevance as a verbal medium as compared with the stilted written English used in outmoded forms of communication. If the radical teacher discharges his responsibility to society by the advancement of the working class, and does so by re-evaluating their culture, his opponent sees this as a deliberate attempt to rob this group of the total cultural heritage, through depriving them of the literacy and literary apparatus which give access to it. The former appears to condemn authority but he is the new anti-intellectual authoritarian who creates the new deprived: the latter will do what he can to universalize intellectual skills (numeracy as well as literacy) but he will probably end up confirming much of the cultural capital acquired in the home rather than in the school. Against this background parental mobilization has increased dramatically through groups like the National Education Association ('Preserve the best: improve the rest'),[155] the National Confederation of Parent-Teacher Associations, CASE and the Advisory Centre for Education which jointly promote a Home and School Council, and many others with specialist concerns — physical punishment, nursery schooling, comprehensive reorganization and so forth. Obviously these reflect different kinds of opinions and cannot be assimilated en bloc to either side of the professional debate. Above all they represent a determination that a debate of such importance should neither be conducted nor concluded by the teaching professional alone, which should not be allowed to define the community's interests for it nor make unilateral decisions about which parts of society it will serve.

Given the high degree of autonomy won by the schools and the firm commitment of different groups of teachers to using internal initiation for the pursuit of different pedagogical values, several consequences follow. Firstly the normative battle will be fought out on the floor of the classroom, and perhaps in the school hall if parental mobilization continues, but it cannot be terminated imperatively, the negotiating strength of the teachers is too great for this. Secondly, therefore, the future direction taken by schooling depends on whether a new professional consensus emerges. At present it seems that the radical politicized trend is gaining ascendancy, and it will probably tend to do so as it is strongest among the young. However, the struggles of the seventies have shown that professional consensus is a fragile mechanism for steering through a consistent policy by means of internal initiation, for the very autonomy on which this process of change relies can immediately be used by dissenting groups to reorient instruction to different goals. At the present time the most likely scenario appears to be an overall development (with temporary reversals, intermittent scandals, affairs and revelations, and pockets of intense resistance), towards the radical pedagogy. Finally, since the assertion of radicalism and the defence of standards both depend upon, and work through, the autonomy of schools the joint effect of the changes they introduce will be increased 'centrifugalism', the avoidance of central controls, repulsion of unification and resistance to the external imposition of systematization. There is no doubt that successive governments have become increasingly concerned about their loss and control and the current employment of the four political tactics against the professional constitutes an attempt to contain internal initiation and increase the importance of political manipulation in directing educational change at all three levels. However, the balance between the respective negotiating strengths of polity and profession is such that although government can intervene to modify 'who' has access to different stages of instruction (e.g. comprehensivization), to different types of institution (e.g. the binary policy and administrative regulation of the Training Colleges), and different kinds of qualifications (e.g. the CNAA); 'what' gets taught in all establishments is defined by the teachers and the ability to do this is defended as their main acquired right. As will be seen in higher education too, the resulting pattern of change is the product of this tense dialectic between internal initiation and political manipulation, although in the universities external transactions do retain something of their old importance.

The Academics, 1965-75

'The 1960s were the most marked watershed in the history of British universities since the rise of the civic colleges in the 1870s and 1880s',[156] but whereas the latter had pulled themselves up by their bootstrings, the new post-Robbins universities were created *de nouveau* with full degree granting powers. They had, unlike any English university before them, not excepting Keele, sufficient resources and autonomy to choose how they would develop and who they would serve. Unlike the civic universities they had no corporate orientation to industry built into their foundations, and, given the freedom to choose, they followed rather different lines. Thus specialization in various directions was one of the major patterns produced by internal initiation at the new universities, but there was also unity in the midst of this diversity.

All of the new institutions also devoted their powers to initiating substantial developments in the social sciences. Partly this resulted from scarcity of resources in relation to the numerical intake targets, for as the Home Universities Conference had forseen with considerable pre-science in 1955 — 'To achieve expansion on this scale without astro-nomic costs, the arts and social studies would have to be encouraged rather than technology'.[157] Partly too it reflected the changing prefer-ences and qualifications of school leavers. But both of these imply a passive university acquiescence to factors and forces beyond their control, whilst in fact there was something a good deal more positive about these decisions: in the professional value system expansion was viewed as an act of social justice in its own right and given priority over any particularistic service to a given sector of society. It was not that the universities despised or rejected industrial transactions at this stage, indeed we have seen that half of the new foundations encouraged them, it was only that given a choice between slower growth with higher per capita costs, which scientific development implied, or more rapid growth of the cheaper social sciences, the professional generally pre-ferred to initiate the latter. Hence the 'paradox that whereas the talk of politicians was the need for technologists and applied scientists the new universities devoted so much of their resources to the arts and social sciences'.[158] In many ways, this paradox was rooted in the Robbins report which had assumed that expansion on grounds of social justice would entail a complementary boost to economic development, with-out clearly specifying the relationship between these two processes. It was also grounded in the alacrity with which industry, commerce and bureaucracy had recruited *all* graduates in the fifties.

There was some mismatch between the lines upon which the uni-versities had chosen to develop and industrial requirements but it was more than this alone which prompted the introduction of the Binary system in the mid-sixties: this was a political judgement on university values as embodied in their recent programmes of internal initiation. Although it was true that industry was unenthusiastic about the social scientists this did not mean firms were deprived of the services they required — after all the Technological Universities (the upgraded CATs) were fully committed to close interaction with industry as were some of the plateglass institutions. At its core, the conflict between the State and the academics was less concerned with a failure to teach the appropriate skills than to socialize into the appropriate values: it was more a question of social control than a problem about academic content. For at precisely the time when outspoken lecturers were advocating social disengagement on the part of the universities, the Labour Party was gearing itself up for new phase of politico-economic intervention which was to culminate in its Industrial Relations Bill. Thus the polity was trying to drive society towards a State 'socialism', predicted on management of the major social institutions, whilst many academics were leading their students to adopt a radical and critical stance whose nurture depended upon the institutional autonomy of universities. The former involved undermining the conditions which permitted internal initiation to hinder social planning, by imposing a higher degree of systematization: the latter on defending them in order to prevent the universities from becoming part of the State apparatus through a move towards greater unification.

However, the debate was not reducible to this simple two-sided conflict. The radicalization of professional values had generated a significant amount of internal opposition on the part of academics who deplored the politicization of university studies and its attendant threat to intellectual standards. But on the whole these opponents of the Critical University were far from being the friends of the State University, and their attempt to found an Independent University of their own collected flack from both sides — the radicals denounced its engagement with industry, the government condemned its disengagement from the political centre, the former blackening its reputation with students, the latter denying it the right to grant degrees. That it survived at all as an act of internal initiation, contributing to the diversity of higher education in England, gives an indication that the encroachment of political control in this period had not fundamentally undermined the freedom of autonomous action on the part of academics, or enmeshed all institutions in its drive towards a new administrative unification. That it was founded and maintained is a pointer to the fact that the profession as a whole has not embraced the new radical orthodoxy.

Political Manipulation

The Education Act, 1918

In the first two decades after the 1902 Act the process of political manipulation was dominated by a struggle over systematization or more precisely by the conflict between those advocating the positive or the negative principle of hierarchical integration. The effect of political interaction during this time was the exact opposite of the changes introduced through the other two processes: whilst the overall result of external transactions was to amplify systemic differentiation and the effect of internal initiation was to increase systemic specialization, political manipulation reduced both of these characteristics. This was partly because the State imposed greater co-ordination but it was also the unintended consequence of the pursuit of other goals, particularly that of educational democratization by the political centre.

The 1902 Act had clearly specified the different types of schools making up the elementary system but had not particularized the components of the secondary level, leaving this to the LEAs as they made provisions suitable to their areas. The building up of the secondary system was thus accomplished by administrative action in the years immediately following the Act. Quantitatively the secondary sector was extremely small — in 1902 the Board recognized 272 secondary schools in receipt of grant aid, with about 30,000 pupils, exactly the same number as the pupil-teachers enrolled that year, though of course in post-elementary rather than secondary institutions.[159] Qualitatively the grammar schools modelled themselves closely on the academic tradition of the *private* sector.

> The cementing of the public school system, under the guidance of the Headmasters' Conference, introduced a new and powerful factor on the educational scene, providing also a rallying point for the remaining endowed grammar schools which were passing through difficult days. It was the continued pressure of such interested bodies that ensured the establishment of a secondary schools department of the Board of Education when this came into being in 1899; that department, staffed by ex-public school and university men, was responsible for administering the regulations governing all other secondary schools. . . these regulations imposed both on the grammar schools and the newly developing municipal secondary schools the academic tradition of education that had been given a new lease of life in public schools.[160]

Hence the 1904 Regulations denigrated the alternative definitions of secondary instruction which had developed in the more practical Higher Grade Schools, quasi-vocational Science schools and Technical Day Schools in favour of a single literary and academic bias. Standardization was the main theme and a great loss of diversity was involved in

> the aggregation of schools which Morant welded, within a few short years, into a recognizable system with considerable unity of purpose: shabby genteel yet incredibly snobbish endowed grammar schools, driven by poverty alone into

the life-giving embrace of the LEAs; private 'secondary' schools, many equally
snobbish, of all grades of quality from excellent to indifferent, or worse;
pupil-teacher centres, some very good, some mere cram shops; higher grade
and higher elementary schools, including 'organized science schools' in which
fifteen hours or more a week might be allocated to scientific subjects; and
entirely new 'municipal' secondary schools conjured out of the rates by the
newly created LEAs.[61]

This effect was intensified, and of course had implications for future
educational reproduction, when the Pupil Teachers Centres were assimilated to the secondary schools:[162] not only did this close another
avenue to working class talent, it acculturated the cleverest pupils,
winning bursarships, into the academic knowledge system of the middle
class. In this connection the scholarship system was taken up by the
Board as a 'capacity catching machine',[163] and this narrow conduit
between elementary and secondary schools was the only concession to
the to the positive principle of hierarchical integration.

In general the negative principle reigned: the great majority of
pupils were restricted to the elementary schools as such, and for the
brighter among them the Higher Elementary school was the place for
further education. As explicitly terminal institutions their curricula
could be much more closely geared to the practical requirements of
employers. Indeed this non-academic orientation was vital for distinguishing the HES from the secondary level: as the Consultative
Committee argued in 1906, the more the former 'approximates to a
secondary school of the real type the less it can be said to meet the
needs of the class of children whose education is in question'.[164] In
their vehement condemnation of this policy the NUT and the Labour
movement attacked *both* the class discrimination implicit in the very
conception (the negative systematization) of the HES and the standardization of the secondary schools (loss of differentiation and specialization) which was entailed. The Labour Representation Committee
sought a broad highway to secondary and *technical* education, paved
with maintenance scholarships for all:[165] the NUT damned the class
policy of the Board, declared there was no place for the HES, and
proclaimed that what was needed was a *varied* system of secondary
schools.[166] In the forthcoming interaction these groups could not
sustain *the two* desiderata, they were forced to choose *between* democratization and diversification in secondary education.

The Board's bifurcated policy for post-elementary instruction did
not alter when the Liberals came to office in 1906. The most the new

government would concede to public and professional pressure was the introduction of the free place system in those grammar schools willing to make 25 percent of their places available to elementary pupils in return for an increased grant. With this went a slight liberalization of the concept of secondary education which was no longer just for those of 'exceptional ability', but now for those 'qualified to profit' from it, although the 'attainment test' soon became indistinguishable from competition for scholarships. Internally the secondary schools continued with their literary and academic curriculum, meeting a demand for clerks and commercial recruits[167] and above all for future pupil teachers,[168] relegating scientific and mathematical instruction to a few hours a week, and excluding technical subjects altogether.

In this context the Labour movement's fight for greater equality of educational opportunity meant in practice that it devoted its efforts to maintaining, and if possible extending, the provision of 25 percent of free places *in this kind of secondary school*. In repudiating the HES because they were a formula for inferiority, attempts to democratize the secondary school also meant accepting the superiority of its definition of instruction, or at least acquiescing to it. Thus the Labour movement, despite its long tradition reaching back to the Halls of Science and Mechanics Institutes, collaborated in the freezing-out of technical instruction. 'It was cold-shouldered by the LEAs who, having to find formidable sums for building secondary schools, were in no position to bear the total cost of buildings and equipment for technical colleges. It was cold-shouldered by the upper and middle classes of a society whose 'whole ethos' it has been said, was directed towards 'respectable white-collar jobs' '.[169] Day Technical Classes, Central Schools and Trade Schools of a vocational orientation, all lived a twilight existence. The rather grudging recognition by the Board in 1913, of the Day Classes as Junior Technical Schools was coupled with the usual injunction to confine themselves to the lower rungs of the occupational ladder (the artisanat), and not to aspire to prepare their pupils for any type of higher education. As a contribution to diversification their recognition hinged on the acceptance of terminal status and of non-integration with secondary education proper. Thus both technical and vocational instruction suffered considerable relegation in the schools and gained no purchase on adult education which was also cast in the mould of liberal generalism.

In the build-up to the 1918 Education Act, the political manipulation of the Labour movement was directed at increasing equality of opportunity: although secondary school intake had increased, only 5% of 10-11 year olds in elementary schools transferred to the former and the odds against such children gaining a free secondary education were 40 to 1.[170] In the Bradford Charter, adopted by the ILP and the Parliamentary Labour Party, secondary education for all meant a common school for all with a common course[171] and showed the supreme priority accorded to positive systematization in the sense that equality was to be bought at the price of uniformity. This left the NUT and WEA as the only pressure groups advocating differentiation amongst *secondary schools themselves,* the former talking about 'different types' of school, the latter agreeing and adding the need for a 'more variable' curriculum.[172] Obviously none of these groups were enamoured of the Continuation School, the most distinctive feature of the Bill, and one which Fisher explained would allow some vocational and regional variation, since once again it associated differentiation and specialization with an inferior and non-secondary branch of instruction. The lack of enthusiasm for the Continuation School on the left was rendered colourless in comparison with the hostility exhibited to it on the part of the FBI, which emerged in the year of revolution 'jaunty and unabashed clamouring that whatever else in shaken, the vested interests of employers in the labour of children of 14 must not be disturbed by so much as eight hours a week'.[173]

Ironically the reactions of the two extremes collaborated in maintaining the status quo: Labour only wished to talk about radical reform of the secondary schools, for which they had no parliamentary support: industry only wanted to kill the novel aspect of the bill, the Continuation Schools, and had just enough parliamentary support to do so, since postponing their introduction turned out to be only a stay of execution. Thus under 'the 1918 Education Act the structure of the education system was not markedly altered'.[174] This was even truer by 1922, when the Cabinet released the LEAs from their responsibility under the Act to plan for Continuation Schools, as part of the cut-back in public spending. The Liberal contribution to change had involved no structural reorganization; they had raised the leaving age to 14, abolished the half-time system and increased the numbers[175] and the free places in secondary schools. The last Education Act of the Liberal Party only abrogated the negative principle of systematization by a slight reinforcement of the frail scholarship ladder. Thus from 1902 onwards the expansion of secondary provisions had meant quite simply an increase in Grammar School places, which in turn spelt wider diffusion of the traditional literary and academic definition of instruction.

The Education Act, 1944

In the interwar period we have seen that the major concern expressed through political manipulation centered on the nature of systematization and the degree of differentiation which should accompany it. When discussing the process of political manipulation it was clear that during the years of economic crisis interest groups made the most intensive use of every official and political channel affecting educational policy as the main, or for many the only, way through which their demands could be met. In now turning to patterns of change it is the complex interplay between these agencies which has to be captured at the points where they shaped educational developments. Here the central/local dimension is of particular importance as far as actual provisions are concerned, for the relative autonomy of the local authorities meant that they could instigate, anticipate, redirect, reinforce, modify or resist central directives. At all times the local politics of education were shaping and reshaping the practicacontext in which central political debates took place, and the characteristics of that context had to be taken into account by any party programme, consultative investigation, Board regulation or of course any piece of parliamentary legislation.

This protracted period of national economy was not rich in large scale changes, the money was simply not forthcoming, especially from the centre, and what happened at the end of the First World War set the financial scene for the interwar years . . . 'it seems evident that what succeeding economy campaigns achieved was the undermining of precisely that central government support for educational development which Fisher had clearly identified as essential. This policy implied negating the one piece of forward-looking legislation passed at the war's end'.[176] The Continuation Schools were the most obvious target in the first economy drive: many authorities were drawing up schemes in conformity with Section 10 of the 1918 Act and seven LEAs were ready to begin when the Cabinet agreed, despite Fisher's protest, to relieve them of this statutory obligation. Certain authorities struggled to start such schools, usually helped by support from employers, but with the abandonment of obligatory attendance most failed to survive the twenties on this voluntary basis, Rugby being the lone exception.[177] However, Section 2 (i) (a) placed a duty on local authorities 'to make, or otherwise secure, adequate and suitable provision by means of central or special classes or otherwise' of practical instruction and advanced instruction for intelligent children or those remaining beyond the statutory leaving age.[178] As a vaguer and more general requirement this did not lend itself to the same systematic stoppage as that inflicted on the Continuation School, and by 1921 158 LEAs claimed to be making some such provision. Probably many did not go very far, and some were doing precious little, but the LCC kept its system of Central Schools going, giving a four year course, and this was followed in Manchester and other northern authorities. Autonomy cuts both ways; it was the case then in 'English Educational Administration that local authorities could with impunity be laggard or reactionary in their provision, thus denying children (and adults) in their areas opportunities available in areas of enlightened and progressive authorities'.[179] However, given the deepest protest on the part of the AEC about the way in which the Geddes cuts had rendered the vital clauses of the 1918 Act inoperative,[180] it is not surprising to find some authorities pushing ahead to make what provisions they could in accordance with the law, but without any political or economic encouragement. Cumulatively 'slight though this provision was, it had an important impact on the future of secondary education in England'[181] for it represented the only concrete challenge to the hegemony of the Morant definition of secondary instruction.

So began a repeat performance of the Higher Grade School sequence. First there were the Central Schools which the LCC had pioneered, and it was now running 51 of them. These were selective schools with a commercial or industrial bias whose courses lasted until 15. Tawney had condemned them as 'cheap substitutes' in relation to 'secondary education for all', but they were a considerable improvement on the all-age schools which more than 90 percent of children attended in 1920. Next there were non-selective Senior Schools recruiting all at 11, as in Leicester, and other variations on the Upper Elementary School or Department. The significance of these developments is not restricted to their experimental character: by 1925 Central and Senior Schools provided two-thirds as many places for those over 11 as did the secondary schools — hence it is not unrealistic to begin to speak of the emergence of an alternative definition of secondary instruction, especially when account is taken of a third development. This was the clutch of Technical Day schools, Junior Technical and Trade Schools, post-elemetary in character and usually offering a two-year course, from the age of 13, geared to some particular trade or industry. At their upper end the Technical Colleges provided a popular form of vocational instruction which succeeded in launching a scheme of National Certificates and Diplomas, initiated by the Institution of Mechanical Engineers with the approval of the Board in 1921. Diplomas could be gained through full-time study, certificates through part-time attendance and both were available at ordinary and higher levels (ONC, OND, HNC, HND). Their initial popularity enabled further schemes to be started, even during the worst time of retrenchment: chemistry (1922), electrical engineering (1923), navel architecture (1927), building (1930), and this 'was one of the few innovations which survived the recurrent economy freezes during the war'.[182] Finally, it was possible for a determined local authority to provide the facilities for full secondary education, and Bradford led the way with nine 'municipal secondary schools', providing for 27 percent of the age group, in addition to its Central Schools.

In other words, local autonomy was harnessed to a new push upwards, to a re-blurring of the distinction between elementary and secondary instruction, and to an increasing diversification and experimentation in the curriculum for those over eleven.

> 'It was precisely because an example could thus be set, that the relative freedom given to local authority planning under the 1918 Act was deprecated by Conservatives and not only because of over-reaching the limits of permissible expenditure. Such independence was the more to be feared as the prospect of important urban authorities falling to Labour opened up. Earlier the cry for economy had served its turn in putting a brake on advance. But in 1925 a second direct attempt to use this argument met with a check, not least because it was coupled with definite plans to curb local authority powers to plan'.[183]

We will return to these financial machinations in a moment, for in 1926 this example which was being set locally received a considerable boost from the publication of the Hadow Report, *The Education of the Adolescent*. Essentially Hadow argued that this outgrowth should be fostered and it endorsed these independent achievements: indeed in some ways the report was 'considerably behind the practice of the most progressive LEAs, and of many teachers in maintained as well as independent schools'.[184] Thus the Consultative Committee reinforced the independent innovations of LEAs and the internal initiation of the professional in the face of governmental antagonism. What is more Hadow reproduced a manoeuvre, classic in decentralized systems, of basing its recommendations for the nation on local precedents which advanced areas has shown to work in practice. In advocating variety in post-elementary education, Hadow not only legitimated these innovations, it actually incorporated them into its organizational proposals — the six types of school held up as recommended models corresponded to the six types in being.[185] (This cycle was duplicated in the same classic form by Circular 10/65, which dealt with comprehensive reorganization). The report was warmly received by the local authorities and it galvanized their efforts to continue with reorganization, adaptation and innovation, especially since there was now a possibility of extracting additional funds from the Board for rebuilding. Hence the County Councils Association recommended all local authorities to formulate schemes for 'Hadow reorganization', thus completing the positive feed-back loop.

The stringent economy cuts of these years were not simply a blanket restriction on educational development throughout the country. Following the halt in 1920, when the obligation on LEAs to implement the 1918 Act in full was removed, the Geddes Committee took another stride into the field of policy when it proposed economizing on free places in secondary schools: 'disapproval continued to be expressed by all sections of the educational world, including Lord Burnham, at the increasing control of the central authority, by means of economic cuts, over educational policy and expenditure. This meant the negation of reforms passed by Parliament'.[186] This attempt to 'stabilize' the grant to the LEAs, a euphemism for pegging the budget to the level of earlier years, was soon followed by a direct assault on the 50 percent grant in 1926. The percentage grant under the Fisher Act had been an undoubted incentive to local initiative and active authorities, for by it the Exchequer guaranteed to match local expenditure on a pound for pound basis. Instead, under the Economy Bill, no grant was to be made towards any LEA expenditure which 'in the opinion of the Board is excessive, having regard to the circumstances of the area of the authority, or the general standard of expenditure in other areas'.[187] Not only was this an increase in central power, it was also a piece of manipulation which reversed the previous incentive scheme by one which would effectively drag all authorities down towards the level of the most laggardly. The AEC and CCA protested in the strongest terms about this attempt to change the law by the back door. They only won a reprieve from this Bill and from a subsequent proposal to replace the percentage grant for education by a block grant for all local authority services, because the General Strike happened to intervene.

The desire not to exacerbate social conflict led to a temporary stay of execution which was prolonged by the Labour interregnum of 1929-31. This government was unable, however, to do more than hold the line: its proposal to raise the school leaving age, providing maintenance payments for needy cases, was rejected by the Lords on grounds of economy. The Party waited too long before deciding to push this through in 1931 under the Parliament Act, for it was itself diplaced during the renewed economic crisis that year. Besides a 10 percent increase in free places at secondary schools and a small growth in university grants, its main achievement was the temporary restimulation of Hadow reorganization. 'Less immediately tangible, but important in the long run, were the improved grants on capital expenditure towards reorganization – of which the more enlightened authorities took immediate advantage and from which many children subsequently profited in reorganized schools'.[188] Within a year the axe fell again, in the form of the May recommendations to the National Government, and again it was the autonomous developments of the most active authorities which were cut most. In their original form these economies were to include the abolition of the percentage grant, a cut in teachers salaries by 20 percent, the raising of secondary fees by 25 percent, and the withdrawal of all free secondary school places in favour of remission of fees on the basis of a strict means test. Only the third suggestion remained totally unimplemented: after a hard fight the percentage principle for the central grant was salvaged, but the 50 percent minimum was lost. At the Labour Party Conference of 1932, Trevelyan argued that the Government's reversal of his policies had thus thrown down a class challenge, and had said to the progressive areas 'you have had your children educated in secondary schools for a generation, but that is now at an end. You shall go down to the level of those backward authorities who know how to keep the working people in their places. Now I say that means class war'.[189] In many areas Hadow reorganization was brought almost to a standstill and this was particularly deleterious for those authorities which had not yet got off the mark and had been too slow to profit from Trevelyan's capital expenditure grants. It is this which accounts for 78 percent of rural schools, usually under Conservative Authorities, still remaining as all-age establishments in 1938, undivided into Junior and Senior institutions.[190]

The effect of these centrally imposed cuts crippled any increase in educational opportunity and imposed a governmental policy of stasis which was diametrically opposed to the dominant orientation of the local authorities. Since they now put up most of the money,[191] and believed more and more sturdily that they should have a strong say in how it was spent – not only did they band together to oppose the cuts, thus becoming a more concerted pressure group in which the non-radical CCA was often found fighting alongside the AEC, but also they increasingly took their place in the anti-government lobby. They had never been less the agents of central government than during this time of retrenchment and these attitudes were to remain when the economic situation improved in the mid-thirties.

Thus the AEC and CCA were prominent in the School Age Council of 1934 where they argued rightly that the failure to raise the leaving age was a major barrier to Hadow reorganization, since it prevented the development of proper post-elementary courses. Certain LEAs were operating in defiance of the secondary school regulations, ignoring restrictions on the proportion admitted free, or at reduced fees, and this was sufficient to prevent a drop in the number of places available in the thirties, though Wales was exceptional in achieving a rate of almost 70 percent. The LCC, under Labour control for the first time, took a stand in 1934 against separate regulations for elementary, technical and secondary instruction, announcing its commitment to introducing the multilateral school in due course. In other words, the local councillors and profession met the end of austerity in combative mood and what they met with were not even half measures. All the National Government would do in 1935 was to legalize defiance of the regulations governing the number of secondary places. A year later the raising of the school leaving age to 15 was conceded, but without maintenance allowances and with exemptions for those in 'beneficial employment' between the ages of 14-15. This was condemned by a joint conference of the AEC, NUT, TUC and WEA, the first of these attempting some local resistance by refusing to grant exemptions. Since the official raising of the leaving age was delayed for three years (and then postponed by the outbreak of war), the main effect of the 1936 Act was financial – additional support for building senior elementary schools and thus for resuming Hadow reorganization.

Thus it was the local authorities which made the running between the wars. Their divergence from central policy is understandable: during 14½ years of Conservative rule (including the National Governments) every President of the Board had been at Eton, whilst the permanant staff of the LEAs were usually the products of elementary schooling. They had got nearly half-way with Hadow reorganization by 1938 (48 percent of schools were now divided into Senior and Junior Departments)[192] working against the centre for most of this time; they had slightly increased opportunities with the help of a declining birthrate (for the percentage of ex-elementary pupils in secondary schools rose from 9.5 percent in 1920 to 14.3 percent in 1938); they had improved the chances of obtaining a free secondary education (30 percent paid no fees in 1920, 47 percent in 1938); and they had attempted to provide and diversify post-elementary schooling and thus sponsored alternative definitions of instruction to the academicism of the grammar school. As far as the latter were concerned Tawney was substantially correct in his harsh judgement on the practical outcome of Hadow reorganization, made in 1934 — 'What has been put in the place of an enlarged system of secondary education is an improvement in the later stages of elementary education'.[193] The main exception, the technical schools which were generating a sound Real definition of secondary instruction, had been contained by a combination of government spending cuts and their higher capital requirements. Thus the Junior Technical Schools catered for only about 3 percent of the age groups,[194] whilst the maintained secondary schools, still of the Morant cast, took in 20 percent;[195] nevertheless, technical schooling did represent a successful element of differentiation which was to survive the war.

In Butler's own view the 1944 Act 'recast' the existing educational system; it did not and was not intended to replace it. Because the processes of change had been at work since 1902, a malintegrated if not chaotic array of provisions had accumulated by the Second World War — the products of weak unification which had permitted their autonomous development. 'The uncoordinated development of primary and secondary, further and university education, and of different categories of schools and colleges has always tended to make the pattern of English Education complicated and overlapping'.[196] The Act itself was mainly addressed to tightening up the administrative framework as a precondition for bringing about a better co-ordination of these component parts. It pinpointed certain inherited administrative characteristics as defective in this respect: at the centre the division of the Board into separate branches, regulating elementary, secondary, technical and university levels in isolation from one another did not lend itself to monitoring the whole of an authority's activities. Similarly the co-existence, in a number of regions, of two separate authorities dealing de facto with secondary education (the Part 111 Authorities, i.e. boroughs and urban councils responsible solely for elementary provisions, which operated alongside the larger county authorities) meant that the former frequently established Central or Senior schools in direct competition with the County Grammar School.[197] These serious barriers to co-ordination were eradicated as part of the main thrust of the Act which was to strengthen the Centre as a means of bringing about the systematization of provisions.

Whilst the Act itself stressed the importance of increased systematization, insisting that education was a progressive process which should be arranged in three end-on stages, rationalizing the boundaries of LEAs and making each responsible for the provision of the three, and enforcing the provision of free secondary education for all which offered a variety of instruction and training, *it did not determine the principles on which co-ordination should be based.* The obligations just specified are of course broad enough to be met by a number of different organizational formulae and most importantly they do not determine the adoption of either the positive or the negative principle of hierarchical integration. For example to insist that the various stages are 'end-on' says nothing about how many will transfer from the second to the third, or whether adjacent stages will be integrated, with one preparing for the next (for the Act remained silent on curriculum), or whether some establishments can be designed as terminal while others lead on to the final stage.

What the Act did do was to make this decision about the principle of systematization a matter largely of Ministerial responsibility. It was his duty under Section I 'to secure the effective execution by local authorities, under his control and direction, of the national policy for providing a varied and comprehensive educational service in every area'.[198] An attempt to move an amendment deleting the words 'under his control and direction' was rejected and Butler successfully retained the clauses which would allow the central authority to 'lead boldly and not follow timidly'.[199] This did not fundamentally destroy the dual central-local control of the decentralized system, but it shifted the balance of power from the latter to the former, who could now make judgements about the overall principles of structural development and also determine which organizational arrangements were compatible with them.

According to Section II, each LEA had to submit a development plan within a year showing *how* they were going to make sufficient primary and secondary provisions in conformity with the Act.[200] It was now of course open to LEAs to submit plans for multi-lateral reorganization, and these were admitted for London and Coventry where substantial new building was required in any case. Bilateral schools were also permitted in certain sparsely populated areas which could not support separate types of schools. In other words, Ministerial discretion was very great, much greater than that enjoyed by the old President of the Board, and sufficient to shape educational policy by encouraging certain local proposals and discouraging others, especially since it was reinforced by the power to intervene when any LEA, or Board of Managers or Governors was acting or proposing to act unreasonably.[201] On the other hand, the initiative for change still resided with the local authorities and Parliament was the immediate arbiter of disputes between the LEAs and the Minister over development plans. Unification had undoubtedly been increased, but some scope remained for the nature of systematization to be thrashed out *between* the central and the local authorities, for the former had not acquired the power to direct change, only to guide it, and the latter remained partners in educational development, not subordinate agents, unlike the distribution of powers in the centralized system.

The struggle over systematization continued in the wake of the 1944 Act and it fell into two distinct phases. In the first both Parties, following one another in office, used the new central powers embodied in the Act. They devoted them to the tripartite reorganization of secondary education and introduced an unprecedented degree of systematization which, during the period of consensus politics, must have appeared as a steady drift towards centralization. However, tripartism was a modified version of the negative principle of hierarchical organization (since it meant that the schools attended by 75 percent of children were intentionally designed as terminal institutions) and egalitarian forces, working through political manipulation at the local level, challenged this by developing the comprehensive school. The second phase then involved a gradual switch to the positive principle, the emplacement of the broad educational ladder spanning secondary education to link the primary to the tertiary stages, but this also involved sloughing off the higher level of unification and of systematization which had followed the Act. The comprehensive movement, based on the initiative of the local authorities, meant that 'moves in Britain towards creating a unified and open system of secondary education appear slow and indecisive, rather than hurried and doctrinaire'.[202] Comprehensive reorganization followed the *incremental pattern* of educational change, but since its building bricks were the diverse experimental schemes generated independently by the local authorities, their summation did not represent a neat and orderly form of systematization. Instead local initiative had again reinforced organizational differentiation and curricular specialization, and the pre-eminence of these two characteristics was once more threatening the overall integration of the educational system.

The 1944 Act had specified nothing about the structure of secondary education, it had merely imposed two organizational constraints — that children must be educated in *separate* primary and secondary schools, and that at the age of 11 *all* must transfer from the former to the latter. Eventually even those limitations were to be swept away in the course of political interaction, but the immediate response was to link the two levels by selective examination which allocated pupils to one of three types of secondary school. Organizationally this involved a nation-wide reintegration of all the autonomous innovations, which had surfaced between the wars, into this tripartite framework — a task accomplished in the first decade after the Act by Labour and Conservative governments working in concert with the Ministry.

Thus the variagated Senior, Intermediate and Central schools were all collapsed into the Secondary Modern School providing a general and practical instruction, but one which led to no examination or qualification — a fierce judgement on the inability of the former to implant a clear and distinctive definition of instruction in the interwar period. In many ways their incorporation into the Secondary Modern School repeated the collapse of the Higher Grade Schools into Higher Elementary schools, in that this too condemned upward striving and confined exploratory ventures by depriving them of the right to award qualifications which others might want or recognize. Secondly, the majority of Technical, Trade and Junior Commercial Colleges became Technical Schools after 1944, and were later brought into line to start at 11 and to run in parallel with the other two types of school. Technical instruction, though historically clear about its educational function, had never been geographically widespread. The higher per-capita costs of establishing Technical Schools which had always held them back continued to do so as top priority was given to 'finishing-off Hadow', that is to abolishing the numerous all-age schools by building separate secondary schools as quickly and cheaply as possible, which in practice meant the construction of secondary moderns. Thus the technical schools never enrolled as much as 5 percent of the age group and remained trapped in a vicious circle in which their unfamiliarity led to a low level of demand, which kept this more expensive provision small and prevented it from acquiring the public status which it was well equipped to earn. In the early fifties Glass found that amongst parents of children in the last year of primary school over half wanted their sons and daughters to enter a Grammar School, whilst those preferring the Technical School (20 percent) were barely greater than those (16 percent) who favoured the Secondary Modern.[203] England remained historically incapable of generating and sustaining a Real definition of education to which prestige was attached. The main reason of course was the endurance of the Morant Grammar School which had sedulously received every structural and cultural support for half a century. The result was to leave the hegemony of academicism unchallenged and this now became the reward for the most intelligent 20 percent of pupils.

These three types of schools, with their supposed parity of status, represented the precise degree of differentiation and specialization which was allowed in the new secondary education. In fact, of course, this entailed a massive reduction of these two characteristics in the system as a whole and involved a more wide-reaching standardization than ever before in English education. Indeed the official tripartite policy became narrower still and was effectively bipartite in many LEAs which contained no technical schools. The priority given to 'finishing Hadow' built up the Secondary Moderns at their expense and thus intensified the segregation between 'grammar school sheep and modern school goats'.[204] Just as the old Board had cleared the middle ground between the primary school and the secondary school after the 1902 Act, so now official policy tidied away any intermediary (except the Technical School) between the Grammar School for the elite and the Secondary Modern school for the mass after the 1944 Act. On the other hand, the academic definition of instruction enshrined in the grammar schools, reached downwards to the junior schools preparing for the 11+, and spread laterally when the secondary moderns copied the grammar schools and prepared for the GCE, thus blurring the distinction between the two types of schools. The fact that many of their pupils succeeded was another nail in the coffin for selection, but at the same time it limited diversity still further for the modern schools never did elaborate an alternative definition of instruction. The initial absence of examinations, intended to allow them to develop freely and to secure parity of esteem through their own efforts, placed them in an impossible position but in trying to break out of it by entering pupils for recognized examinations, they were condemned to a thoroughly second rate status.[205]

Both political parties had fostered this standardization and in doing so had often overriden the preferences of local authorities. Whilst only a small number of LEAs had so disregarded Ministerial advice as to plan for multilateral schools (though about 5.5 percent of schools in the postwar reorganization plans were designed as comprehensives), nevertheless few wanted the tripartite system in its unadulterated state.[206] Moreover, the handful of multi-lateral schools which were admitted by the Ministry had to be very large so as to accommodate grammar, technical and modern streams within them — thus they were merely to carry tripartism into one building and not to develop something different (Circular 144, June 1947). It was on these grounds that the Labour government rejected both the Middlesex and North Riding plans since they proposed the small comprehensive school of American experience which could be introduced quickly by using existing buildings. When Labour left office in 1951 there were only twelve comprehensive schools in being (and some more 'approved'): when the Conservatives finished their first term of office there were less than fifty and the first purpose built comprehensive had only opened in 1954. It was not building costs per se which restrained this development. In Coventry where bombing had necessitated rebuilding, the Conservative Minister insisted on the experimental nature of the new multilateral schools and of their construction in such a way that they could later be split up on tripartite lines.

Comprehensive Reorganization

Thus any innovations outside the tripartite framework in these years were due to the influence of a few committed LEAs, working against the centre. The comprehensive ideal recruited significant support from amongst teachers and administrators well before the 1944 Act and for this reason some of the earliest reorganization plans embodied this principle. The LCC had pursued this ideal from 1934 onwards. A number of rural areas (Westmorland, Anglesey and the Isle of Man), presumably encouraged by official references to the special problems of sparsly populated areas, dating back to the Spens Report, proposed smaller comprehensive schools. In addition various county boroughs

(Bolton, Oldham, Reading and Southend) planned for a single secondary school. By the mid-fifties the LCC and Coventry plans were being implemented (both had awaited rebuilding), the rual areas had been operating their comprehensive schools for a few years (Windermere was the first to open in 1945), and a number of experimental schools, like the two salvaged from the rejected Middlesex plan and the Calder High School which the West Riding had been able to open because it possessed a building erected immediately before the war, were now in action and accumulating experience. All these developments represented hard won concessions from both parties in government, and most had only got through with a label reading 'experimental status' or 'special circumstances' attached to them.

From the mid-fifties onwards, however, the local assault on central tripartism began to snowball. Once multilateral schemes were underway, the very political controversy which had surrounded their introduction, guaranteed a flood of visits from other LEAs. Organized parties of visitors were booked to capacity to view Kidbrooke School (the first of the LCC plan) with its five gymnasia, six science laboratories, and nine housecraft centres.[207] The importance of these concrete experiments of comprehensive education in action cannot be exaggerated in terms converting, convincing or clinching the attitudes of other Local Authorities. Mutual influence and imitation amongst the LEAs has continued to be of enormous importance and the fact that the schools are there to be seen has removed the whole debate from airy speculation of an idealistic or pessimistic kind as well as adding to the ranks of comprehensive supporters, for the public relations of the early schools were good. Thus one observer commends the influence of the Leicestershire Plan (the first LEA to become fully comprehensive):

'An enormous number of visitors from England and Overseas have been received and welcomed. One school in less than two years of existence had been visited over 1000 times. Representatives of other LEAs, academics, civil servants, teachers, politicians, are among those who have wished to see for themselves how the Leicestershire schools work in practice. The evidence is that they have been impressed, thus creating a climate of opinion favourable to the policies pursued. The result is that not only have the people inside the system been convinced of the value of the advanced practices but many influential educationalists outside it have seen that they can be generalized throughout a system.[208]

In addition the success of the Leicestershire experiment also demonstrated to many LEAs that given a determined Chief Education Officer,

a well designed plan using existing facilities, and the continuous involvement of all those affected or interested, it was possible to steer through
macroscopic change without ministerial confrontation and despite
certain seemingly discouraging features like a Conservative controlled
County Council.[209]

The actual number of comprehensive schools was still small by the
late fifties, but with the Local Authorities now straining at the leash
'the significant factor — as those responsible for both central and local
administration were now aware — was not so much the number of
schools which has been established as the example that had been set, at
a time when it was becoming more and more difficult to maintain
confidence in the process of selection'.[210] The selection procedures
were the Achilles heel of secondary education, for they were not
supposed to be a competitive examination but a scientific process of
matching child to school. If this claim for accurate allocation could not
be sustained, then the main prop for tripartism fell to the ground and
with it the official rationale which justified restraining public demand
for a longer and better secondary education.

Already with the first wave of comprehensives in the fifties it was
clear that 'innovations are related, one creating the conditions in which
the other could flourish. First was the reorganization . . . of the pattern
of secondary schooling. From this followed a new freedom in the
schools that led to curriculum developments and the use of new
teaching methods'.[211] Certainly the earliest schools felt compelled to
stress that they could compete with the grammar schools in terms of
the *same kinds* of academic attainments, but even here a new note was
sounded — the comprehensives with their larger intakes could offer a
wider range of subjects to their pupils. Even where the smaller rural
schools were concerned the same claim held good and the Headmaster
of the first Anglesey comprehensive school argued that by 1953 his new
sixth form 'has not only increased in numerical strength but has
broadened its field of *specialist* studies.'[212] Equally when summing up
internal changes in school practices in 1955, Pedley highlighted the fact
that 'the whole structure of today's schools of comprehensive type is
based on *differentiation of courses and classes*'.[213] The salience of these
two characteristics was becoming more pronounced as the new schools
struggled out of the bipartite straight-jacket. Early on they rejected the
minimal differentiation into grammar, technical and modern sides[214]
which the polity sought to impose throughout the school, in favour of a
common course at the beginning which led on to a variety of branching

alternatives – in London, for example, technical, craft and commercial courses of different kinds ran in parallel to an 'academic' course.[215] Ultimately this involved a challenge to the exclusively academic definition of instruction, particularly beyond the compulsory leaving age. 'As courses became established more pupils stayed on beyond the leaving age and there began to develop what became known as "the new sixth form". In other words, it was not only pupils staying on to take 'A' level GCE who made up sixth forms but others following secretarial, pre-nursing, or other courses and taking 'O' level subjects at 17. In general more varied sixth forms were developing than those in the traditional grammar schools'.[216] These organizational and curricular developments were pioneered by the Local Authorities against Central resistance – even the Labour Party, which now supported comprehensive reorganization, was still arguing in 1958 that the new schools would preserve the old tradition and give 'grammar school education for all'.[217] It was the local authorities who led the way, a new clutch of plans for reorganization being hatched in the industrial North during the early sixties. When the Labour Government came to power in 1964 committed to introducing the positive principle of hierarchical integration, these LEAs were ready to harness their own innovations in organizational differentiation and curricular specialization to this policy.

After 1964 'all the pointers were in one direction – away from the long advocated road of diversity by means of broad divisions into separate types of school, and towards unification of the administrative system allowing for a genuine diversity within the single school'.[218] Because all the Centre insisted upon was the new form of systematization (from tripartism to comprehensivization), but left the local authorities with the initiative on how they reorganized in conformity with it, this meant official acceptance of great organizational diversity and internal variety.

Until 1964 the age of transfer from primary to secondary education remained at 11+, in conformity with the 1944 Act. That year, in response to local demands to be allowed to experiment with different kinds of schools, the Secretary of State lifted this restriction and opened the way for a new range of reorganization plans. The Labour Government thus allowed regional experimentation rather than insisting on one particular structural pattern. Circular 10/65 merely collated the different types of organization already underway, though it was positively discouraging about Scheme 5 (Sixth Form Colleges) and 6 (the Middle School), for which statutory approval would be restricted. Clearly the

> flexibility of Middle School arrangements would add immeasurably to the range of choices open . . . Despite the damp discouragement of 10/65, so many areas submitted these schemes that a bare nine months afterwards the Secretary of State had to relent from his 10/65 position and announce that approval would be given to Scheme 6 as to any other . . . Once again it was local initiative that pressed ahead with Middle School planning, mostly of break-at-thirteen schemes – initiatives that made the Plowden Council's recommendation of transfer at age twelve obsolete long before it was made.[219]

The development of Middle Schools, straddling primary and secondary levels, and the emergence of Sixth Form Colleges were only the most obvious elements of a growing organizational heterogenity which continued to characterize the comprehensive movement. Thus by 1972 Benn and Simon could list twenty-one different age ranges in schools, which represented an enormous shift away from the standardized pattern of which had characterized tripartism.[220]

The new organizational diversity again encouraged less standardization in curriculum, teaching methods, and pupil assessment. The gradual abandoning of the selective examination at 11, which had placed such a brake on progressive techniques, coupled with the emergence of middle schools and departments, allowed the new informal methods to move up through the age range rather than being confined to primary level. Thus the existence of comprehensive schools gave a new freedom to primary schools in the same area, which could now branch out 'in quite new directions, in the teaching of the 'new mathematics', French, art and music; a richer variety of activities was possible now that the formal teaching required for the eleven plus tests was no longer essential'.[221] Similarly within the comprehensives themselves experiments were launched with team teaching, the integrated curriculum, and special subject teaching. There was a general tendency to seize on the opportunity presented by the Mode III CSE, which allows a school to design its own curriculum and which thus prevented specialized developments from being straight-jacketed by uniform external examinations. Diversification of contents, methods and assessment went hand in glove with comprehensive reorganization and were encouraged by both the Newsom and Plowden Reports. Thus the comprehensive movement, emerging through political manipulation, and the internal initiation of the teaching profession, guided by its progressive pedagogy, came together and became mutually reinforcing during the sixties.

Circular 10/65 catalysed action which was already underway; it encouraged those then moving in the comprehensive direction, it perhaps convinced some waivering areas, but it could do nothing to those LEAs which determinedly set their faces against this form of reorganization. The Circular set no date by which schemes must be started or completed, its policy was at the mercy of changes in local politics and although it set the official seal of approval on what was becoming a new popular philosophy of education, the impetus for change had to come from below rather than above. 'Where reorganization was successful, it was once again due to strong local initiative. This meant that there would either have had to be a strong-minded and fair-minded Chief Education Officer, whose views were definite and whose judgement was Solomon's, and/or a particularly determined and knowledgeable leader or group on the education committee. They could be Labour or Conservative, although more often they were Labour'.[222] Through this patchwork of local changes, the number of comprehensive schools rose from 189 at the time of the Circular to 1,145 five years later.[223] By the same date nearly 30 LEAs had abandoned the 11+, whilst another 100 had decided to do so, but the patterns of reorganization were the products of mutual inspiration not of national policy. In consequence 'the total approach was uneven and unsystematic and suffered from the lack of any real "central guidance" '.[224] This situation, instigated by Circular 10/65, was exacerbated by the failure of the Labour Party to pass legislation in 1970 which would at least have encouraged the universalization of the comprehensive school, although it would still have been a school taking many different forms. This inability to introduce further unification meant that once again strident differentiation and specialization were threatening the overall integration of the educational system.

Hence

the most crucial point, the real problem left by the policy of Circular 10/65 was not uniformity, but the very opposite. By 1970 observers were saying 'The present education is near anarchy' and was in fact 'chaotic'. What was needed was not yet more licence but order at last. Soon after 10/70 was issued the Chief Senior HMI gave his opinion that the rampant variety in school types which had been allowed to develop was a problem for secondary education and that some day a government would have to step in to take some 'hard decisions . . . about the limits with which experimentation with organizational limits can be accepted'. He tactfully put the date in the late 1970s for this, but his worries about unlimited permissiveness had relevance to the situation in 1970 and to the aftermath of a policy of under-coordination and under-directed development of secondary education in the years 1965 to 1970.[225]

Thus the Conservative policy, launched in 1970, only intensified the situation for it reinforced the local autonomy which had given rise to these diverse and uncoordinated developments in the first place. Furthermore the fact that it was *individual schools* rather than *complete schemes* which the Secretary of State now examined also implied a lower level of uniformity within each LEA, and not simply between different areas. Tory policy did not involve outright opposition to the comprehensive system — indeed by 1972 Mrs Thatcher had approved 2,300 proposals and rejected only 92.[226] However, it was increasingly clear that the schools excepted from comprehensive schemes were grammar schools and that a policy of co-existence was being pursued — between an enlarged comprehensive sector and a reduced, but now protected, grammar school sector. Thus the Conservative Circular like the previous Labour circulars 'was an unequivocally party political move, but it was also, as 10/65 rather less dogmatic than it might have been. It tended to reinforce existing administrative arrangements rather than make a new direction. It did not specifically object to comprehensives but withdrew the encouragement of central government for them, restating the autonomy of LEAs'.[227]

In other words, Conservative Government had done nothing to restrain the predominance of differentiation and specialization and nothing to restore the integration of the system in the face of such diversity and lack of co-ordination. When Labour returned to office it was with the intention of universalizing the comprehensive school, although it still took some months for this to harden into a resolve to increase systematization and unification. In order to strengthen systematization and generalize the positive principle of hierarchial organization, the Secretary of State first concentrated on removing an obstacle to full comprehensivization — the Direct Grant Schools — which created exigencies for the new secondary policy by creaming off some of the best pupils and perpetuating pockets of privilege within the public system. In 1970 the Donnison Commission had recommended that they should be phased out, being given the option of going fully independent. When in government, the Conservatives had ignored this proposal, now in Opposition they fought it vehemently, but by mid-1975 the Direct Grant Schools were forced to choose between complete independence (meaning the end of government grants) and full integration into the publicly maintained sector. This represented a coercive move and mirrored the conviction of the Secretary of State that further persuasion would be fruitless: since only two Direct Grant Schools had been assimilated into comprehensive schemes by 1972, it was probably true that few more would voluntarily associate themselves with this form of reorganization. Significantly the Labour Government was also resolved that the same kind of imperative measure was essential to bring recalcitrant authorities into line. Legislation to increase unification was promised in late 1975. By this time, however, it was only with the greatest superficiality that the problem of integration could be reduced to the dozen or so LEAs who were holding out against comprehensive reorganizationn – the real problem lay with the dozens who had done something, and been allowed to do something, called 'going comprehensive'.

The difficulty was that once again unification and systematization were to be superimposed on a system (this time of secondary education) in which differentiation and specialization were already strongly rooted and developed. Given the predominance of the latter characteristics it again seems unlikely that the first pair can be grafted on top of them – there are too many vested interests conditioning rejection. Take, for example, the attempt to improve the co-ordination of public secondary schooling by eliminating the Direct Grant School. Obviously this measure was intended to remove a source of obstruction and of contradiction from the theory and practice of comprehensive schooling. However, in 1975 more than 100 of these schools opted for complete independence out of a total of 174, and the remainder was largely made up of Roman Catholic Schools, which accepted 'voluntary-aided' status.[228] In other words, the net effect of trying to increase systematization in this area was to drive the Direct Grant Schools into the private sector of education: its unintended consequence then was to strengthen those institutions whose very independence allows them to create the most serious exigencies for public policy. Similarly it seems just as improbable that a substantial increase in the degree of unification can be achieved in the face of resistance from the local authorities. In the past they have jealously guarded their autonomy from central encroachment: 'It is clear that LEAs of any political persuasion are disposed to follow a strong lead from the DES but that, where they feel unable to, even a determined Secretary of State had great difficulty in securing compliance. Despite the battery of financial and legal powers he possesses, an adamant LEA is no mean opponent'.[229] With local government reorganization and the creation of larger administrative units in the seventies, they should be in a stronger position from which to protect their vested interests and to defend their place in educational decision-making from the threatened incursion of central powers.

If this is the case then, as seems most likely, that the superimposed factors — unification and systematization — will be weak in comparison with the entrenched characteristics — differentiation and specialization, there will never be a uniform and standardized comprehensive school, only a label which covers a diversity of practices and sanctions a variety of ongoing experiments. The most political manipulation appears likely to achieve at the moment is the universalization of the positive principle of hierarchical integration in *public* secondary education. So far each step towards it has cost the centre something in terms of concessions to local authorities over organizational and curricular freedom. Even if the promised legislation means another step in this direction, then progressive systematization will still go hand in hand with the progressive segmentation which has already taken place through three decades of political interaction and negotiation.

THE PRODUCTS OF CHANGE
IN CENTRALIZED SYSTEMS:
FRANCE AND SOVIET RUSSIA

The importance of political manipulation in centralized systems has been examined exclusively in terms of the way in which it shapes the stop-go pattern of change. The sequence of polity-directed changes has been analysed with reference to the socio-political interaction which gave rise to them and to their own effects on subsequent interaction. Thus it remains to assess the cumulative effects of these changes over time and to establish how far they represent a departure from the original structure of these systems at the time of their emergence. In particular this is to ask whether these two systems are still centered around a leading part, such that a small change in this part will be reflected in considerable changes throughout education. In other words, are they still centralized systems, do unification and systematization continue to be their dominant characteristics, and will the sto-go pattern persist in the foreseeable future?

In both countries the effects of political manipulation have been consistently centripetal in nature: such developments have shown no tendency to escape central control or to foster unresponsiveness to the central authority. Polity-directed changes have been standardized in character and well co-ordinated with other parts of the system: such developments have shown no anarchic tendency, threatening the overall integration of the system. Instead the changes brought about through political manipulation have maintained and strengthened unification and systematization over time: and they have done so with extraordinary tenacity in the face of all kinds of counterpressures from wider society. Nevertheless the fact that these polity-directed changes have reinforced the main formal characteristics of the system in no way implies that little change has taken place, that the emergent structures have proved ultra-stable, or that the current systems bear much resemblance to their prototypes.

Formal continuities in educational control and co-ordination have survived far reaching changes, which have themselves been extremely discontinuous in nature. The political action (and inaction) producing these 'go' phases has already been examined earlier in the chapter. There it was seen that large-scale change was associated with alterations in politico-educational priorities which occurred most obviously, but not exclusively, with changes in elite leadership or political regime. Furthermore, new educational policies were frequently prompted by changing circumstances represented externally by alterations in world markets and international relations, and internally by factors like industrial development, agricultural crises and modification of the occupational structure. The two have often been interrelated. For example, educational change in nineteenth century France represented the sequential application of rival programmes rather than the slow evolution of consensus, but each regime had to face the fact that the speed of industrialization outstripped the capacity of education to meet the demands of the new economic elite.

Secondly, these formal continuities have themselves created the need for further change. The pursuit of centrally defined goals through uniform measures entails a systematic inflexibility which precludes adaptation or adjustment at the periphery. Moreover, since educational standardization multiplies miscalculations nationally, these errors necessarily represent large-scale problems (surpluses and shortages of skills, inflated expectations, disfunctional attitudes and the hardening of new lines of stratification). 'The making of non-optimal decisions quite clearly influences the development of a system, and consequently in the process of development the necessity arises to make additional decisions which will decrease the variation from the optimum'.[230] Thus polity-direction involves optimization procedures, and it is no surprise that both France and Soviet Russia eventually adopted intricate forms of educational planning, which have no counterparts in the two decentralized systems. In addition optimization necessitates self-correction (the modification of non-optimal decisions), in the light of experience, and it is to this task that many of the polity-directed changes are directed. (In the decentralized system the central authorities are much more preoccupied with correcting undesirable developments which stem from *other* sources *outside* the polity.) Thus change here is partly the result of a hunt by the political elite for a better (or better and better) educational formula to meet their requirements. Oppositional groups often tend to suppose that given educational control they could obtain all they wanted from education. In reality this is more difficult, for even when an elite has clearly defined goals, it still has the problem of framing the educational policy which will meet them: and this is only to highlight the difficulties of drawing up the appropriate plan, further problems arise over the implementation of such a blueprint.

Thirdly, then, there are always practical limitations on the exercise of educational control, and these can prevent the centre from receiving the full services it requires, even if it had made the correct judgement of appropriateness in the first place. These in turn necessitate further adjustments and create new problems for the system to solve — by further changes. Thus, to take an example from Soviet Russia, places in higher education are determined by forecasts of manpower requirements, but students at one time showed an annual drop out rate of 5 percent.[231] Given courses of a five year duration, this meant that one quarter of the students failed to graduate. The shortfall could be dealt with by an upward adjustment of place quotas in the following years, but the employment of these drop-outs was an intractable problem which distorted manpower targets and educational planning at lower levels. Because of the continuity of unification and systematization these sytems remained highly responsive, but no system is perfectly responsive, especially when operating in a country of the size and complexity of Soviet Russia, or when buffeted by internal and external forces which defy repression as in France.

Thus in the centralized systems there was a continuous state of tension between education and its environment. The basic problem was to construct a system whose operations blended harmoniously with its environment, and hence enabled those inputs, processes and outputs to be produced which corresponded to demands which had been deemed politically legitimate. However, the strength of standardization and centripetalism militated against this harmony. In fact the very tenacity with which the central authorities clung to unfication and systematization, for purposes of control, produced an endless sequence of mismatches with the environment. The inflexibility of such an educational system meant that any change of circumstances promptly threw it out of alignment. The Russian system 'rather like the French system, . . . is a neat blueprint in which regularity of outline and orderliness of procedure outweigh the uncertainties of the historical ebb and flow'.[232] A period of growing political dissatisfaction with the way in which education was functioning would finally culminate in a thorough overhaul. Stasis would follow, the alignment would again begin to slip, dysfunctional consequences to build up, and the cycle would then repeat itself. Thus while problems of integration were experienced in the decentralized system as tensions between the central authorities and the centifugalism of other parts of the system: with centralization the problem of integration arose between the system as a whole and its social environment. It was a periodic problem of external maladaptation rather than a imminent threat of internal anarchy.

Why then are unfication and systematization maintained with such tenacity if their concomitant inflexibility generates major problems at regular intervals? One suspicion it is important to disabuse is that educational centralization is nothing more than a reflection of authoritarian politics. This might well arise given that Russia and France have both undergone extensive periods of political closure, whether these involved autocracy, bonapartism, totalitarianism or imperialism. Nevertheless, it is crucial to stress that the maintenance of these two characteristics, unification and systematization, was no less pronounced during the intervening periods when more open political structures prevailed, whether these took the form of bourgeois monarchy, republicanism, government by assembly, or a parliamentary presidential system. The fact that France has tried out most of these types of government twice-over gives ample evidence that these educational characteristics are not narrowly associated with a particular kind of regime. Indeed, the protestations of republicans like Jules Ferry, cited earlier, about the essential role of education in protecting the republican State and consolidating republican society, provide the key to this tenacious continuity. For any incoming regime or government the inheritance of a highly responsive educational system was extremely advantageous: and the more the new regime differed from the old in structure and ideology, the more welcome was centralization since education could immediately be harnessed to legitimating and re-inforcing the new polity. Thus the Soviet regime accepted the structure of the Tsarist system with alacrity, whilst the basic structure of Napoleon's *Université Impériale* was passed unaltered from hand to hand through the whole spectrum of political organization. In brief unfication and systematization remained the predominant character-istics because they facilitated the achievement of political goals and protected these from interference by other agencies. Consequently education was consistently harnessed to the tasks of political socializa-tion, political integration and political recruitment from the inception of the centralized system in both countries.

The course of change itself was moulded between the two factors just discussed: the intermittent need to re-establish harmony with the environment and the consistent defence of centralization. But neces-sarily the first task had to be accomplished within the framework of the second, otherwise a loss of control and of responsiveness would have been the result. It follows therefore that if the course of change was undercontrolled in the decentralized system (being initiated from the periphery and barely rationalized or contained by the central authori-ties), it was overcontrolled in the centralized systems, where adjust-ments and adaptations were instrumented from the top down. Once the need for such changes had been negotiated through political manipula-tion, they were carefully introduced from the centre and closely co-ordinated with other components of the system so as not to prejudice the provision of other politically sanctioned services.

Thus, for example, 'modernization' always figured amongst the top priorities of the central authority in France, i.e. it acknowledged to the economic elite that a series of adjustments were needed to match the rapid changes in the industrial environment. But the educational changes introduced always fell short of the moving target and did so because of their inflexible implementation and rigid coordination. Accepting the need for a shorter and more practical instruction, several formulae were tried out during the Second Empire (a policy of bifur-cated secondary instruction, experiments with Technical Schools and finally the introduction of Special education at secondary level). All of these merely served to prove that the State's educational ideal could not be reconciled with the vocational specialization that professional education entailed. The Third Republic inherited the problem and made three different attempts at adaptive modernizatioṇ. The policy of developing modern technical training failed largely because the centre would abandon no authority to local industrialists, enabling them to adjust it to their diverese requirements. The policy of updating secondary studies and diluting the hegemony of *culture générale* foundered because it was based on extending Special education, marrying it to the Baccalauréat, and making it operate alongside classicism in the lycée, rather than in a differentiated institution. Consequently modern education assumed an inferior status and the main result was that Special education lost its distinctive character when assimilated to the same methods and mode of examination as traditional secondary instruction. Finally, the attempt to found Real universities, as specialized centres of teaching and research, failed because all faculties were elevated in the same standardized fashion, spreading resources too thinly for specialization.

These examples serve to illustrate a common feature of changes in the centralized system, namely that since every attempt to re-establish harmony with the environment must take place within the framework of central control, the former is consistently subordinated to the latter. In other words, compatibility with the environment involves differentiation and specialization (since no aspect of it is ever uniform, it can only be matched by provisions which are adapted, or which can be adjusted, to local variations, special circumstances and unique configurations). Yet this kind of change has to be accommodated in an educational system whose unfication and systematization are already strong and which the central authorities are determined not to relax. Thus in the course of change the two pairs of characteristics, unification/systematization and differentiation/specialization have to develop conjointly, but the latter remain the weaker pair as they were upon the emergence of the system. It is they which have to do the accommodating, have to take second place and have to accept the precedence of the first pair.

Nonetheless, in its own interests the central authority cannot afford to let education slip grossly out of alignment with its environment, as this threatens it own goal attainment. Consequently it has to make periodic efforts to introduce the requisite degree of differentiation and specialization in order to produce the services required. (Namely those sought by the elite itself or negotiated by others through political

manipulation.) What follows therefore is that progressive systematization and progressive segmentation develop simultaneously in a process
of guided change — that is within a context of strong unification. In
modern terms this would simply be called planning, but it was practised
in education long before it was conceptualized in this way, and without
any of the advanced techniques now denoted by the term. The course
of change thus represented a succession of reintegrations of the system
at higher and higher levels of complexity.

Progressive segregation, through which diversification is
accomplished, entails a successive division into sub-systems which is
accompanied by a differentiation of their functions and a specialization
of their activities. Progressive systematization consists in the strengthening of pre-existing relations between parts, the linkage of parts
previously unrelated, and the gradual addition of new components and
relations to a system. The two take place simultaneously under the
guidance of the centre and develop by a series of jerks during each 'go'
phase. To call these 'progressive' is only to reflect on the overall
tendency of the system to become more complex in these respects over
time. The term carries no evaluative connotation nor does it preclude
periods of structural inertia or of regression to simpler forms of organization. The history of the French and Russian systems witnesses to the
conjoint development of segregation and systematization over time, but
also demonstrates the predominance of the latter — these systems have
always been, and they remain, extremely neat in form compared with
their decentralized counterparts.

In this context the Second Empire, which inherited a system sub-
divided into two levels unlinked to one another (the negative principle
of hierarchical organization), was mainly notable for its attempt to
diversify secondary education with the eventual introduction of a
shorter differentiated course of 'special' education. The Third
Republic retained and reinforced the basic segregation of the primary
from the secondary level, which was such that the design and development of these two sub-systems could proceed almost independently of
one another — fulfilling totally different functions and enrolling very
different social strata. Within each sub-system, however, segregation
and systematization both took a big step forward. On the one hand the
lycées and collèges were integrated more closely and linked more
tightly with the facultés and grandes écoles. Within the secondary level
the aim was to diversify, to introduce the degree of differentiation and
specializaion commensurate with modernization. Yet, as we have seen,

the priority accorded to systematization meant that Special education was the vehicle used for this, and although it was intended to grow in importance when awarded its 'own' Baccalauréat (for this was designed to sub-divide the examination itself, thus increasing specialization), it in fact lost its distinctiveness. Its demise was complete in 1902 when 'Special' education disappeared altogether.

Then a further re-integration was attempted: a single secondary education now led to a Baccalauréat with four different sections. This was meant to be a realization of the unity of education which at the same time afforded a greater variety of instruction. In other words, systematization and segmentation were to go hand in hand, but as usual there was no doubt about which one led. Modern studies were confined to the fourth (inferior) option and lost their distinctive character between pressures to imitate the prestige branches and to prepare for university entry. In tackling the same problem, the same sequence was repeated in the twentieth century with the creation of the technical Baccalauréat in 1946. There was also an additional difficulty that this then exerted a powerful downward influence, standardizing lower levels of technical instruction, which had previously been able to diversify satisfactorily because they were part of the segregated primary network. Thus these attempts to achieve a higher level of reintegration, which included differentiated courses of modern subjects, made some progress but always suffered from the fact that systematization acted as a straight-jacket which denied distinctiveness, diluted specialization and thus demoted diversification. Exactly the same story was repeated at the primary level, with successive attempts to introduce more differentiated and specialized courses of vocational or pre-vocational instruction only really succeeding in rare cases when these institutions broke away from the Ministry of Education altogether. Otherwise their practical orientation steadily gave way to general education the longer they remained part of the system — the fate not only of full-time institutions like the EPS but also of the part-time training courses for working youth, introduced immediately after the First World War.

As the Third Republic entered the twentieth century, the system required considerable democratization and modernization in the view of many whose demands bombarded the National Assembly. Nothing but very tentative moves were made towards the most fundamental of structural changes — the linkage of the primary and secondary subsystems. Not until the Fifth Republic did both demands receive serious attention. Grudgingly, at first, the government tried to get away with the most minimalistic link between the two levels (the weakest form of positive hierarchical organization). This merely entailed the *harmonisation* of programmes at the end of the first degré and the start of the second, the orientation, at least in principle, of pupils to different types of further instruction on the basis of their performance, and the establishment of *classes passerelles* allowing for the transfer later on of those who had taken the wrong route. This involved no audacious change and the creation of no new self-standing institution. Because of this the old segregated institutions continued to recruit from different parts of the social structure and to confer different life chances upon their pupils. Continuing pressures gave rise to a more thorough-going policy of systematization which consisted in the creation of differentiated institutions, the CES, standing between primary and post-primary schooling and performing the task of orientation, i.e. of allocating pupils to more specialized courses. These included entry to secondary schools, to various types of full-time vocational instruction and to apprenticeship schemes or short courses preparatory to employment, each of which carried a different qualification.

Progressive systematization and segregation had gone forward together and produced a reintegration of parts at a higher level of complexity. Nevertheless the way in which this development was designed by the centre betrayed the usual reluctance to experiment with wholly new institutions (which were unpredictable in relation to central control and might traduce vested interests). Instead the differentiation of the CES was accomplished by the regrouping of existing components (the final class of primary, the first cycle of secondary and the CEGs). To a large extent these elements resisted re-integration and refused to collaborate in a purposeful manner. The introduction of the positive principle of hierarchical organization, the biggest rupture yet with the Napoleonic structure, needed to be articulated by a forceful institution committed to overthrowing a century and a half of socio-educational discrimination – like the original conception of the école unique: instead the task was entrusted to this weak and divided amalgam – the CES.

The composition of the political elite made it considerably more sympathetic and creative in relation to modernization at secondary and higher levels. The same device was used to introduce greater diversification in both – the differentiation of cycles of studies, giving more chance for vocational and academic specialization. Each cycle which was segregated in this way was also systematized with those below and above it, although distinctiveness was protected by each cycle awarding a separate diploma. Thus secondary education was divided into two cycles, a short and a long, whilst the historical influence of the Baccalauréat as a force for standardization was reduced by its division into numerous sub-sections, related to different occupational outlets and higher educational inlets. At the higher level the differentiation of the IUT replicated the segregation of short and long alternatives. University education was itself subdivided into three cycles, each with specialist options and a diploma at the end of it. Thus in a technocratic fashion the Fouchet reforms had brought about a re-integration at a much greater degree of complexity. What partly betrayed it, at least at the higher level, was the superordinate insistance on systematization – the reforms were imposed uniformly and universally from the centre, their rigidity defying local or institutional adaptation. Only the outburst of the May events led to the concession of sufficient university autonomy for differentiation and specialization to be defined in situ rather than at the centre – but even here the subordinate characteristics have not grown well on the old tree.

The course of change in Twentieth Century Russian education displays similar developments, if starker in form. It demonstrates the same disadvantages attaching to overcontrol, yet a similar reluctance to abandon central guidance. The Unified Labour School of the post-revolutionary period, devoted to the creation of the egalitarian society, deliberately excluded every vestige of differentiation and specialization. It was a single institution, covering all grades, eliminating primary/secondary distinctions and abandoning divisive specialization and qualifications – as such it embodied the naked principle of hierarchical organization and nothing else. The revolt against this polytechnic education at the end of the twenties involved no diminution in central control and co-ordination, but sought to reintegrate that degree of differentiation and specialization which was then required for planned economic growth. Central educational planning therefore re-introduced selection, specialization and vocationalism to the precise extent required by the national economic plans. In servicing the economy with such single-mindedness, this reform was held to have gone too far in the opposite direction. It had encouraged differentiation and specialization to a point at which education was re-creating social divisions, just as the polytechnic principle had sacrificed utilitarian to egalitarian considerations.

The next two policies were attempts to recombine the four characteristics in ways which avoided mutual obstruction by the two pairs. The 1958 reform represented the first formula for bringing about progressive systematization and progressive segmentation in conjunction. The eight year compulsory school with its standardized curriculum was predominantly egalitarian in aim. It was, however, regarded as the *incomplete* Labour Polytechnic School, and the multi-track institutions which stood end-on to it were to introduce the necessary amount of diversification without proving socially divisive, since each branch would involve periods of useful manual work. Examination determined entry to one of the several differentiated institutions — vocational shift schools for working and rural youth, Polytechnical Schools attached to a plant or collective farm, and the specialized Technikums. Whilst the lower levels of training could be allowed some scope for adjustment to local agricultural or industrial requirements, the higher levels were more closely systematized under the Ministry of Higher and Secondary Specialized Education. As a formula it proved neither egalitarian nor particularly efficient, for the inflexibility with which it was applied served to magnify deficiencies in the planning of manpower training.

By 1964 this policy had been abandoned in favour of a new attempt at reintegration at a still higher level of complexity, embracing further specialization, on utilitarian lines, and institutional differentiation of a kind which moved away from the common one-block basic school. In principle this reform seemed to indicate that more flexibility was accepted and that greater curricular diversification and institutional independence were its concomitants. However, the wording of the resolution by the Central Committee and Council of Ministers, which introduced the reform, was revealing about the future courses of change: it referred to 'measures to improve the training *of specialists* and *perfect the guidance* of *higher* and *specialized* education *in the country*' (my italics). In practice then the process of diversification has been directed and monitored from the centre; it has not involved devolution of authority or an increase in institutional autonomy. Instead unification has been increased, with the creation of a single Ministry of Education for the USSR, the full scale inspection of higher education, and the Ministry assuming direct control over a number of these institutions in order to run them as models. In other words, systematization has increased ahead of segmentation, so that the ensuing differentiation and specialization can in no way threaten central control. As in France the pair of characteristics which predominated when the educational system first emerged still retain their pre-eminence.

THE PRODUCTS OF CHANGE IN DECENTRALIZED SYSTEMS: ENGLAND AND DENMARK

So far the discussion of change has focussed on its patterning in these two countries, rather than on its contents. Thus although we have noted that the three processes of negotiation all contributed to this *incremental pattern,* and have described the ways in which they did so, no attempt has been made to assess their cumulative impact on the nature of the decentralized educational system. It is to this that we now turn. Firstly, the overall effect of the three processes operating along-side one another in the twentieth century must be examined in order to discover what changes they wrought between them (i.e. *how* they interwined and *what* they produced). Secondly, this leads directly to an assessment of whether the initial parity of importance between these processes has been destroyed or maintained in the course of interaction (i.e. did the changes which have taken place combine to reinforce or to remove the systemic conditions upon which each process of negotiation is predicted?). This is tantamount to asking if the two countries still possess decentralized educational systems, and any further questions about prospects for future change obviously hinge on the answer given here.

When the three processes for negotiating change are considered in relation to one another over time (in fact exactly the same period is involved for the two countries — the first three-quarters of the twentieth century) certain long-term regularities become apparent in the types of changes which they have produced. In particular External Transactions and Internal Initiation have operated as forces for diversification, which have strengthened the *differentiation* and the *specialization* of the educational system over time. By contrast Political Manipulation has represented a consistent force for standardization which has defended the *unification* and *systematization* of national education during the same period. These two influences will be examined in turn, before discussing the products of the different forms of negotiation in conjunction, for the latter are shaped by this continuous tension between diversification and standardization.

External Transactions, Internal Initiation
and Diversification

The historical fluctuations in the relative importance of these two processes have already been charted for England and Denmark; what will be stressed now is the *nature* of the changes that they introduced *when* they could contribute significant modifications at different levels. Most of these served to strengthen differentiation and specialization over time and since these two characteristics were already pronounced at the start of the system, their intensification had serious consequences for systemic integration. In effect they represented *centrifugal* tendencies, whether considered alone or in conjunction with one another. This centrifugalism manifested itself in three main ways, all of which undermined central control and organizational co-ordination and thus were a continual challenge to unification and systematization which had never been strong.

Firstly, the changes which stemmed from these processes constantly threatened to escape administrative control. Such developments were products of autonomy whose effect was to increase autonomous action at either the professional or the institutional level. Autonomy in turn spelt unresponsiveness to the centre, a lack of concern for systemic problems and instead a self-absorption in sectional problems and interests. In brief, the independence of different components of the system was accentuated as a direct consequence of successful internal initiation or external transactions. Thus, for example, in both countries there was considerable and growing dissatisfaction on the part of the central authorities with developments in higher education and its resistance to regulation from the centre. In Denmark the internal initiation of academics served to reproduce intellecutal traditionalism, to intensify the pursuit of pure knowledge in long courses unrelated to social or political demands and to repulse overtures, invectives and threats which asked them in different tones of voice to abandon their academicism. Similarly in England the universities have recently proved extremely unresponsive (a joint consequence of external transactions and internal initiation) at just the time when Government is attempting to extend its control over the major institutions and seeks their active contribution to the mixed economy and managed society. In sum this kind of development accentuates the *undercontrolled* nature of the decentralized system, as well as adding to it.

Secondly, such developments can threaten central educational policy in a number of ways. Thus the English Public Schools, maintained and extended through external transactions, vitiated the tripartite and comprehensive policies in turn, by perpetuating differentiated enclaves of elitism. In a different way the outgrowth of Senior Schools (the product of internal initiation and local action after the Great War) involved forms of institutional differentiation and of curricular specialization, on scientific, technical and vocational rather than literary subjects, which blurred the official distinction between Elementary and Secondary schooling and undermined the official definition of instruction at either level. Equally the Danish Folkschool teachers' commitment to Grundtvigian values (an education differentiated on practical lines), which they have implemented whenever possible, has at times contradicted the official policy of achieving egalitarianism through uniformity. Basically then these developments damage central policy because they involve differentiation and specialization in directions which are incompatible with it. They stress the absence of a leading part, as well as preventing its emergence.

Thirdly, such developments are anarchic and endanger the overall integration of the system. The changes introduced through external transactions satisfy the parties involved, and their specialization in particular is consistently in advance of public policy. Correspondingly, however, the parties involved are uninterested in the consequences of this for the rest of the system. Thus Danish vocational education developed in parallel to public post-compulsory schooling, but its inputs, processes and outputs, being geared to practical life, bore no relationship to mainstream standards, practices or qualifications. Similarly postwar developments of further and higher education in England were officially held to have involved a chaotic array of overlapping and uncoordinated provisions, entailing wastage of public resources. Equally the products of internal initiation can threaten systematization from within the mainstream institutions, rather than by the differentiation and addition of new elements. Thus the transformation of the English primary school along progressive lines is held by some to have undermined integration between levels by not inculcating the skills or values needed later on, thus jeopardizing a high standard of secondary and vocational instruction. These changes disrupt the system by failing to dovetail with other parts or activities. They serve to emphasize the fragility of co-ordination, as well as making this task more difficult.

Political Manipulation and Standardization

Polity-directed changes showed a strong tendency to reinforce unification and systematization over time. It is not that they operated to conserve the type of administrative framework or organizational co-ordination which characterized the system at its start. On the contrary, there have been major changes in the form and in the functions which these two characteristics serve. Nevertheless, the determination to introduce centrally defined policies has entailed their defence. In particular the fact that the polity in both countries was increasingly preoccupied with the quest for educational democratization, especially after the Second World War, meant that both needed to defend a degree of unification sufficient to ensure the national implementation of a new form of systematization, based on the principle of the educational ladder. Nor was this motive for reinforcing unification and systematization merely a matter of contingency: it arose from the structural predisposition for the lower and working classes to make great use of political manipulation, the other processes of negotiation being much less accessible to them. However, because the very introduction of polity-directed changes was itself predicated on maintaining the weaker pair of characteristics in the decentralized system, these were constantly reinforced by most governments, and not just by the political representatives of labour. Consequently polity-directed changes involved a consistent *centripetal* trend. This centripetalism manifested itself in various ways, all of which sought to contain and restrain the forces encouraging diversification and thus accentuating the predominance of differentiation and specialization which had always been strong.

Firstly, the changes stemming from political manipulation were both uniform and universal in conception. Because this process for negotiating change was preoccupied with the relationship between education and social stratification, the policies to emerge from it were necessarily universalistic, whatever the colour of government, and were to be standardized in their application. Thus, for example, the English tripartite policy, which had been preceded by a strengthening of central control under the 1944 Act, was to universalize the selective system and specified the precise degree of institutional differentiation compatible with it. The 1937 Act introducing the Practical Middle School in Denmark had exactly the same characteristics. Furthermore, such was the committment of the Left in both countries to the introduction of the positive principle of hierarchical organization, that the equalization of educational opportunity took priority over any other goal. Thus when confronted by a conflict between promoting democratization or maintaining diversity, as the Social Democrats and the Labour Party were, they both determined to purchase equality at the price of uniformity. In policy terms, a single school with a common curriculum was the best defence against the perpetuation of privilege and worth the sacrifice of freedom of choice, practical relevance, or local adaptability. In practice, polity-directed changes of this scope were less than easy to implement, but they were buttressed in two further ways.

Secondly, then, the effects of changes introduced through political manipulation are to minimize other developments which threaten to disrupt central policy. This involves the pruning and elimination of those institutions and activities which are not complementary, and a corresponding increase in standardization. In England there were three different phases in which such developments were pruned back hard to prevent their interference with a politically sponsored institution and to ensure the latter pride of place. Successively the Higher Grade Schools were cut down and replaced by the Higher Elementary Schools at the incorporation stage; the outgrowth of a wide range of differentiated post-elementary institutions were weeded out in favour of the uniform Morant Grammar School; and the Senior, Central and Municipal schools proliferating between the wars were forced, root and branch into the Secondary Modern format. Training and containing are alternatives to pruning and eliminating, but have the same consequences in terms of loss of diversification. Thus, for example, adult education was trained along 'non-partisan' lines in England, the WEA being unified under the Board of Education and subordinated to university direction. Similarly the burgeoning development of technical schools at intermediate levels was contained: in 1913 Junior Technical Schools were reluctantly recognized providing they operated as terminal institutions, unintegrated with the secondary level. Again after 1944 they were trained into line (by adjusting ages of entry etc.) with the tripartite policy, then condemned to inertia through lack of positive official encouragement. The loss of a strong practical, Real or technical definition of instruction was the price paid for the defence of central policies.

Thirdly, the changes stemming from political manipulation operate to maintain the integration of the system, by ensuring that the component parts and levels dovetail with one another. This again buttresses central policy but does so by co-ordinating and incorporating those kinds of developments which are both disruptive but also unamenable to the harsh pruning measures detailed above. Hence, for example the attempt to co-ordinate the traditional Danish universities, too autonomous to be forced into line, through successive advisory committees of representative composition. In a different way the three networks of agricultural, technical and commercial training, which enjoyed immunity because of their private status, were successively incorporated by a series of Acts between 1954 and 1960. In this way the centre at least gains overall rationalization and co-ordination with its own policies, but the system increases in complexity because the new elements retain their specificity: this in turn invites future problems of integration and will not be resorted to unless public policy can be defended in no other way.

The Joint Products of the Three Processes of Negotiation.

Clearly the products of internal initiation and external transactions on the one hand, and those of political manipulation on the other, are in a continuous state of tension. Centrifugalism is a perpetual threat to the integration of the system and the achievement of central goals: centripetalism barely contains these diverse developments and separatist tendencies. The changes which actually take place are shaped and reshaped between these pushes and pulls. They are woven by a ceaseless dialectic between the forces for diversification and pressures towards standardization.

From the start of these two systems at the beginning of the century change has assumed an undulating gait. Straight away changes fanned out from both external transactions and internal initiation and brought about an immediate increase in institutional differentiation and curricular specialization. *This intensified the pair of structural characteristics which were already predominant and threatened the weak unification and systematization which had been superimposed on the networks at the time of incorporation.*

The central response arising from political manipulation was to rationalize through a re-systematization and an increase in unification.

But the central authorities, as we have seen, could not proceed like a general, deploying and disposing at his will in order to achieve a grand planned strategy, because the parts fought back to defend their autonomy. Instead the centre more often had to work like a sheepdog patrolling the periphery, giving a nip here and a nip there, herding developments on the right trail. Moreover, although unification and systematization are mutually supportive when strong, the two here had frequently to be traded-off against one another on the part of the centre. Thus systematization was often bought at the price of unification, especially when the incorporation of independent elements meant the admission of new partners to control and therfore spelt educational power sharing. Equally systematization sometimes had to be sacrificed as the only way in which to bring about some important unified change, such as the acceptance of a plethora of local arrangements in order to achieve national comprehensivization.

Consequently, although unification and systematization were reinforced, they were not strong, and though they held diversification back for a time, they themselves were gradually sloughed off by the combined effects of local initiative, external transactions and internal initiation. As they gradually slipped, more and more changes would accumulate and these would again accentuate systemic differentiation and specialization. Another bout of central intervention would then take place, confining and reordering these changes as unification and systematization were re-established. So the two systems proceeded in undulating fashion, with changes swelling out and then being squeezed in, only to bulge out again as the phases of diversification and standardization alternated with one another. The phases, however, did allow for progression. They involved no return to the status quo, and though they were sometimes conservative in their effects, this represented no structure-maintaining mechanism. Instead it was much more common for progressive segmentation and progressive systematization to go hand in hand, with each new stage of reintegration being achieved at a level of greater complexity. Although this was the dominant tendency, morphogenesis must not be elevated to the status of an automatic or inevitable process; for in the course of development of these two systems some elements were killed and remained permanently excluded from twentieth century education.

In both countries the major Education Acts signalled the main phases in which unification and systematization were reinforced: differentiation and specialization expanded in the interval between them, and of course precipitated re-intervention on the part of the centre. Thus in England the 1902 settlement was followed not just by the spread of the Higher Elementary School and Morant Grammar School, which were officially approved, but by the growth of diverse institutions (Science Schools, Technical Day Schools, Pupil Teacher Centres, Trade Schools, Vocational Schools etc.). The 1918 Act which confirmed the structural and cultural hegemony of the academic Grammar School intended to crowd most of these developments into the Continuation Schools, which would be allowed some practical orientation but would remain firmly elementary. Effectively this Act was weaker than usual as a concrete affirmation of unification and systematization because of the intervention of the depression and the suspension of many of its provisions. Consequently, despite austerity, a variety of intermediary institutions again proliferated and these Central, Senior and Technical schools represented a real challenge since they enrolled two-thirds as many pupils as the 'official' grammar school. Thus a chaotic array of provisions had accumulated by the outbreak of war, and the application of the 1944 Act again crammed them into the inferior part of the system, this time the Secondary Modern School. This Act which had greatly strengthened unification was also to produce an unprecedented degree of systematization, as the tripartite policy took root and achieved the closest integration between the primary and secondary levels. Almost immediately, however, local initiative began to push forward with multi-lateral developments which gathered speed with Labour encouragement and became even less uniform with the Conservative policy of co-existence. Once again the Minister threatened another round of legislative intervention in 1975 and made it clear that this would involve strengthening the powers of the centre. This final phase only serves to illustrate the endurance of a phenomenon which characterized the very inception of the decentralized system, namely that unification and systematization must always be superimposed on component elements which are already highly differentiated and specialized.

Changes in higher and further education followed the same scenario, although as far as the universities were concerned the central authorities were content to work through incorporation until after the Second World War. Following that, as we have seen, the phases in which the centre sought to tighten its grasp on higher education (re-ordering further education, creating the CATS, the CNAA, the Binary Policy) and in which the component institutions twisted themselves free, succeeded one another with increasing speed.

The same pattern was repeated in Denmark and reveals substantive as well as formal similarities with .the sequence of events in England. Thus the 1937 Act imposing the non-examination middle school, which prefigured the secondary modern in almost every way, had the same standardizing effects and involved the same close integration with junior schooling. Unification and systematization thus increased in relation to the Folkschool, just as they had done with respect to the English primary school. The Act was followed by two decades in which teachers steadily used internal initiation to diversify the curriculum and increase its practicality, whilst employers turned to external transactions with the private networks for vocational instruction, in preference to absorbing the unqualified middle school leaver. The 1958 Act was the point at which the Social Democrats felt compelled to choose between diversification (with its imminent status differentials) and democratization. They opted for the latter, extending the unified and undivided Folkschool until 14 and minimizing internal curricular specialization. Consequently most practical, applied, pre-vocational, experimental or branching courses and options were confined to the two voluntary classes which continued after the school leaving age. In its wake however, diversification again fanned out. Real education developed more forcefully in the Folkschool, teachers experimented with pre-vocational courses and awarding certificates which made each additional year's schooling both valuable and popular, and the Gymnasia teachers ironically decided that with a shortened course the only salvation for high standards lay in differentiated courses and subject specialization. The 1970 Act largely concentrated on systematizing these developments more closely since the principles underlying them were unobjectionable to a government of the right.

Thus the course of change in the two countries has steadily increased differentiation and specialization at all three levels as has been mirrored in a proliferation of curricula, courses, departments and institutions, each of which has retained or acquired sufficient autonomy to preserve its distinctiveness. Nevertheless, the last quarter of a century has also witnessed the development of progressive systematization in the two countries. In particular this has consisted in a strengthening of pre-existing relations amongst the parts, particularly the primary and secondary levels, by reinforcing and widening the ladder between them. At first this still represented a modified version of negative hierarchical organization, for it consigned the bulk of pupils to schools which were terminal in character. The subsequent reorganization on comprehensive lines was a great step forward in terms of systematization for it linked all three levels together and eliminated those parts, like the Secondary Moderns or the non-examination Middle Schools, which had never been and were never intended to be related to the upper reaches of secondary schooling, let alone higher education. Simultaneously the gradual addition and incorporation of parts and components into the system throughout its growth represented a progressive reintegration at higher and higher levels of complexity.

Nonetheless, systematization consistently trailed in the wake of segmentation and the central authorities often presented the picture of running behind and tidying up after the forces producing diversification. Even when the centre tried to take the initiative it could not do so imperatively and categorically but had itself to negotiate the implementation of such policies with the appropriate local authorities and institutions; and negotiation spelt concession, compromise, exception, exemption, re-interpretation, modification, dilution and every other antithesis of standardization. Consequently, although progressive systematization has grown considerably, structural elaboration in the decentralized system remains an untidy process. This has led one North American observer to comment of the Danes that 'rather than re-organize their schools, they simply add further educational appendages as the need arises'.[233] His further characterization of the system as 'jerry-rigged' has considerable justification for any decentralized system of education, where order and co-ordination are always superimposed with difficulty on parts and activities which are already differentiated and specialized. And this will always be the case whilst-ever the three processes through which change is negotiated continue to operate alongside one another and to retain their rough parity of importance.

PROSPECTS FOR CHANGE

Examination of the course of change in the centralized and decentralized systems led to the conclusion that in both a progressive segmentation and a progressive systematization had developed side by side since the initial emergence of these systems. Does this mean that structural convergence has taken place between them? To a certain degree this is undoubtedly the case. From their beginnings the centralized systems have been subject to pressures to reduce their standardization and to meet a multiplicity of demands with greater precision, by introducing more differentiation and specialization. When such demands were successfully negotiated through political manipulation (and of course many were not) they were carefully co-ordinated by the central authorities into polity-directed changes which were transmitted to education from the top down. Sequentially these added up to a multi-purpose system of much greater complexity, whose new sub-divided parts permitted this differentiation of services. Sub-division was the key mechanism: through it levels could be broken down into cycles, cycles into differentiated branches, and branches into specialized courses – all without loss of control or co-ordination. Sub-divisions broke up the stark outlines of the original systems, whose simplicity reflected the limited goals of their founders and the equally limited concessions they had been forced to make to get these systems off the ground.

In the decentralized systems, the initial phase of incorporation which brought them into being did not finish there. The processes of external transaction and internal initiation continued to generate new developments, in response to the demands of professional and external interest groups, which were characterized by their specificity. These took place with scant attention to the central authorities beyond the need to evade them, dissimulate to them and sometimes to propitiate them. Nevertheless, the summarivity of these developments did gradually give way to wholeness. The integrative role of the central authorities worked to contain, connect and co-ordinate these anarchic changes. It reduced the internal chaos and contradiction between parts in order to increase responsiveness to central direction and to ensure complementarity between the great variety of services provided. The move towards wholeness increased the coherence of these systems, tidying up their ragged outlines, streamlining their main components, and simplifying the tangle of provisions which mirrored the diverse goals which education had undertaken to service over time.

Thus *to stress convergence is to emphasize the growth of progressive segmentation in the centralized system and of progressive systematization in the decentralized system.* Both have indeed taken place but they only represent one part of the story. When discussing the products of change there was also cause to accentuate the way in which the pair of characteristics which dominated these two kinds of systems at their emergence have retained their pre-eminence over time. In other words,

it was important to stress that the segmentation progressively introduced into the centralized system involved no diminutition of systematization or unification. On the contrary the very introduction of these
sub-divisions was planned, orchestrated and monitored *by* the central
authority, which thus strengthened its position as the leading part.
Equally the systematization progressively introduced into the decentralized system entailed no loss of differentiation and specialization. On
the contrary the coherence produced was an ordering of changes
already brought about autonomously by the parts which then retained
their capacity to instigate change independently of the centre. In other
words *not only did the two kinds of system remain very different in
these structural respects but the mechanisms which generated these
differences remained largely intact.*

The earlier discussion of legislative changes in Russia did indicate
that recently there were some tentative signs that the political elite was
beginning to experiment with increased flexibility and a slight devolution of authority at lower levels of vocational training. However, the
overall formula that they still appear to endorse is one in which
segmentation and systematization are encouraged to develop simultaneously, but within the context of very strong unification. The Soviet
elite seems unwilling to dilute the central political control of instruction, even if this is not the totally unmitigated asset it was once thought
to be. Thus unless the elite goes further in destroying the predominance
of unification and systematization, only the transformation of the
political structure itself can bring the 'stop-go' pattern of change to an
end.

In France, too, it appears that the structural conditions for a
continuation of the 'stop-go' pattern of change remain largely unaltered
and will continue to do so unless and until the polity manifests a
thoroughgoing willingness to relax central controls over education.
Otherwise,

plus augmentant les dimensions du système, plus cette administration risque, si
les principes actuels sont maintenus, de se perdre dans les détails au détriment
de ses tâches essentielles, de s'épuiser à vouloir maintenir dans un cadre rigide
des situations qui ont chacune leur spécificité et, en définitive, de paralyser par
son impuissance le fonctionnement général de l'ensemble. Il est donc urgent de
décentraliser. C'est au niveau d'autorités régionales et locales que peuvent,
selon les cas, être réglés les principaux problèmes concernant l'organisation
matérielle et le fonctionnement courant du service public de l'éducation. C'est
au niveau de chaque établissement, non seulement dans le supérieur mais aussi
dans le premier et le second degré, que, dans le cadre d'objectifs clairement

définis, les contenus et les méthodes pédagogiques peuvent être adaptés à la situation concrète de la population desservie.[2][3][4]

Yet as the Fifth Republic has now survived two potential crises of Presidential succession and as the immediacy of the educational outburst has retreated historically and will not be repeated until students and the left recreate solidarity, there is little ground for expecting a new move towards decentralization. One of the best substantiated of comparative generalizations is that no governing elite voluntarily renunciates a centralized educational system. If there are few signs that the leading part is abdicating any of its powers in the centralized systems, it is equally the case that decision-making powers remain dispersed in the decentralized systems. In both countries the three processes of negotiation have maintained themselves over time and one has not continuously won out at the expense of the others. In particular there is no consistent tendency for political manipulation to have increased in importance, relative to external transactions and internal initiation, thus spelling a drift towards centralization. On the contrary, in Denmark the trend is if anything in the opposite direction.

Taking the period as a whole it appears that power resources in Denmark have been somewhat devalued in relation to professional expertise and liquid wealth. As a consequence educational changes have become less polity-directed, standardized and unified over time. On the one hand, the consistent success of external transactions has meant that educational control has progressively been shared with other institutional elites, who used their financial resources to produce diverse specialized services from new educational establishments, founded or developed for this purpose. On the other hand, the profession has made important steps towards becoming master in its own house, especially in the postwar period, and this too has meant a less unified system more receptive to the values of teachers and, at primary level, to those of the community.

The significance of this trend should not be exaggerated, for in both decentralized systems the relative importance of the three processes has been subject to temporal variations. The more important point to stress is that the rough parity between them has been preserved during the twentieth century as a whole. Thus, for example, in England when the 1944 Act signalled an unprecedented degree of unification and systematization, this did not imply supremacy for the process of political manipulation. On the contrary the postwar period was one of the richest for internal initiation, with the teachers gaining mastery over curricular development, and for external transactions, especially at the various terminal points — vocational, further and higher education. Because the three processes of change have maintained their rough parity over time, the incremental pattern of change is likely to continue in the foreseeable future. Certainly it is true of both countries that their respective centres would like to gain more control, particularly over higher education at the moment. But desire and attainment are two different things, and there has probably never been a time at which the central authorities in a decentralizaed system have not wanted greater control over one level or another in order to redirect its activities. What is much more important to emphasize is that they cannot achieve such control at will: the acquired rights of the profession and of external interest groups are defended and retained.

Furthermore, we must resist the temptation to endow the most recent events with a greater significance than their predecessors. It is certainly the case in England at the present time that the centre seems poised to intervene more roughly at both secondary and higher levels, but this is better interpreted as one of the periodic re-orderings conducted by the central authorities than as a dramatic change in the nature of educational control. After all the 1944 Act seemed at the time to indicate a great lurch towards centralization, but it was in fact followed by the most active period of external transactions and internal innovations which effectively undermined any such convergence. Exactly the same is expected now, not only because a legislative act of that magnitude is not even on the horizon, but also because the rights acquired by professional and external interest groups have taken a number of additional steps forward in the intervening decades since the war.

In other words, both the centralized and the decentalized systems continue to exert different structural influences on educational interaction in their respective countries, despite the fact that some convergence has taken place between them. Does this mean then that they will continue to condition different patterns of educational change and to produce different kinds of systemic modications? In answering this question in the affirmative, let it be absolutely clear that I am talking about structural conditioning and not about structural determinism.

There is no logical necessity about this, for neither in principle nor in practice is there any factor or force which ultimately prevents the appropriate decision-makers in both types of system from deciding to alter the structure of those systems. Thus logically there is nothing to stop a governing elite from passing an act which would transform a centralized system into a decentralized one, hence destroying the conditional influences which have reproduced the 'stop-go' pattern of change over time and preserved structuration around a 'leading part'. In reality, however, structures distribute vested interests in their maintenance and it is the fact that groups do defend these which makes patterns of interaction and change durable in the long-run. In our discussion of centralized systems we have examined numerous political elites with the most diverse ideological orientations and have found them unanimous in their support for and defense of the centralized structure. There is not a single counter-example in which centralization itself (rather than the purposes to which it was put) was thrown over by a governing elite, whether reactionary or revolutionary, which was willing to sacrifice the political advantages of educational control. It is because of the endurance of this vested interest that the centralized system is expected to condition its own maintenance in the foreseeable future.

Exactly the same is the case with the decentralized system. Again, logically the appropriate decision-makers, here the profession and the external interest groups, could decide to terminate their independent initiatives and autonomous innovations. Indeed in our empirical discussion we did encounter examples of groups which ceased such activities for reasons of financial hardship and others where these transactions were repressed or discouraged. However, this was never a systematic phenomenon, and at the very time that such examples occurred other groups were taking up these processes of negotiation for the first time. In other words, the initial structure again invites its own continuation. There is nothing deterministic about this, it is simply that over time the decentralized structure conditions small localized changes which intensify the autonomy which allowed them to occur in the first place. This in turn distributes vested interests in educational control more and more widely throughout society and outside the central authorities. It is the defence of these interests from within and without the educational system which conditions the endurance of the 'incremental pattern' of change and will prevent the central authority from assuming the position of a 'leading part' in the foreseeable future.

The lasting structural differences between the two kinds of system, which still allow them to be characterized as centralized or decentralized, mean that the present cycle is not yet over. In other words, structural conditioning continues to shape interaction in different ways in the two systems; interaction itself still follows two distinctive patterns; and the structural elaboration which results re-confirms the differences between the two systems which caused one to distinguish between centralization and decentralization in the first place.

Thus the prospects for change are that future educational inter-action will continue to be patterned in dissimilar fashions in the two systems and that the products of change will reproduce the main features of centralization or decentralization. The force of this argu-ments rests on the endurance of differences in the structural con-ditioning of interaction and change between the centralized system and the decentralized system. In opposition to this it might be objected that such an argument neglects cultural factors whose contribution encourages educational convergence. The latter is incontestable. There is no doubt that the postwar period has witnessed a growing inter-nationalization of student culture and of pedagogical approaches: nor is there any doubt that because students, teachers and academics read the same books, repeat the same arguments and respond to the same values the world over, they thus represent a force for convergence — a force which pushes national systems to address similar problems, to adopt similar methods and to accept similar solutions. Nevertheless, cultural forces, however international they may be, still have to contend with the established structures of the different national systems of education and the vested interests associated with their maintenance. In other words, the cultural forces for educational convergence are working against the structural forces which condition the endurance of different educational systems. Yet, as was argued at the very start of this book whatever the project which is in view, it is always advantageous to have structural factors working for it rather than against it. The differences between the centralized and the decentralized systems of education may ultimately give way, but not yet, and not without tremendous resistance from those who benefit from these two different types of educational control.

NOTES

1. G. Z. F. Bereday, W. W. Brickman, G. H. Read, *The Changing Soviet School*, Cambridge, Mass., 1960, p. 7.

2. Amitai Etzioni, *The Active Society*, New York, 1965.

3. G. Z. F. Bereday, W. W. Brickman, G. H. Read, *The Changing Soviet School,* op. cit., p. 5.

4. Jaan Pennar, Ivan. I. Bakalo, G. Z. F. Bereday, *Modernization and Diversity in Soviet Education,* New York, 1971, p. 98.

5. V. I. Lenin quoted in A. P. Pinkevitch, *The New Education in the Soviet Republic,* New York, 1929, p. 375.

6. See V. I. Lenin, *The Impending Catastrophe and How to Combat It,* in his *Collected Works,* Vol. 25, London, 1960, pp. 323-65.

7. V. I. Lenin speaking at the 9th Congress (1920) quoted by Carew Hunt, *The Theory and Practice of Communism,* Harmondsworth, 1963, p. 184.

8. See I. I. Kaplan, 'The Influence of Education on Labour Output', in H. J. Noah (ed.), *The Economics of Education in the USSR,* New York, 1969.

9. See N. Hans, *The Russian Tradition in Education,* London, 1963, p. 156 ff.

10. Quoted in G. Z. F. Bereday, W. W. Brickman, G. H. Read, *The Changing Soviet School,* op. cit., p. 69.

11. Ibid, p. 164.

12. N. Hans, *The Russian Tradition in Education,* op. cit., p. 184.

13. G. Z. F. Bereday, W. W. Brickman, G. H. Read, *The Changing Soviet School,* op. cit., p. 19.

14. G. Z. F. Bereday, 'Class Tensions in Soviet Education', in G. Z. F. Bereday and Jaan Pennar, *The Politics of Soviet Education*, London, 1960, p. 72.

15. G. Z. F. Bereday, W. W. Brickman, G. H. Read, *The Changing Soviet School,* op. cit., p. 245.

16. Quoted by Richard V. Rapacz, 'Polytechnic Education and the New Soviet School Reforms', in G. Z. F. Bereday and J. Pennar, *The Politics of Soviet Education,* op. cit., p. 28 ff.

17. G. Z. F. Bereday, W. W. Brickman, G. H. Read, *The Changing Soviet School,* op. cit., p. 6.

18. An earlier more extreme proposal that all students should undertake two or three years of productive work at the end of the eight year school would have freed 2½ million to join the labour force. Ibid, Ch. 10.

19. G. Z. F. Bereday, 'Changes in Soviet Educational Administration', *School and Society*, January, 1958, pp. 37-39.

20. Cf. V. A. Zhamin, 'Contemporary Problems of the Economics of Education', in H. J. Noah (ed.), *The Economics of Education in the USSR*, op. cit.

21. For example, in the specialization 'sewing and sewing machine operators' as many workers were training between 1959-63 as would be needed for a complete replacement of the entire workforce engaged on such jobs. Ibid.

22. N. G. Feitel'man, 'The Tasks of Planning Education', ibid, p. 170.

23. Jaan Pennar, Ivan I. Bakalo, G. Z. F. Bereday, *Modernization and Diversity in Soviet Education,* op. cit., p. 102.

24. Nigel Grant, 'USSR', in Margaret Scotford Archer (ed.), *Students, University and Society,* London, 1972, p. 85.

25. Jaan Pennar, Ivan I. Bakalo, G. Z. F. Bereday, *Modernization and Diversity in Soviet Education,* op. cit., p. 103.

26. N. Hans, *The Russian Tradition in Education,* op. cit., p. 157.

27. Nigel Grant, 'USSR', op. cit., p. 100.

28. R. D. Anderson, *Education in France 1848-70,* Oxford, 1975, p. 96.

29. F. Buisson, *L'enseignement primaire supérieur et professionnel,* Paris, 1887, p. 11.

30. R. D. Anderson, *Education in France 1848-70,* op. cit., p. 218.

31. Ibid., p. 44.

32. M. Reclus, *Jules Ferry, 1832-93,* Paris, 1946, p. 174. See also: Réné Martin, *La vie et l'oeuvre de Jules Ferry, 1832-93,* Montelimar, 1931; Ferdinand Buisson, *Jules Ferry et l'ecole laique,* Paris, 1911; Edouard Cavailhon, *La France Ferrycide,* Paris, 1888; Thomas F. Power, *Jules Ferry and the Renaissance of French Imperialism,* New York, 1944.

33. Louis Legrand, *L'influence du Positivisme dans l'oeuvre scolaire de Jules Ferry,* Paris, 1961, p. 188.

34. John E. Talbott, *The Politics of Educational Reform in France,* Princeton, 1969, p. 6.

35. Antoine Prost, *L'enseignement en France 1800-1967,* Paris, 1968, p. 273.

36. To Ferry 'L'égalité consiste, ici, à réaliser l'égalité morale des fonctions dans l'inégalité réelle et obligatoire des situations'. Cited by Louis Legrand, *L'influence du Positivisme dans l'oeuvre scolaire de Jules Ferry,* op. cit., p. 115.

37. Ibid., cited p. 222, (Part of Jules Ferry's 1870 'Discours sur l'égalité d'éducation')

38. Antoine Prost, *L'enseignement en France 1800-1967,* op. cit., p. 340.

39. Luc Decaunes and M. L. Cavalier, *Réformes et projets de réformes de l'enseignement Français de la Révolution à nos jours (1789-1960),* Paris, 1962, p. 44.

40. Louis Legrand, *L'influence du Postivisme dans l'oeuvre scolaire de Jules Ferry,* op. cit., p. 149.

41. Antoine Prost, *L'enseignement en France 1800-1967,* op. cit., p. 292-93.

42. L. Liard, cited by Luc Decaunes and M. L. Cavalier, *Réformes et projets de réformes,* op. cit., p. 50.

43. Antoine Prost, *L'enseignement en France 1800-1967,* op. cit., p. 337.

44. Ibid., p. 239.

45. Ibid., p. 240.

46. Jacques Fournier, *Politique de l'éducation,* Paris, 1971, p. 210.

47. Luc Decaunes and M. L. Cavalier, *Réformes et projets de réformes,* op. cit., p.154.

48. Ibid., p. 81.

49. Antoine Prost, *L'enseignement en France 1800-1967,* op. cit., p. 314.

50. Ibid., p. 338.

51. Antoine Prost, *L'enseignement en France 1800-1967,* op. cit., p. 422.

52. F. Ponteil, *Histoire de l'enseignement en France: Les grandes etapes, 1789-1965,* Paris, 1966, p. 374.

53. Jacques Fournier, *Politique de l'éducation*, op. cit., p. 66.

54. Jean Guilhem cited in Luc Decaunes and M. L. Cavalier, *Réformes et projets de réformes,* op. cit., p. 224.

55. W. R. Fraser, *Reforms and Restraints in Modern French Education,* London, 1971, p. 131.

56. Antoine Prost, *L'enseignement en France 1800-1967,* op. cit., p. 424.

57. Jacques Fournier, *Politique de l'éducation,* op. cit., p. 184.

58. W. R. Fraser, *Reforms and Restraints in Modern Frecnch Education,* op. cit., p. 41.

59. See P. Bourdieu and J. C. Passeron, *Les héritiers,* Paris, 1964. See also their *La reproduction,* Paris, 1970.

60. F. Ponteil, *Histoire de l'enseignement en France,* op. cit., p. 388.

61. W. R. Fraser, *Reforms and Restraints in Modern French Education,* op. cit., p. 163.

62. Ibid., p. 86.

63. Maurice Duverger, 'Les contradications de l'Université Nouvelle', *Le Monde,* 12 September 1969.

64. *Le Monde,* 4 February 1969.

65. *Le Monde,* 6 February 1969.

66. As Professor Bredin (from the University of Paris – Dauphine, who had contributed to the drafting of the loi d'orientation) commented in September 1969, 'starting from parity which they had conquered for themselves, reassured by the promise that they would retain this parity, the students found themselves reduced to a ratio of 1:3 in the new councils without knowing quite how this happened. The proportion was not a bad one. Most of them would have accepted it, had it been admitted openly and loyally. But this proportion had only been arrived at after complicated calculations based on inaccurate statements about parity which in fact they distorted. By the operation of percentages, social classes were created within the representative councils. Each within his bracket was likely to defend not the common interests of his university but – by a vaguely intellectualized Poujadism – the interests of his own category'.

67. E. Terray, *Le Monde,* 12 February 1969.

68. Minister Faure condemned it explicitly as undemocratic during the parliamentary debate on the loi d'orientation in October 1968, 'selection would be a breach of the explicit commitment of the Law and the implicit commitment of the State towards those who sent their children to secondary schools. How could we explain to these parents that we refuse (to their children) the access which we had promised to them. Would not the victims be those families deprived of money and connections? Selection would also mean a breach of the commitment entered into by the State after the Liberation when natality was encouraged'.

69. These 'stages' are either incorporated in UERs comprising other courses or – less frequently – constitute discrete units. They are compulsory and linked to a recommendation which is not binding upon the student – either to continue on the course of his (her) choice, or to opt alternatively for a shorter cycle of studies within the same university. If the advice is heeded, the student has a right to be re-registered in accordance with the guidance given to him. However, he is free to disregard it and to proceed according to his initial intent, but should he

fail at the end of the first year, he may have to undergo another multi-disciplinary 'stage' whose conclusions are then binding upon him. Hence the freedom of secondary school leavers to register is a constraint upon the universities and can only be minimized by redirecting the least promising entrants towards shorter courses, designed for vocational ends.

70. To each university the ministry grants a fixed credit per square meter of the campus (30 frs. in 1971) and per student (100 frs. in 1971). Moreover a credit whose amount varies with the subject matter is intended to cover special costs of tuition (e.g. 40 frs. per student in law and economics, 60 in letters and social sciences, 220 in medicine and pharmacy, 600 in science). These latter credits are increased by 30 percent in the case of the Parisian universities. Predictably the criteria for differentiating between disciplines are challenged by specialists who maintain for instance that teaching mathematics to scientists is not intrinsically more expensive than teaching methodology to social scientists. Efforts are being made by the advisory bodies of the Ministry and the conference of university chairmen to devise new criteria less closely connected with the former faculty structure and better able to incorporate the requirements of innovation.

71. J. Mandrin, *Enarchie; Les Mandarins de la société bourgeoise,* Paris, 1967.

72. C. Debbasch, *L'université désorientée,* Paris, 1971.

73. Michalina Vaughan, 'Gaullism', pp. 108-37 in M. Kolinsky and W. Patterson, *Social and Political Movements in Western Europe,* New York, 1976.

74. Maurice Duverger, *La Cinquième République,* Paris, 1963, p. 250.

75. Michalina Vaughan, 'Gaullism', op. cit., p. 133.

76. W. R. Frazer, *Reforms and Restraints in Modern French Education,* op. cit., p. 169-70.

77. Eigil Thrane, *Education and Culture in Denmark: A Survey of the Educational, Scientific and Cultural Conditions,* Copenhagen, 1958, p. 29.

78. Ibid., p. 36.

79. S. Tovborg Jensen, 'Agricultural Training', in Royal Danish Ministry of Foreign Affairs, *Denmark,* Copenhagen, 1964, p. 268.

80. Erik Tøttrup, 'The Training of Non-Skilled Workers', in Royal Danish Ministry of Foreign Affairs, *Denmark,* op. cit., p. 288.

81. Danish Ministry of Education, *Higher Education in Denmark,* Copenhagen, 1954, p. 28.

82. Erik Langsted 'Commercial Training', in Royal Danish Ministry of Foreign Affairs, *Denmark,* op. cit., p. 277.

83. Erik Tøttrup, *'The Training of Non-Skilled Workers',* op. cit., p. 289.

84. Willis Dixon, *Education in Denmark,* Copenhagen, 1958, p. 145.

85. William W. Brickman, *Denmark's Educational System and Problems,* Washington, 1967, p. 13 f.

86. OECD, *Study on Teachers: Denmark Italy, Luxembourg: Training. Recruitment and Utilization of Teachers,* Country Case Studies, Paris, 1968, p. 30.

87. Ole B. Thomsen, 'Governments and Universities: A Danish View', in D. F. Dadson (ed.), *On Higher Education,* Toronto, 1966, p. 108.

88. Ibid., p. 110.

89. Loc. cit.

90. Ibid., p. 124.

91. Ibid., p. 121.

92. Cf. Willis Dixon, *Education in Denmark*, op. cit., p. 136.

93. The National Union of Teachers, cited ibid., p. 145.

94. Jørgen Jørgensen, the Minister of Education introducing the 1935 Bill. Cited ibid., p. 153.

95. Jørgen Jørgensen, cited loc. cit.

96. Paedagogisk-Psykolgisk Tidsskrift, August 1966, cited ibid., p. 200.

97. Loc. cit.

98. Loc. cit.

99. Cited ibid., p. 221.

100. F. C. Kalund-Jørgensen, 'The Relation between Secondary Schools and Universities – Denmark', in G. Z. F. Bereday and J. A. Lauwerys, *The Yearbook of Education*, London, 1959, p. 474.

101. See William W. Brickman, *Denmark's Educational System and Problems*, op. cit., p. 18 f.

102. Aksel Nelleman, 'The Gymnasium School in Denmark', in Danske Selskab, *Schools and Education in Denmark*, Copenhagen, 1972, p. 79.

103. See William W. Brickman, *Denmark's Educational System and Problems*, op. cit., p. 20 f.

104. Aksel Nelleman, 'The Higher Leaving Examination' in Danske Selskab, *Schools and Education in Denmark*, op. cit., p. 105.

105. Candidates who have passed the Higher Leaving Examination qualify for entry to:
   a) A primary school teacher training course at a Teacher Training College.
   b) Training as a social worker at the Social High School of Denmark.
   c) Training as a hospital laboratory assistant (if the physics and chemistry option has been taken).
   d) Training in agriculture/dairying at the Royal Veterinary and Agricultural High School of Denmark.
   e) Training in veterinary medicine at the above (if maths, physics and chemistry options taken).
   f) Training in dentistry at the Copenhagen Dental College (if physics and chemistry options taken).
   g) Training as a physiotherapist (if physics and chemistry options taken).
   h) The Academy of Fine Arts' School of Architecture.
   i) Courses of business economics at Commercial Colleges (exemptions given).
   j) Certain graduate courses at Danish Universities (depending on options studied and supplementary entrance exams).
See Aksel Nelleman, 'The Higher Leaving Examination', op. cit.

106. Cited in James Murphy, *Church, State and Schools in Britain, 1800-1970*, London 1971, p. 104.

107. 'Of students in colleges of education in 1963-64 about one-fifth were in colleges connected with the Church of England and about one-tenth in colleges organized by the Roman Catholic Church; a small proportion were in colleges run by Methodists, the Free Churches, and undenominated organizations; but more than three-fifths were in colleges wholly maintained and controlled by public authorities. Of the students who began training for teaching in 1964 about one-seventh were in the departments of education of universities, and these are undenominational. In 1967 there were in England and Wales fifty-three colleges

of education controlled by voluntary bodies, thirty university departments of education and 128 institutions controlled by local education authorities.' Ibid, p. 125

108. Ibid., p. 111.

109. R. J. W. Selleck, *English Primary Education and the Progressives, 1914-39*, London, 1972, p. 75.

110. Ibid., p. 126

111. Willem van der Eyken and Barry Turner, *Adventures in Education*, Harmondsworth, 1975, p. 8.

112. See A. Griffiths, *Secondary School Reorganization in England and Wales*, 1971, p. 75.

113. Caroline Benn and Brian Simon, *Half-Way There*, Harmondsworth, 1972, p. 63.

114. Ibid., p. 64.

115. Brian Simon, *Education and the Labour Movement; 1870-1920*, London 1965, p. 319.

116. Ibid., p. 341.

117. Michael Sanderson, *The Universities and British Industry, 1850-1970*, London, 1972, p. ix.

118. Ibid., pp. 88-89.

119. Ibid., p. 93

120. Ibid., p. 391.

121. B. Tipton, *Conflict and Change in a Technical College*, London, 1973, p. 23.

122. Ibid., p. 20

123. See Michael Sanderson, *The Universities and British Industry, 1850-1970*, op. cit., p. 370.

124. Loc. cit.

125. Ibid., p. 384.

126. Ibid., p. 387.

127. Ibid., pp. 104-05.

128. Ibid., p. 119.

129. *Report of the Committee on Education for Salesmanship* (Goodenough Committee), 1931, p. 65.

130. Michael Sanderson, *The Universities and British Industry, 1850-1970*, op. cit., p. 212.

131. Ibid., p. 94.

132. R. J. W. Selleck, *English Primary Education and the Progressives, 1914-39*, op. cit., p. 35.

133. By 1926 2000 schools were said to be using the Dalton Plan, ibid., p. 41 ff.

134. See Asher Tropp, *The School Teachers*, London 1957, p. 235.

135. Michael Sanderson, *The Universities and British Industry, 1850-1970*, op. cit., p. 260.

136. Ibid., p. 275.

137. Harold Perkin, *Key Profession: The History of the Association of University Teachers*, London, 1969, pp. 93-94.

138. Ibid., p. 94.

139. See ibid., pp. 126-27.

140. Ibid., p. 130.

141. R. J. W. Selleck, *English Primary Education and the Progressives, 1914-39,* op. cit., p. 156.

142. Ibid., p. 143.

143. William Taylor, *Society and the Education of Teachers,* London, 1969, p. 12.

144. 'Parents have no real place in the management structure; many of the managing bodies are short of the authority to do a real job and, if they had it would not really be representing anybody but the local council which appoints them . . . officially, the managing body has the 'control' of the conduct and curriculum of the school. In practice, this control is a mere form and the true authority relationship rests between the headteacher of the primary school and his Chief Education Officer and the Chief Education Officer's staff.' Maurice Kogan, *The Government of Education,* London, 1971, p. 26.

145. Cf. Maurice Kogan, *Education Policy-Making,* London, 1975, p. 127.

146. Maurice Kogan, *The Government of Education,* op. cit., p. 32.

147. *Higher Education,* (Robbins Report), 1963, p. 127.

148. Harold Perkin, *Key Profession,* op. cit., p. 234.

149. Ibid., p. 235.

150. Joseph Ben-David and Awraham Zloczower, 'Universities and Academic Systems in Modern Societies', *European Journal of Sociology,* 1962, Vol. 31, pp. 45-85.

151. Graeme C. Moodie and Rowland Eustace, *Power and Authority in British Universities,* London, 1974, p. 68.

152. Harold Perkin, *Key Profession,* op. cit., p. 214.

153. Maurice Kogan, *Educational Policy-Making,* op. cit., p. 144.

154. Ibid., p. 109.

155. See Michael Locke, *Power and Politics in the School System,* London, 1974, p. 46 f.

156. Michael Sanderson, *The Universities and British Industry, 1850-1970,* op. cit., p. 360.

157. Ibid., p. 372.

158. Michael Beloff, *The Plateglass Universities,* London, 1968 p. 39.

159. H. C. Dent, *1870-1970 Century of Growth in English Education,* London, 1970. p. 61.

160. Brian Simon, *Education and the Labour Movement, 1870-1920,* op. cit., pp. 359-60.

161. H. C. Dent, *1870-1970 Century of Growth in English Education,* op. cit., p. 61.

162. 'In the year 1905-06, of a total of 482 recognized pupil-teacher centres 283 were integral parts of secondary schools and 192 were separately organized. Four years later, in 1909-10, of 603 recognized centres 512 were integrated in secondary schools, and only 80 were separately organized'. Ibid., p. 65.

163. In advocating the extension of the scholarship system Sidney Webb argued for a reform which 'would organically connect the scholarship system with all the public elementary schools, instead of, as at present, only about a third of them; and would bring London's 'capacity-catching machine' to bear on every

promising child'. Sidney Webb, *London Education,* London, 1904, p. 26 f.

164. *Report of the Consultative Committee upon Higher Elementary Schools,* 1906, p. 27.

165. See Brian Simon, *Education and the Labour Movement, 1870-1920,* op. cit., p. 255.

166. Ibid., p. 268.

167. 'The shortcomings of the old higher grade schools, with their excessive emphasis on scientific subjects, was condemned by HMIs and professional associations of teachers as one-sided, and detrimental to more humanistic and literary studies. Moreover, there was a growing demand for clerks, pupil-teachers and commercial recruits. So after a Commons debate in July 1903, new regulations were issued to ensure that such an imbalance should not recur'. W. H. G. Armytage, *Four Hundred Years of English Education,* Cambridge, 1970, p. 187.

168. Cf. Olive Banks, *Parity and Prestige in English Secondary Education,* London, 1955, p. 44 f.

169. H. C. Dent, *1870-1970 Century of Growth in English Education,* op. cit., p. 73.

170. Brian Simon, *Education and the Labour Movement, 1870-1920,* op. cit., p. 273.

171. 'A sound foundation of general education for all is envisaged; only in the final year of the secondary course should there be any technical, professional or commercial bias, and then as part of a continuing general education'. Ibid., p. 384.

172. Ibid., p. 349.

173. R. H. Tawney, *The Radical Tradition,* London, 1964, p. 50-51.

174. Lawrence Andrews, *The Education Act, 1918,* London, 1976, p. 77.

175. By 1923, under the stimulus given by the 1918 Education Act, the number of pupils in secondary schools on the grant list had increased from 216,765 pupils in 943 schools in 1917 to 327,601 pupils in 1,137 schools in 1923-24. The number of free places in these secondary (grammar) schools had also increased after the passing of the 1918 Education Act. In 1915 the number of free places had been 65,799, or 33.1 percent of the total number. By October, 1922, this number had risen to 113,405, or 34.2 percent. Ibid., p. 85.

176. Brian Simon, *The Politics of Educational Reform, 1920-40,* London, 1974, p. 298.

177. Cf. Lawrence Andrews, *The Education Act, 1918,* op. cit., pp. 74-75.

178. Cf. H. C. Dent, *1870-1970 Century of Growth in English Education,* op. cit., p. 87.

179. H. C. Dent, *The Education Act, 1944,* London, 1969, pp. 5-6.

180. See Brian Simon, *The Politics of Educational Reform, 1920-40,* op. cit., p. 42.

181. H. C. Dent, *1870-1970 Century of Growth in English Education,* op. cit., p. 87.

182. Ibid., p. 91.

183. Brian Simon, *The Politics of Educational Reform, 1920-40,* op. cit., p. 122.

184. H. C. Dent, *1870-1970 Century of Growth in English Education,* op. cit., p. 100.

185. Brian Simon, *The Politics of Educational Reform, 1920-40,* op. cit., p.

129.
186. Lawrence Andrews, *The Education Act, 1918,* op. cit., p. 72.
187. See Brian Simon, *The Politics of Educational Reform, 1920-40,* op. cit., pp. 110.
188. Ibid., p. 167.
189. Cf. Ibid., p. 185.
190. Ibid., p. 191.
191. Between 1921 and 1938 the costs of education fell more heavily on the rates than on taxes: whilst Exchequer Grants rose by 13 percent, local authority expenditure grew by 44 percent. This was direct result of the cuts, for during the brief operation of the 1918 Act, the central contribution rose from 47 percent in 1914 to 56 percent in 1920, this was reversed and by 1938-39 the figure had still only crept back to 49 percent. Ibid., pp. 296-99.
192. Ibid., p. 289.
193. R. H. Tawney, *Juvenile Employment and Education,* Barnet House Papers, No. 14, 1934, p. 17.
194. David Rubinstein and Brian Simon, *The Evolution of the Comprehensive School,* London, 1969, p. 35.
195. H. C. Dent, *The Education Act 1944,* op. cit., p. 12.
196. H. C. Dent, *1870-1970 Century of Growth in English Education,* op. cit., p. 125.
197. P. H. J. H. Gosden, *The Development of Educational Administration in England and Wales,* Oxford, 1966, p. 194 f.
198. H. C. Dent, *The Education Act 1944,* op. cit., p. 5.
199. Loc. cit.
200. Ibid., p. 16.
201. Ibid., p. 46-47.
202. Caroline Benn and Brian Simon, *Half Way There,* op. cit., p. 38.
203. David Glass (ed.), *Social Mobility in Britain,* London, 1954, p. 160 f.
204. D. E. Regan, *Local Government and Education,* London, 1977, p. 47.
205. David Rubinstein and Brian Simon, *The Evolution of the Comprehensive School,* op. cit., p. 55.
206. Ibid., p. 45.
207. Ibid., p. 69.
208. Brian Holmes, 'Leicestershire, United Kingdom', in Centre for Educational Research and Innovation, *Case Studies of Educational Innovation, II At The Regional Level,* Paris, 1973, p. 99.
209. Ibid., p. 30.
210. David Rubinstein and Brian Simon, *The Evolution of the Comprehensive School,* op. cit., p. 87.
211. Brian Holmes, 'Leicestershire, United Kingdom', op. cit., p. 11.
212. Cf. Caroline Benn and Brian Simon, *Half Way There,* op. cit., p. 49.
213. See David Rubinstein and Brian Simon, *The Evolution of the Comprehensive School,* op. cit., p. 76. Emphasis added.
214. London County Council, *The Organization of Comprehensive Secondary Schools,* London, 1953, p. 7.
215. See London County Council, *London Comprehensive Schools; A Survey of Sixteen Schools,* London, 1961, p. 55 ff.

216. David Rubinstein and Brian Simon, *The Evolution of the Comprehensive School,* op. cit., p. 79.

217. See Michael Locke, *Power and Politics in the School System*, op. cit., p. 87.

218. David Rubinstein and Brian Simon, *The Evolution of the Comprehensive School,* op. cit., p. 93.

219. Caroline Benn and Brian Simon, *Half Way There,* op. cit., p. 219.

220. Ibid., p. 92.

221. David Rubinstein and Brian Simon, *The Evolution of the Comprehensive School,* op. cit., p. 97.

222. Caroline Benn and Brian Simon, *Half Way There,* op. cit., p. 72.

223. Cf. D. E. Regan, *Local Government and Education*, op. cit., p. 50.

224. Caroline Benn and Brian Simon, *Half Way There,* op. cit., p.72.

225. Ibid., p. 92.

226. See Michael Locke, *Power and Politics in the School System*, op. cit., p. 91.

227. Ibid., p. 90.

228. See D. E. Regan, *Local Government and Education*, op. cit., p. 42.

229. Ibid., p. 53.

230. Iu. I. Saenko, 'The allocation of Capital Investment for School Construction', in H. J. Noah (ed.), *The Economics of Education in the USSR*, op. cit., p. 87.

231. Nigel Grant, 'USSR', op. cit., p. 92 f.

232. G. Z. F. Bereday, W. W. Brickman, G. H. Read, *The Changing Soviet School,* op. cit., p. 4.

233. John F. Ohles, 'Danish Education – General or Specialized? ' *School and Society,* Vol. 85, No. 195, p. 41.

234. Jacques Fournier, *Politique de l'éducation,* op. cit., pp. 309-10.

INDEX

Margaret S Archer

was an undergraduate at the London School of Economics and went on to postgraduate work there and at the Ecole Pratique des Hautes Etudes, Paris. She has been Reader in Sociology at the University of Warwick since 1973. Her first research on the development of national educational systems, carried out with Michalina Vaughan, appeared as *Social Conflict and Educational Change in England and France: 1789-1848*, Cambridge, 1971. This was followed by an edited symposium entitled *Students, University and Society*, London 1972. She has also edited two collective volumes with Salvador Giner: *Contemporary Europe: Class, Status and Power*, London and New York, 1971, and *Contemporary Europe: Social Structures and Cultural Patterns*, London, 1978. Margaret Archer is Editor of *Current Sociology*, the journal of the International Sociological Association.